ANDRÉ LEON TALLEY

STYLE IS FOREVER

Rizzoli Electa

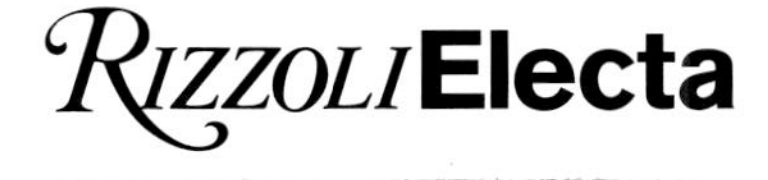

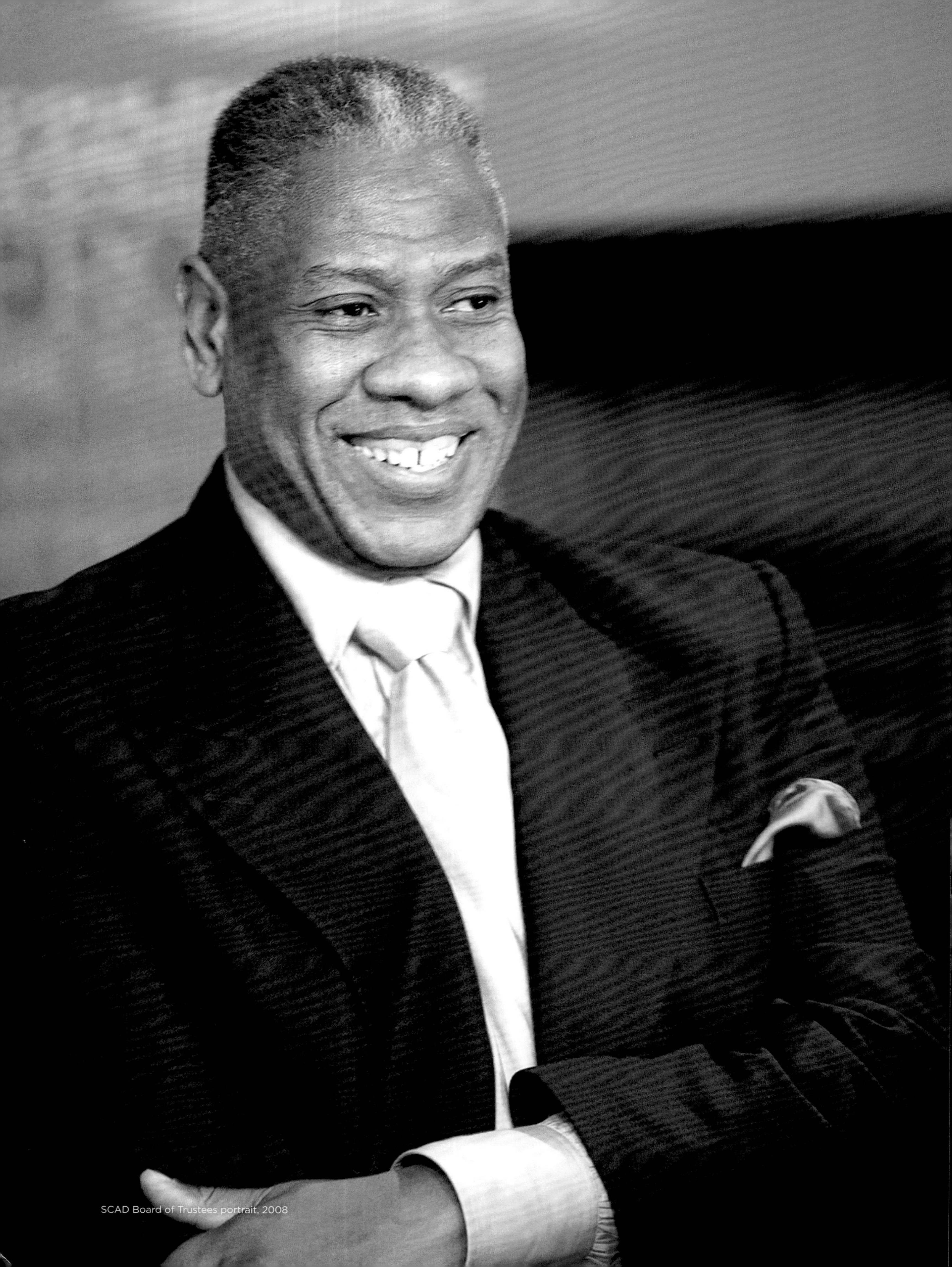

SCAD Board of Trustees portrait, 2008

“I’d like to be **remembered** as someone who made a difference in the lives of young people—that I **nurtured** someone and taught them to **pursue** their **dreams** and their careers, to leave a **legacy**.”

André Leon Talley

(1948–2022)

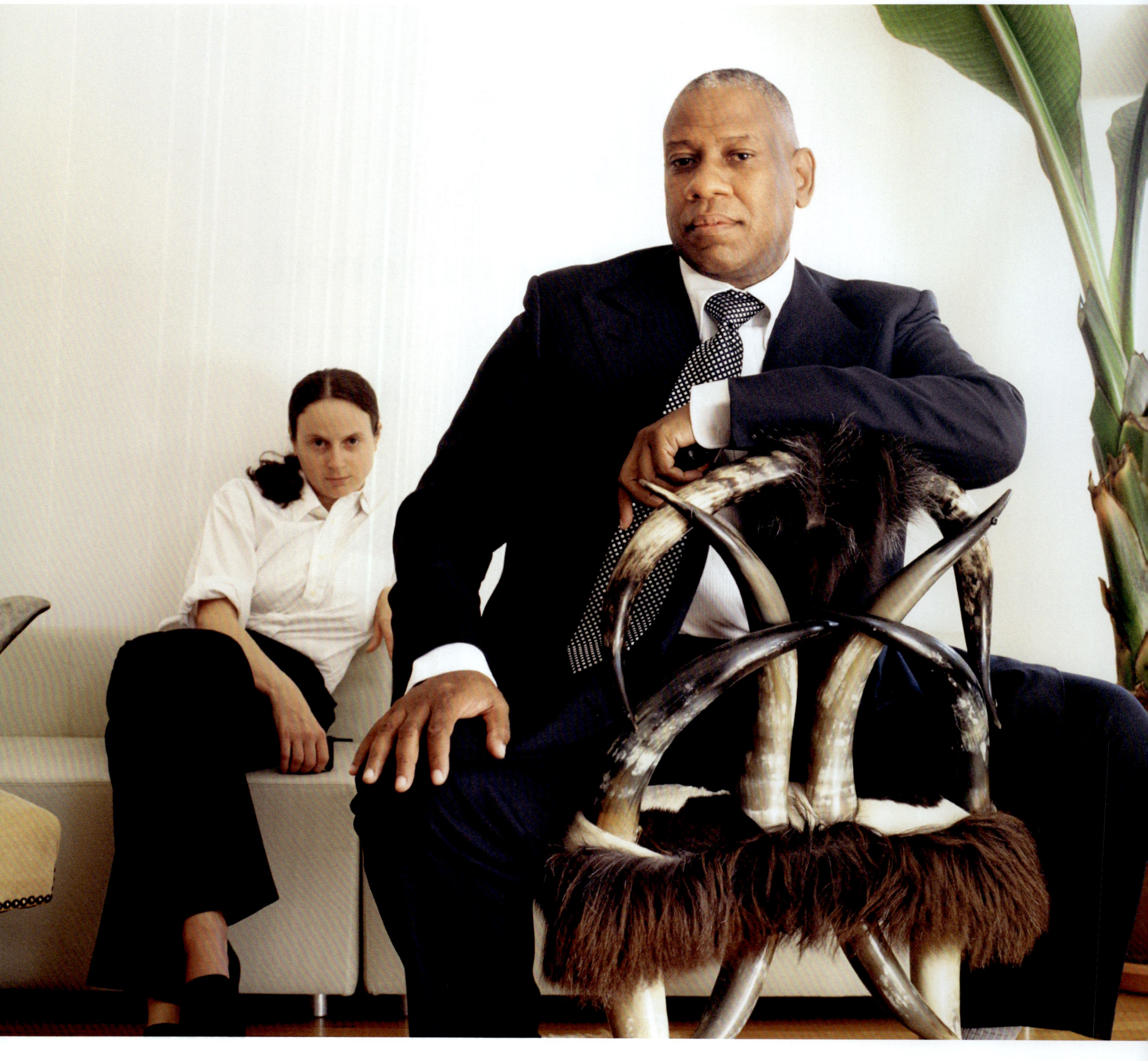

André with Alexandra Kotur on assignment for *Vogue*, September 2002.
Photographed by Jonathan Becker.

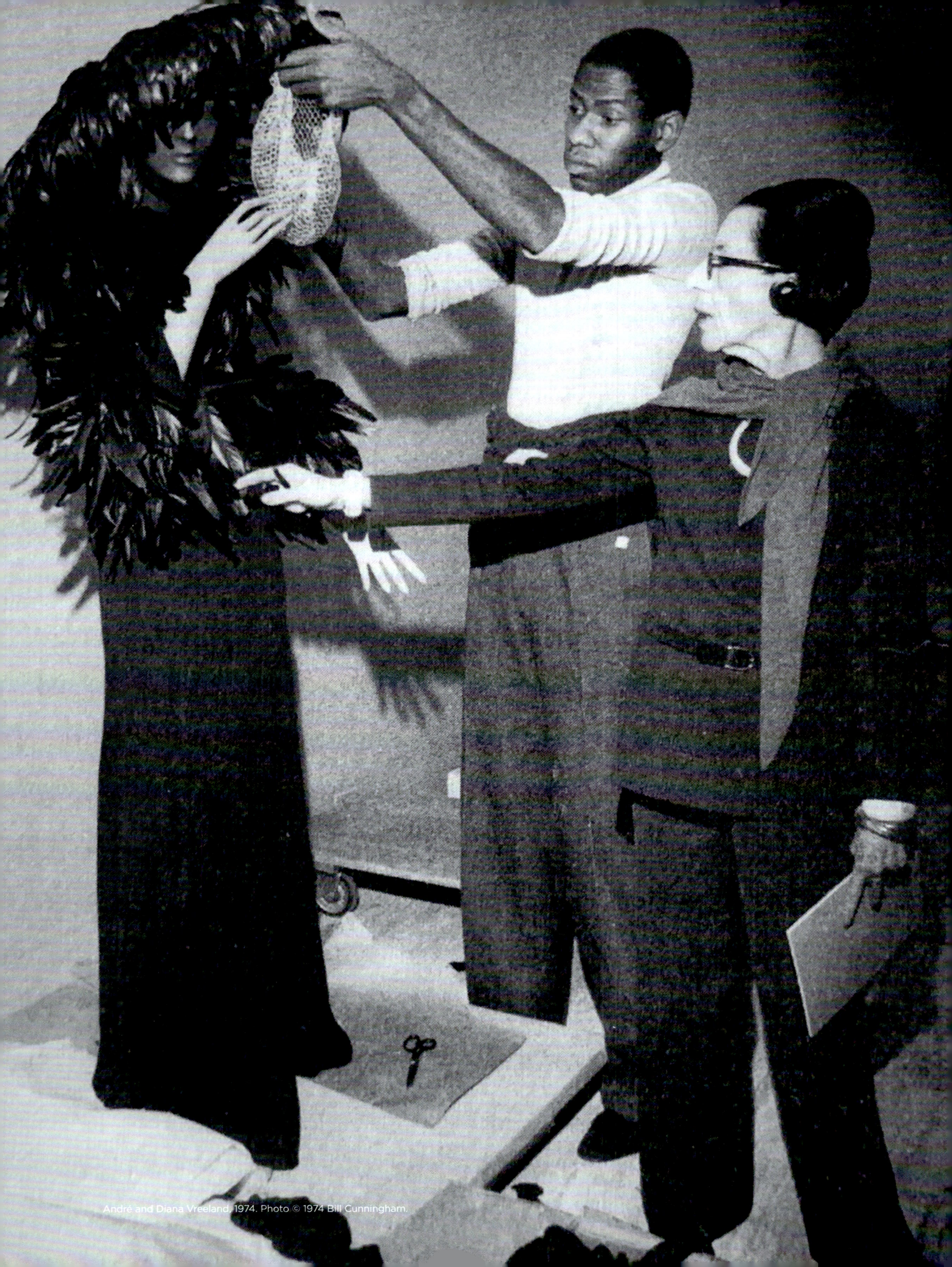

André and Diana Vreeland, 1974. Photo © 1974 Bill Cunningham.

BECOMING ANDRÉ

In André's youth in Durham, North Carolina, his grandmother emphasized the importance of a neatly starched shirt and taught him to model her own immaculate style. As André rose, through sheer grit and scorching talent, from a promising scholar to the great eminence of the fashion industry, a crisp, pressed shirt would remain a staple of his looks. Even in his early years as a master's student at Brown University in Providence, Rhode Island, André was fond of grandeur, knotting yards of striped crepe de chine at his shoulder and strutting around his apartment as if it were a catwalk, with a hat sourced from Harlem and a tasseled necklace from Kenya—dressing lavishly simply to dine in with friends.

After graduation, André alighted in New York, taking on an apprenticeship at the Costume Institute of The Metropolitan Museum of Art, where his innate gifts were nurtured by Diana Vreeland. In New York, André favored slim suits and tailored trousers, eye-catching ensembles but only glinting at the persona to emerge. Impressed by André's passion and panache, Vreeland introduced him to Andy Warhol, who hired him at *Interview*, bringing André new standing in the city's creative and social scenes. From Warhol's Factory to the dance floor of Studio 54, André embraced a more elaborate visage: seersucker suits with straw boaters, sable coats with fedoras, shorts with silk scarves in vivacious colors—a presence not to be ignored.

And he was truly seen, not only as he partied with the New York elite but also as he devotedly honed his craft. In the late 1970s, André sent shock waves through the worlds of fashion and publishing with his appointment as Paris bureau chief of *Women's Wear Daily*. Swept up in the pulse of his work in Paris, he scandalized the savoir faire with his industry-shaking dispatches and his boundary-pushing looks, breezing into Maxim's in a black cashmere dressing gown—filched from Karl Lagerfeld's closet—a portent of the many flowing capes, caftans, and kimonos yet to come.

André continued to break barriers with his historic appointment at *Vogue*, where he served as the first Black creative director and later editor at large, making space in the world of fashion for those who had never before felt represented. In his years at *Vogue*, André's style effused with experimentation and adornment. He believed unquestionably in his originality, and he dressed accordingly, becoming an icon not only within his own industry but in popular culture and the popular imagination, as his personality and purpose shined ever brighter—and remain forever radiant.

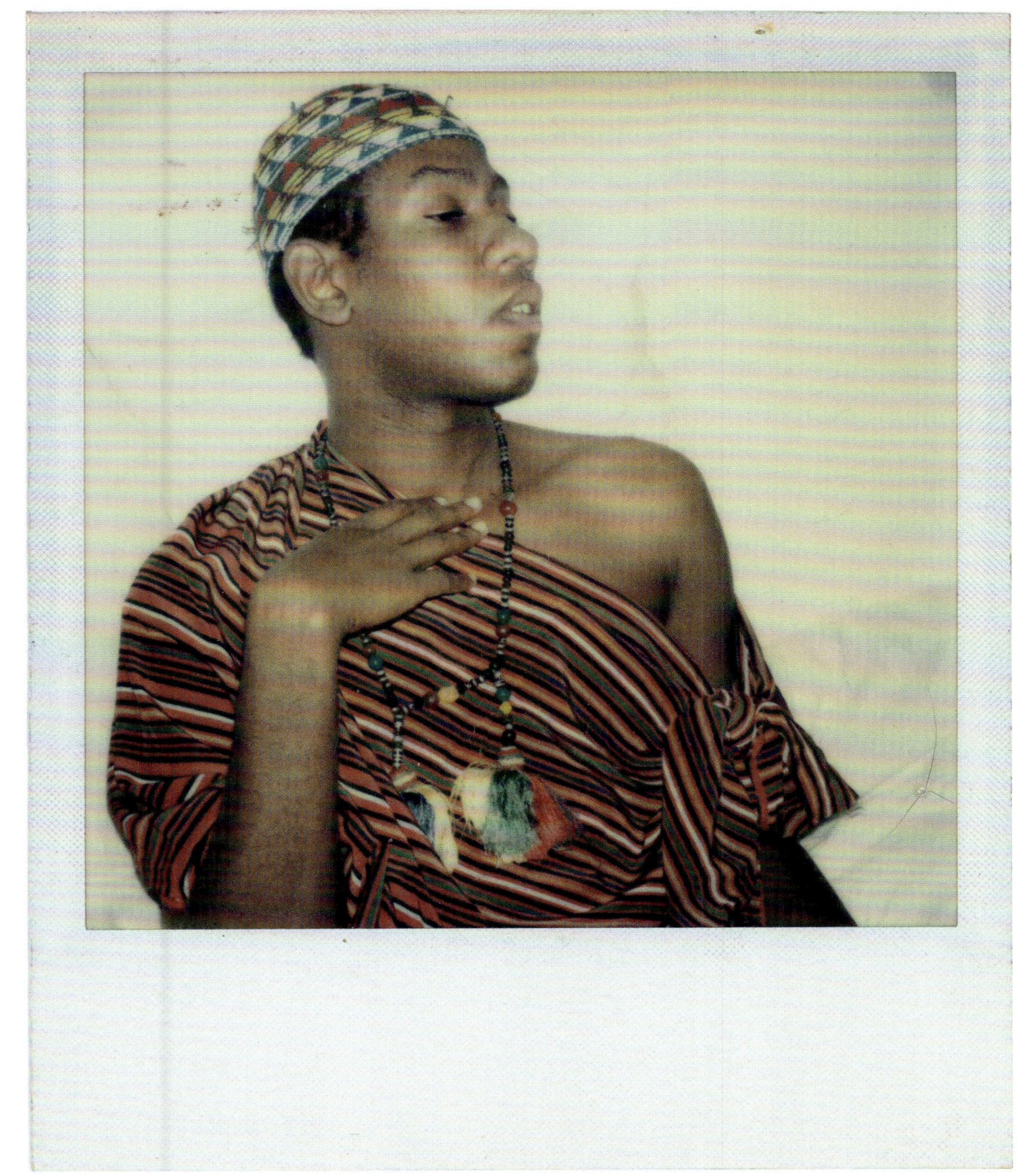

André, 1974. Photo © Reed Evins. Image © The Metropolitan Museum of Art/Art Resource, New York.

CONTENTS

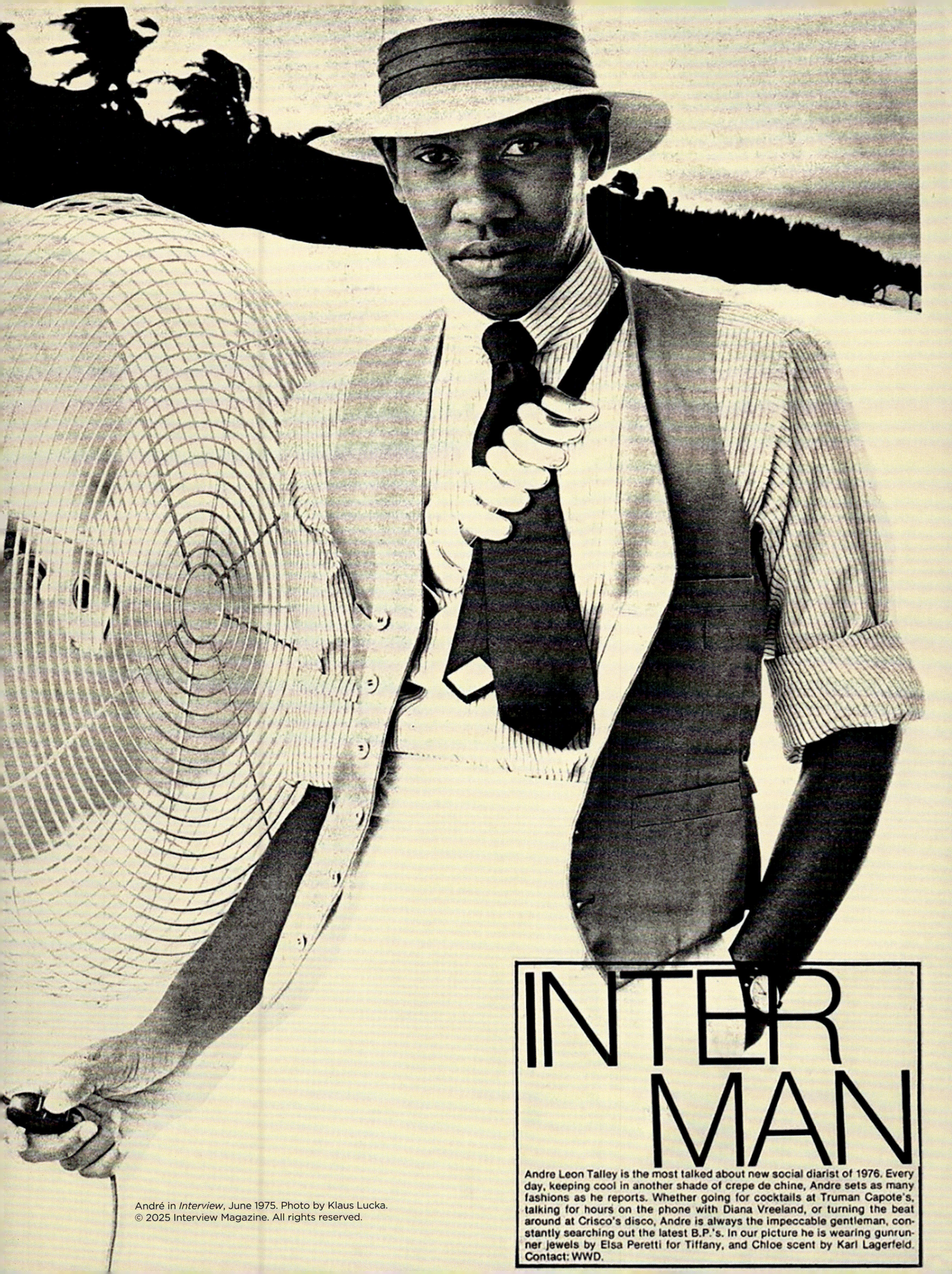

André in *Interview*, June 1975. Photo by Klaus Lucka.

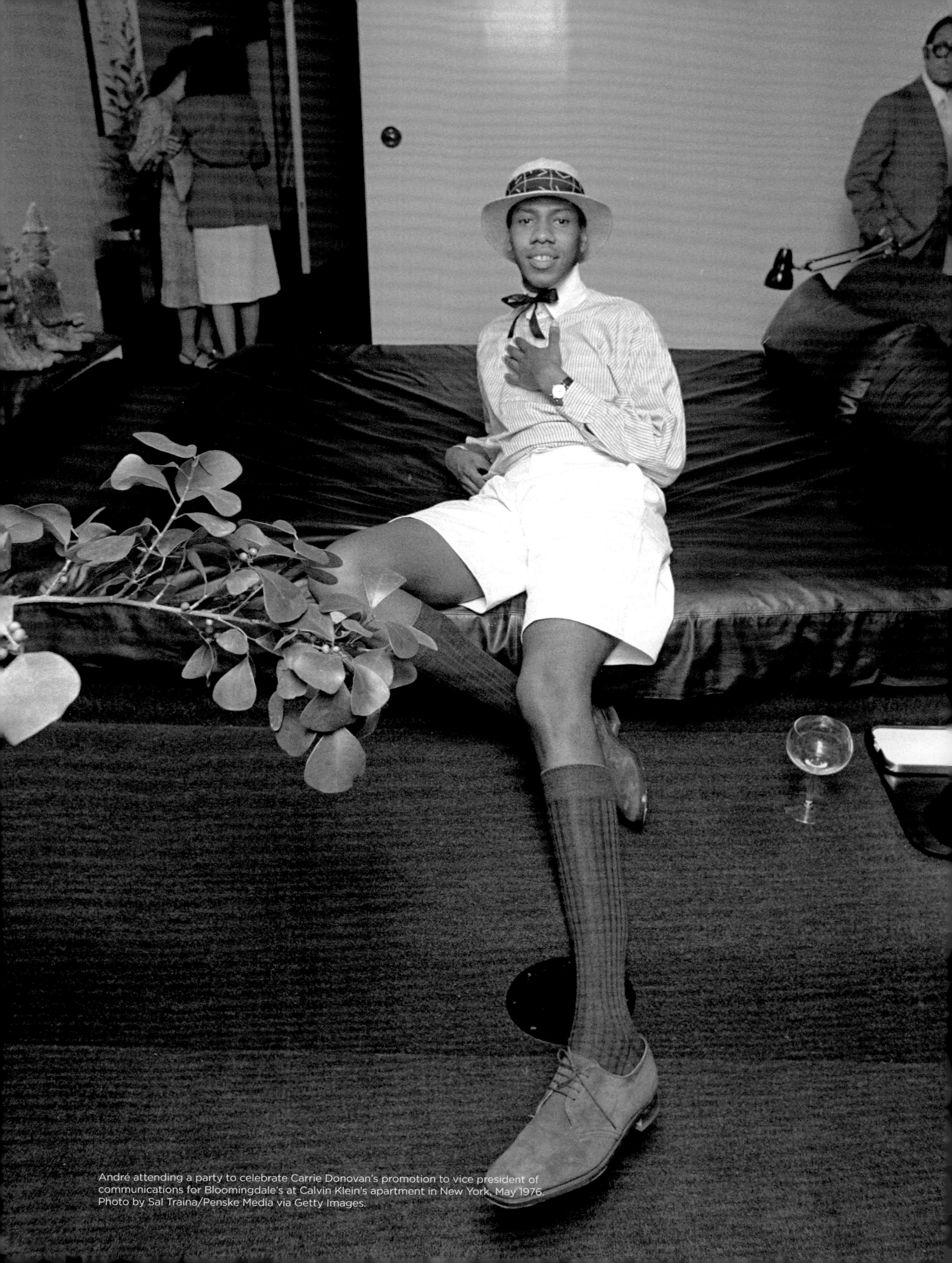

André attending a party to celebrate Carrie Donovan's promotion to vice president of communications for Bloomingdale's at Calvin Klein's apartment in New York, May 1976. Photo by Sal Traina/Penske Media via Getty Images.

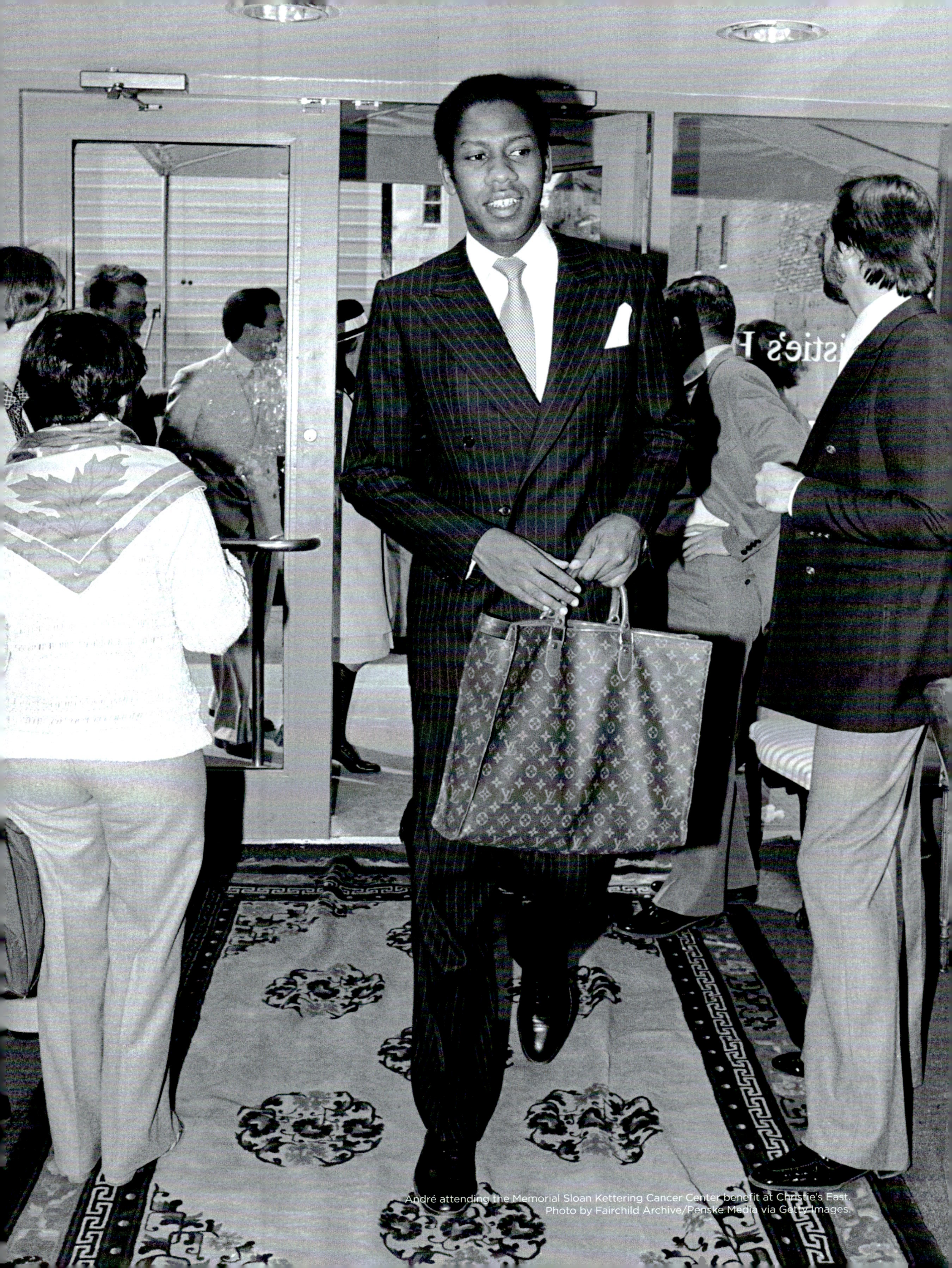

André attending the Memorial Sloan Kettering Cancer Center benefit at Christie's East.
Photo by Fairchild Archive/Penske Media via Getty Images.

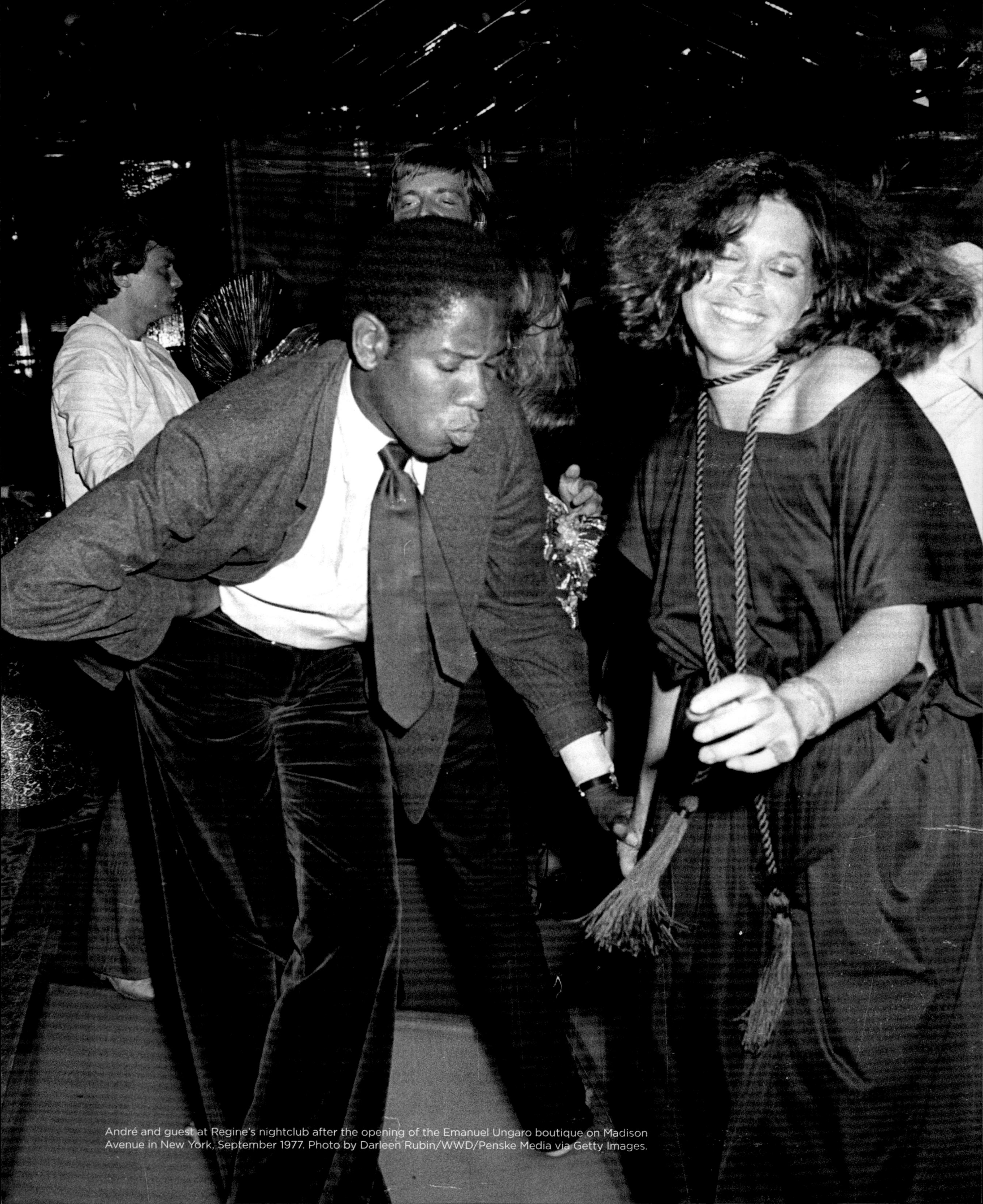

André and guest at Regine's nightclub after the opening of the Emanuel Ungaro boutique on Madison Avenue in New York, September 1977. Photo by Darleen Rubin/WWD/Penske Media via Getty Images.

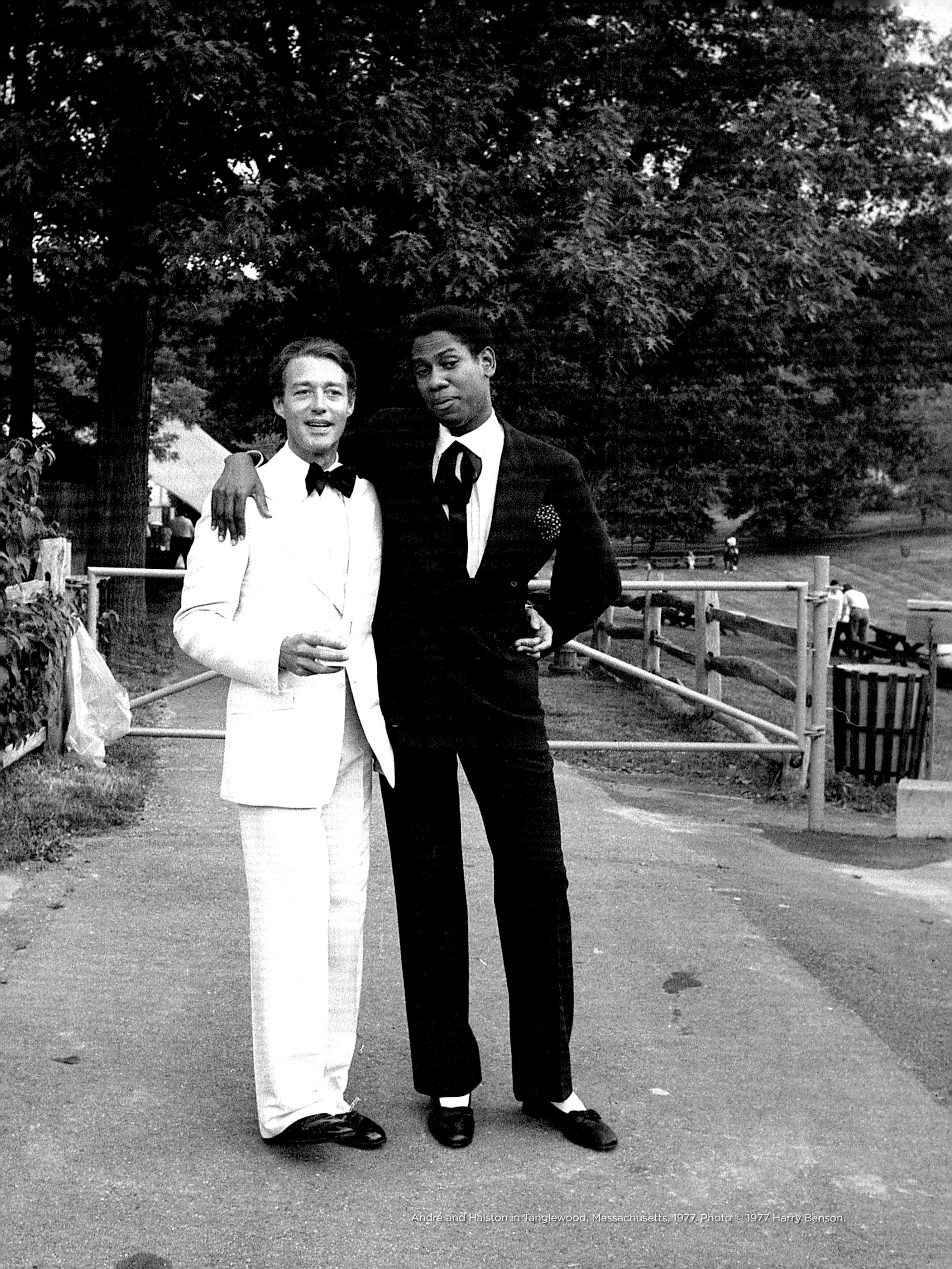

André and Halston in Tanglewood, Massachusetts, 1977. Photo © 1977 Harry Benson.

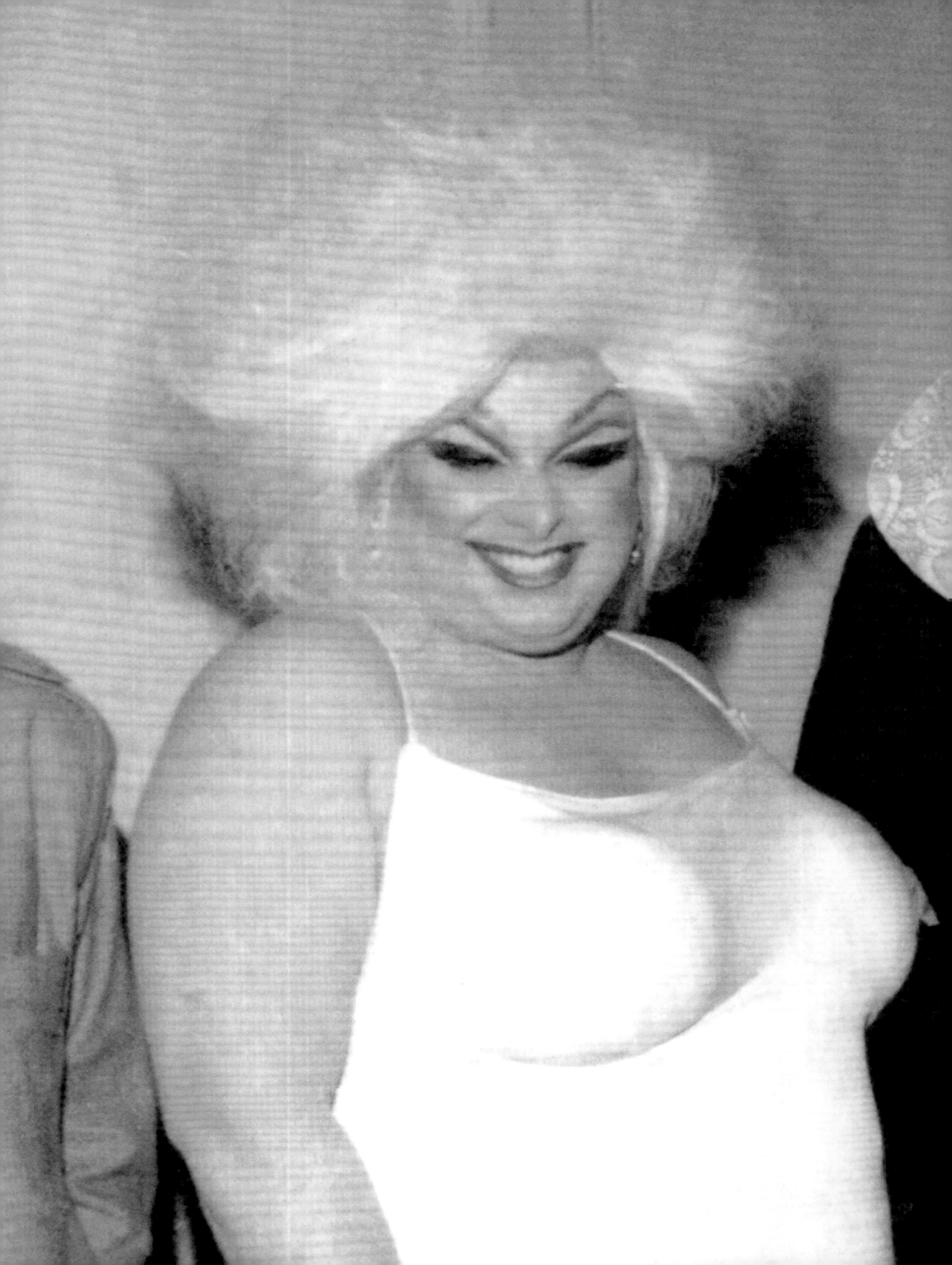

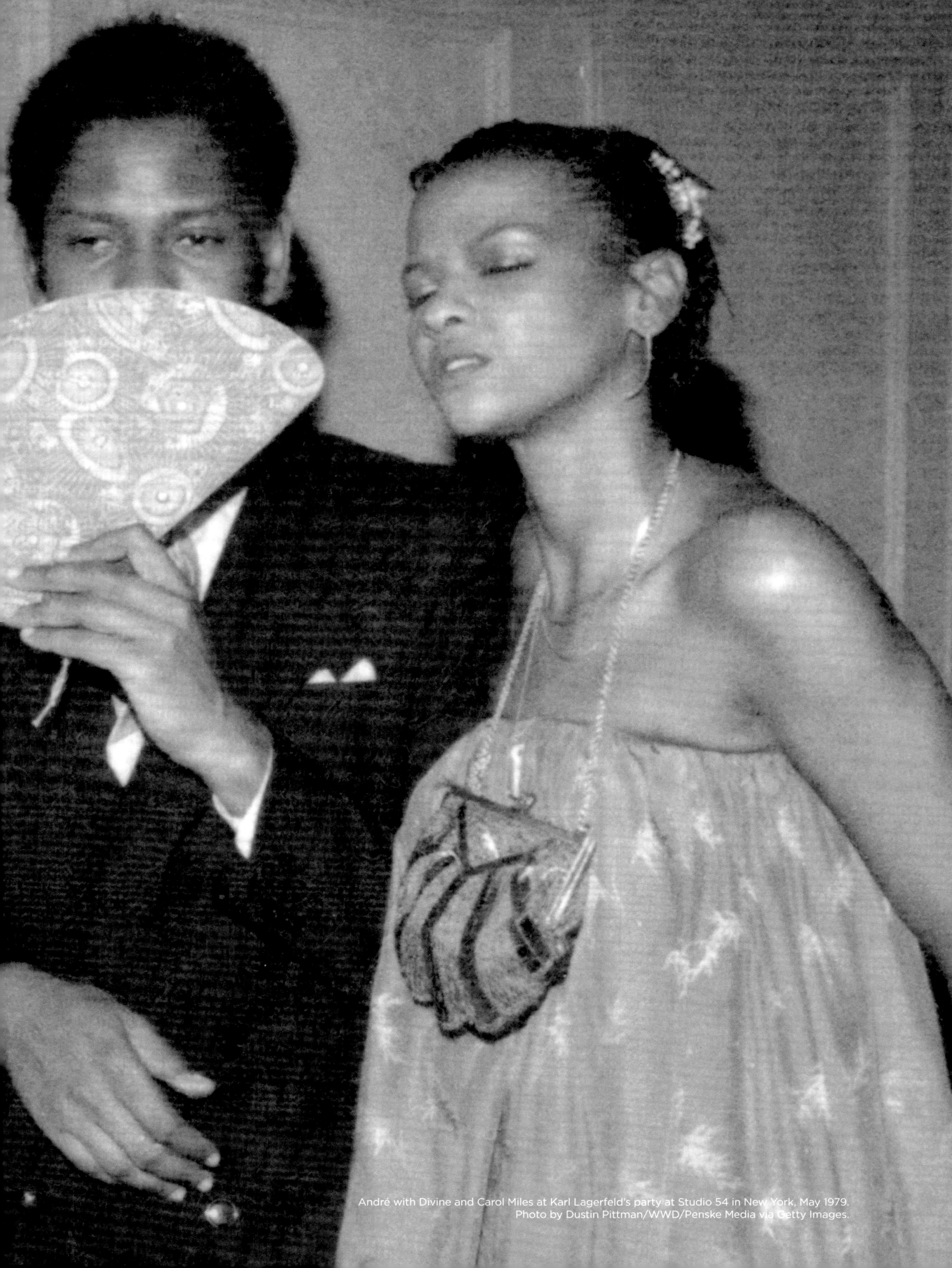

André with Divine and Carol Miles at Karl Lagerfeld's party at Studio 54 in New York, May 1979.
Photo by Dustin Pittman/WWD/Penske Media via Getty Images.

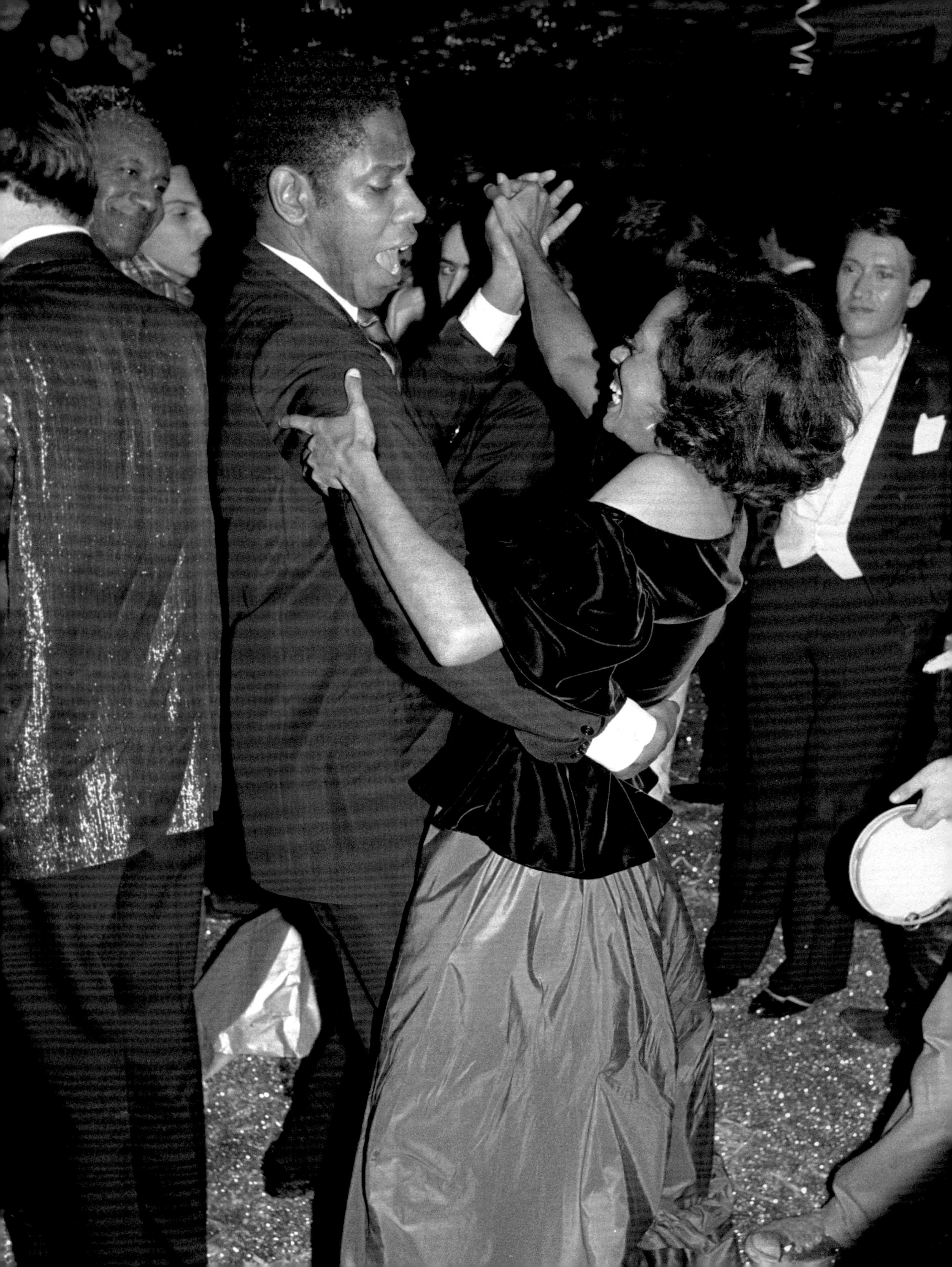

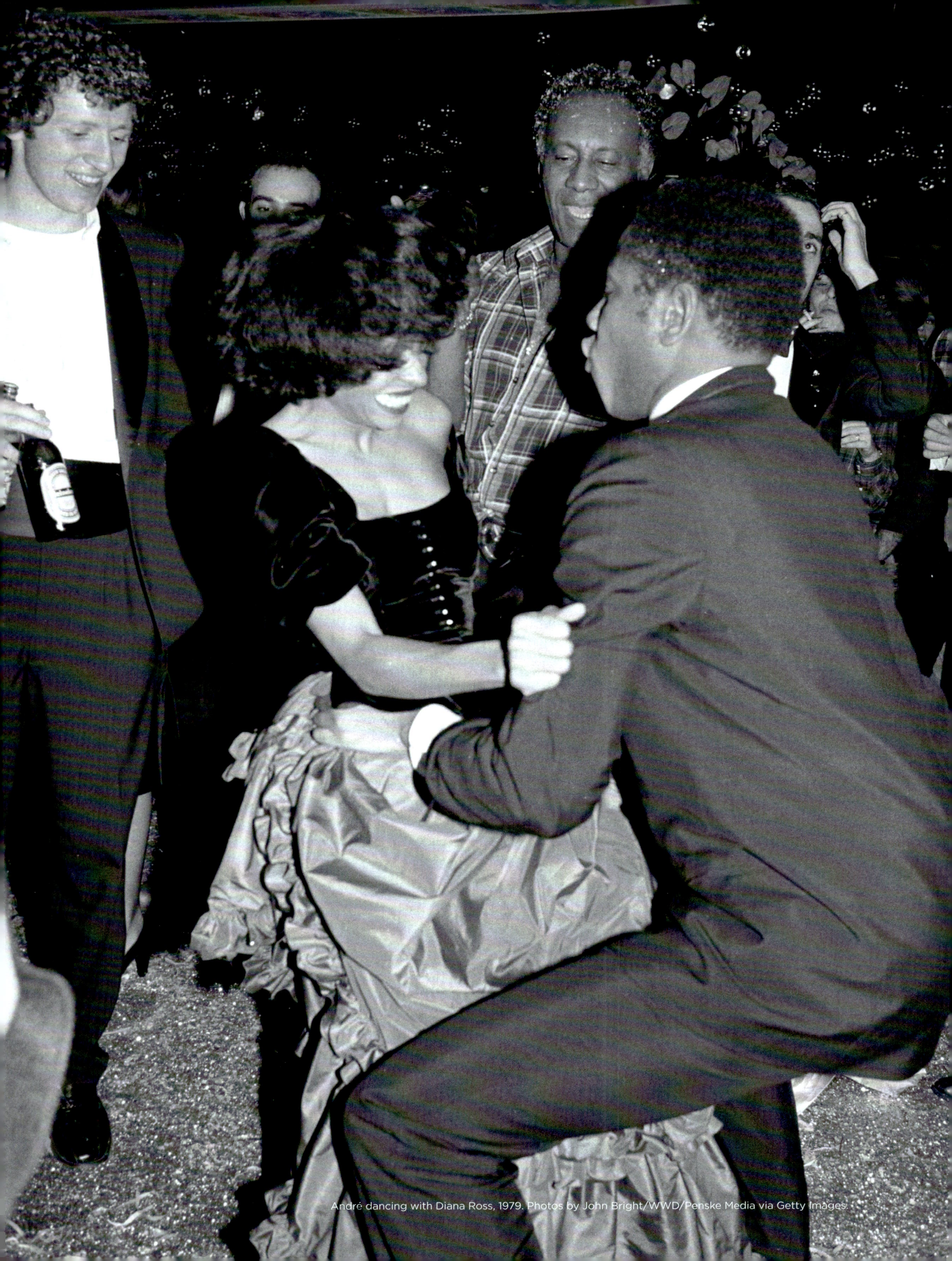

André dancing with Diana Ross, 1979. Photos by John Bright/WWD/Penske Media via Getty Images

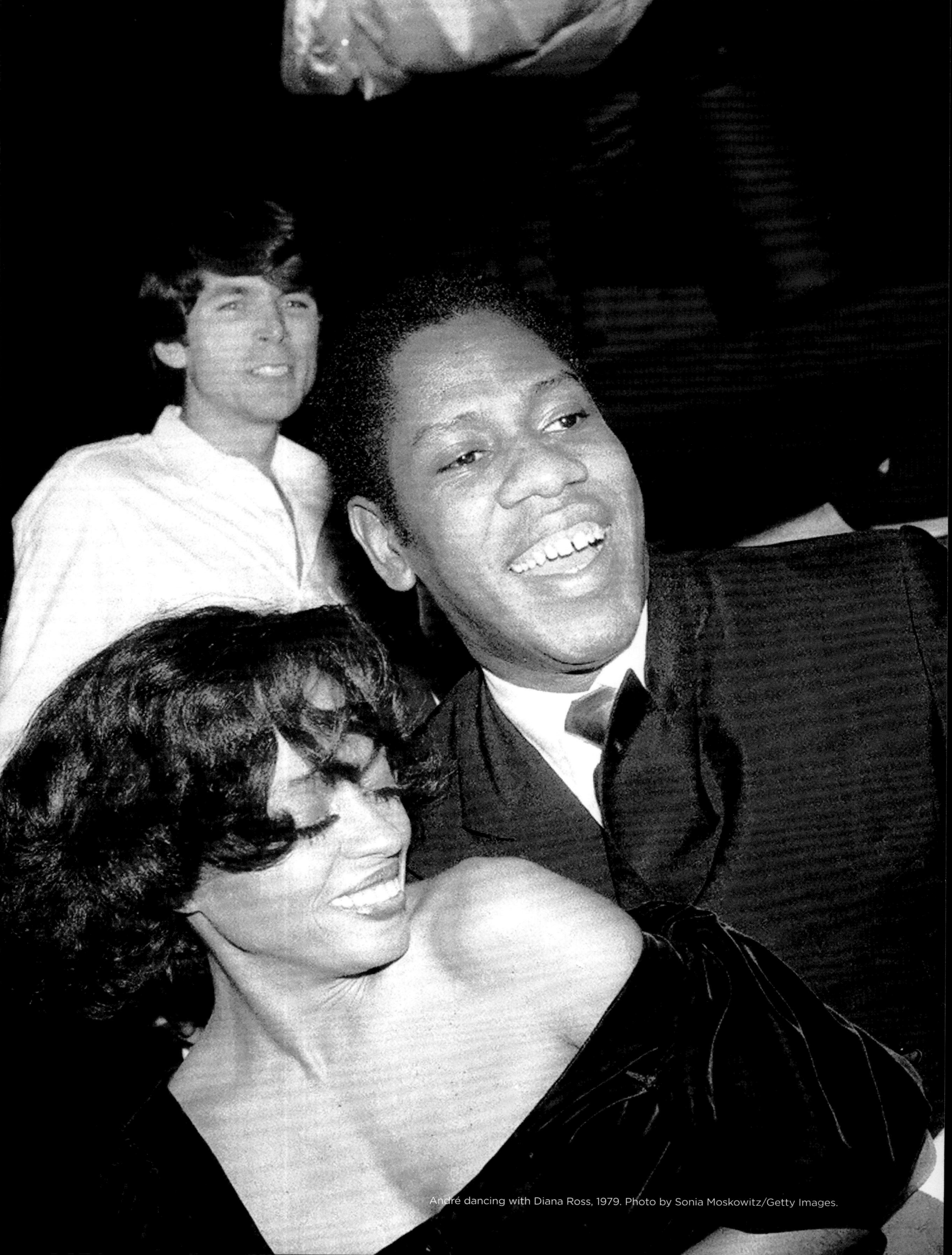

André dancing with Diana Ross, 1979. Photo by Sonia Moskowitz/Getty Images.

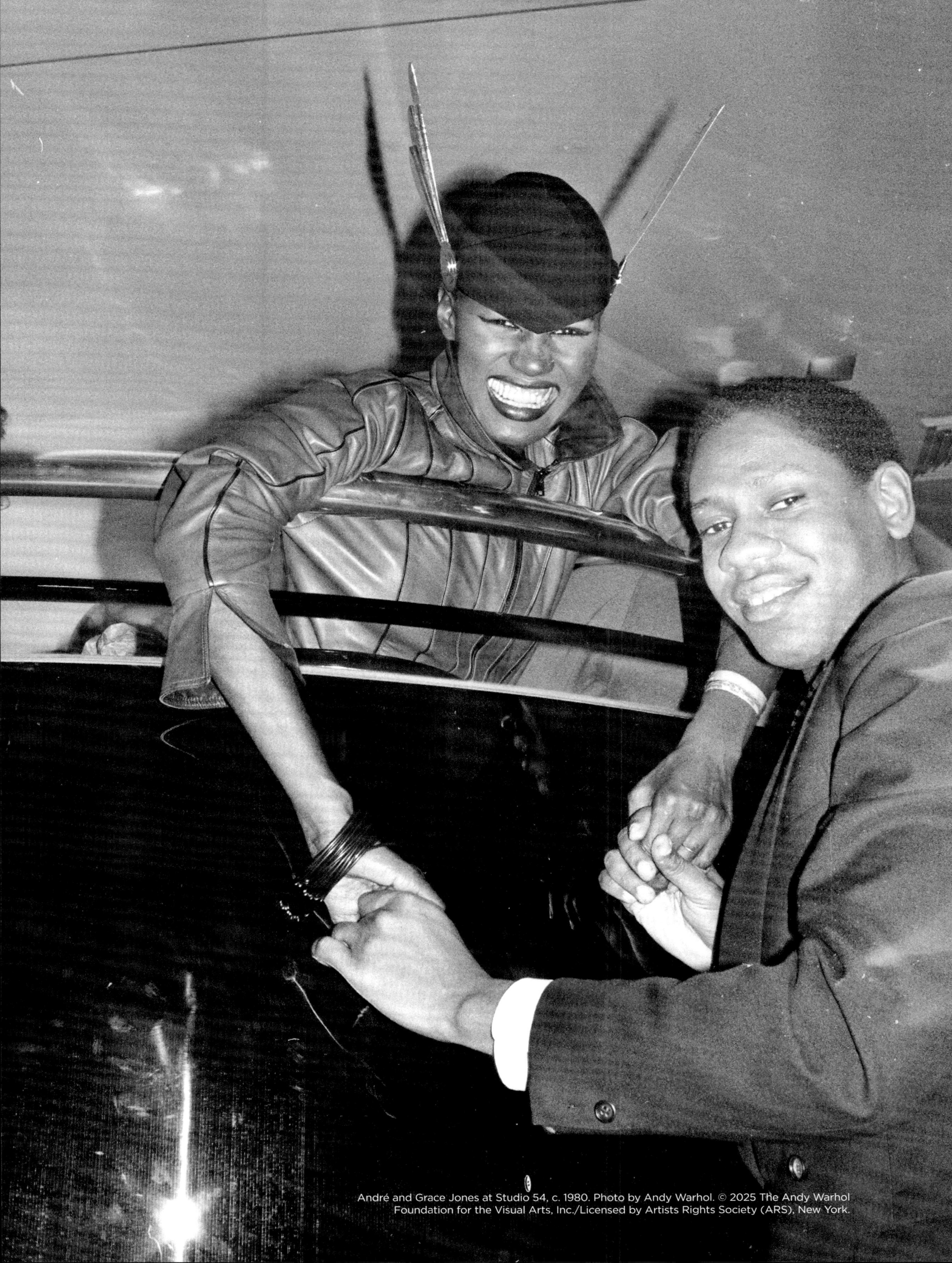

André and Grace Jones at Studio 54, c. 1980. Photo by Andy Warhol.

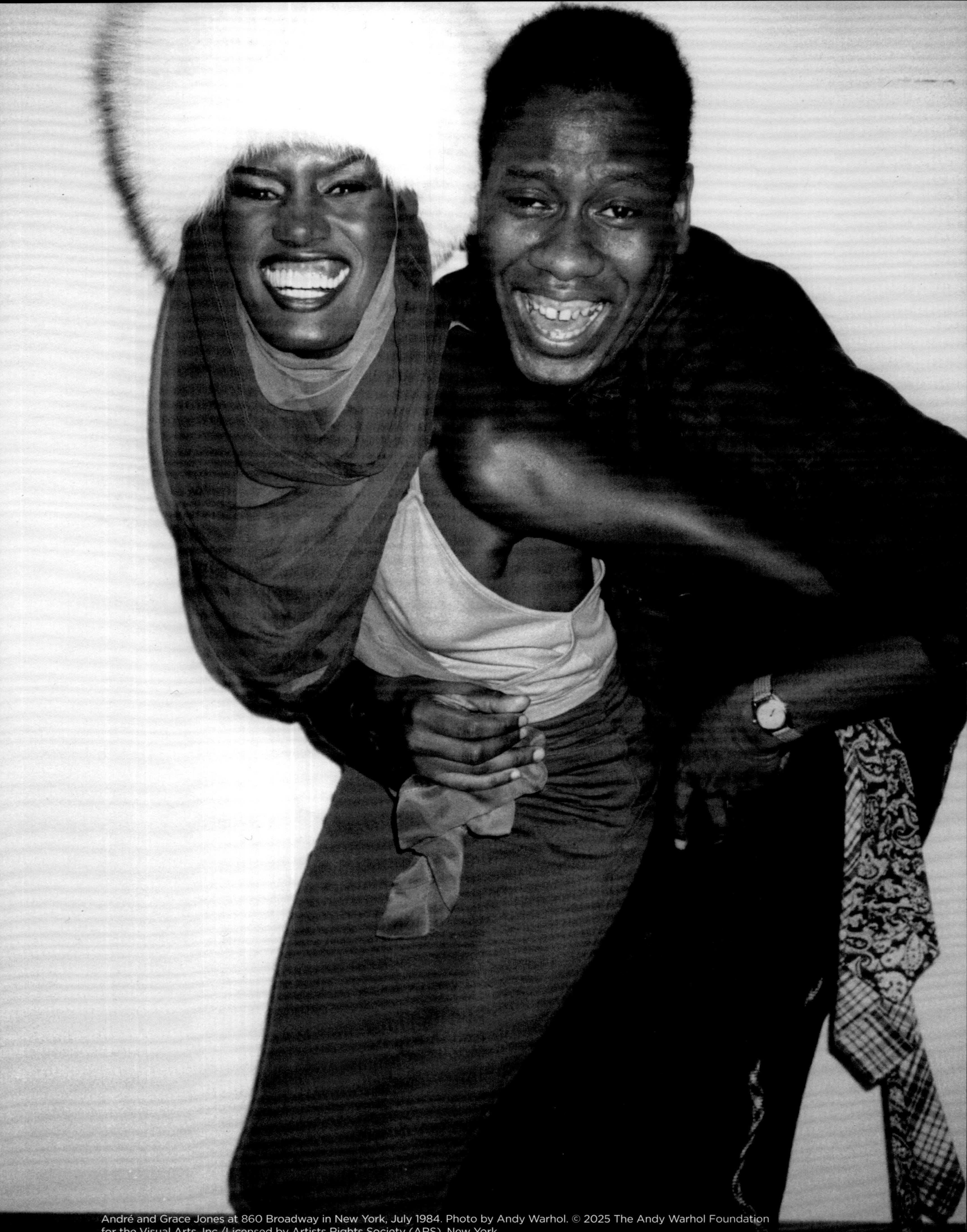

André and Grace Jones at 860 Broadway in New York, July 1984. Photo by Andy Warhol.

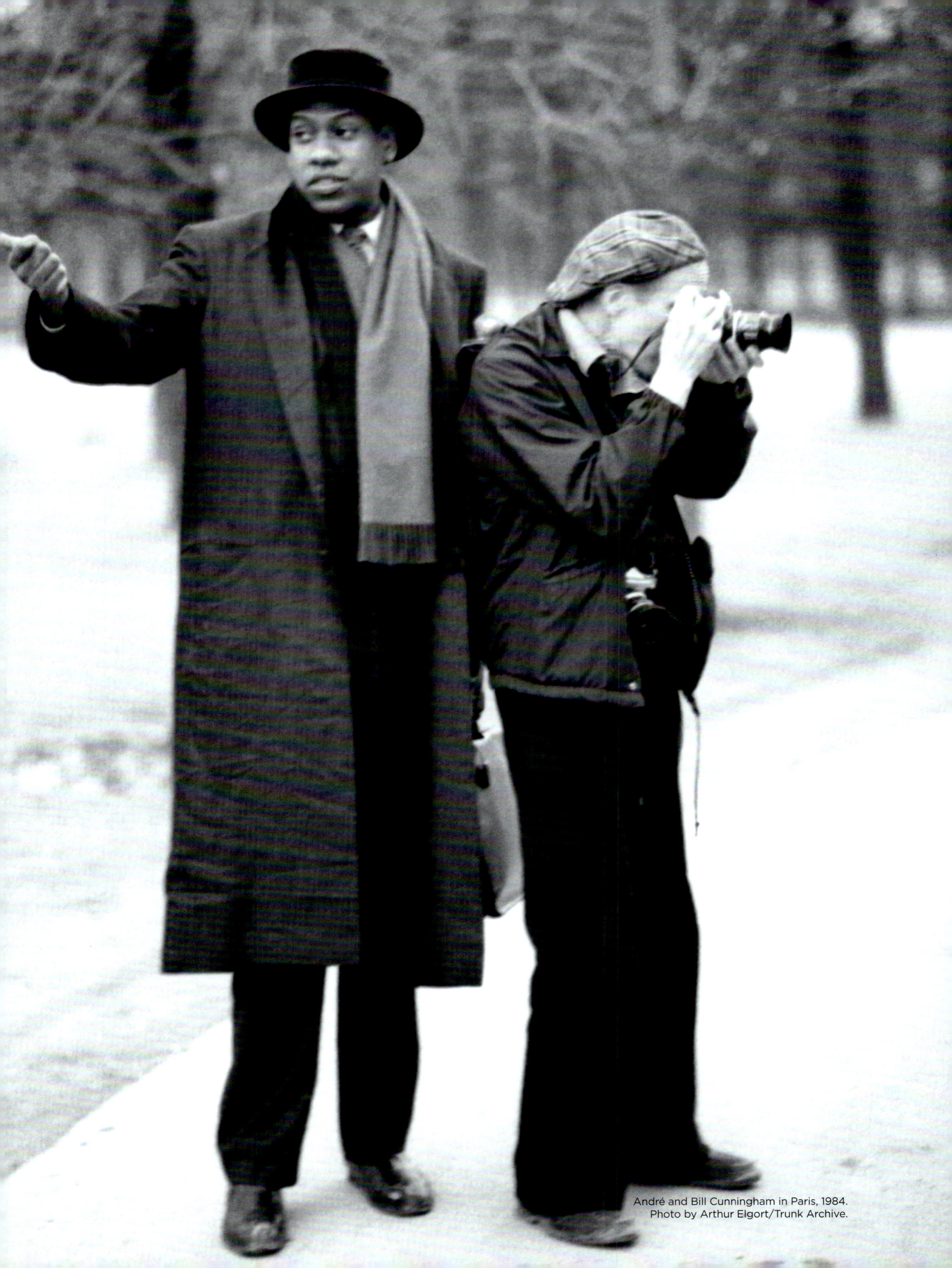

André and Bill Cunningham in Paris, 1984.
Photo by Arthur Elgort/Trunk Archive.

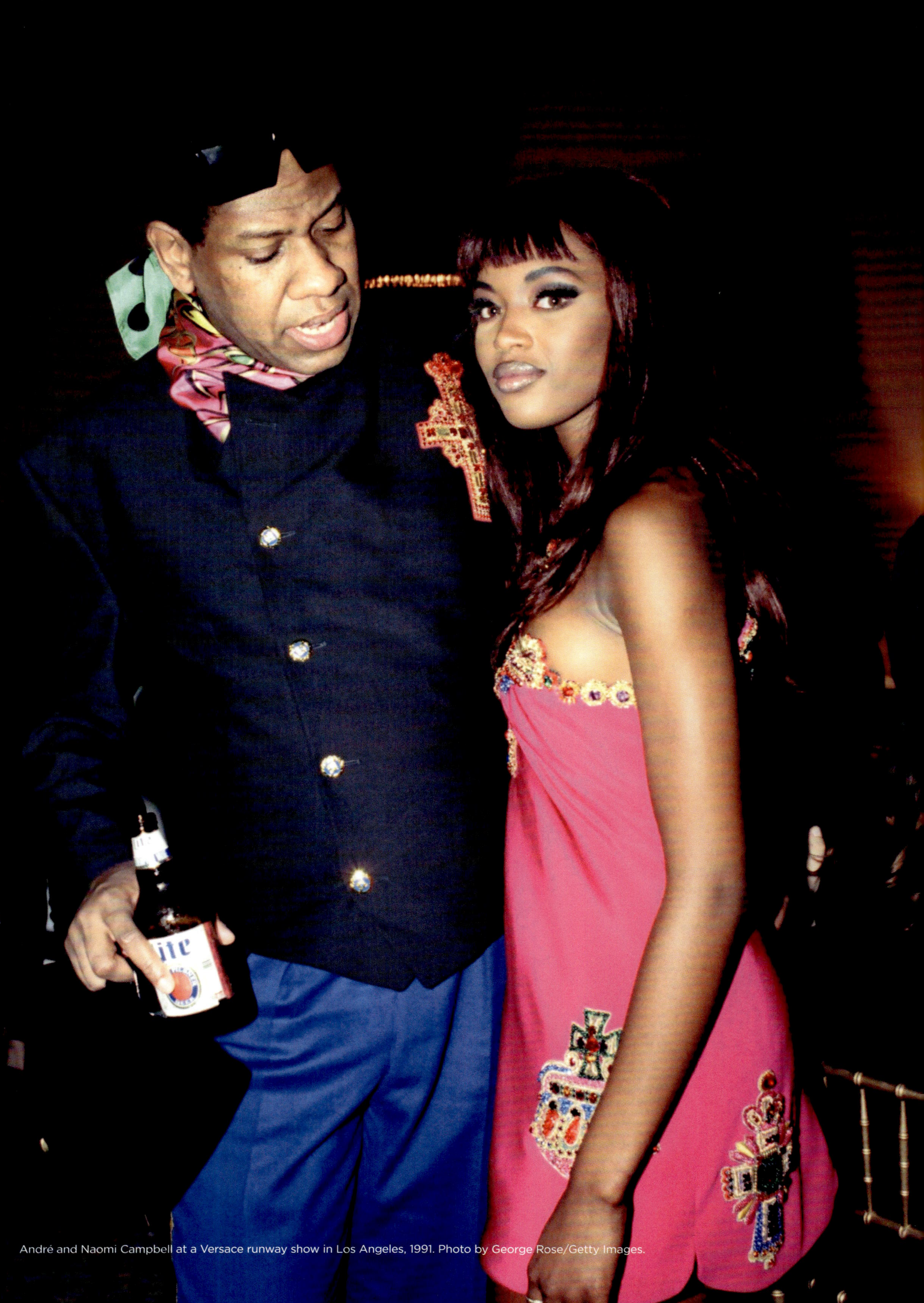

André and Naomi Campbell at a Versace runway show in Los Angeles, 1991. Photo by George Rose/Getty Images.

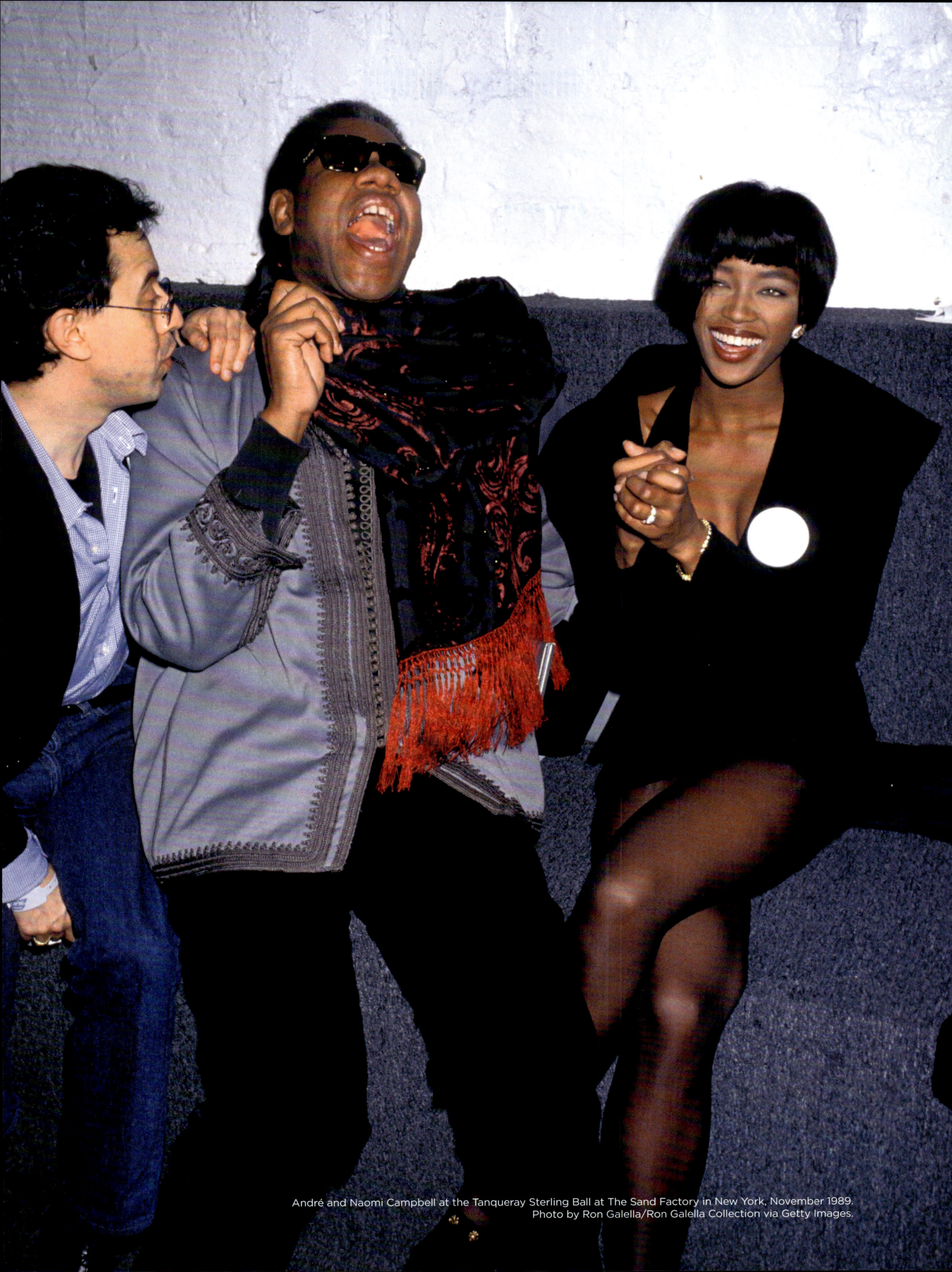

André and Naomi Campbell at the Tanqueray Sterling Ball at The Sand Factory in New York, November 1989.
Photo by Ron Galella/Ron Galella Collection via Getty Images.

ANDRÉ AND SCAD: THE IMMORTALITY OF INFLUENCE

Paula Wallace

Late on a Tuesday night in January 2022, I got the call that André Leon Talley — fashion's truest oracle, heir to James Baldwin and Alice Walker, a Goliath of intellect and influence with a wondrous heart — was gone. Many know of his legendary, picaresque career with Diana Vreeland at The Metropolitan Museum of Art's Costume Institute, Andy Warhol at The Factory, Anna Wintour at *Vogue*, the New York days and Paris nights, turning heads in his caftan and bejeweled turban, his gift for language, his long reign as fashion's kingmaker, his columns and covers that altered cultural history. For me, André was much more: a treasured friend and ally who profoundly shaped the Savannah College of Art and Design, where we first met a quarter-century ago.

By then, I had been reading his *Vogue* column for years and invited him in 2001 to receive a Lifetime Achievement Award at our annual SCAD fashion show. Knowing André loved spectacle, we greeted him at the airport with a gospel choir singing "Swing Low, Sweet Chariot."

"A choir of angels! My jaw is officially on the tarmac!" he said, laughing in that unmistakable voice, earthy and deep and supersonic all at once.

André loved SCAD, and we loved him right back, fusing his creative obsessions and fascinations with a Southern setting that reminded him of home. He once told me that when he welcomed guests to SCAD, he always prioritized a pilgrimage with them to the Candler Oak, one of the region's oldest living landmarks, growing for 300 years in front of what is now the Deloitte Foundry of SCAD.

"You can feel the voices in the branches," he mused lovingly, "in the elegant, almost crinoline-like bounce of the branches, the decades, the years."

He spoke in poetry, even over email, rhythm and color in every syllable. Like his favorite Savannah tree, André's presence was larger than life, towering and regal and imbued with wisdom and grace.

André befriended everyone at SCAD, especially our students, with whom he loved to hold court before runway shows, after film screenings, or in the midst of exhibitions he curated for the university. He shared his breadth of knowledge democratically across majors: fashion, writing, photography, graphic design, accessory design, furniture design, jewelry, art history. He led students on frequent trips across the world for atelier visits with elite designers who hired — and continue to hire — SCAD graduates, and he summoned a train of luminaries to SCAD: Tom Ford, Miuccia Prada, Stephen Burrows, Marc Jacobs, Vera Wang, Ruben and Isabel Toledo, Manolo Blahnik, Oscar de la Renta, Vivienne Westwood, Diane von Furstenberg. These legends crossed oceans and continents at his invitation, soon finding themselves under the happy enchantment of SCAD students, drawn to their unfettered imagination and all-enveloping *joie de vivre*.

André's boundless enthusiasm for our university led to his longtime service on the SCAD Board of Trustees (2002–2014) and, through his encouragement, to memorable gifts for the SCAD Permanent Collection from so many, including Pat Altschul and Anna Wintour, whose own tribute you can find in these pages. He introduced SCAD to writers like Robin Givhan and Maureen Dowd and to Darren Walker at the Ford Foundation, resulting in generous support for SCAD museums.

We created so many beautiful collaborations together: SCAD exhibitions, books (including *Little Black Dress*, a perennial favorite), and films like *Ovation for Oscar*, a documentary

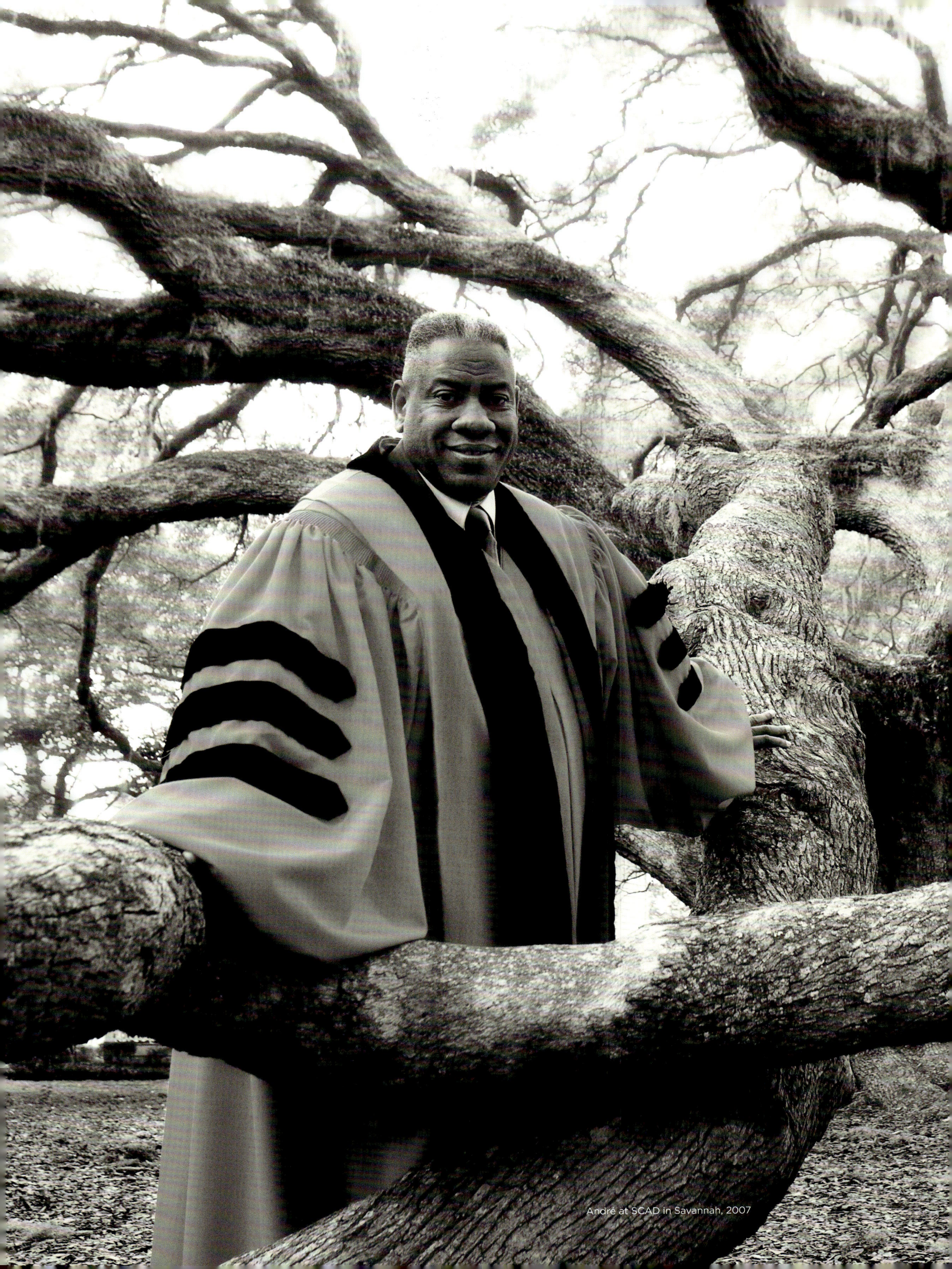

André at SCAD in Savannah, 2007

tribute to Oscar de la Renta starring André and SCAD students as they prepared an exhibition honoring the designer's life and legacy—winning Best Fashion Documentary at the London Fashion Film Festival.

Like so many brilliant creatives, André blazed with wonder, curious and open to every new experience. One year during the SCAD Savannah Film Festival, on a halcyon afternoon, André, who, in his later years, found walking difficult, said how perfect it would be to ride a bike around Savannah's Forsyth Park. An hour later, we'd found him an enormous red tricycle. "Très chic!" he said as he rang the little bell and pedaled around the park, giddy, laughing, happy.

When André set foot near the runway, he was supernaturally gifted, missing nothing, his keen eye roving, taking everything in: details he would later remember with remarkable precision from his encyclopedic, photographic memory. In one of his many letters, he confided in me with impish glee and a note of pride: "Oral history is all I have. I never take notes or write journals. I have never taken a notebook to a fashion show!" He evinced this same gift time and again over the years, including at SCAD fashion shows. His astute recall was wizardly. I was fortunate to attend several shows at his invitation over the years: Oscar de la Renta, Valentino, Marc Jacobs, Chanel, the Dior show at Versailles. In New York, he invited me to one of his "Miu Miu Musings," a series of parlor discussions right out of Bloomsbury.

My fondest moments with André took place in SCAD's Magnolia Cottage, where, after long days of studio visits with students, he and I would retreat to watch films until the wee hours. I made truffle popcorn and André chose the films, movies like Tallulah Bankhead's *Lifeboat* or Joan Crawford's *The Women*. Those evenings together, discussing film, fashion, history, and education, were magical. He was a movie date nonpareil and truly had a teacher's heart. Once, after a screening of *The Gospel According to André* at SCAD Atlanta, he held forth onstage for hours, taking selfies with at least a hundred eager students, making each one feel heard and seen.

I sometimes wonder why he chose SCAD as the beneficiary of his love and learning. I think he found here the outward manifestation of all the worlds that lived inside him. SCAD was André's happy place, the marriage of Southern charm (evoking the best of his childhood in North Carolina) to a design sensibility, cosmopolitan taste, and the everlasting pursuit of wisdom. He rejoiced in the warmth of the Georgia sun and hospitable nature of our community. We were kindred. Family. He often called SCAD his "Zen zone of divine wonder." And he loved dressing to the nines when he was on campus: custom suits, capes, and turbans. When our Bees remarked with awe and curiosity about his wardrobe, André beamed: "I always bring the jewels out of the vault for my SCAD!"

When I created the André Leon Talley Gallery at the SCAD Museum of Art—a moment of prodigious joy for my dear friend; he cheerfully referred to it as his "wing" of the museum—he made even more visits to campus to collaborate with our curators and teach lessons about the meaning and import of true luxury. (André often said his definition of luxury was "crisp white sheets on the clothesline, blown dry by the breeze and warmed by the sun.")

His vast wardrobe served as fitting armor for André, and his sanctuary, his tabernacle. When I proposed an exhibition of his personal collection of garments and accessories, a veritable encyclopedia of twentieth- and twenty-first-century design, he agreed: "It must be done," he said. André often reminded me of his wish that many of his most celebrated looks would live forever in the SCAD Permanent Collection and that the SCAD Museum of Art would present an exhibition for the benefit of countless future SCAD students and museum guests. He never stopped thinking about our Bees.

So often over the years, countless alumni have written to me about how much André's presence at SCAD meant to them, including designer Bradley Bowers, who wrote of the courage he drew from experiencing "the magnificent force of nature that he personified." André, he said, gave others hope "to be themselves fearlessly and unapologetically."

In 2008, SCAD awarded André an honorary doctorate, and he wore his new title and regalia (in his signature cardinal red) with pride. "If I can help others," he once said, "then my life will not have been in vain." This catalogue is a testament to his gift for sharing his brilliance with new generations of designers—Dr. André Leon Talley, a teacher forevermore. He famously did not take notes, but we did (along with many sumptuous images), and here memorialize his manifold gifts and storied life.

After his passing, per his Last Will and Testament, he posthumously invited SCAD curators into his hallowed sanctum of closets—teeming with bespoke mantles, caftans, impeccably tailored suiting, a magnificent menagerie he loved—and we assembled a panoply of André's most iconic looks, which you find here immortalized.

André's plentitude of treasured possessions featured in this book now belong to SCAD students for all time, so that all who visit SCAD museums can step into the wardrobe of fashion's knightly bon vivant: Charlemagne of the Chiffon Trenches. His life and legacy eternally endure at SCAD, his influence as immortal now as my dear friend's sensitive soul. A legend for the ages.

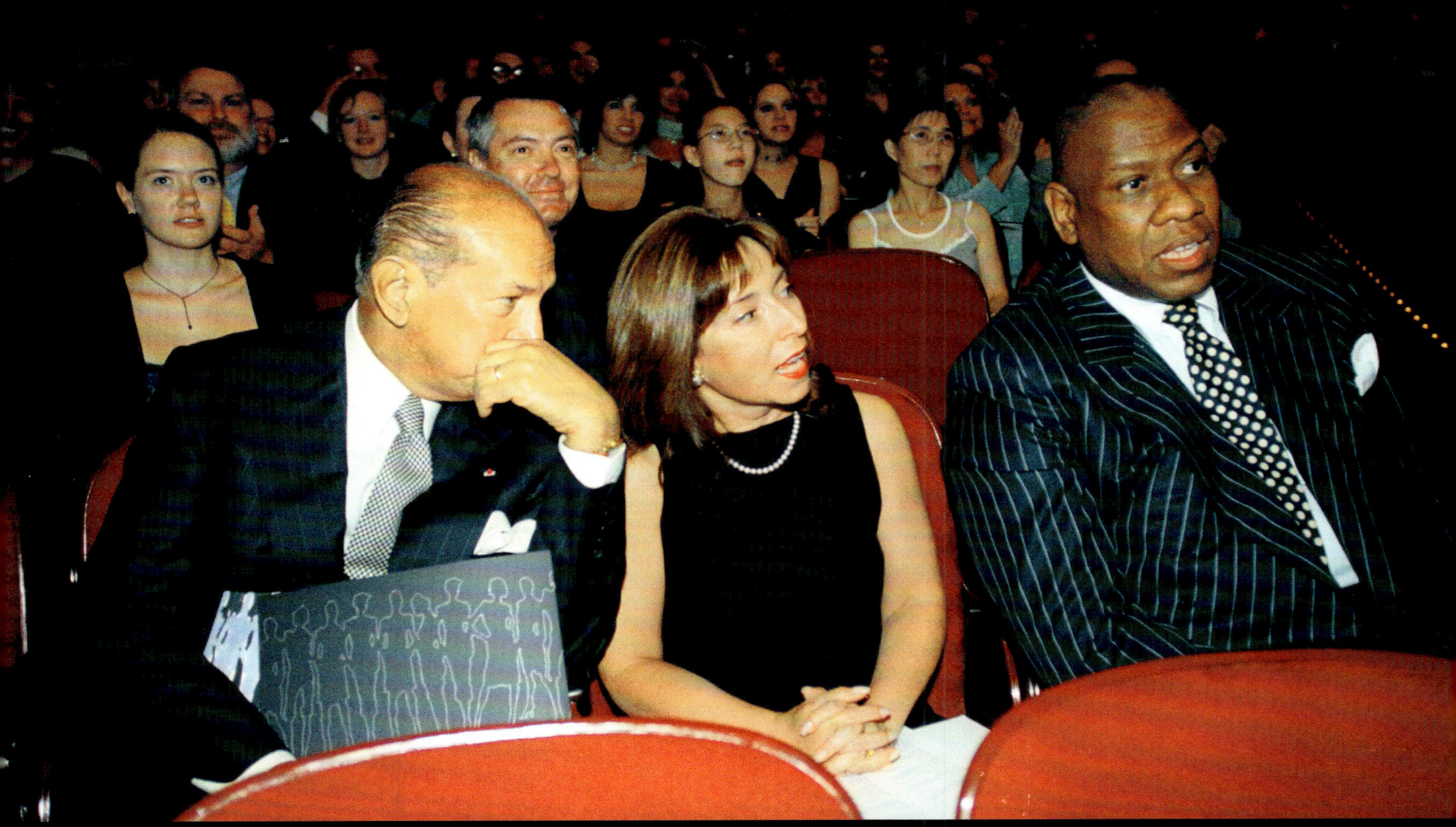

André at the annual SCAD fashion show in 2001 with Oscar de la Renta and Paula Wallace

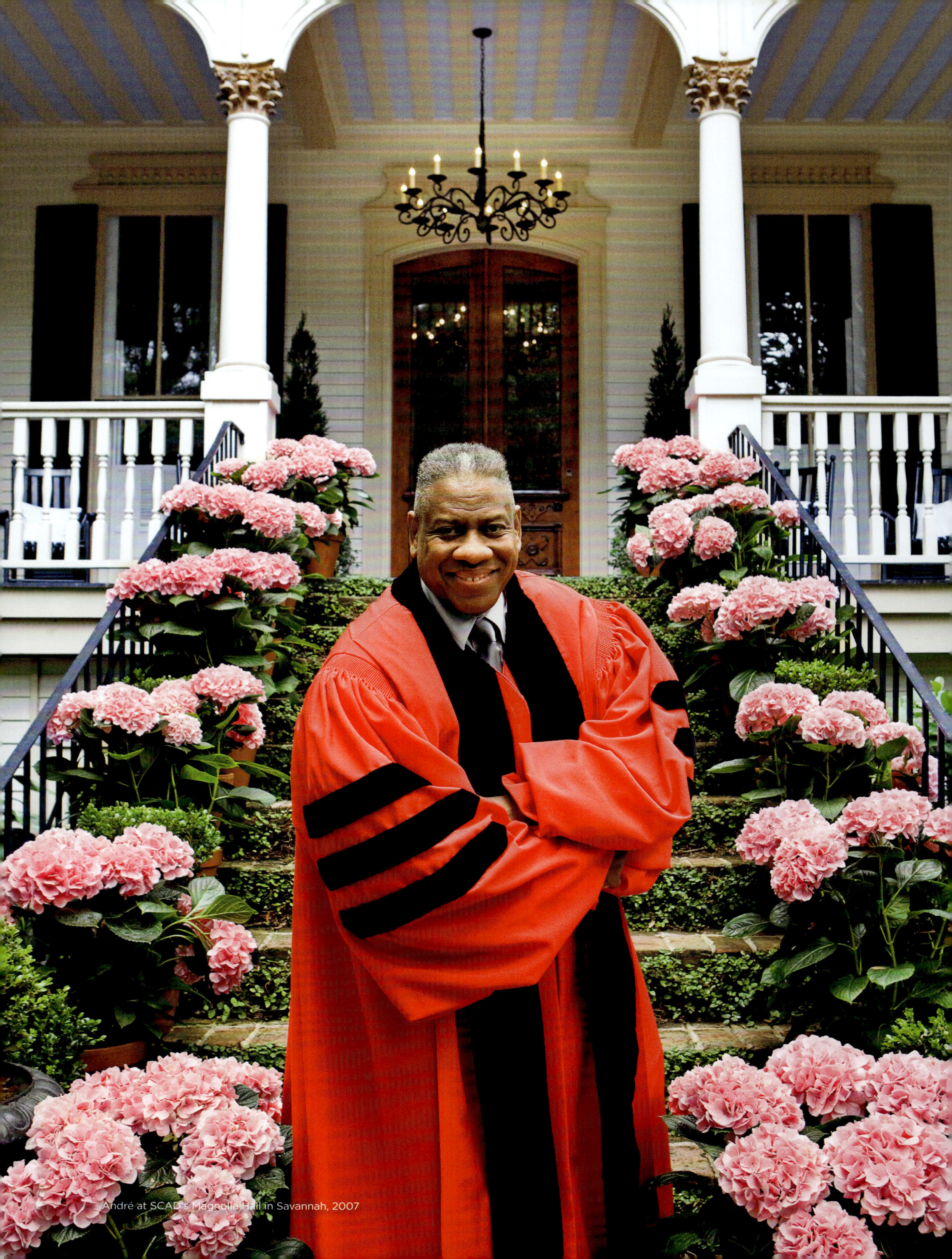

André at SCAD's Magnolia Hall in Savannah, 2007

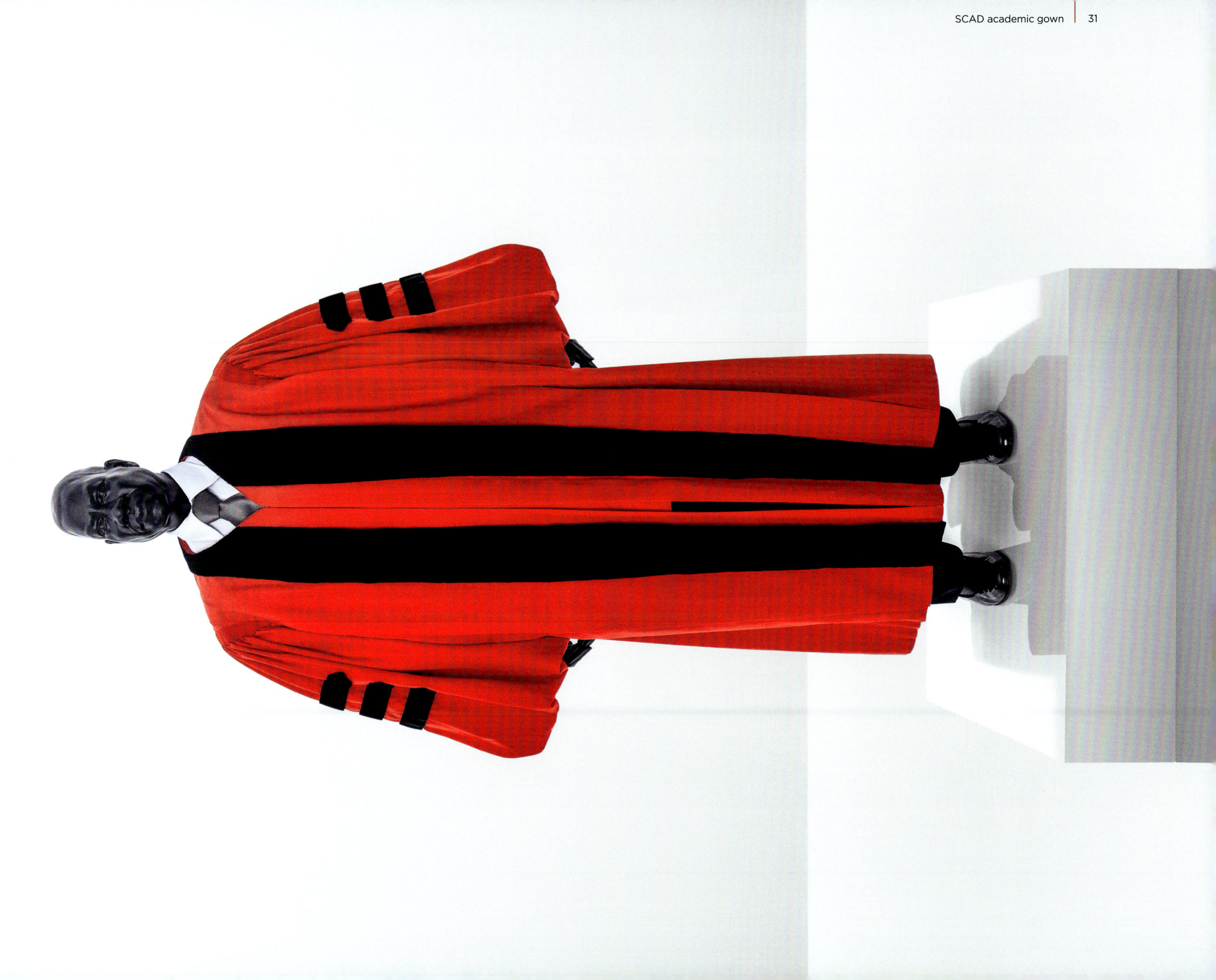

SCAD academic gown

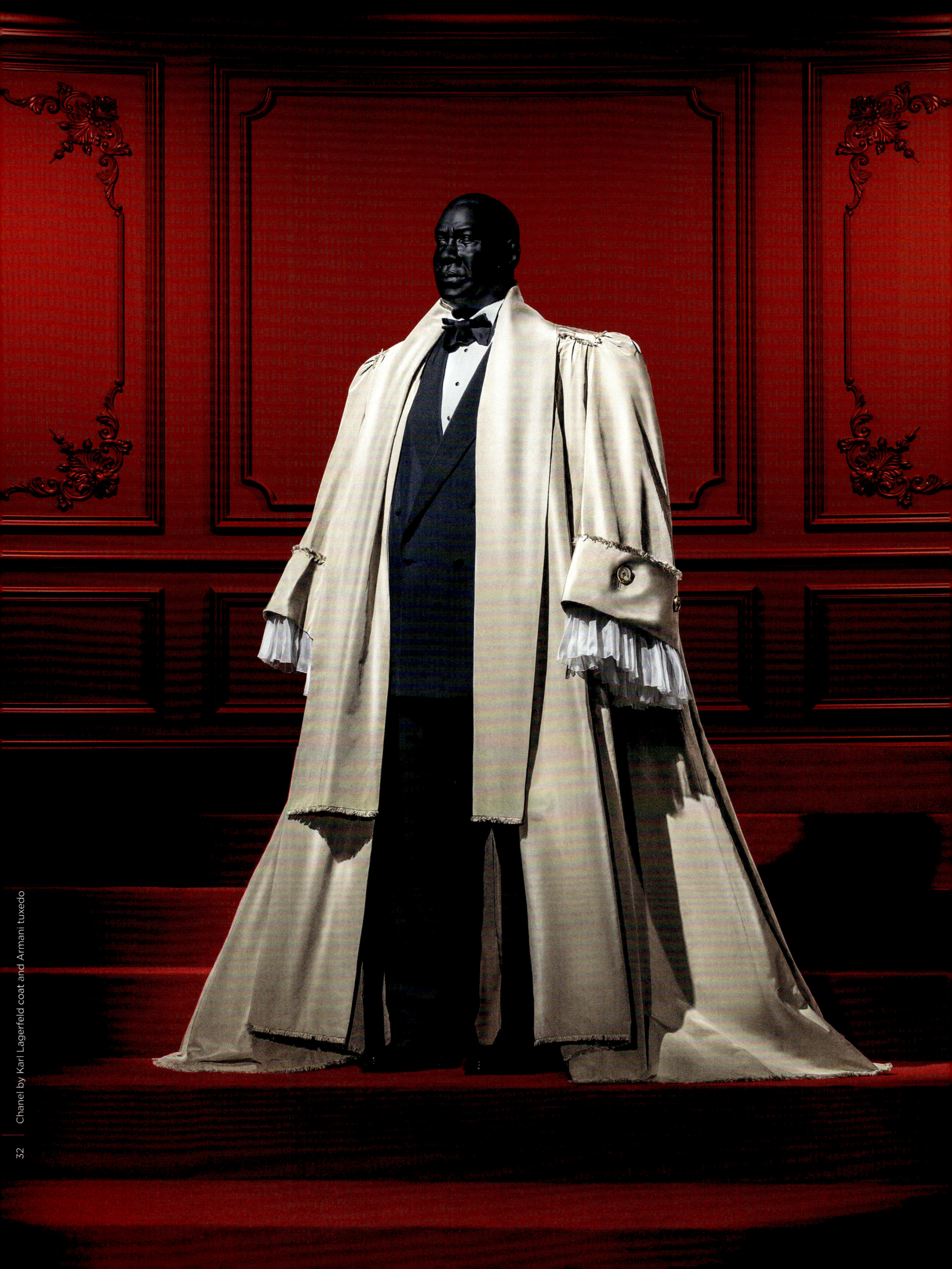

Chanel by Karl Lagerfeld coat and Armani tuxedo

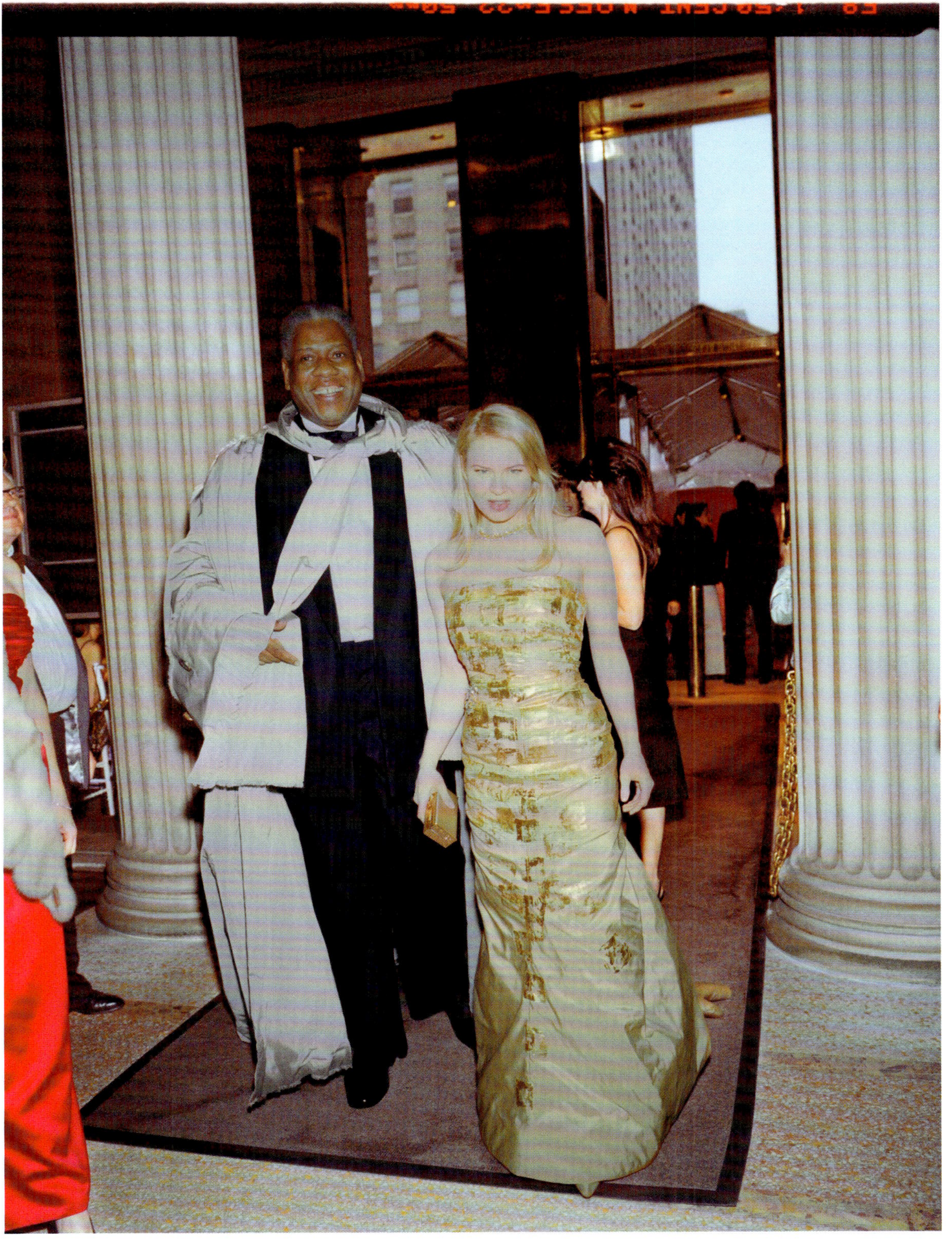

André and Renée Zellweger arriving at the Met Gala for *Dangerous Liaisons: Fashion and Furniture in the Eighteenth Century*, May 2004. Photo by Robert Fairer.

Hand-painted eighteenth-century button

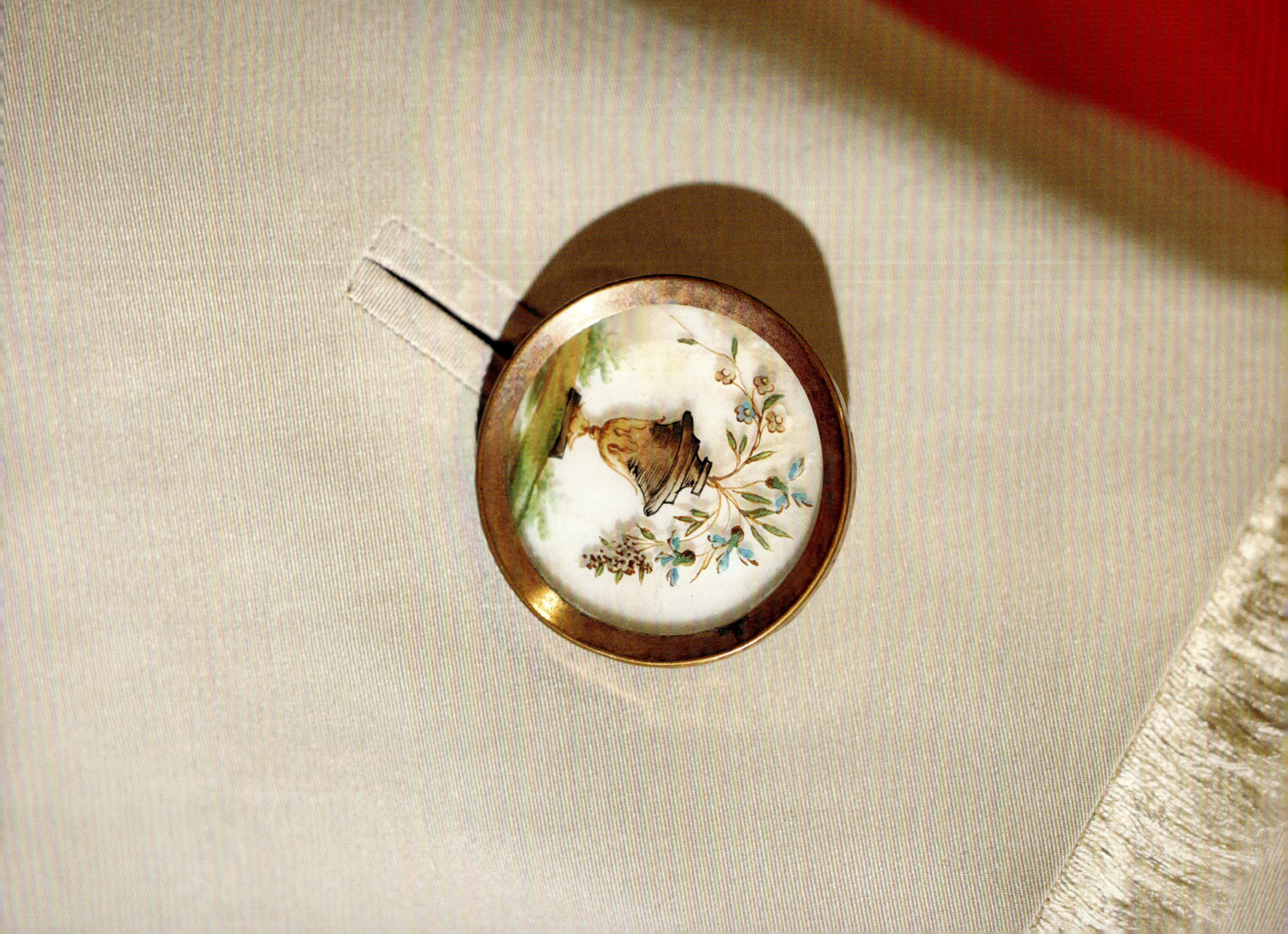

“

You had to hire André. He was the only person who knew **more about fashion** than I do.

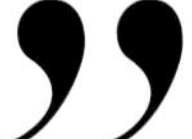

DIANA VREELAND

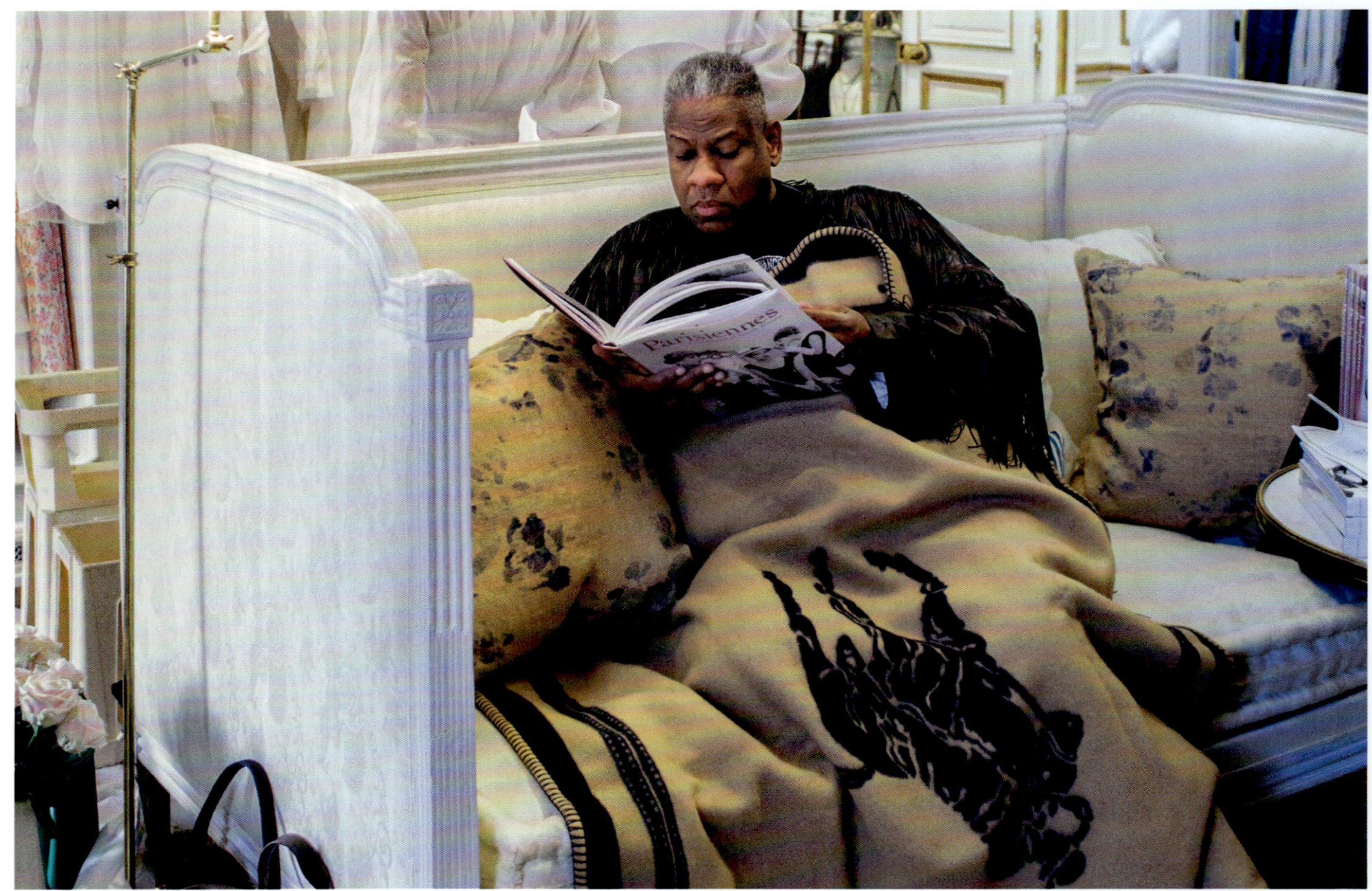

André at Ralph Lauren in Paris on assignment for *Vogue*, April 2010. Photo by Robert Fairer.

FASHIONING A LEGACY

Antoine Gregory

In the world of fashion, where trends come and go, there are rare figures whose presence transcends style, becoming a beacon of culture, resilience, and change. André Leon Talley, the legendary trailblazer and first Black creative director and editor at large of *Vogue* magazine, is one such figure. Born in North Carolina in the 1940s, Talley beat a path from the rural, segregated U.S. South to the upper echelons of the fashion industry, earning his place as a formidable icon. Produced on the occasion of *André Leon Talley: Style Is Forever*, this catalogue is dedicated to André's life and the gift of his wardrobe to the Savannah College of Art and Design. More than just a collection of clothing, this gift—like the exhibition and catalogue it has inspired—is a testament to a life lived boldly, unapologetically, and with a profound understanding of fashion and its power to reshape the world.

Fashion is many things, but most of all, it is a connector of communities and their shared stories—the celebration and commemoration of our lives and the visual voice of our people. It is a way to document the present, preserve the past, and design the future. As André once eloquently expressed, "Fashion is not just about looking pretty. It's about looking forward." His life was a reflection of this philosophy. André did not merely participate in fashion, he embodied it, transforming the way we understand and interact with clothing. For André, fashion was a language—a way to communicate identity, challenge dogmas, and assert self-hood in spaces that often sought to marginalize people like him. He used fashion as a tool to push boundaries and craft narratives that were as rich and complex as the garments he wore. André's way of navigating in the fashion world was a revolutionary act that he carried with great honor. He resisted industry norms not just by his position but by the sheer force of his personality and the depth of his knowledge. He brought a generosity to fashion that extended beyond aesthetics, infusing it with history, art, and a nuanced understanding of culture. Through his work, he evolved fashion from commodity to a form of social dialogue that could speak to issues of race, representation, and empowerment.

André wielded fashion as both a shield and a weapon. Every piece of clothing was deliberate. Each garment was a carefully chosen armor that allowed him to navigate and conquer spaces that were, at times, hostile to his very existence. The dramatic capes that enveloped him were his fortress, a barrier between himself and a world that didn't always understand his brilliance. His custom-made clothes, including the many caftans of his later years, referenced the regal robes of kings and the garb of Roman statesmen, invoking a sense of formality. In the rooms where few who looked like him held any power, and on his body, André's clothes were a declaration of sovereignty over his identity.

Through his style, André taught us that clothing is not just what we wear — it is how we present our hopes and dreams to the world, how we challenge perceptions, and how we leave our mark. It is a reflection of ourselves that we get to choose. As he poignantly remarked, "You can be aristocratic without having been born into an aristocratic family." For him, this idea wasn't about wealth or status. It was about a state of mind, a way of presenting oneself with dignity, elegance, and confidence regardless of background. In an industry that often prioritized lineage and exclusivity, André defied those standards. He proved that true aristocracy lies in one's bearing and ability to command space. Through his grand opulence and intellectual mastery of fashion history, he demonstrated that aristocracy was not something inherited but something earned through an unwavering commitment to self-expression and authenticity.

André's archives chronicle his own history — and not only by way of aesthetics. André's history is also evident in the circle of designers who crafted his garments, among them longtime friends and colleagues. Many of his shoes were by Manolo Blahnik, a friend he vacationed with on Fire Island and danced with on the parquet floors of Studio 54. The garment André wore to the 2004 Met Gala, an imposing taffeta trench coat with iridescent plissé pleated cuffs emerging from the sleeves, was a custom Chanel design by Karl Lagerfeld — a close friend and decades-long collaborator who, even after the two had a falling out, continued to ask after André. And the names go on: Dapper Dan, the Harlem-based couturier who, through a partnership with Gucci, offered up caftans in rich golden brocades, as well as designers like Tom Ford and Miuccia Prada, who have both spoken about the valued messages André would write to them after their runway shows each season. Through André's clothes, a network of influential creatives is found, bound by this singular figure.

But more than that, through this archive I got to see André the person: the young boy from the Jim Crow South whose style was inherited and nurtured by the women in his life, and who — because of his grandmother Bennie Frances Davis and dear friend Diana Vreeland — believed in the power of dressing. Through the faith these women placed in him, André built upon the foundation of wearing your Sunday best, even if it wasn't Sunday. In his garments, I was able to better understand his triumphs and his tragedies — how the voluminous silhouettes were as much a weapon to take up space as they were a shielding mechanism for his fluctuating weight.

I felt a closeness to André — one that, in many ways, I had always felt. They say you should never meet your heroes and, for the most part, I do believe that. But André was bigger, louder, and better dressed than any hero I've ever had. I looked up to André not just for his sartorial genius but for the way he carried his Blackness with so much pride and resilience. And, of course, with no famine of beauty. The way in which he lived was an example that I, too, could be the maker of my own life. I could decide who I wanted to be in this world of fashion and beyond. In André, I see my biggest dreams but also my greatest fears.

Though his choices were often subtle, I came to understand their profoundness. From designer to fabric, everything had a place and a reason — even in the smallest details, like the buttons of a coat in a hand-painted still life design. Clothing, as André showed us, is not just something we put on; it's something that lives with us, moves with us, and shapes the people we want to be. I am only one keeper of his legacy, which extends far beyond the pages of *Vogue*, the red-carpeted stairs of the Met Gala, or the runways of New York, Paris, Milan, and London. His legacy lives on in every young Black boy, like myself, who dares to exist in an industry that not so quietly lets us know *we do not belong*.

Documenting André's contributions to fashion in this archive is not the final mark of his life but a cultural keepsake for the next generation of fashion enthusiasts and all the generations behind them. His legacy will not be confined to the past. It is a living, breathing force that continues to inspire, to challenge, and to uplift. I thank André for what he has given me and the indelible mark he has left on an industry. I thank him for facing the "Chiffon Trenches," often alone, and surviving. It is because of this I am reminded to have hope — to never underestimate the power of our own presence and the limitless possibilities of what we can achieve.

My hope is that *you* are reminded of the joy of getting dressed and that clothing lives too. That you show up as your best self, embracing the boldness and elegance that André Leon Talley embodied so fiercely. Let the clothing you choose be an echo of his belief that style is a transformative act — a celebration of identity, history, and dreams.

Because that is what it means to be a fashion icon.

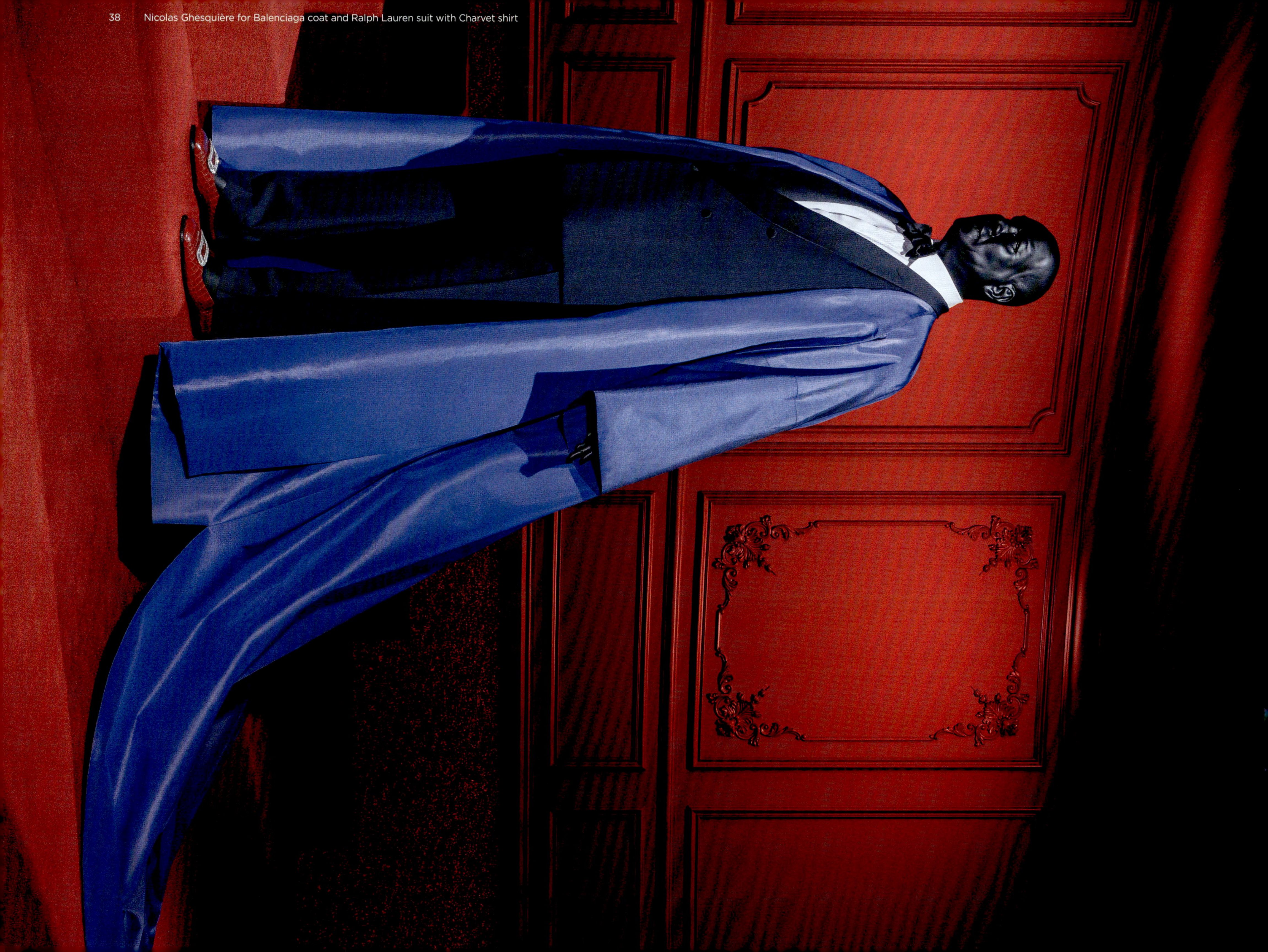

Nicolas Ghesquière for Balenciaga coat and Ralph Lauren suit with Charvet shirt

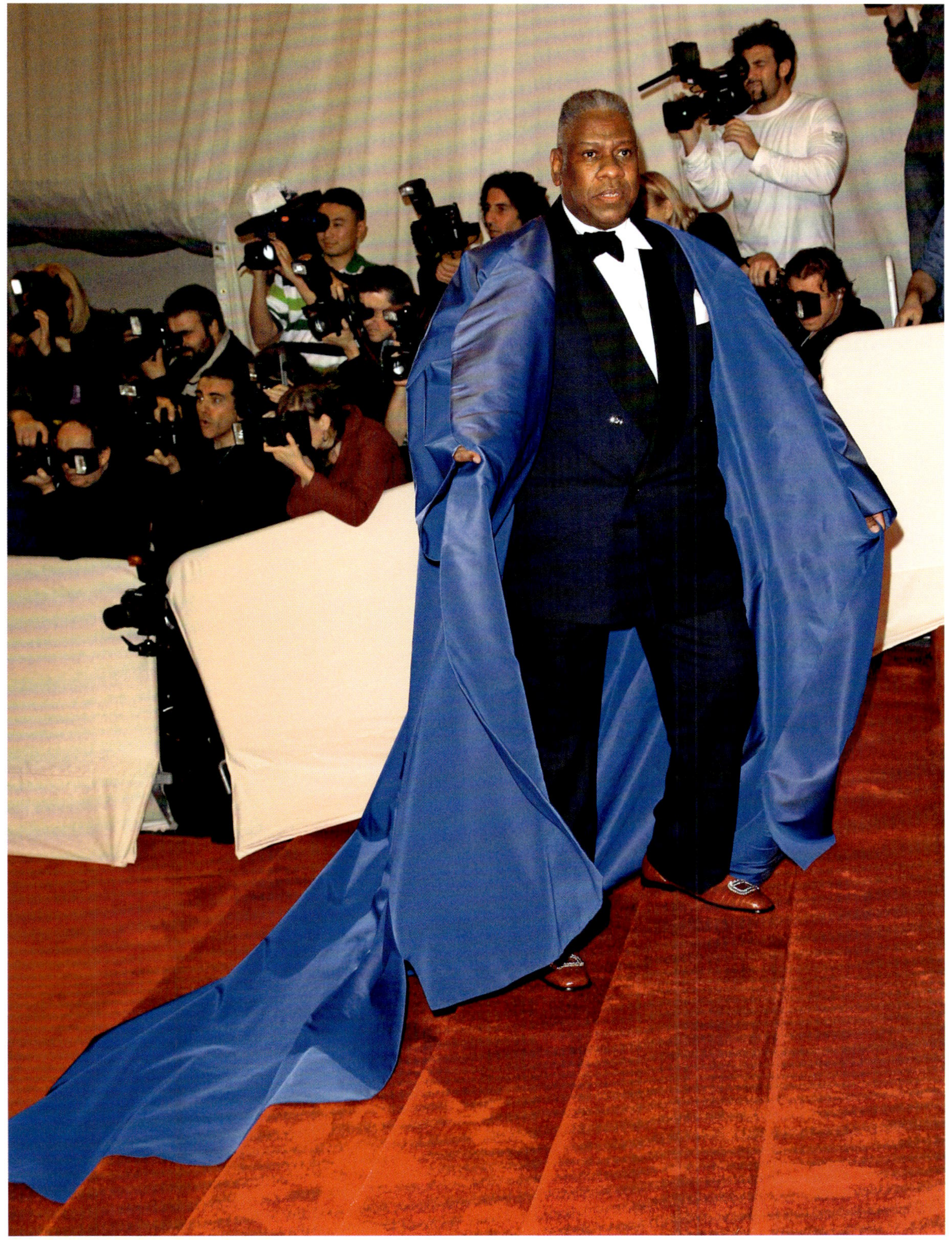

André at the Met Gala for *Alexander McQueen: Savage Beauty*, 2011. WENN Rights Ltd./Alamy Stock Photo.

No label coat and Chanel haute couture gown

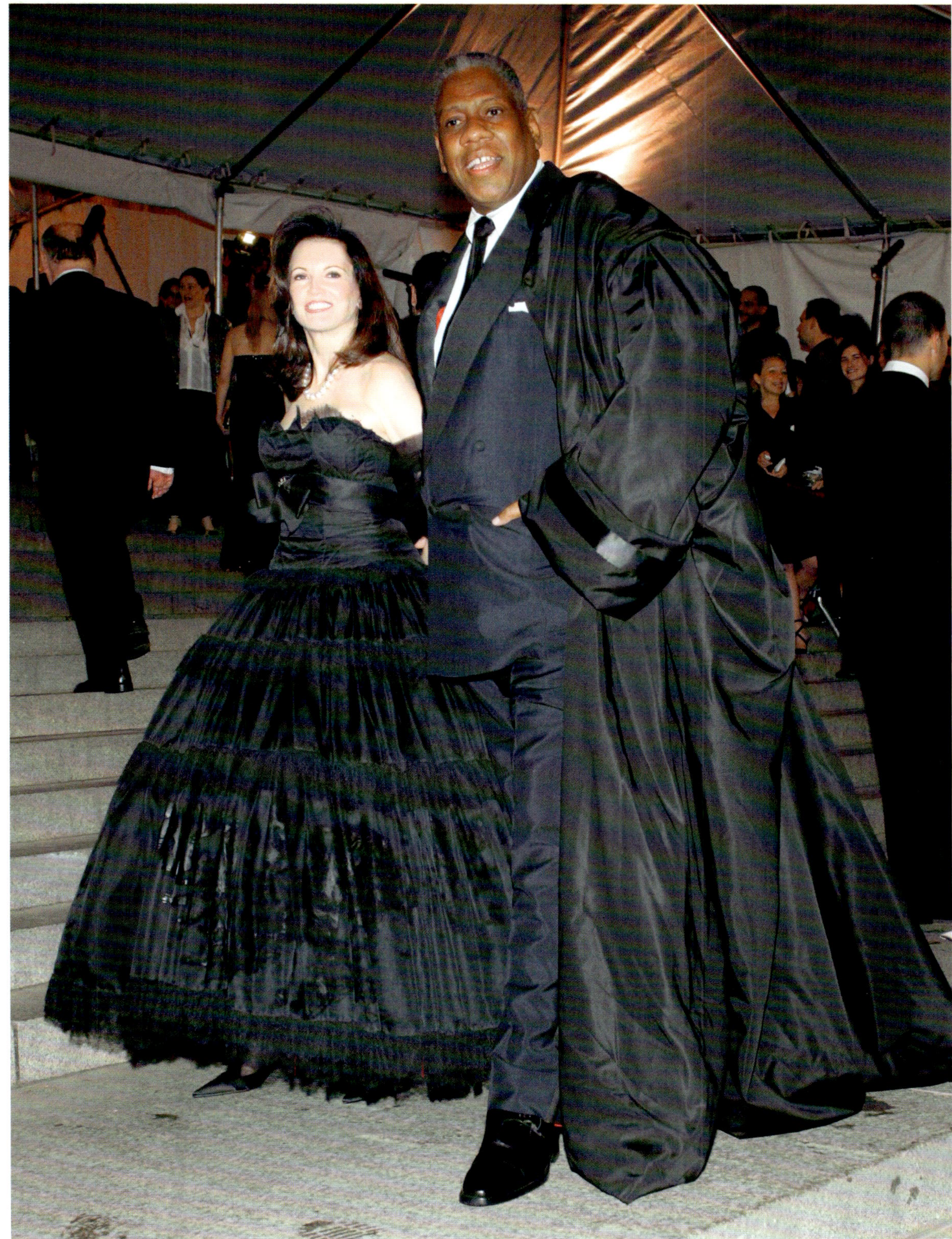

André escorting Patricia Altschul to the Met Gala, 2005. Photo by Steve Eichner/WWD/Penske Media via Getty Images.

Chanel by Karl Lagerfeld cape

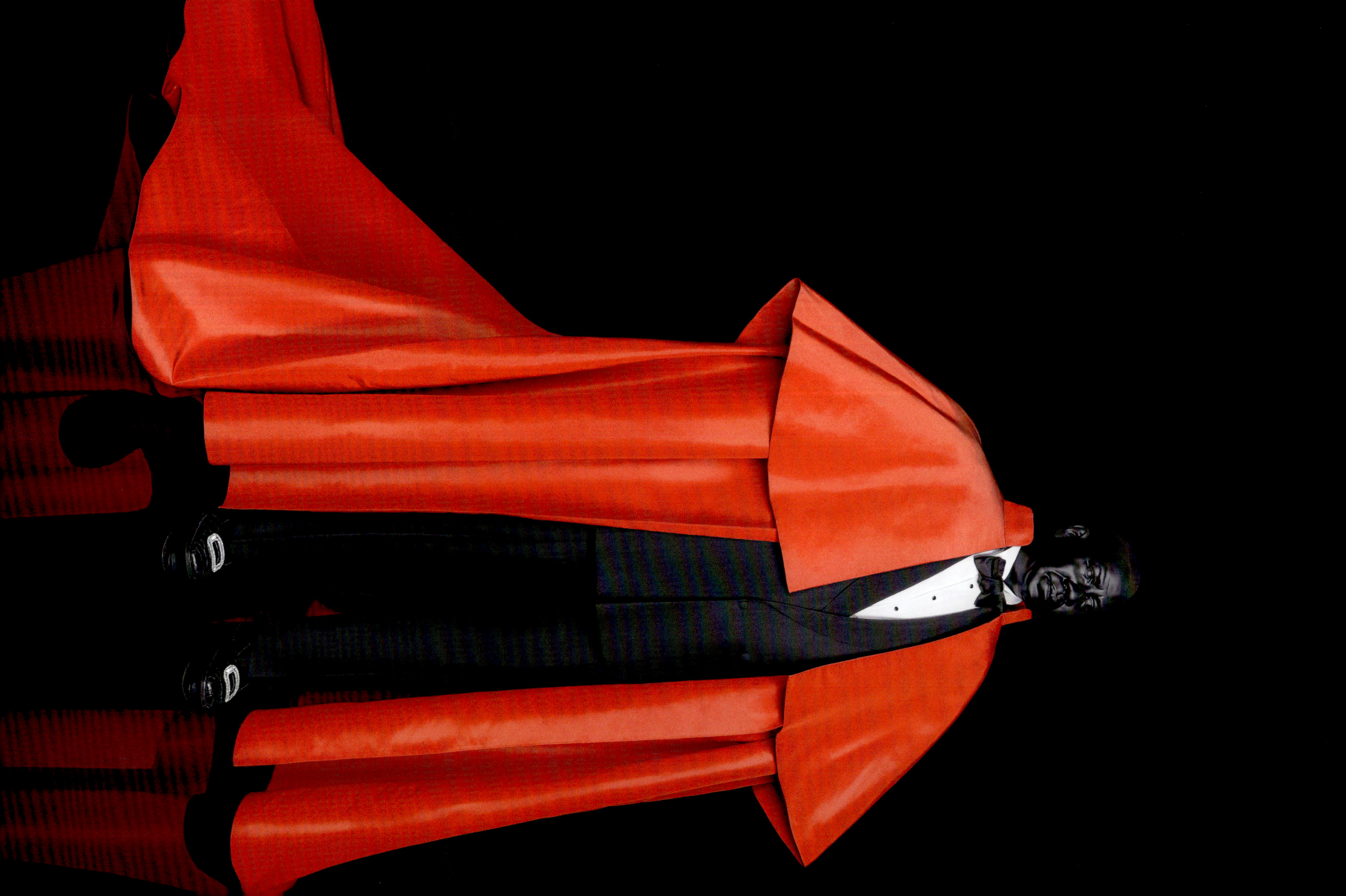

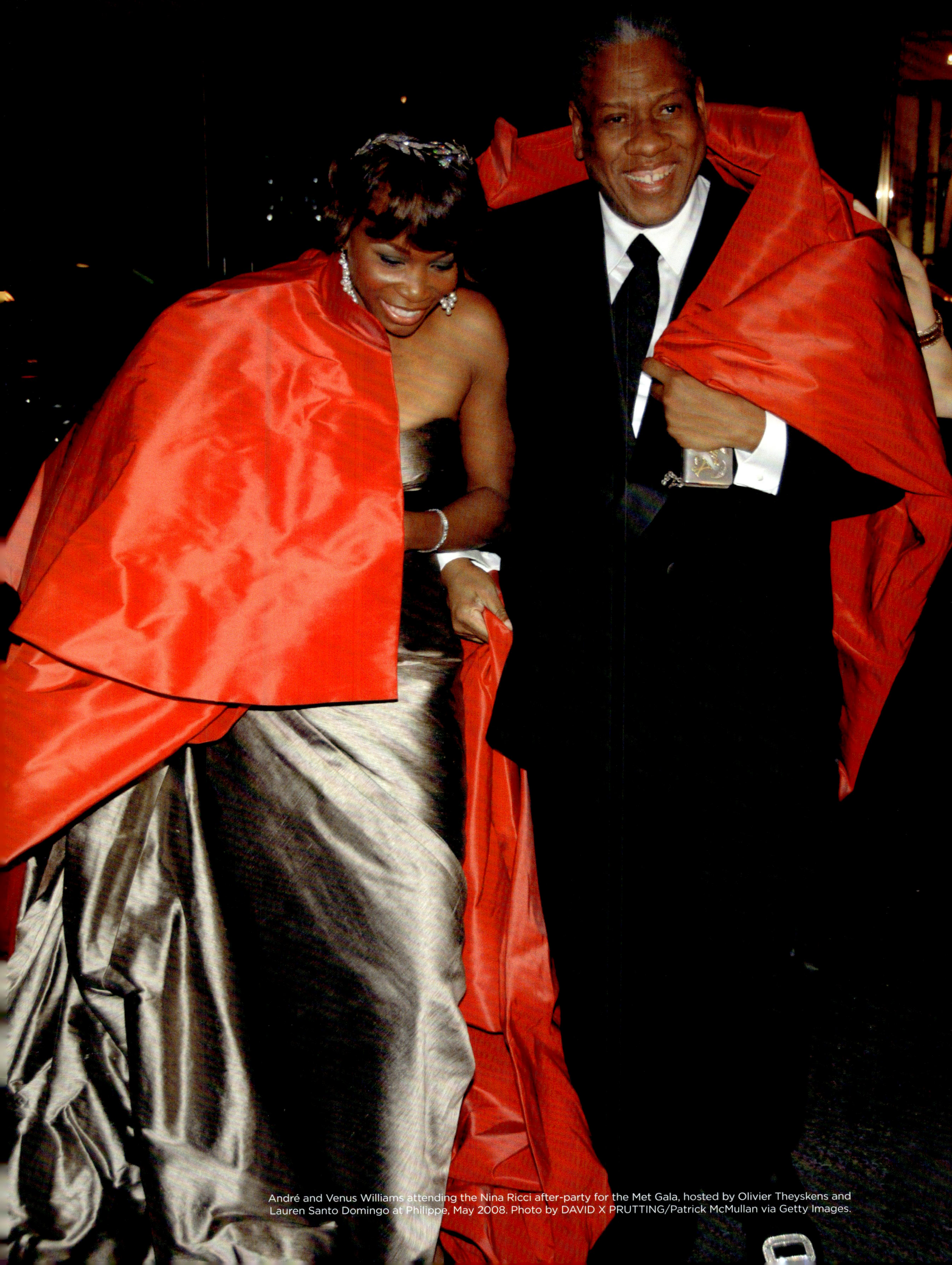

André and Venus Williams attending the Nina Ricci after-party for the Met Gala, hosted by Olivier Theyskens and Lauren Santo Domingo at Philippe, May 2008. Photo by DAVID X PRUTTING/Patrick McMullan via Getty Images.

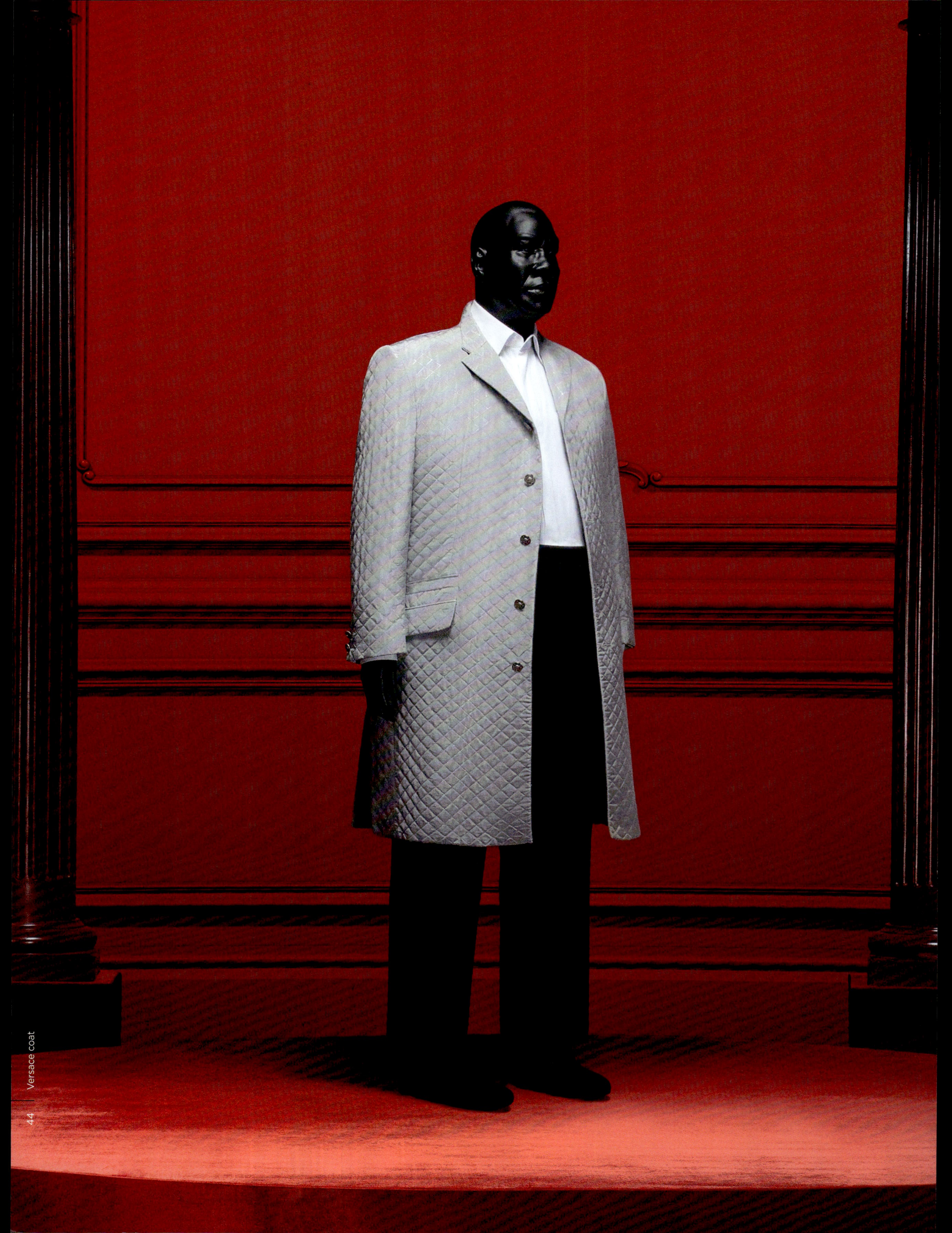

Versace coat

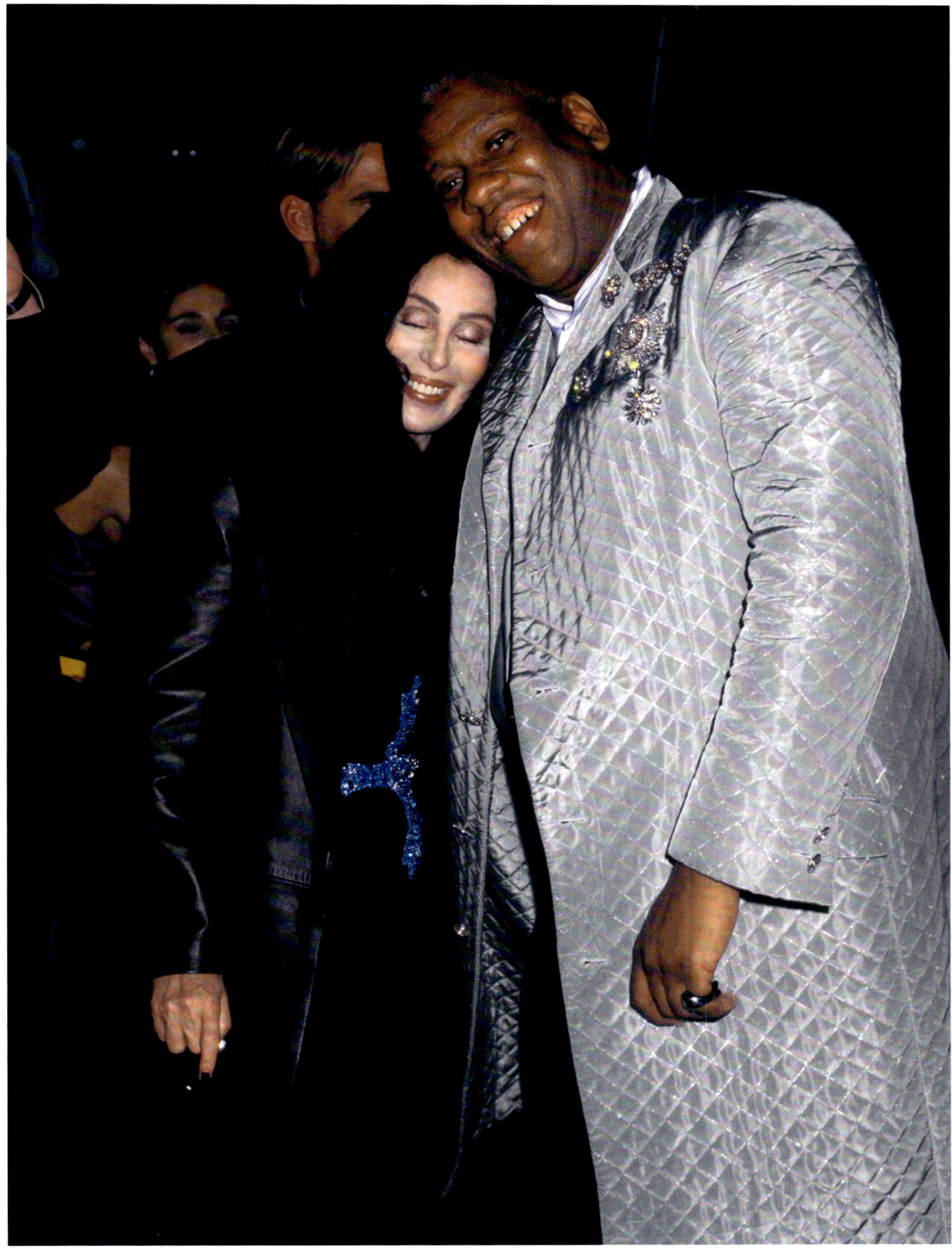

André and Cher attending the Met Gala for the Gianni Versace retrospective, December 1997.
Photo by Ron Galella/Ron Galella Collection via Getty Images.

GRAND GESTURES

Rafael Brauer Gomes

André Leon Talley was a titan of the fashion industry whose contributions to journalism, impeccable sense of style, exuberant personality, and willingness to speak his mind left an indelible mark on the world. André was, for me and many others, a profound influence and a guiding light. From the very beginning, our paths would frequently intertwine, especially during my years as archive director with Vivienne Westwood, when I was honored to work alongside him on a retrospective exhibition he was curating for the Savannah College of Art and Design.

André's relationship with SCAD was special. He found a warmth here, and he shared his knowledge and connections freely, invigorated by the energy of the students and the university community. Our Vivienne Westwood exhibition, *Dress Up Story—1990 Until Now*, opened at the SCAD Museum of Art in 2015, marking the beginning of a prolific collaboration. With André's mentorship, I was invited to join SCAD as the creative director of the university's new fashion museum in Atlanta. Working closely with André on exhibitions for SCAD over the years, I was constantly in awe of his passion and creativity. Our friendship was deeply rooted in a love for visual storytelling.

Before his passing in 2022, André and I were busy at work, pouring our hearts into planning an exhibition of his personal collection, spanning the most important designers and cultural moments of our time. André was particularly insistent that we create a catalogue to accompany the exhibition, emphasizing the importance of documenting history. In the wake of his passing, we were deeply honored to learn that André had bequeathed these cherished pieces to SCAD.

This exhibition and the catalogue André so enthusiastically envisioned serve in tribute to his genius, his enduring influence, and his unparalleled contributions to fashion. Each of the featured looks, accessories, and memorabilia exemplifies André's rarefied personal aesthetic. They also reveal the heart of his mutual respect and care for the designers who crafted them expressly for him.

André's dramatic capes and garments by Karl Lagerfeld for Chanel speak to the myriad common threads in the complex weaving of their friendship, holding layers of significance within their own relationship and within the histories of art and design. André's riches of caftans by Ralph Rucci luxuriate in their own synergistic appreciation for splendor and comfort, dazzling with their knowledge of craft. André's pride in his culture finds expression in several extraordinary garments by Tom Ford, Dapper Dan, John Galliano, Valentino, Diane von Furstenberg, and many other outstanding names. And André's "heaven on earth," Norma Kamali's candy-red sleeping bag coat, soothes the incomparable loss of our grandest friend.

André's legacy lives on in his brilliance, his elegance, and his unwavering devotion to beauty. He opened doors and created opportunities for countless among us, tirelessly advocating for our voices and our talents on a global platform—and he continues to inspire current and future generations, at SCAD and around the world, through his generosity. I firmly believe André secured immortality with everything he accomplished—a legend for all time. His spirit lives on in us.

He is a gift we will cherish forever.

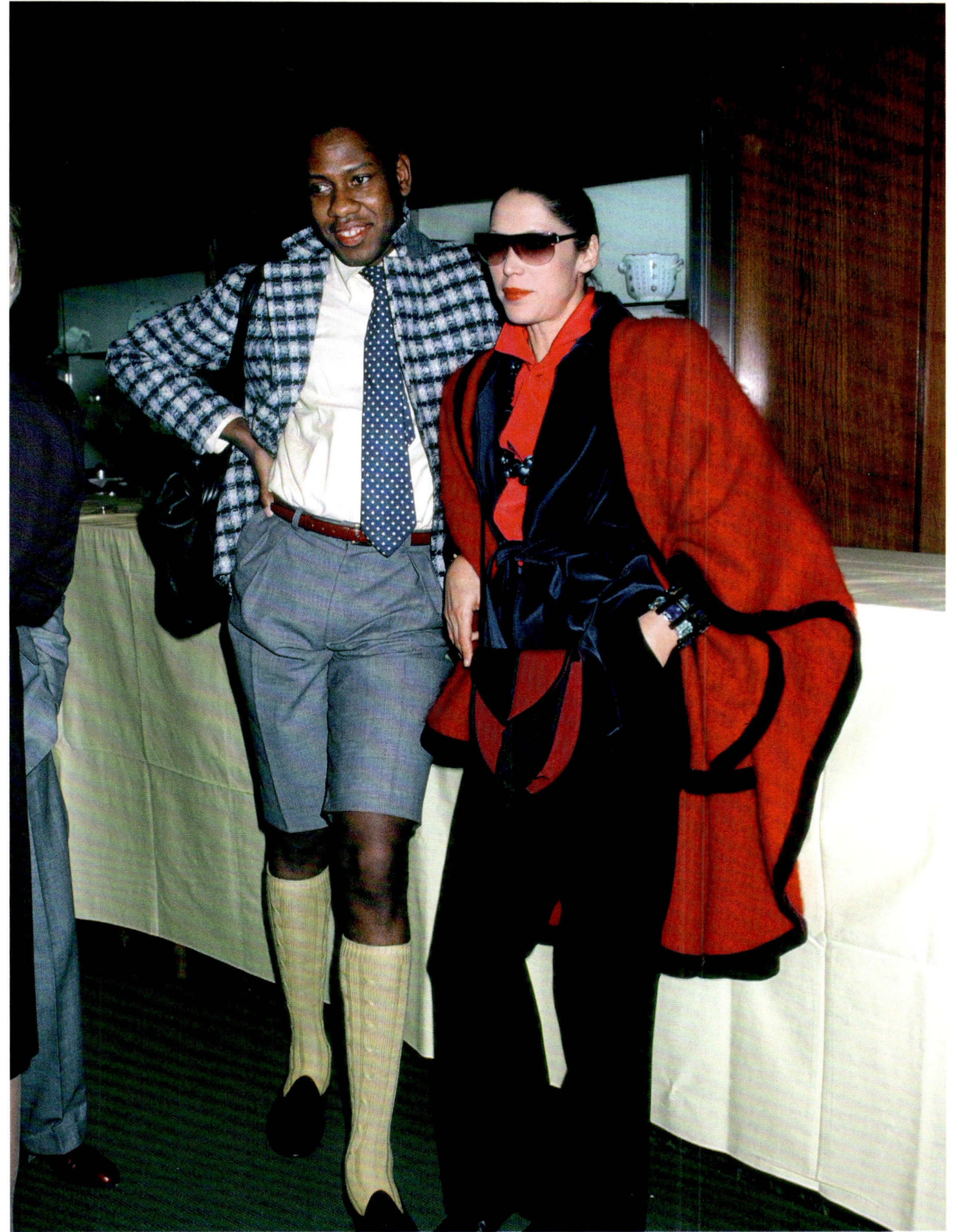

André and Marina Schiano in New York, c. 1980. Photo by PL Gould/IMAGES/Getty Images.

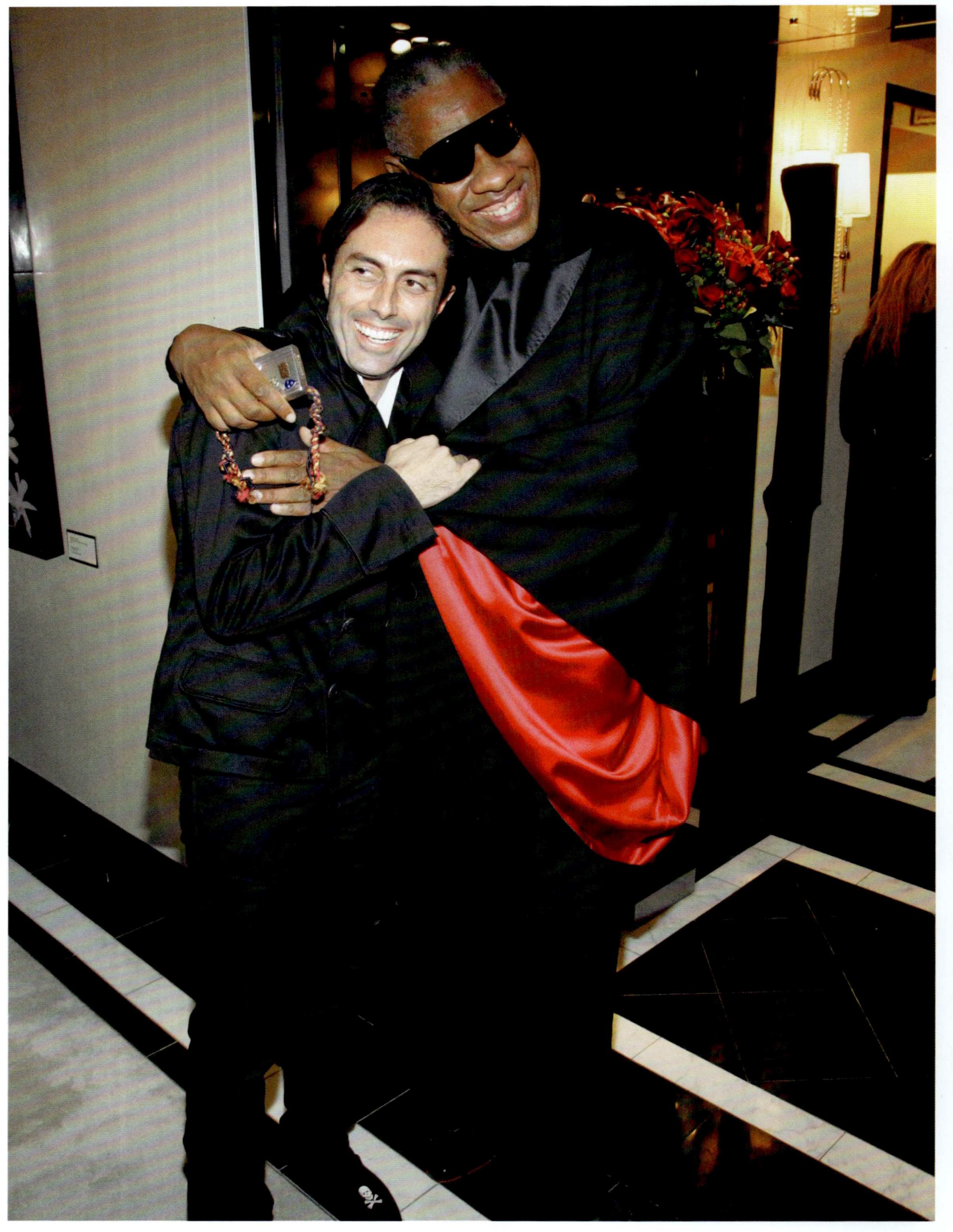

André and Giambattista Valli attending a party for the designer at Bergdorf Goodman, October 2006. Photo by Zack Seckler/WWD/Penske Media via Getty Images.

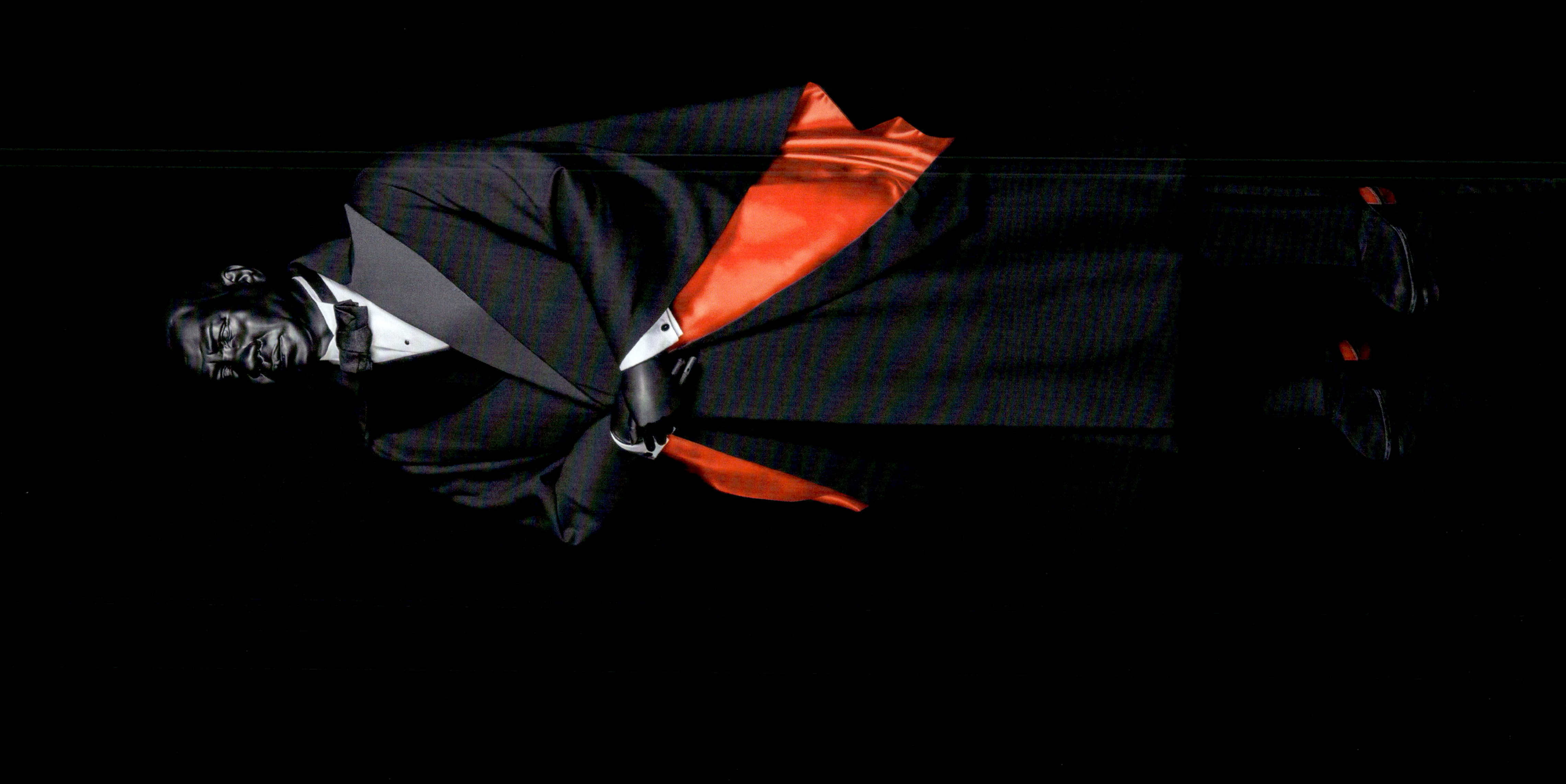

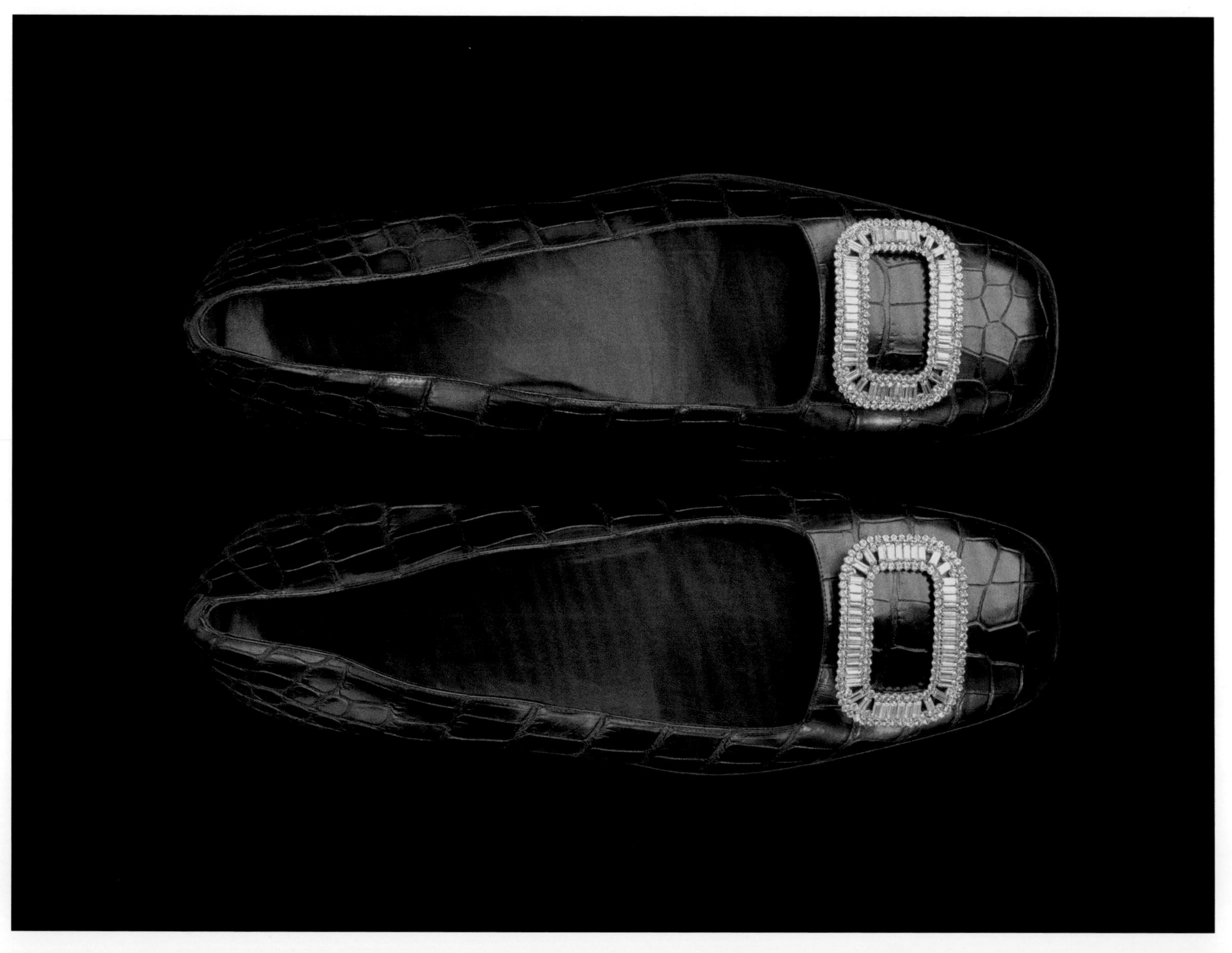

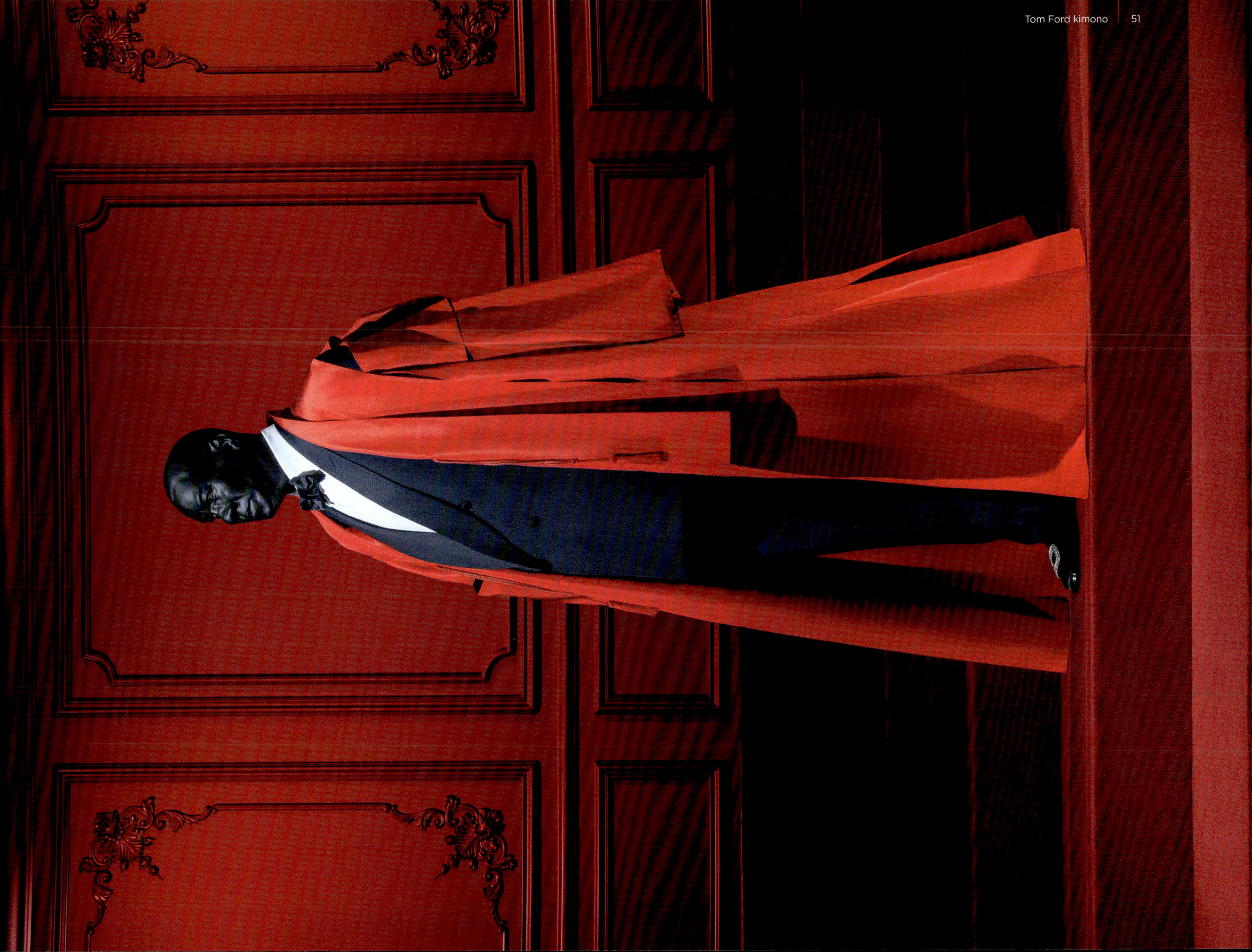

Tom Ford kimono

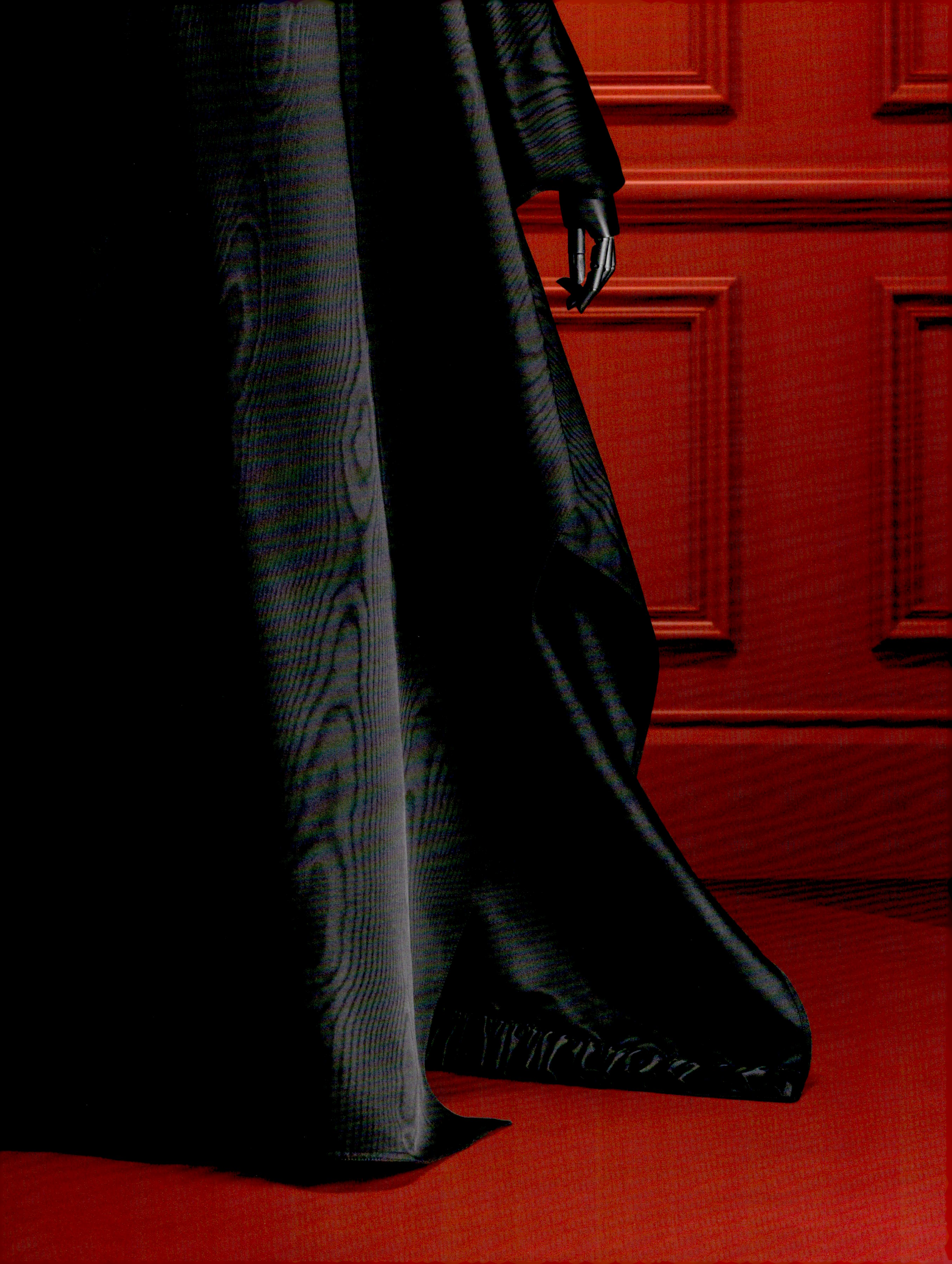

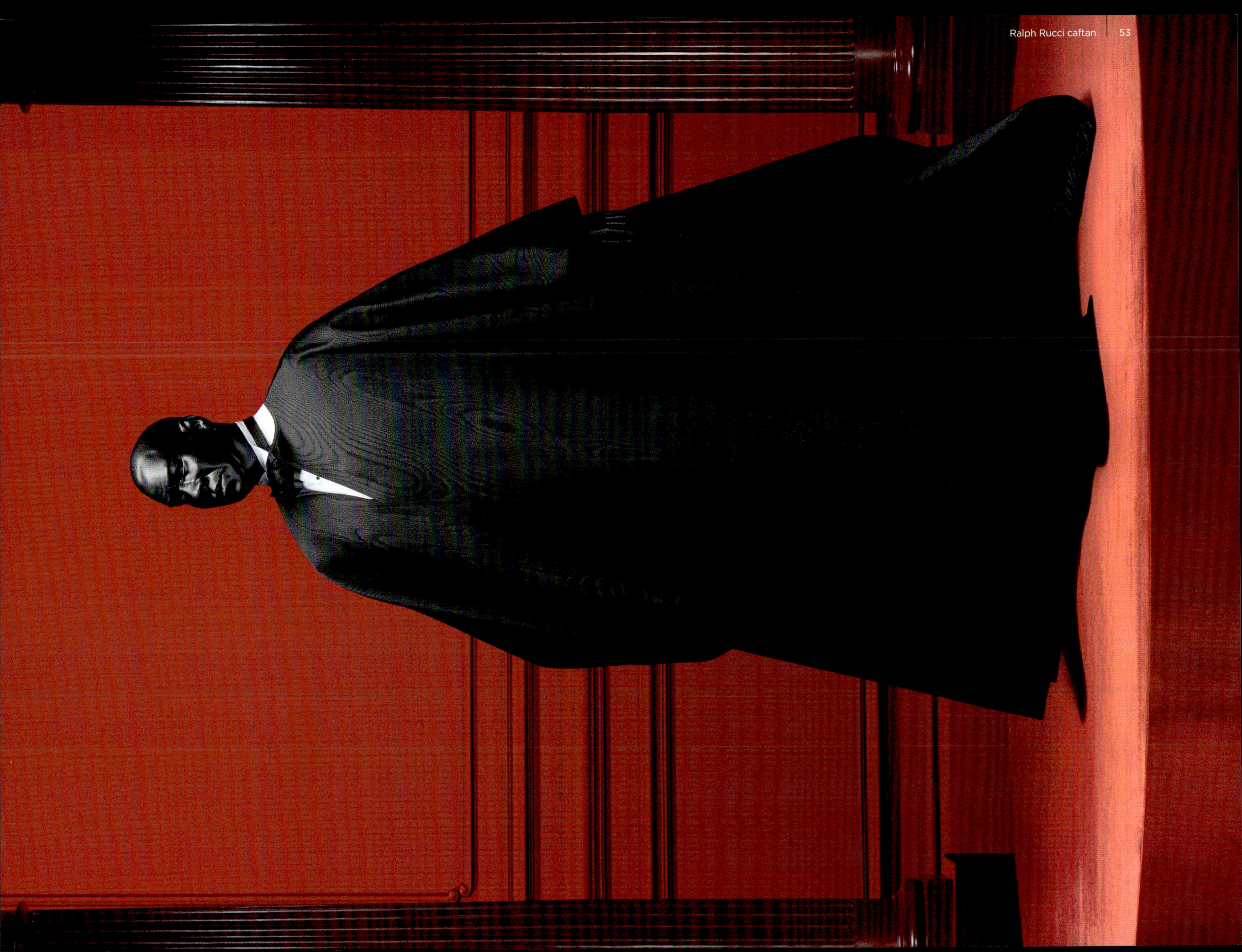

Ralph Rucci caftan

ALT x SCAD
Anna Wintour

My dear friend and colleague André Leon Talley was, rather famously, not a man of half measures in anything he did, including his work for the Savannah College of Art and Design. André loved being at SCAD—not just because it reunited him with the South of his childhood, but also because he responded so deeply to its students' pure and unabashed love of fashion, their excitement at being on the very cusp of their adult careers. André never failed to be moved by absolute enthusiasm—the very quality, of course, that had powered so many of his own achievements in his remarkable life.

The establishment of the André Leon Talley Award in 2001 allowed André to bring designer after designer to SCAD. Who, other than André, could summon the likes of Diane von Furstenberg and Vera Wang, Vivienne Westwood and Miuccia Prada—who flew in and out from Milan in a single day, arriving mere hours before the ceremony—to tell their life stories in real and honest terms to a packed crowd of excited students? These students, he reasoned, simply needed the opportunity to dream of where fashion could take them. After all, it was an approach that had worked magnificently for him, and André, always generous to a fault, simply wanted to share that dream with just about everyone he could.

André and Anna Wintour attending the Met Gala, 1999. Photo by Rose Hartman/Getty Images.

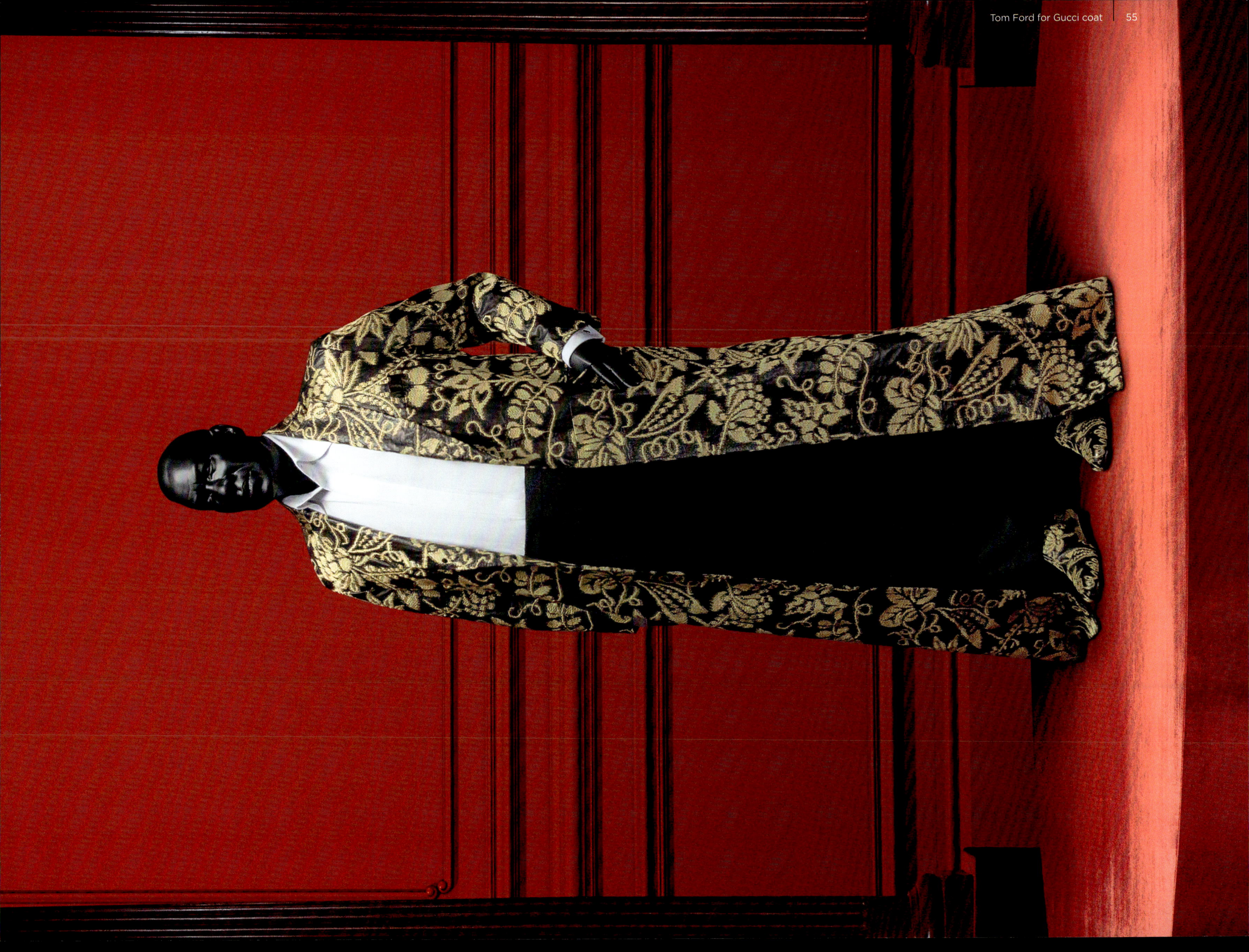

Tom Ford for Gucci coat

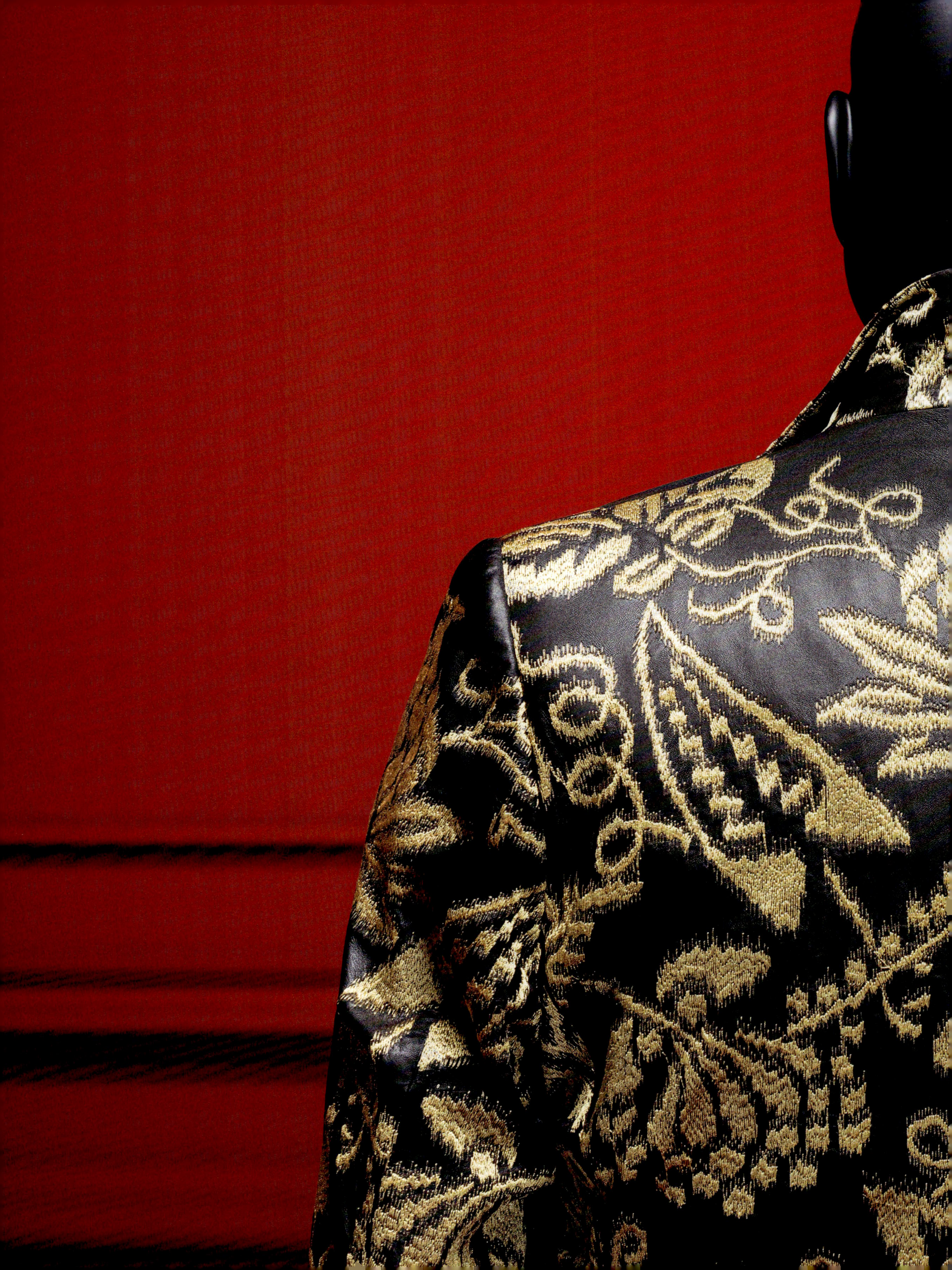

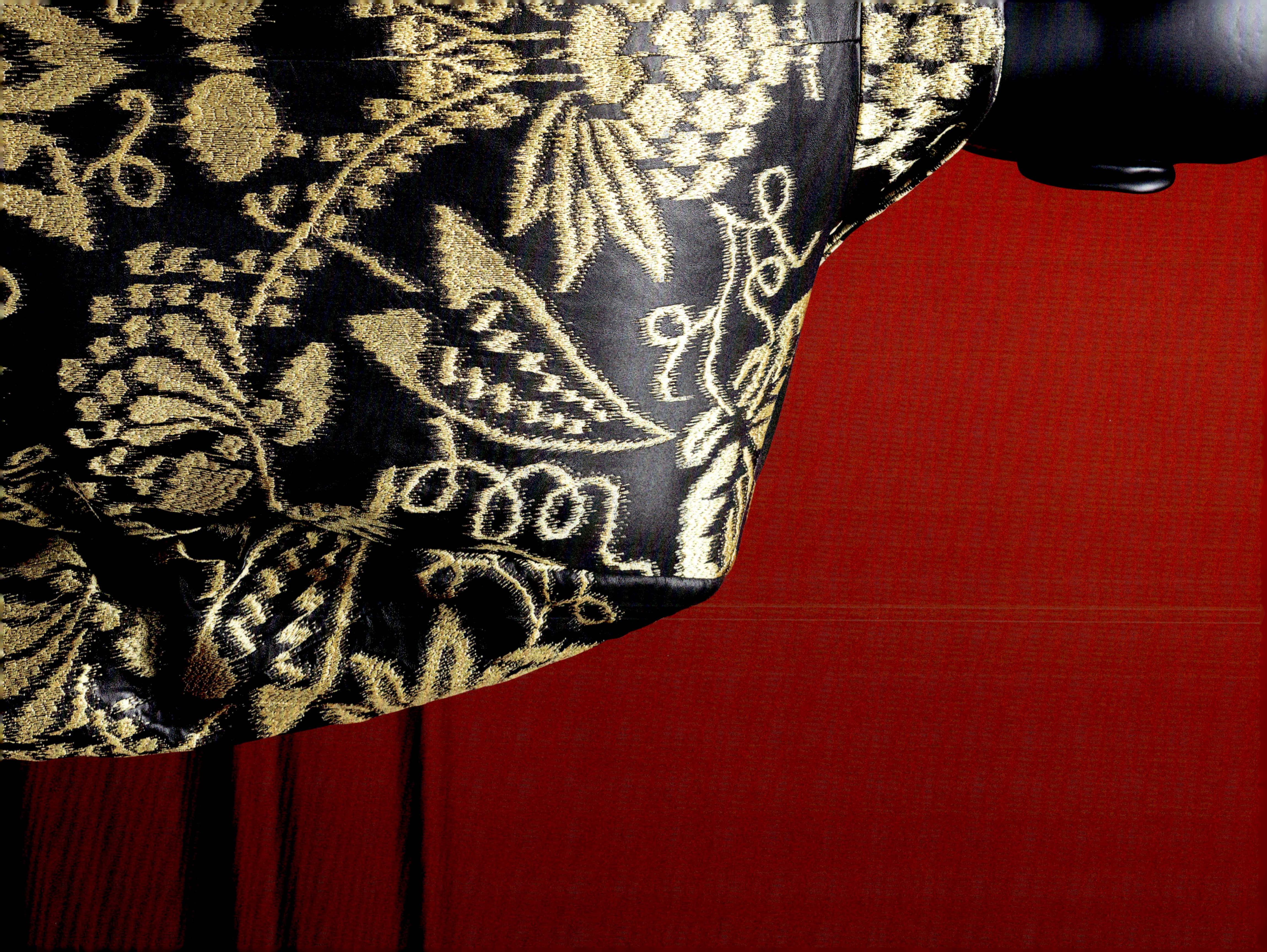

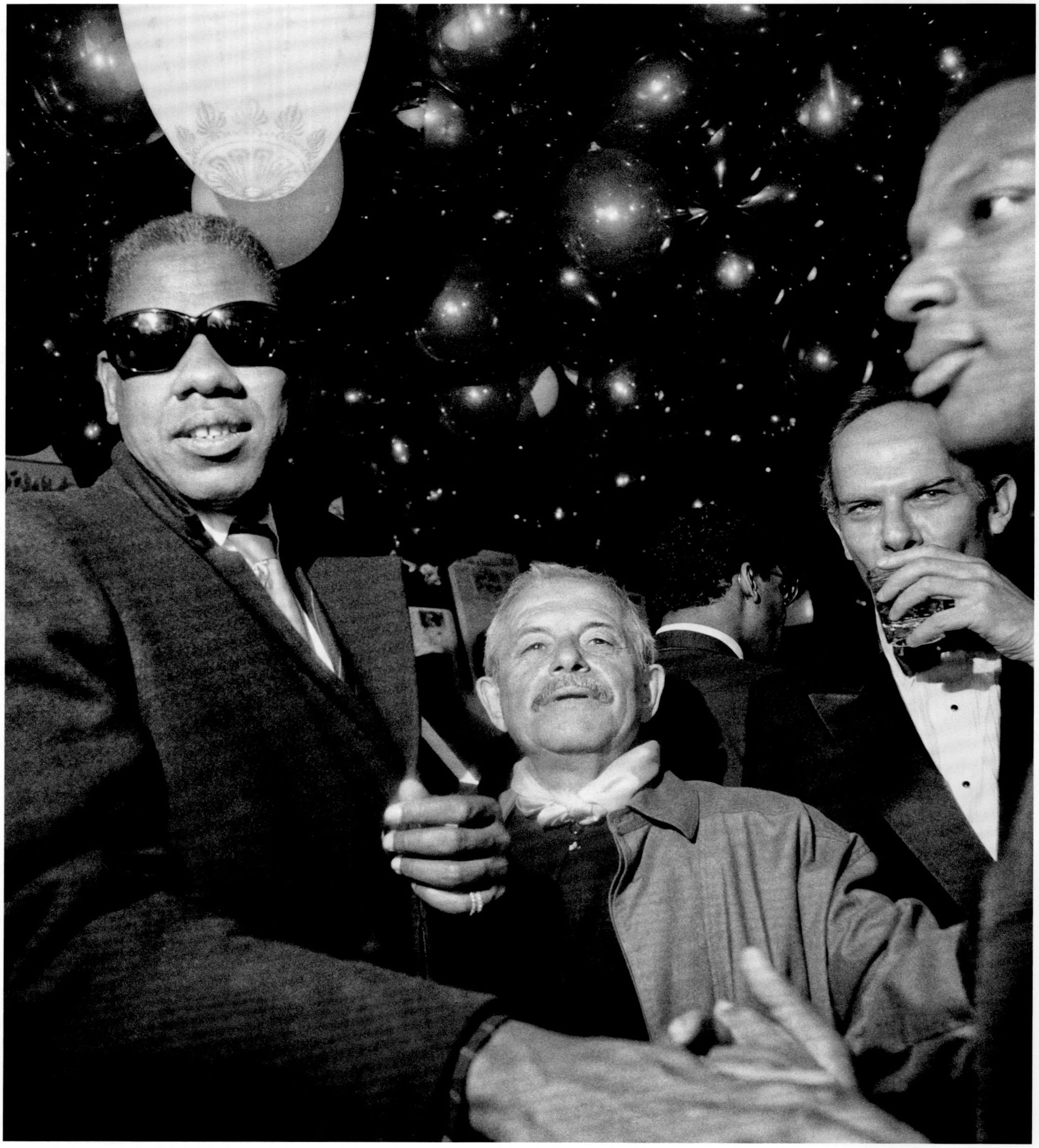

André at Elaine's for the restaurant's twenty-fifth anniversary, April 1988. Photographed by Jonathan Becker.

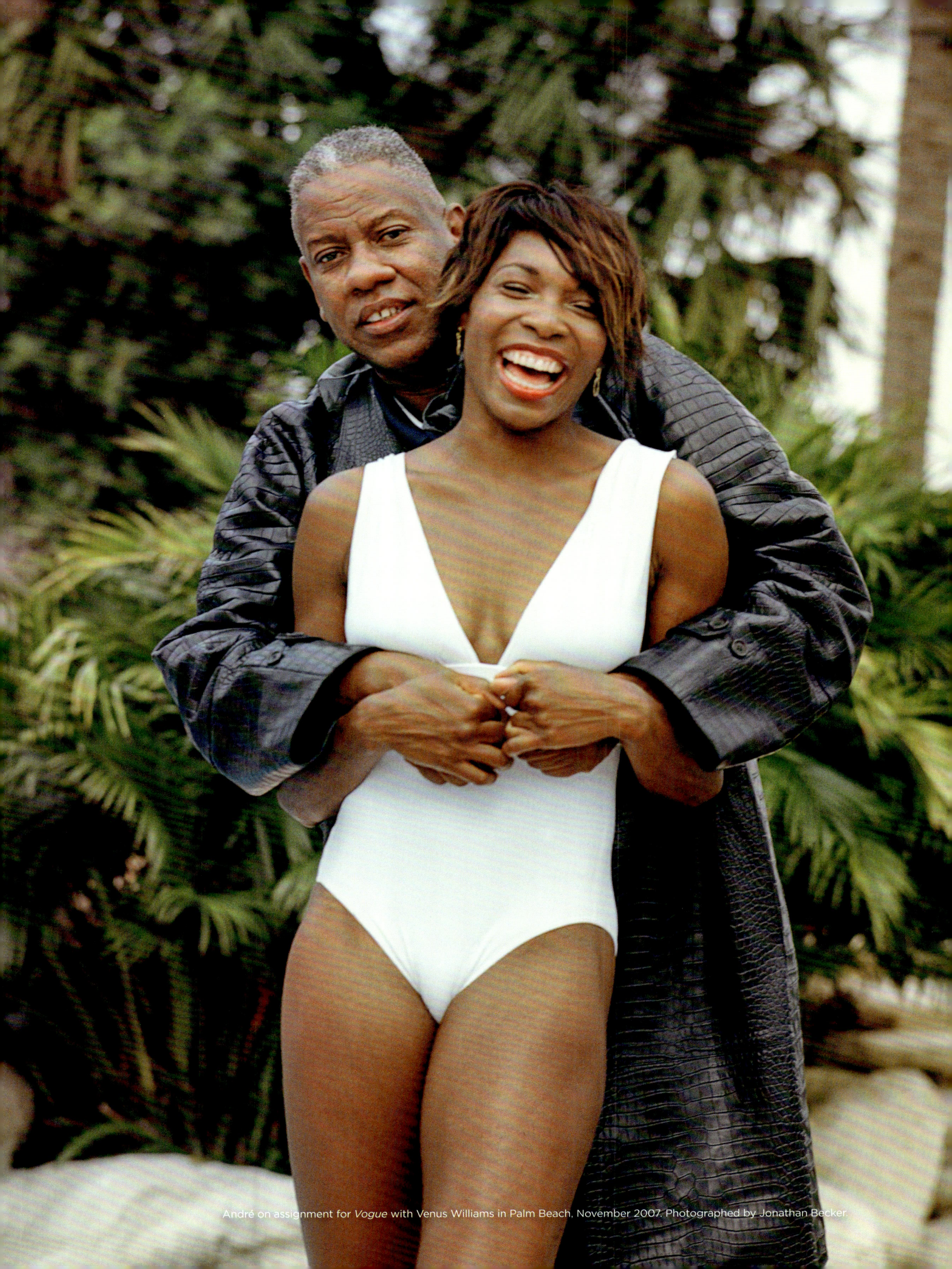

André on assignment for *Vogue* with Venus Williams in Palm Beach, November 2007. Photographed by Jonathan Becker.

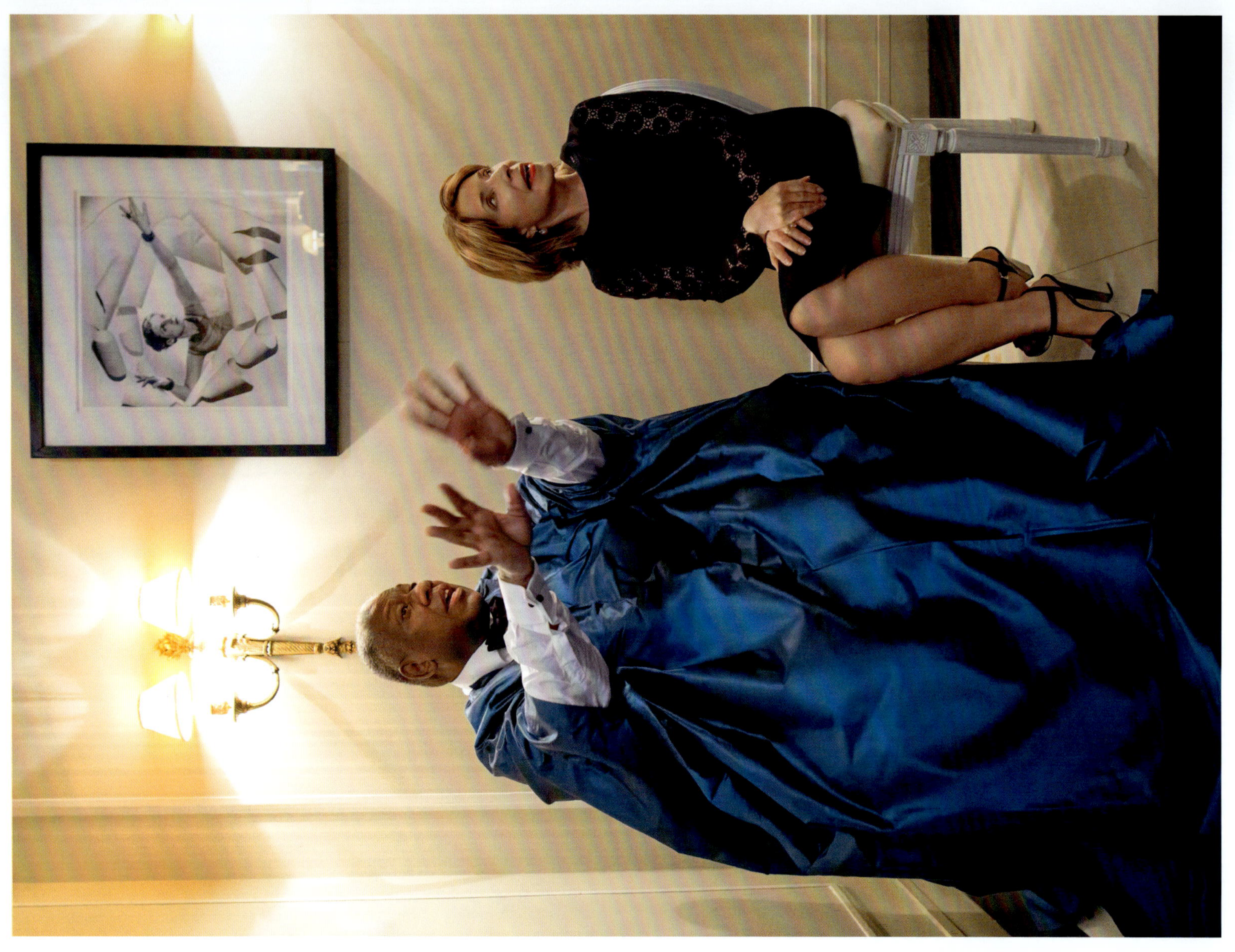

André and Paula Wallace at the *Little Black Dress* opening reception at the Mona Bismarck American Center in Paris, July 2013

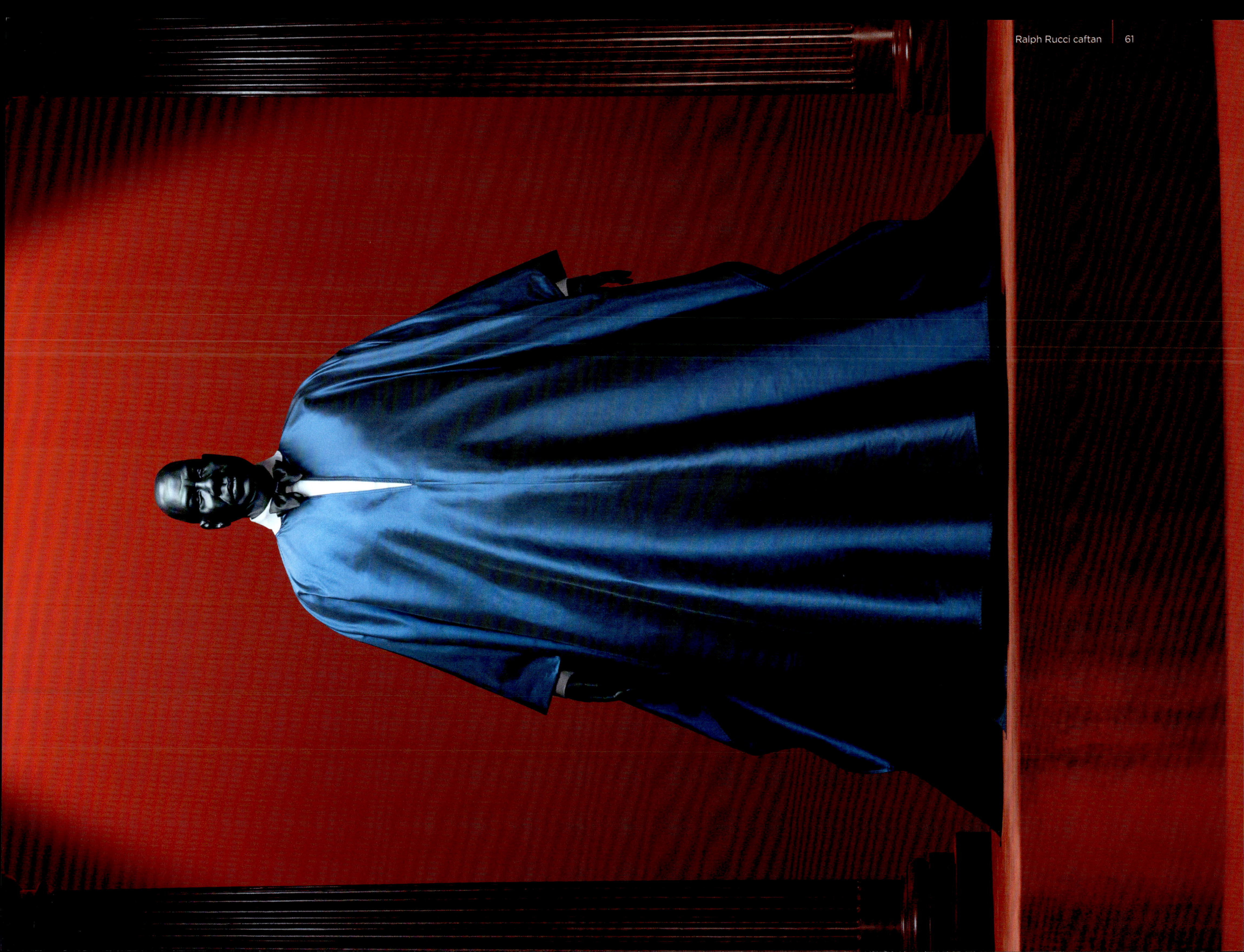

Ralph Rucci caftan

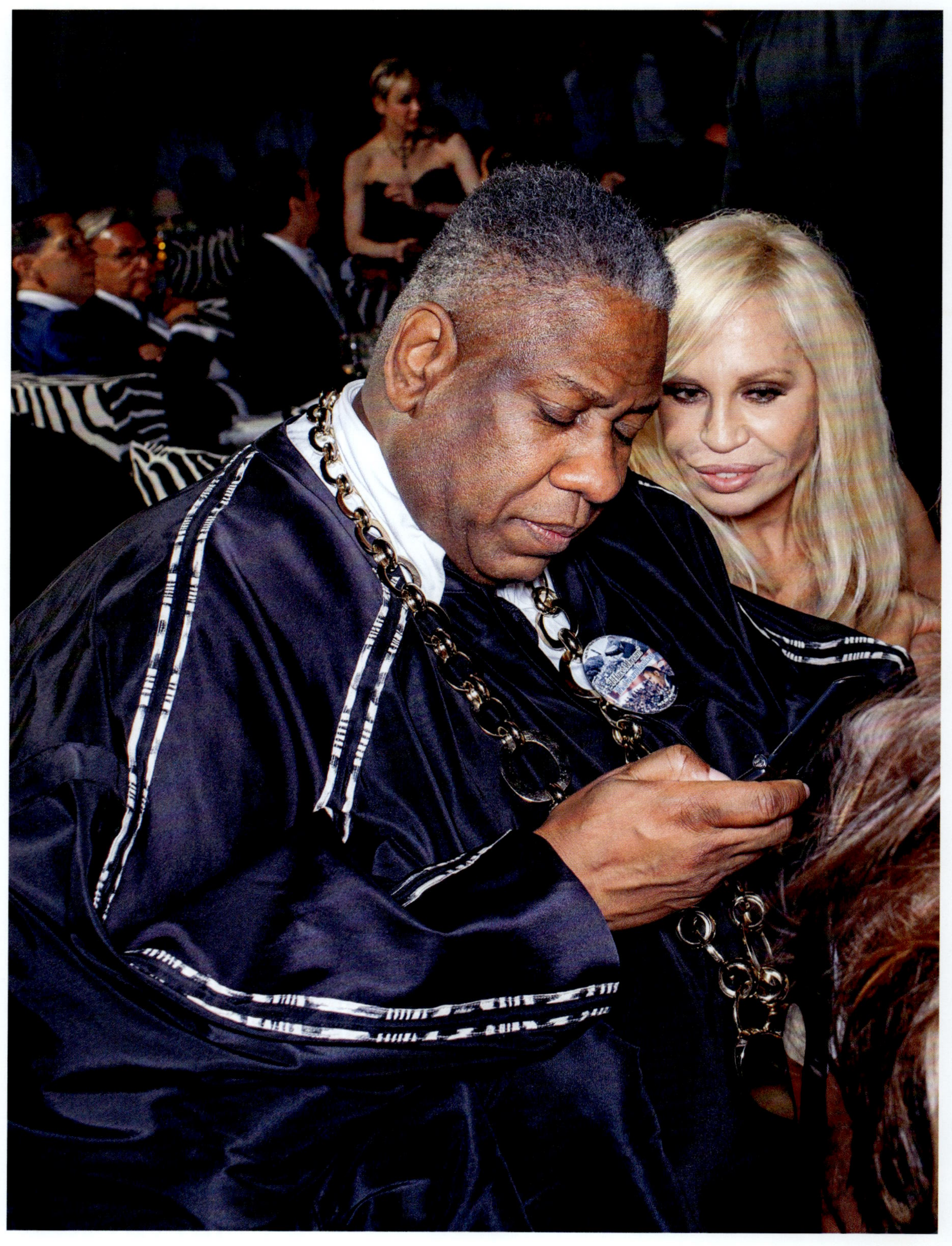

André and Donatella Versace at the Met Gala for *The Model as Muse: Embodying Fashion*, May 2009. Photo by Robert Fairer.

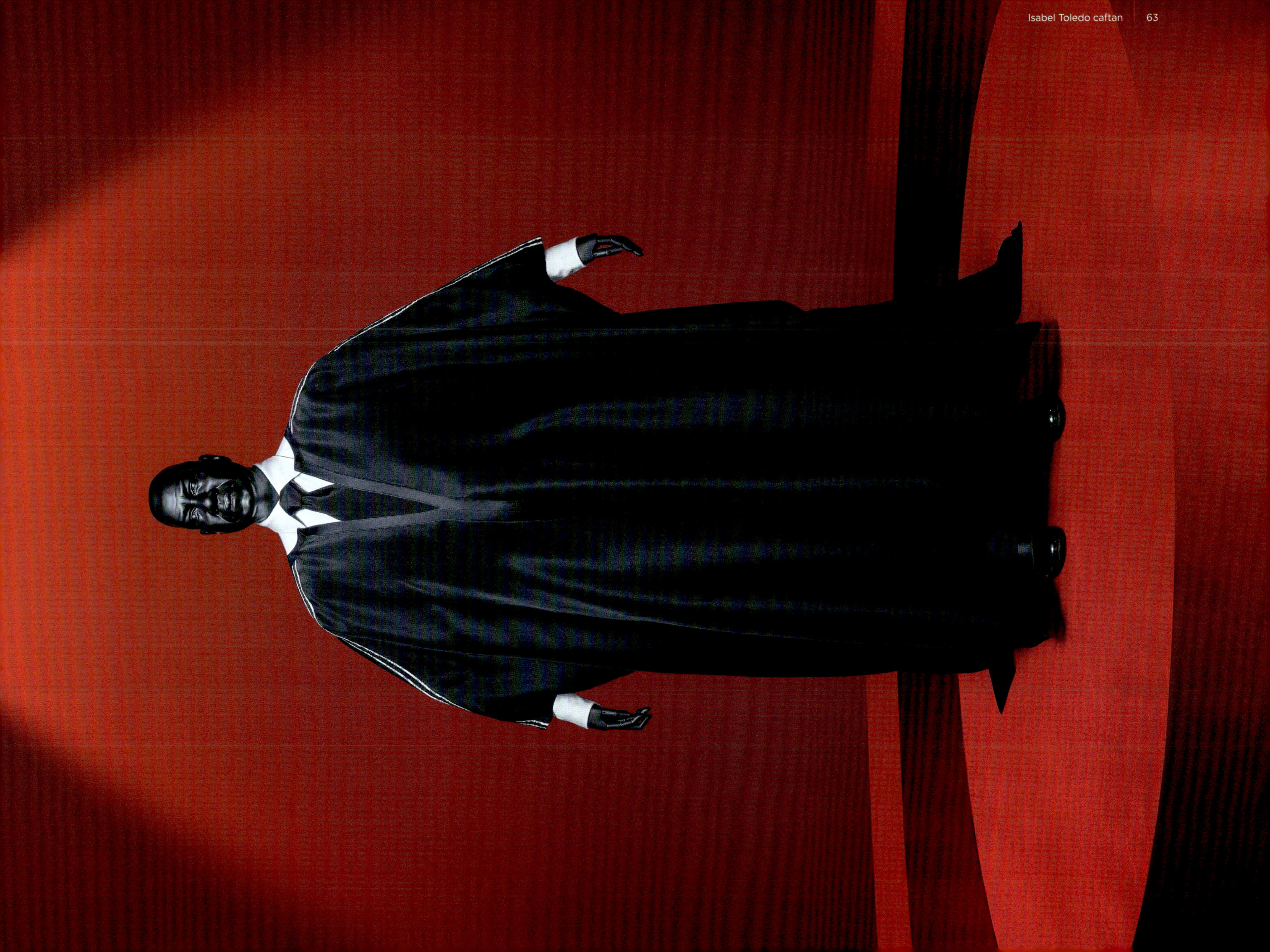

Isabel Toledo caftan

 Nicolas Ghesquière for Balenciaga cape

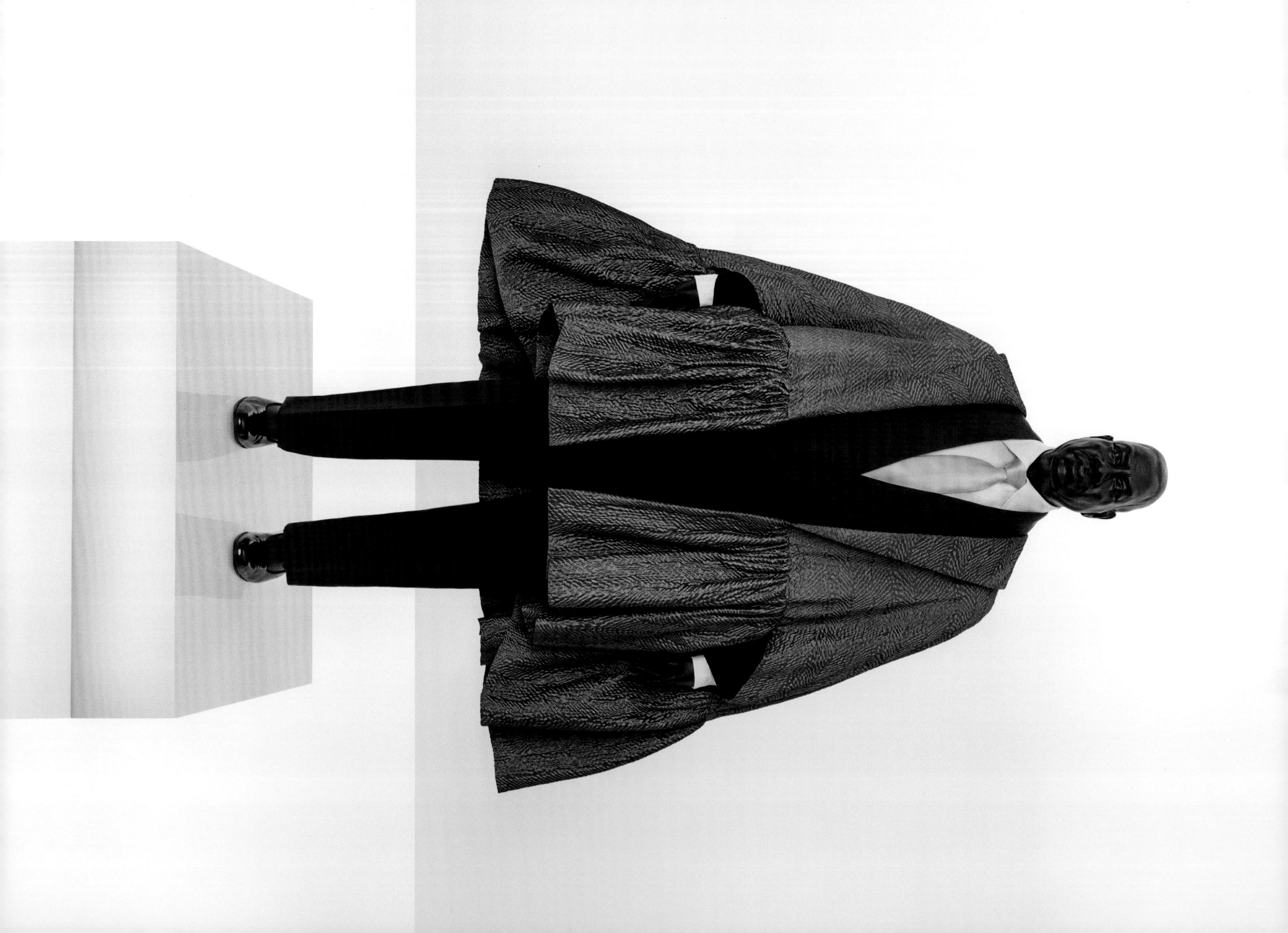

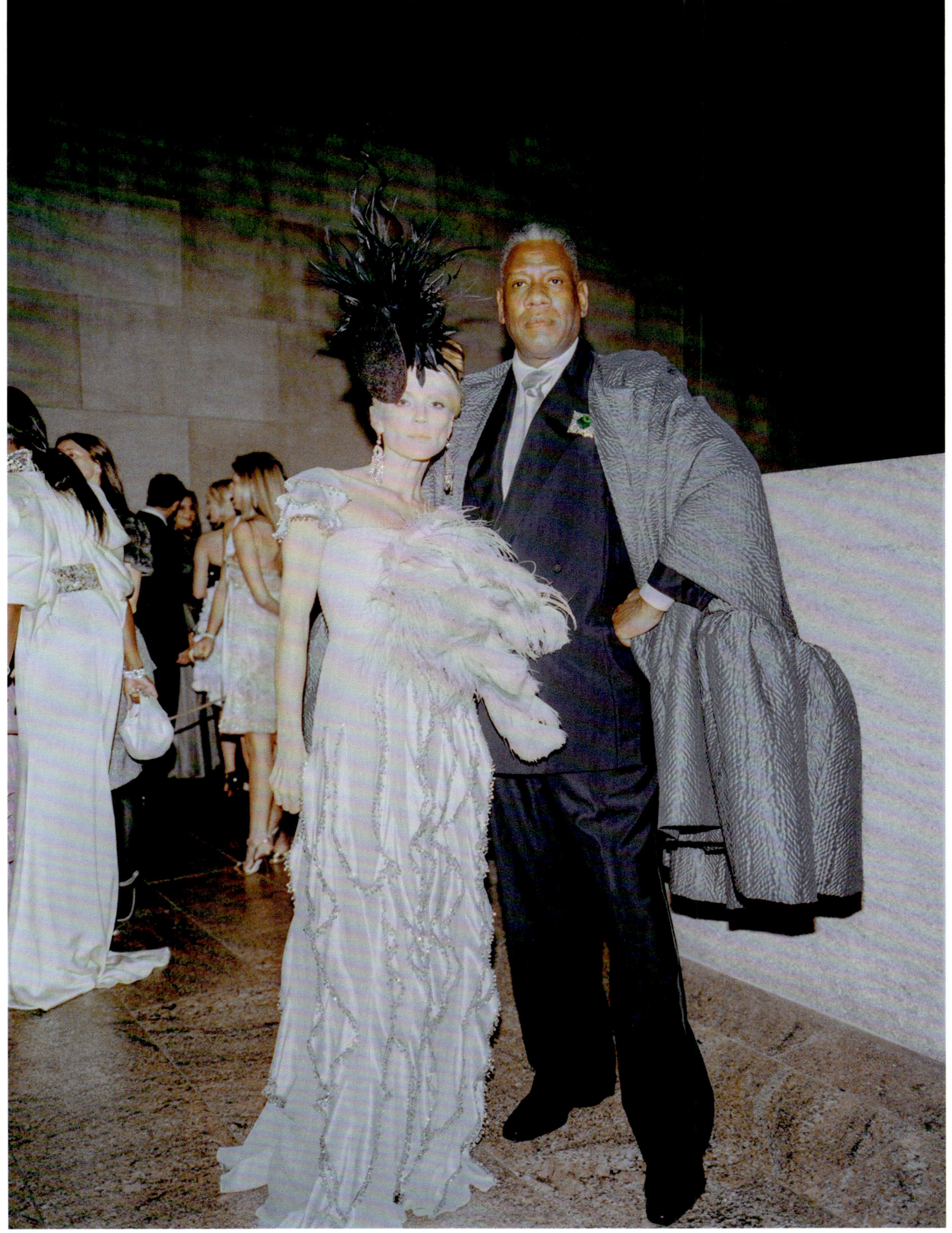

André and Daphne Guinness arriving at the Met Gala for *AngloMania: Tradition and Transgression in British Fashion*, May 2006. Photo by Robert Fairer.

THE ENDURING GIFT

Darren Walker

André Leon Talley was a singular force — brilliant, fierce, unapologetic. Yet, to reduce André to his fashion-world persona would be to miss the extraordinary fullness of his story.

André was a man of complexity and contradiction — a celebrated genius, a misfit and outsider. And his legacy transcends fashion — giving powerful testimony to his faith, activism, and love for his community.

I met André in 1995 at Harlem's Abyssinian Baptist Church, the institution that transformed my own life. He and I were fast friends; we shared a language. And through the years, I came to know him as a man of unconditional, if unconventional, faith, who understood the power of symbols, both aesthetically and spiritually. So, it was little surprise to me that, in the end, he chose to turn the objects he cherished into acts of meaning.

André's final act of generosity — and reciprocity — was his gift to the community that had sustained him: Abyssinian, the place where we found each other, and the Mt. Sinai Missionary Baptist Church in Durham, North Carolina, his hometown. He sold his singular fashion collection — Tom Ford caftans, Valentino capes, and Prada crocodile coats — to support these Black churches and bolster their ability to continue serving neighbors in need.

As I reflect on this profound expression of philanthropy, among others, I'm struck by how André always carried a deep consciousness of history — not just fashion history, which he knew better than anyone, but the history of race and resilience, and of the Black church's indispensable role in the American story. And, of course, he always held close his own personal history. In his heart of hearts, André was a queer Black man raised in the segregated South by his grandmother, a maid. One of his most important contributions was making the crooked path to dignity and opportunity a little smoother, a little more level for all those whose journeys began like his own.

Before Christie's auctioned André's prized belongings, the Abyssinian choir sang Nina Simone's "To Be Young, Gifted, and Black." Its words are fitting: "In the whole world you know, there are a million boys and girls who are young, gifted, and Black, and that's a fact." They seemed to echo André's deepest hope: to inspire others to see their worth, even in a world that might overlook it.

André Leon Talley was an original, sui generis, one of a kind. More importantly, he was a friend, a trailblazer, and a man who believed in the transformative power of love. Fashion, almost by definition, is temporal and ephemeral. But André's legacy endures in and through all of us — and will through the generations.

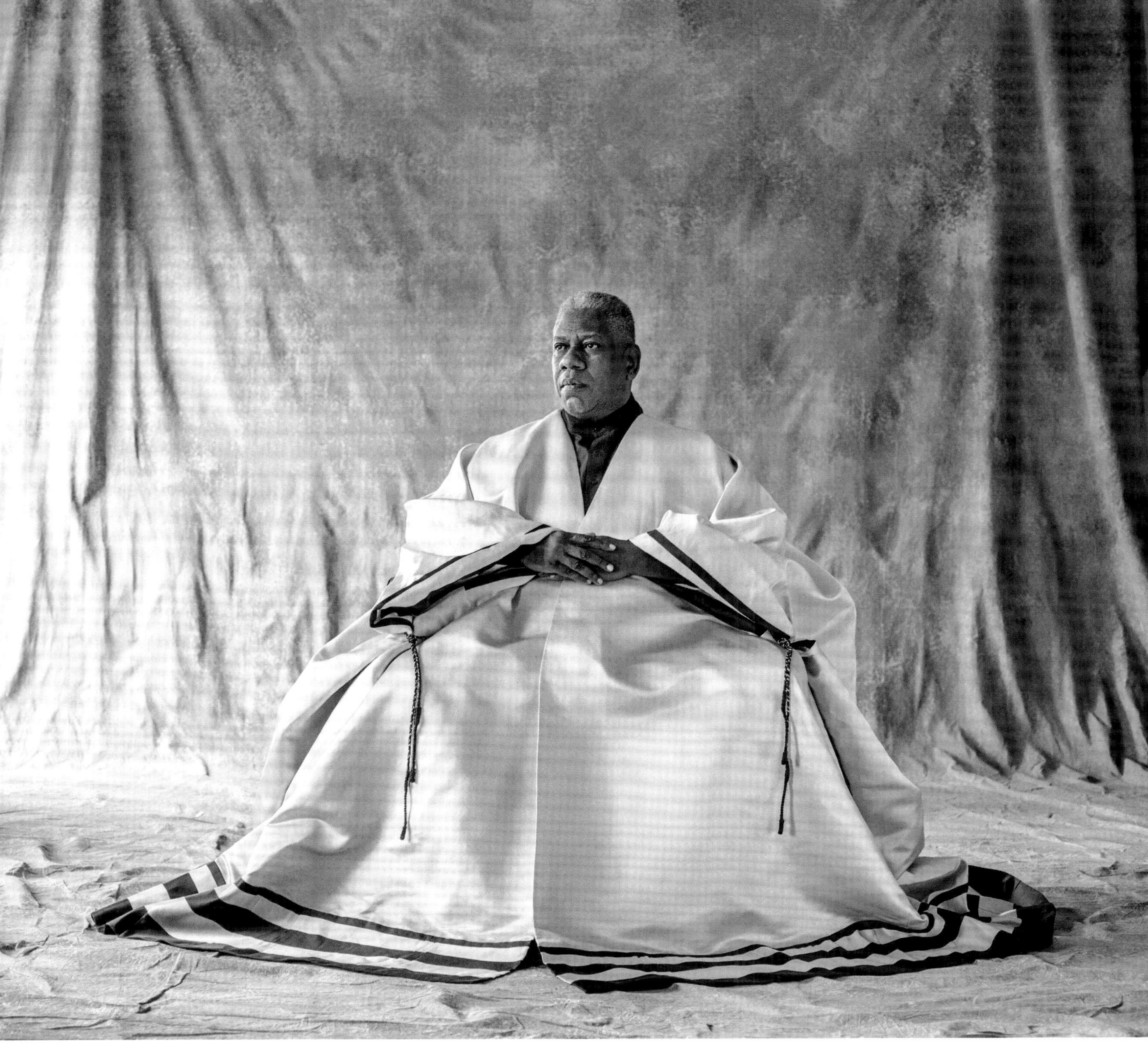

André at SCAD in Savannah, August 2013. Photographed by Jonathan Becker/Contour by Getty Images.

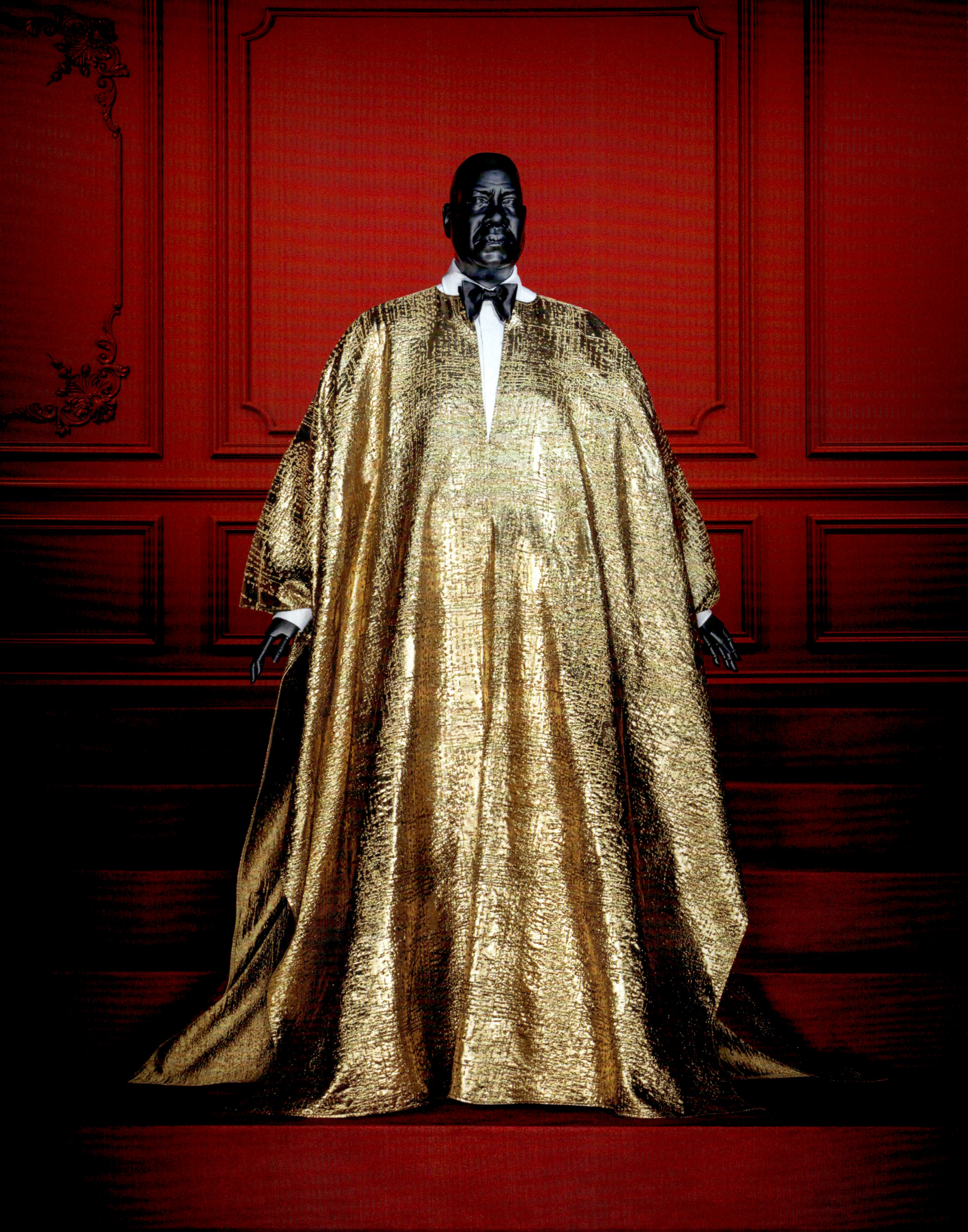

Ralph Rucci caftan

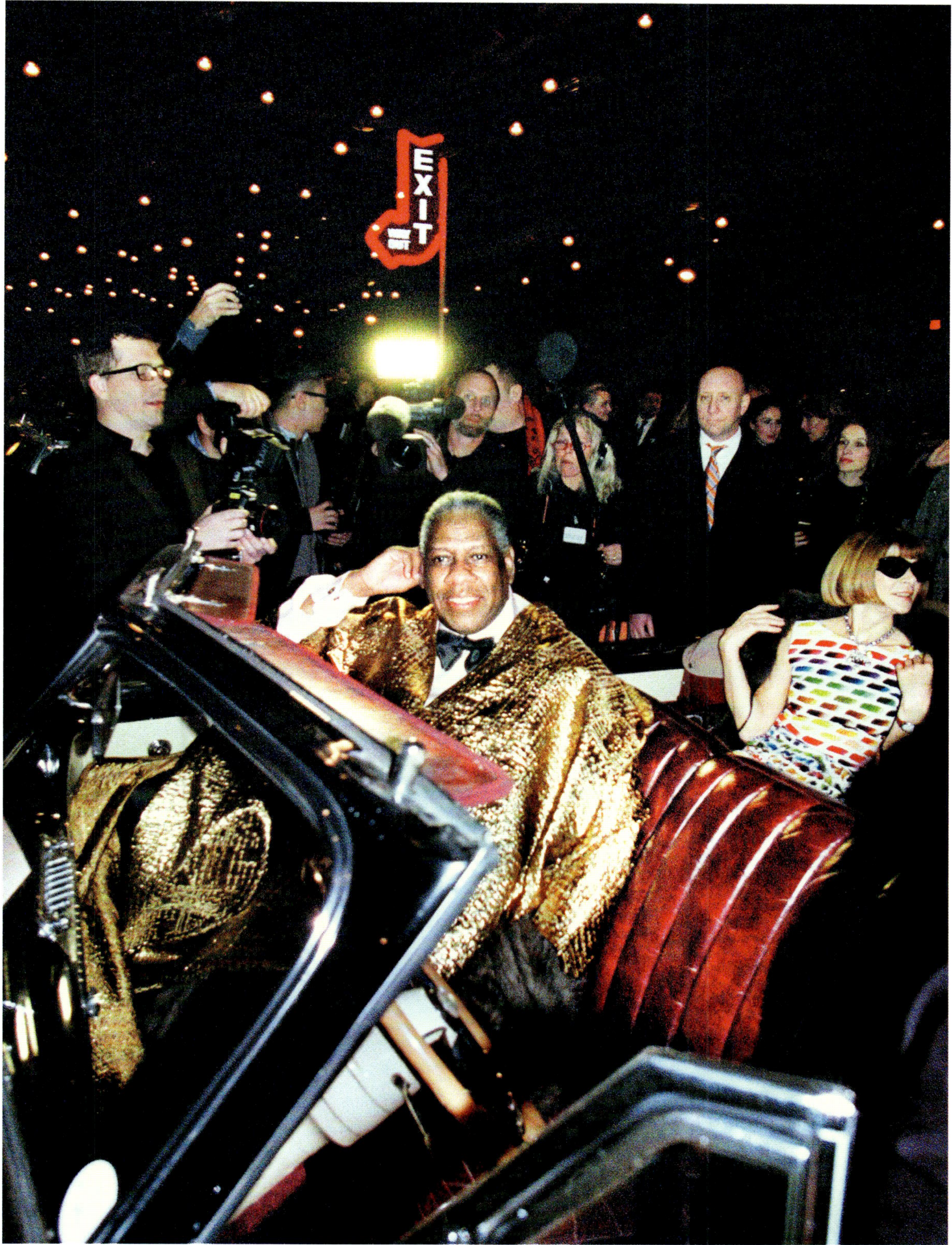

André and Anna Wintour at a Chanel runway show, 2013. Photo by Pari Dukovic/Trunk Archive.

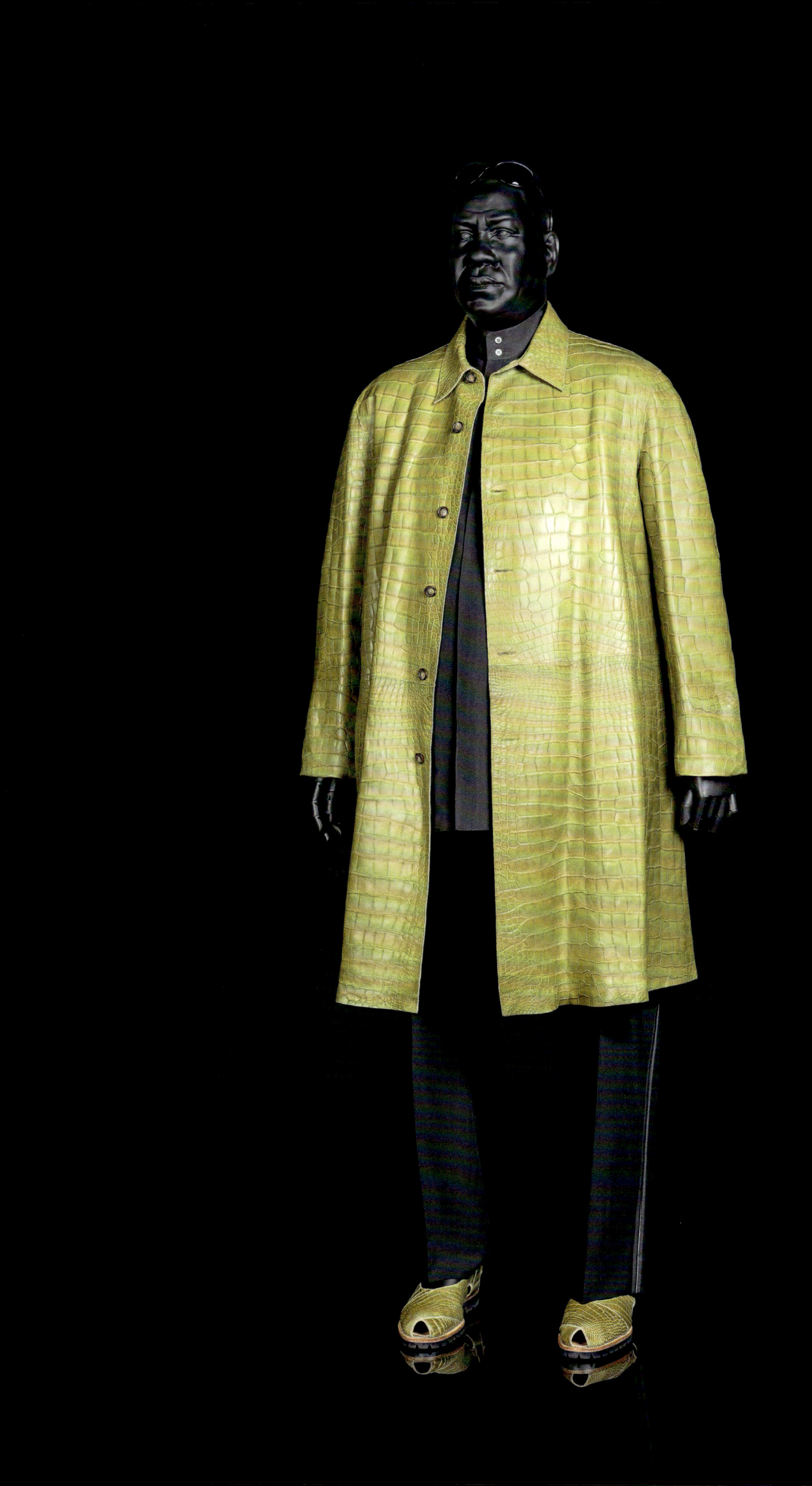

Prada balmacaan and Ralph Lauren trousers

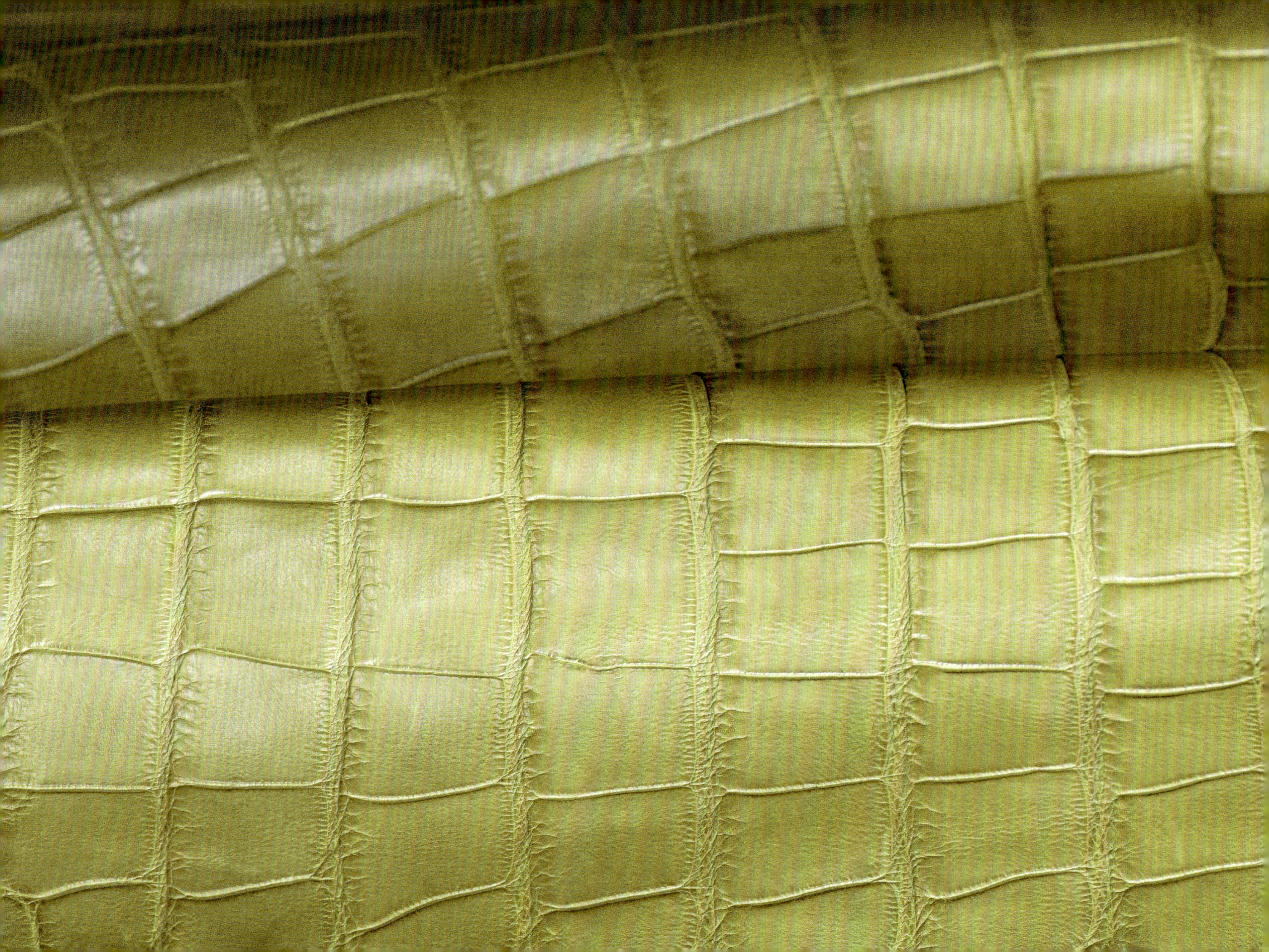

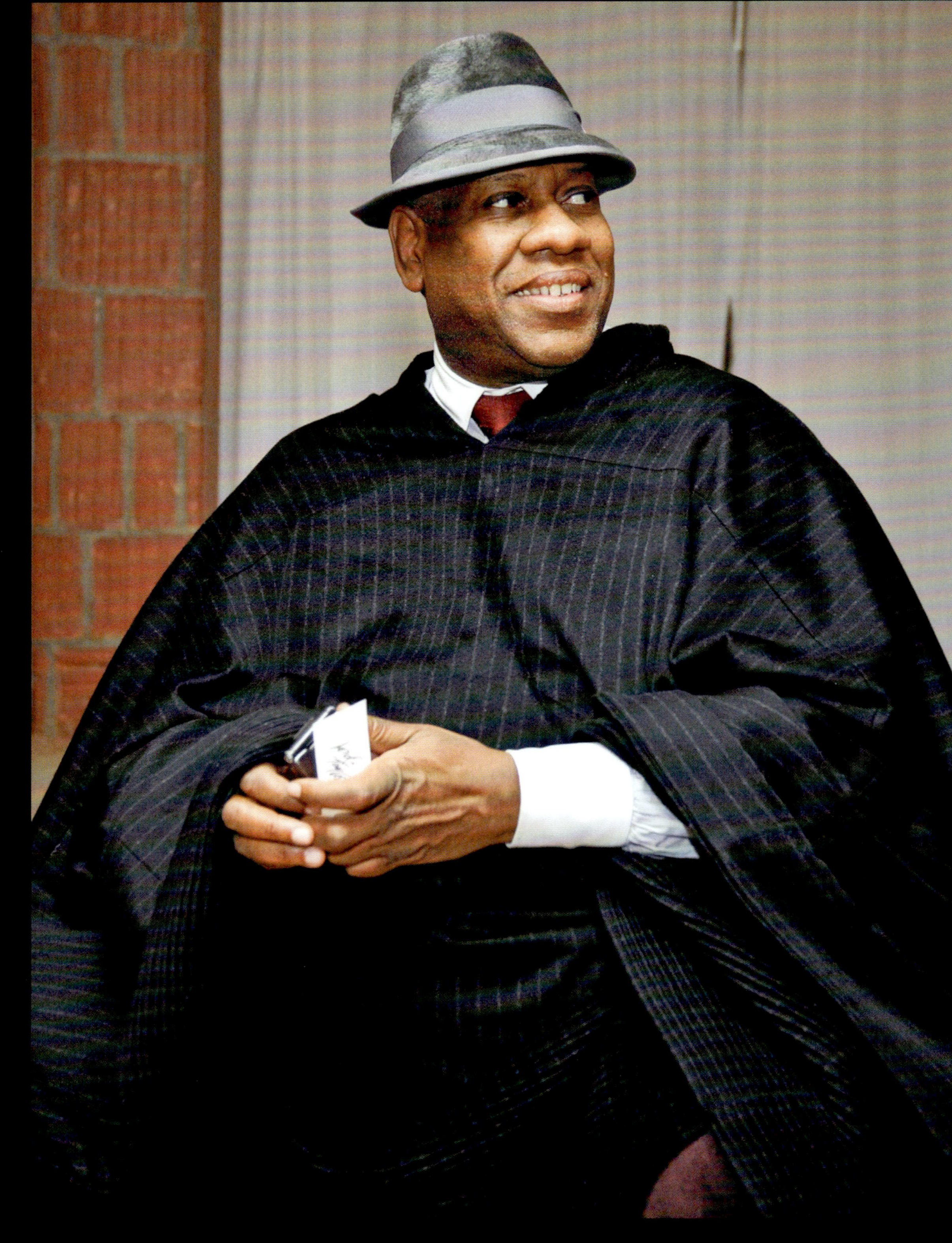

André at the Stephen Burrows Fall/Winter 2011 runway show. Photo by Ryan McCune/PMC. © Patrick McMullan.

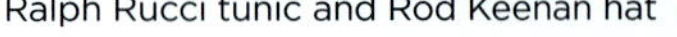

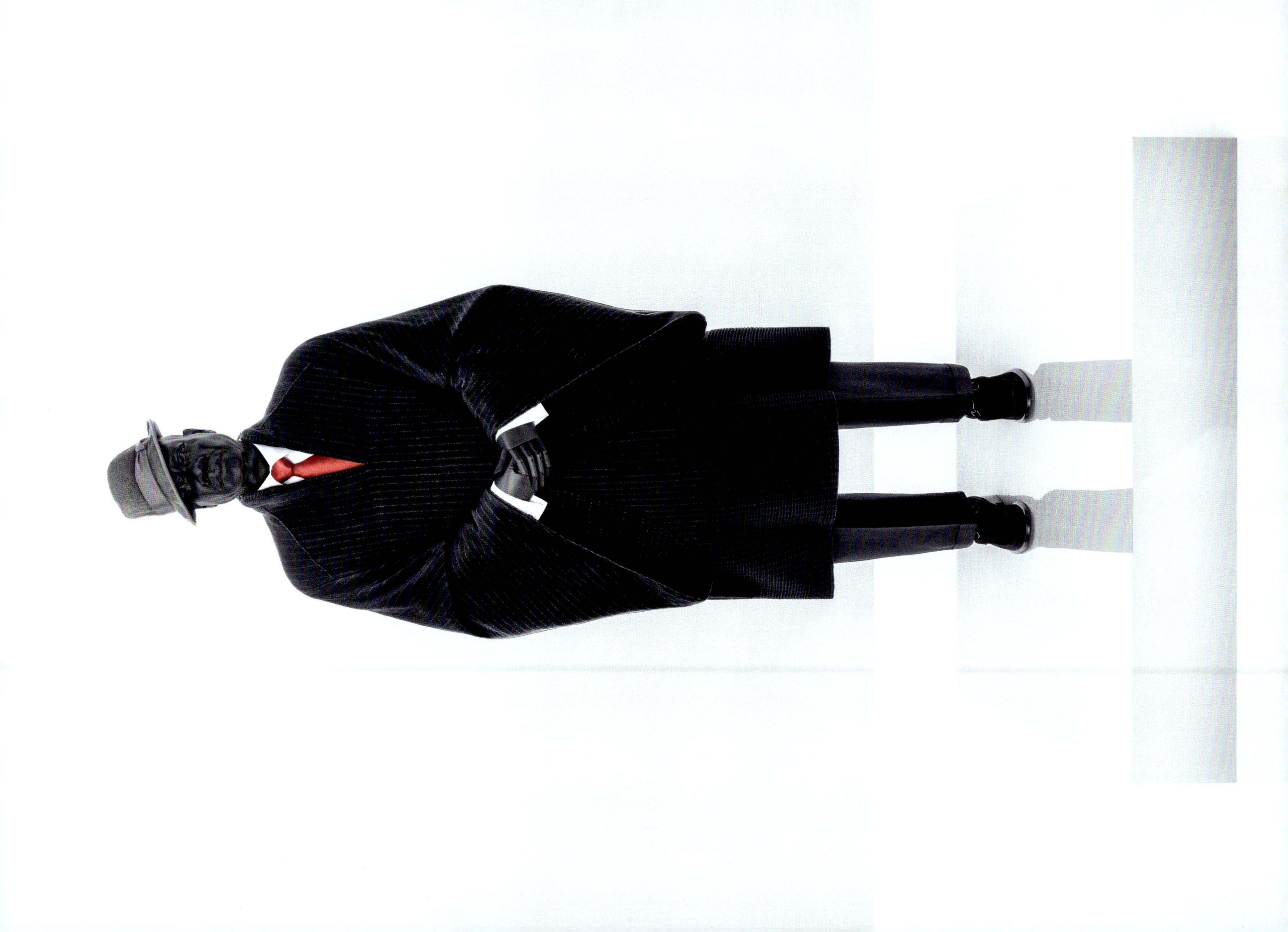

Ralph Rucci tunic and Rod Keenan hat

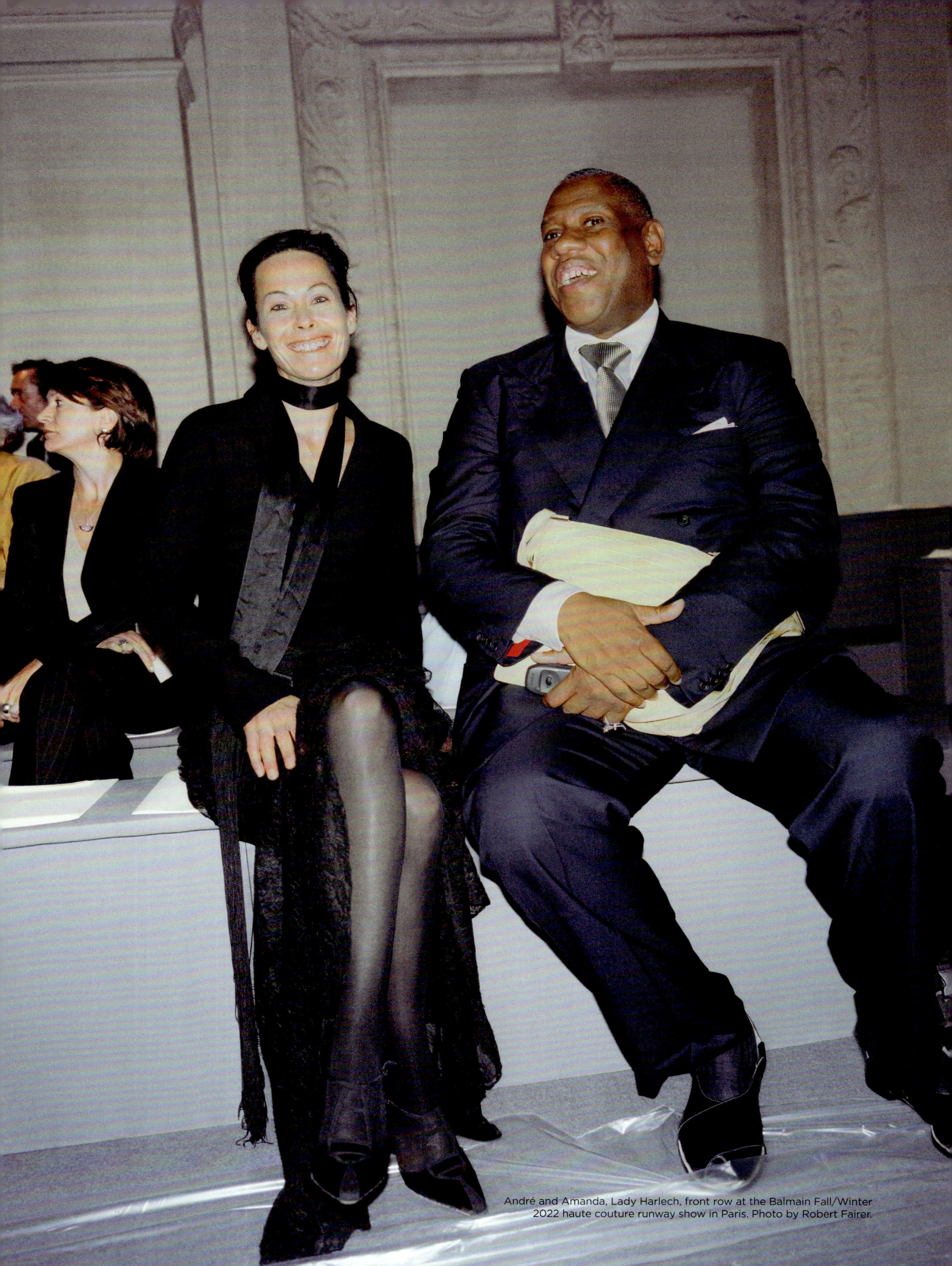

André and Amanda, Lady Harlech, front row at the Balmain Fall/Winter 2022 haute couture runway show in Paris. Photo by Robert Fairer.

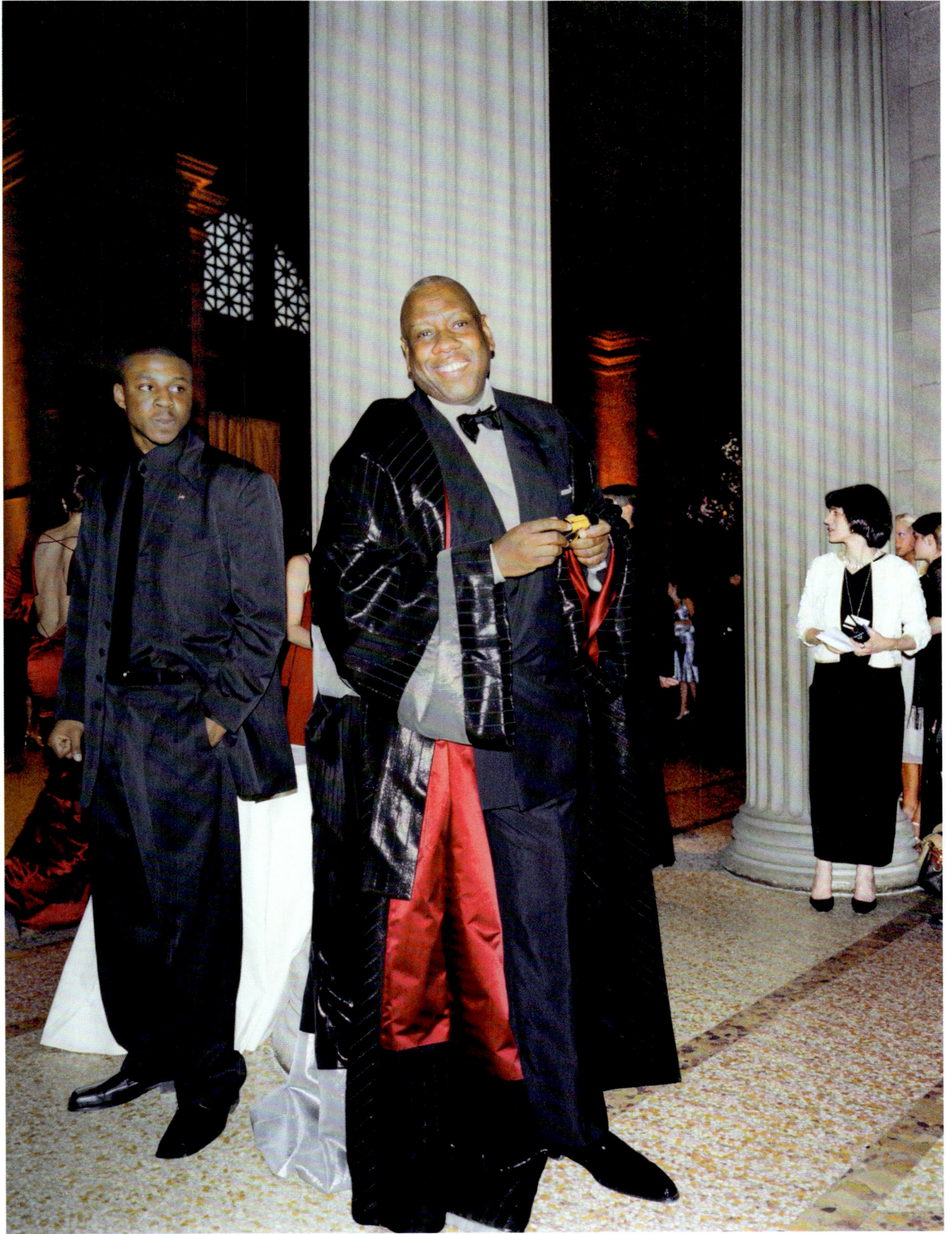

André at the Met Gala for *Goddess: The Classical Mode*, May 2003. Photo by Robert Fairer.

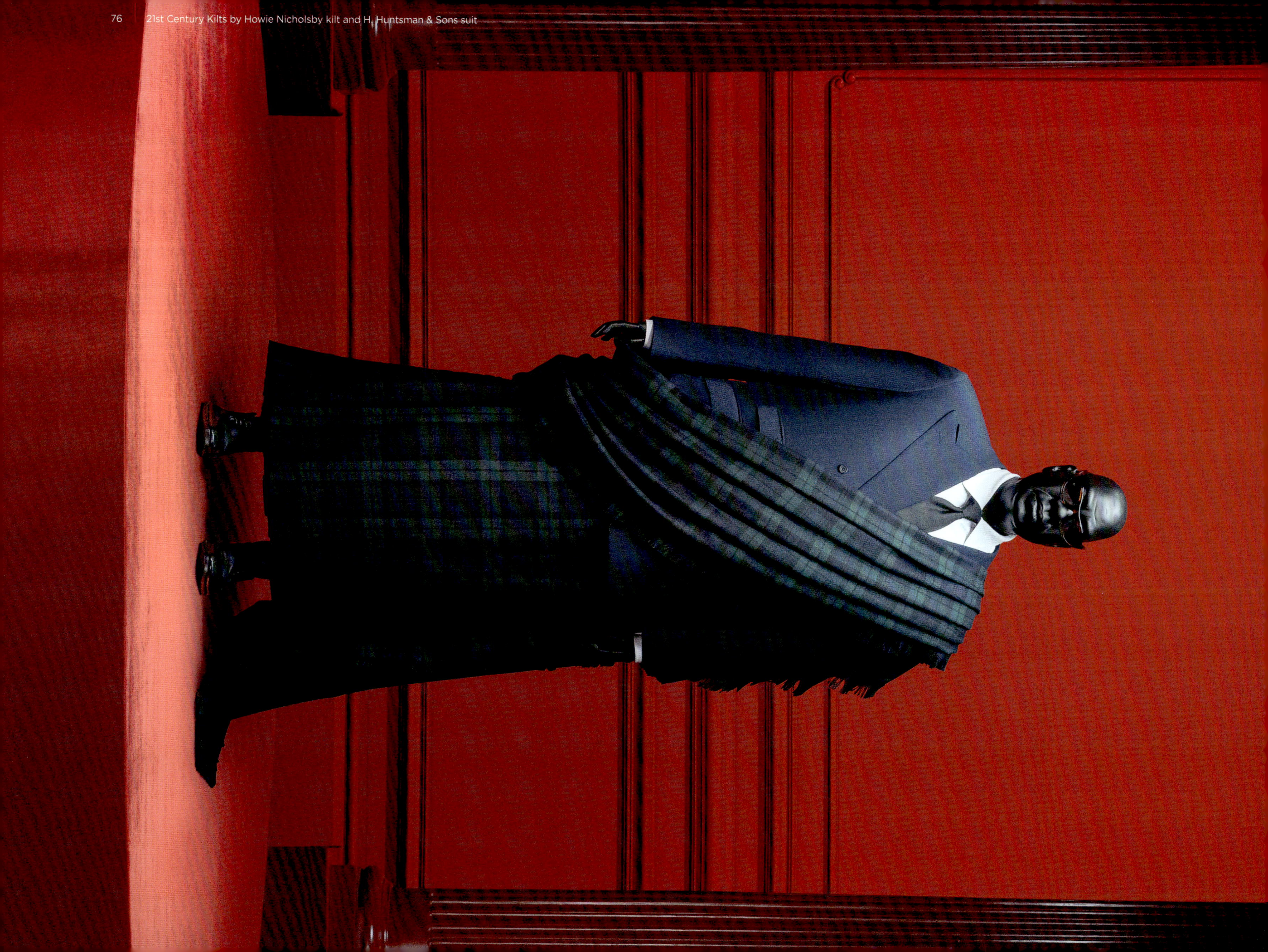

21st Century Kilts by Howie Nicholsby kilt and H. Huntsman & Sons suit

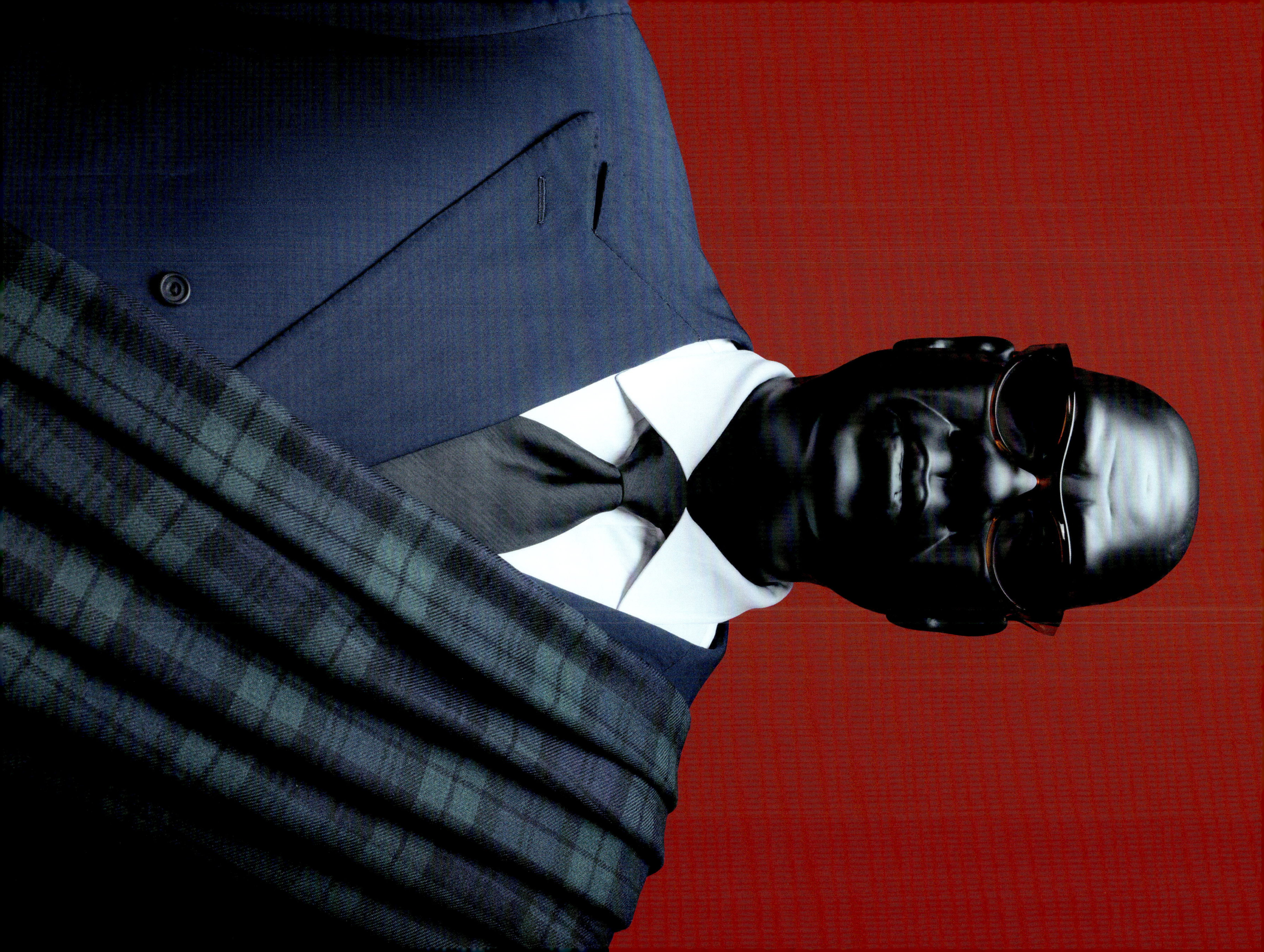

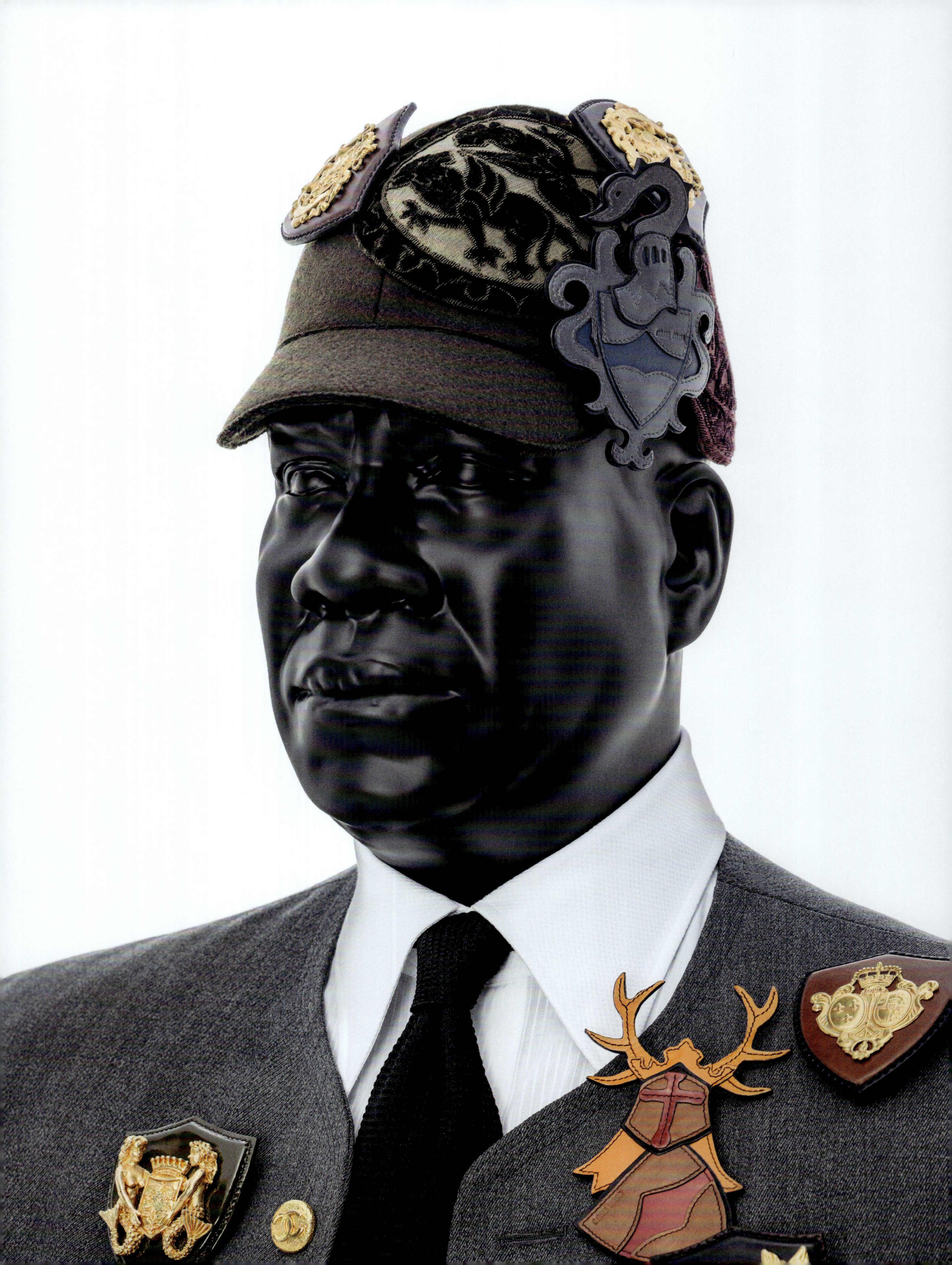

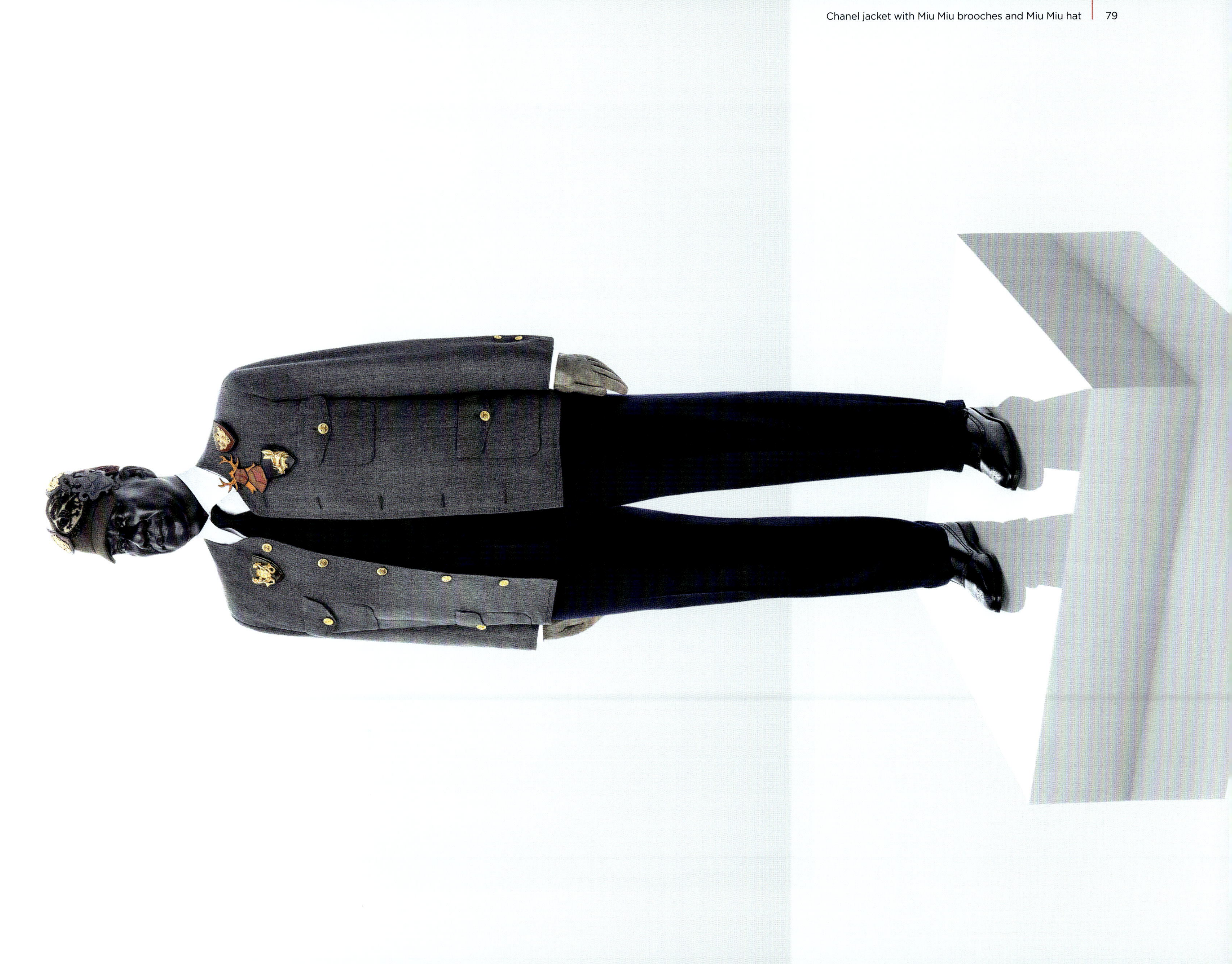

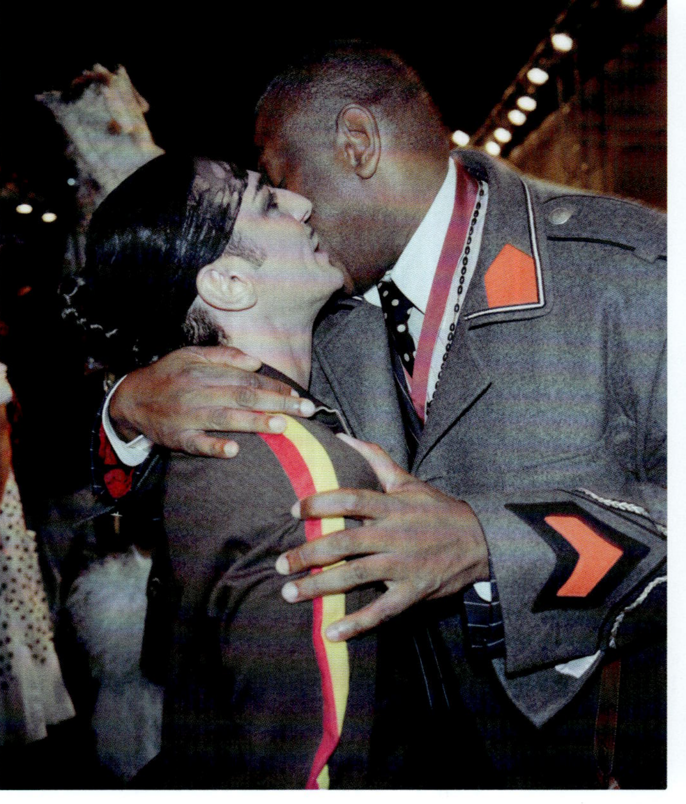

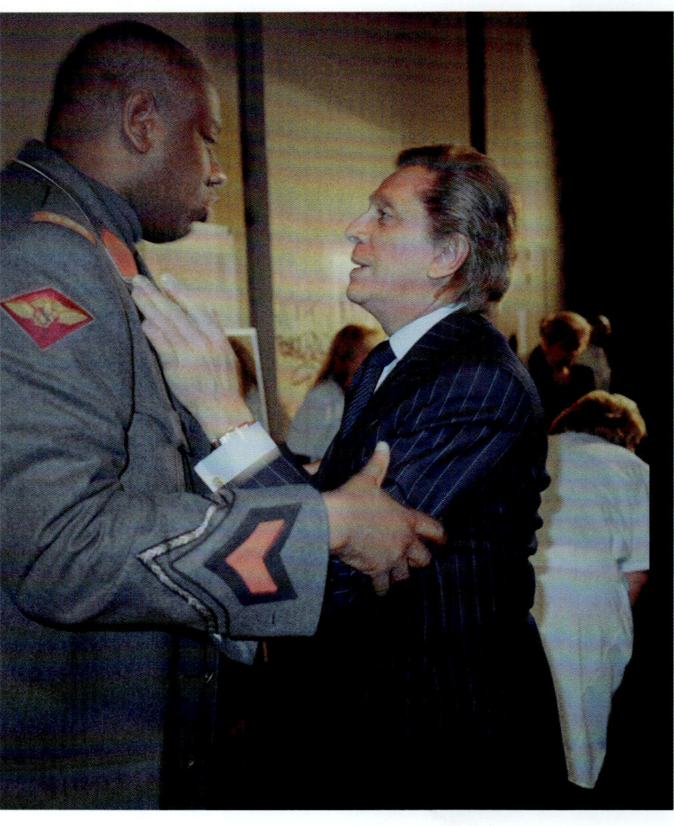

Left: André and John Galliano backstage at the Dior Spring/Summer 2002 haute couture runway show. Right: André and Valentino Garavani backstage at the Valentino Spring/Summer 2002 haute couture runway show. Photos by Robert Fairer.

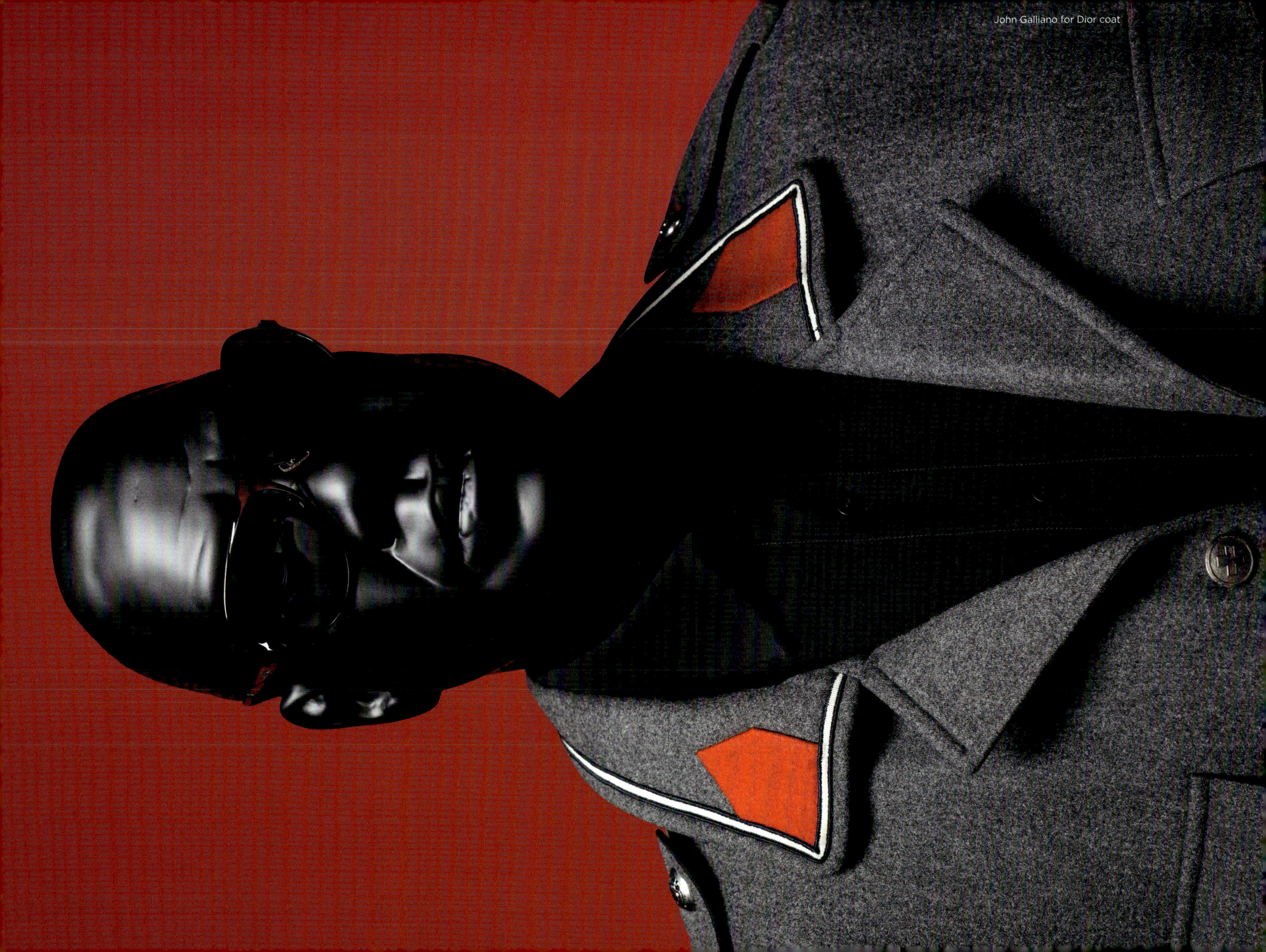

John Galliano for Dior coat

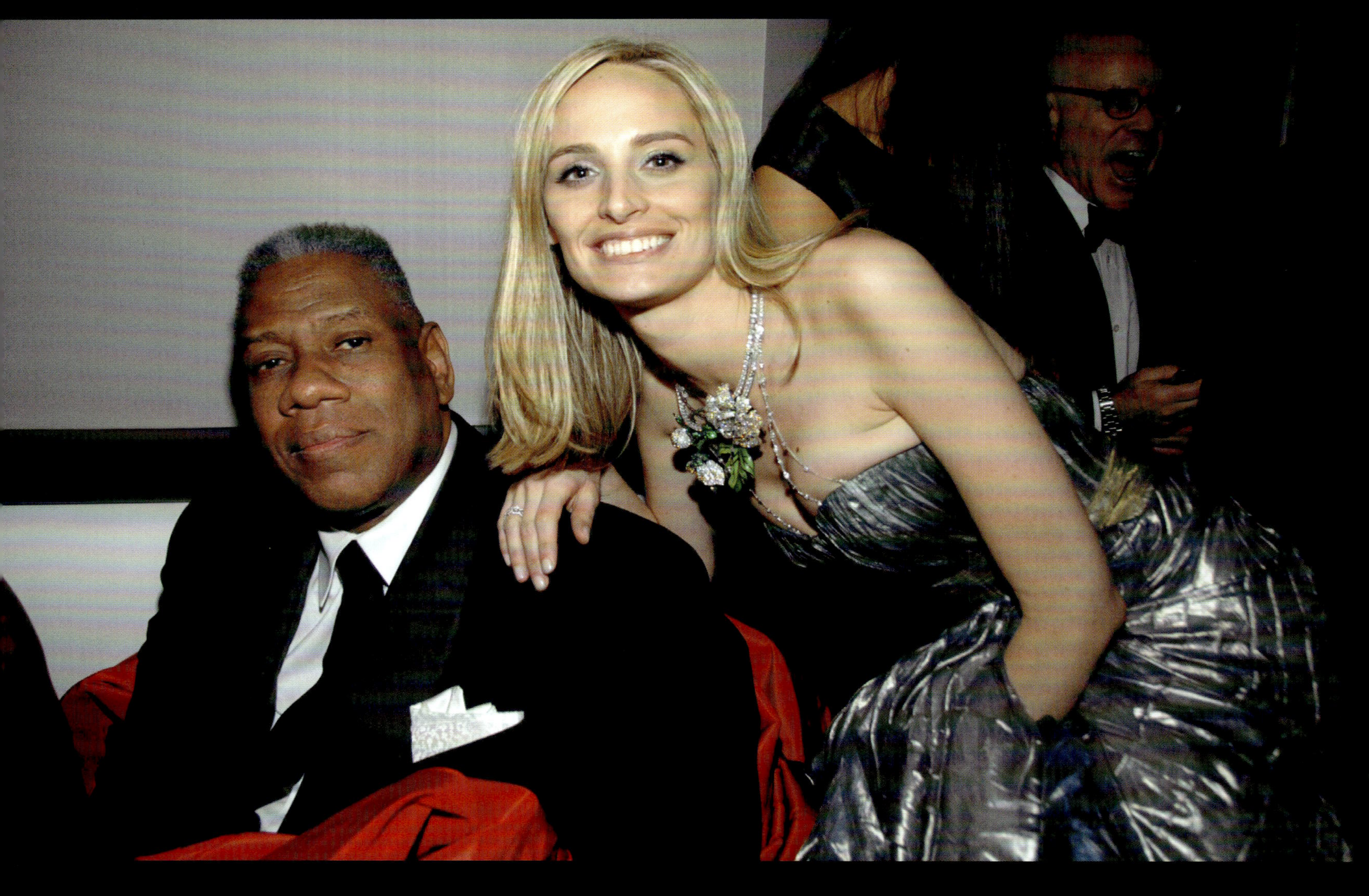

André and Lauren Santo Domingo at the Nina Ricci after-party for the Met Gala at Philippe in New York, May 2008. Photo by DAVID X PRUTTING/Patrick McMullan via Getty Images.

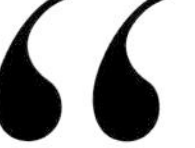

André had an encyclopedic **knowledge** of fashion history. He knew every **moment**, every trend, every designer, every look.

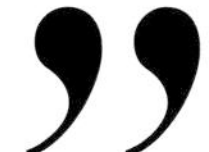

LAUREN SANTO DOMINGO

Tom Ford kimono, Dior haute couture shirt, and Chado Ralph Rucci trousers

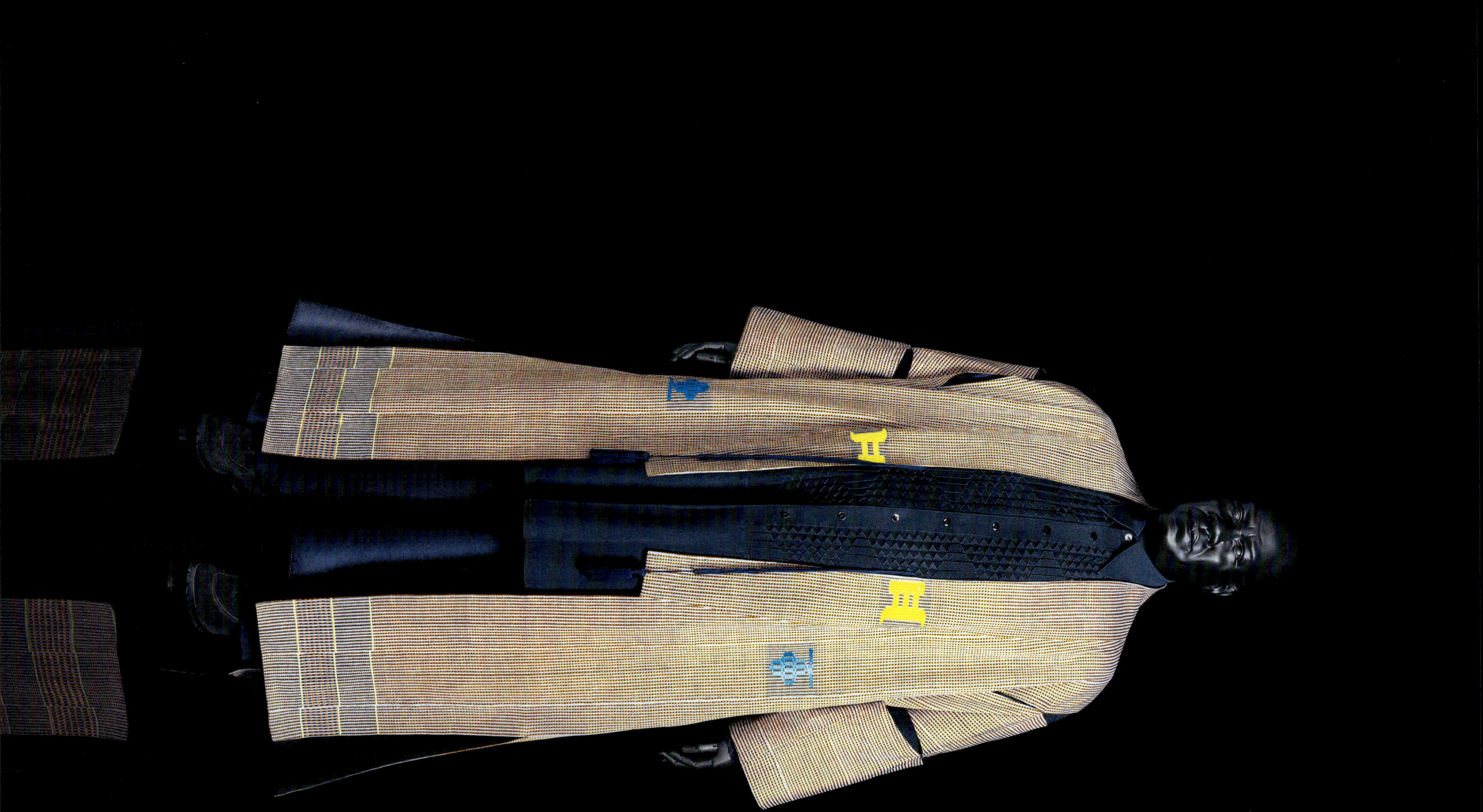

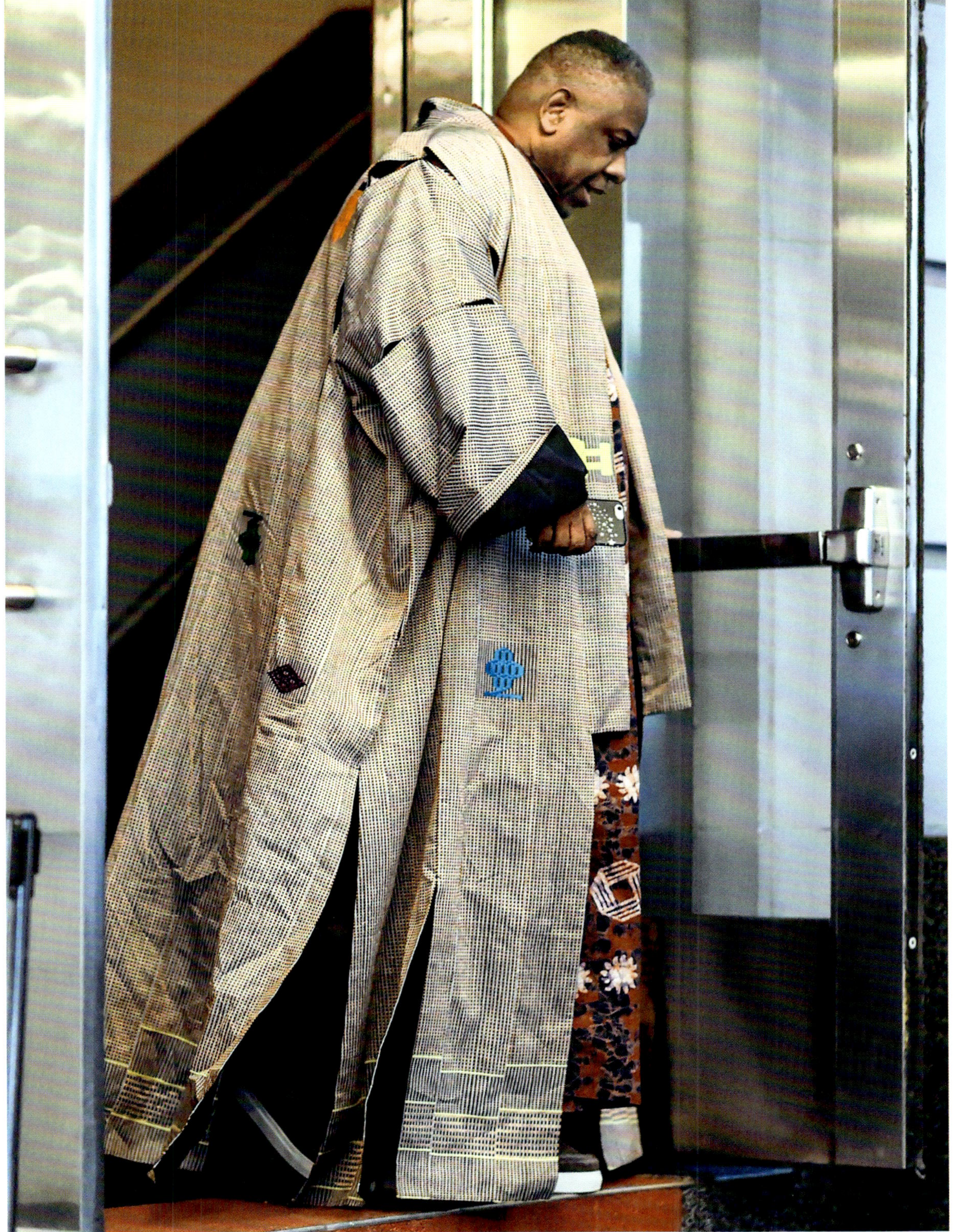

André outside the Marc Jacobs Spring/Summer 2017 runway show during New York Fashion Week. Photo by Daniel Zuchnik/Getty Images.

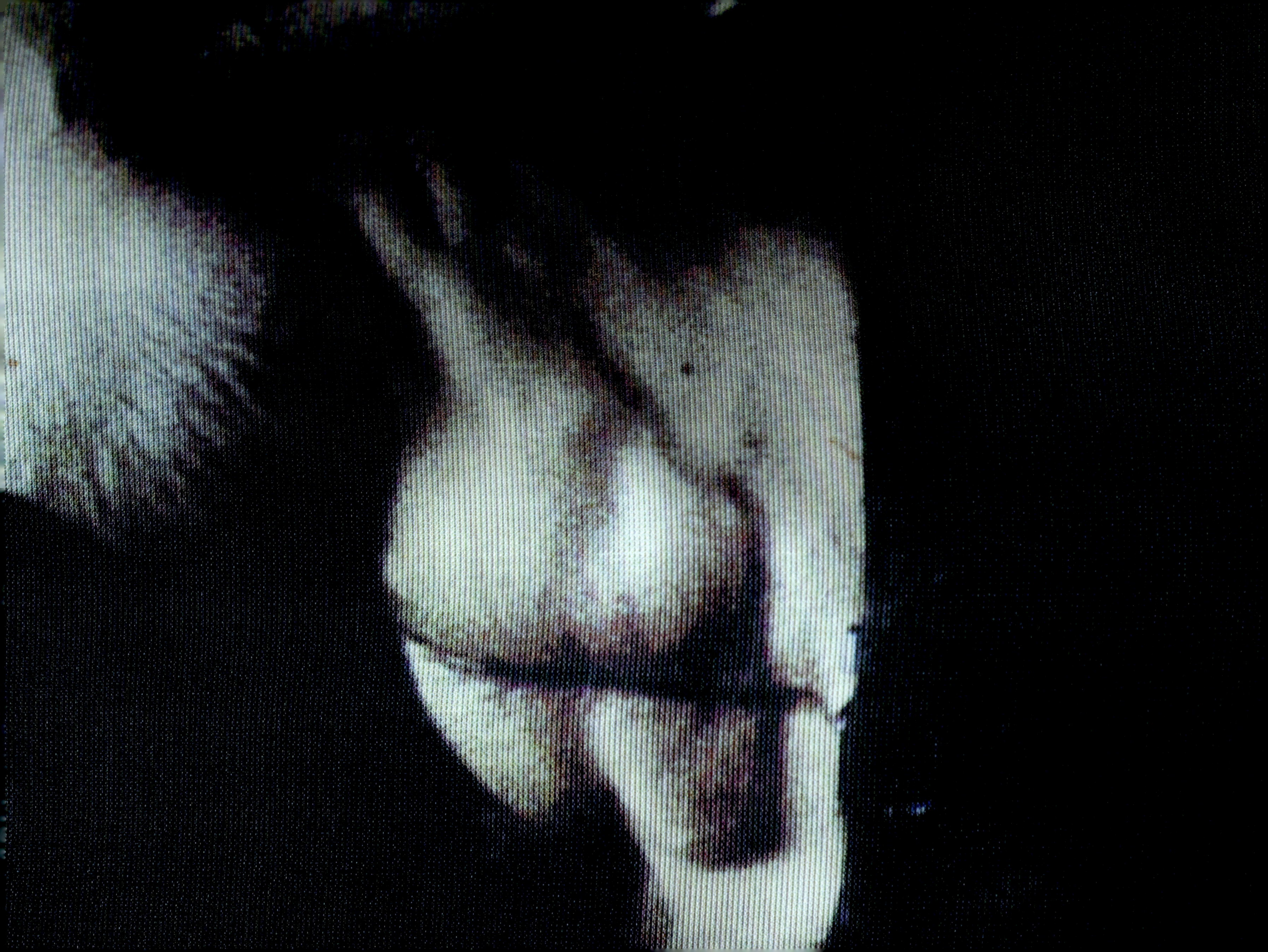

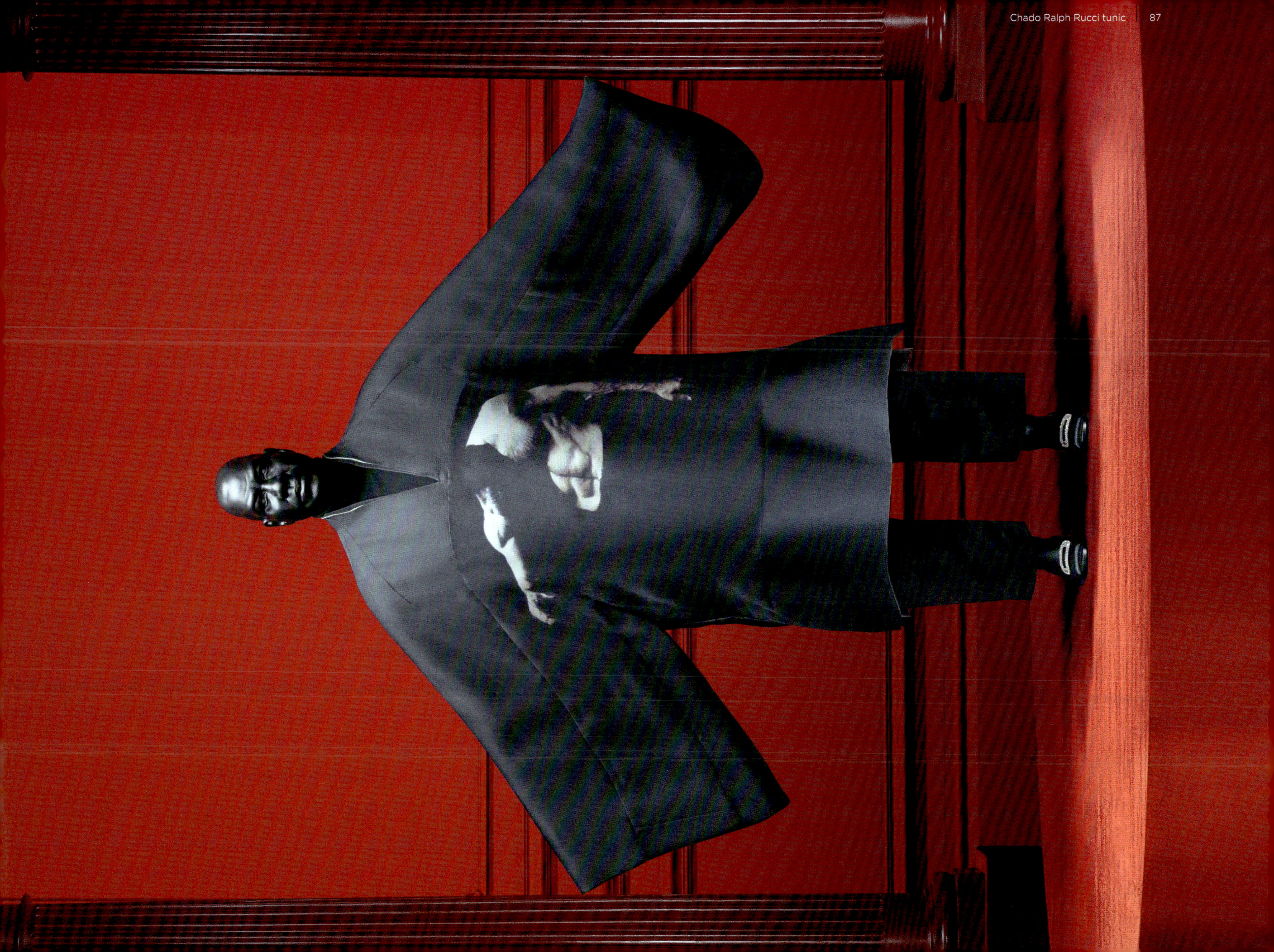

Chado Ralph Rucci tunic

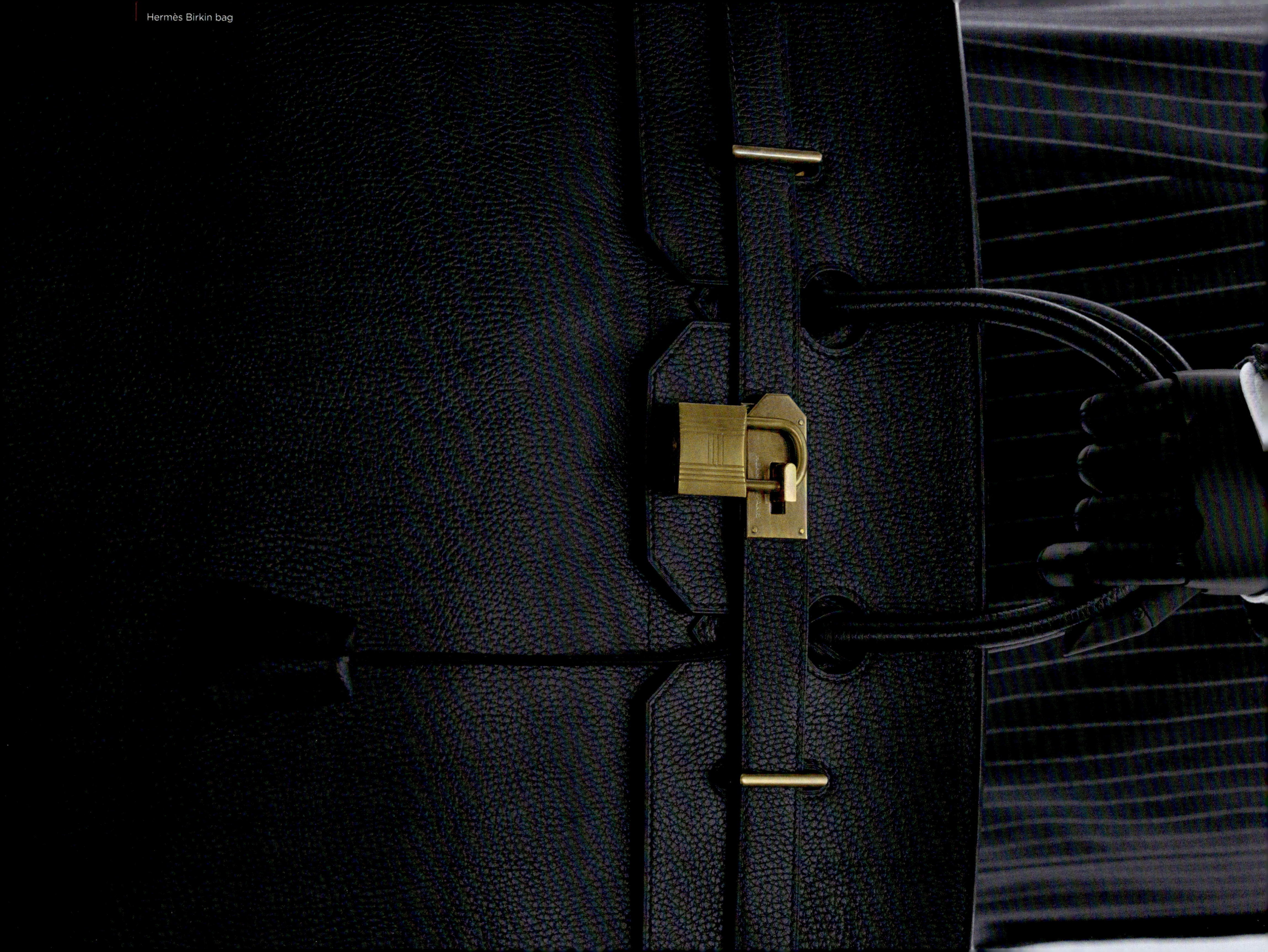

Hermès Birkin bag

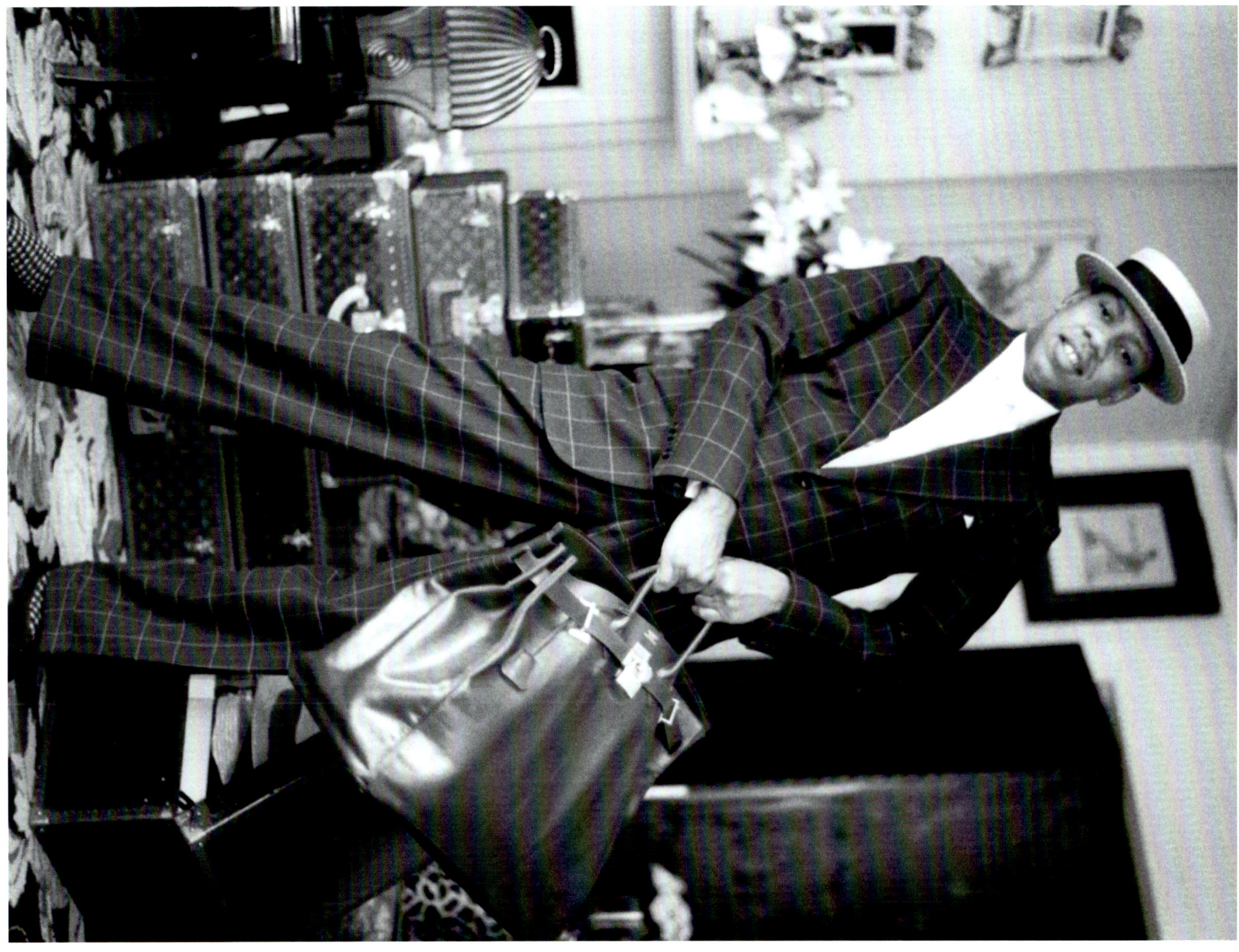

André, date unknown. Photo by Arthur Elgort/Trunk Archive.

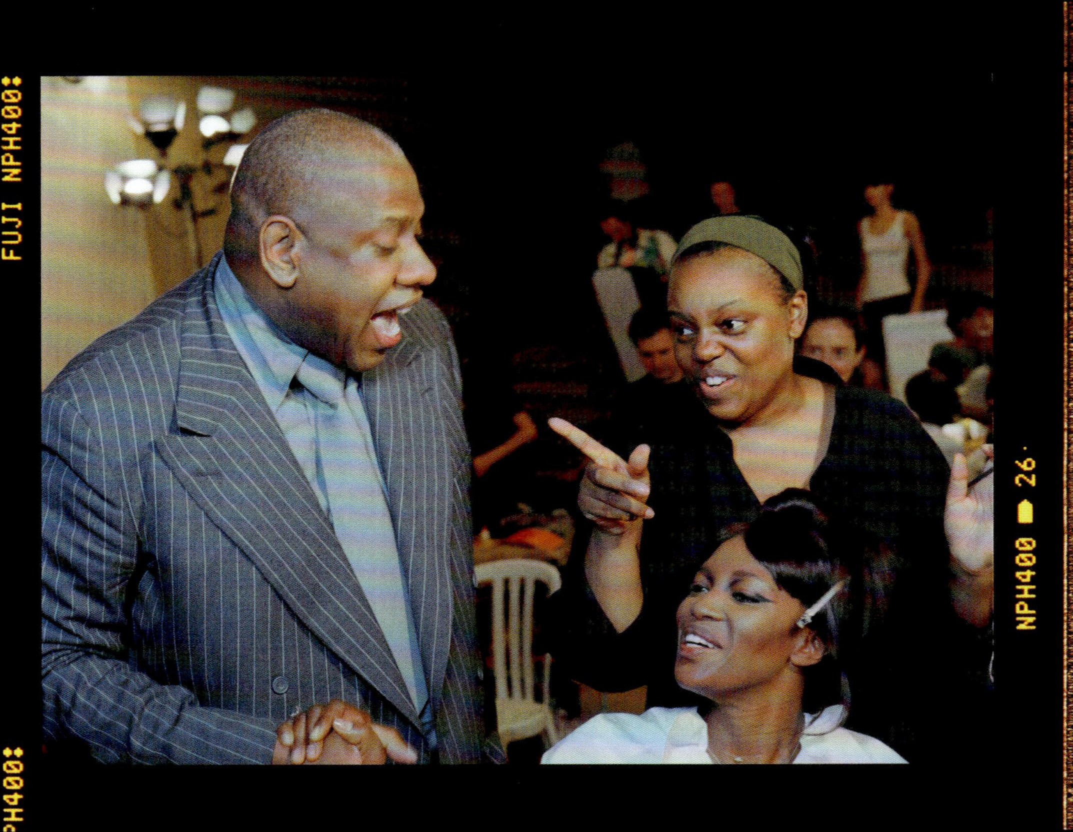
FUJI NPH400
NPH400 26
PH400

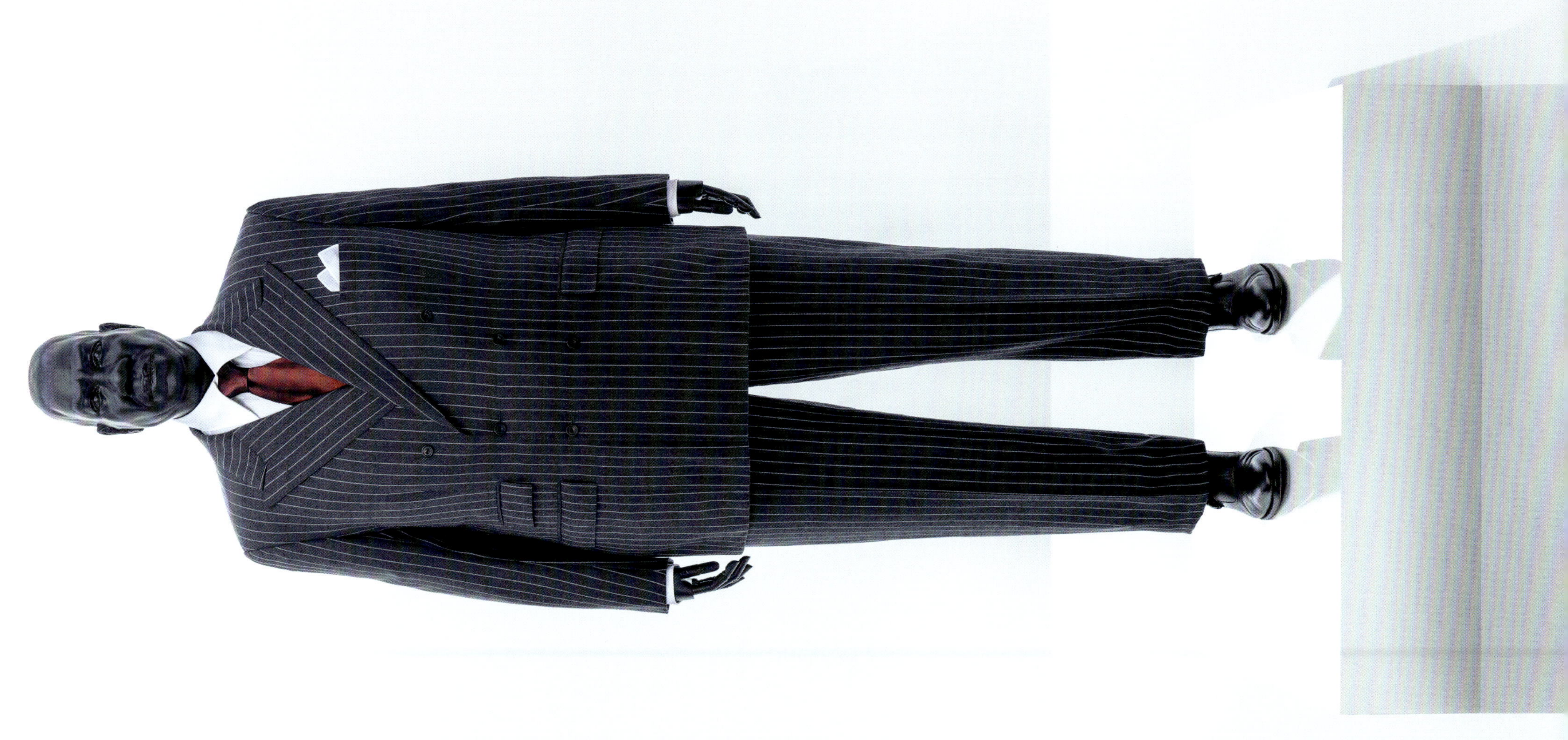

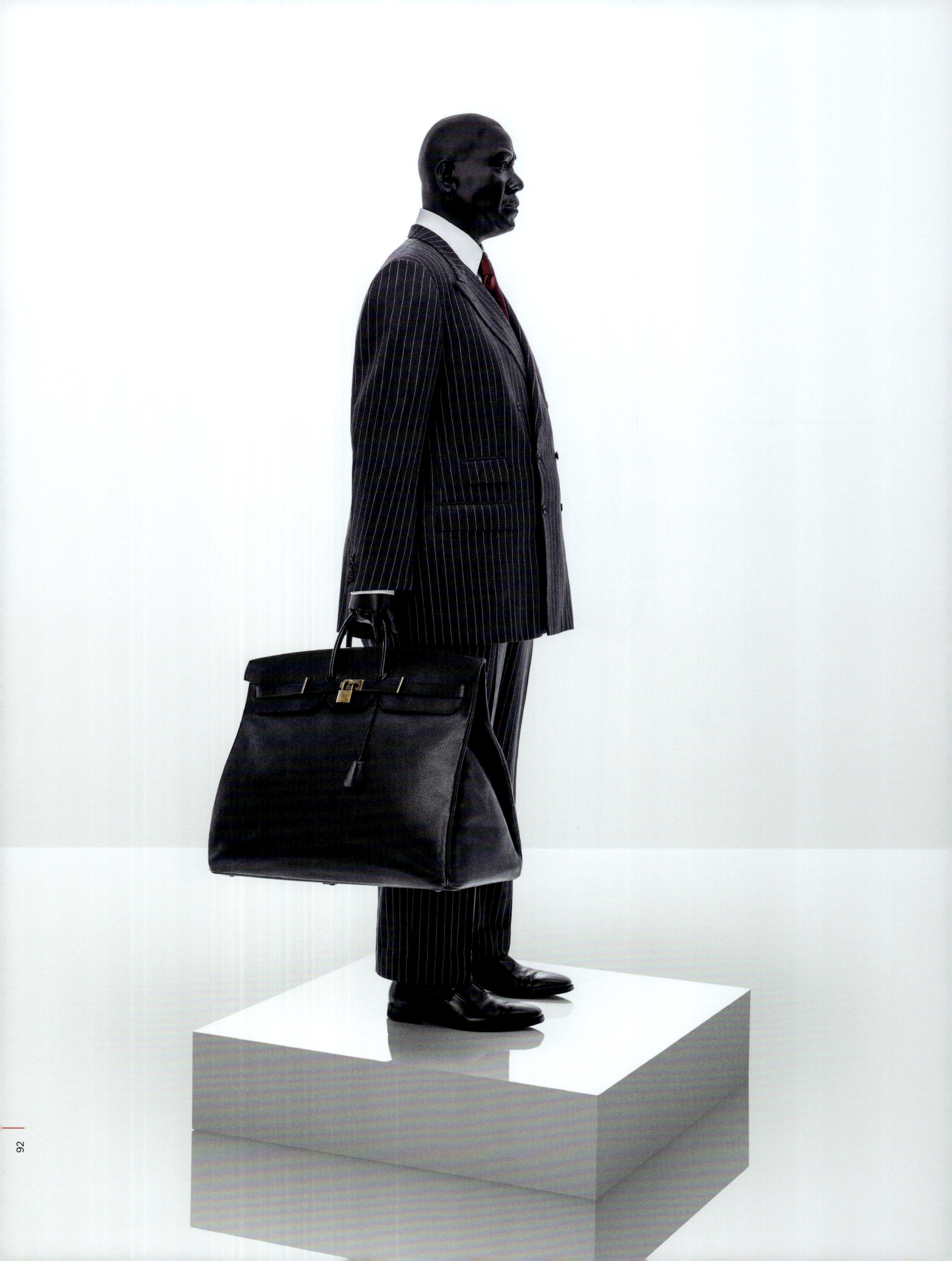

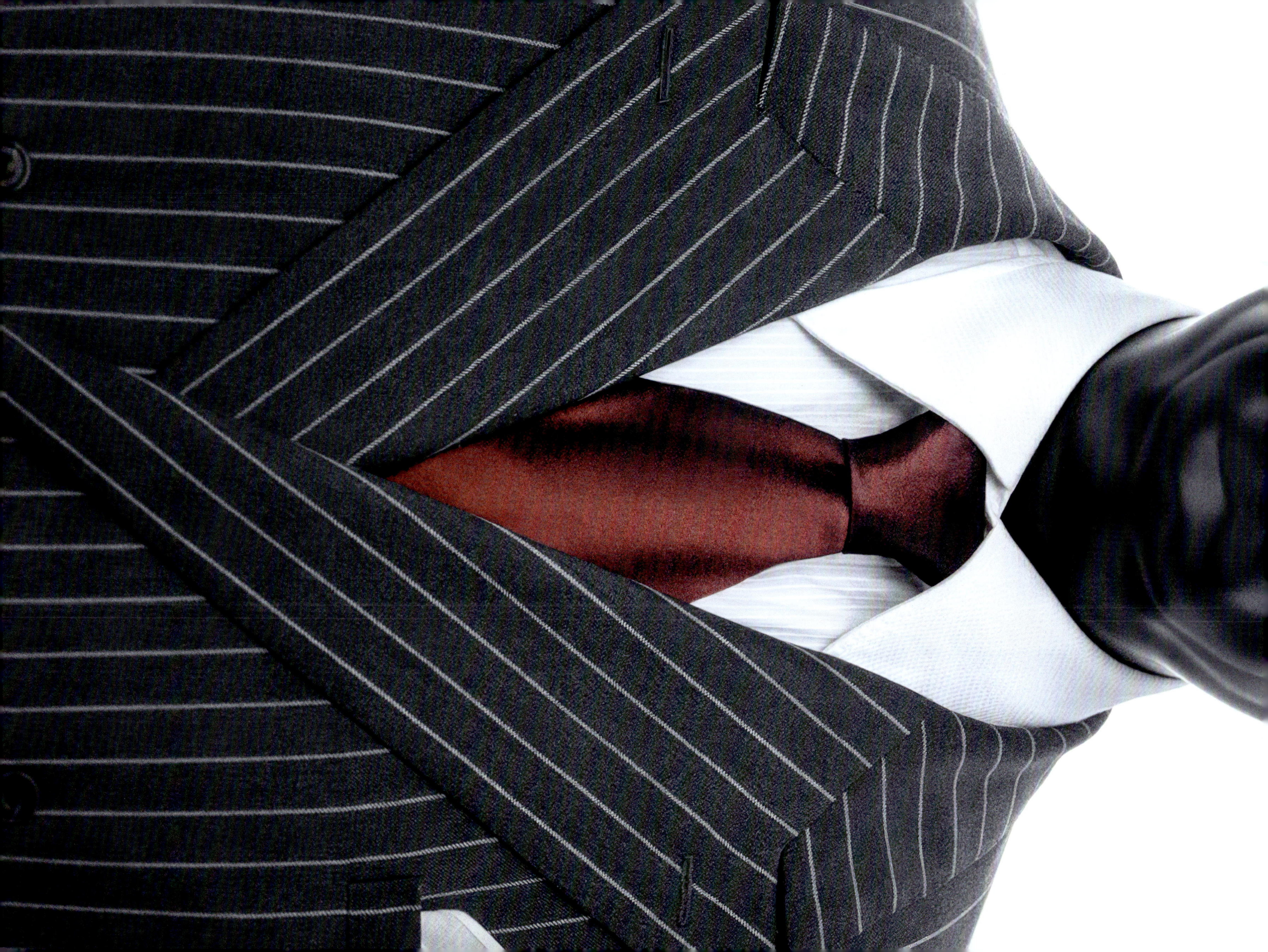

“

Fashion is **not just** about looking **pretty**.
It’s about **looking forward**.

”

André Leon Talley

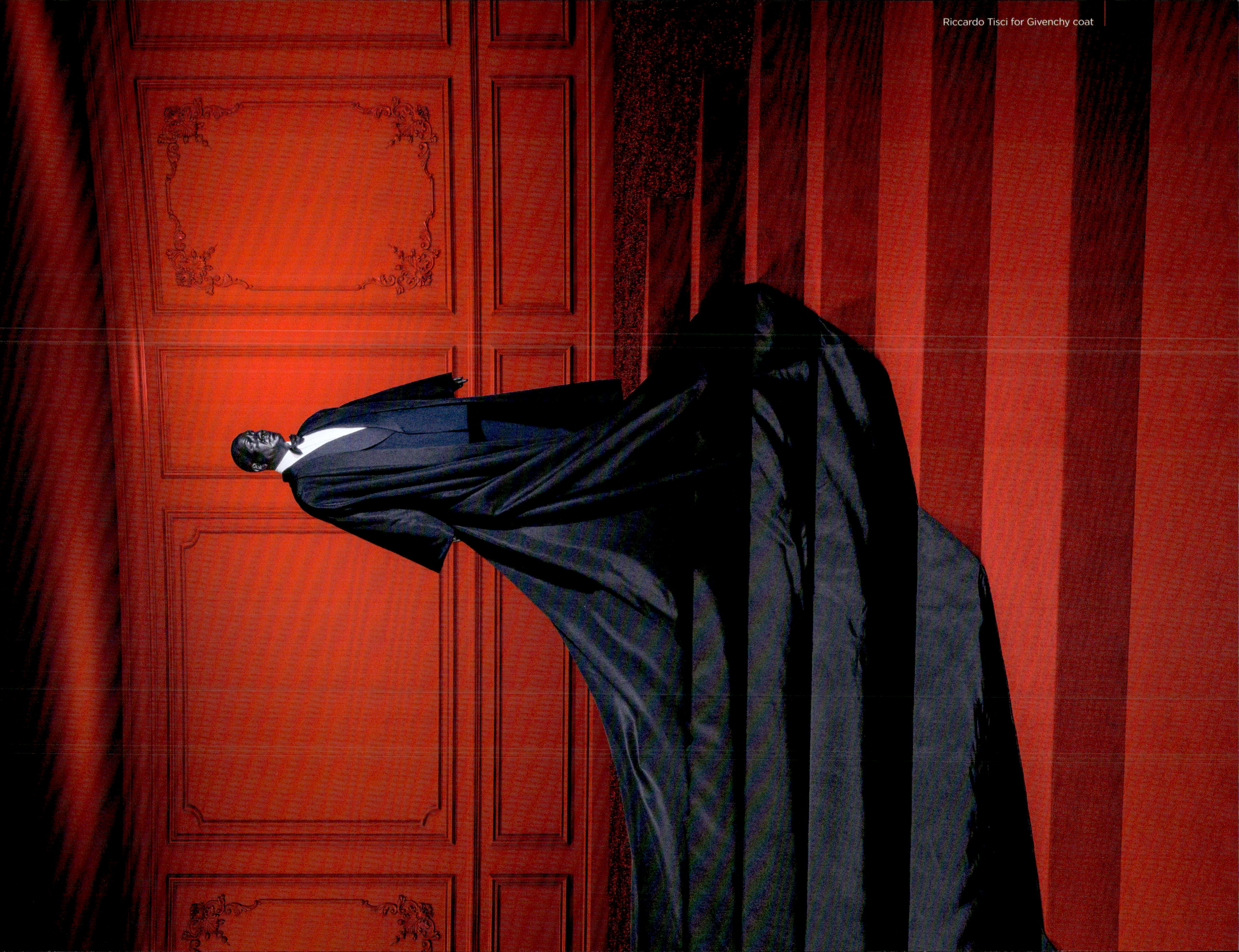
Riccardo Tisci for Givenchy coat

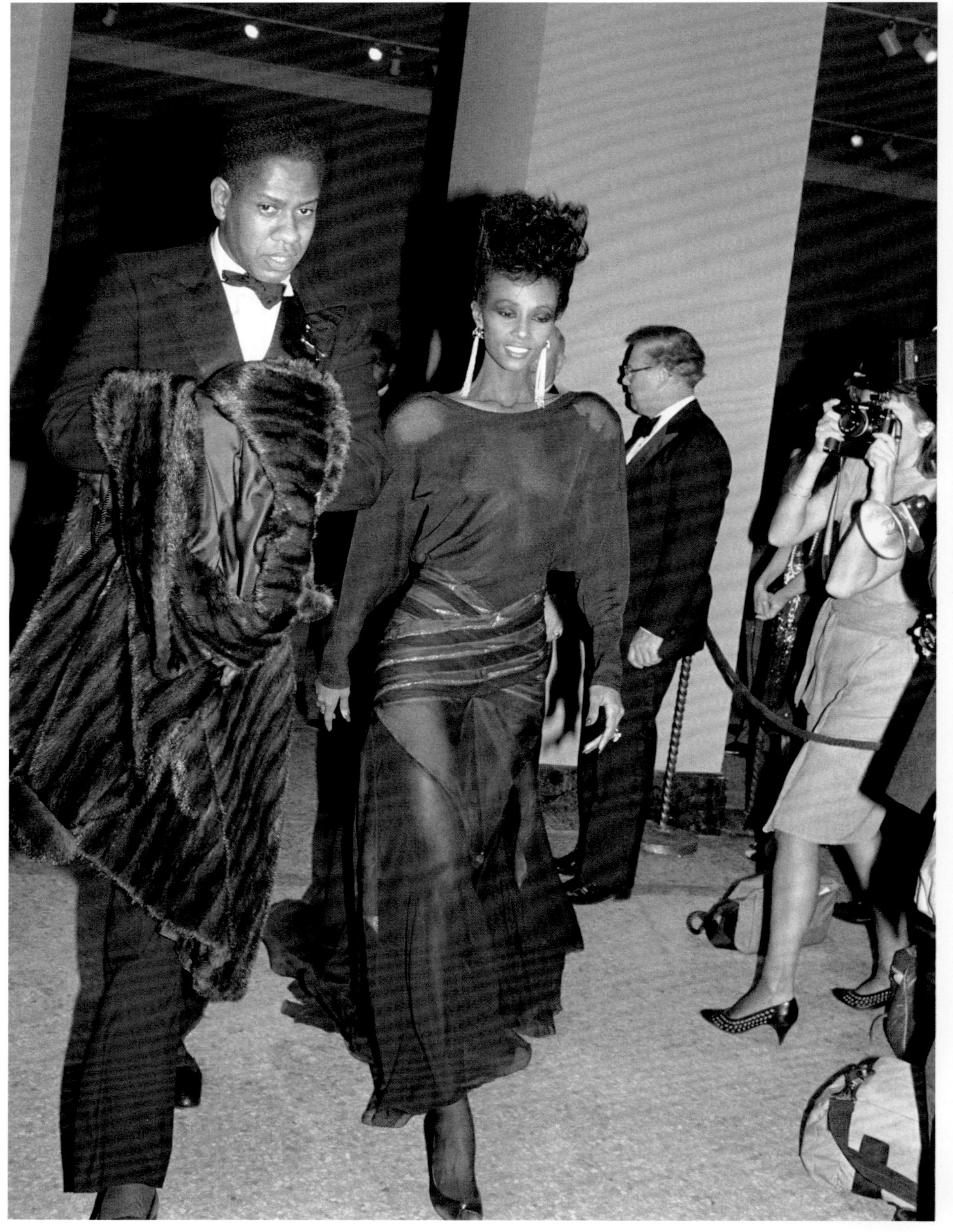

André and Iman arriving at the Met Gala for the Yves Saint Laurent retrospective, December 1983. Photo by Tony Palmieri/WWD/Penske Media via Getty Images.

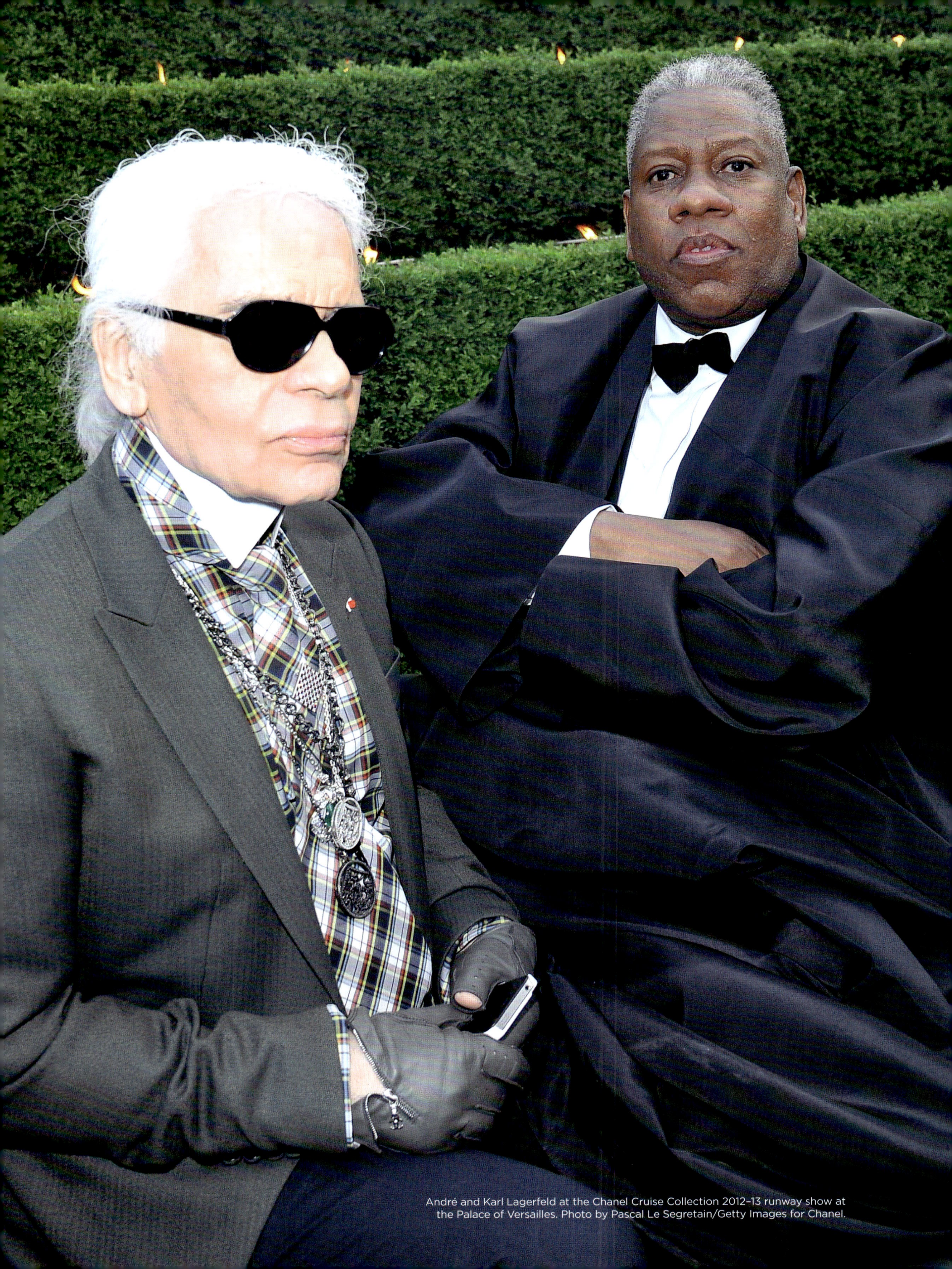

André and Karl Lagerfeld at the Chanel Cruise Collection 2012–13 runway show at the Palace of Versailles. Photo by Pascal Le Segretain/Getty Images for Chanel.

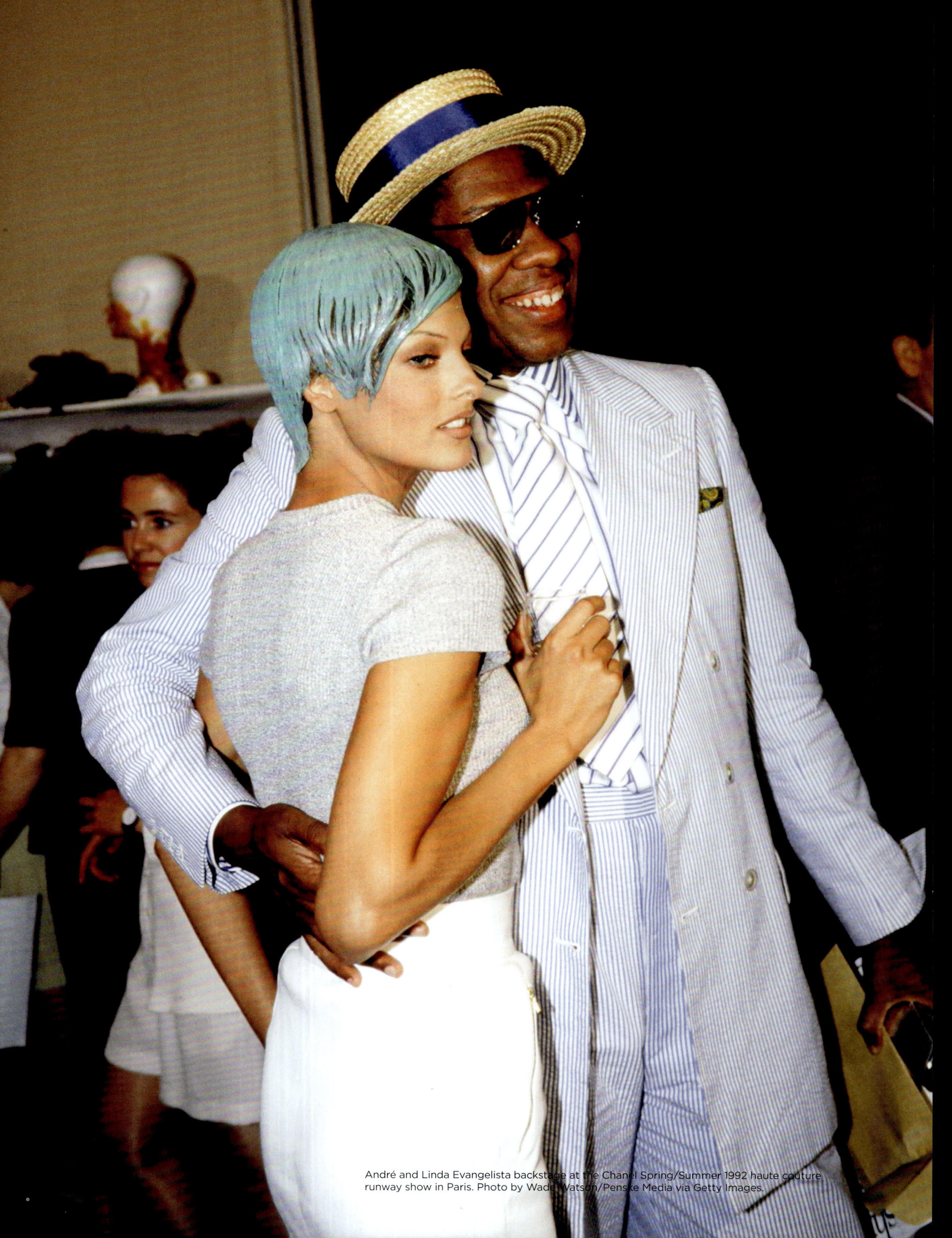

André and Linda Evangelista backstage at the Chanel Spring/Summer 1992 haute couture runway show in Paris. Photo by Wade Watson/Penske Media via Getty Images.

Richard Anderson suit with Alex Hitz tie and no label boater hat

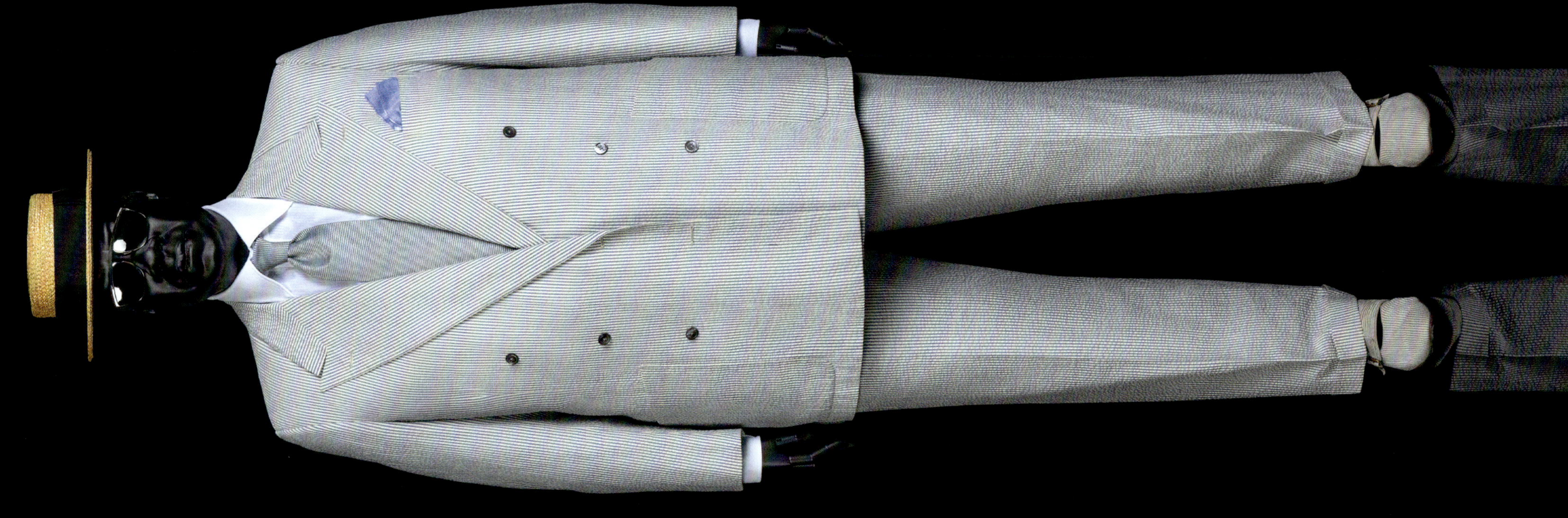

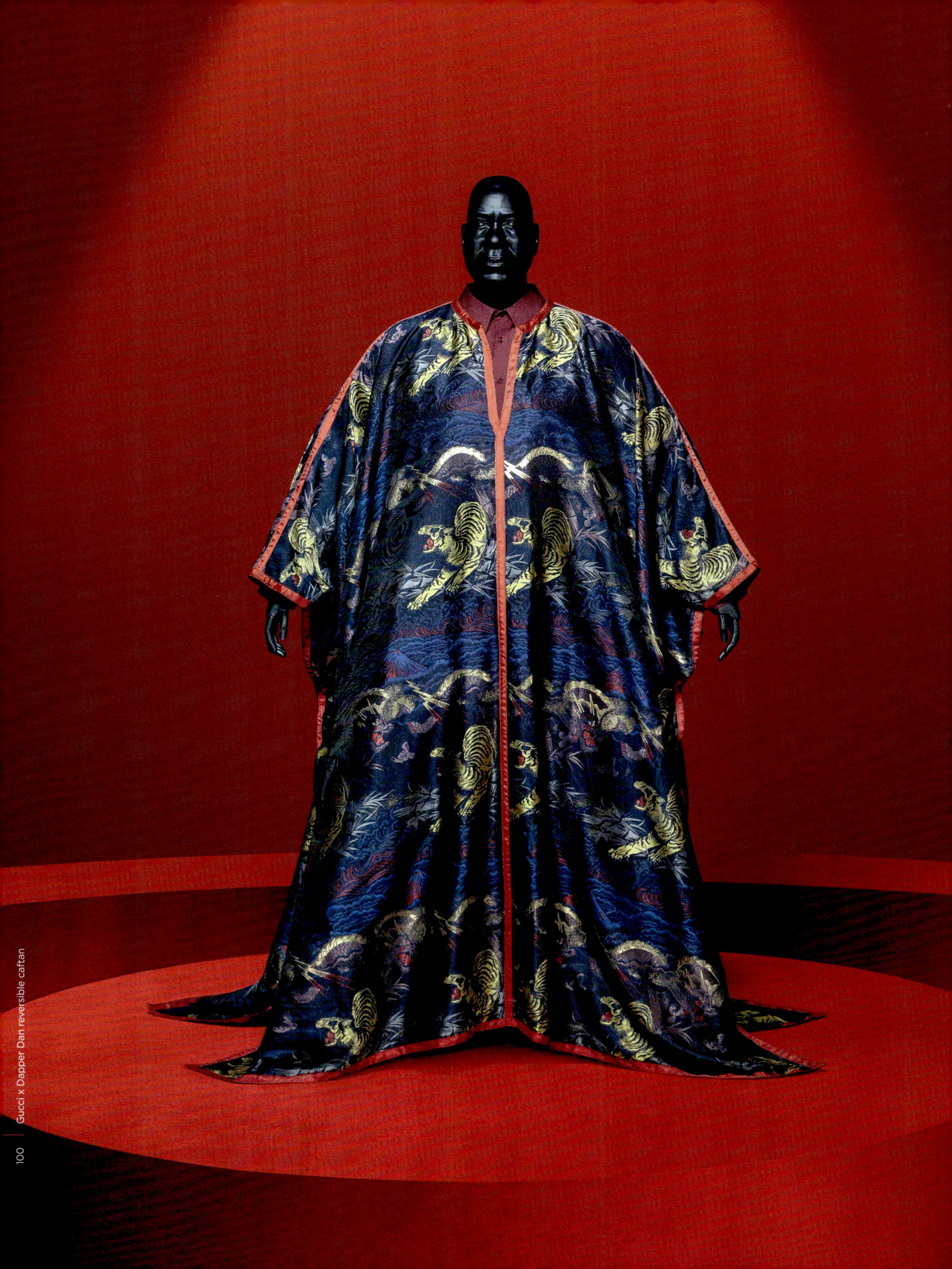

Gucci x Dapper Dan reversible caftan

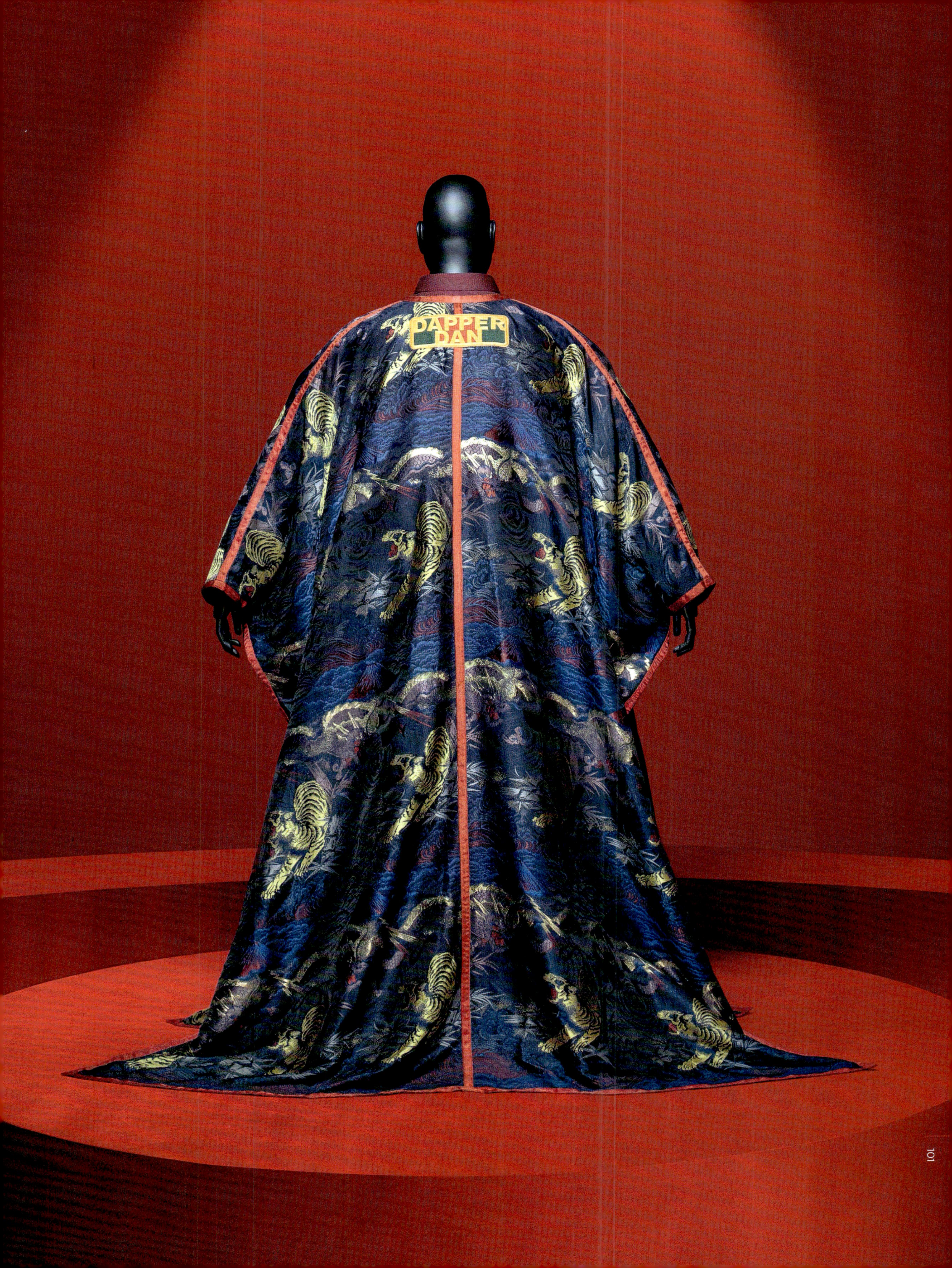
DAPPER
DAN

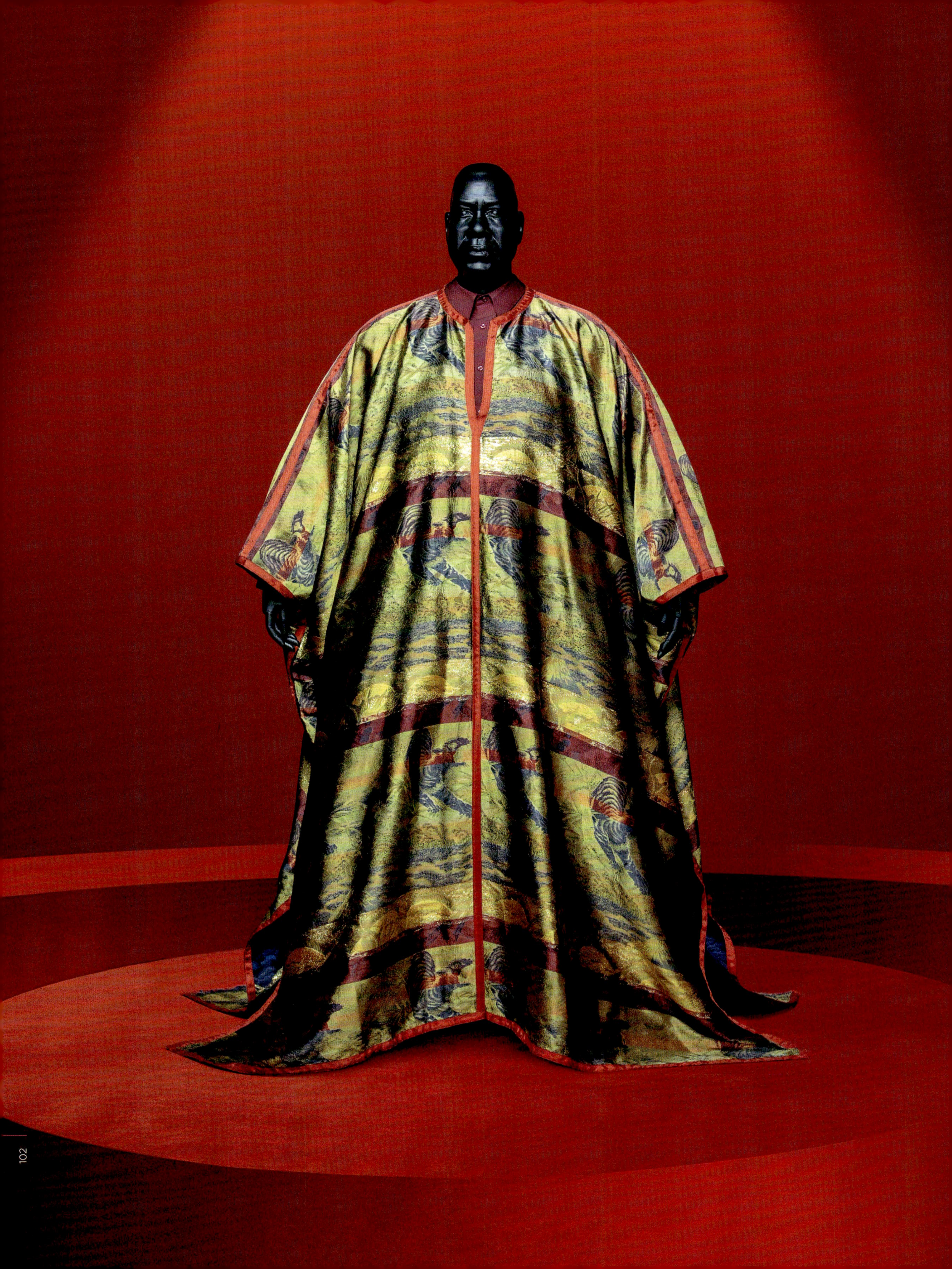

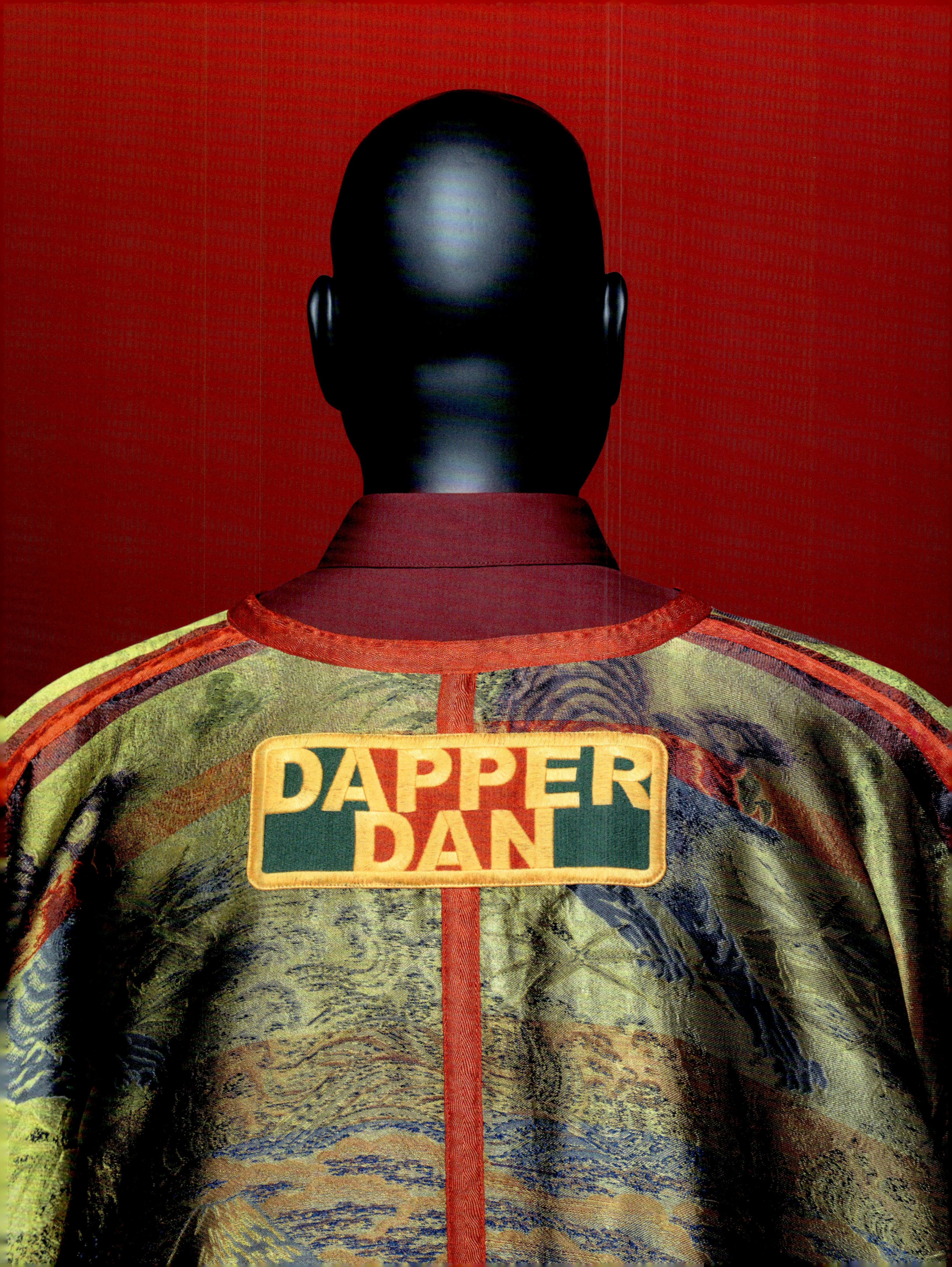
DAPPER
DAN

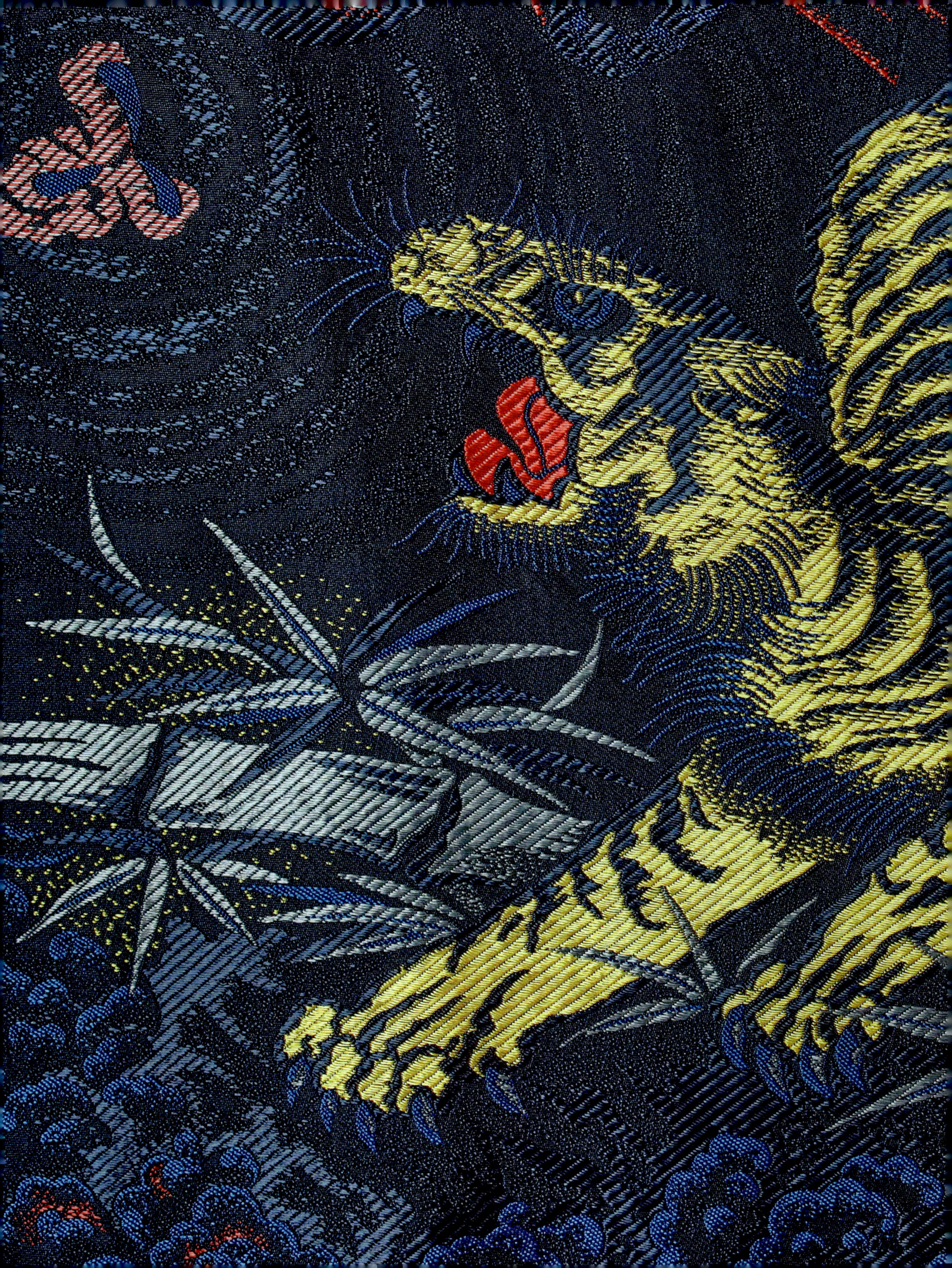

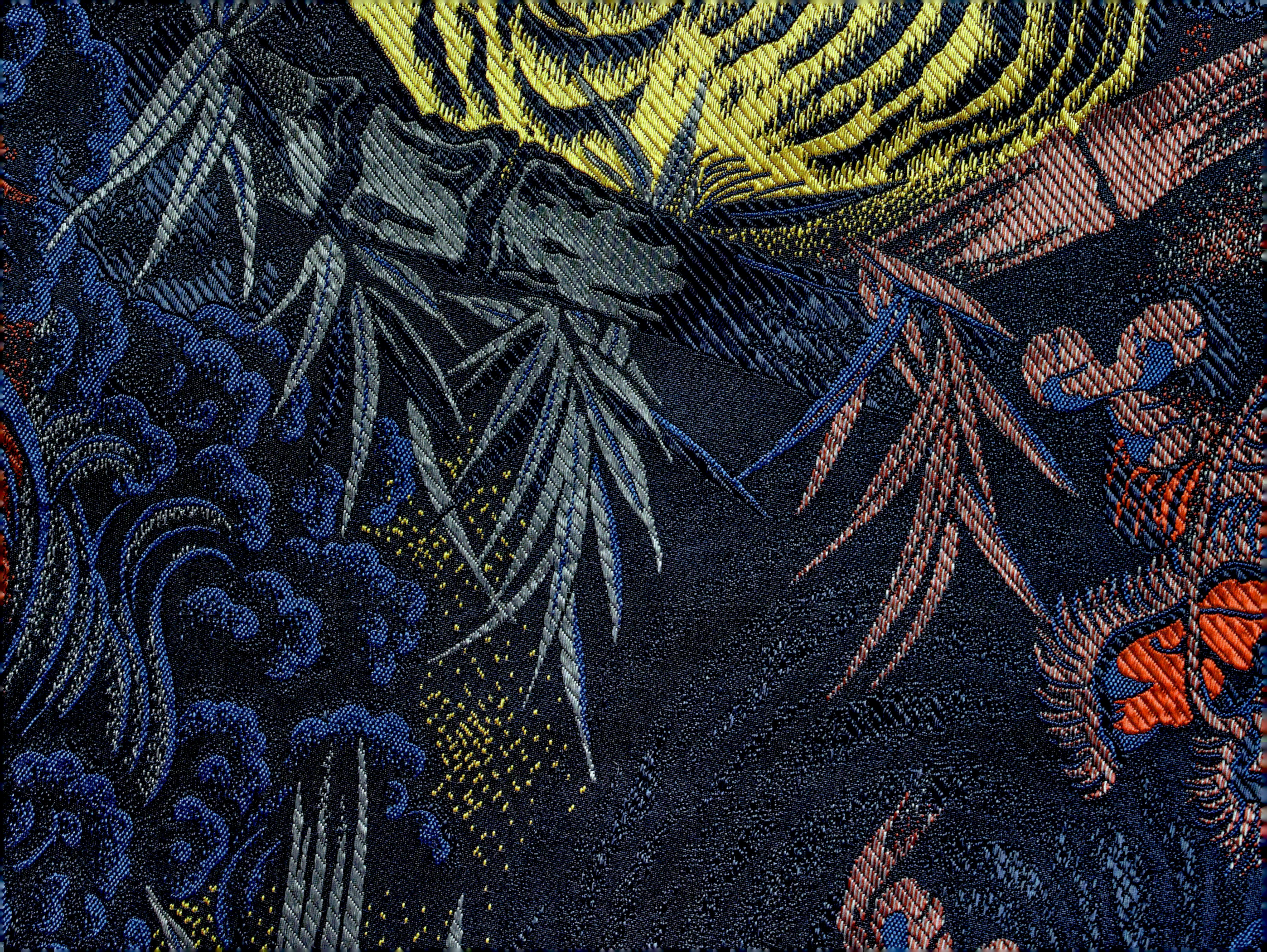

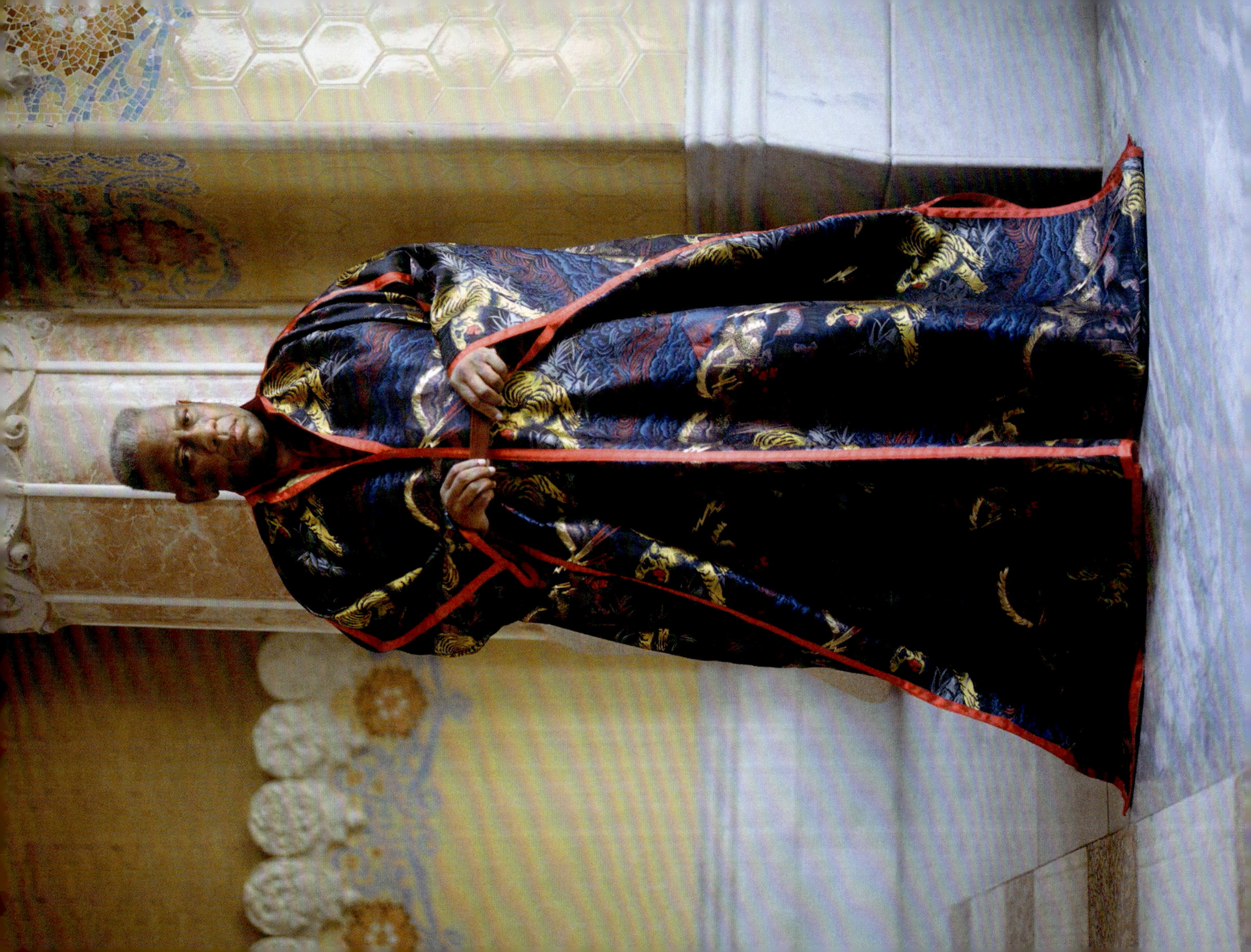

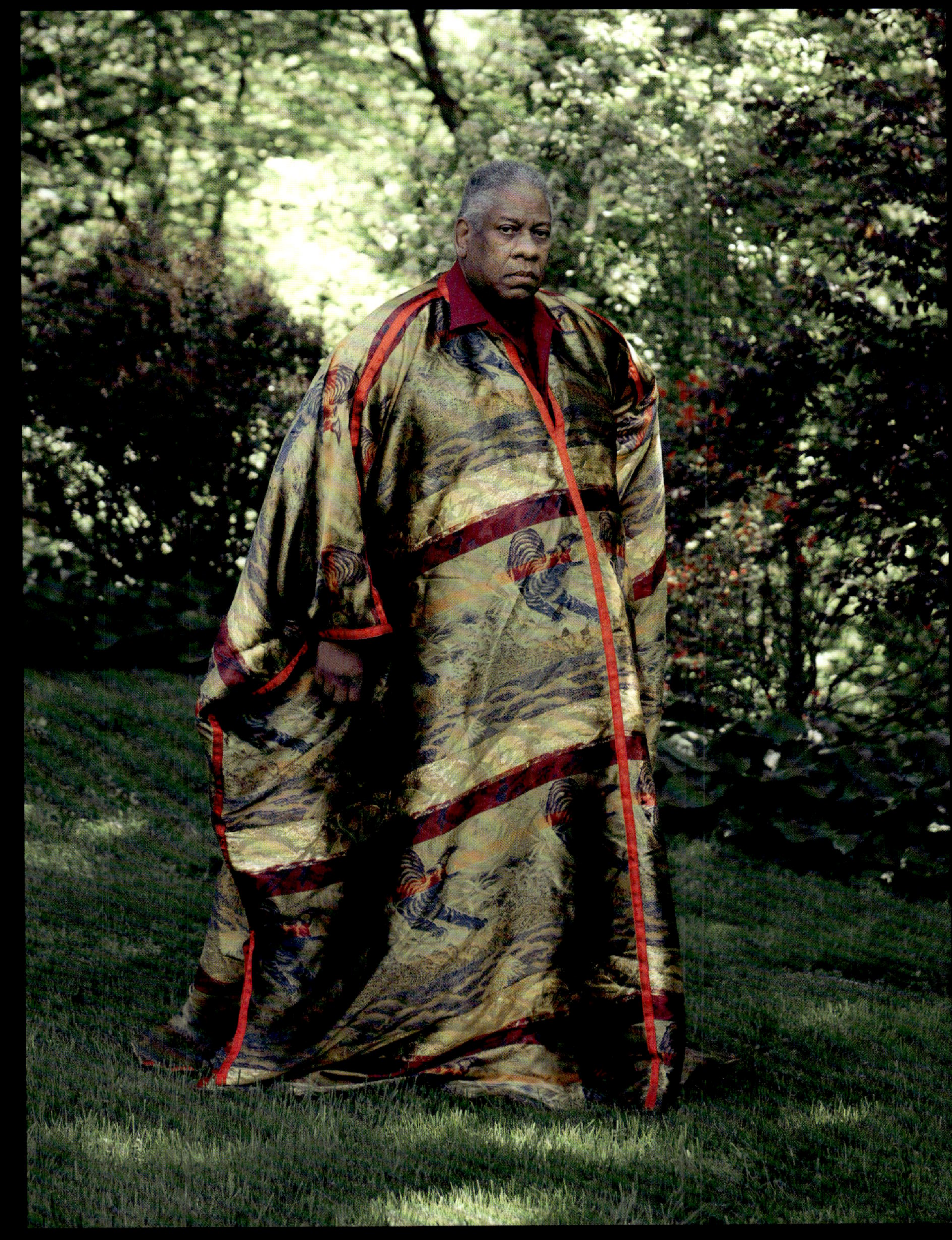

André at his home in White Plains, New York, May 2018. Photo by George Etheredge/The New York Times/Redux

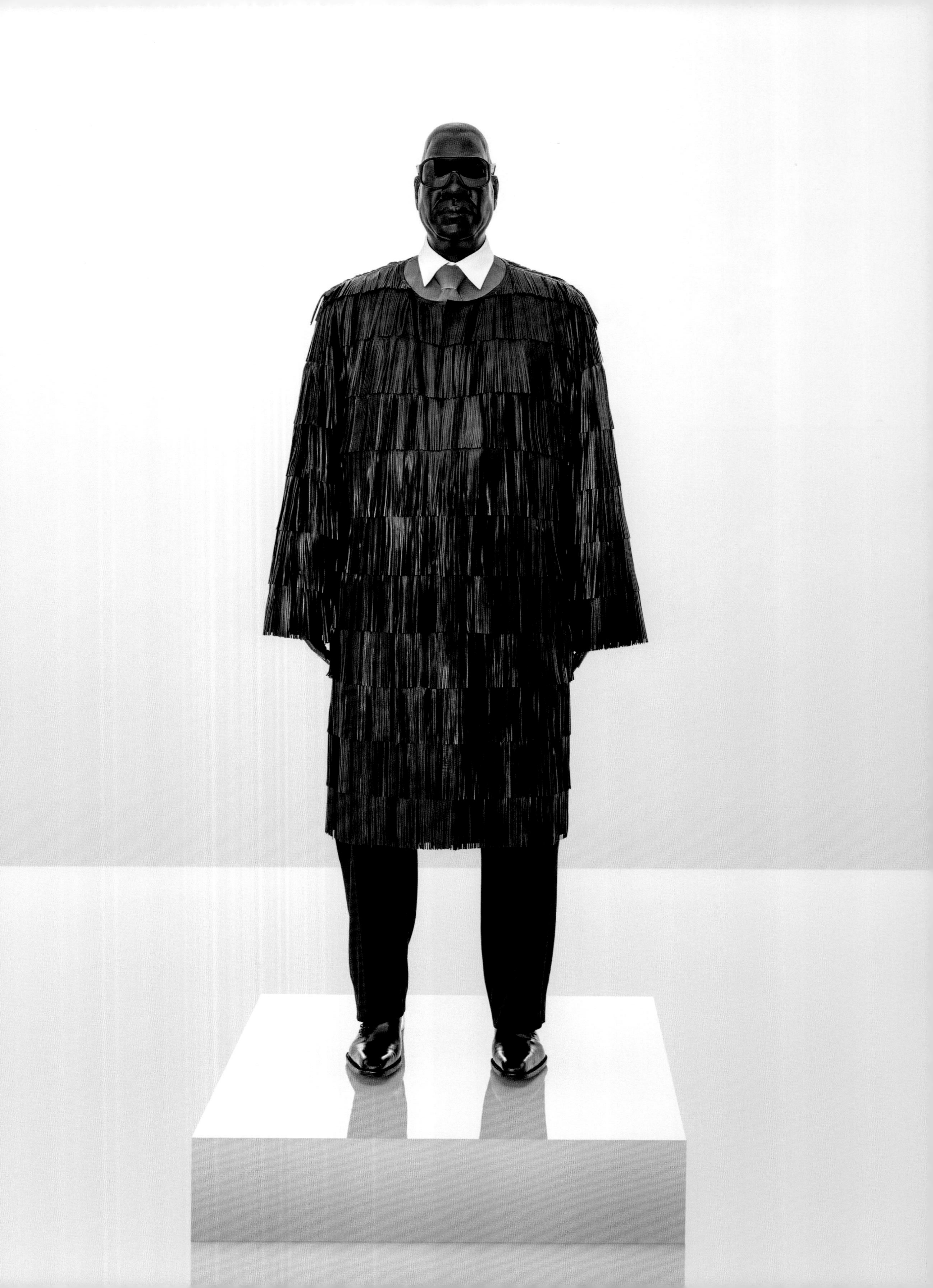

Prada coat with Charvet shirt and tie

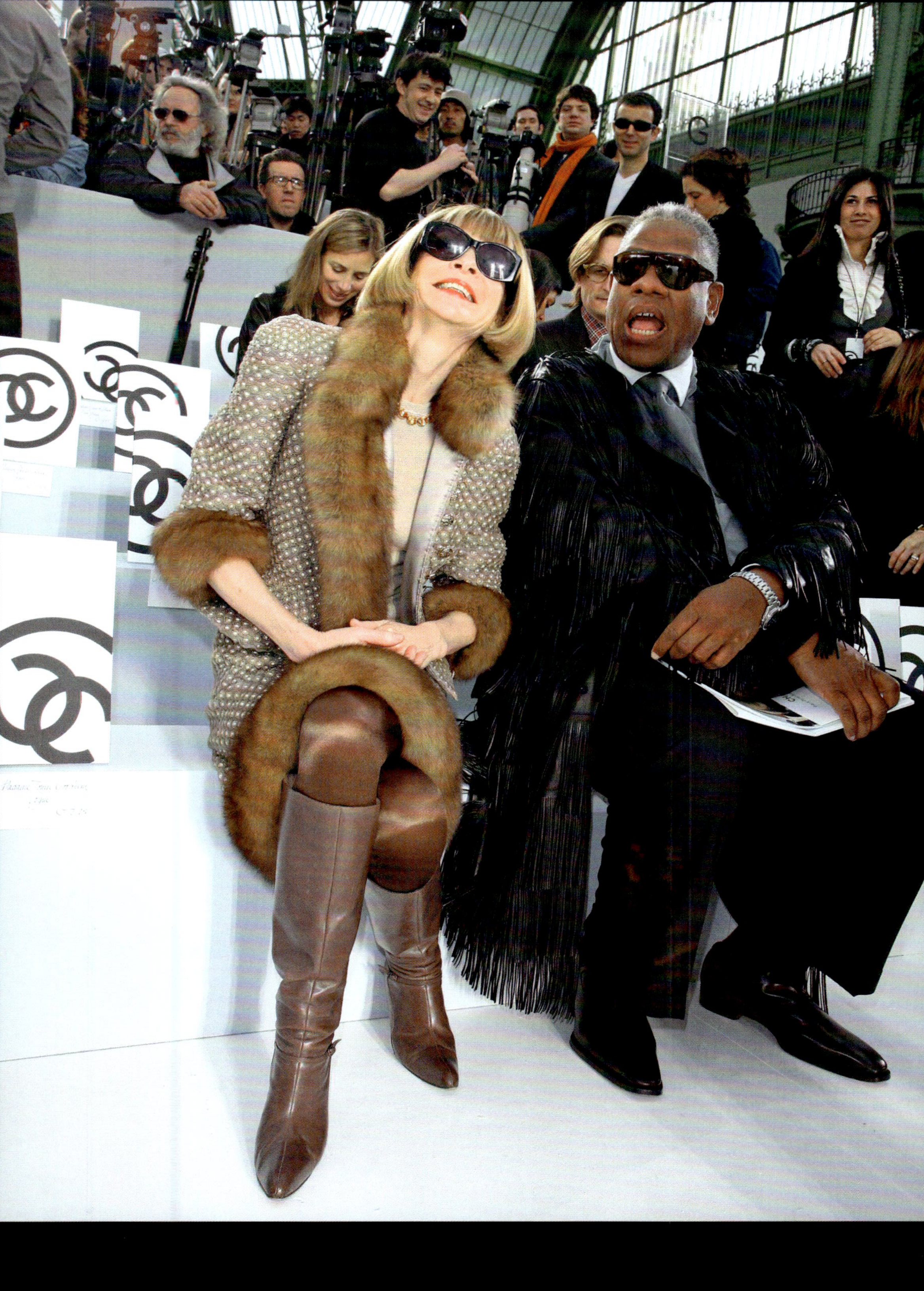

André and Anna Wintour at the Chanel Fall/Winter 2007 ready-to-wear runway show a
Palais in Paris. Photo by Guignebourg-Khayat-Taamallah via Abaca Press/Alamy S

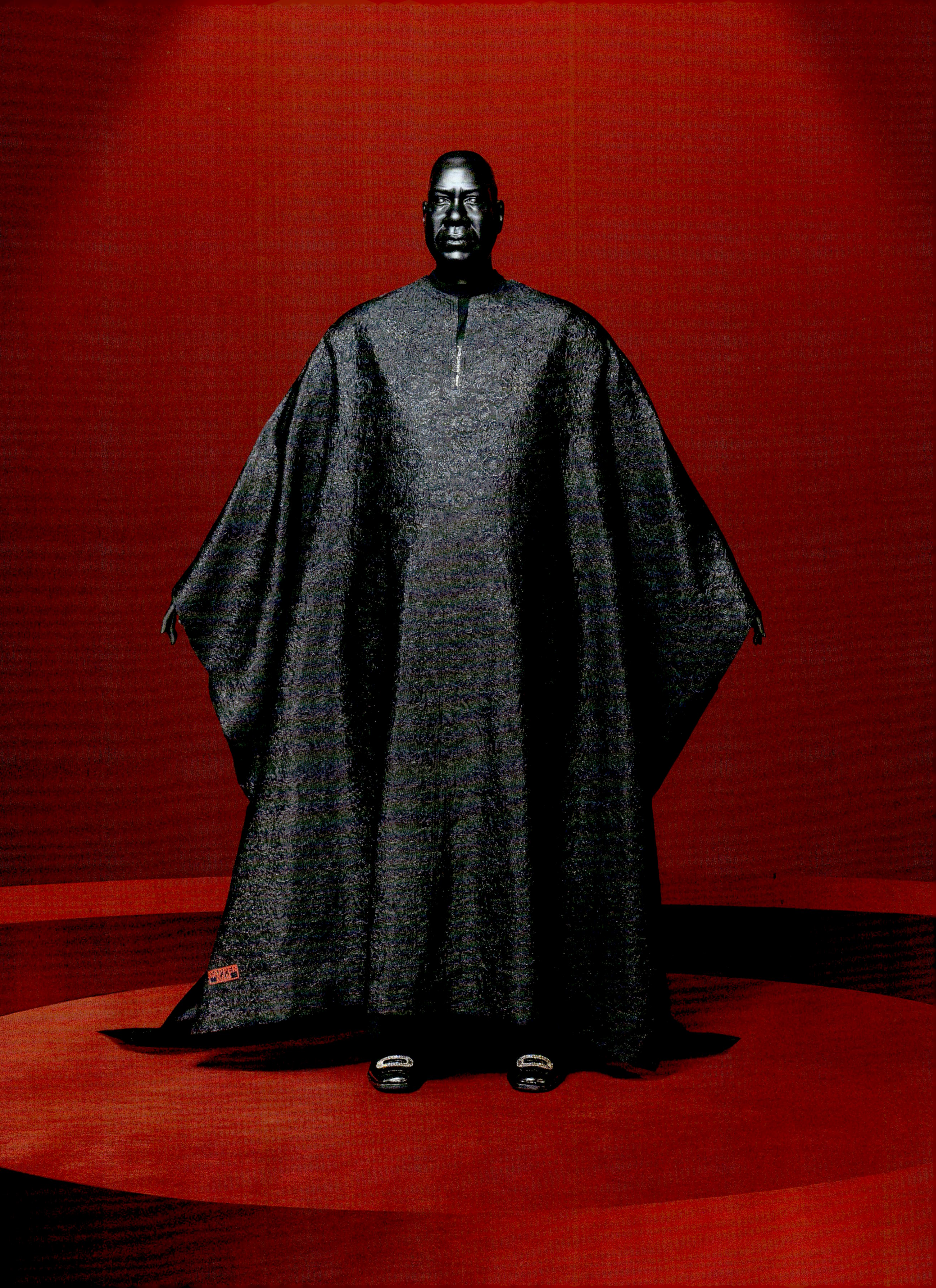

Dapper Dan caftan

“

André Leon Talley is the **texture** that defines the cloth of fashion. Studying him allowed me to drape my own ideas of fashion. The day he came to my Gucci atelier in Harlem was my birthday to the global world of fashion. He is the **father of fashion** identity.

”

DAPPER DAN

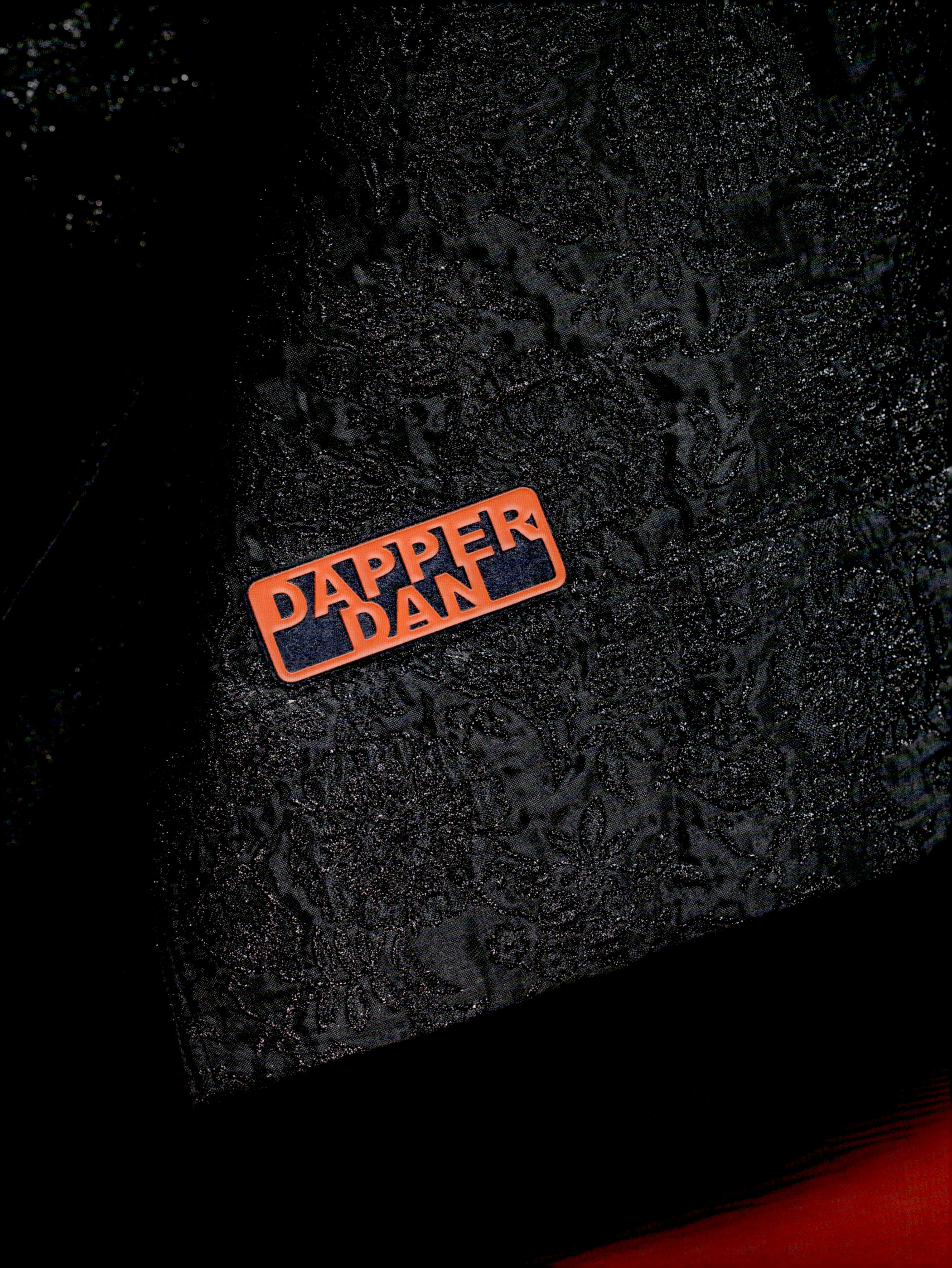
DAPPER
DAN

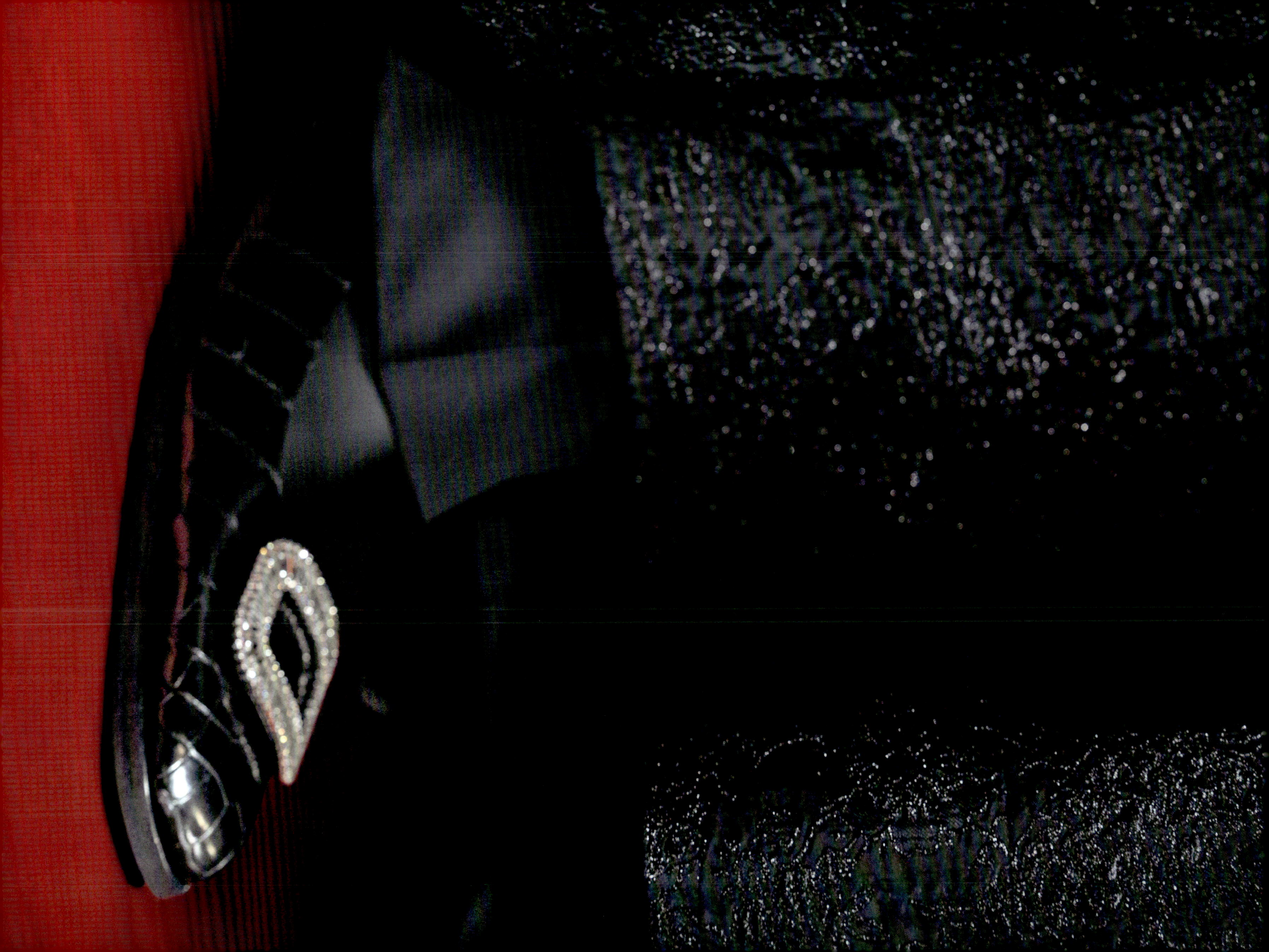

Chado Ralph Rucci tunic

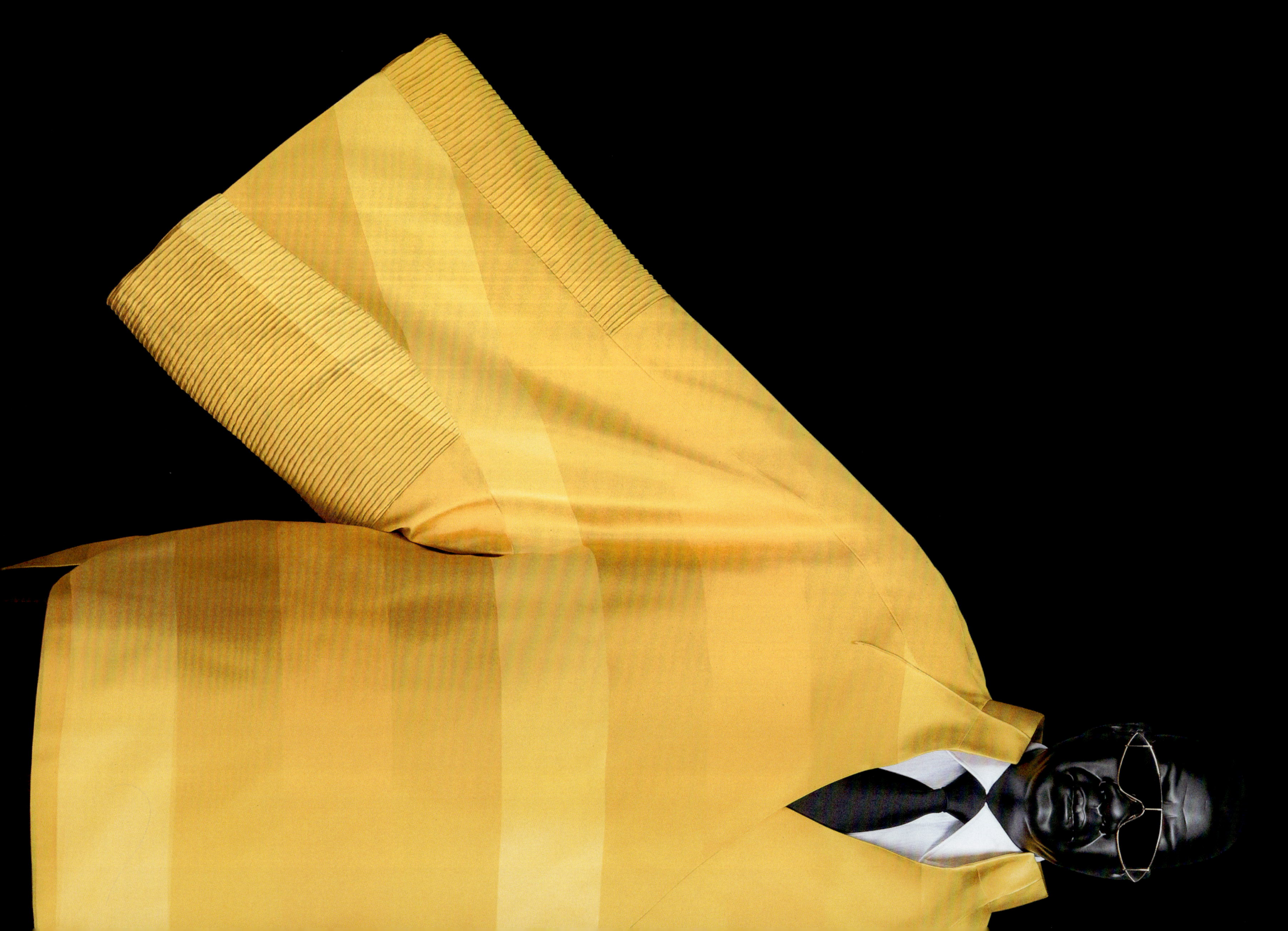

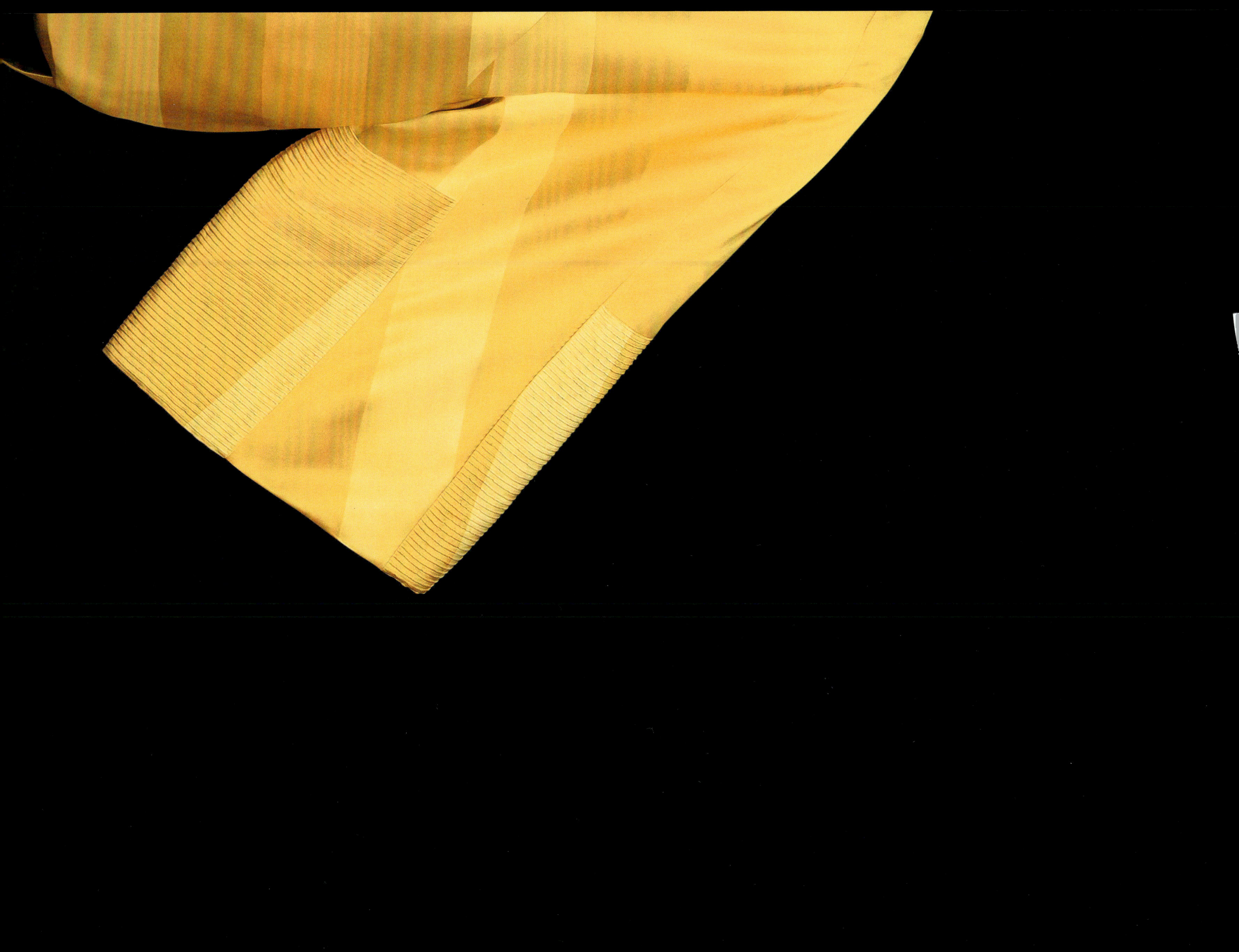

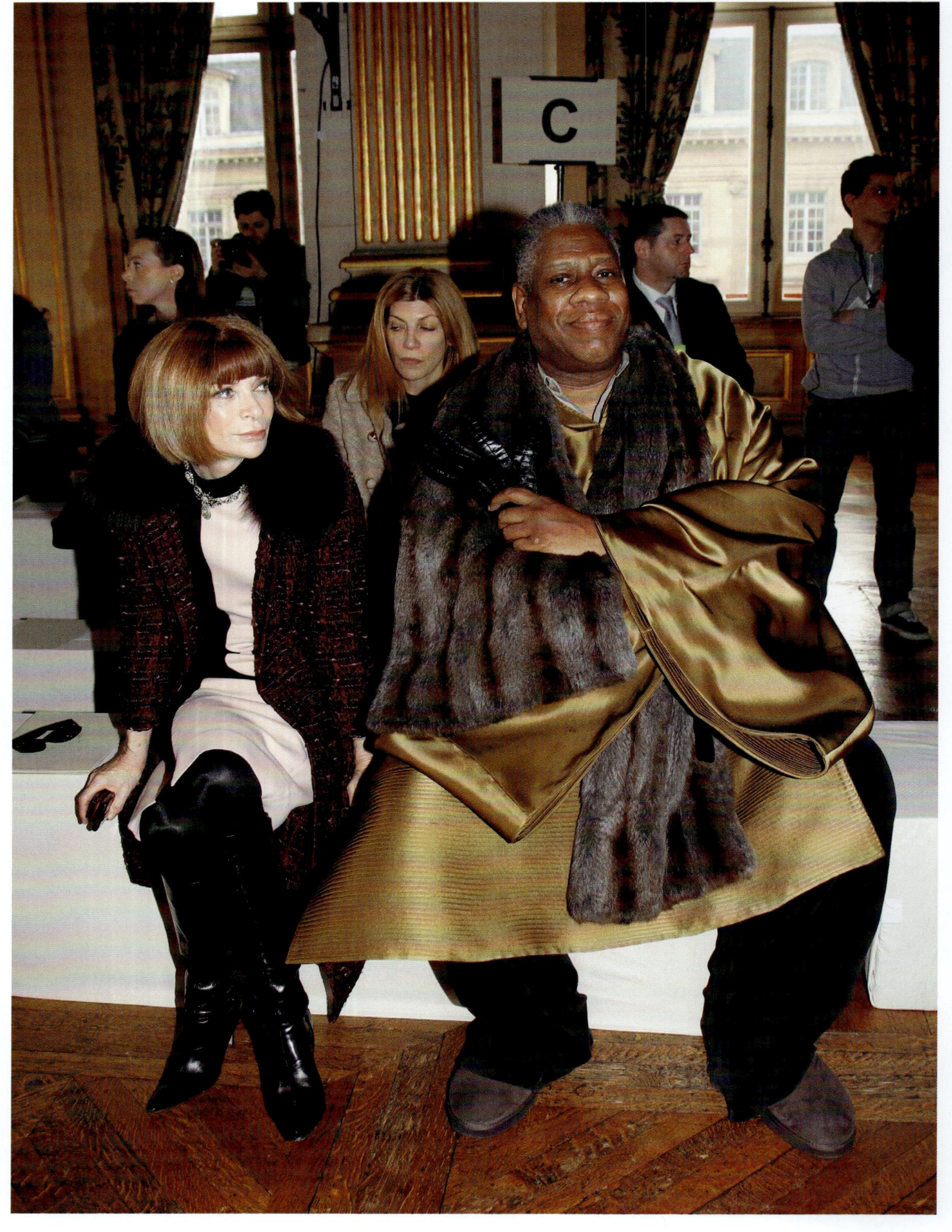

André and Anna Wintour at the Stella McCartney Fall/Winter 2012 ready-to-wear runway show during Paris Fashion Week. Photo by Michel Dufour/WireImage/Getty Images.

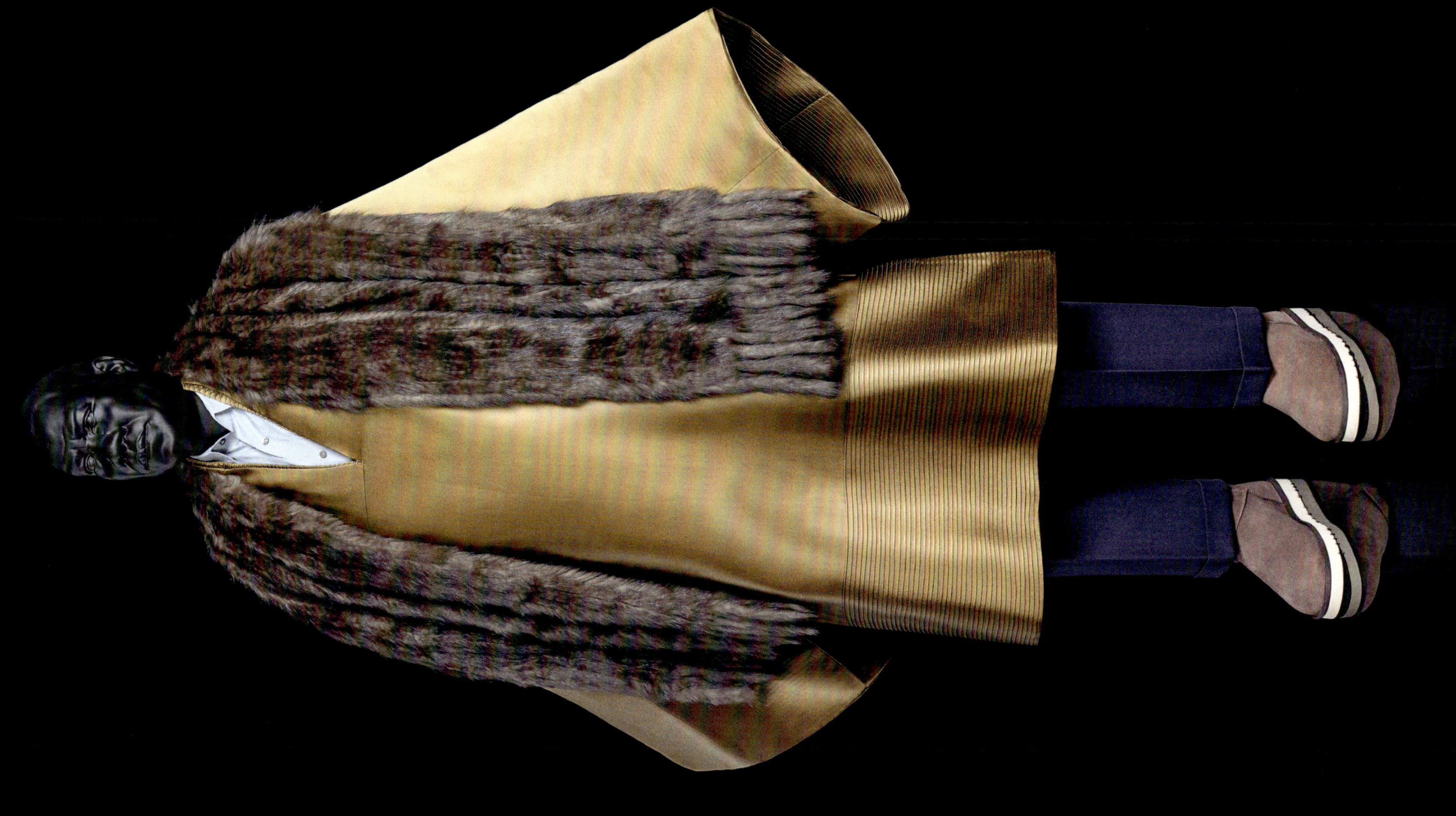

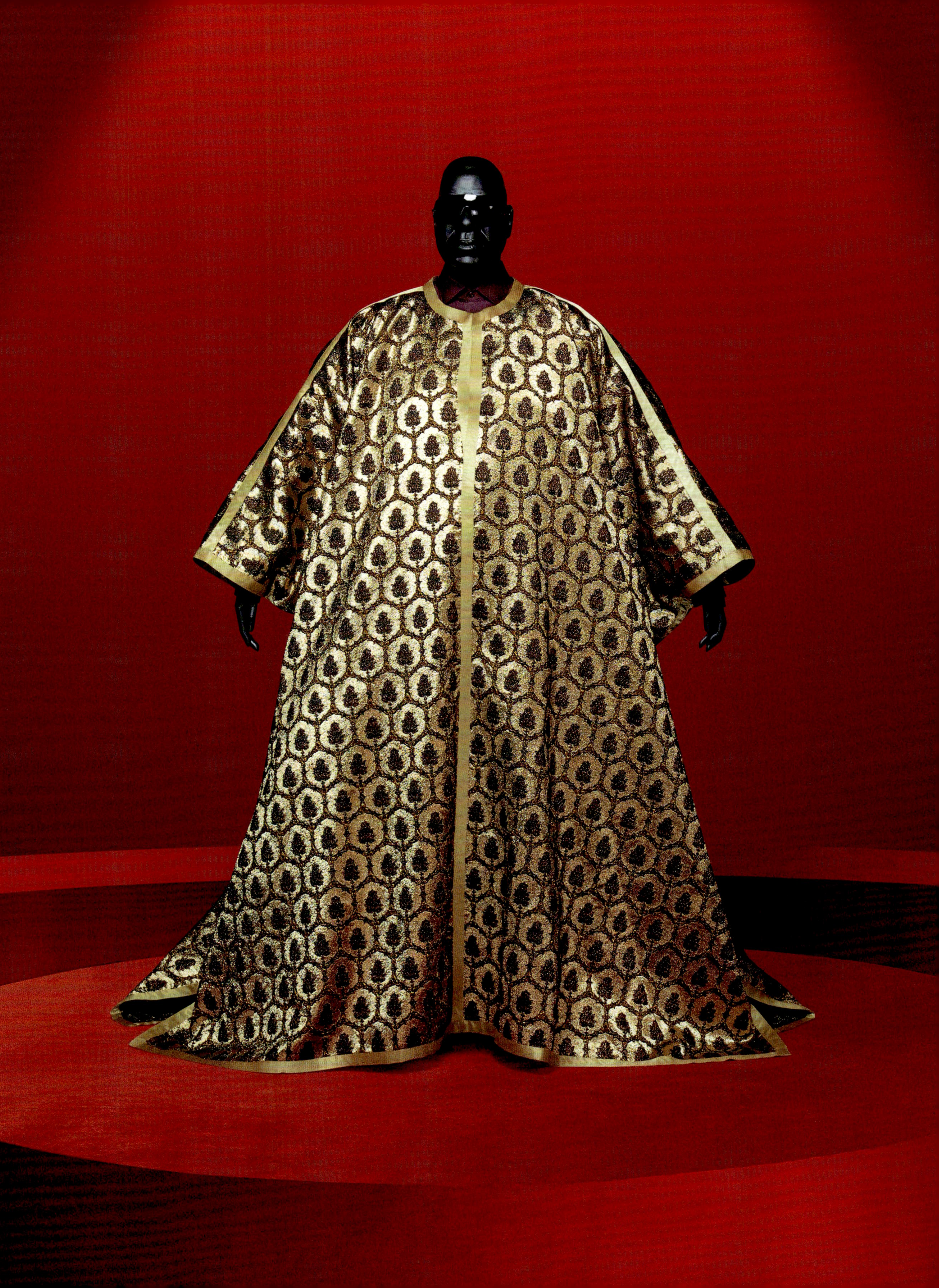

Gucci x Dapper Dan caftan

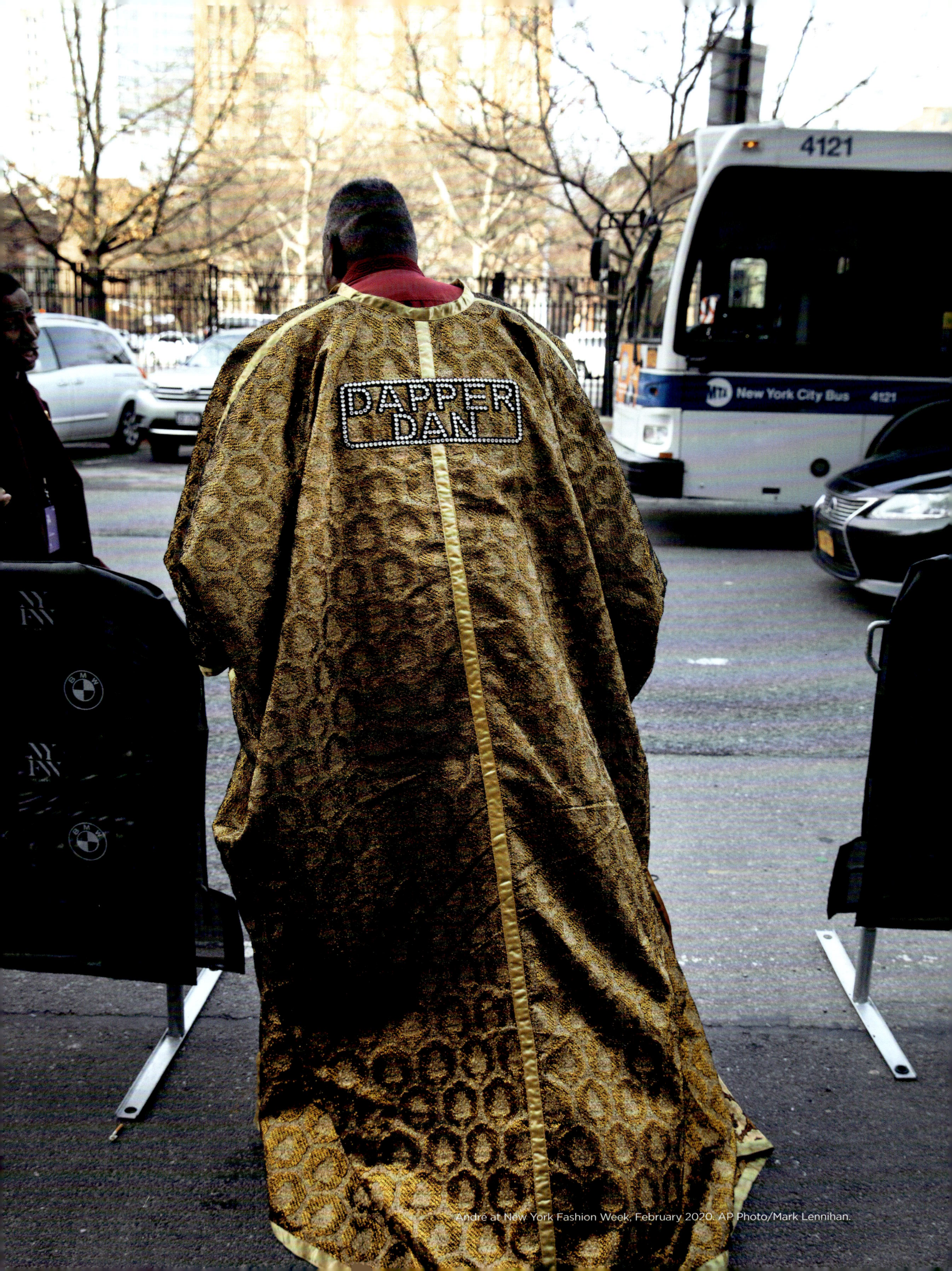

Andre at New York Fashion Week, February 2020. AP Photo/Mark Lennihan.

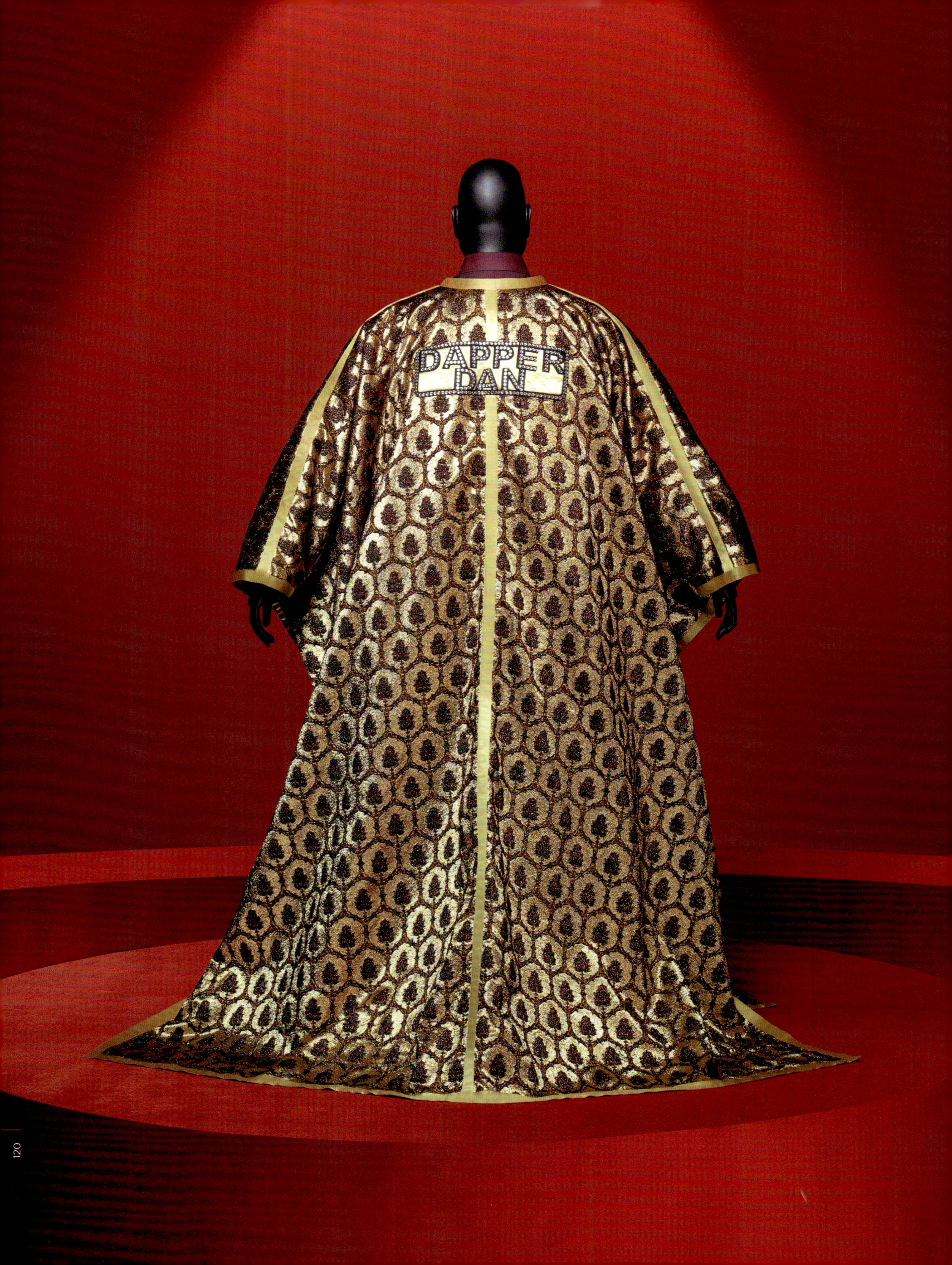
DAPPER
DAN

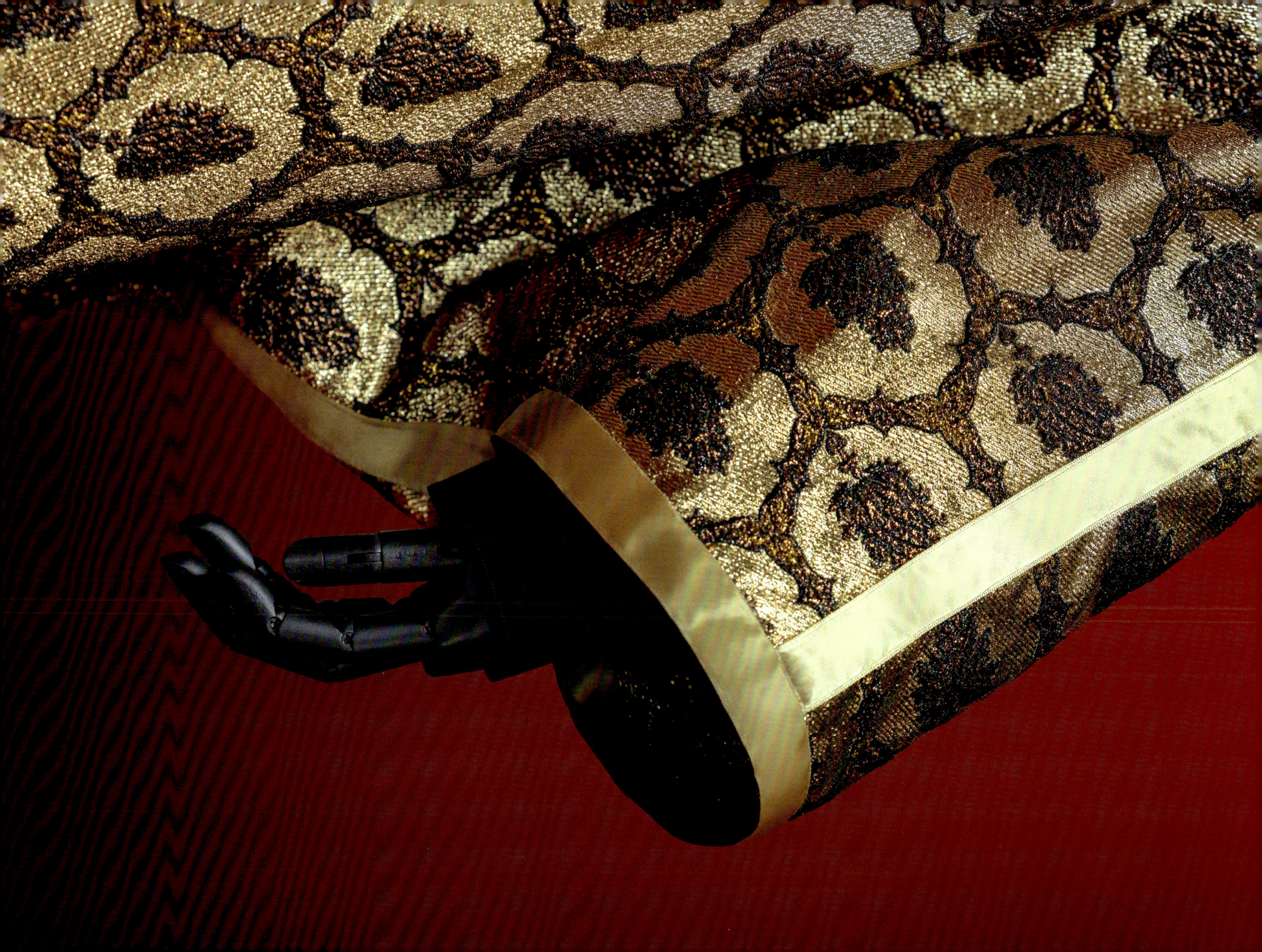

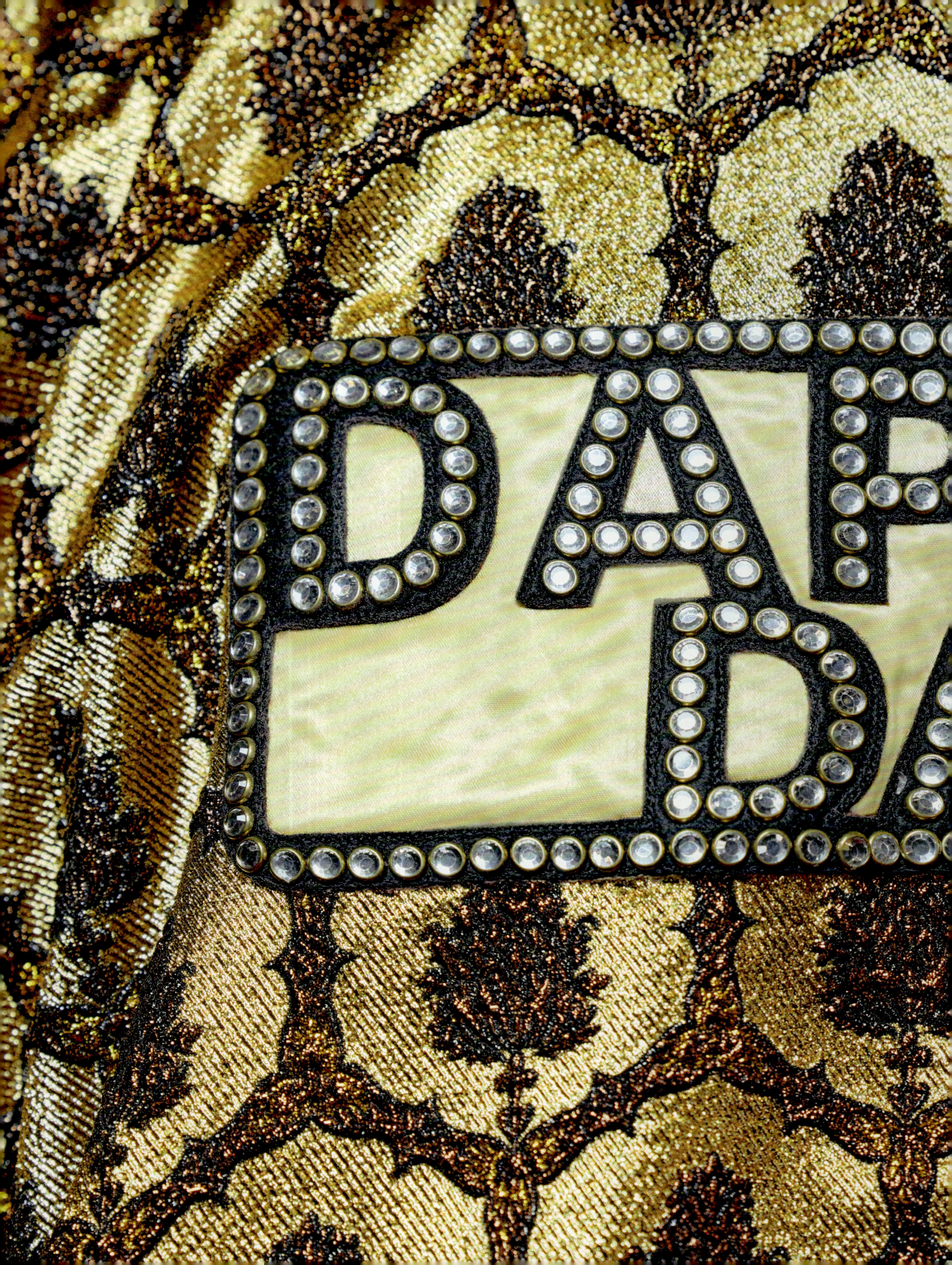
DAP
DA

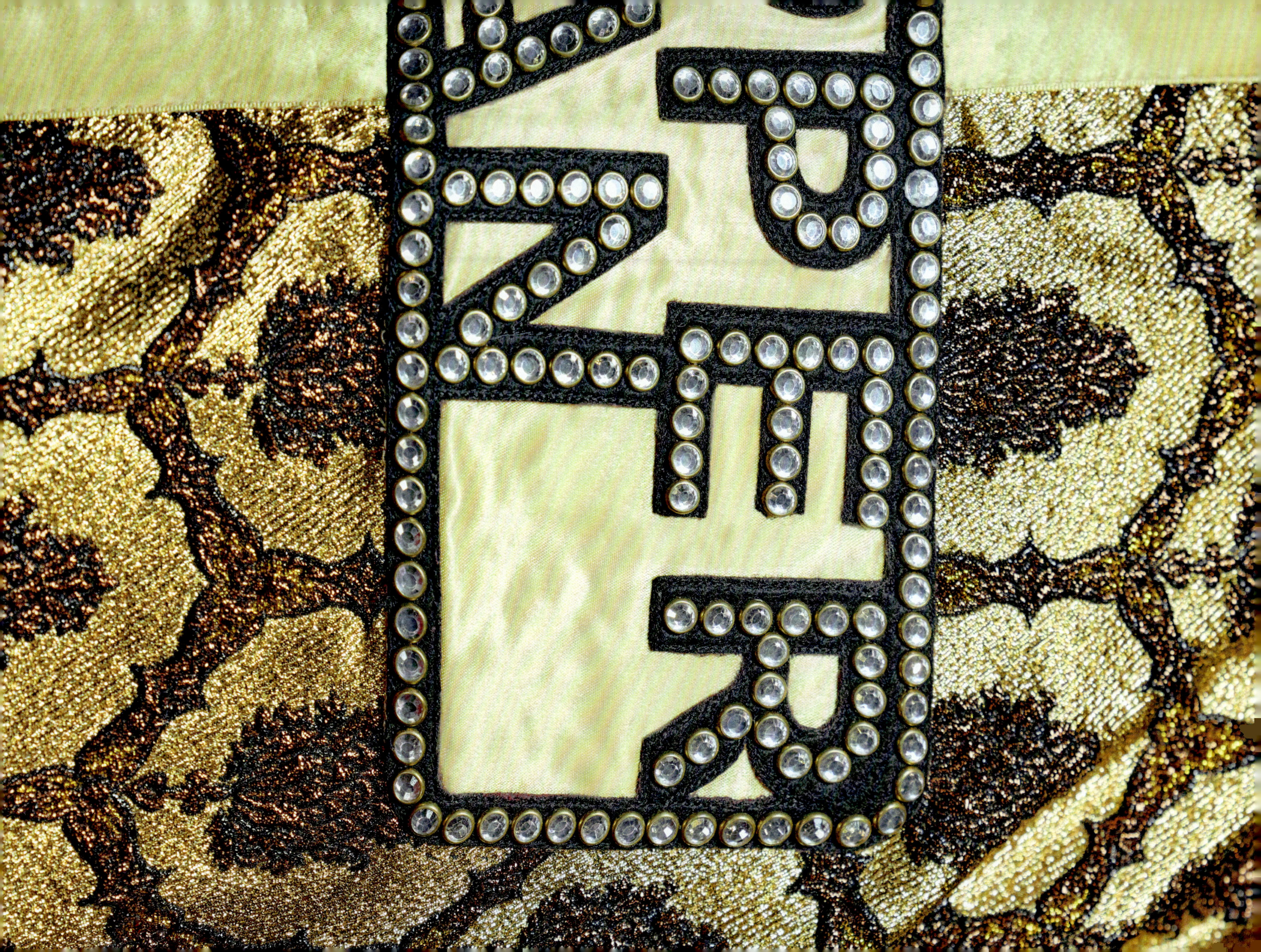

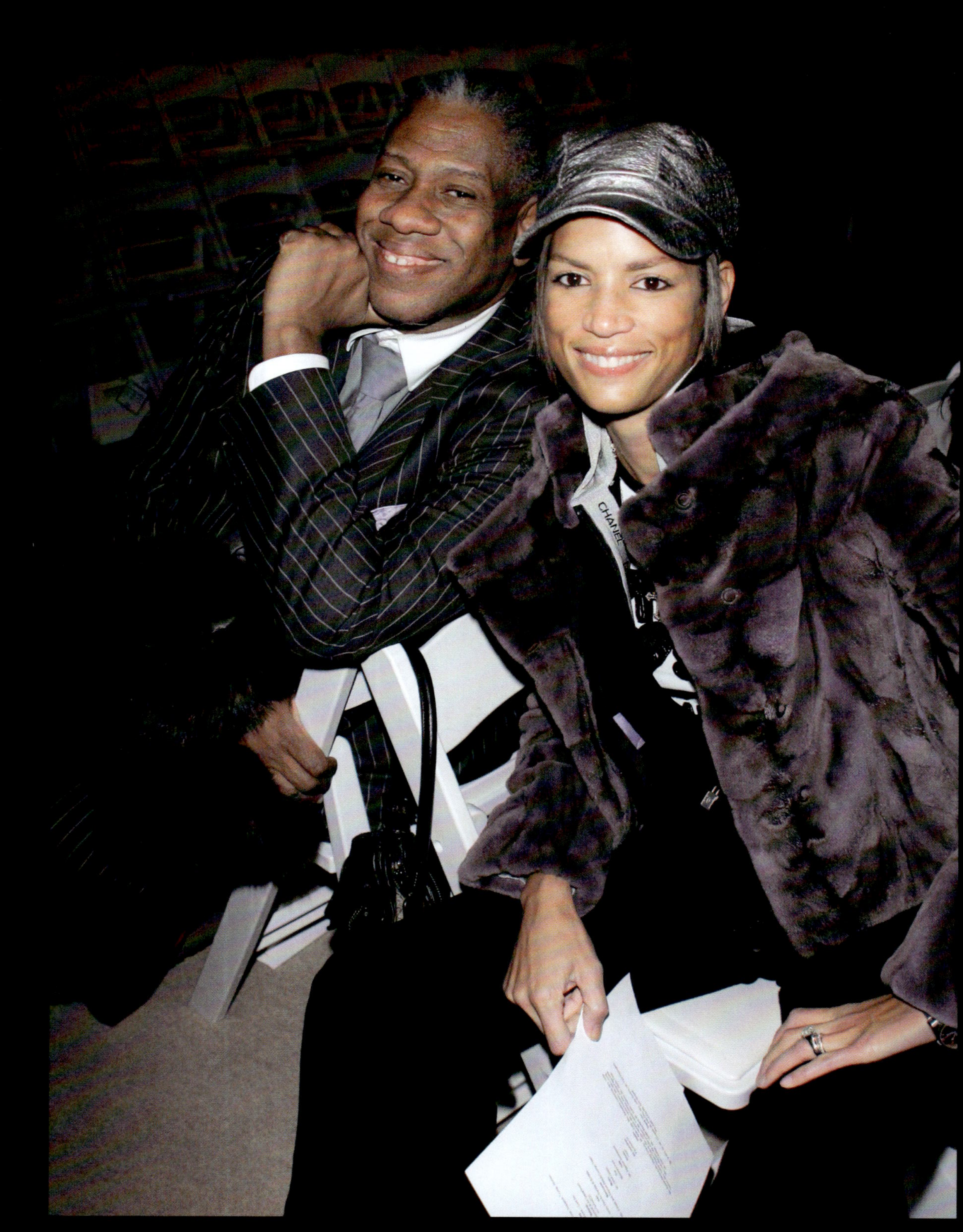

André and Veronica Webb front row at the Tuleh Fall/Winter 2007 runway show at The Promenade during New York Fashion Week. Photo by Jemal Countess/WireImage/Getty Images.

“

André convinced people that photographers, models, writers, designers of color, who wouldn’t have gotten a **chance**, who wouldn’t have been taken seriously otherwise, were **valid**, creative, and deserved to be seen. I’m here because André **believed** in me.

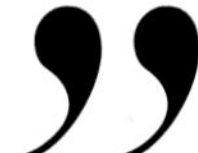

VERONICA WEBB

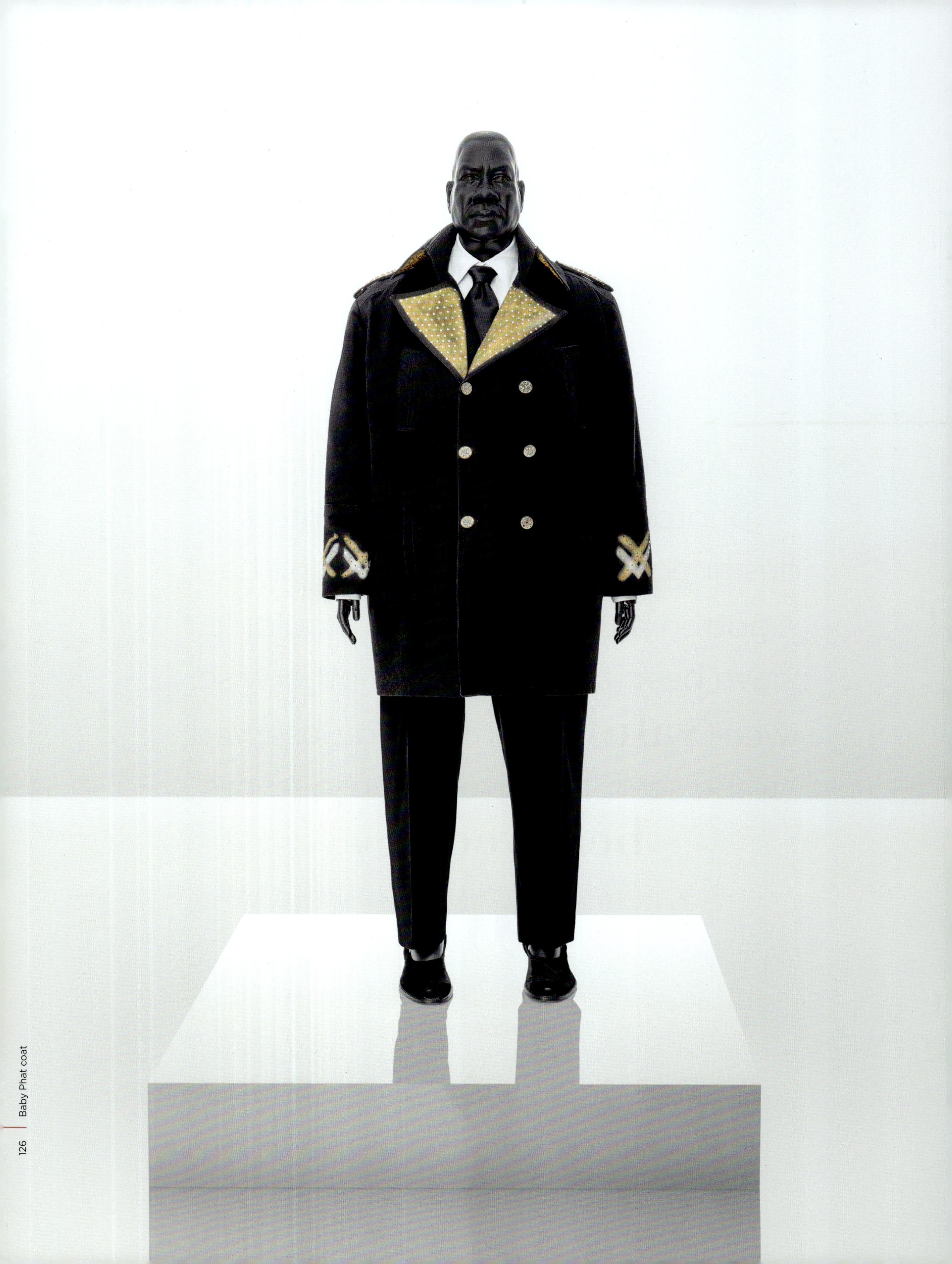

126 | Baby Phat coat

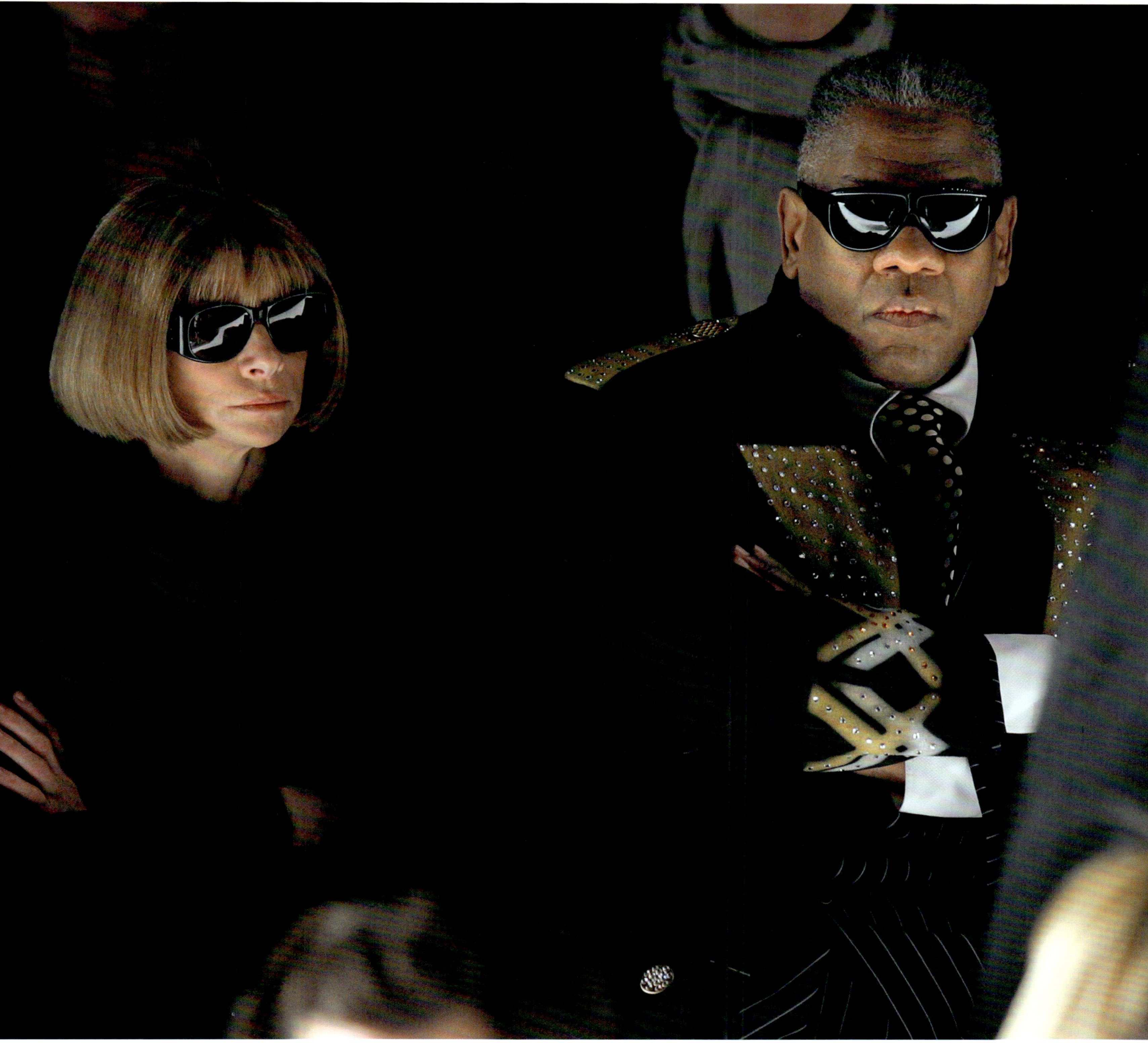

André and Anna Wintour front row at the Carolina Herrera Fall/Winter 2007 runway show during New York Fashion Week. Photo by Peter Kramer/Getty Images for IMG.

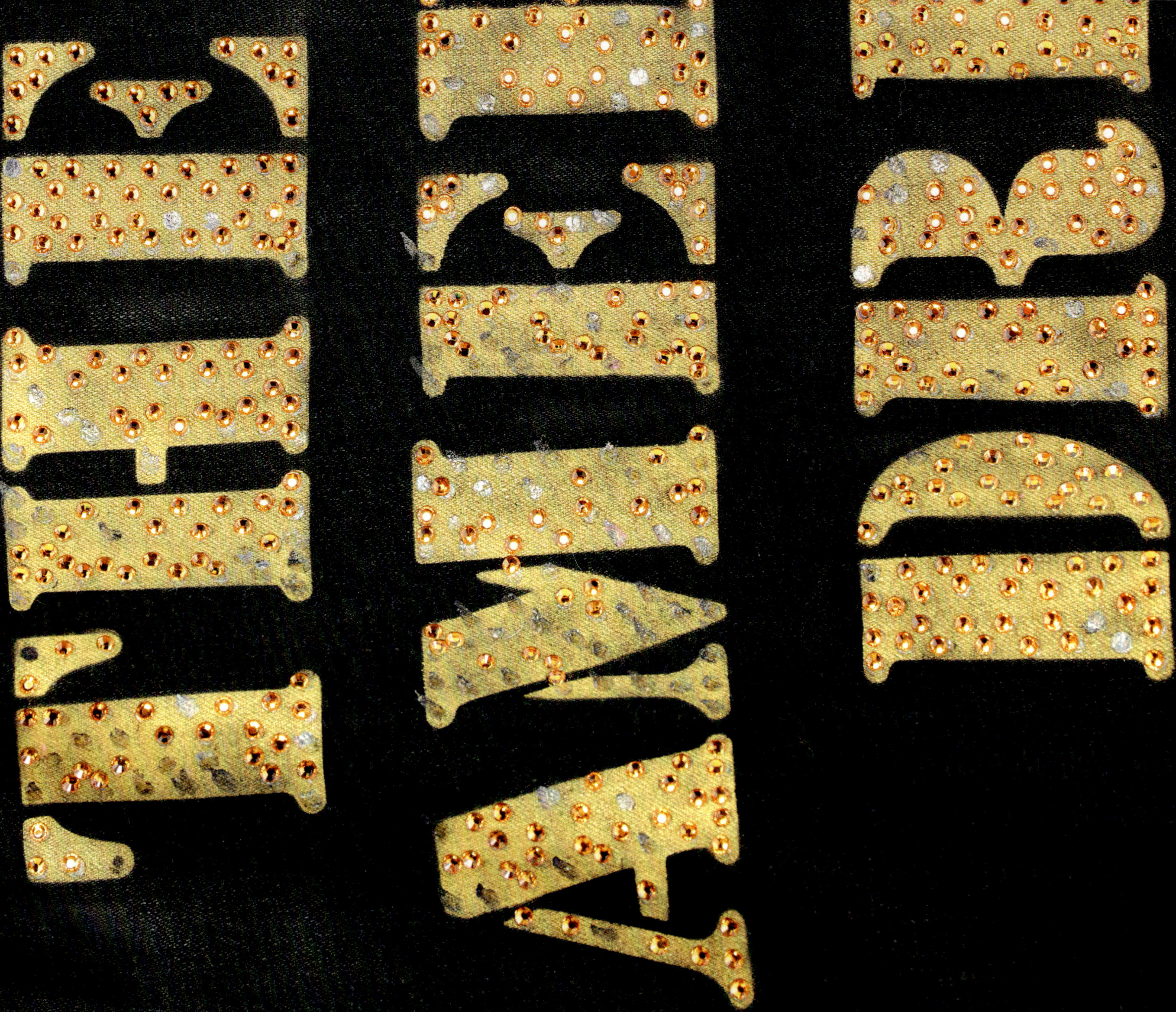

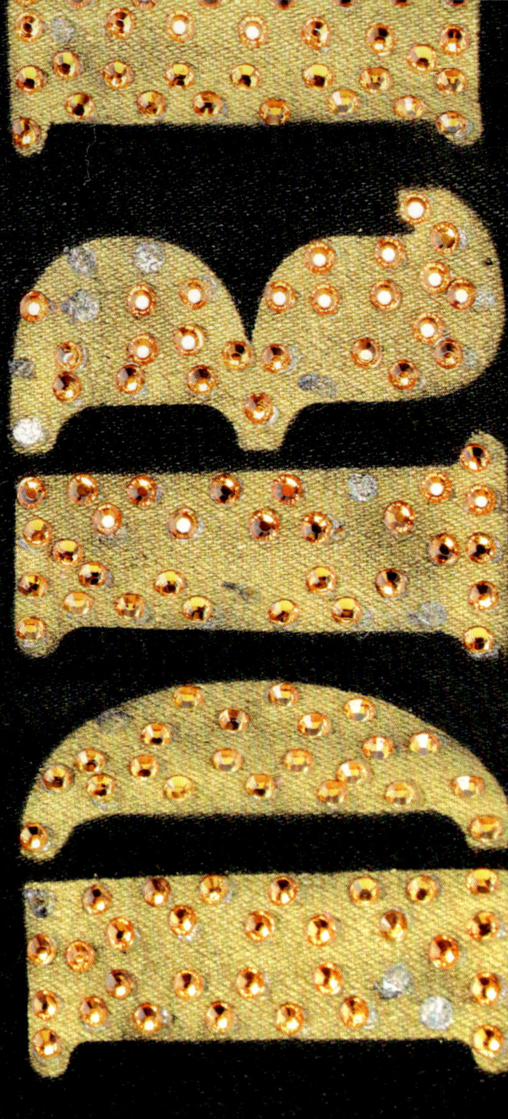
THE
AME
DR

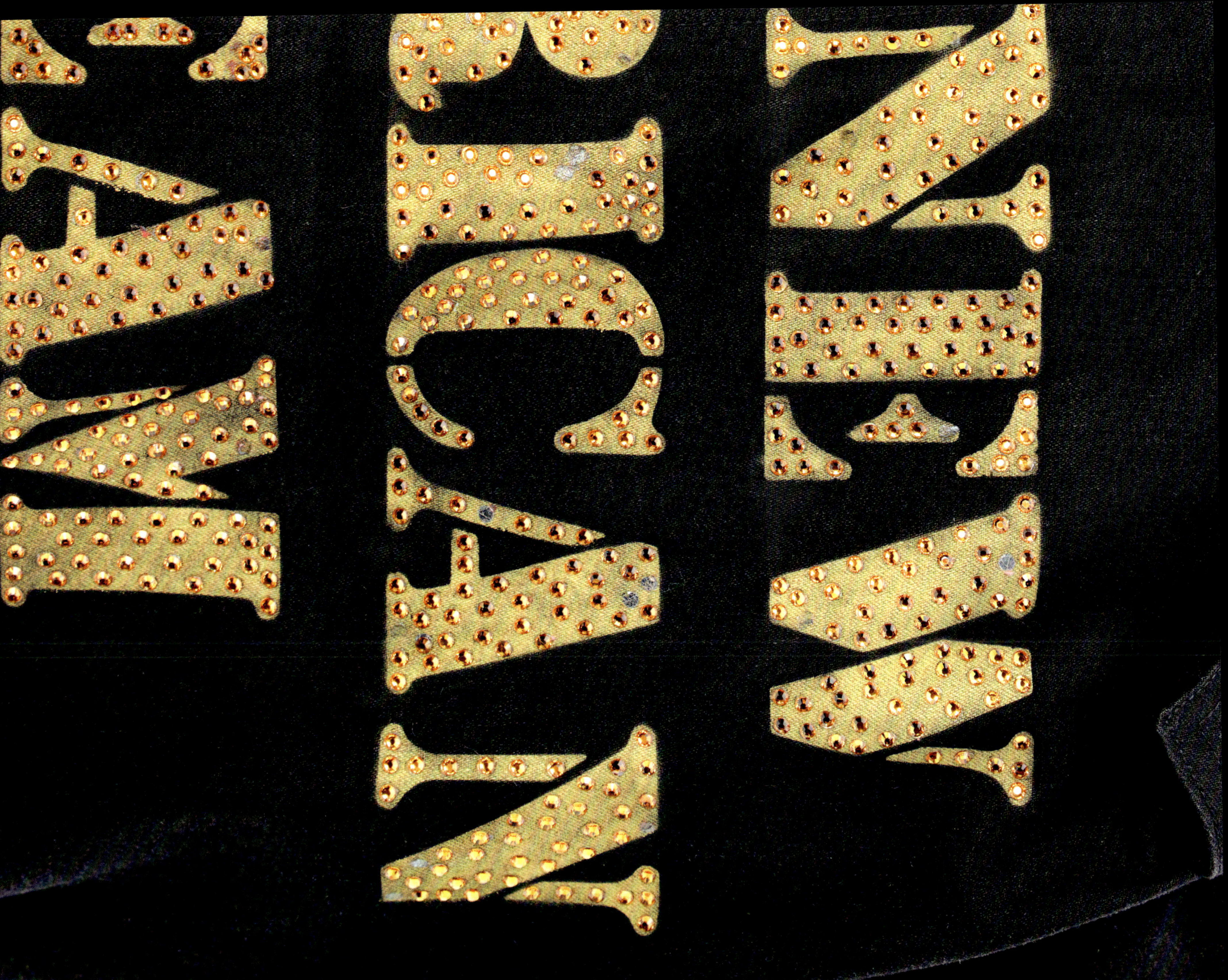

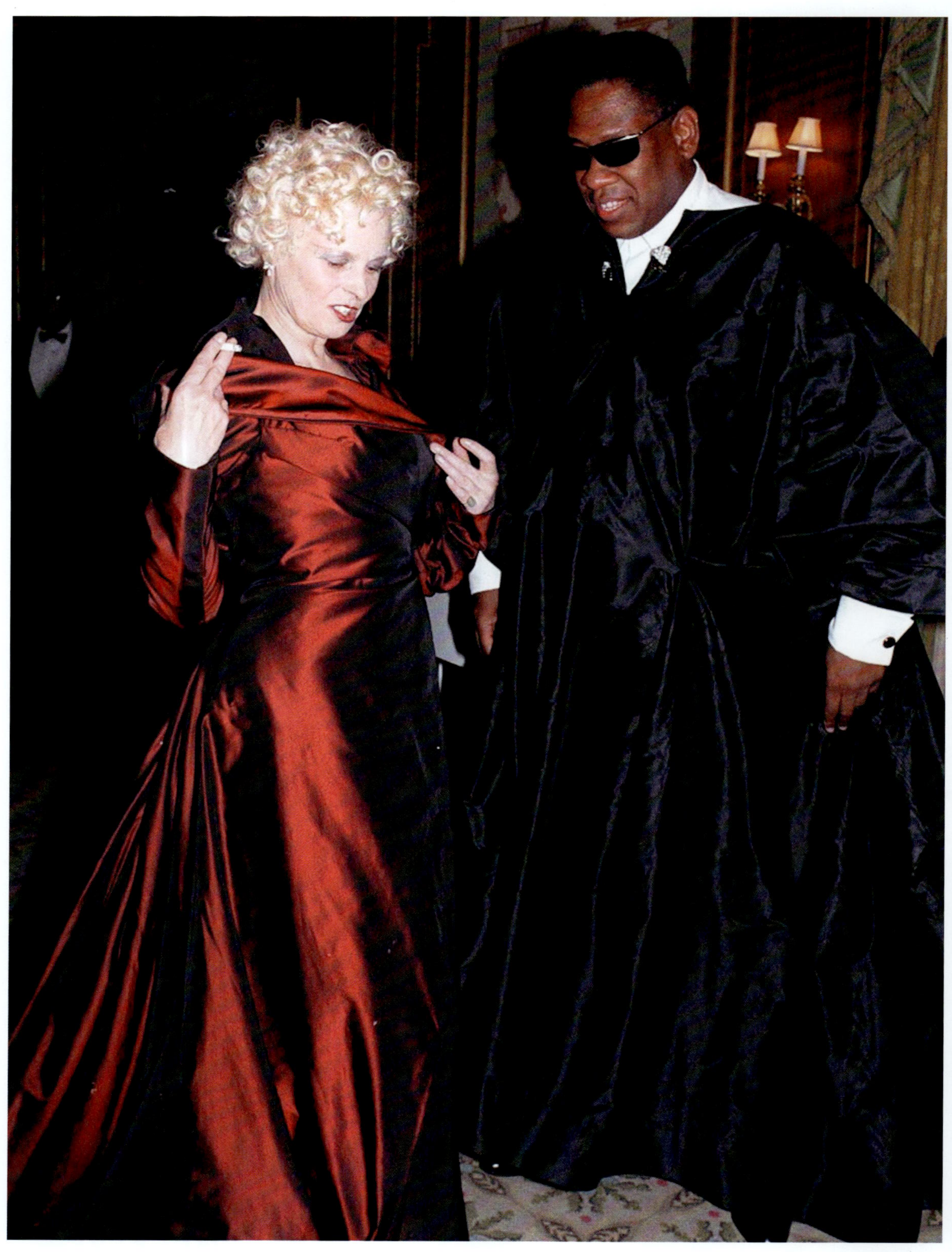

André and Dame Vivienne Westwood at a gala in New York, September 1996. Photo by Bill Cunningham/The New York Times/Redux Pictures.

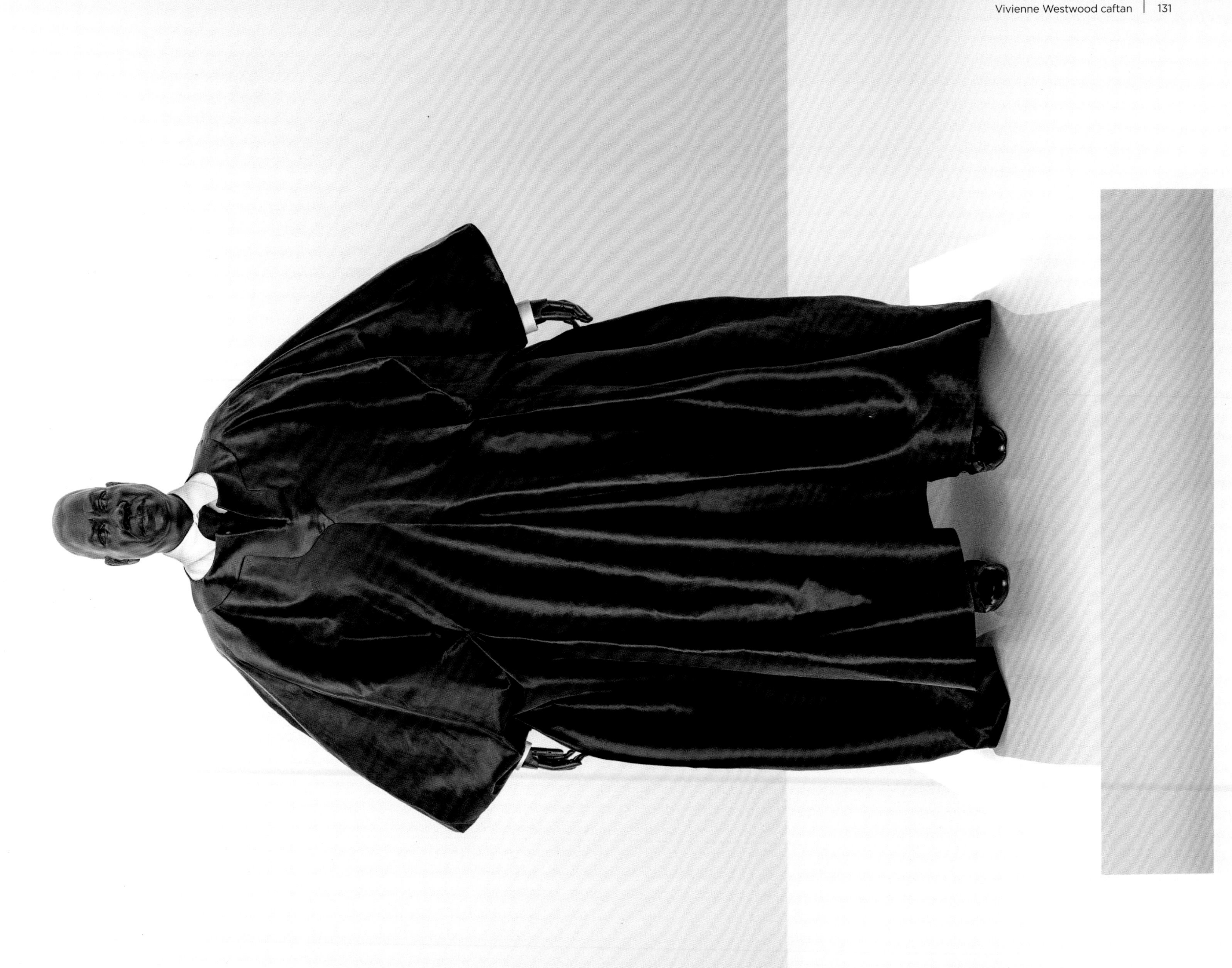

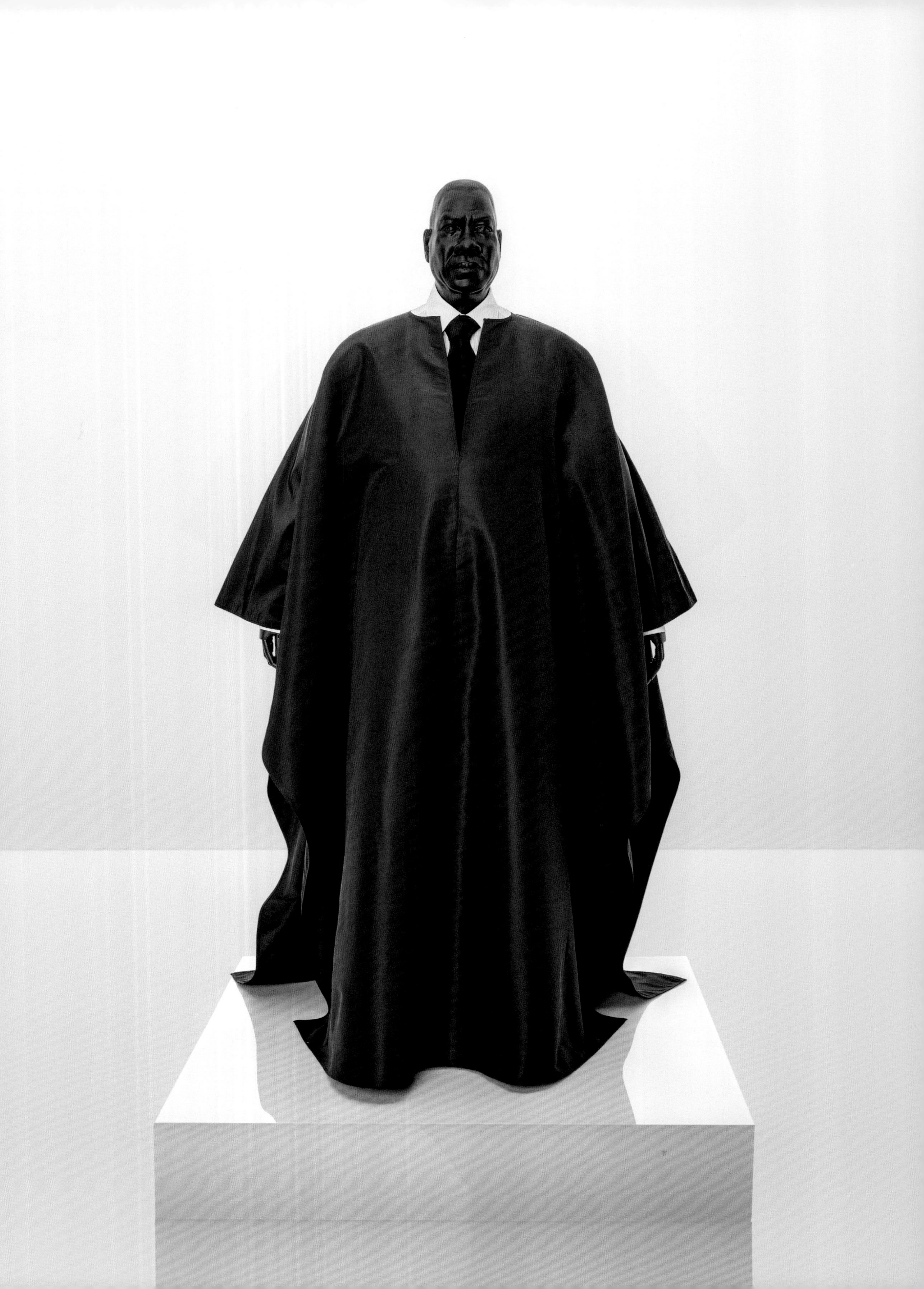

Ralph Rucci caftan

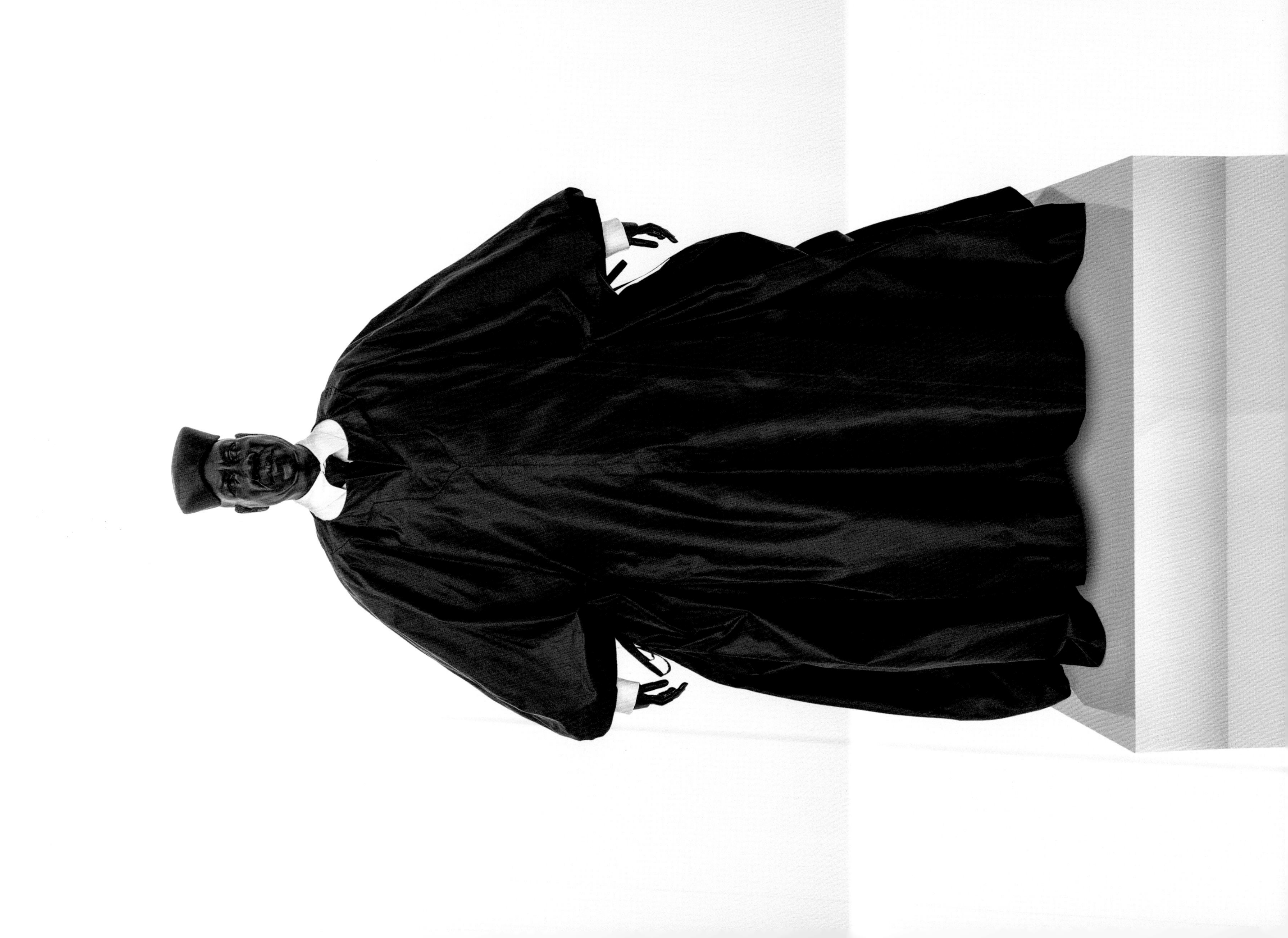

“

I miss not being able to talk with André about whatever we witnessed or heard that day. I miss, too, our trusted conversations about the things that disappointed or hurt him. André was very sensitive and protective of himself. His retort could be lethal. For those who never experienced being in his presence, blessed you are that there are so many photos and videos, but even those cannot capture all that he was: a **brilliant human** with extraordinary taste, skill in languages, and an understanding of luxury or how one should be dressed. He would often tell me to ‘put on a bit of red lipstick,’ even though I hated red lipstick. He was a **great friend** if he loved you; painful if he felt unloved or disrespected. He would often say to me, ‘I know I am difficult.’ It pleased me that he knew and would admit that. Many can’t and don’t. He was **truly my brother**, good, bad, and otherwise. He will be forever missed.

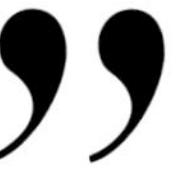

BETHANN HARDISON

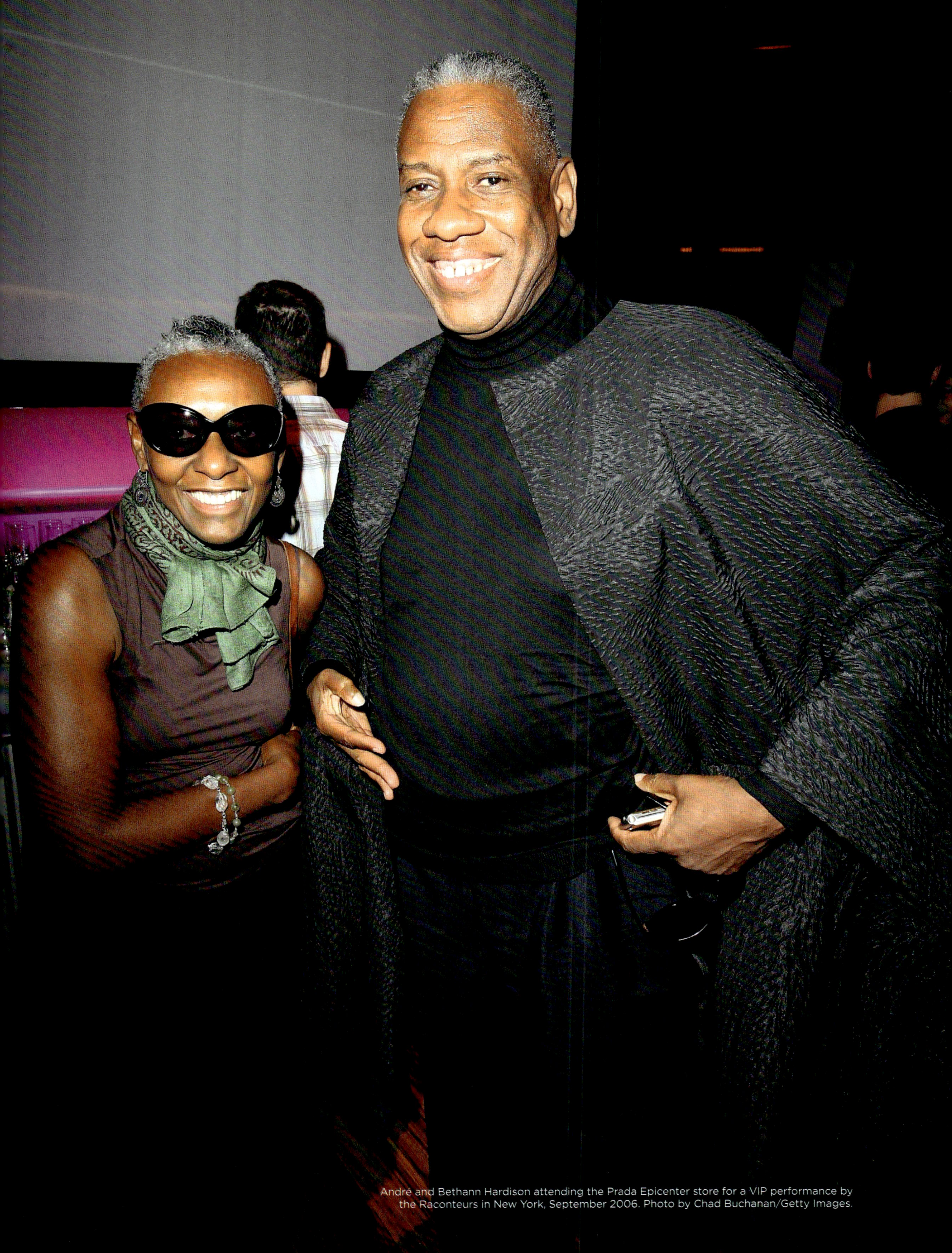

André and Bethann Hardison attending the Prada Epicenter store for a VIP performance by the Raconteurs in New York, September 2006. Photo by Chad Buchanan/Getty Images.

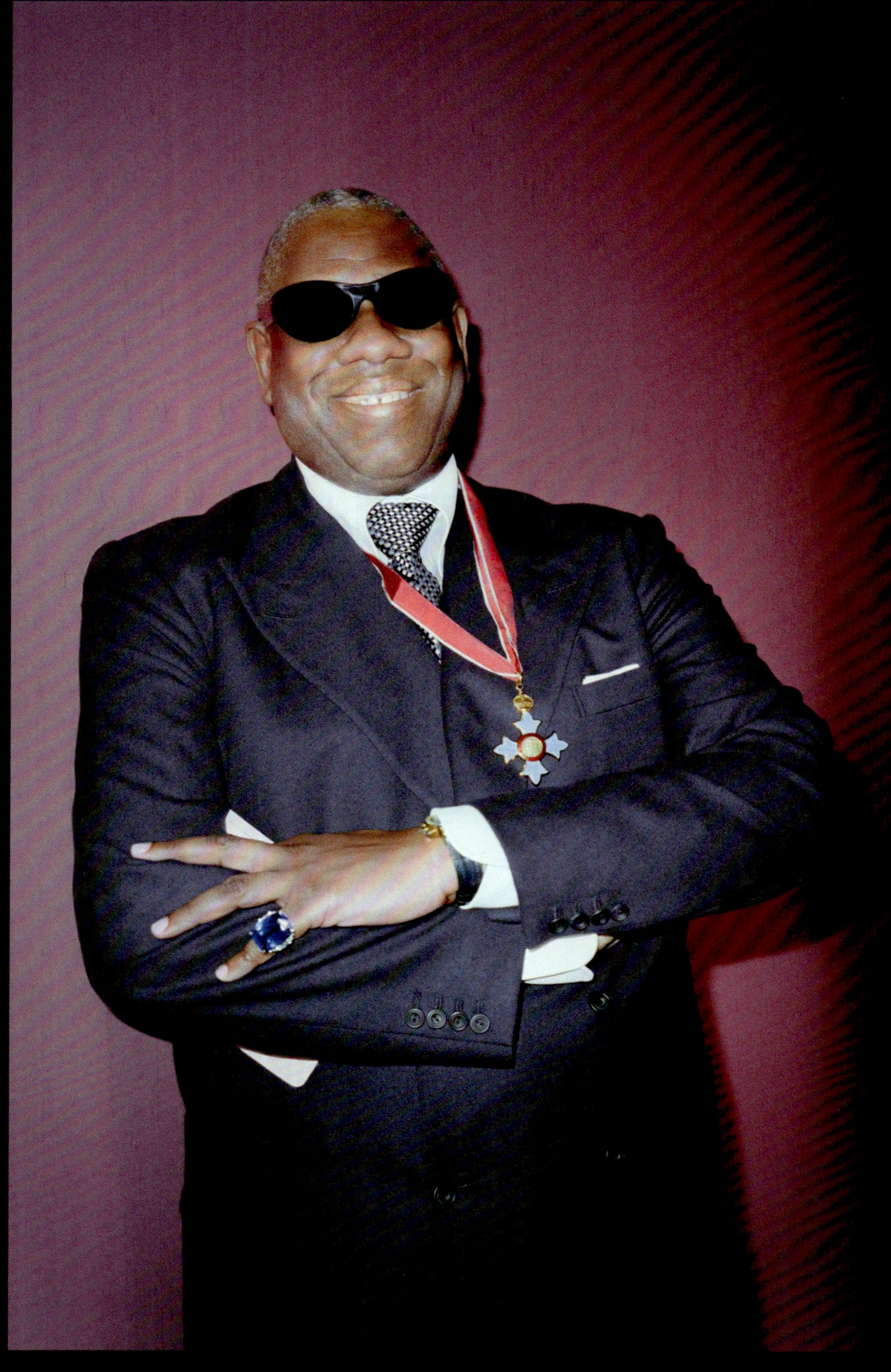

André backstage at the Christian Lacroix Spring/Summer 2002 haute couture runway show in Paris. Photo by Robert Fair

© R.FAIRER C.LACROIX
COUTURE S/S2002 1130*161

Contact sheet from backstage at the Christian Lacroix Spring/Summer 2002 haute couture runway show. Photos by

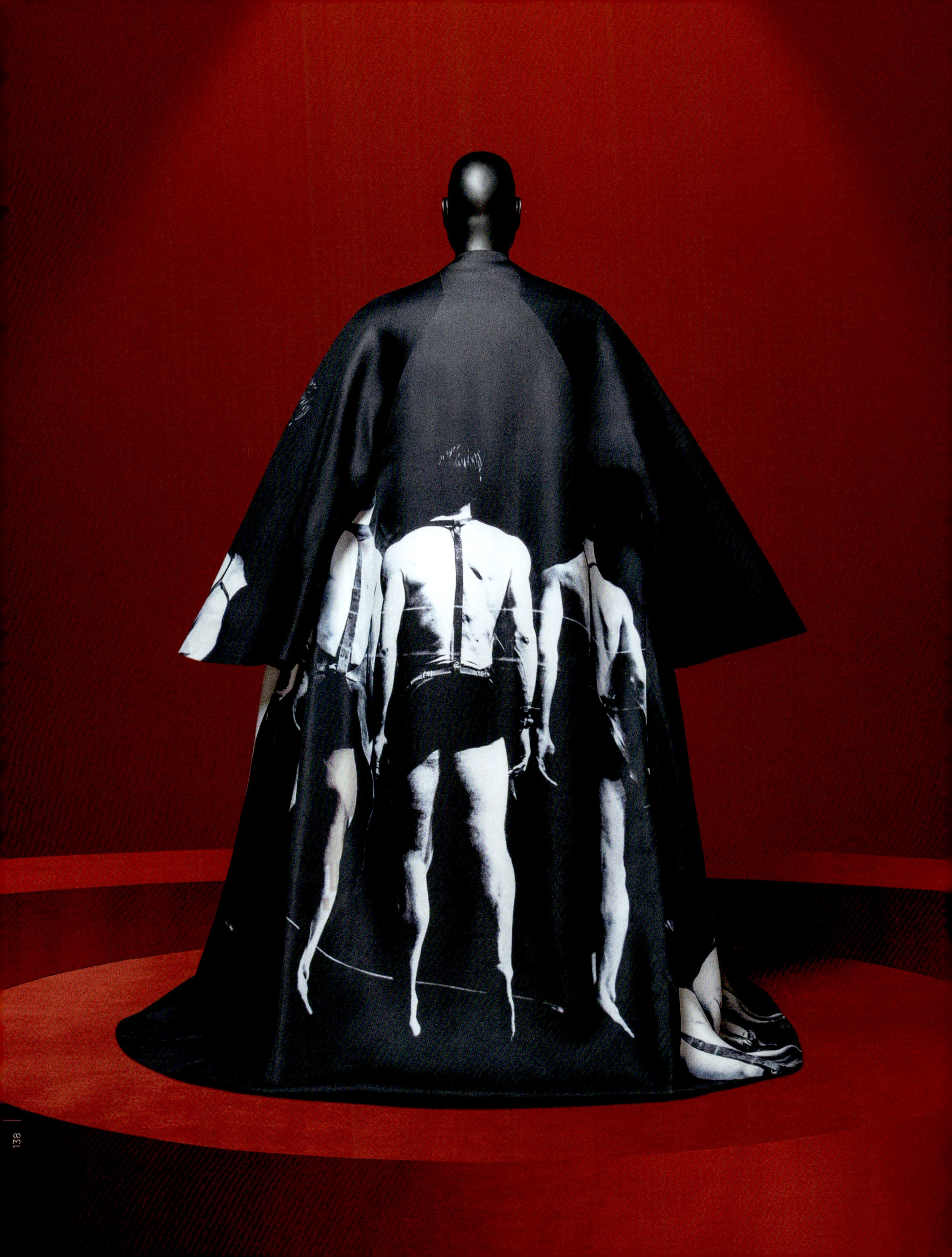

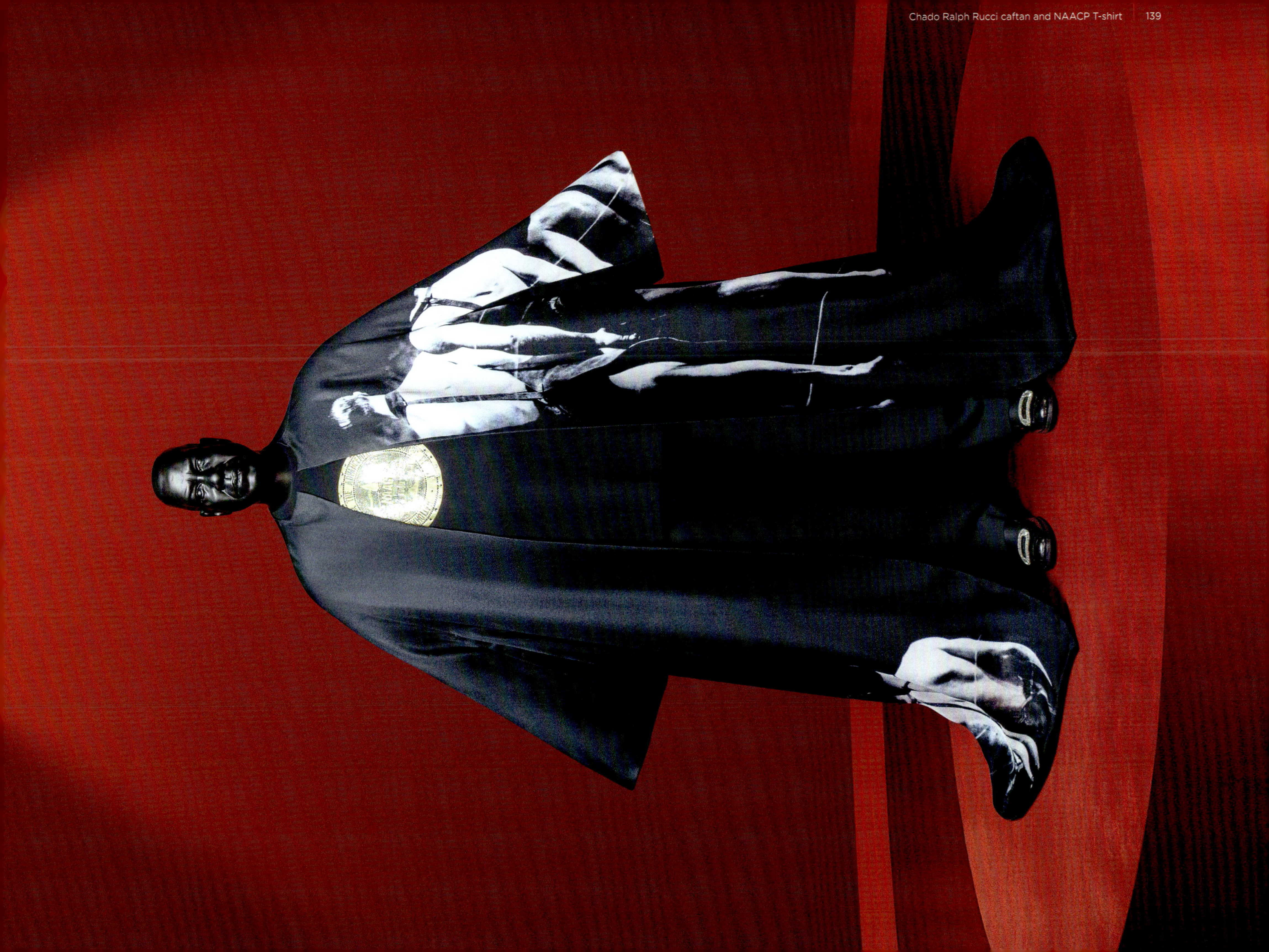

Chado Ralph Rucci caftan and NAACP T-shirt

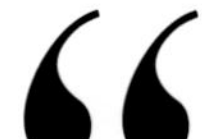

André laid the groundwork for us to **keep moving forward**, and we will keep moving.

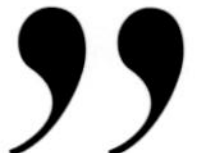

ZACH STAFFORD

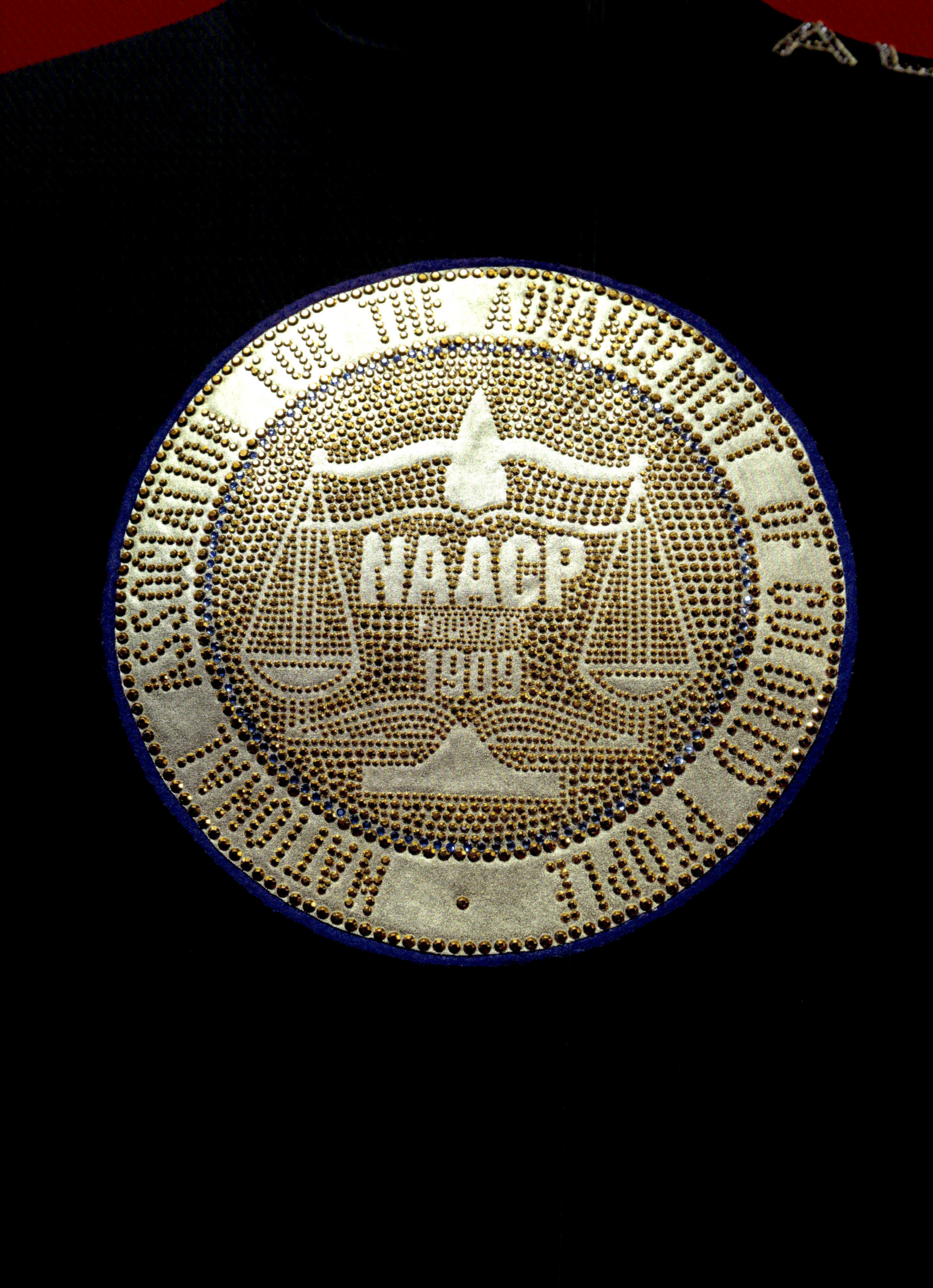
NATIONAL ASSOCIATION FOR THE ADVANCEMENT OF COLORED PEOPLE
NAACP
1909

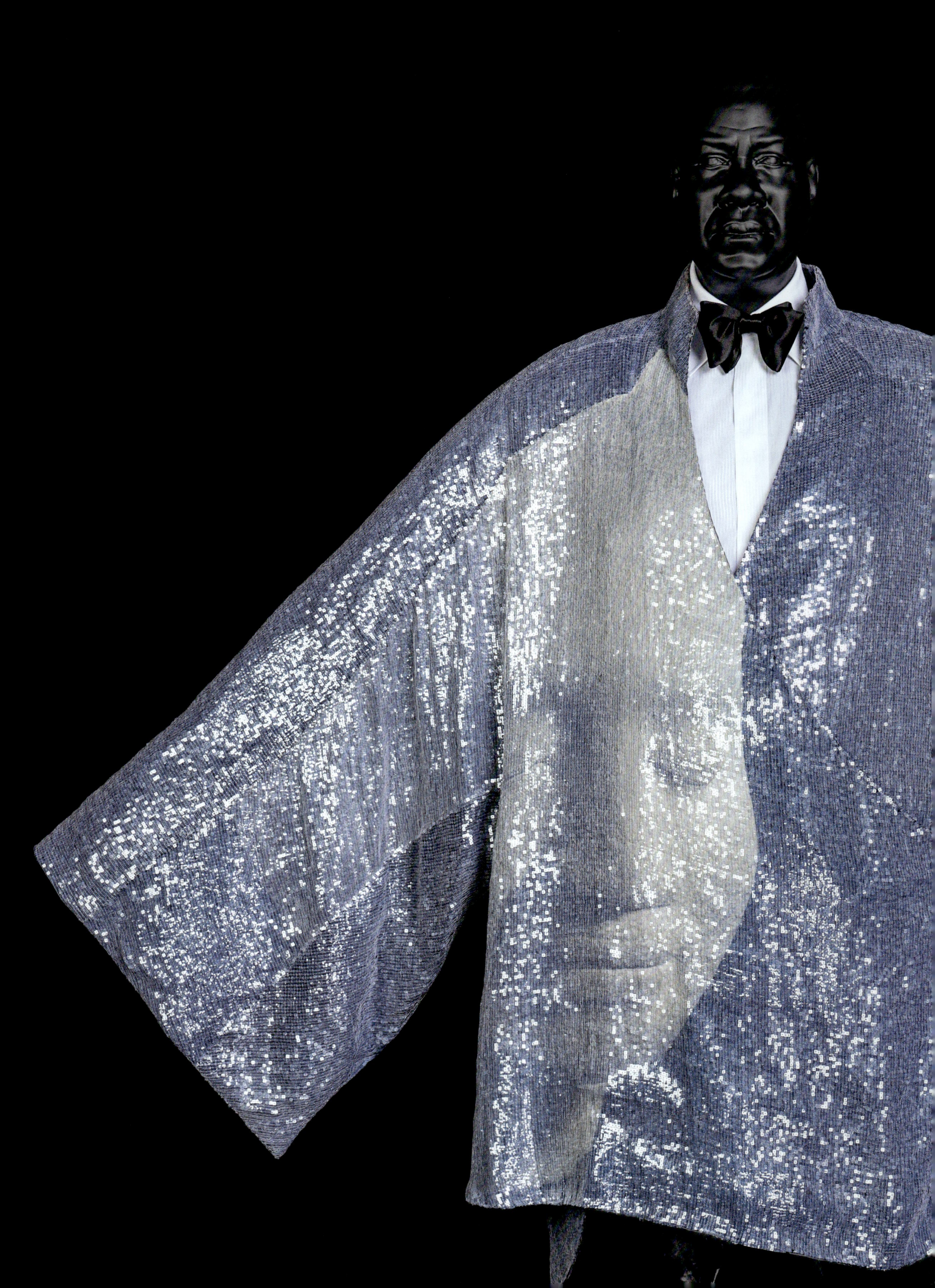

Chado Ralph Rucci tunic

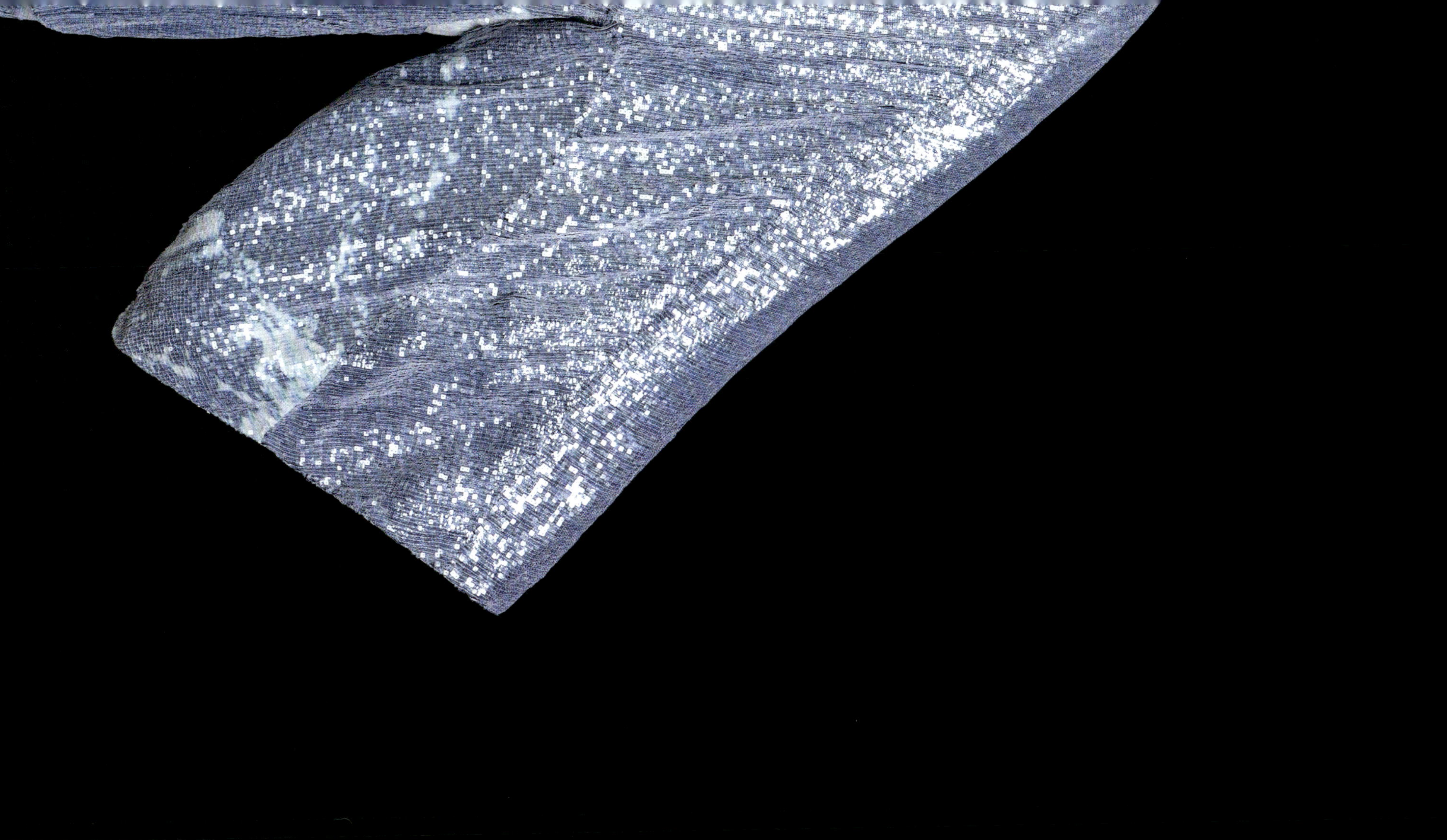

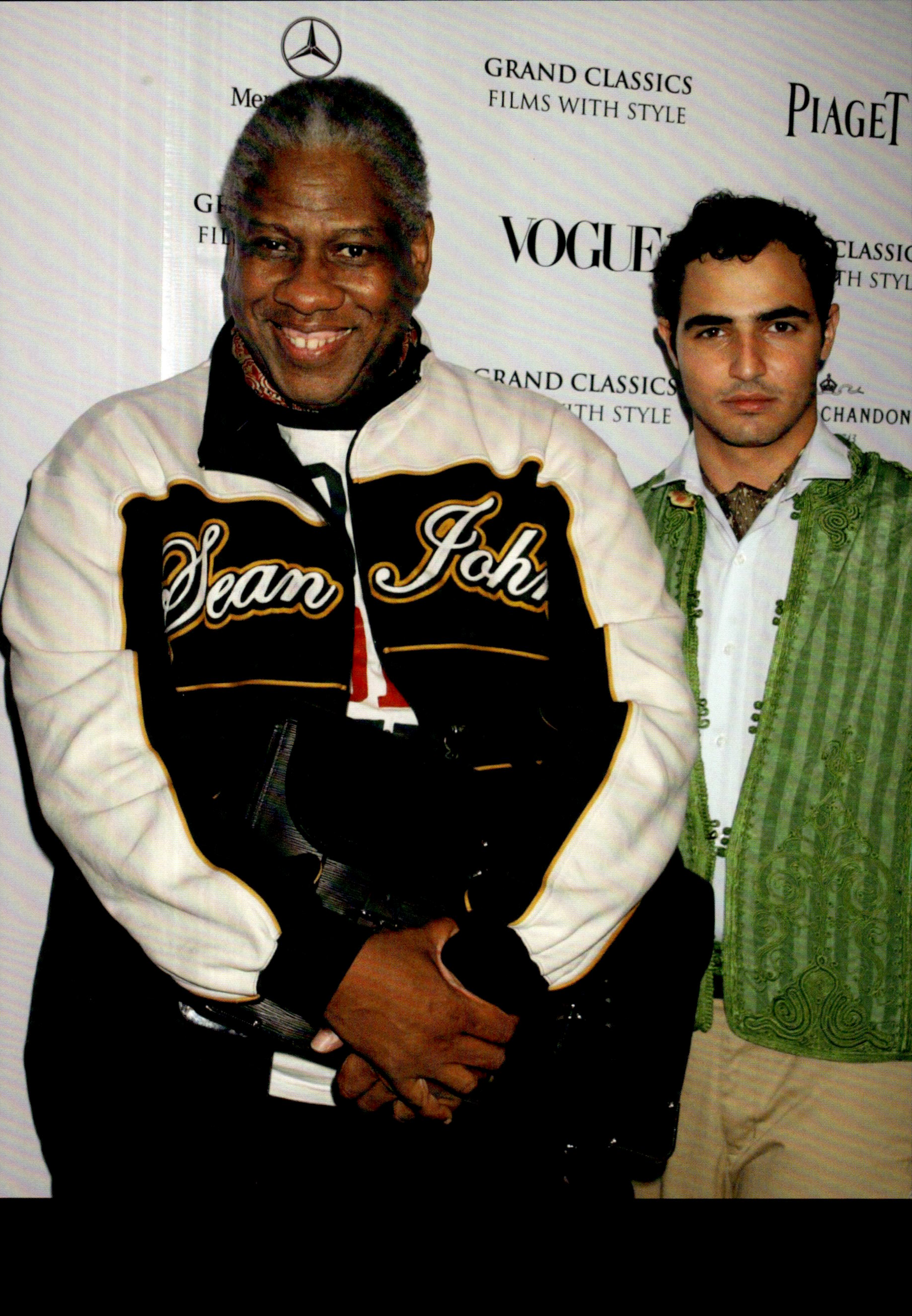

Zac Posen at the Grand Classics: Films With Style screening of *The Women*, hosted at Soho House in New York. Photo by Sylvain Gaboury/FilmMagic.

“

André’s **power** was his real relationship with **creators**.

”

ZAC POSEN

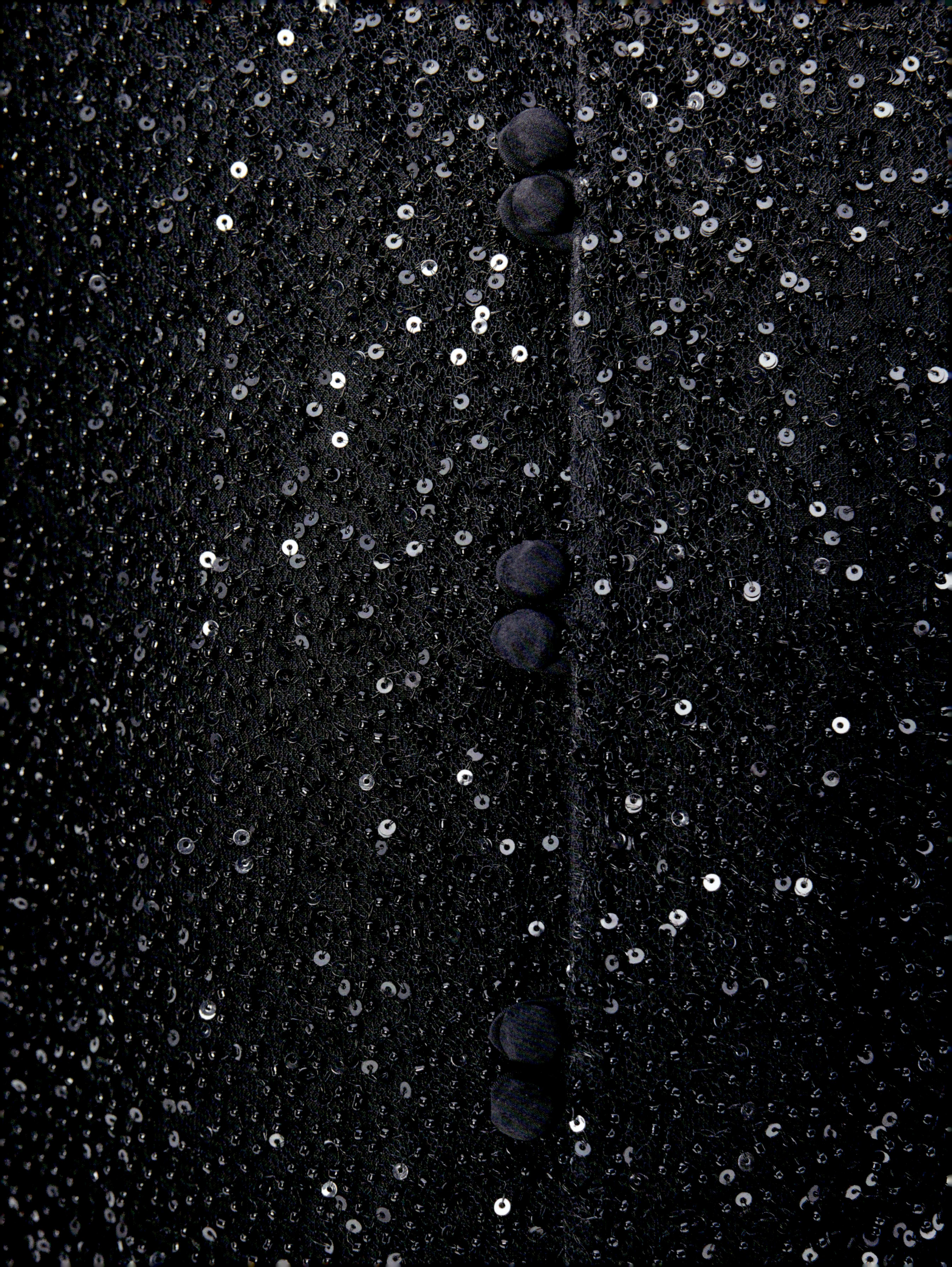

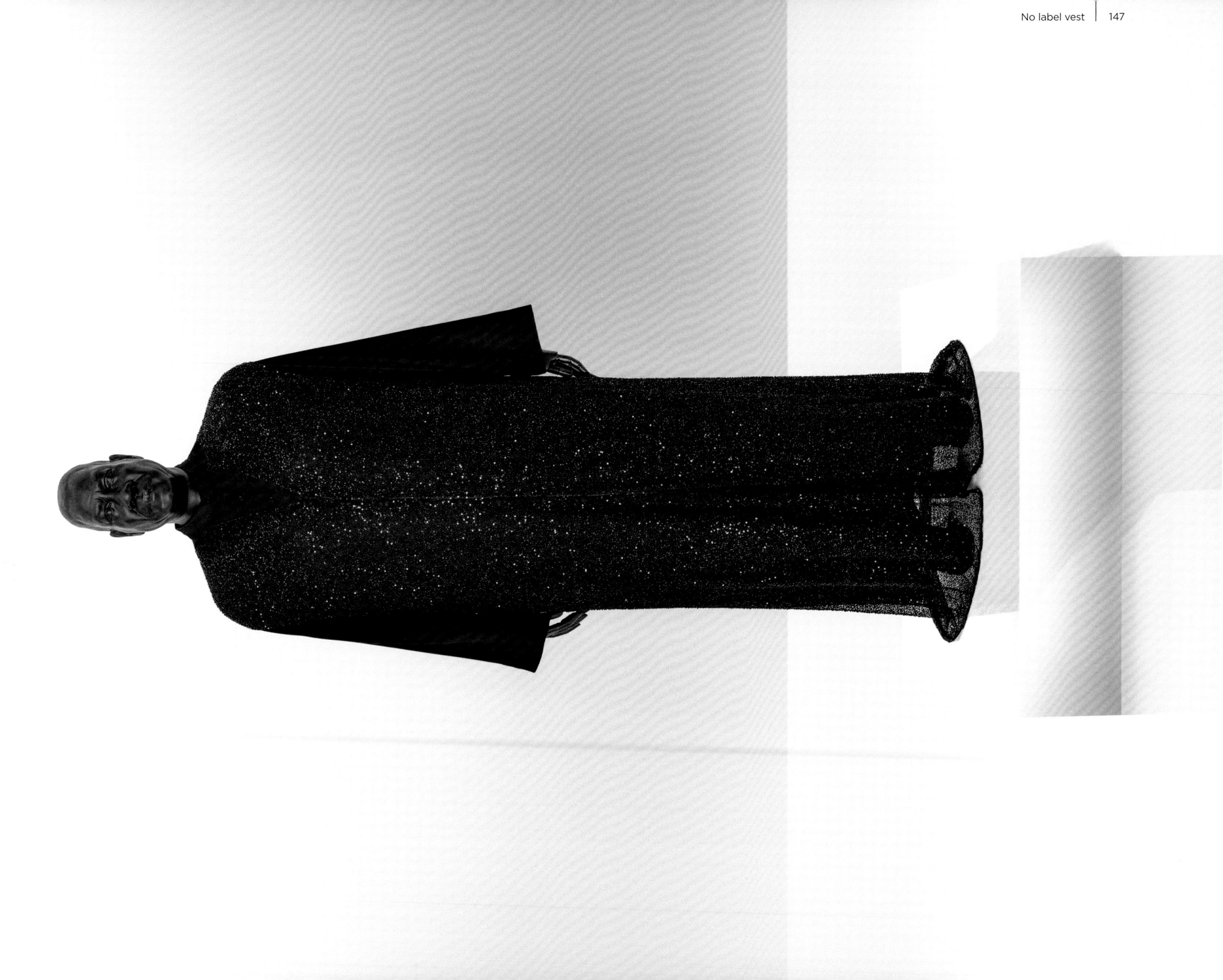

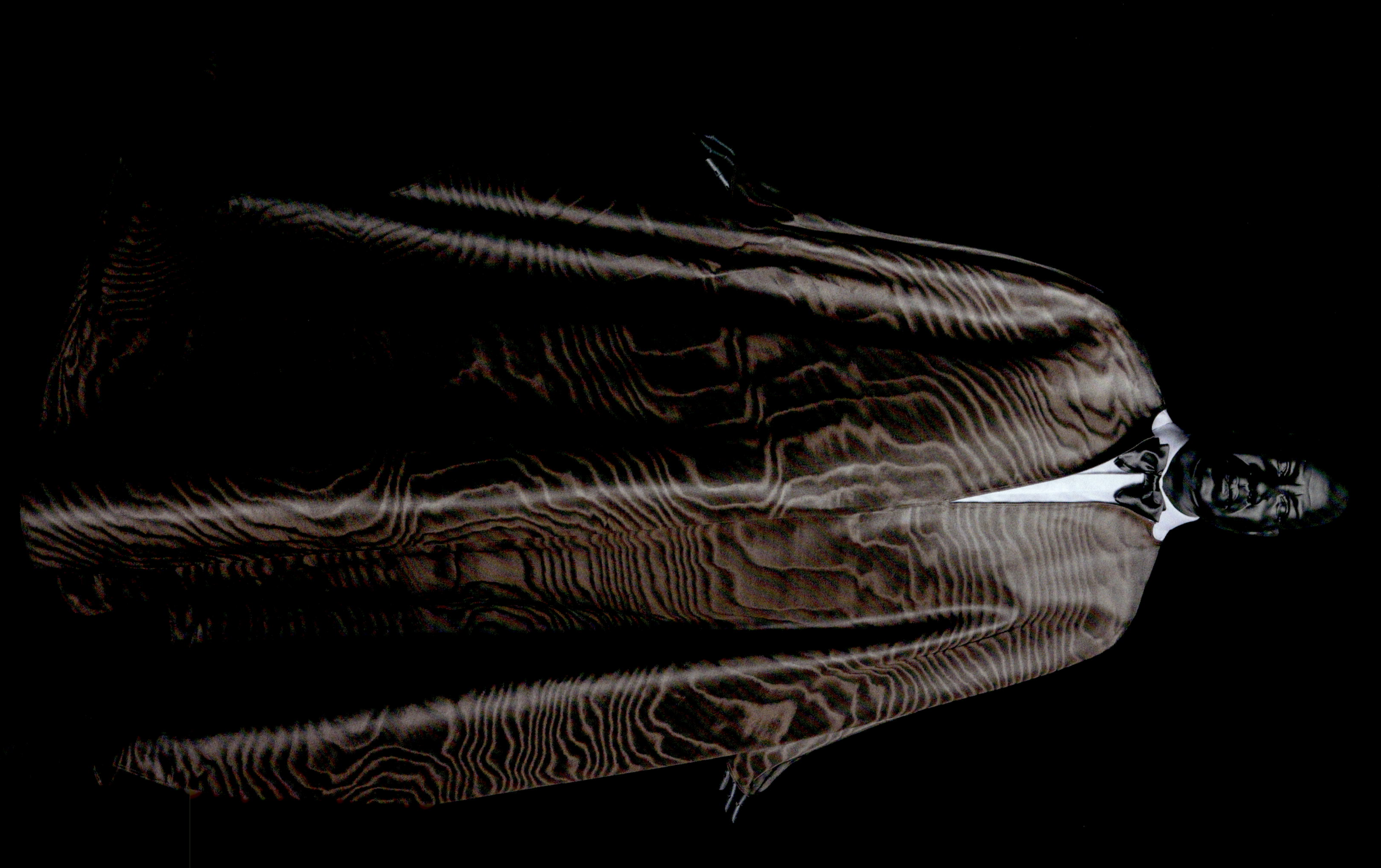

Ralph Rucci caftan

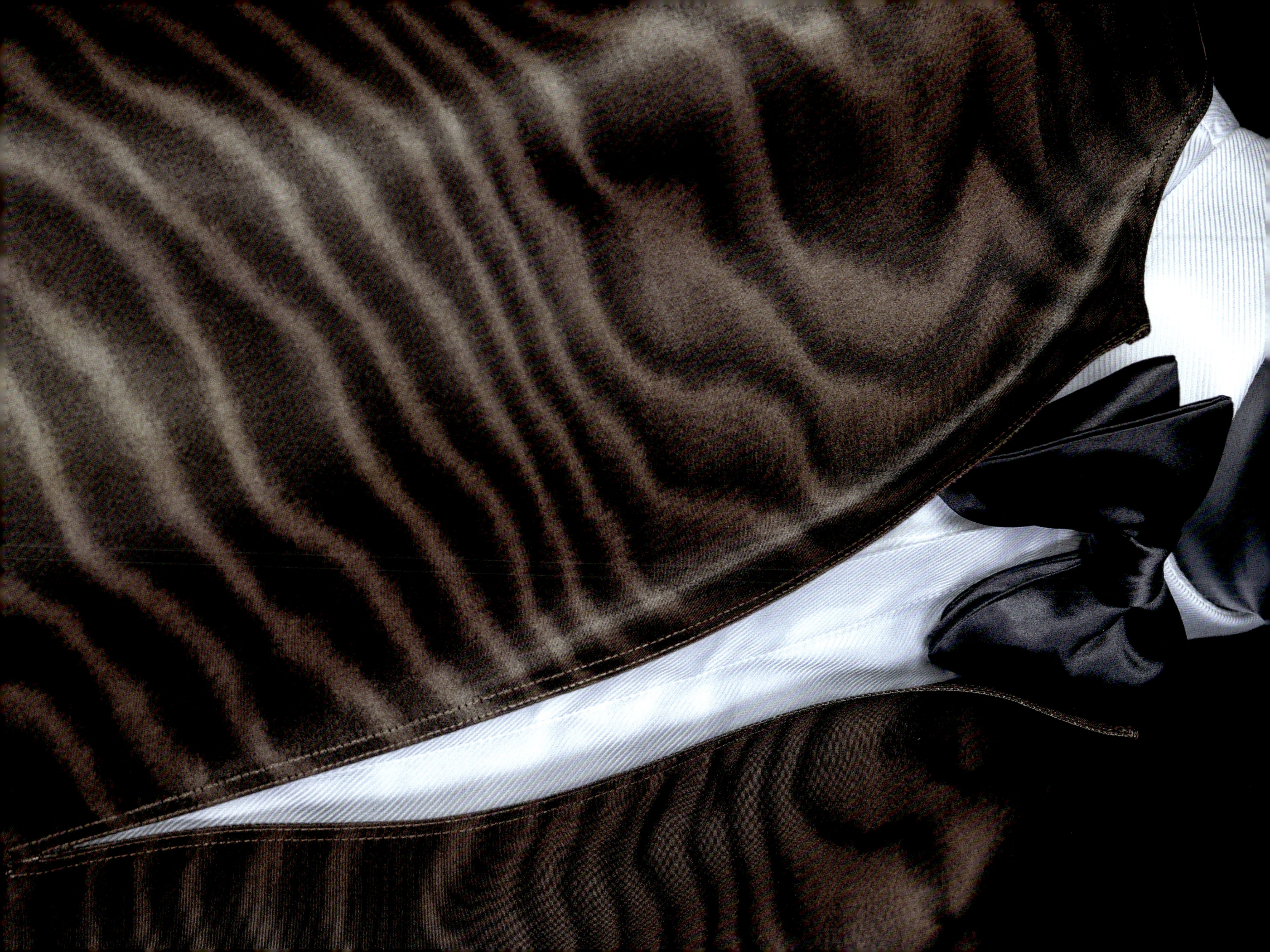

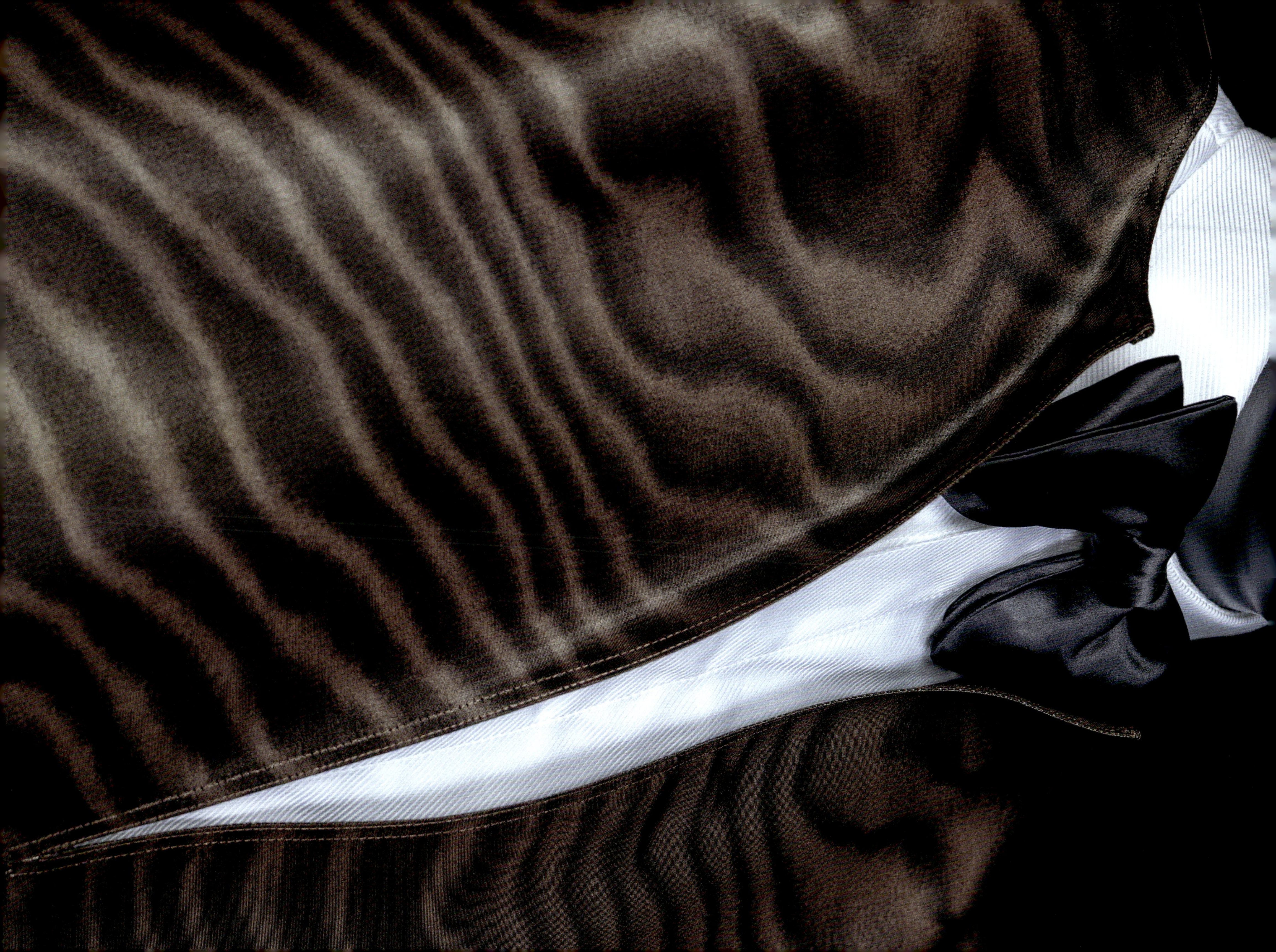

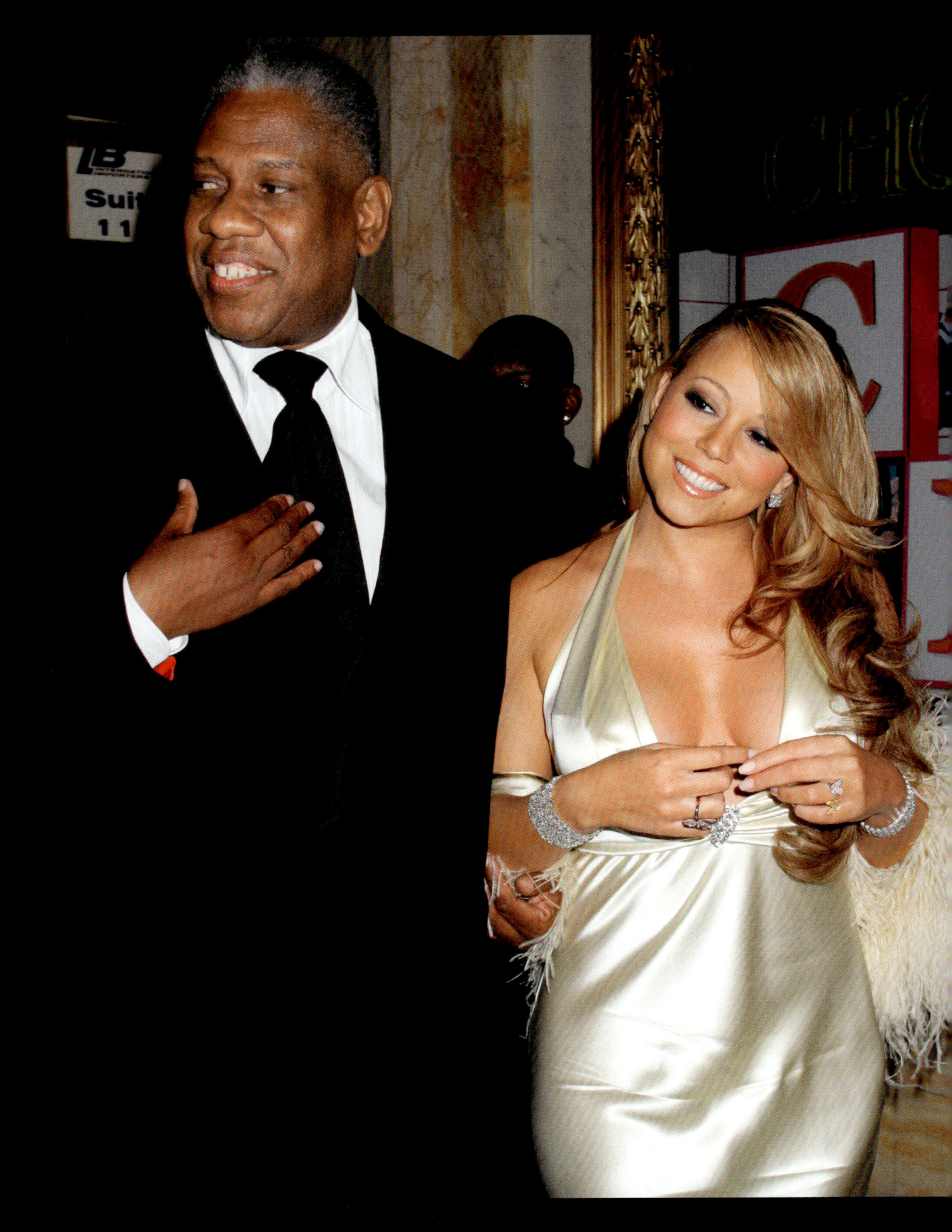

André and Mariah Carey at the launch party for her album *The Emancipation of Mimi* at Cipriani in New York, April 2005. Photo by Steve Azzara/Corbis via Getty Images.

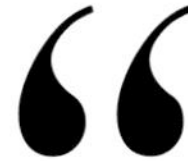

André Leon Talley was one of the most unique people on the planet. You knew he was **in the room** before he even walked in. André had a robust, mirthful, and whimsical personality. He was beloved worldwide and had an incredible **zest for life**, beauty, and fashion. He will surely be missed by myself and scores of others. I love you, **we love you**—there will never be another human like you!

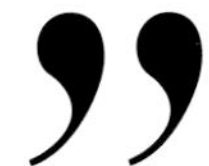

MARIAH CAREY

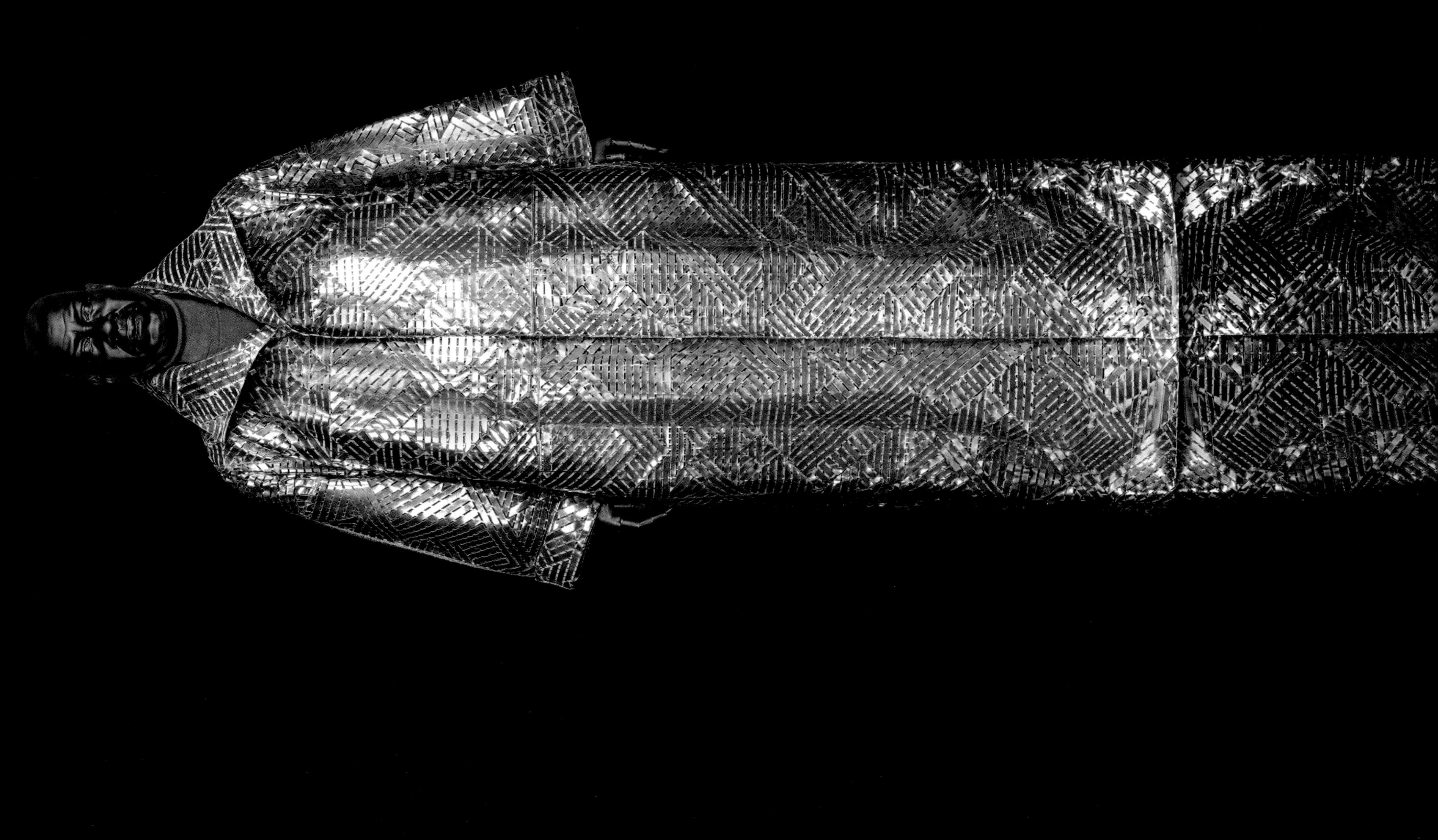

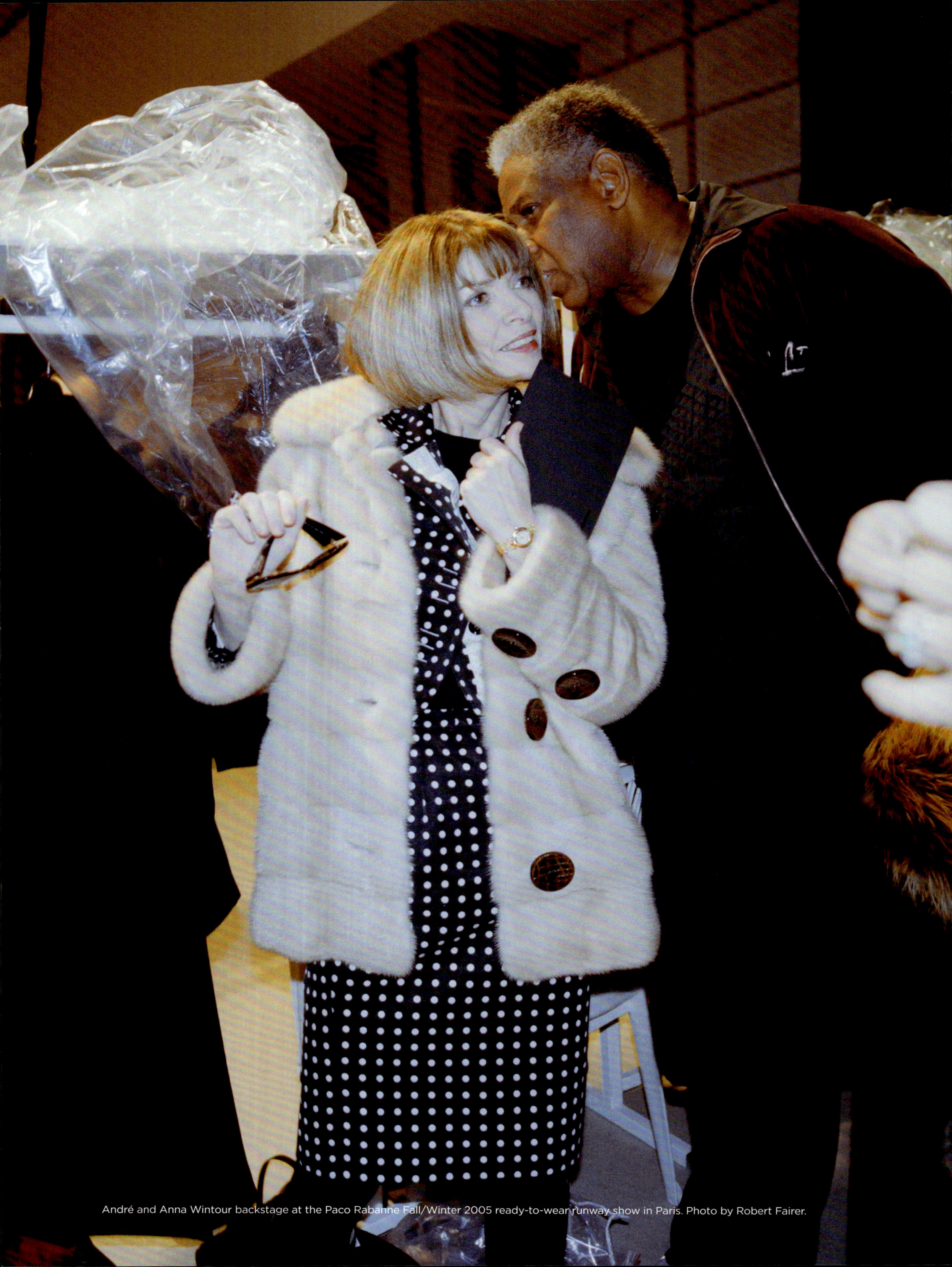

André and Anna Wintour backstage at the Paco Rabanne Fall/Winter 2005 ready-to-wear runway show in Paris. Photo by Robert Fairer.

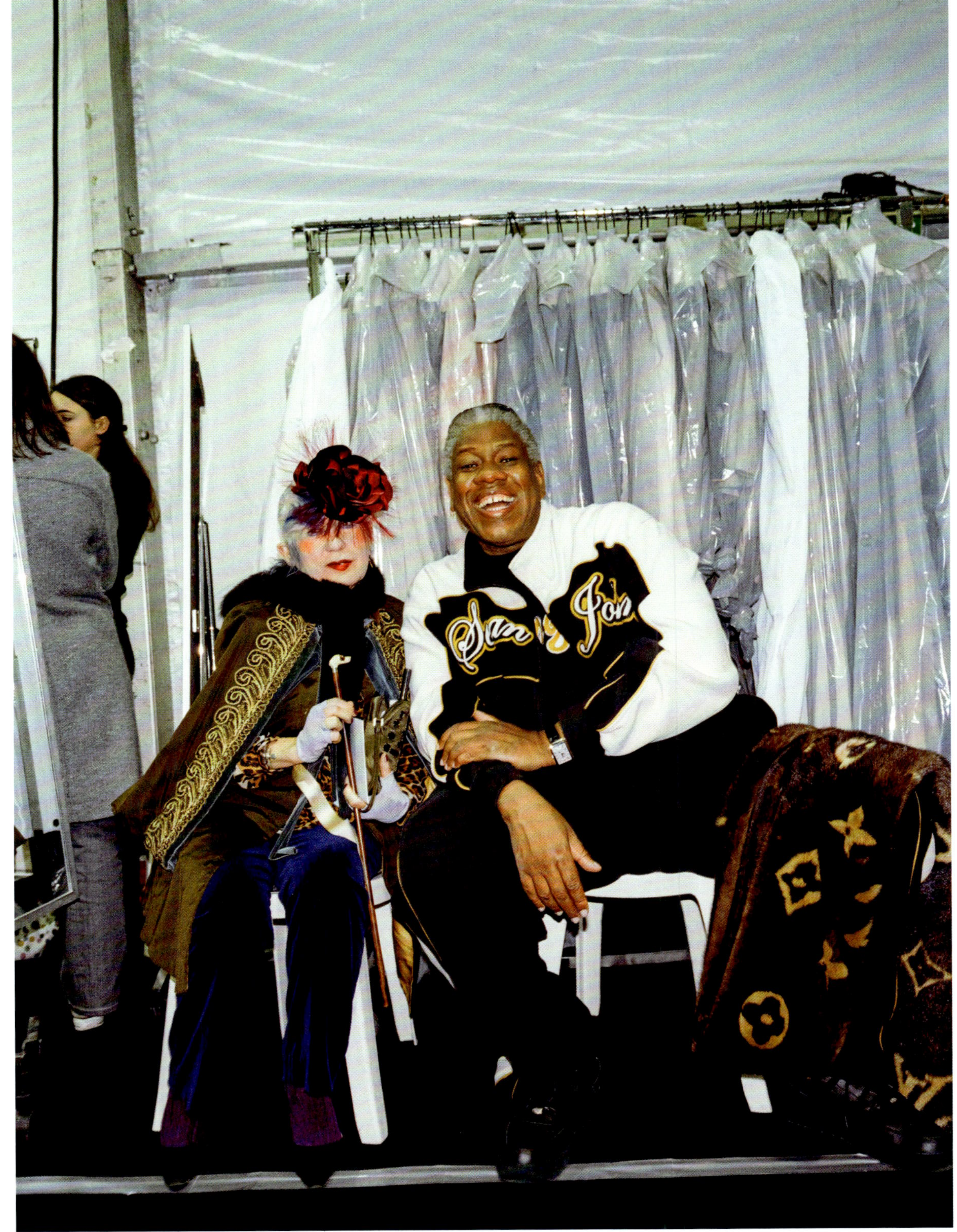

André and Anna Piaggi backstage at the Rochas Spring/Summer 2005 ready-to-wear runway show in Paris. Photo by Robert Fairer.

Brooks Leather Sportswear vest with Chrome Hearts accessories

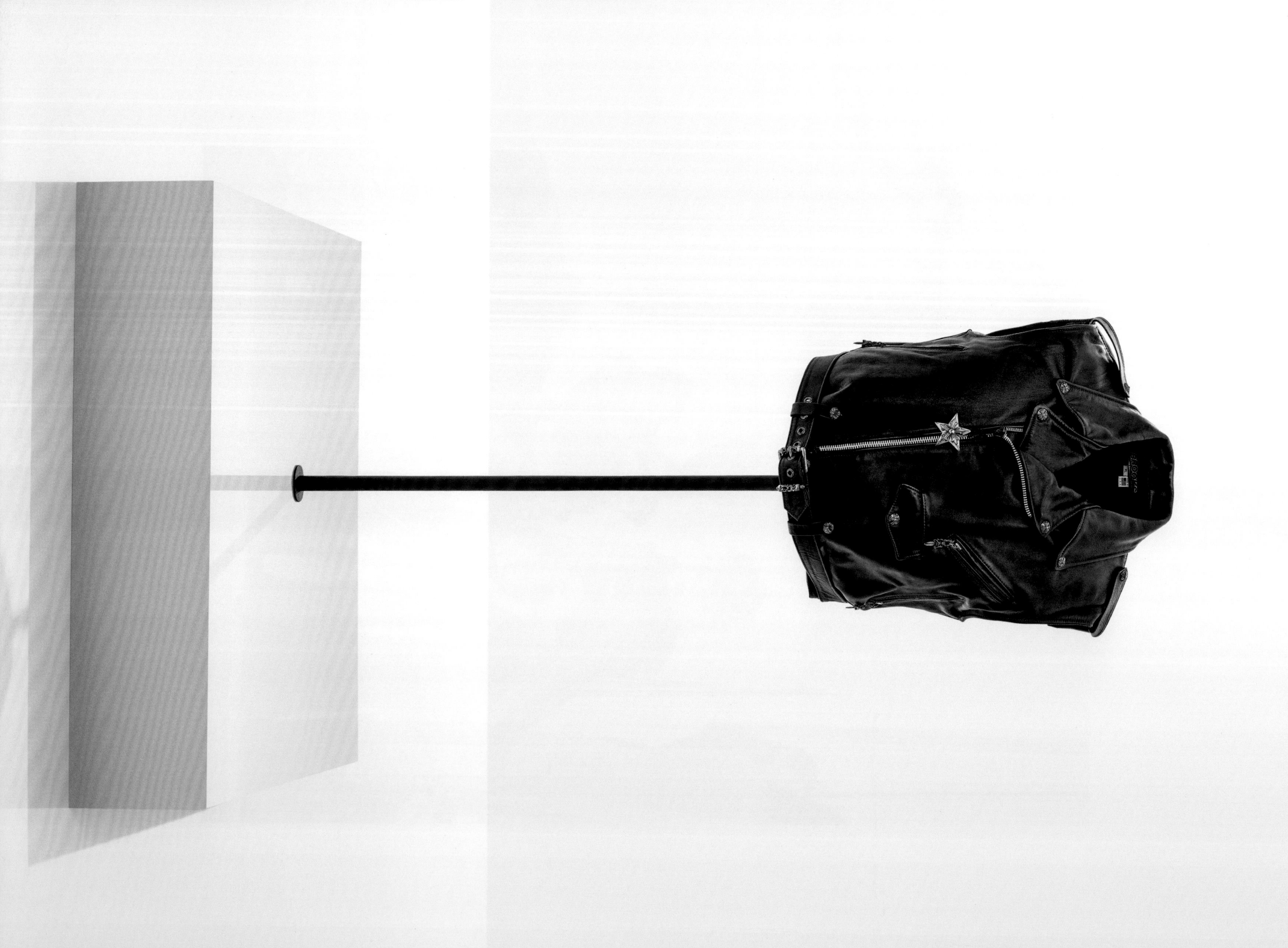

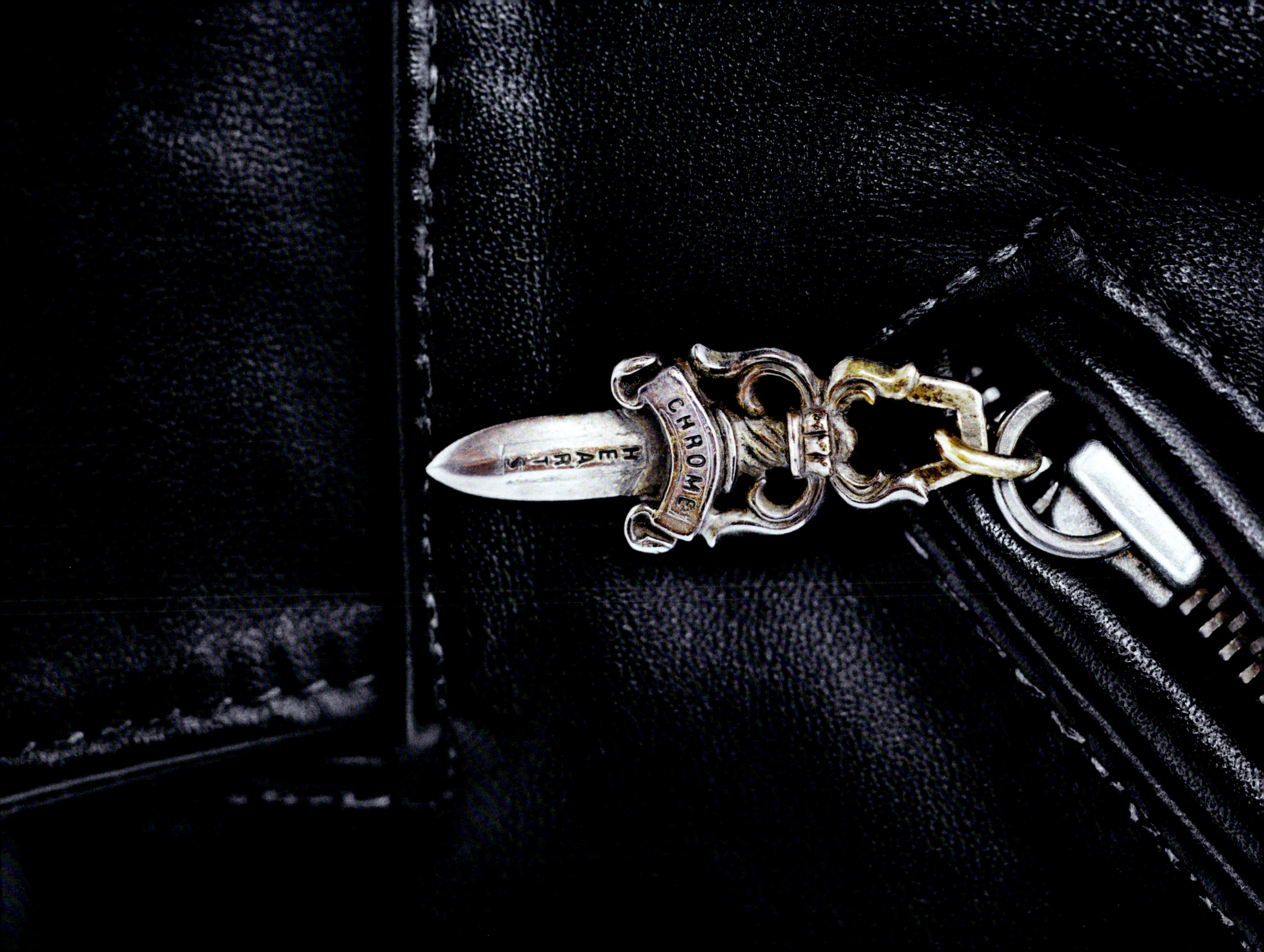
CHROME
HEARTS

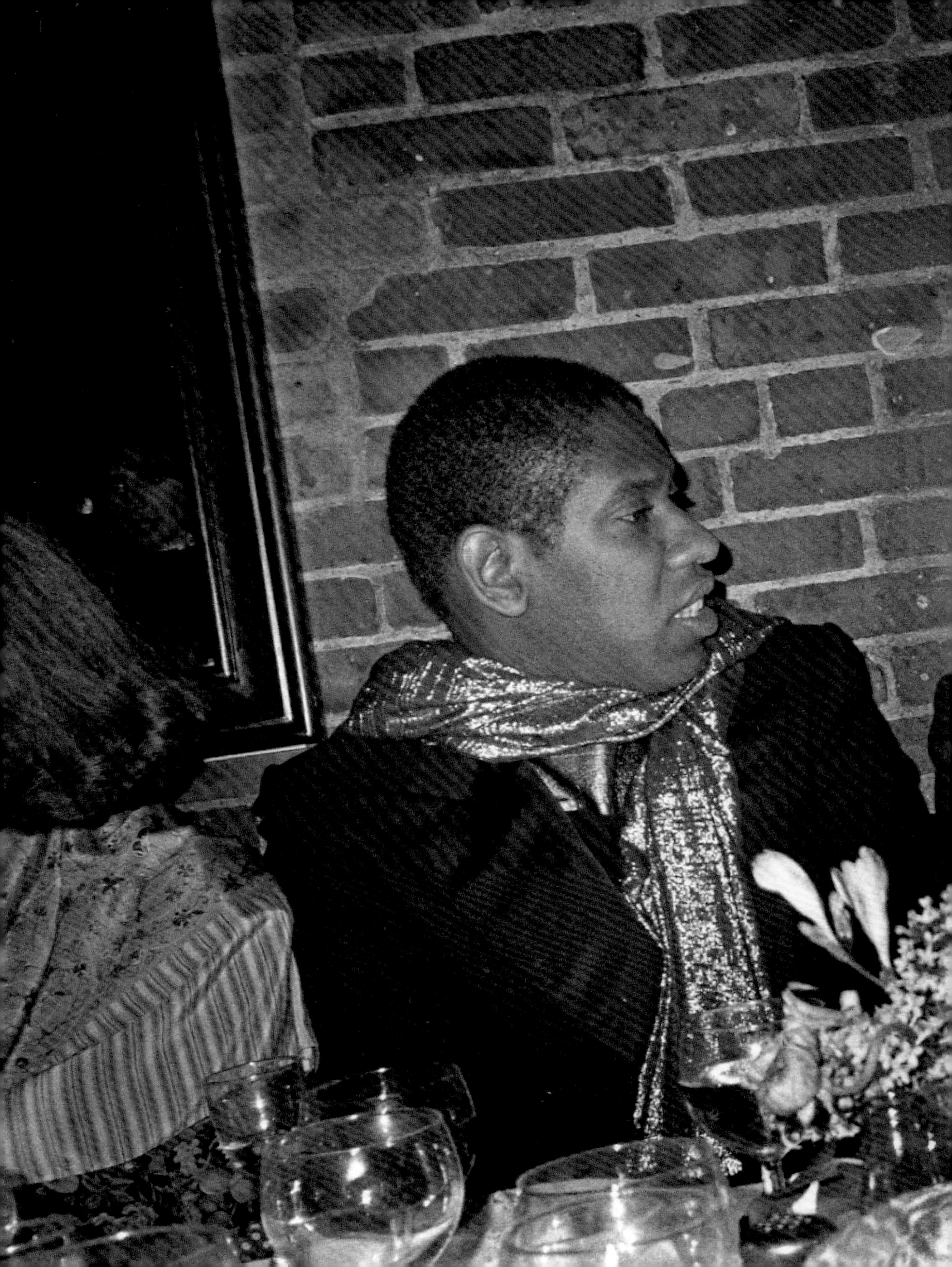

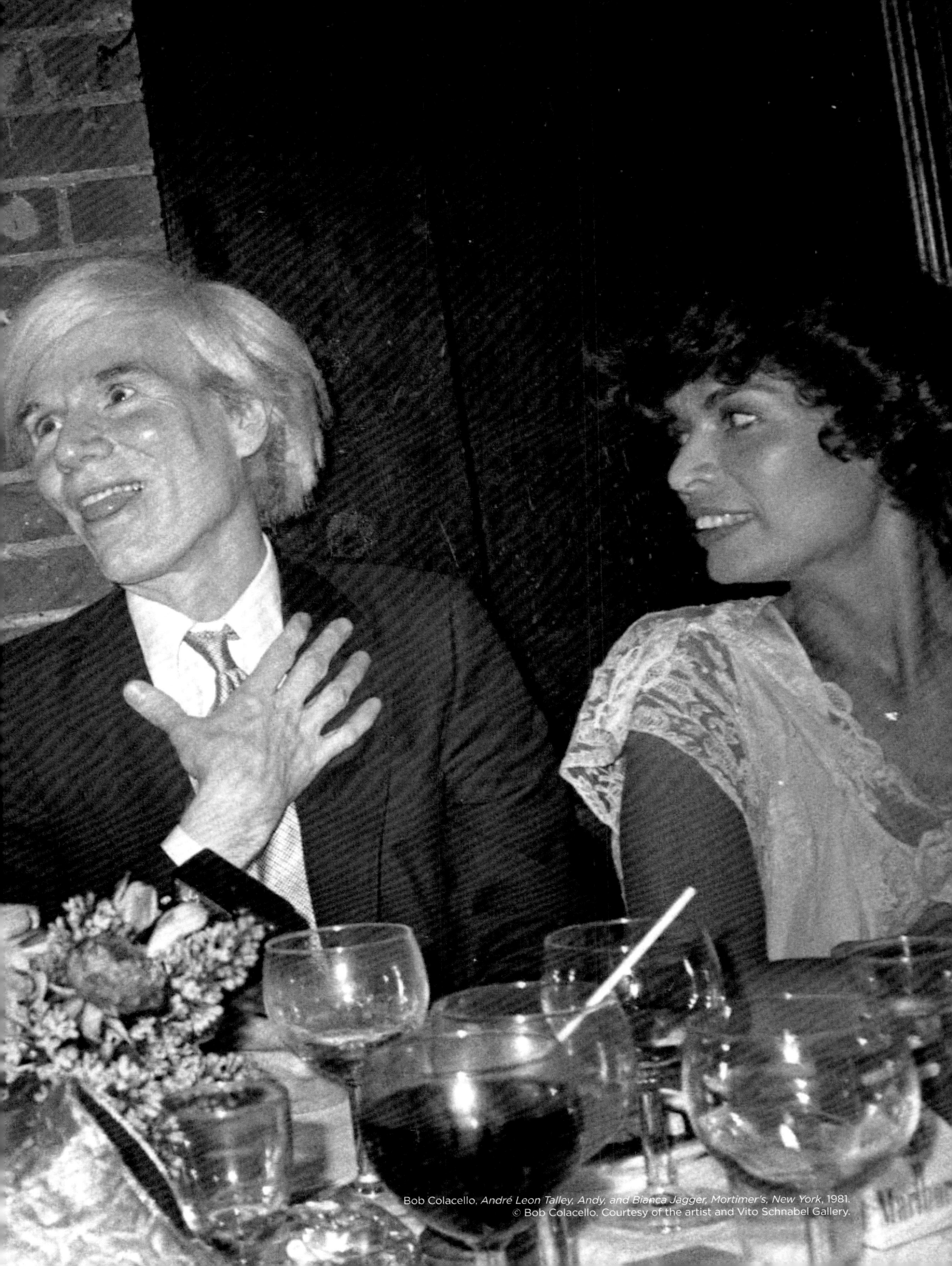

Bob Colacello, *André Leon Talley, Andy, and Bianca Jagger, Mortimer's, New York*, 1981.

LETTERS FROM ANDRÉ

Tom Ford

André always said exactly what he thought. Sometimes his words could sting, but they could also inspire. The way that he spoke, like the way that he wrote, was dramatic and passionate. Overblown, but powerful. His words were large and sweeping. There was nothing ever meek about anything André did or said.

In Milan, we usually stayed at the same hotel, and after a collection I would wait to see if a note from André would be slipped under my door. If there was no note, it meant that he did not like the collection and I would be crushed. If there was a note, it was often pages and pages of effusive writing in his beautiful script. His knowledge of fashion was so broad and so deep that he was perhaps the only journalist who could write about one of my collections and tell me literally everything that had been on my inspiration board. He could see every reference and understood every nuance. This was what made his opinion so valuable.

As a friend, the same honesty applied. When André said something to you, he meant it. If he was angry, he made that clear, and if he was happy or grateful or simply wanted to tell you that he cared, he meant that too. I miss him in so many ways.

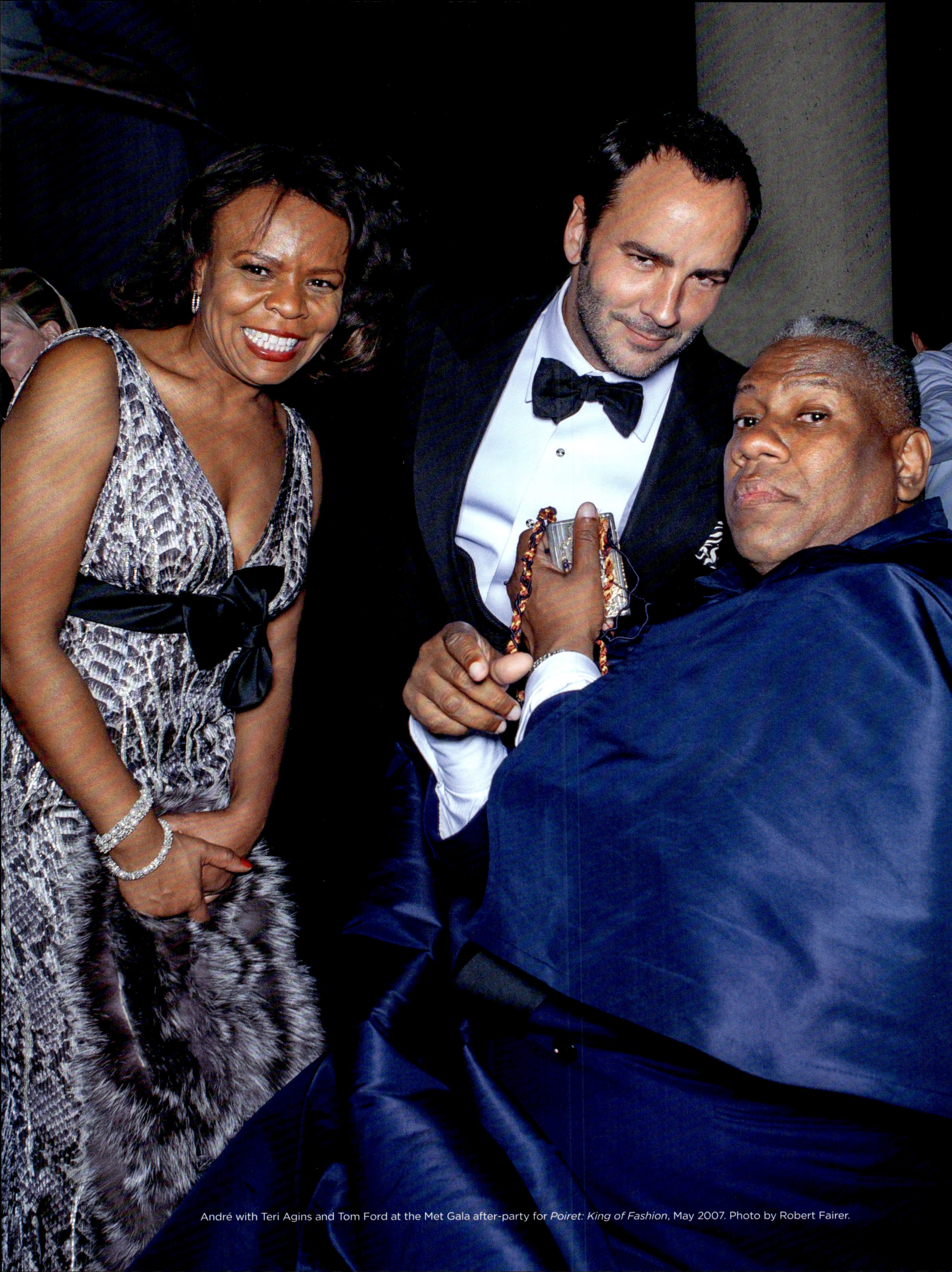

André with Teri Agins and Tom Ford at the Met Gala after-party for *Poiret: King of Fashion*, May 2007. Photo by Robert Fairer.

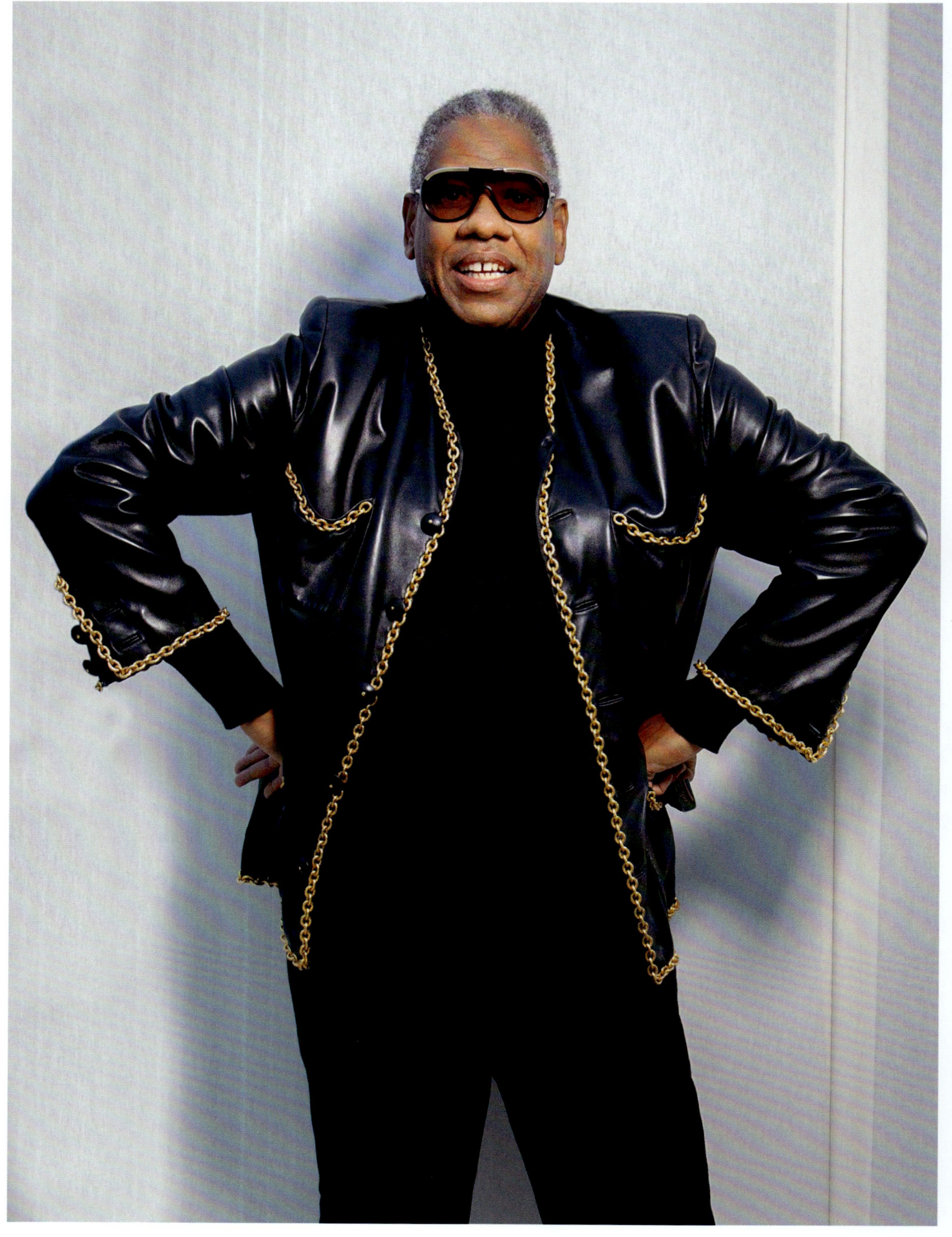

André backstage at the Chanel Spring/Summer 2007 haute couture runway show. Photo by Robert Fairer.

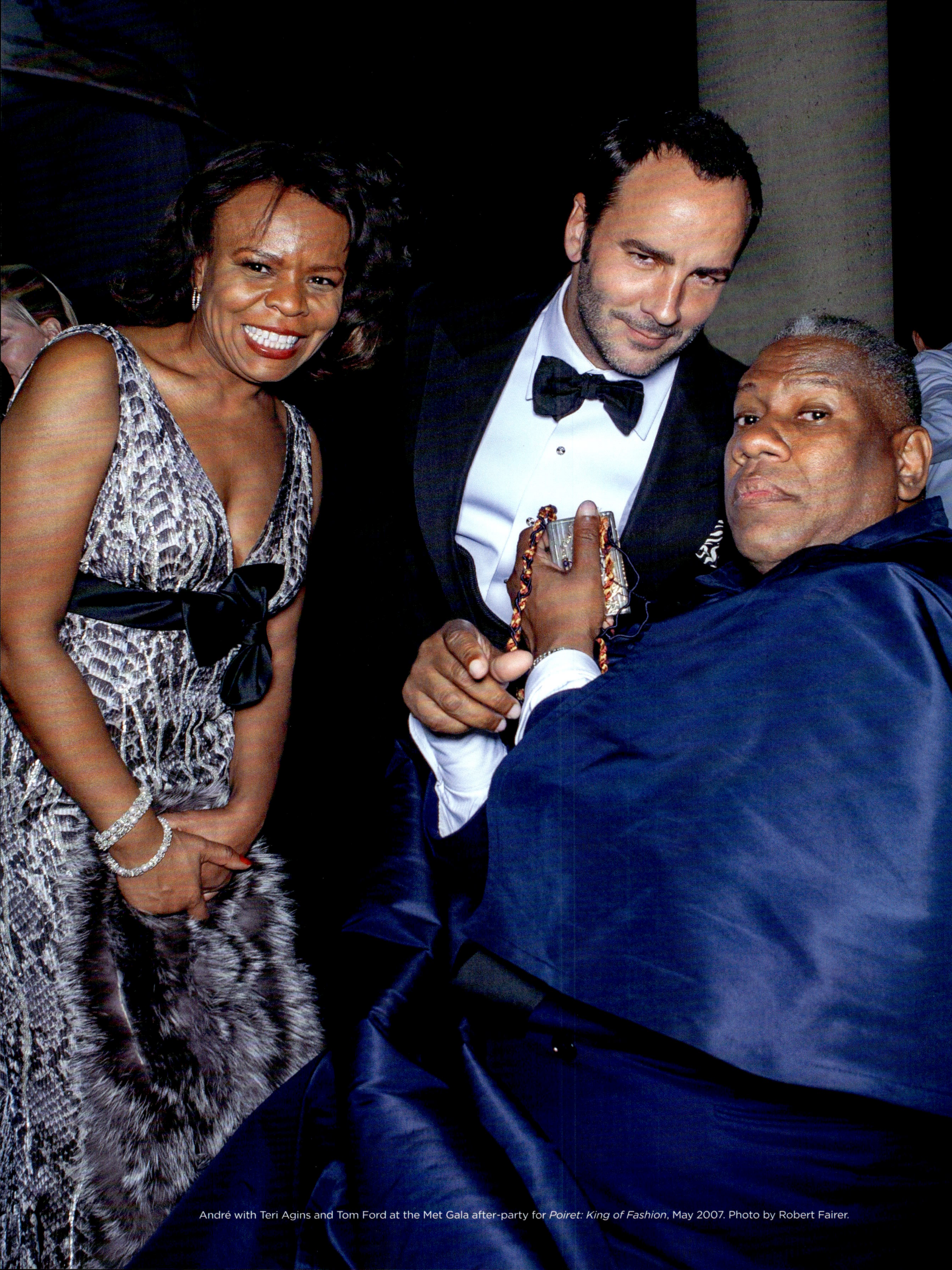

André with Teri Agins and Tom Ford at the Met Gala after-party for *Poiret: King of Fashion*, May 2007. Photo by Robert Fairer.

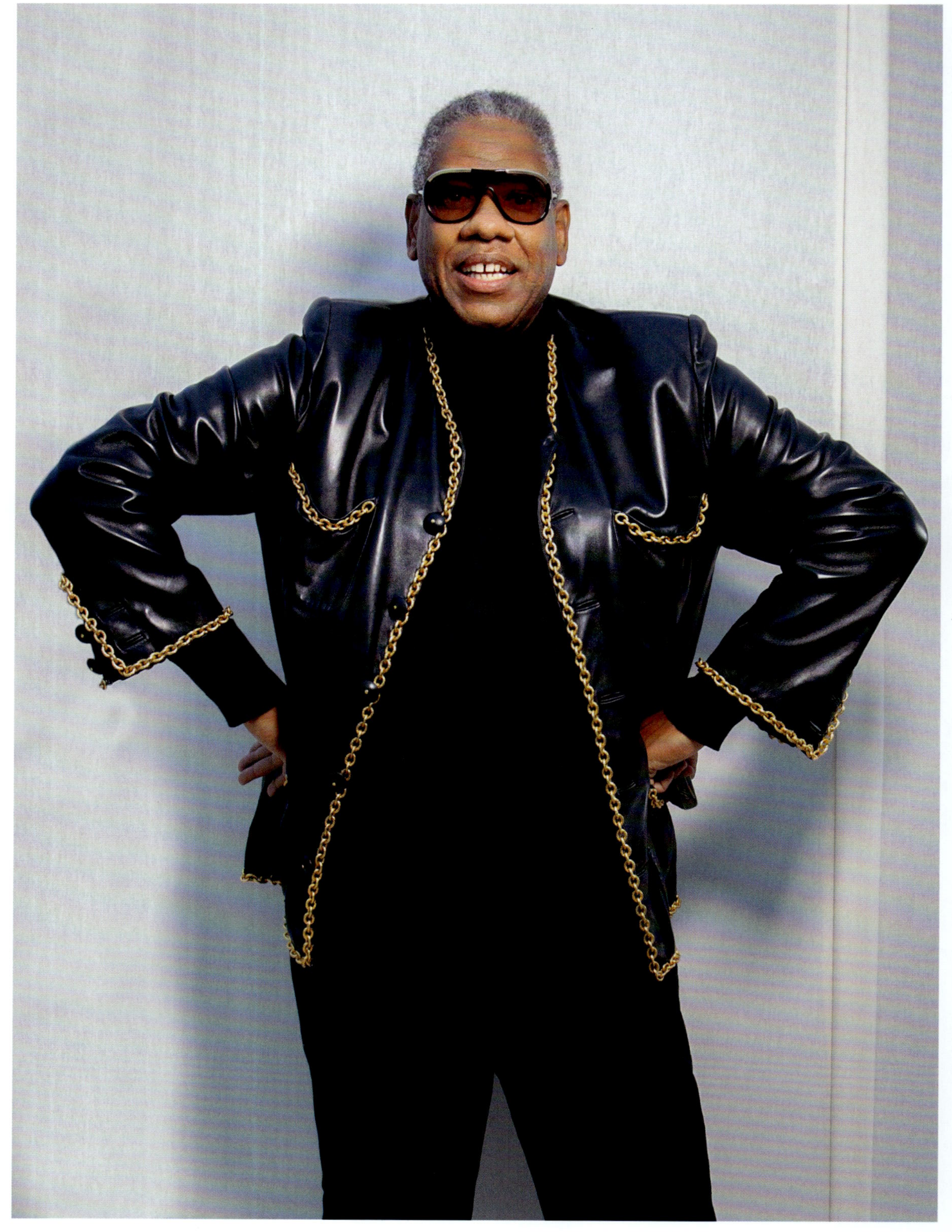

André backstage at the Chanel Spring/Summer 2007 haute couture runway show. Photo by Robert Fairer.

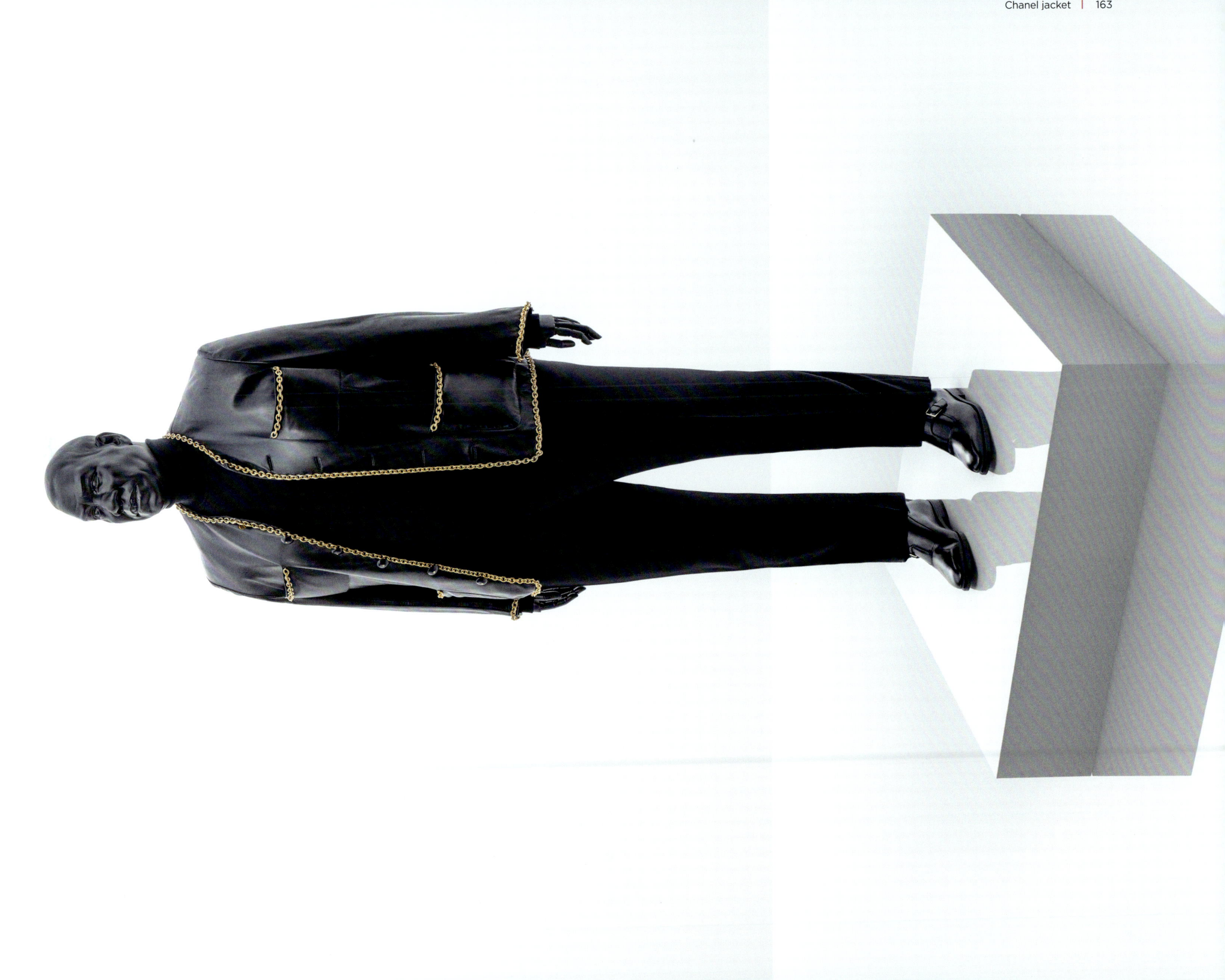

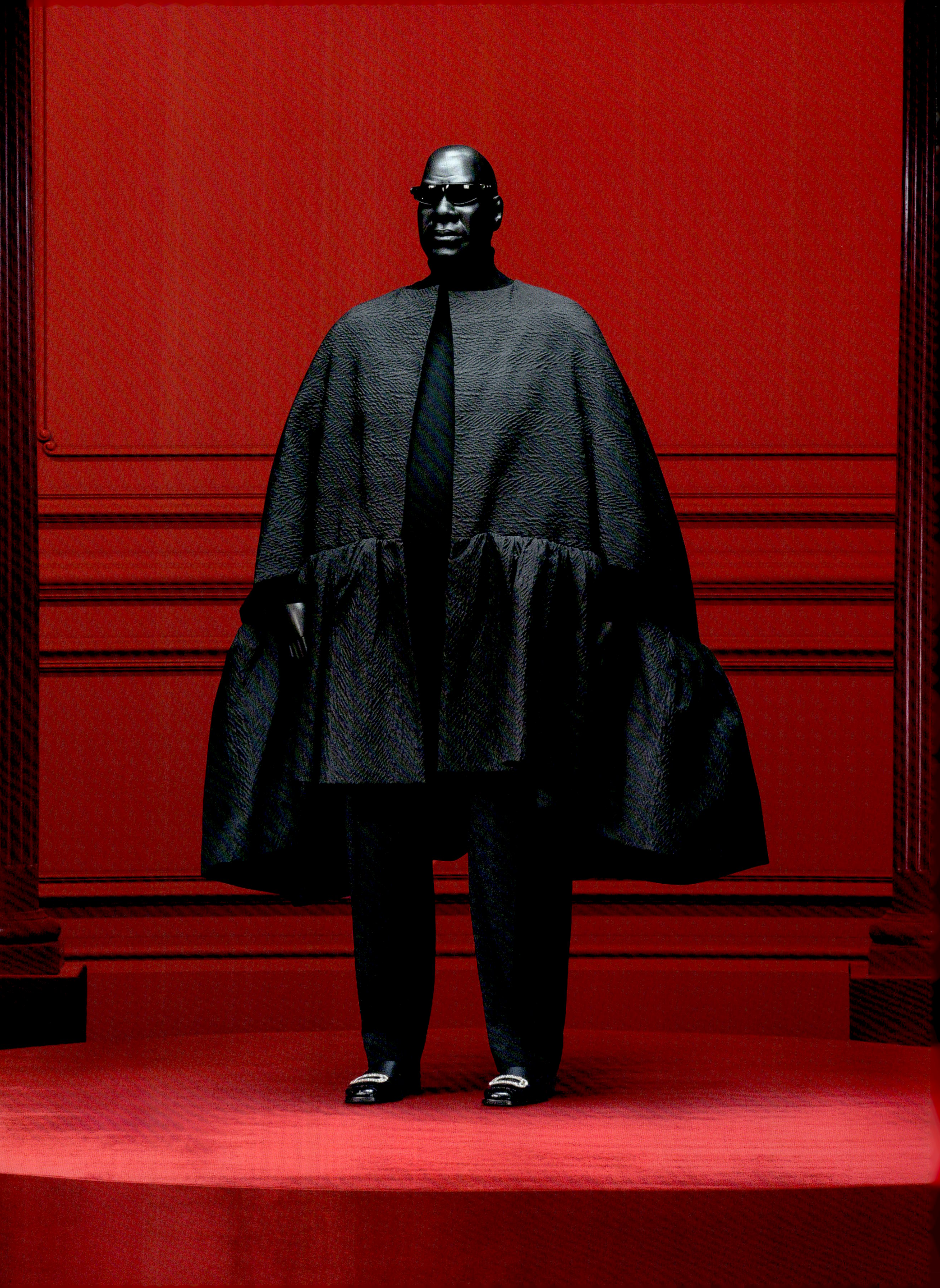

Nicolas Ghesquière for Balenciaga cape

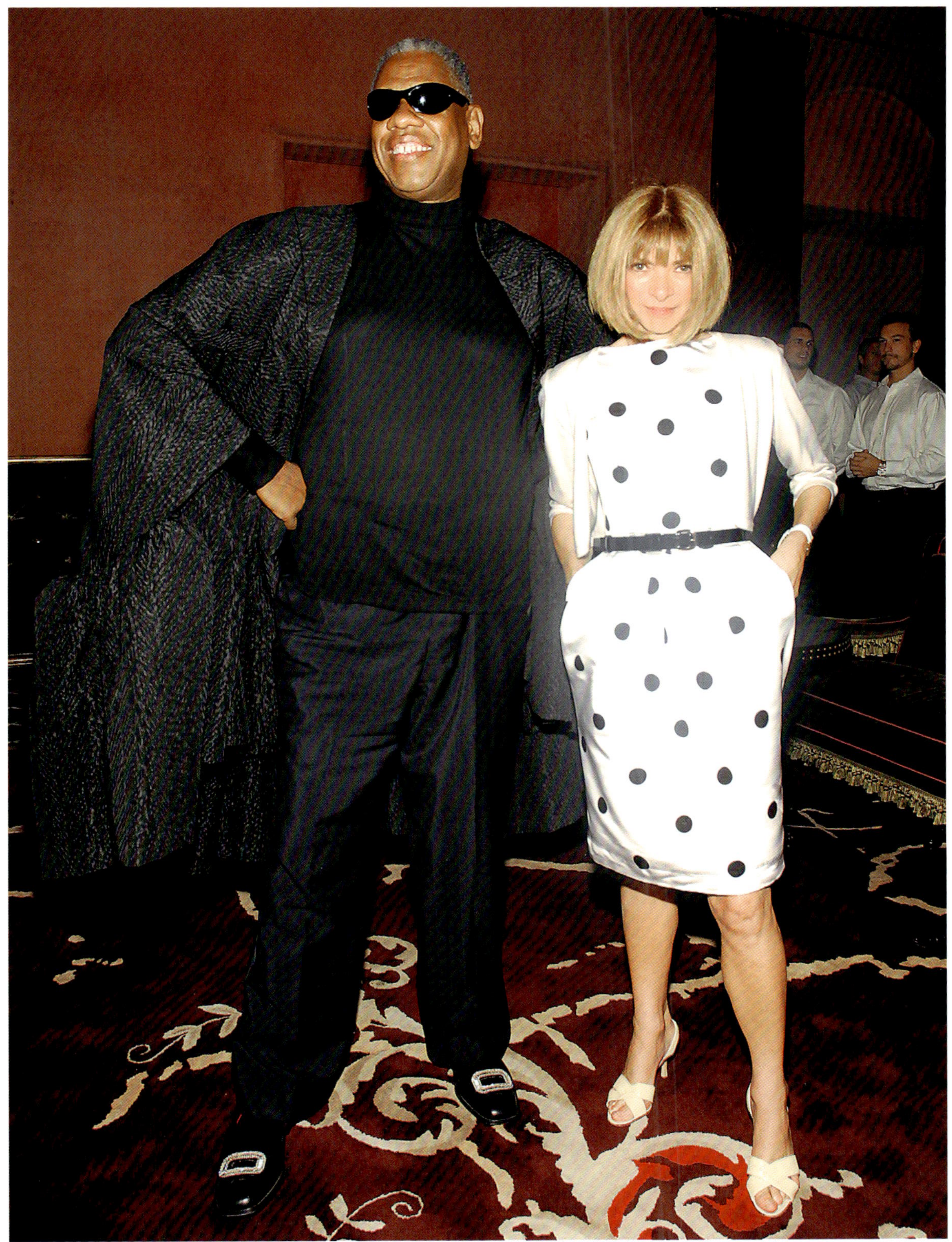

André and Anna Wintour attending the CFDA/Vogue Fashion Fund party at the Gramercy Park Hotel, 2006. Photo by Fairchild Archive/Penske Media via Getty Images.

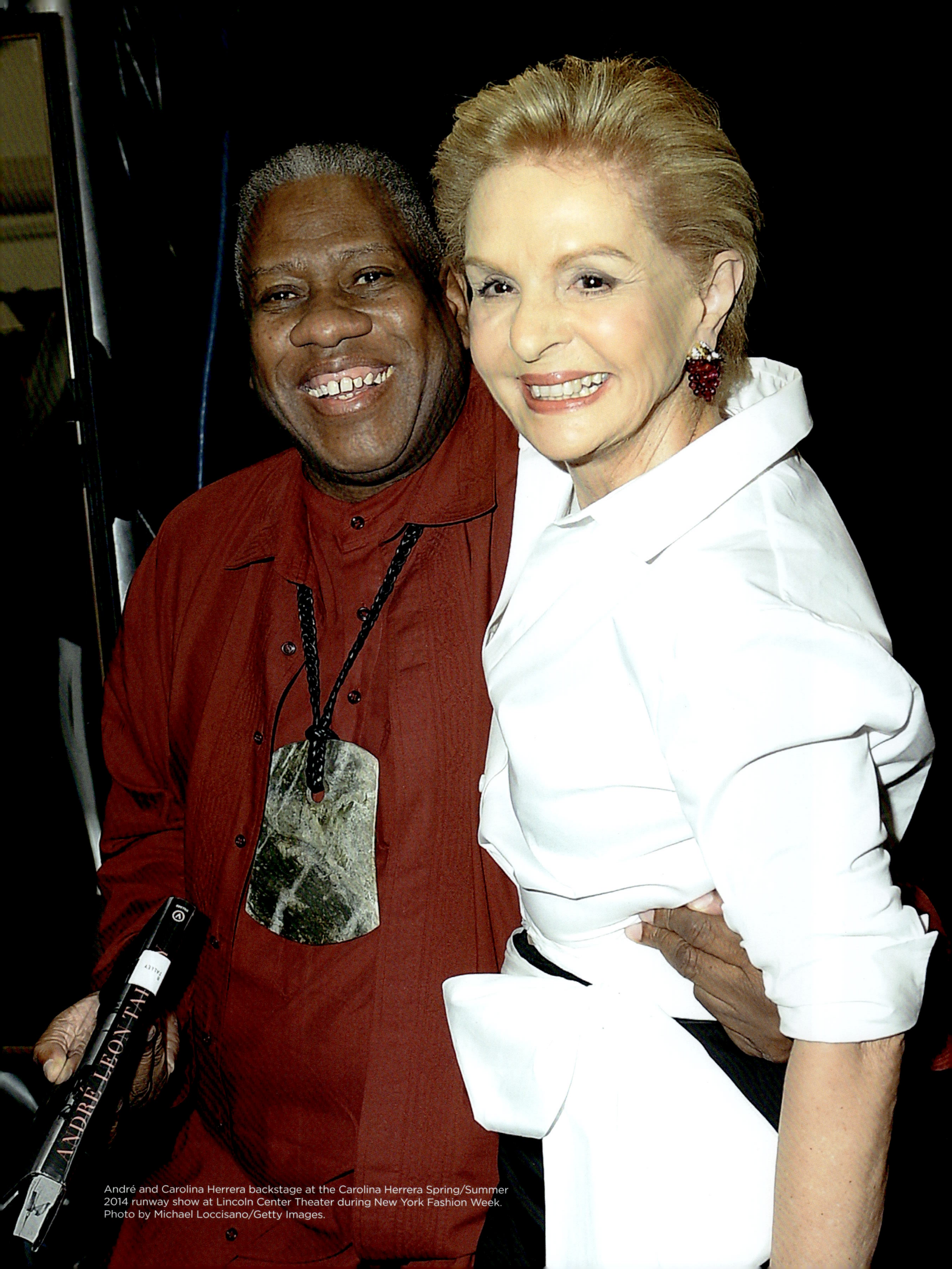

André and Carolina Herrera backstage at the Carolina Herrera Spring/Summer 2014 runway show at Lincoln Center Theater during New York Fashion Week. Photo by Michael Loccisano/Getty Images.

André Leon Talley was the most passionate critic of fashion. He was the fashion **historian** of our days, and his legacy is vital. I always remember him dressed in a very **distinctive** way, especially when he was wearing his **fabulous** caftans. He was always around when you needed him and gave the best fashion advice. He was **unique** and he will never be replaced by anyone. He was my dear **friend**, and I loved him.

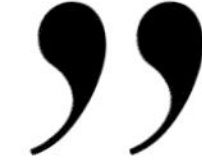

CAROLINA HERRERA

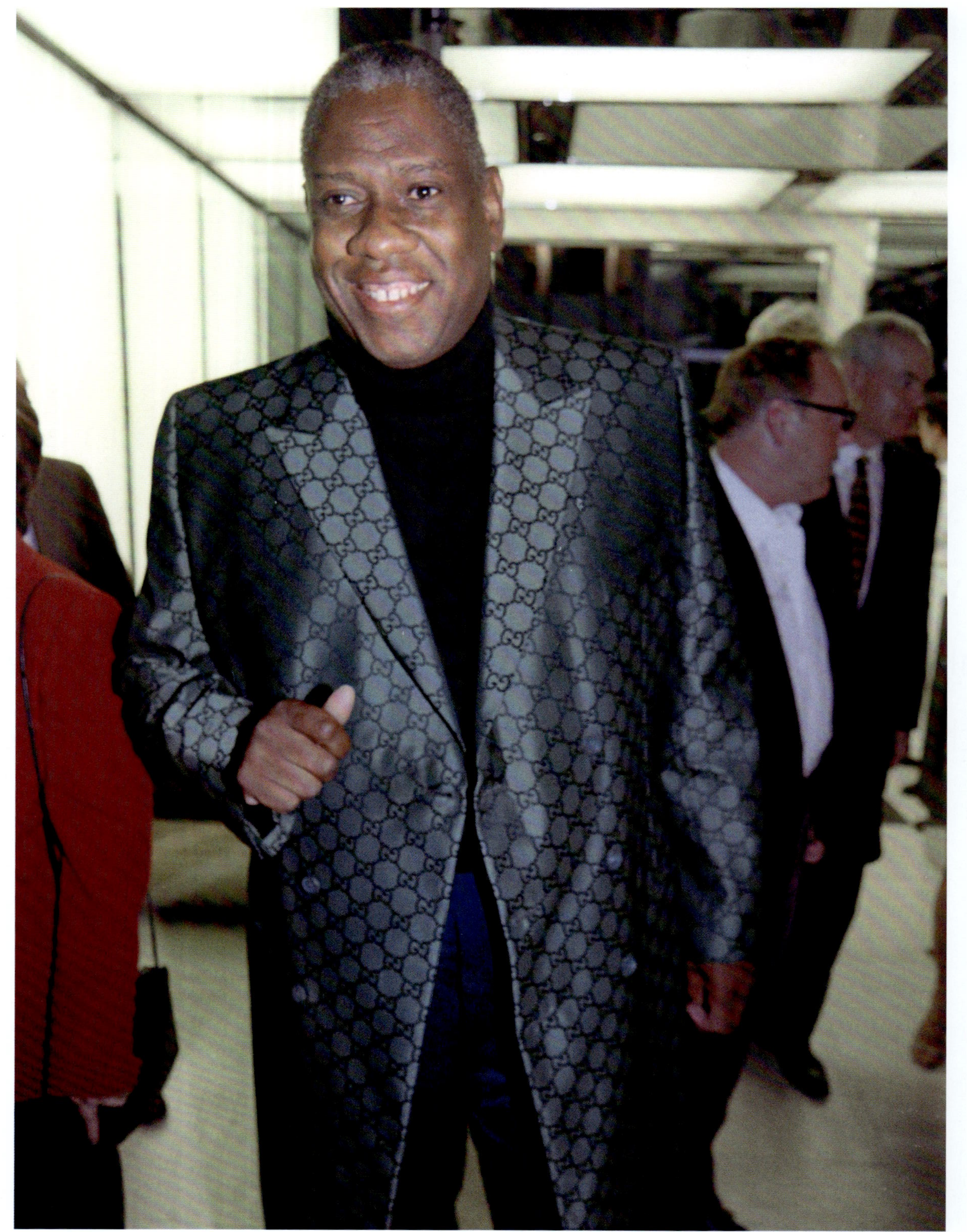

André at the opening party for the Gucci Fifth Avenue storefront. Photo by Steve Eichner/WWD/Penske Media via Getty Images.

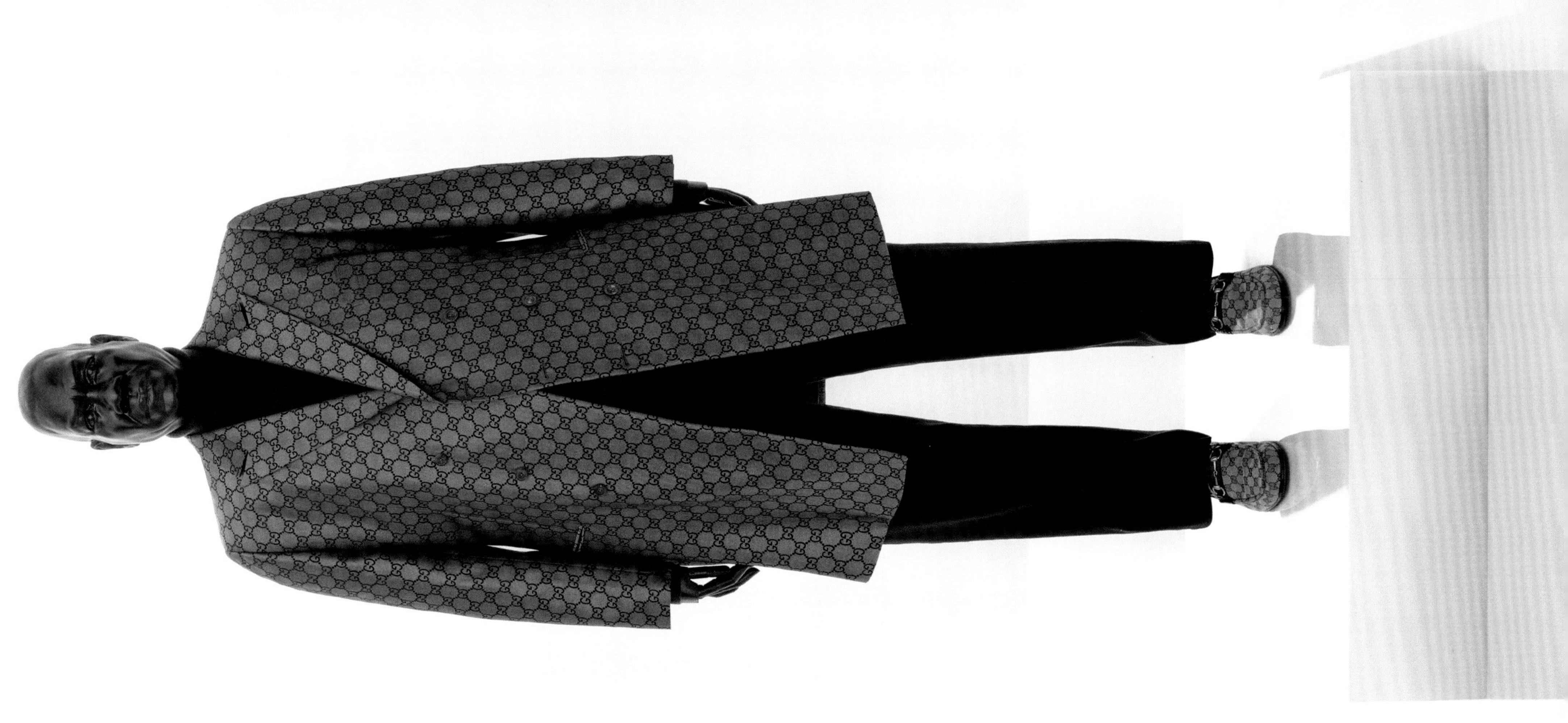

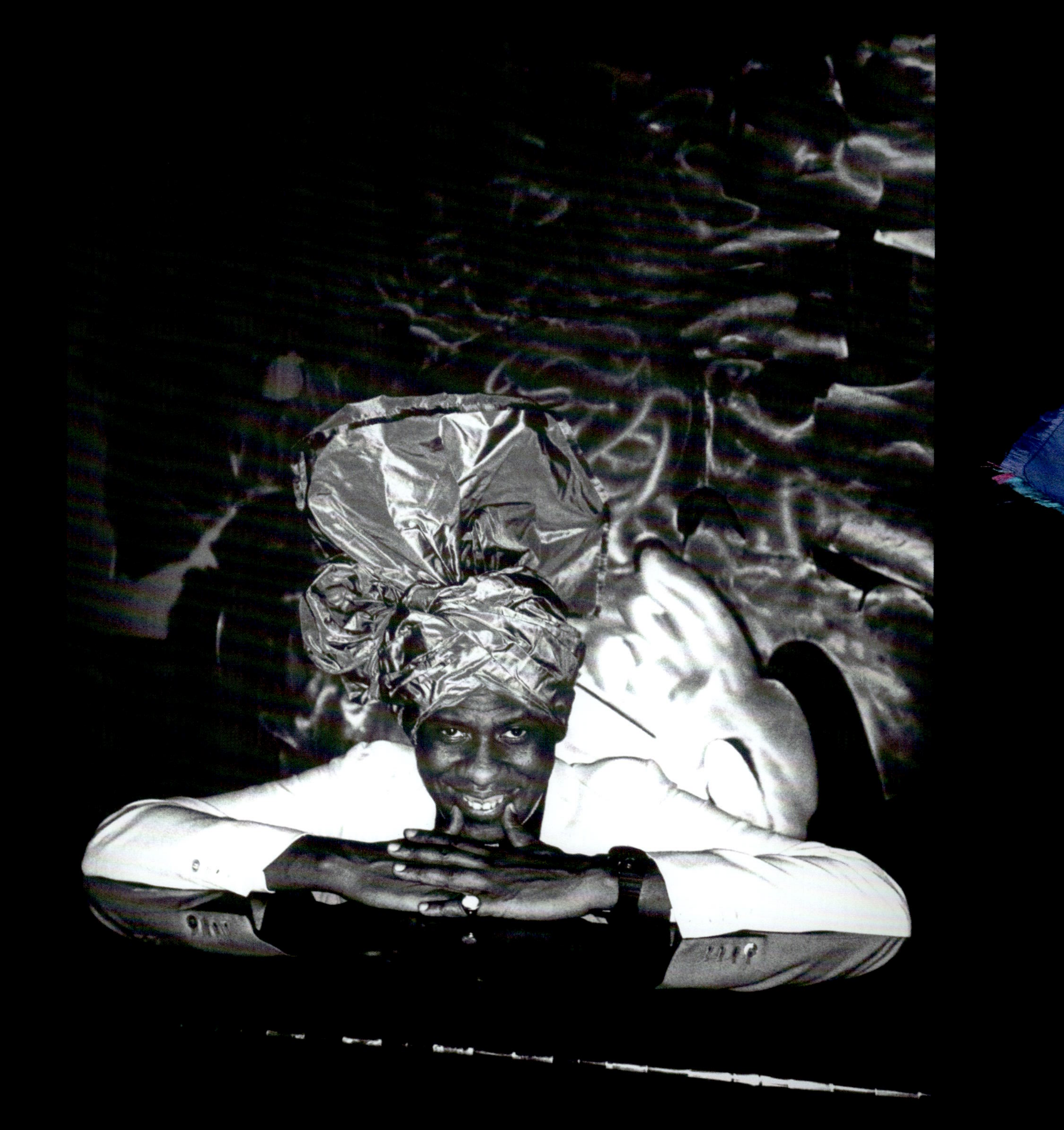

André, 1992. Photo by Karl Lagerfeld.

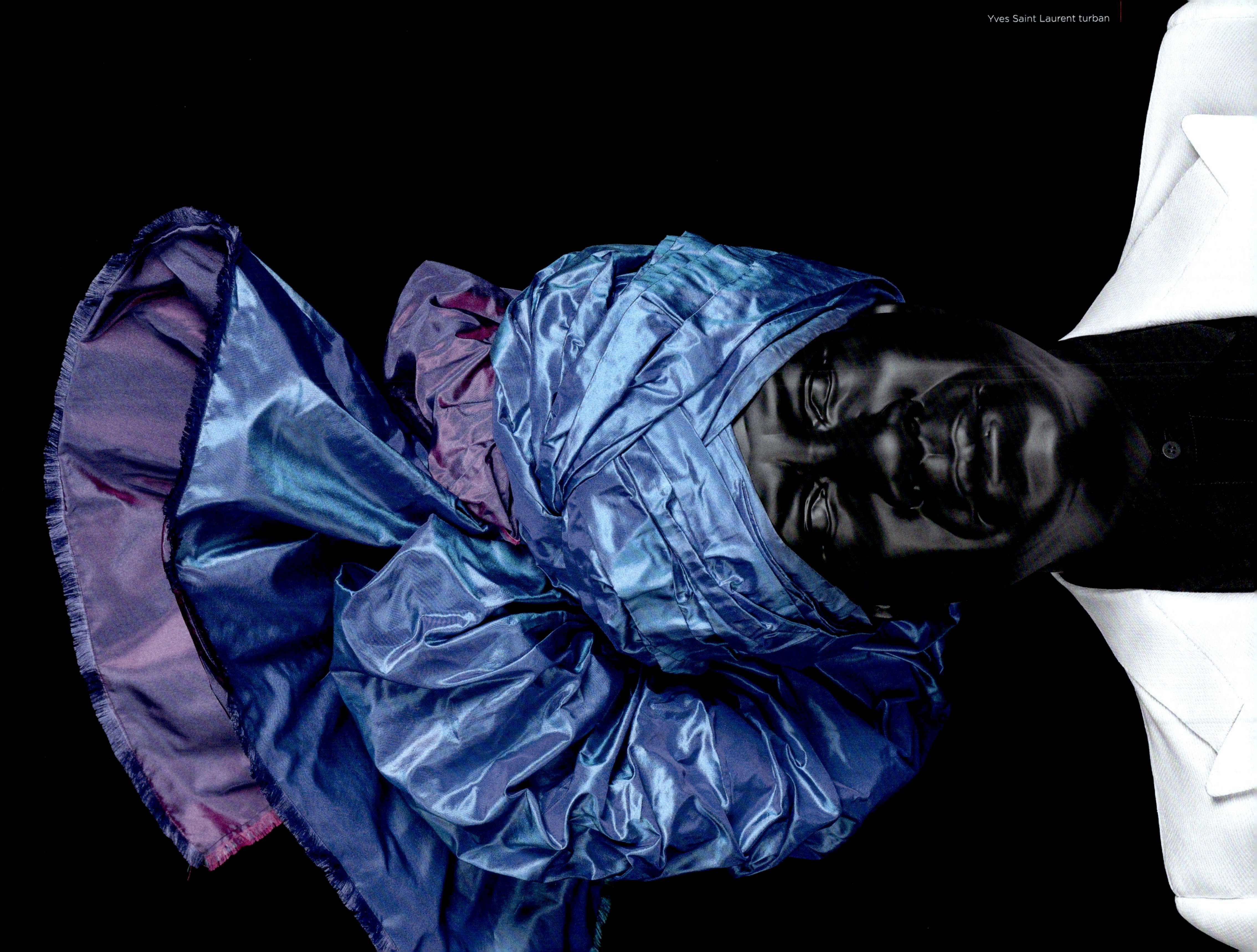

Yves Saint Laurent turban

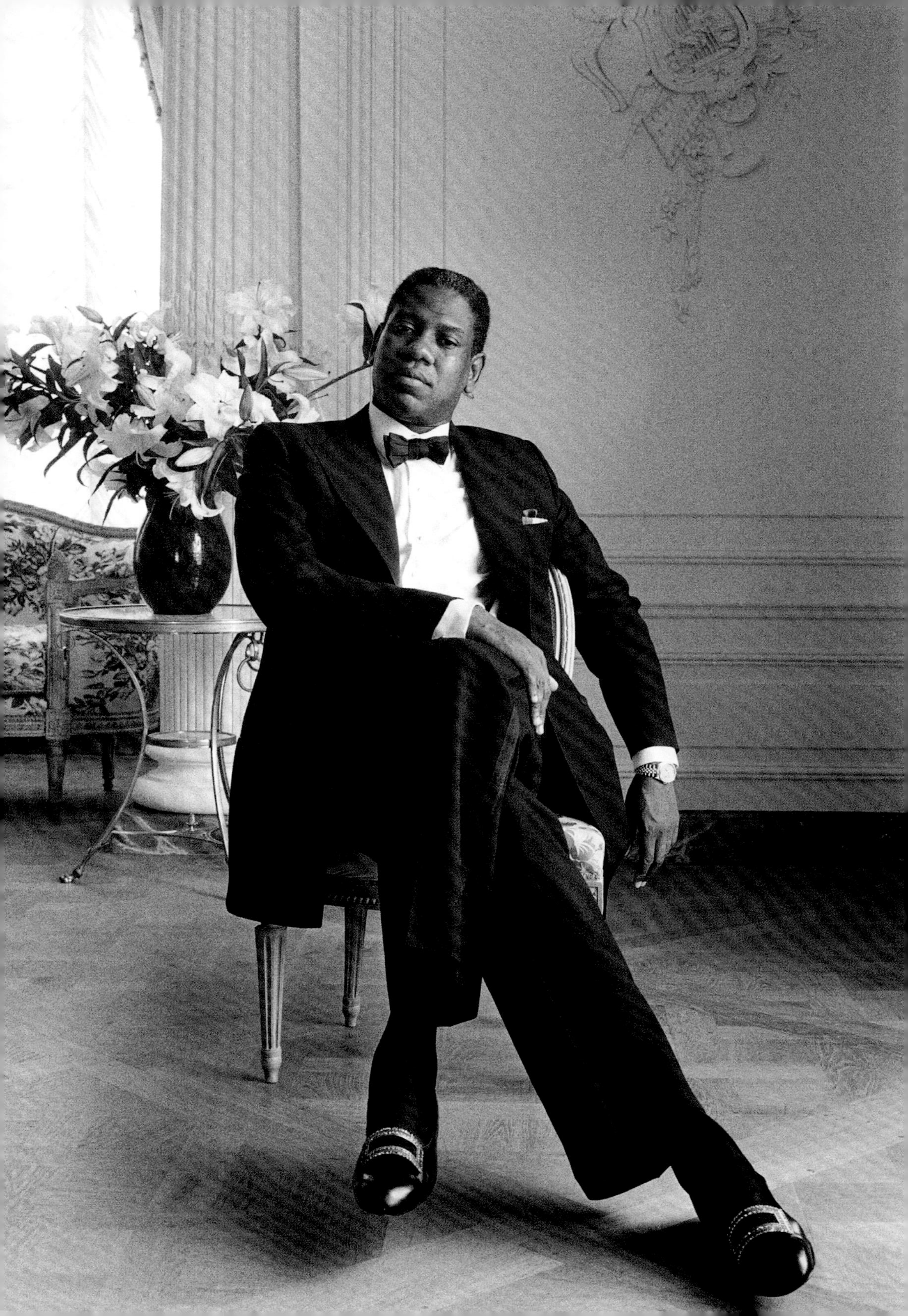

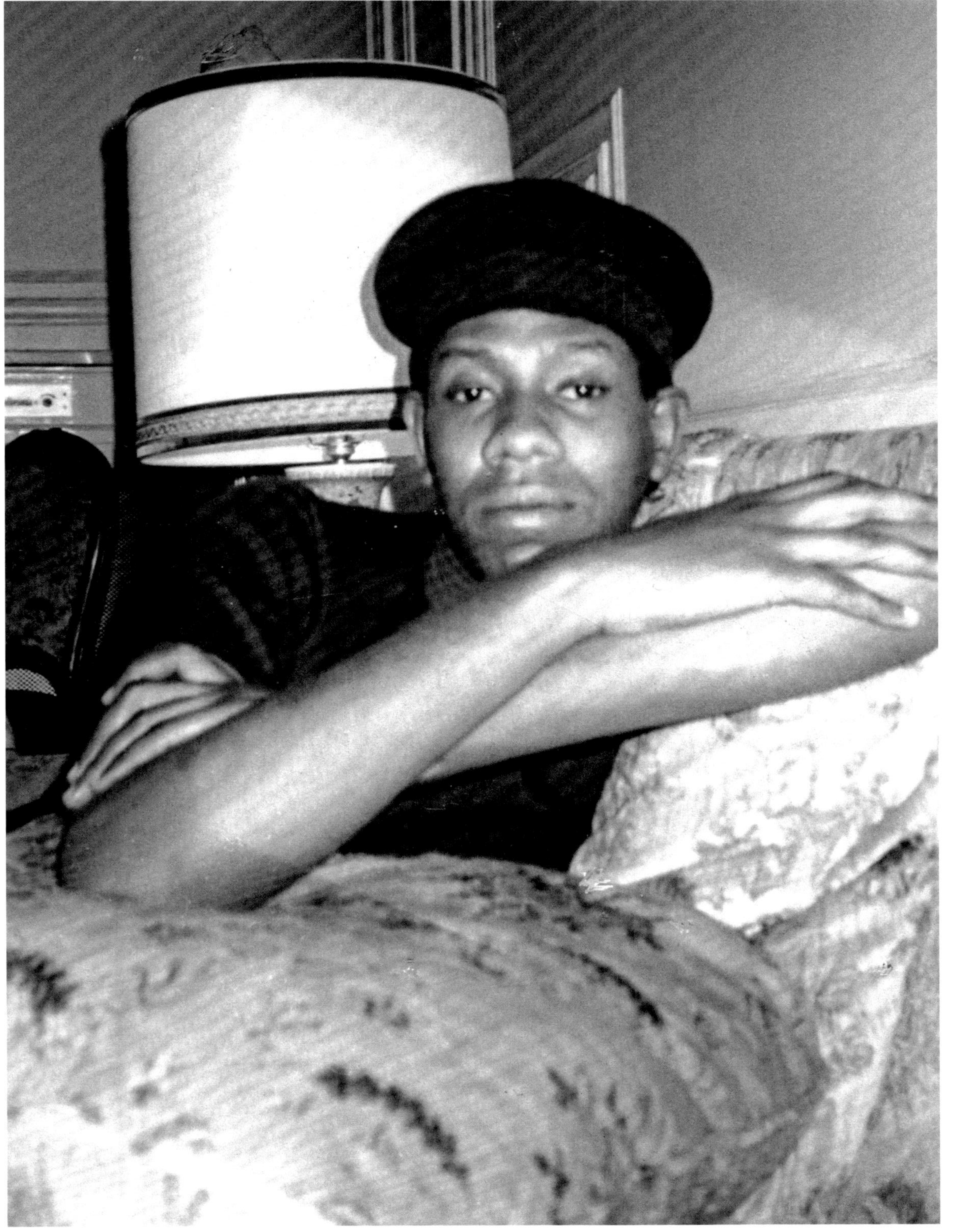

André, date unknown. Photo by Diane von Furstenberg.

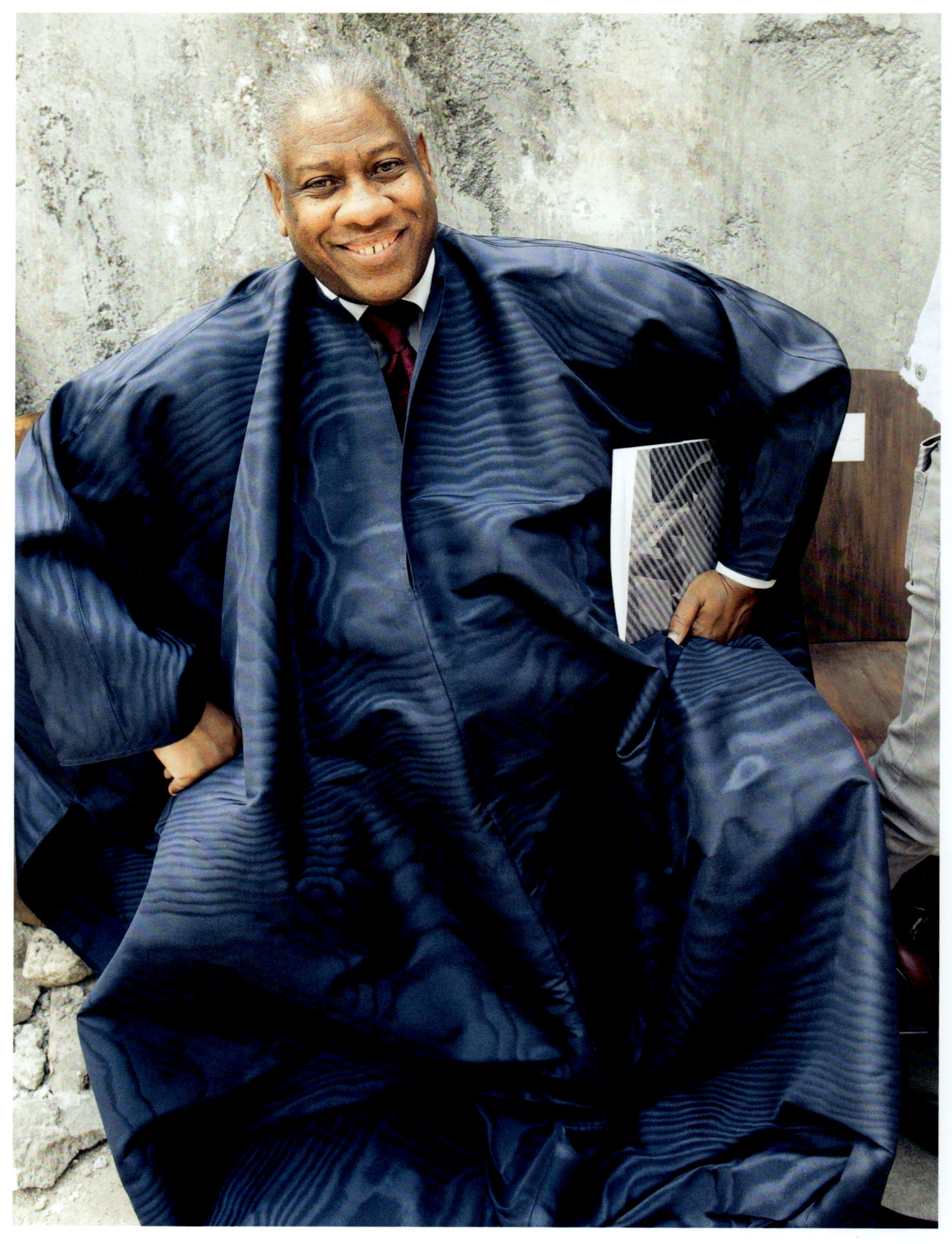

André, date unknown. Photo by Coveteur/Trunk Archive.

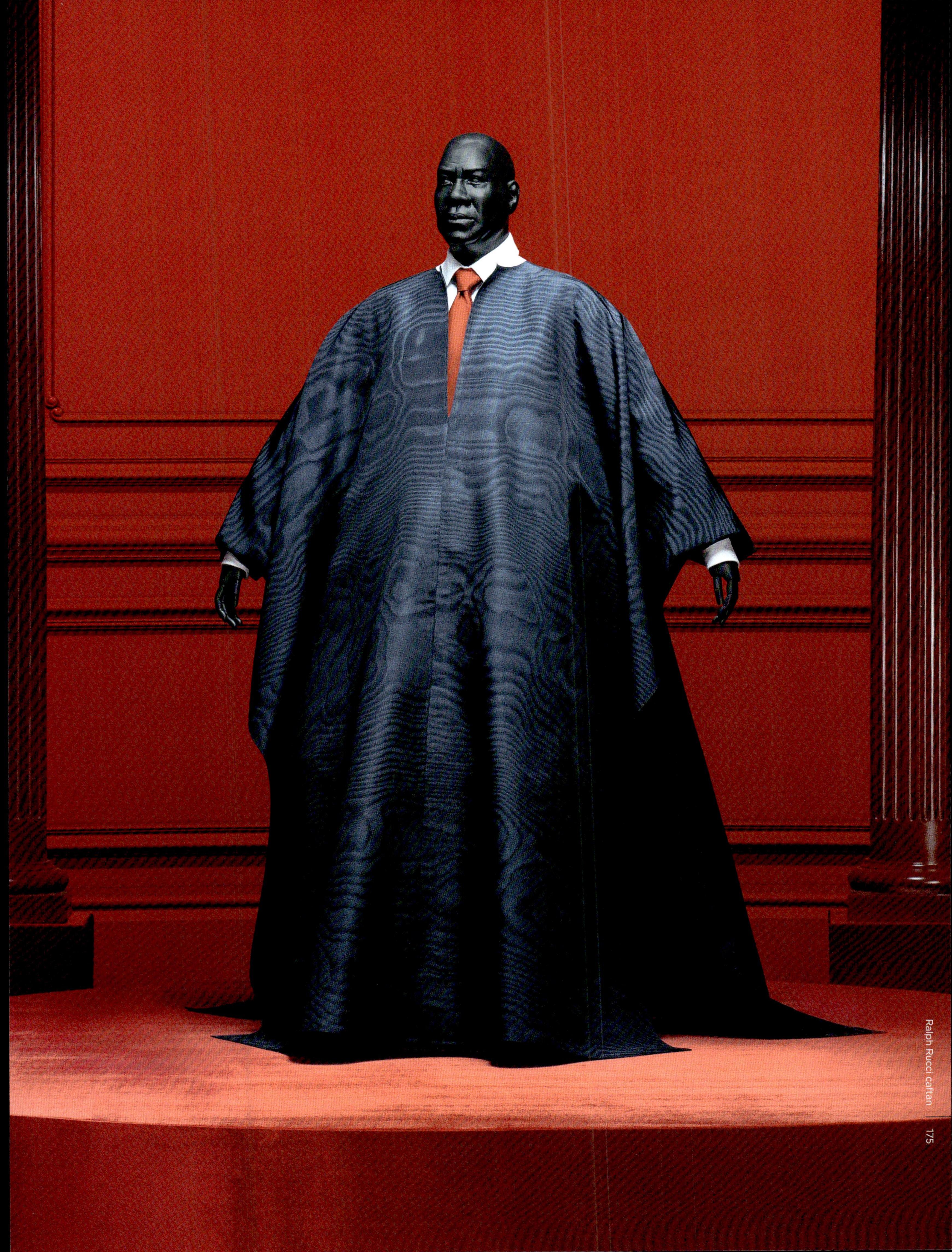

Ralph Rucci caftan

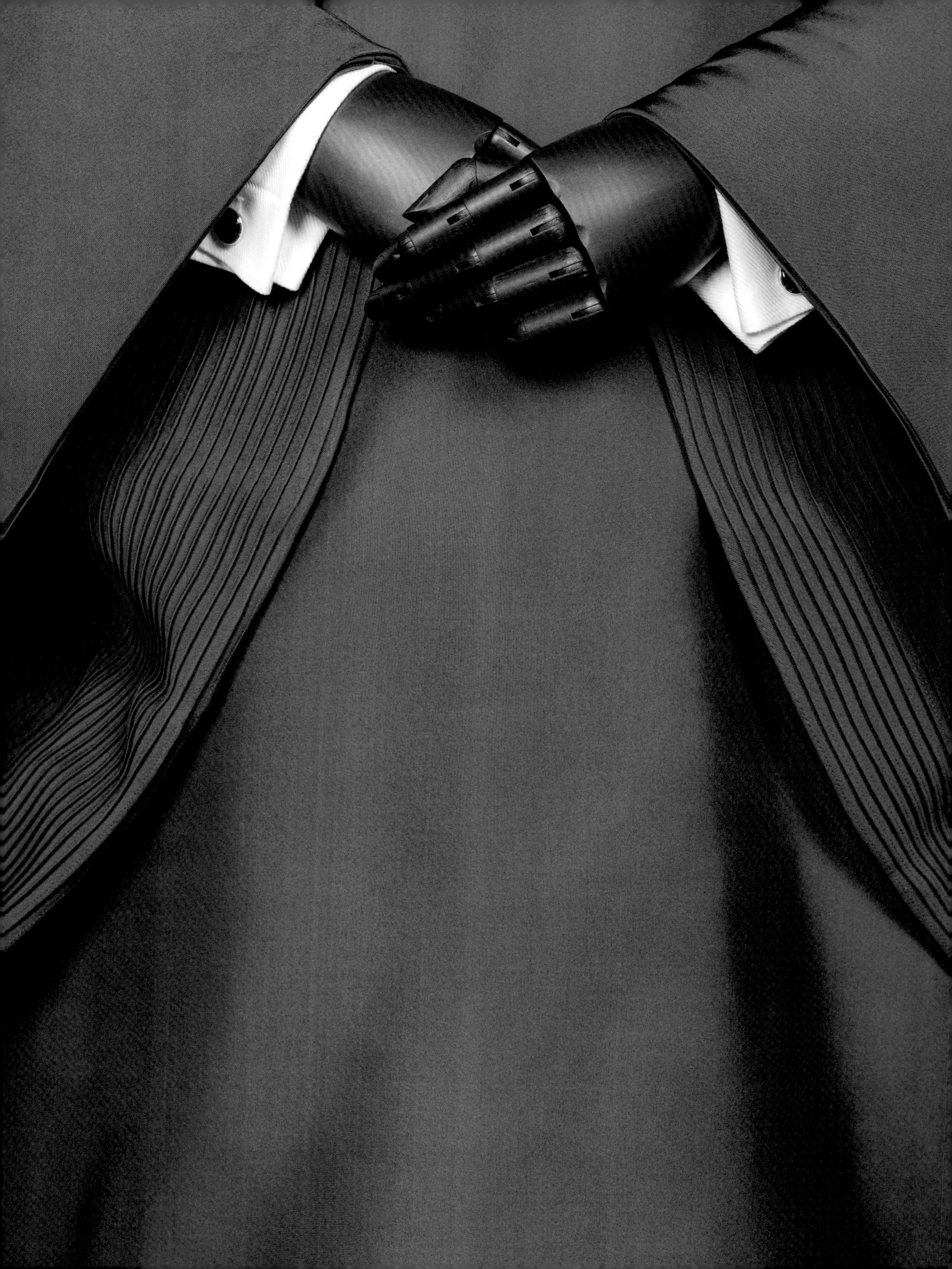

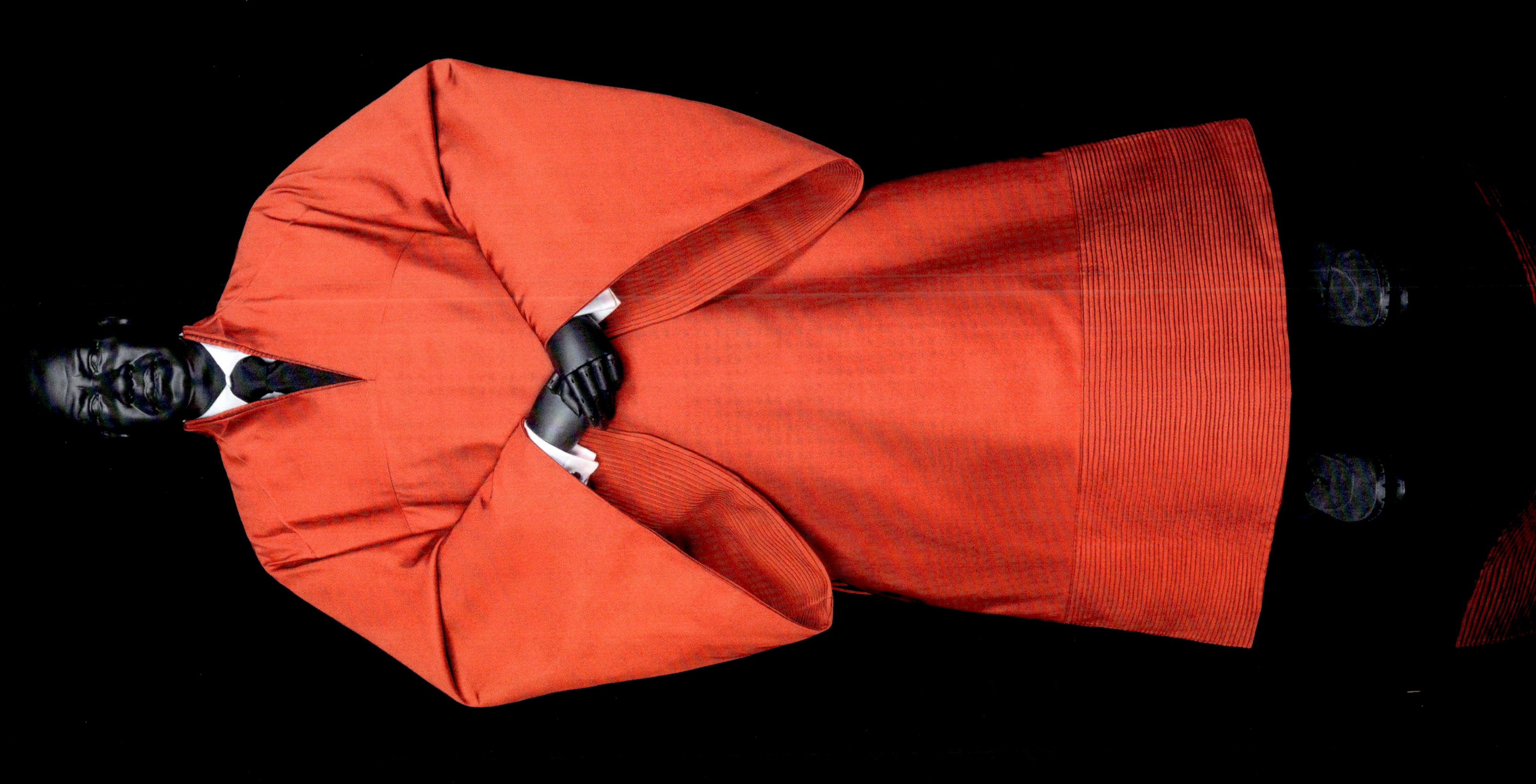

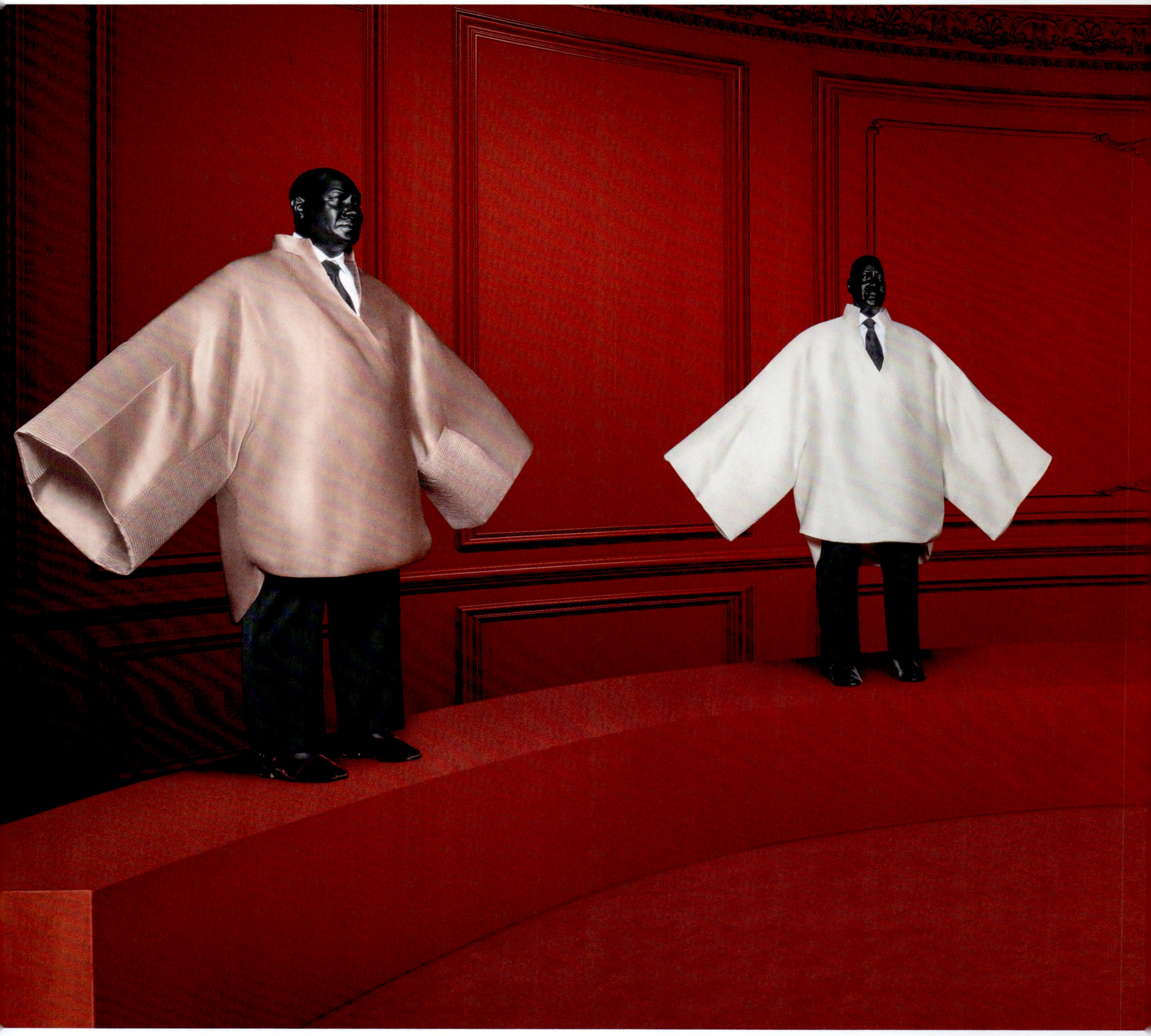

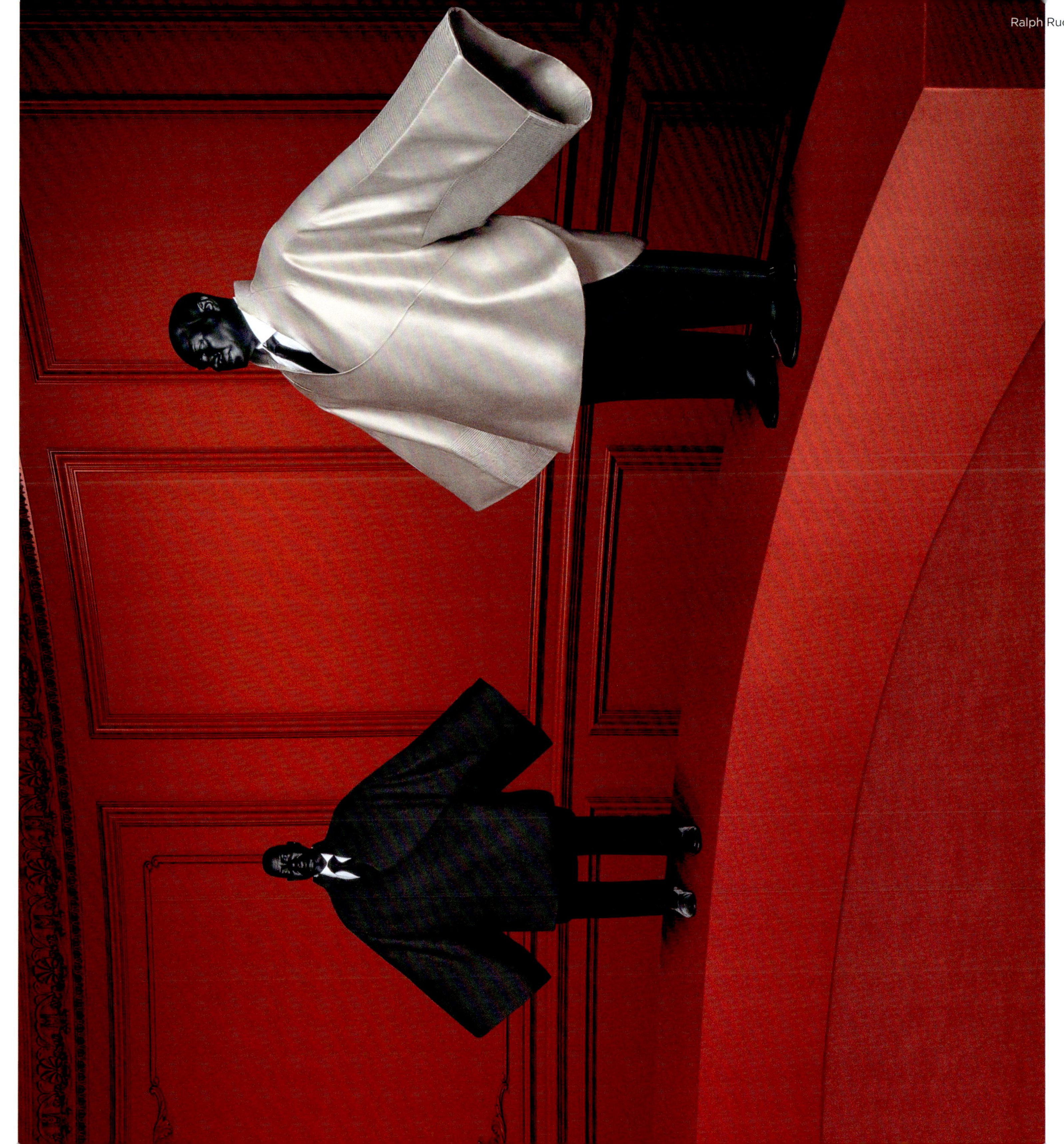

Ralph Rucci tunics

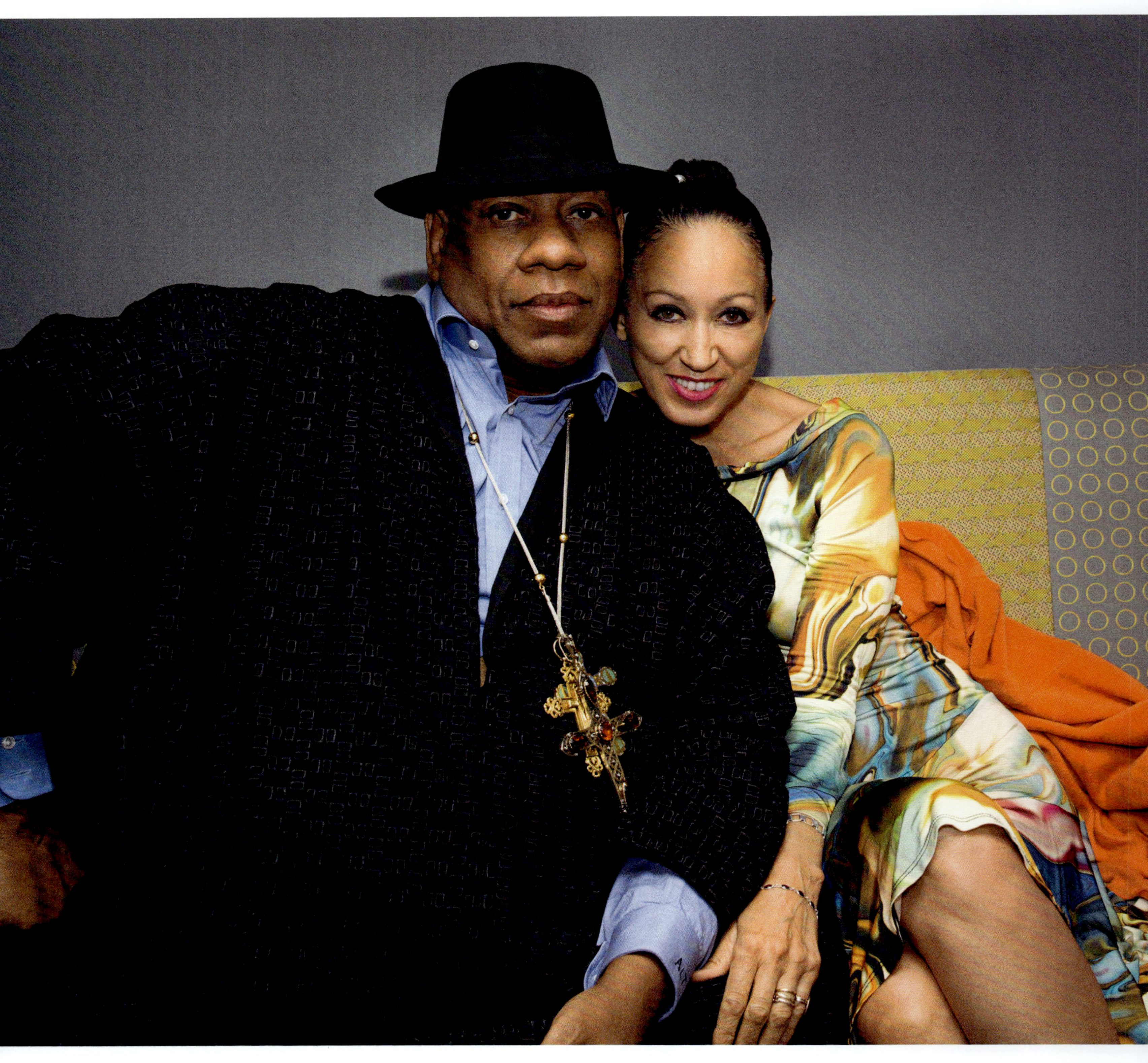

André and Pat Cleveland, 2014

I first met André in Paris in 1971. I think he had just gotten out of university. He said he was a fan from seeing pictures of me in magazines. I appreciated that. We were both so young then, but the best part is I got to know him as my very tall, **smart friend** who loved fashion—and he turned out to be a great chronicler of fashion history, and on top of that an **advocate** for diversity and inclusion within the fashion world. What vibrant style he had with his **unique** voice. He was eloquent both in French and English. He became a beacon of light at *Interview*, then Condé Nast for *Vogue*, inspiring fashion lovers around the world. I'm proud to have him in my heart for always.

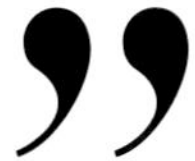

PAT CLEVELAND

FOR ANDRÉ
Jonathan Becker

Even if he were the reverend, a preacher of fashion, it was just a denomination. André's broad scholarship and understanding of culture at large encompassed, spotlit, and inspired any artistic endeavor of integrity inasmuch as those endeavors inspired him. Our native roots, André's and mine, couldn't have been more incongruous and disparate. I, white from the Upper East Side of New York; he, Black and deeply Southern. We met at Andy Warhol's *Interview* in 1974 during Bob Colacello's reign and continued to collide at work to great advantage at the magazines to which we both committed our lives and derived our livelihoods: *WWD*, *Vanity Fair*, *Vogue* and its European editions.

One pivotal encounter came in 1979 at Diana Vreeland's apartment where I was sent to make her portrait by John Fairchild for *W*. André, as the sittings editor and writer, was almost irrepressibly disappointed that an unknown photographer, whom he knew to be a taxi driver, would be assigned to a portrait of such significance to him. In any event, however, we collaborated intensely, and the result was what DV wrote in ardor, passionately, to say was her favorite portrait ever. As André and I bonded that day, our own common root was planted.

Myriad collaborations and crisscrossing at magazines and many fallings out and reconciliations later, the subject of our portrait in 2013 for *Vanity Fair* was André himself. We met at the high point of the ornate Pont Alexandre III at dawn, Tour Eiffel in the background, an ecstatic morning—a personal high point, too, as we grew ever closer with time.

André's post-*Vogue* salvation came at SCAD where, thanks to the generosity and foresight of the president and founder, Paula Wallace, he channeled his heroine Diana Vreeland's salvation at The Metropolitan Museum of Art's Costume Institute in New York. André lived a halcyon time in Savannah, idyllic years in Magnolia Cottage, an antebellum house all to himself overlooking the glorious Forsyth Park surrounded by long-armed live oaks draped gracefully with Spanish moss. Fashionable trees. There, André could focus with academic intensity on pure fashion in exhibitions at his namesake gallery in the SCAD Museum of Art to glamorous and international acclaim.

In the postbellum of the magazines' brutal demise, as we were both reinventing ourselves, André rewarded me with his last curated show—he called it *A Fashionable Mind*—of my portraits, and SCAD became a great respite and salvation to me, too, as my many decades of work at magazines wound way down.

President Wallace, with André's encouragement, also awarded me, or rather requited me, with an honorary doctorate. For one who had fled conventional education at seventeen, it was an unimaginable, magical honor. But my greatest good fortune was to have shared time with André, to have been accepted in his flock, to have experienced his daily enthusiasm. His legacy remains now of faith and encouragement that still permeate the zeitgeist powerfully.

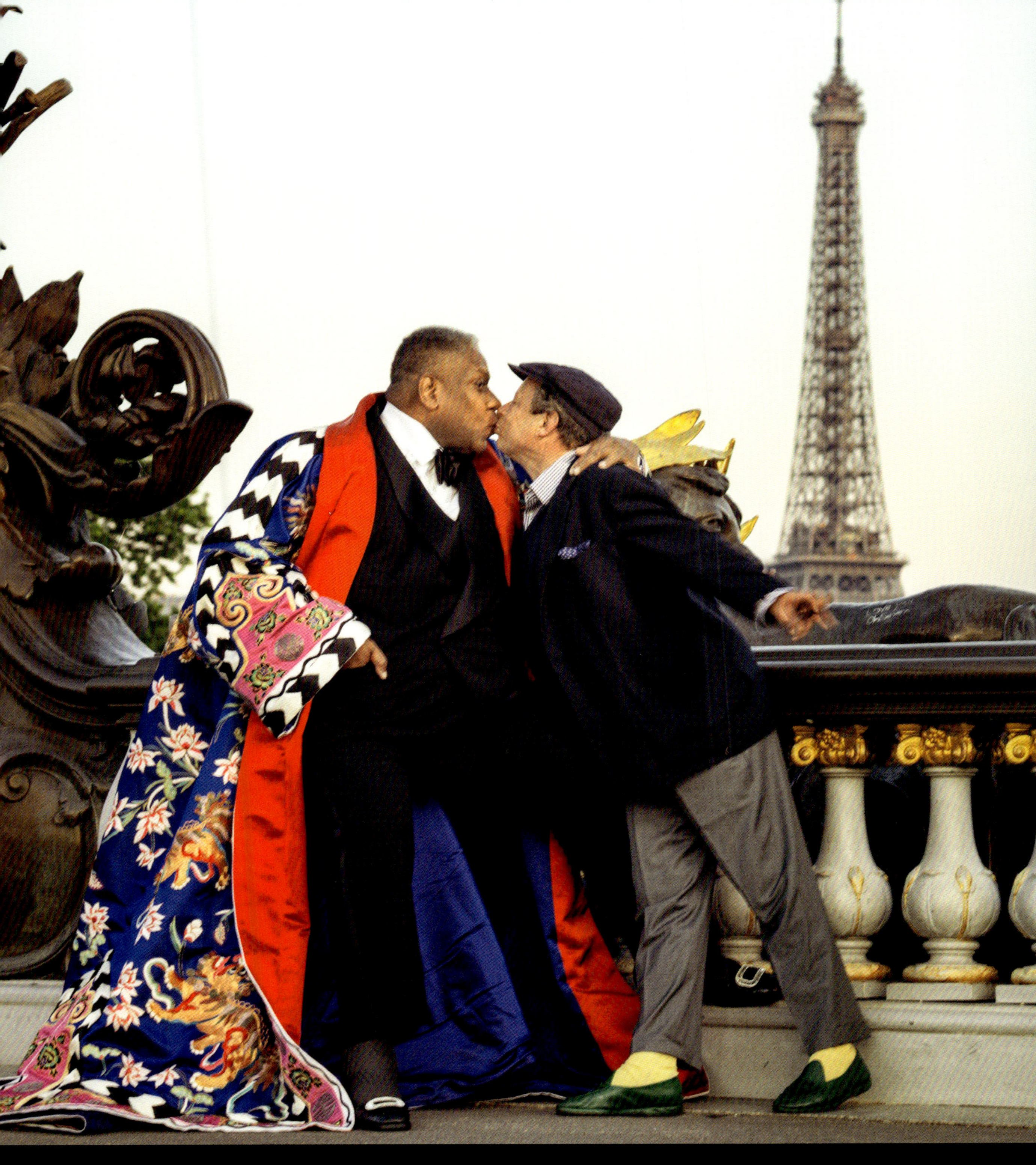

André with Jonathan Becker for *Vanity Fair* at the Pont Alexandre III in Paris, June 2013. Photographed by Jonathan Becker

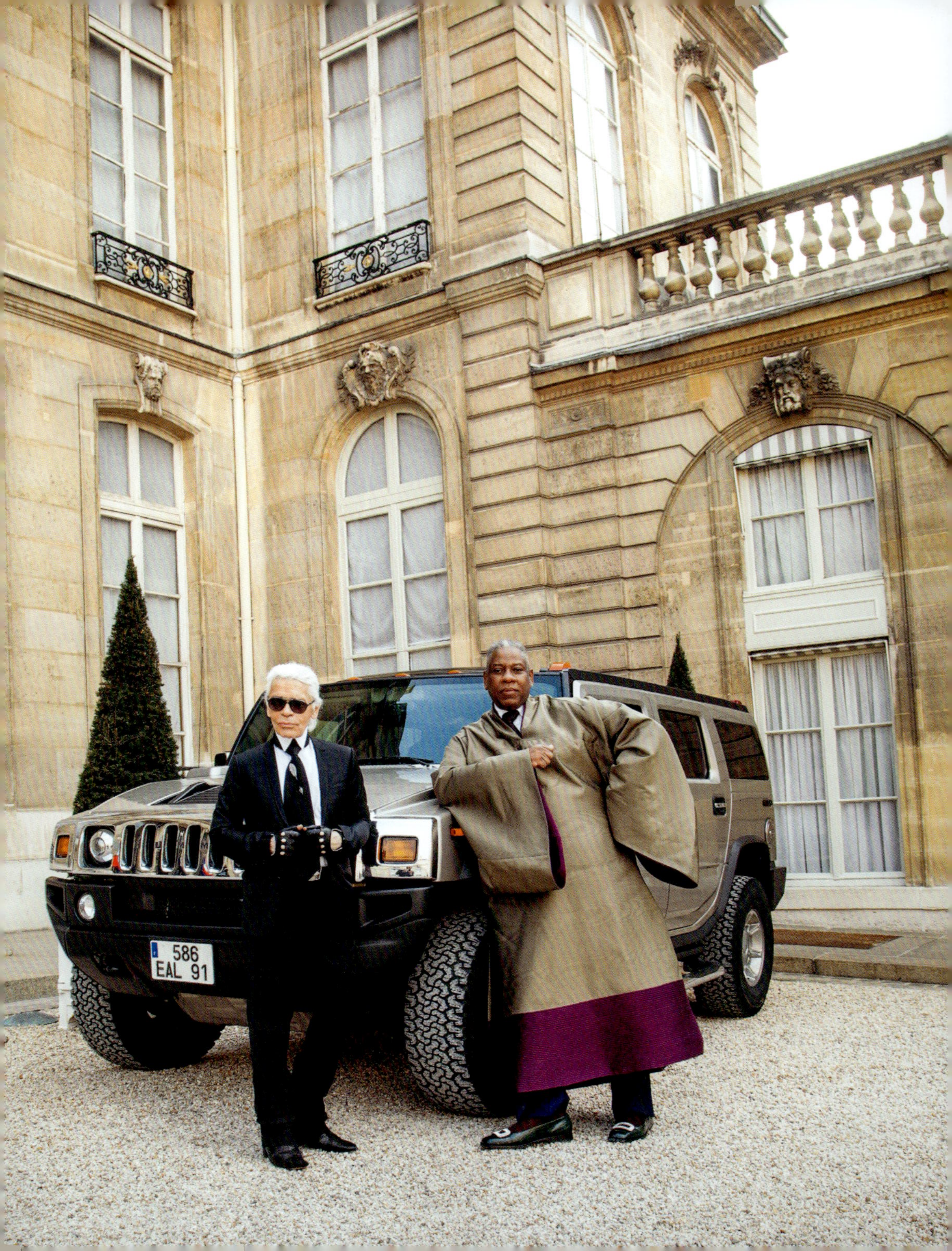
586
EAL 91

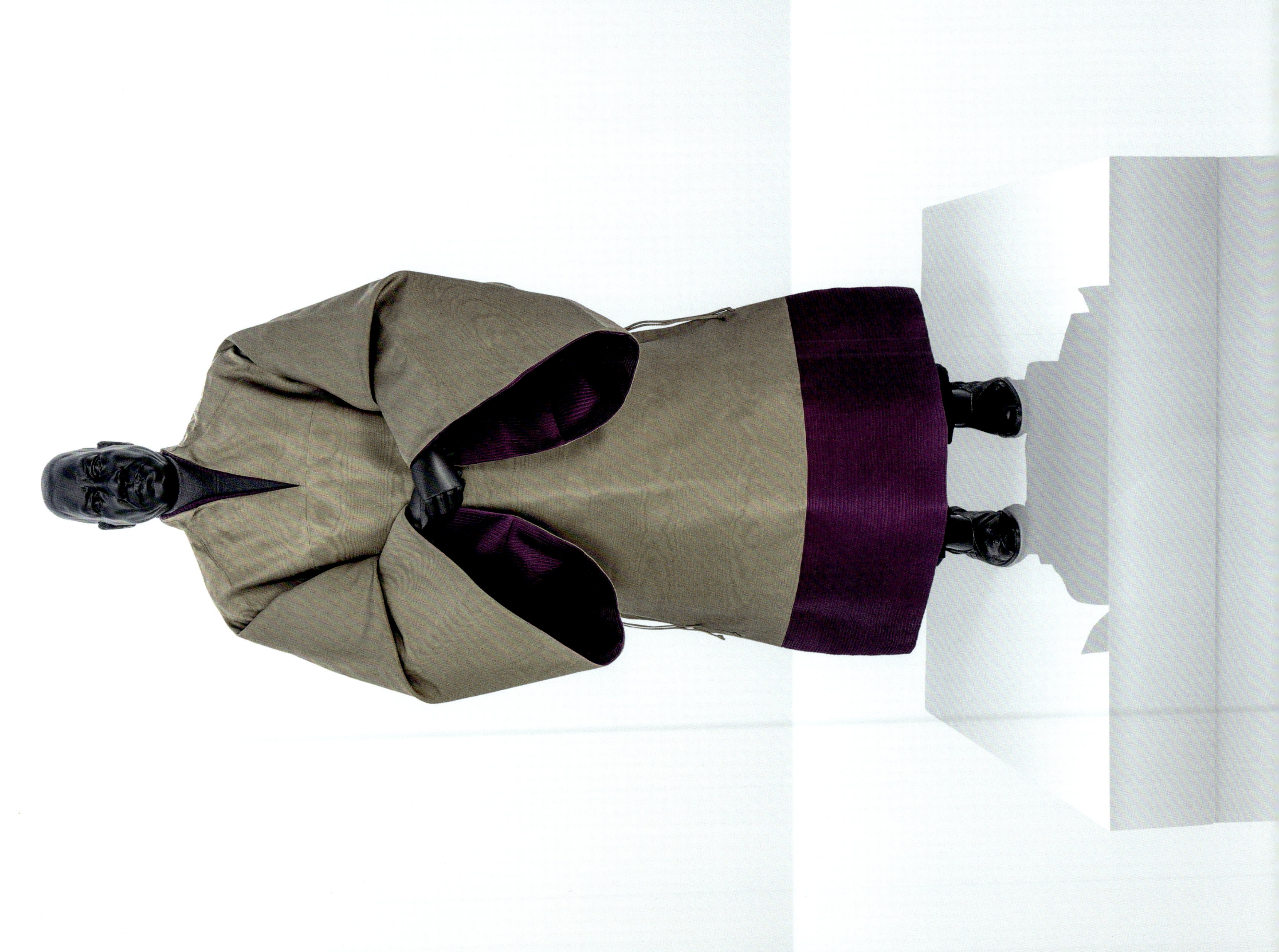

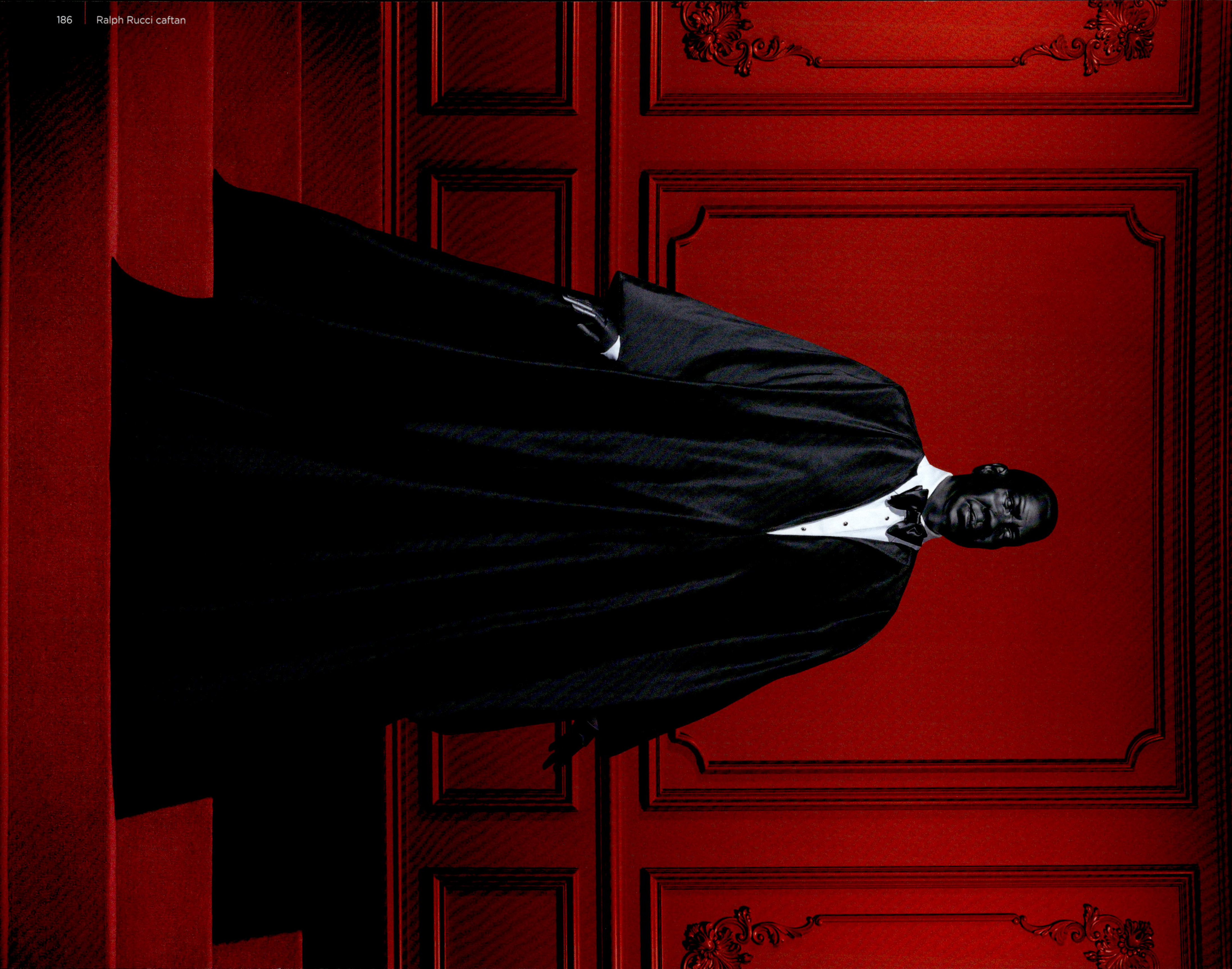

Ralph Rucci caftan

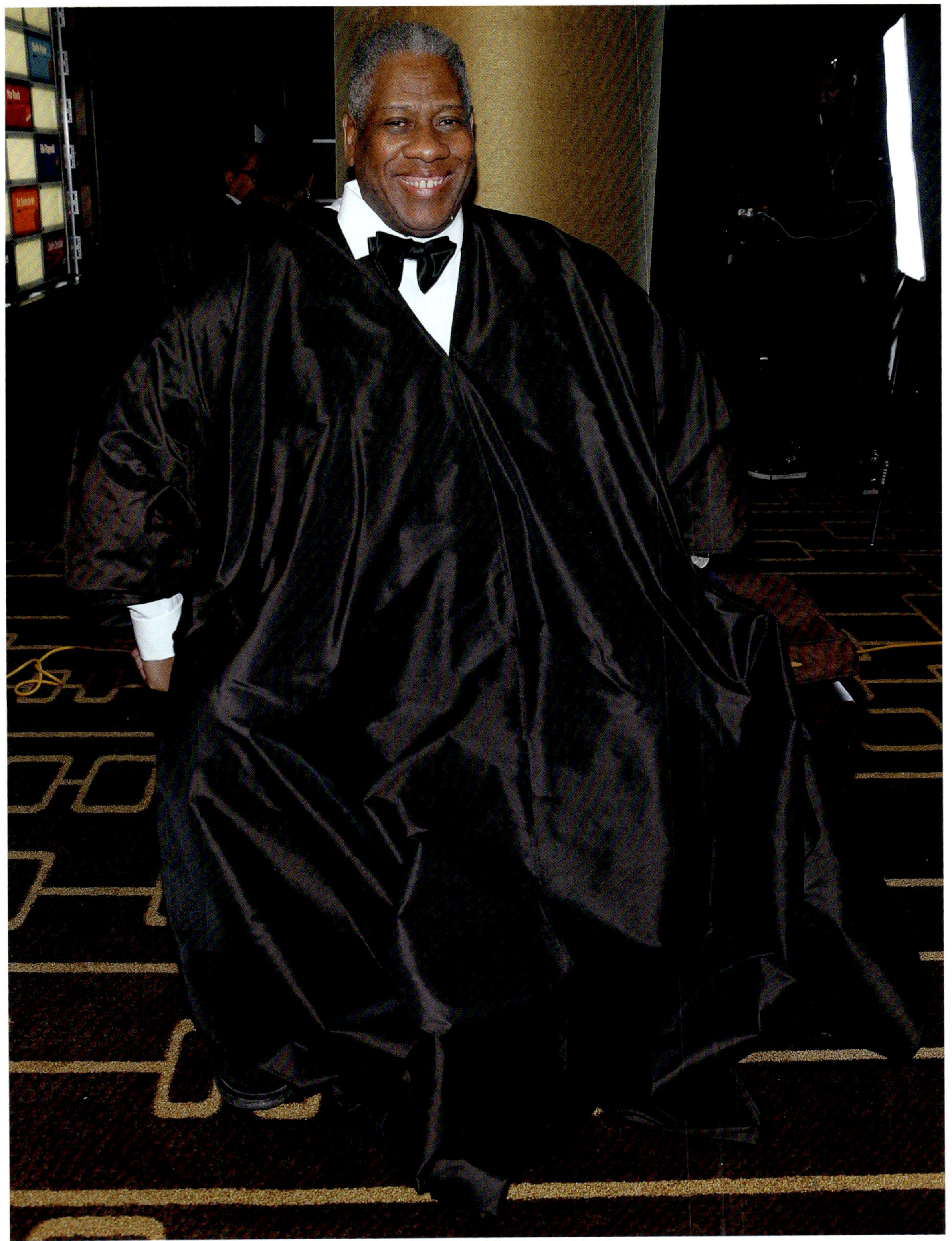

André attending the Triumph Awards at Rose Theater at Lincoln Center in New York, October 2013. Photo by J. Countess/Getty Images.

Valentino caftan with Gianfranco Ferré shirt

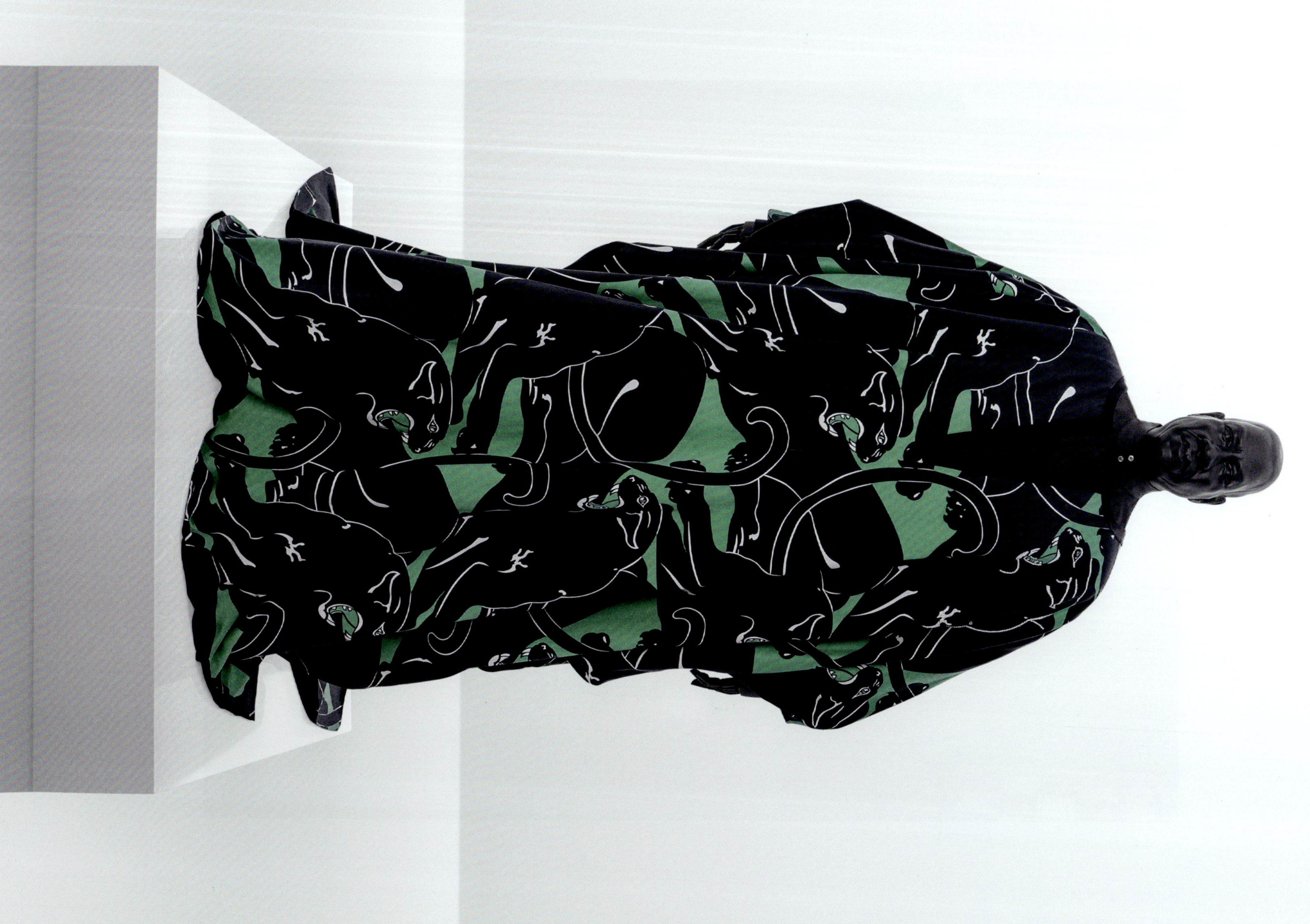

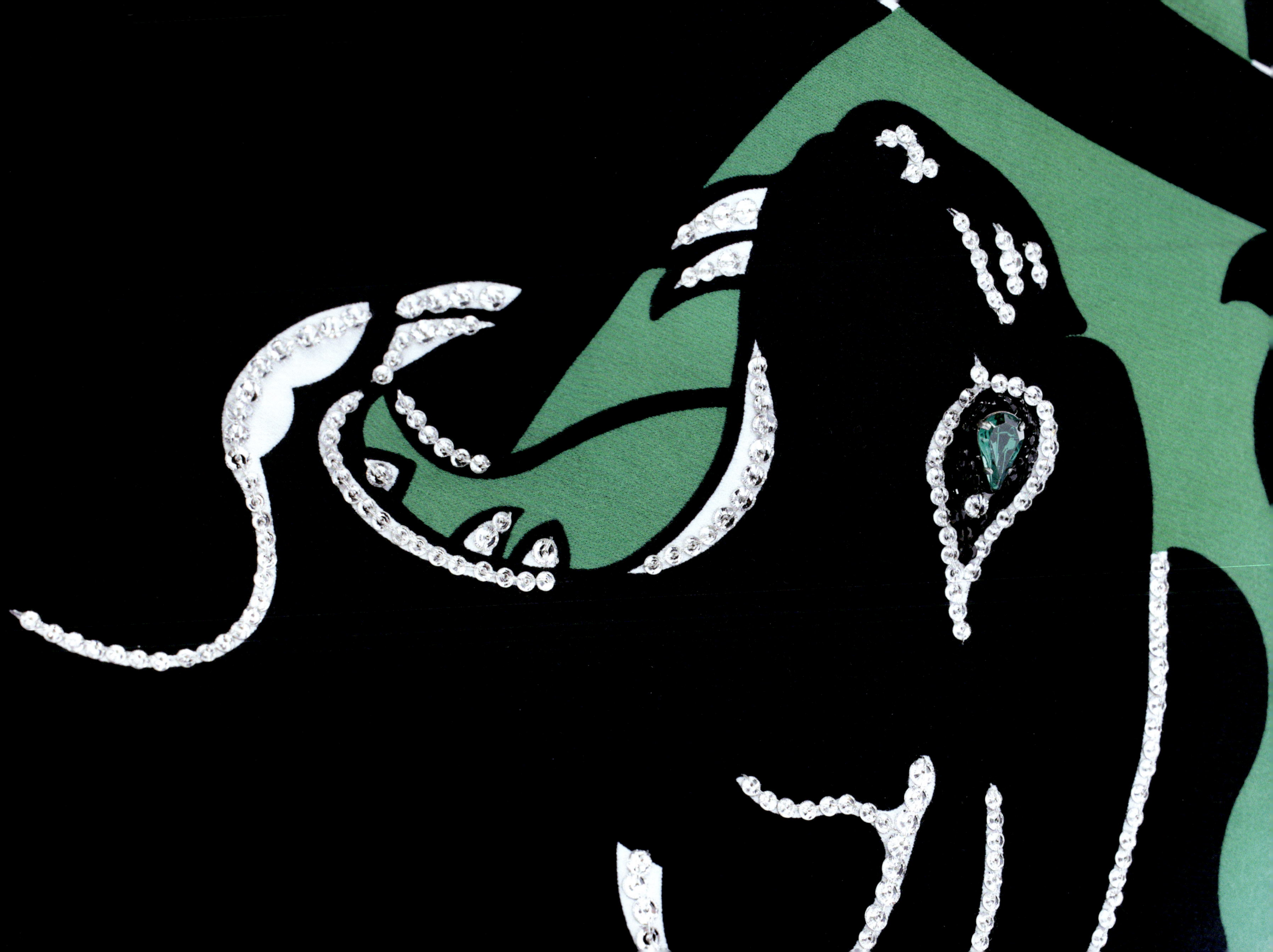

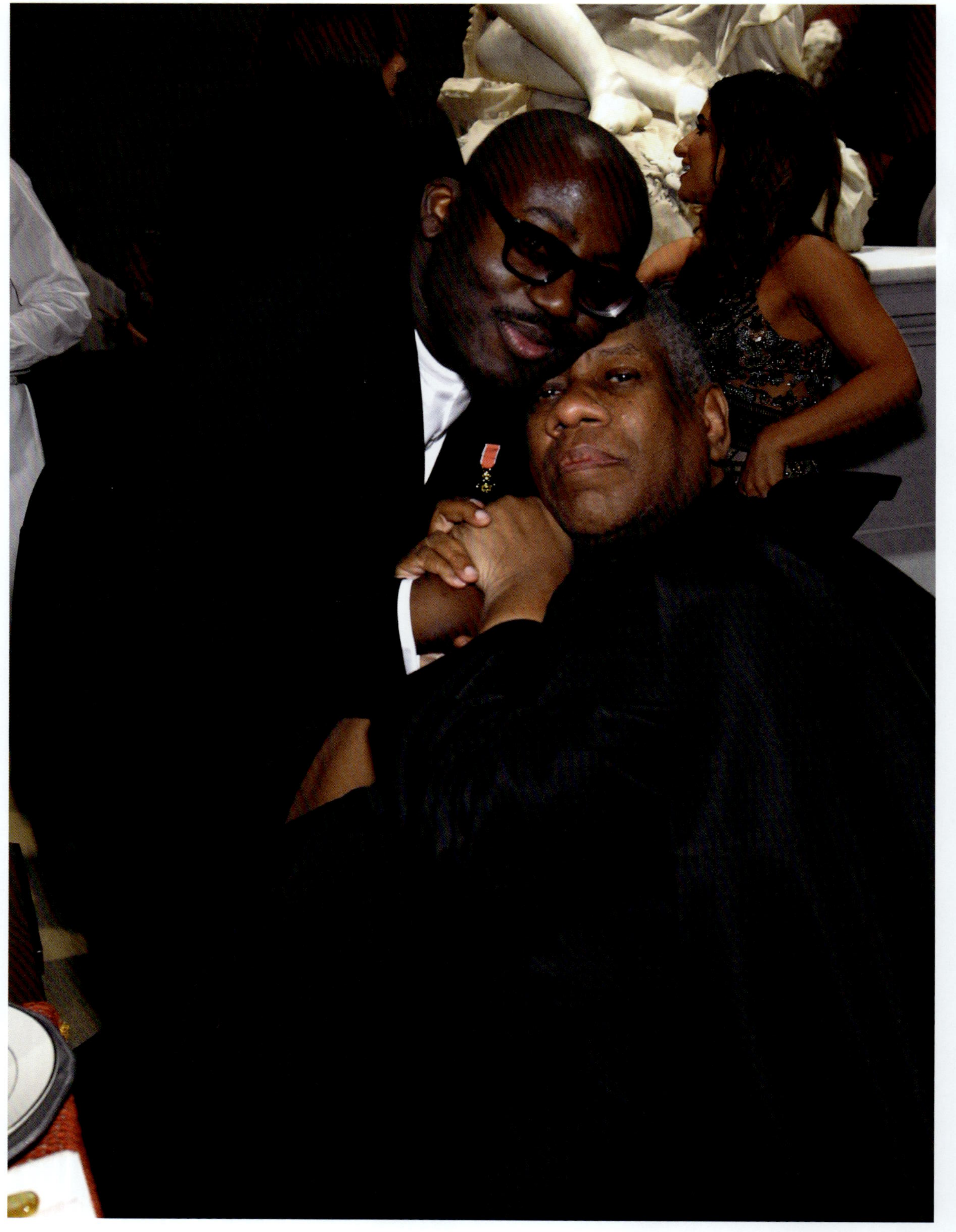

André and Edward Enninful at the Met Gala for *Heavenly Bodies: Fashion and the Catholic Imagination*, May 2018. Photo by Dimitrios Kambouris/MG18/Getty Images for The Met Museum/Vogue.

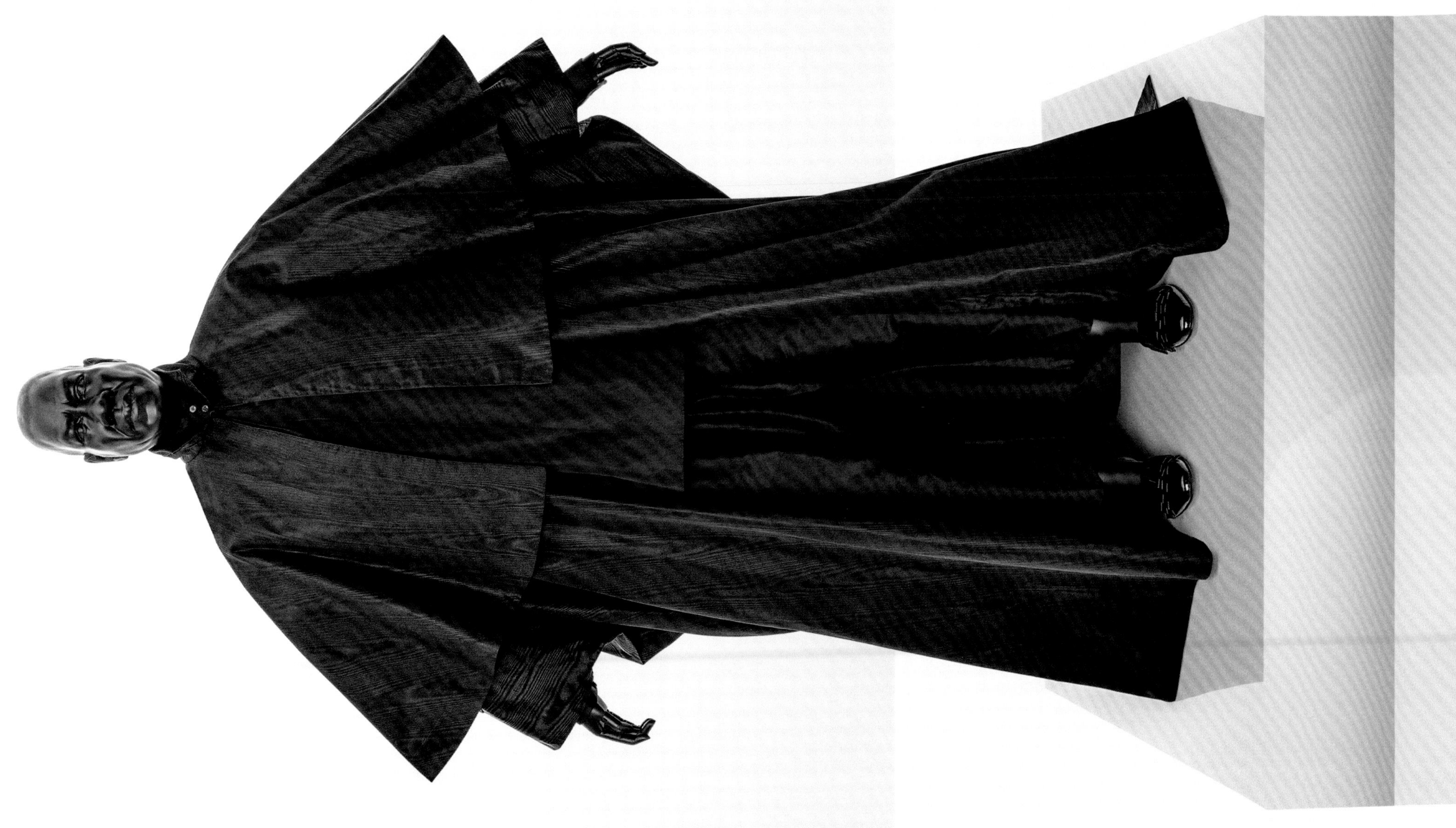

SCOOP DU JOUR
Teri Agins

"Girl, that coat is MAJOR," André Leon Talley boomed to supermodel Naomi Campbell as she twirled around in her vintage leopard coat with bona fide Hollywood provenance: its lining was monogrammed *Ann-Margret*. I was the intrepid reporter backstage, hours before Isaac Mizrahi's runway show in New York in 1997, when André beamed as he spotted me eavesdropping. That scene made a delicious opening for my first nonfiction book, *The End of Fashion*, in 1999. André, *Vogue*'s editor at large, rewarded me with a glowing back-cover blurb: "This is a landmark book that reveals the complexities inside fashion in an original and entertaining way."

André was himself a most entertaining fashion original and a savvy journalist who steered me by example. We first met in 1977 at the office of our mutual employer, Fairchild Publications, on 7 East Twelfth Street, when the towering, bespoke-suited André—then *WWD*'s Paris bureau chief—blew through the newsroom. I was an ambitious newbie reporter for the menswear trade daily *DNR* and so psyched to meet a fellow Black staffer, and the most glamorous writer at Fairchild at that. André held forth, brandishing his kid glove in my face: "Teri, you must be out! OUT, OUT all the time. Before and after the runway shows. The private designer dinners that go LATE. You must be OUT to report accurately about what's IN-side."

He knew so well that access always leads a reporter to the juiciest stories. André, the North Carolinian francophone with a haughty swagger, worked the "Chiffon Trenches" with panache. He was a Manolo Blahnik–wearing shoe-leather scribe, driven by daily deadlines. In Paris, he burned the midnight telex, tapping out reams of hot copy. "André, your reporting on Yves' brilliant collection is one of the best things I've ever read," John Fairchild telexed in reply in 1978 to André's marveling at the sharp Yves Saint Laurent tailoring that Mr. Fairchild dubbed "The Broadway Suit."

André was well-read, well-traveled, always curious, with an informed vision that elevated him to his storied career at *Vogue* alongside editor in chief Anna Wintour. In 1990, when *The Wall Street Journal* charged me to develop the fashion business beat, I dug deep to turn out investigative industry articles that created impact and buzz. I was the protégé André egged on. He extended me a prized invite to a formal dinner for twenty at Karl Lagerfeld's mansion in Paris during the July 1997 couture shows, where I sat between Gianfranco Ferré and Donatella Versace—and later, after dessert, I dished with Karl in the kitchen. After several years of applauding my *WSJ* Page One scoops, André, the 2003 winner of the coveted Council of Fashion Designers of America Award for Fashion Journalism, predicted that my turn was coming soon. And sure enough, I won in 2004, just as André foretold.

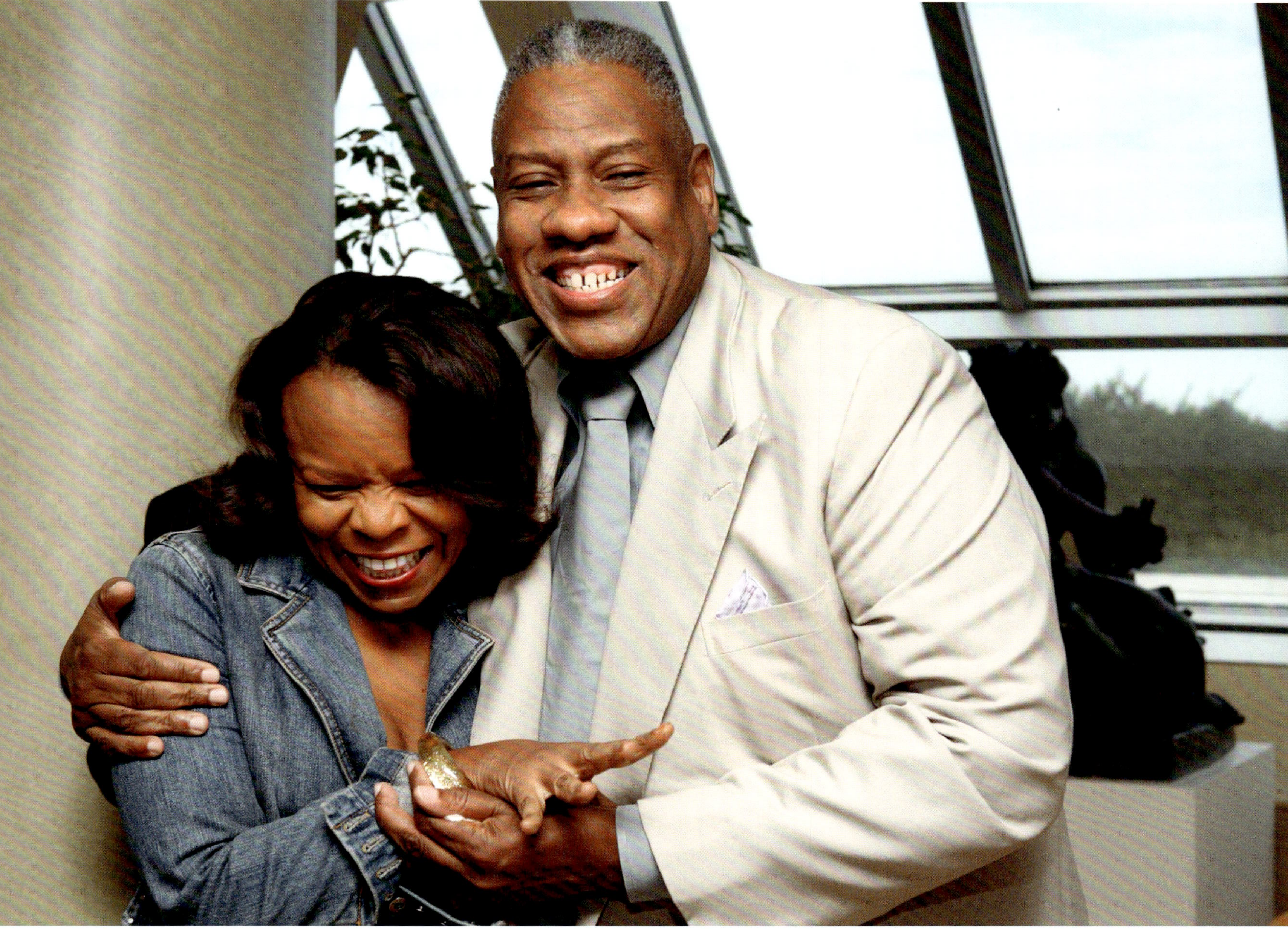

André and Teri Agins attending a breakfast for Harriette Cole and *Ebony* hosted by The Metropolitan Museum of Art in New York, September 2007. Photo by Amy Sussman/Getty Images.

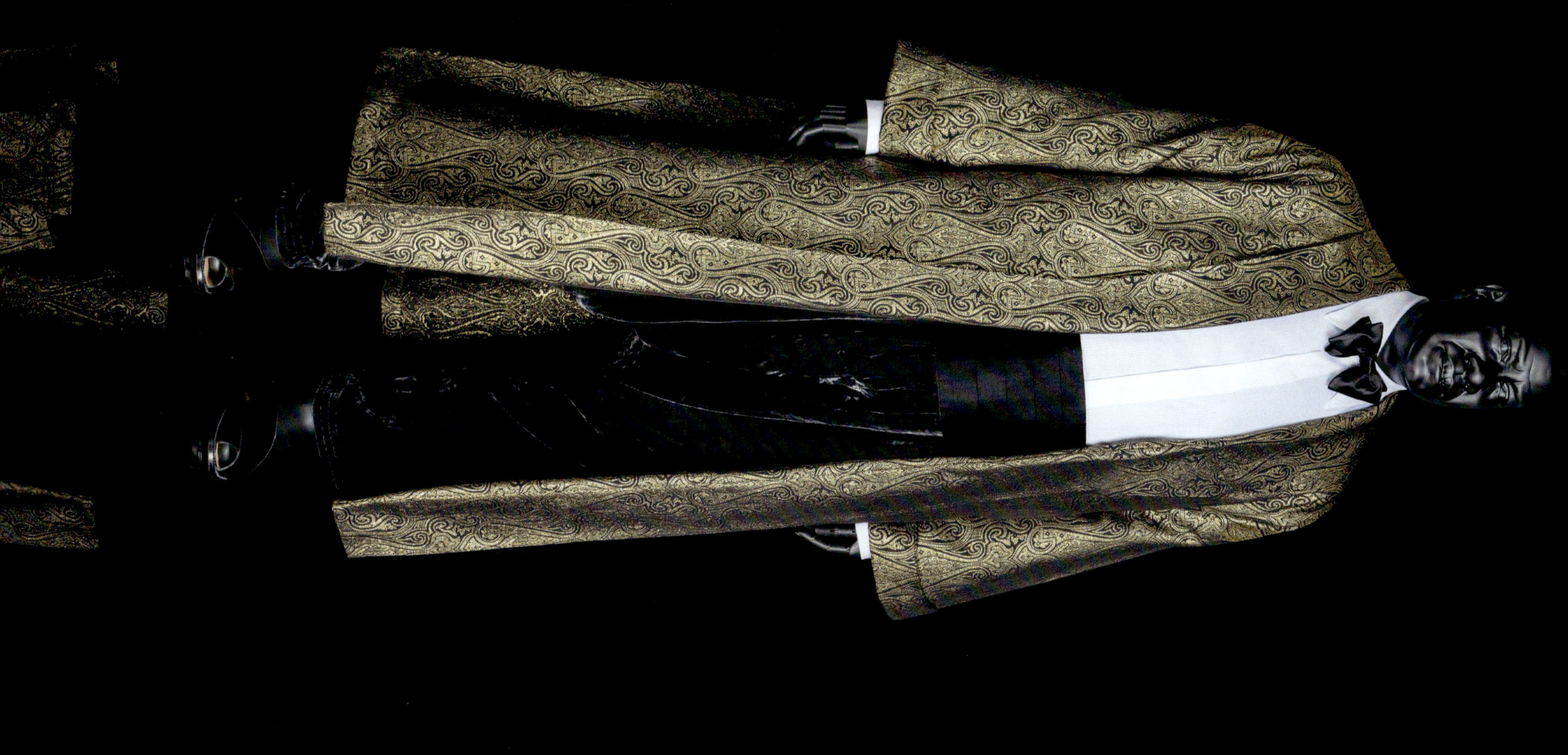

Versace coat

“

I scorched the earth with my **talent**
and I let my light **shine**.

”

André Leon Talley

Ralph Rucci caftan with Diane von Furstenberg charms and Accessocraft NYC chain

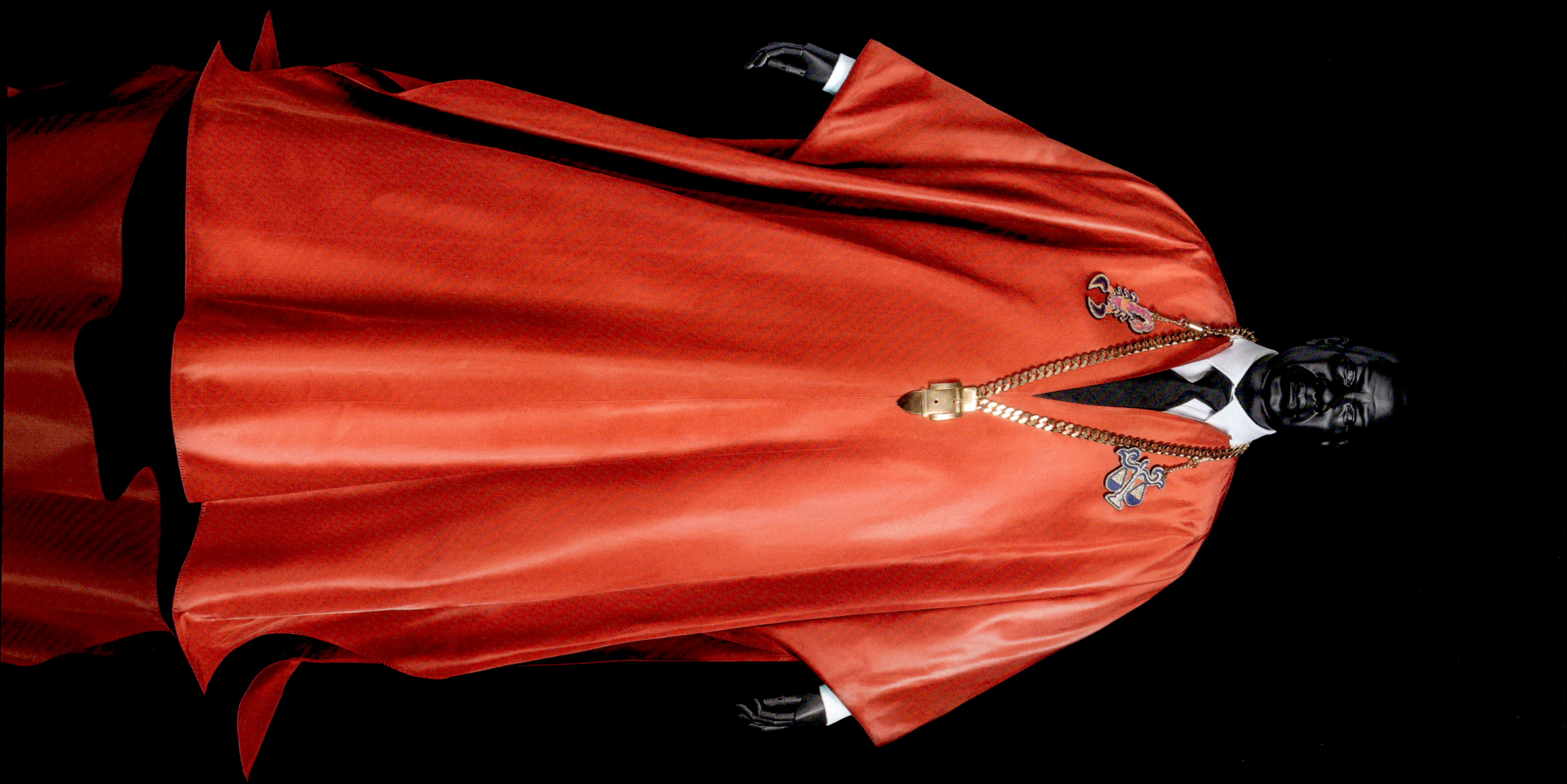

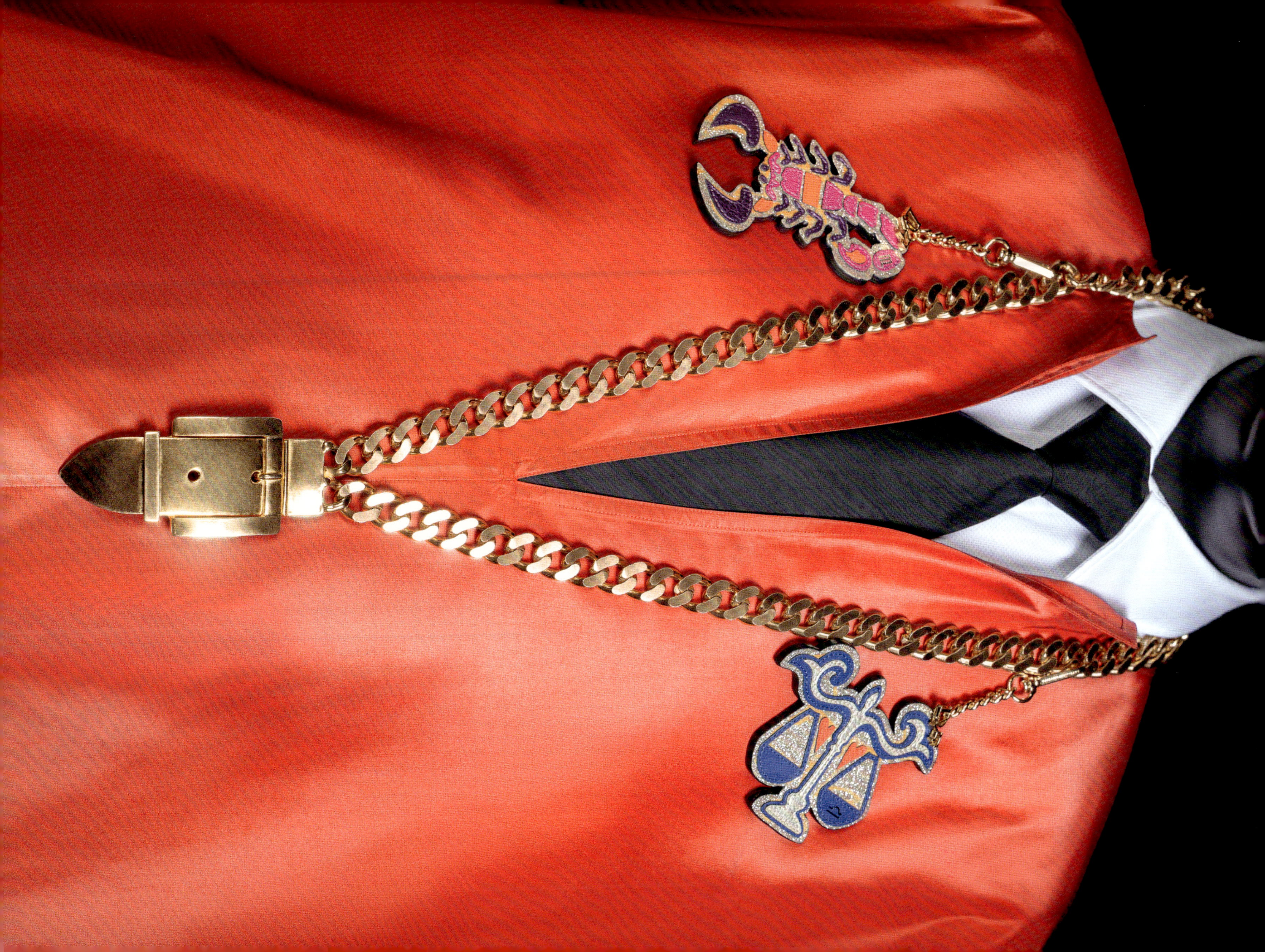

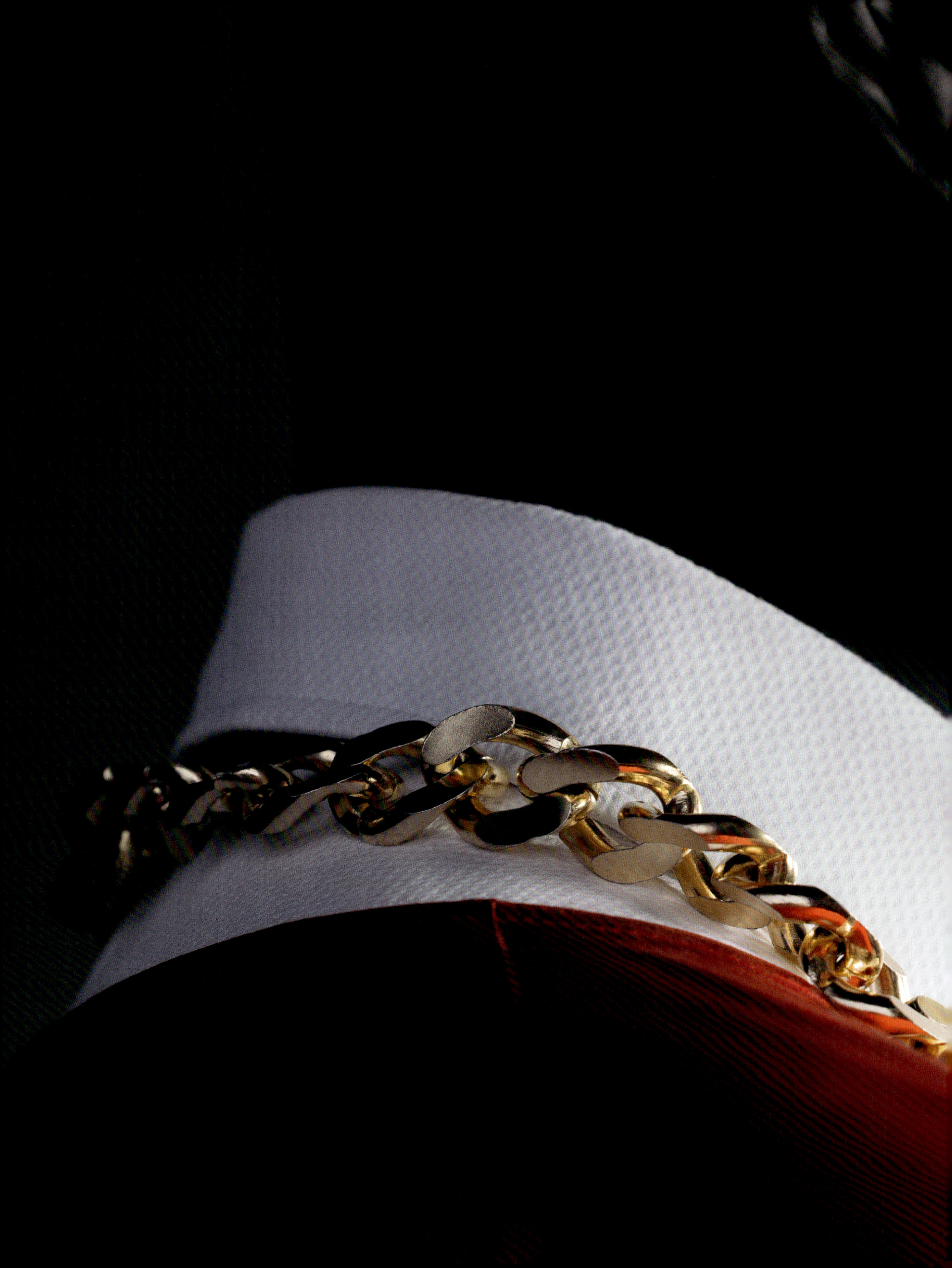

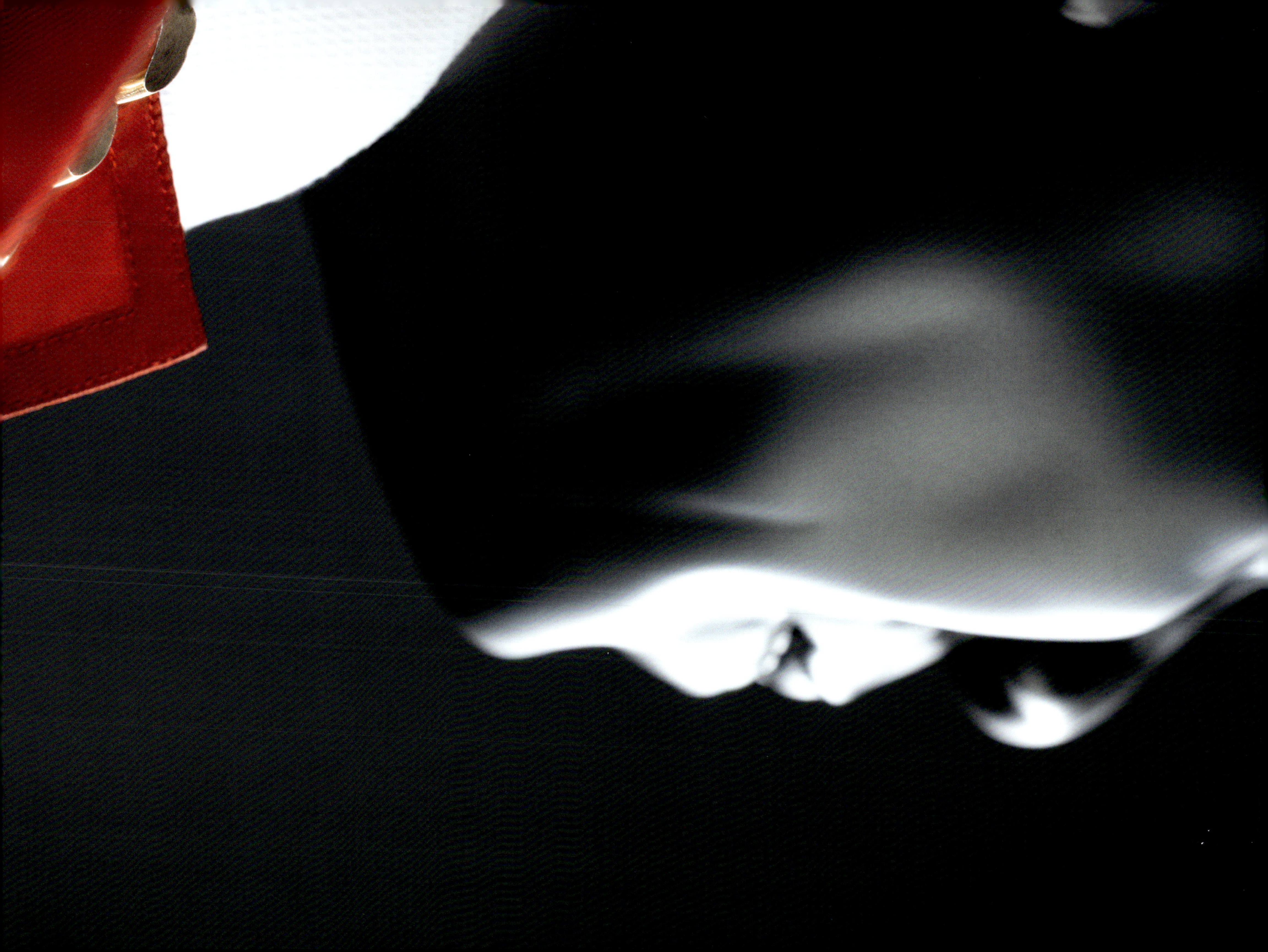

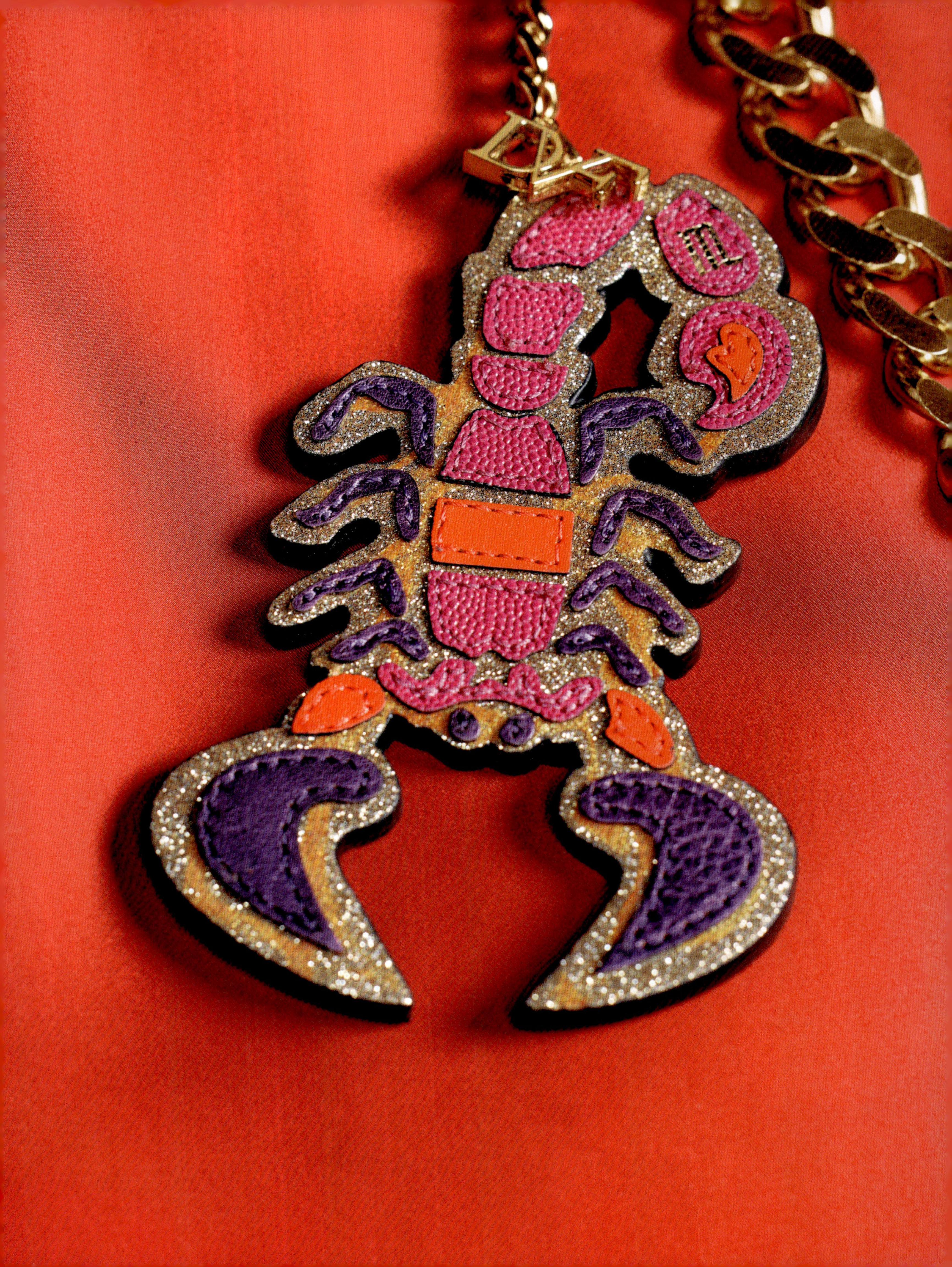

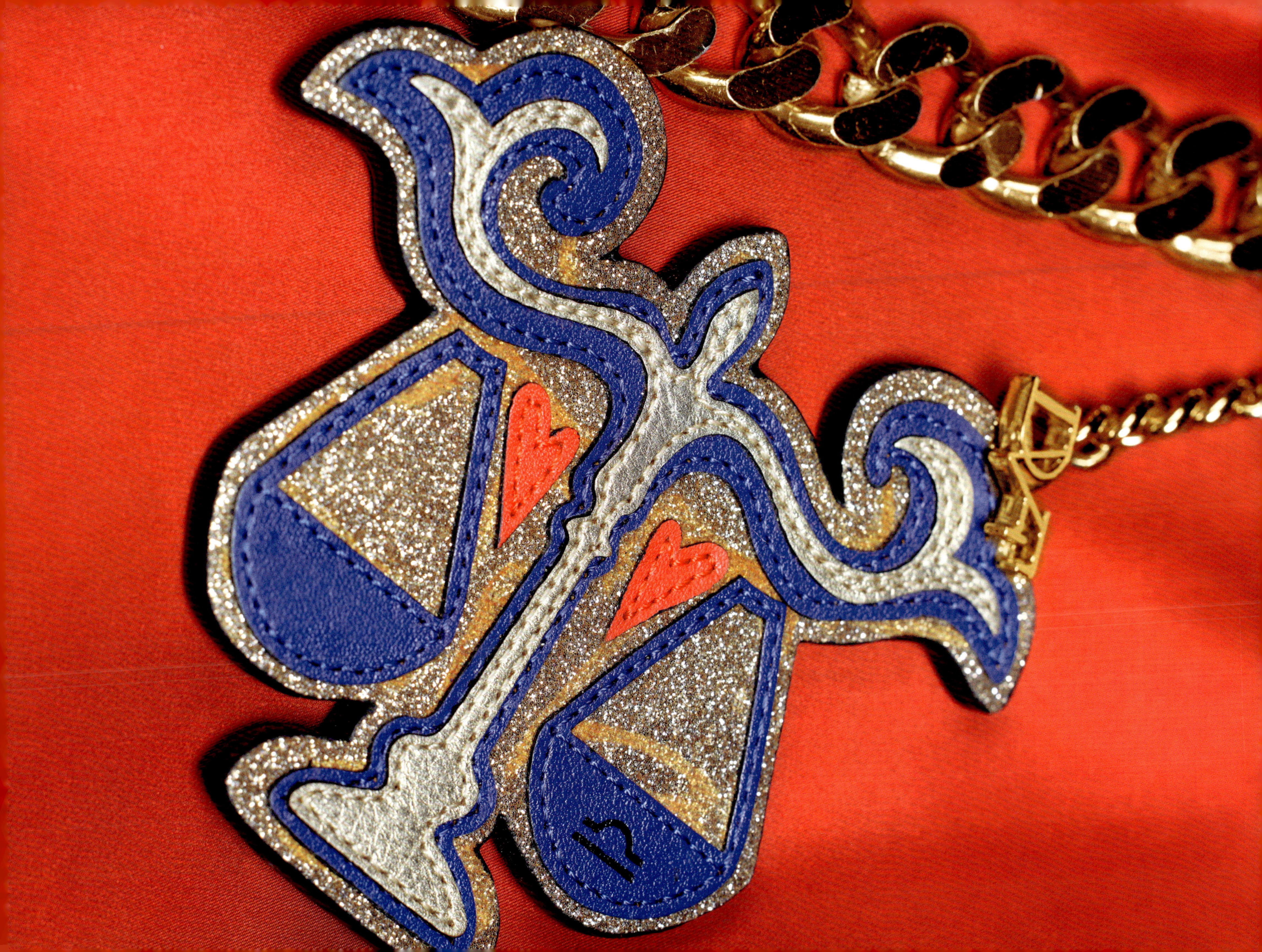

JOURNEY OF LOVE

Diane von Furstenberg

I believe the secret to life is being true to yourself, and my dear and loving friend André Leon Talley was always true to himself. André and I met in our early twenties. He had earned a scholarship from Brown University, spoke fluent French, and was obsessed with Paris and fashion. He was determined to become a famous personality, and he did, indeed, manifest his dreams. In New York, André apprenticed for the Doyenne of Fashion herself, former *Vogue* editor in chief Diana Vreeland, who was by then leading the Costume Institute for The Metropolitan Museum of Art. She immediately took interest in him and taught him everything she knew about style, etiquette, and the fashion industry. André later interned at *Interview* for Andy Warhol, who became another fabulous mentor. With a tiny camera in his hands and dressed in the most flamboyant colors, André met and photographed all the beautiful people of New York. He then caught the attention of John Fairchild, the publisher of *Women's Wear Daily*, which was the most important magazine in fashion at the time.

Fairchild ruled fashion media and could be quite a terror. He was always very provocative but he shocked everyone when he named André the official *WWD* correspondent in Paris. André, too, was in awe. He had achieved one of the most powerful jobs in the fashion industry and lived in his beloved Paris. But that was only the beginning of his legendary career, which, of course, included a very long and successful tenure at *Vogue*, as consiglieri to editor in chief Anna Wintour. André loved fashion but, perhaps more importantly, through this love he uplifted so many designers and creatives, sharing the opportunities he had boldly claimed for himself with countless others. He loved SCAD, too, with a passion that rivaled almost any other in his life, and he brought so much joy and inspiration to the students there. He welcomed me to SCAD to receive his namesake award in 2010 and honored me with my own exhibition, *Journey of a Dress*, which became yet another treasured moment together with my friend. I loved André unconditionally and without hesitation. I will miss him forever.

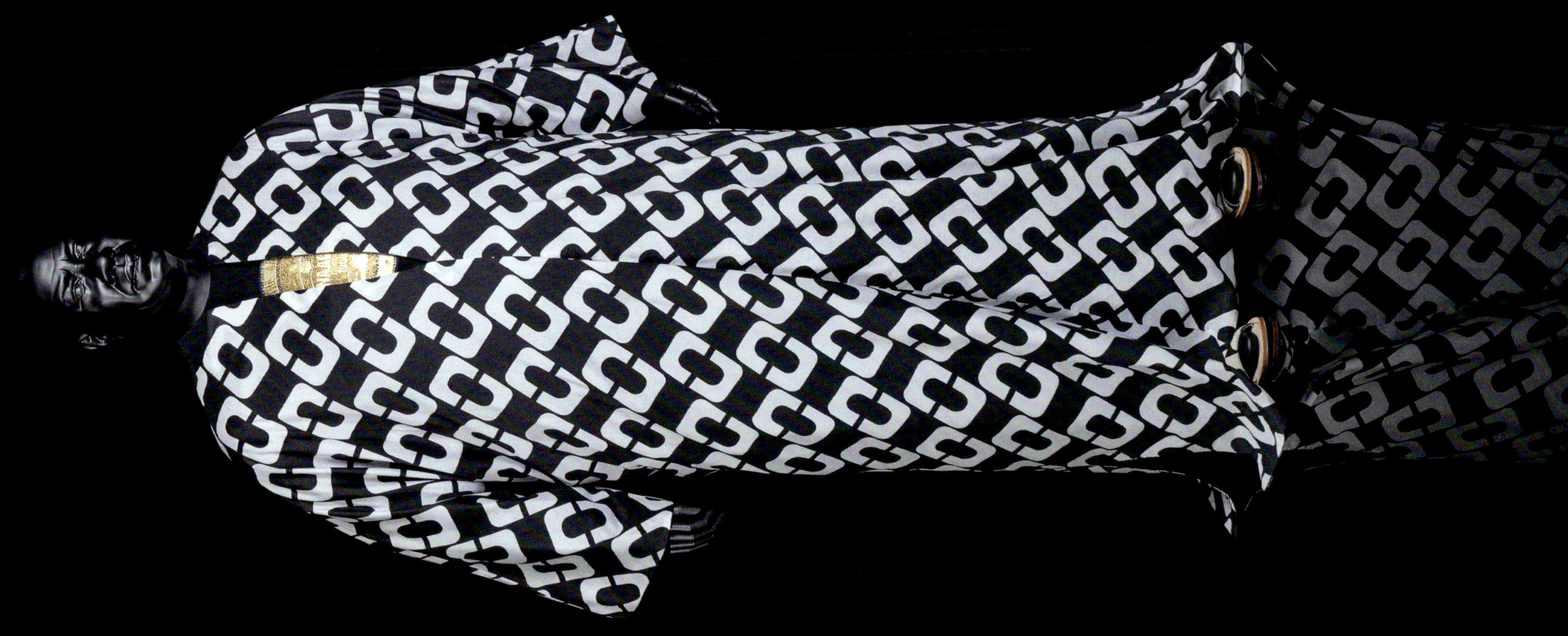

André's elephant trinket by Diane von Furstenberg

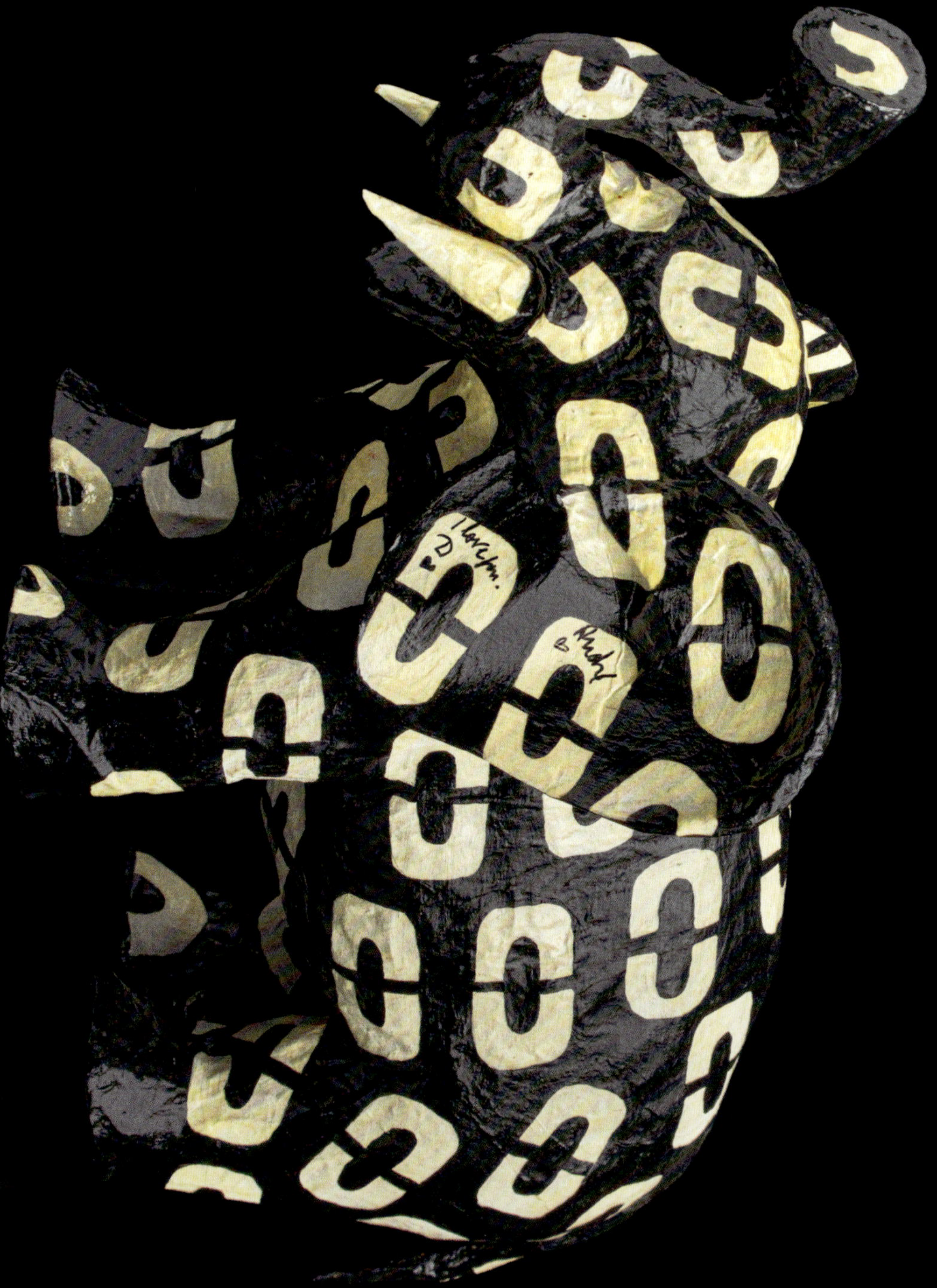

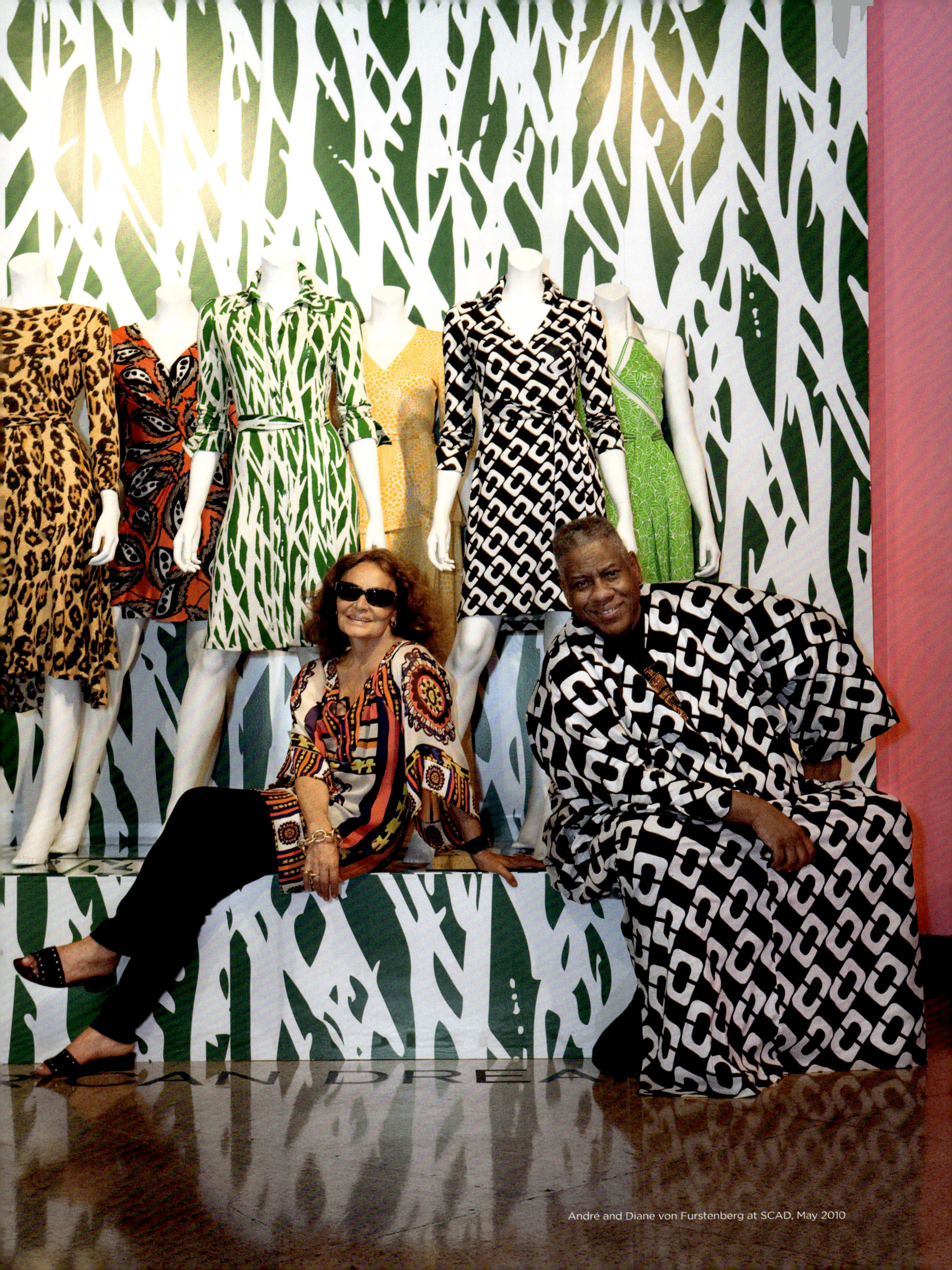

André and Diane von Furstenberg at SCAD, May 2010

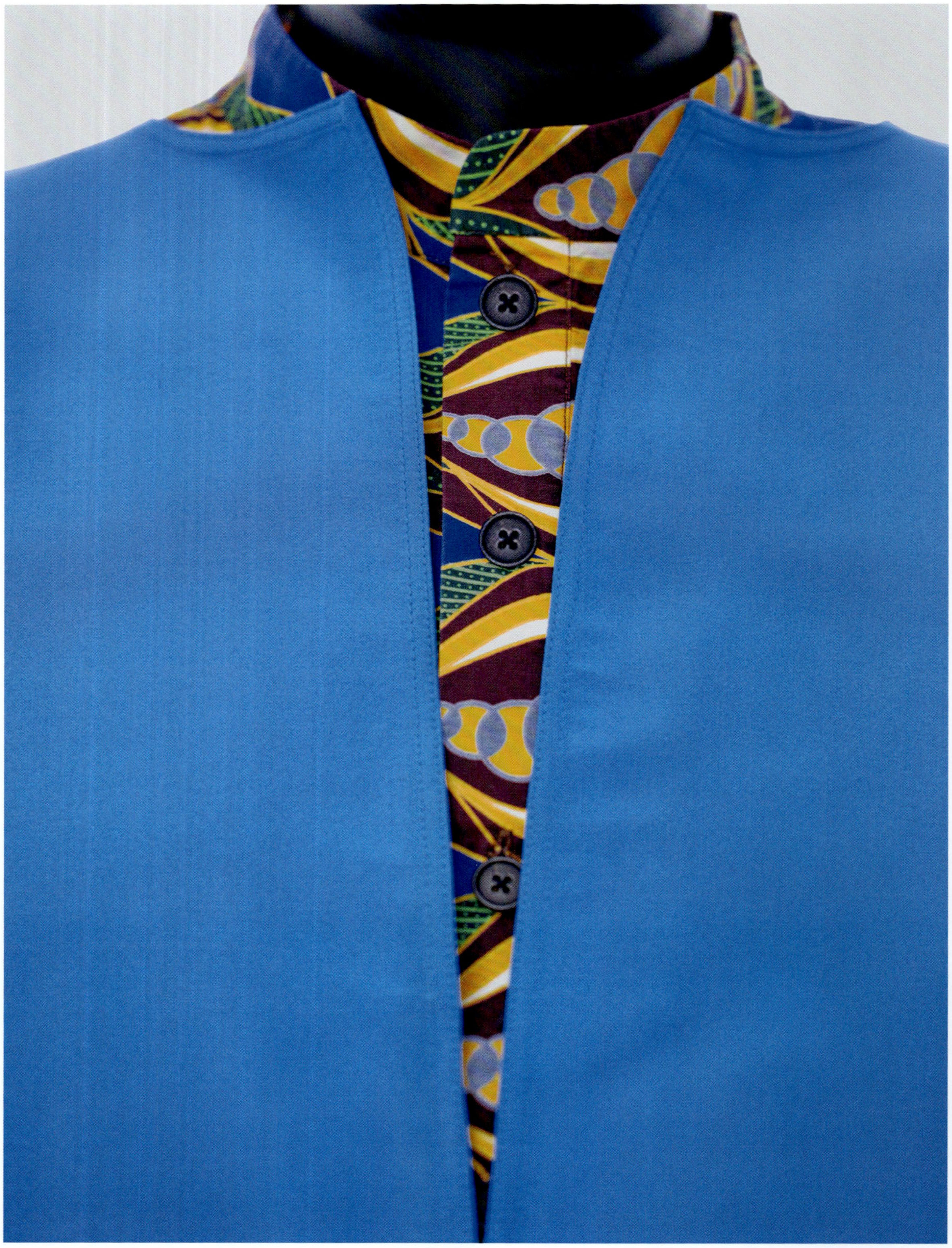

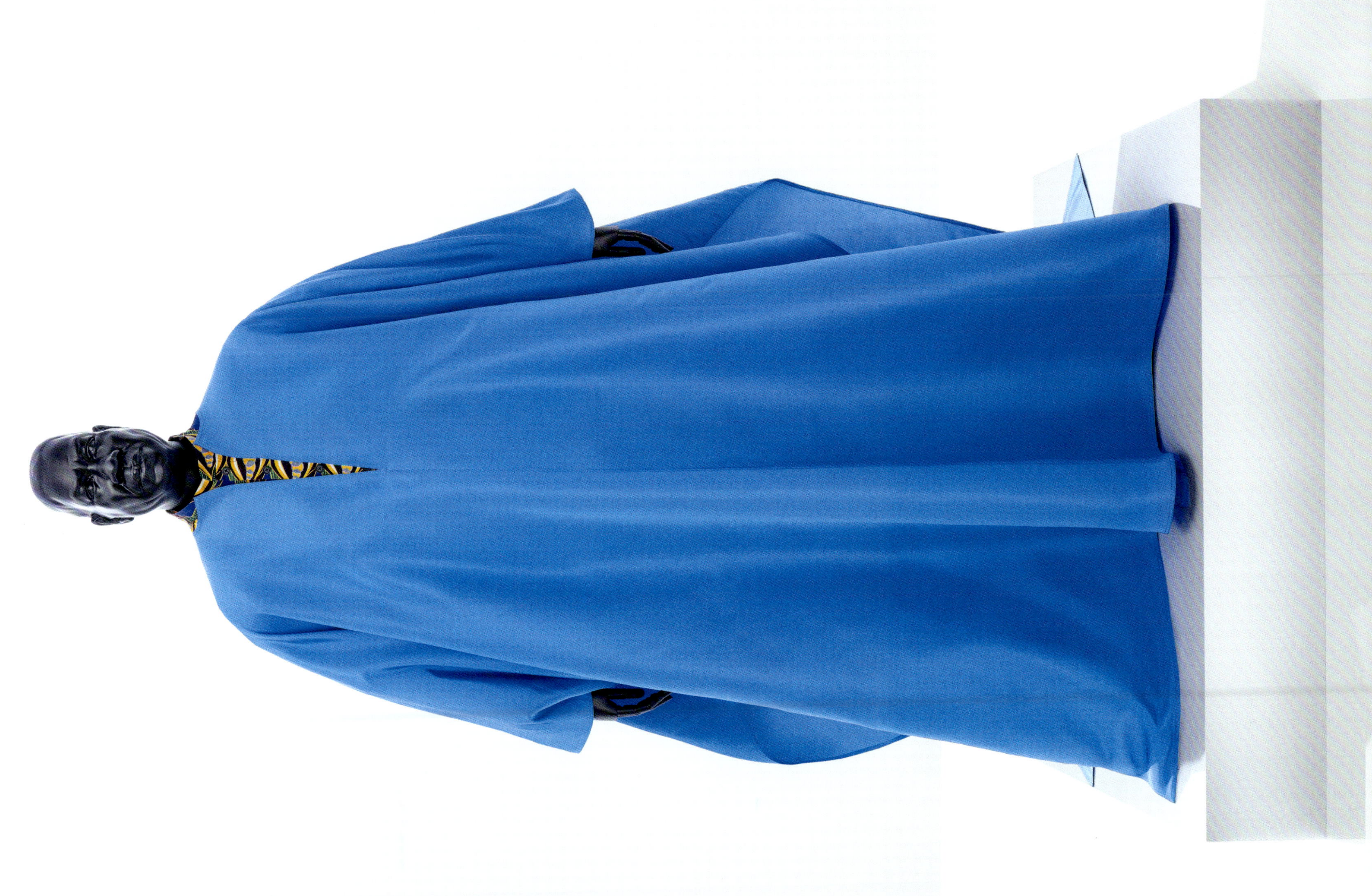

Ralph Rucci caftan with Demestik by Reuben Reuel tunic

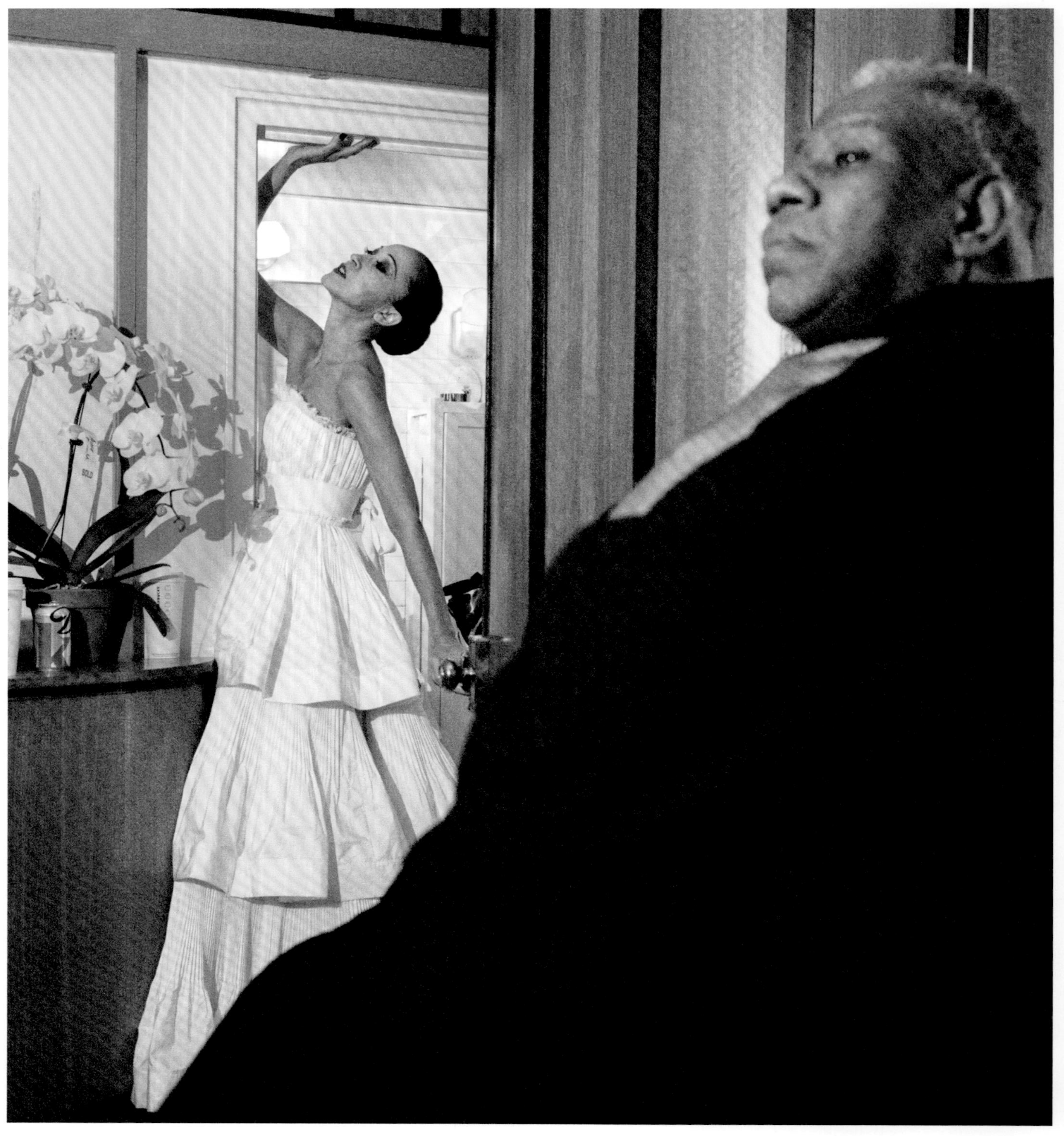

André and Pat Cleveland at Jonathan Becker's Sutton Place studio, 2013. Photographed by Jonathan Becker.

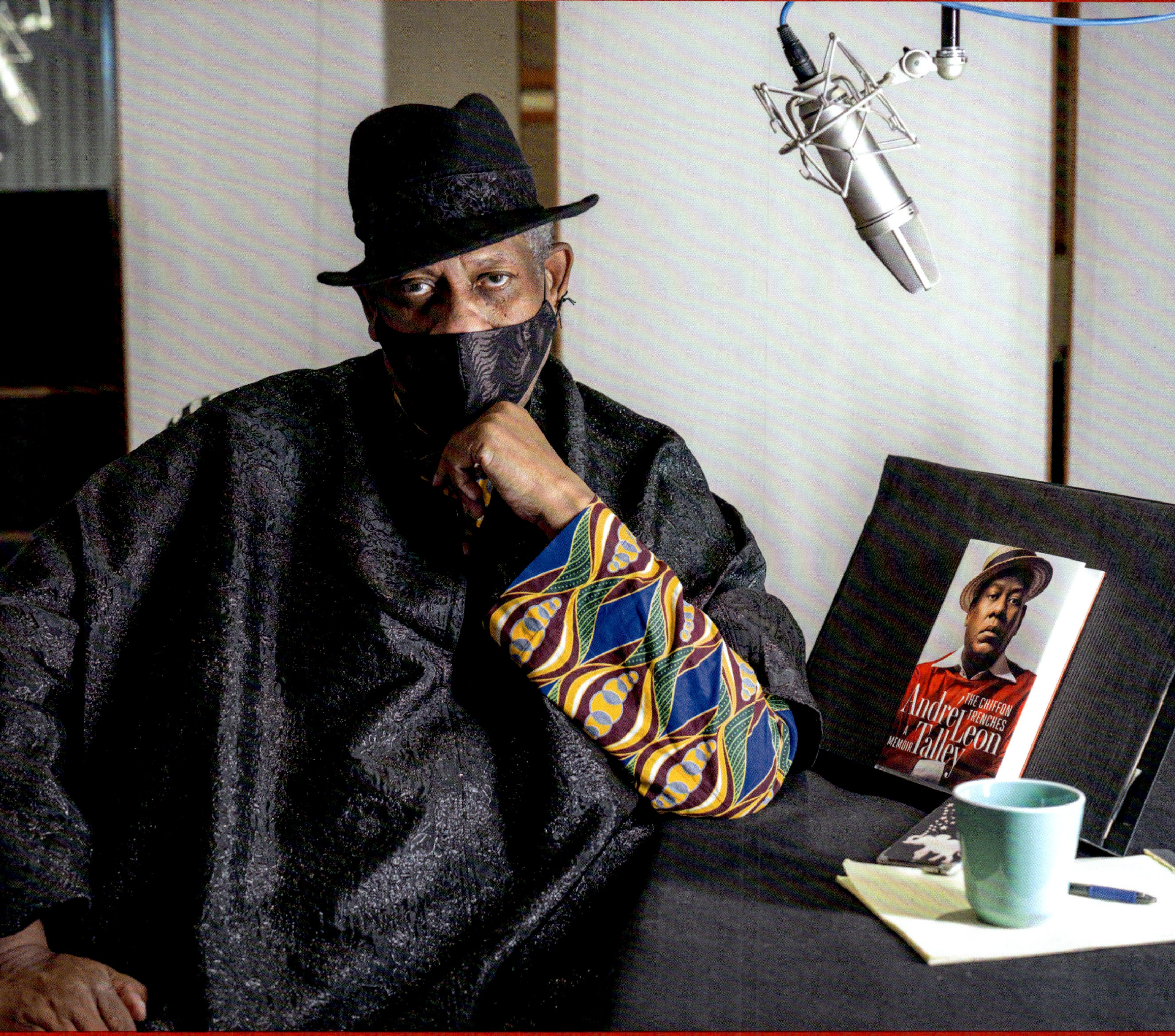

André at a studio in Katonah, New York, recording his book *The Chiffon Trenches*, October 2020. Photographed by Jonathan Becker.

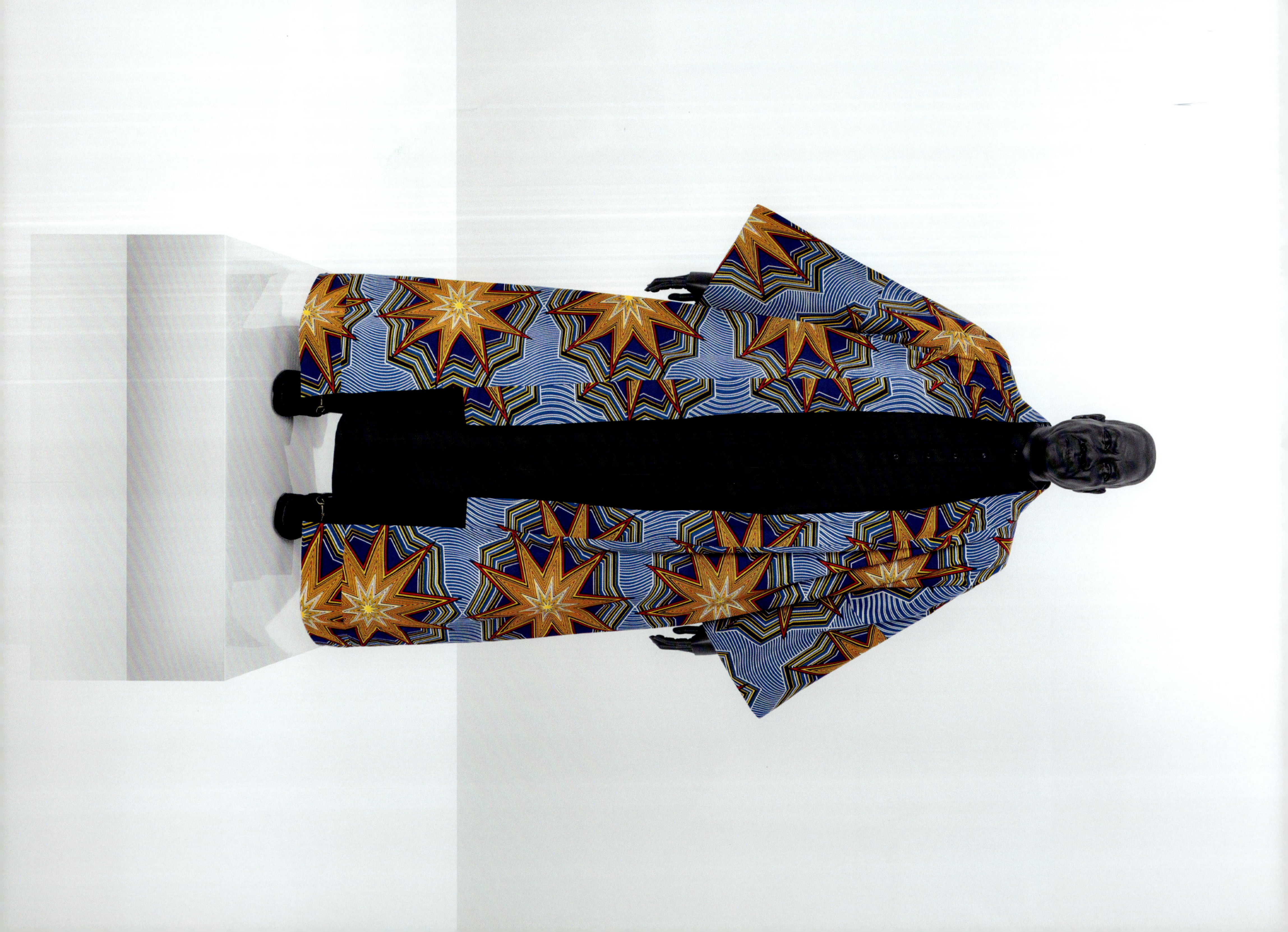

Demestik by Reuben Reuel kimono

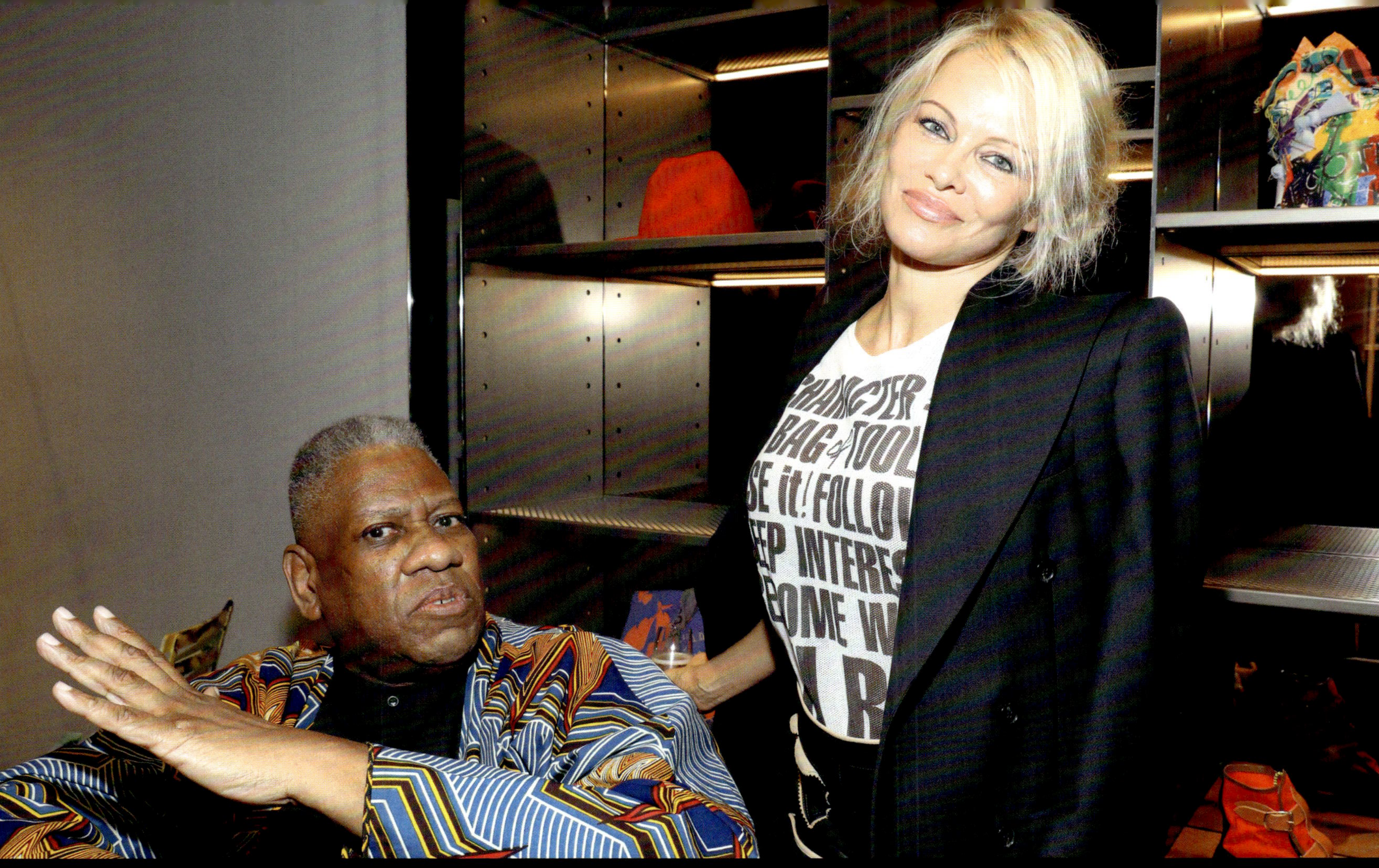

André and Pamela Anderson at the Vivienne Westwood x Juergen Teller exhibition opening during Spring/Summer 2018 New York Fashion Week. Photo by Amy Sussman/WWD/Penske Media via Getty Images.

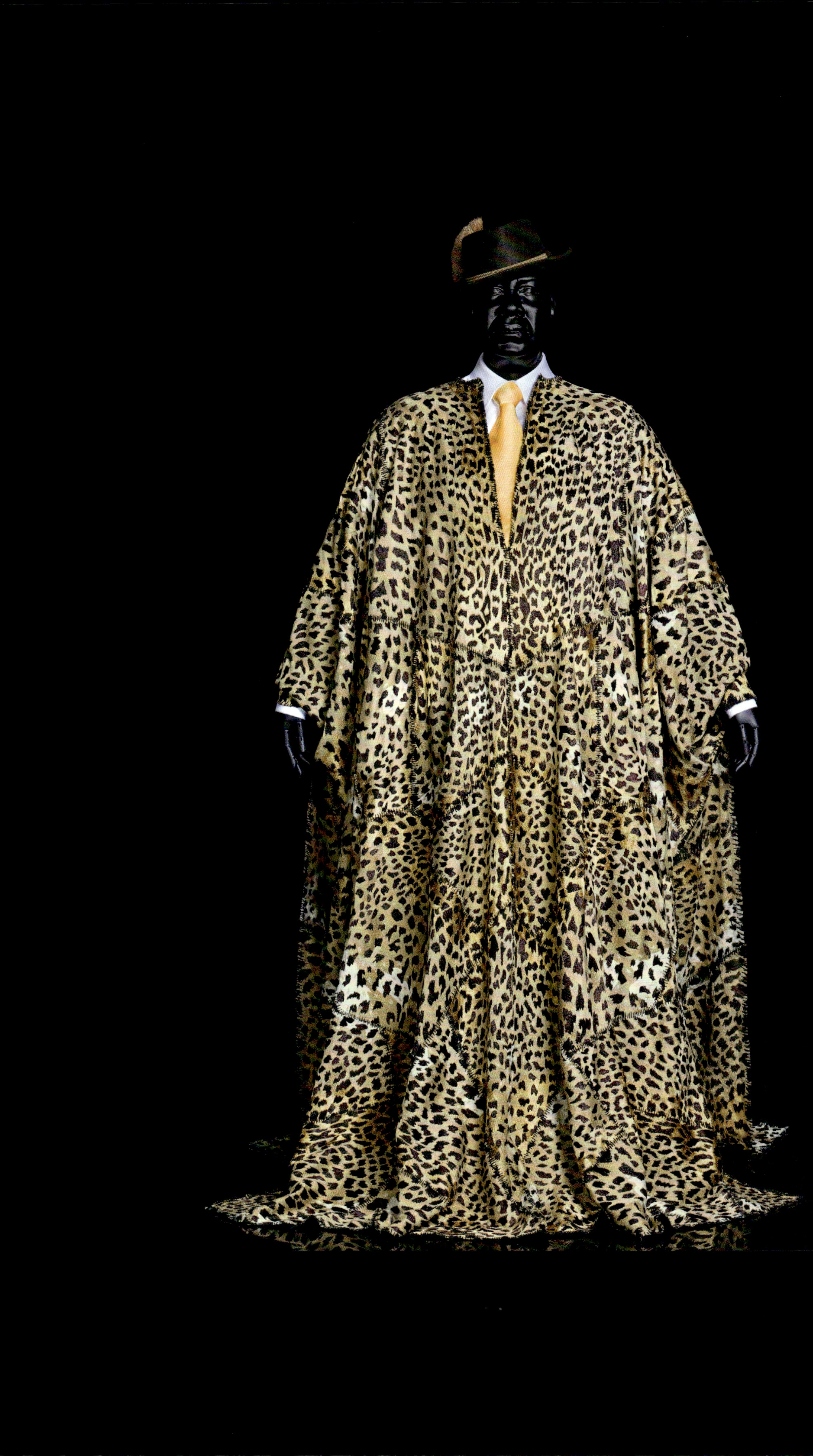

Tom Ford for Yves Saint Laurent caftan and Hutkönig Regensburg hat

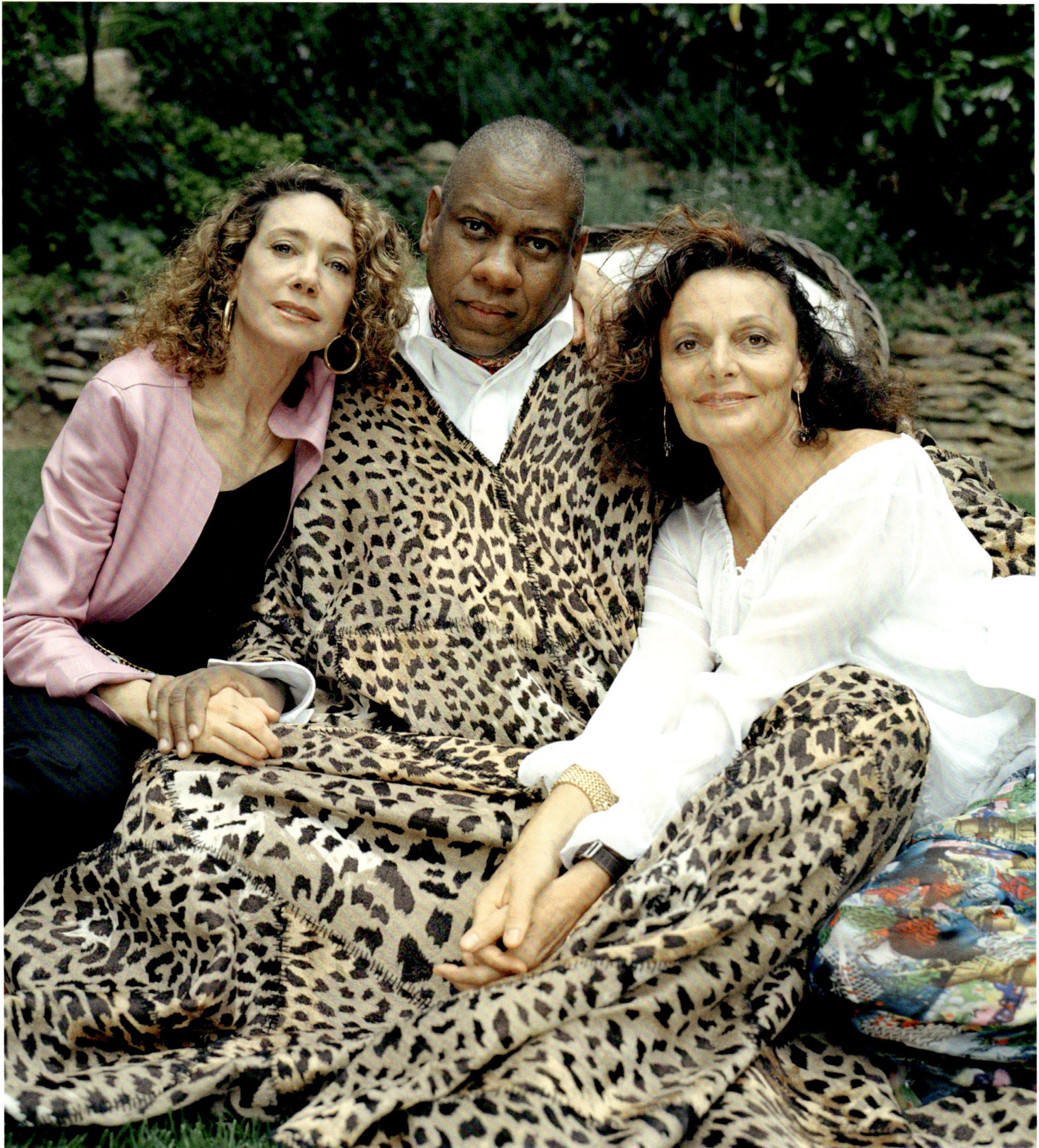

André with Marisa Berenson and Diane von Furstenberg at Canyon Park in Beverly Hills, California, March 2002. Photographed by Jonathan Becker/Contour RA by Getty Images.

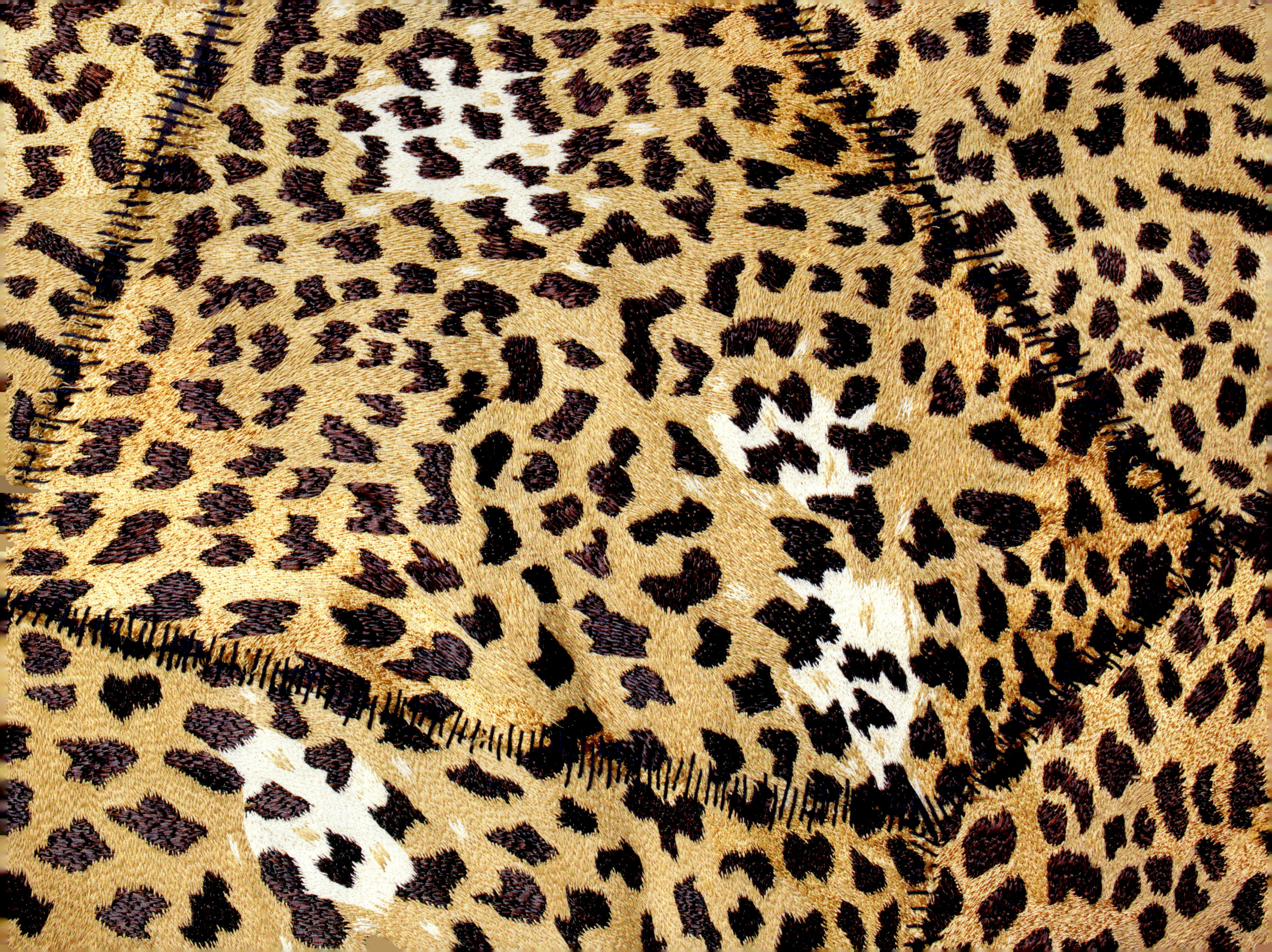

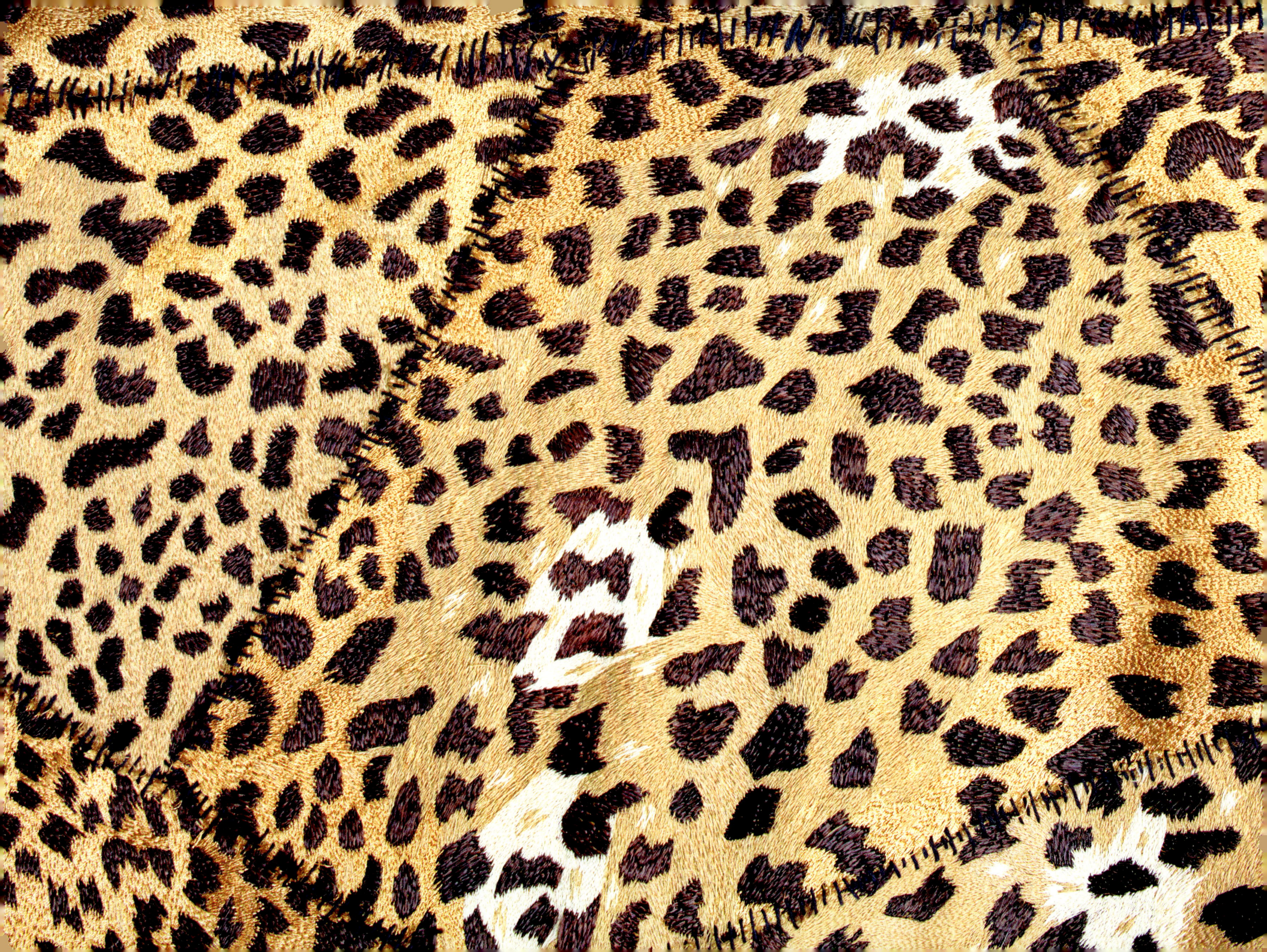

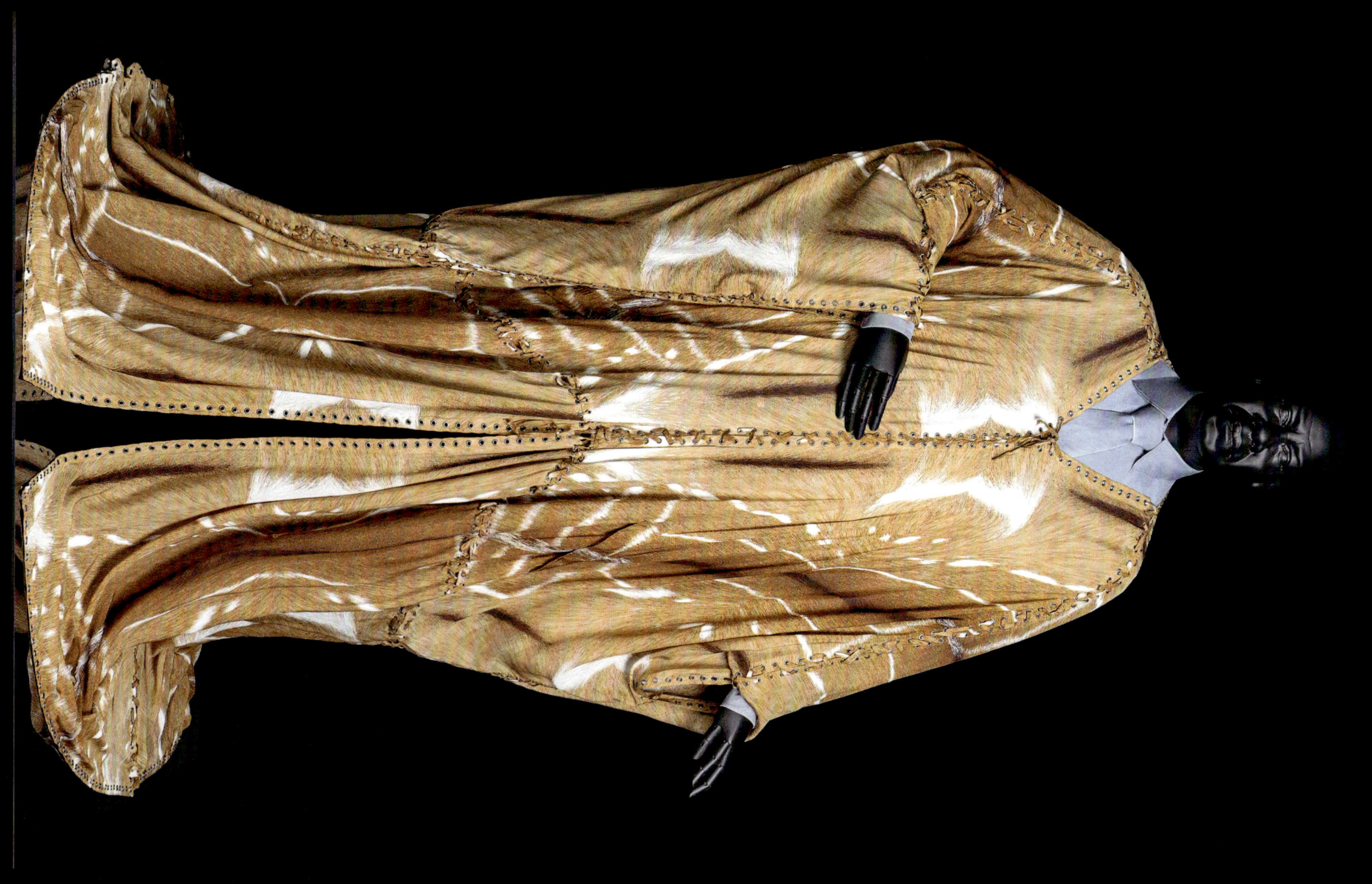

Tom Ford for Yves Saint Laurent caftan

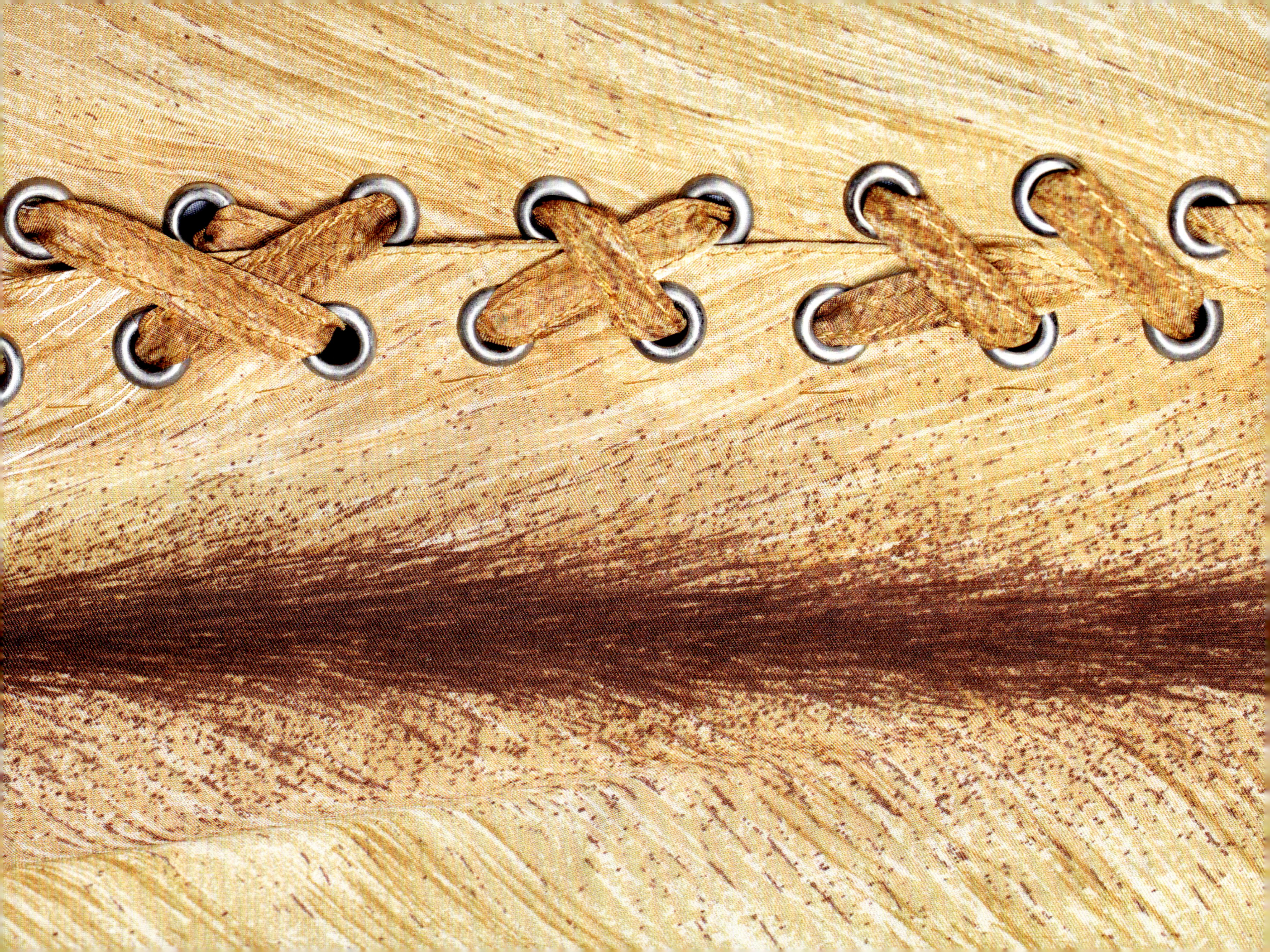

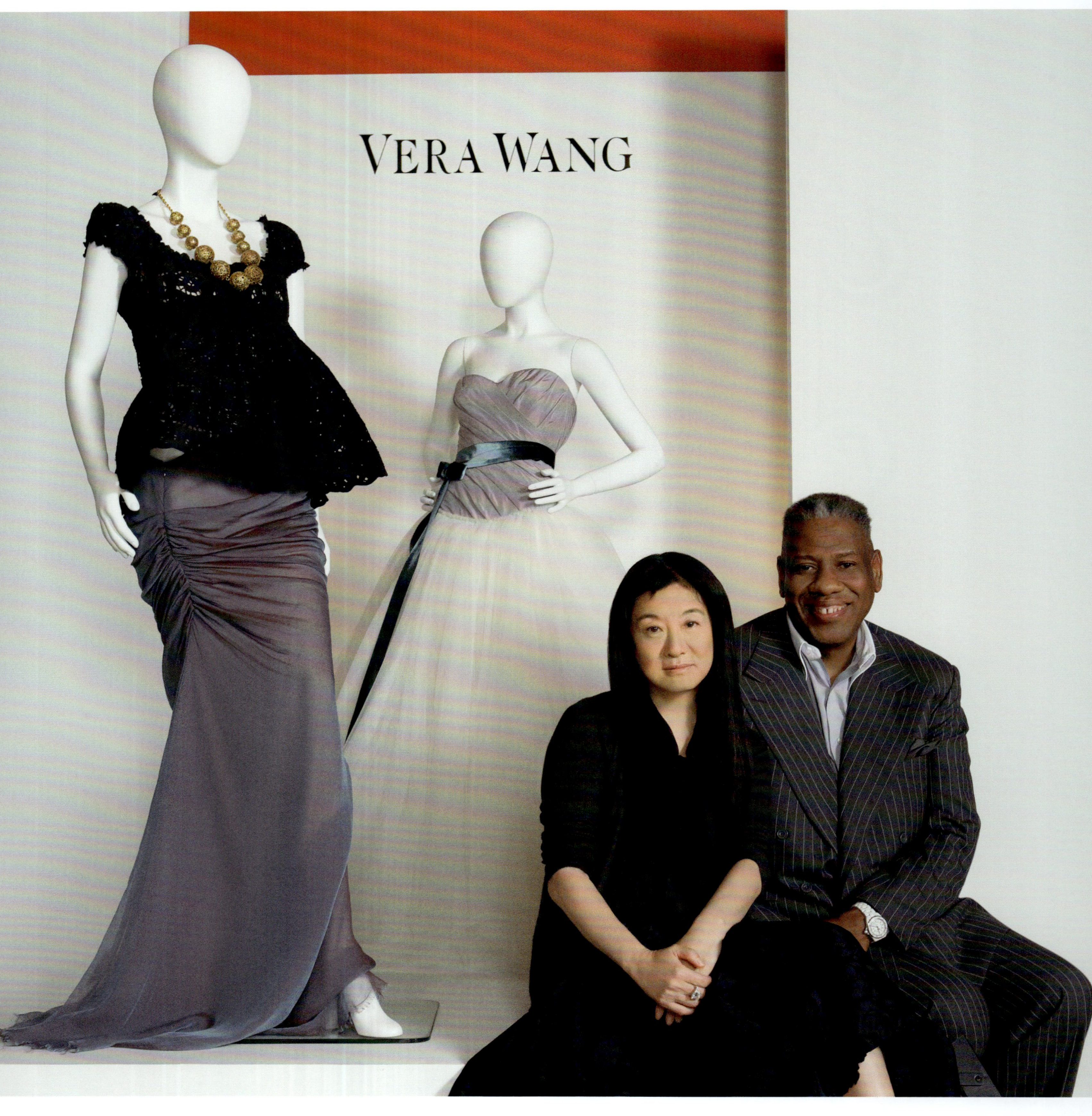

André and Vera Wang at SCAD, 2008

“

You couldn’t ignore André, **nor** did André **wish** to be ignored.

”

VERA WANG

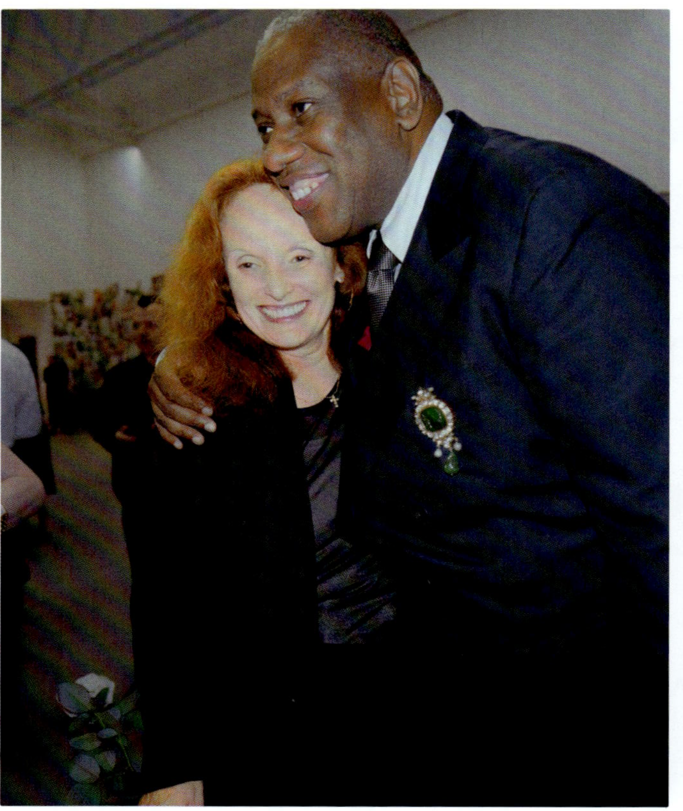

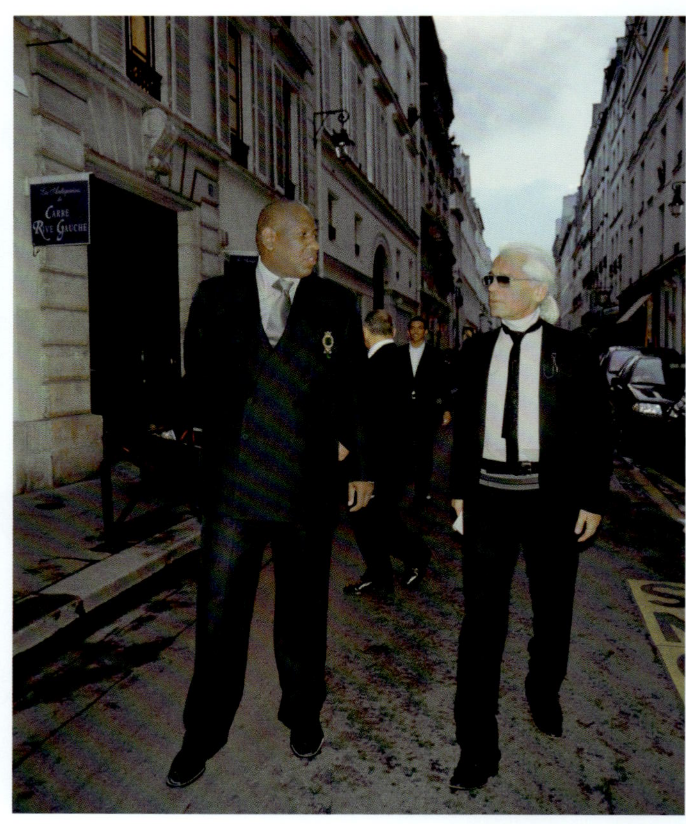

Left: André and Grace Coddington at her book launch in Paris, Summer 2002. Right: André and Karl Lagerfeld on rue de Lille in Paris, 2002. Photos by Robert Fairer.

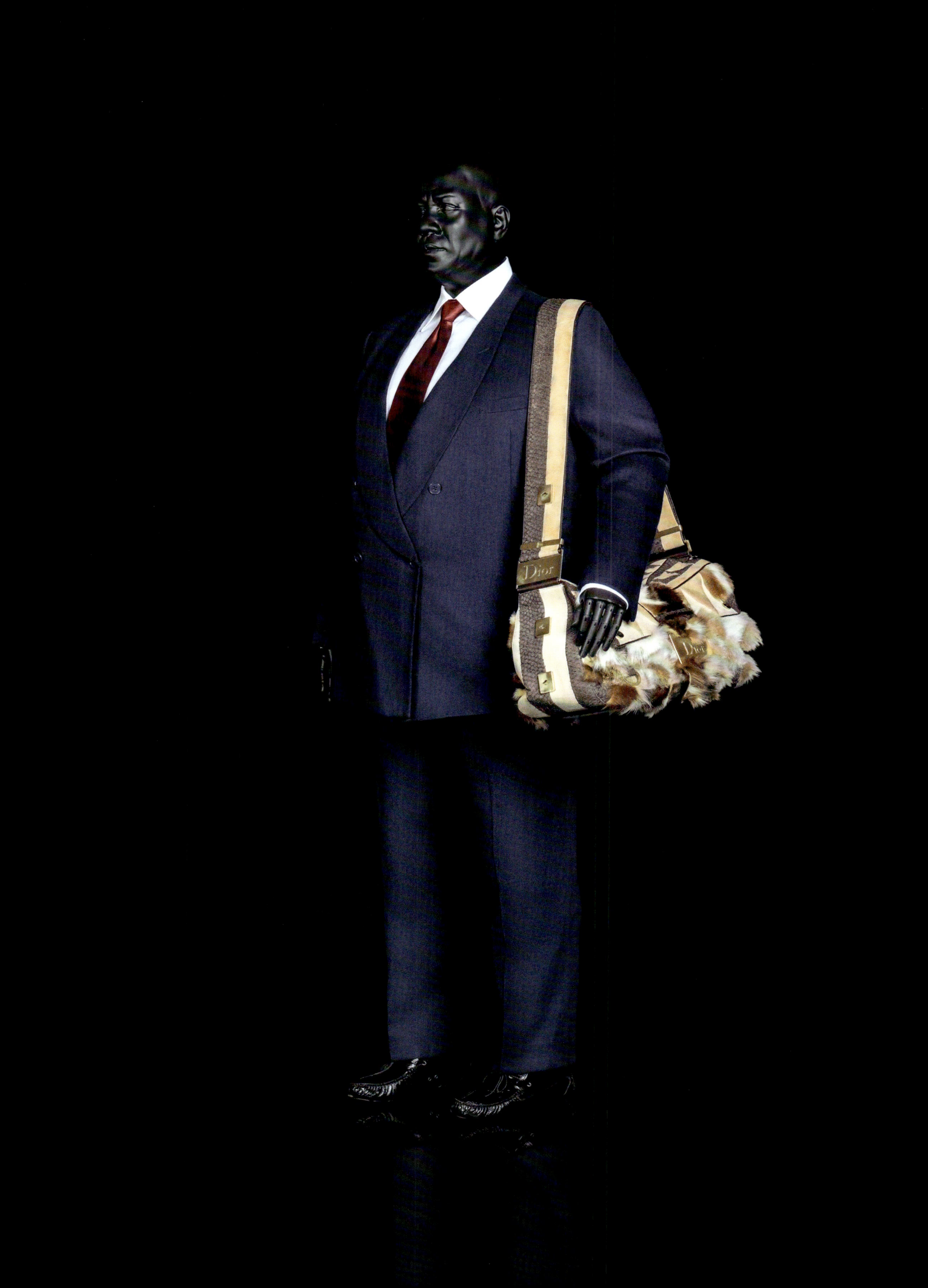

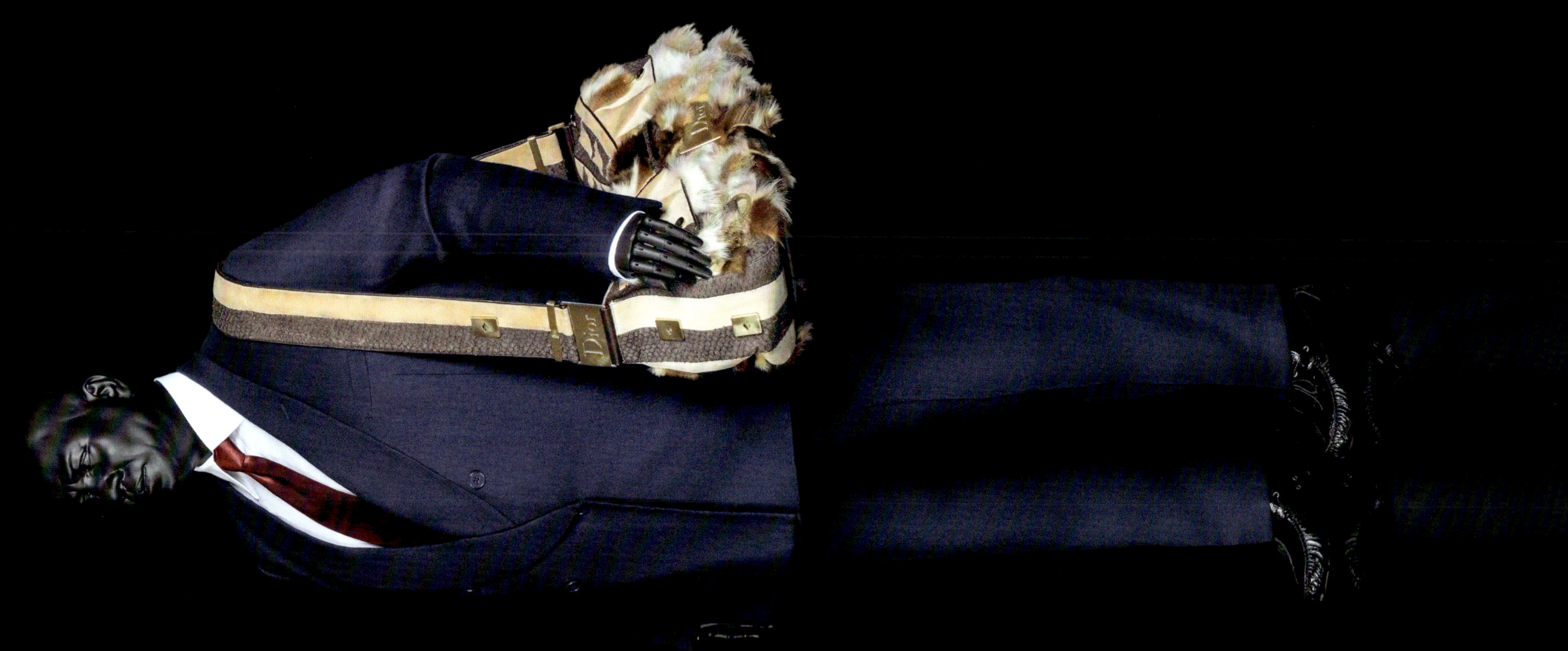
Dior

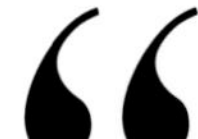

André had such an **exuberance** to him and a vibrance. He wanted to build you up, and he **wanted you to win**, and he wanted you to succeed.

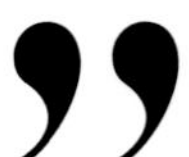

KIMORA LEE SIMMONS

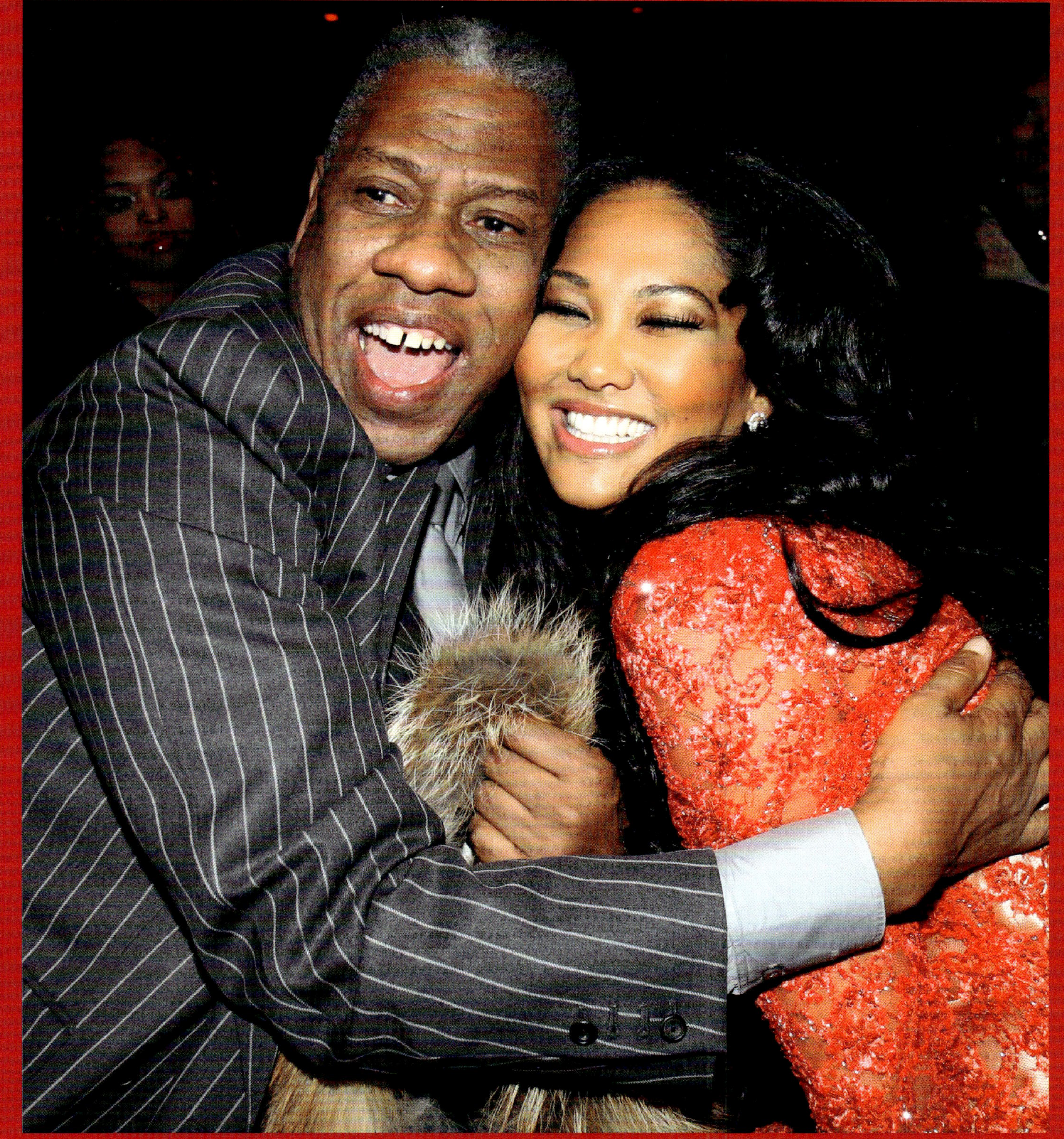

André and Kimora Lee Simmons backstage at the Baby Phat Fall/Winter 2007 runway show at Roseland Ballroom during New York Fashion Week. Photo by Johnny Nunez/WireImage.

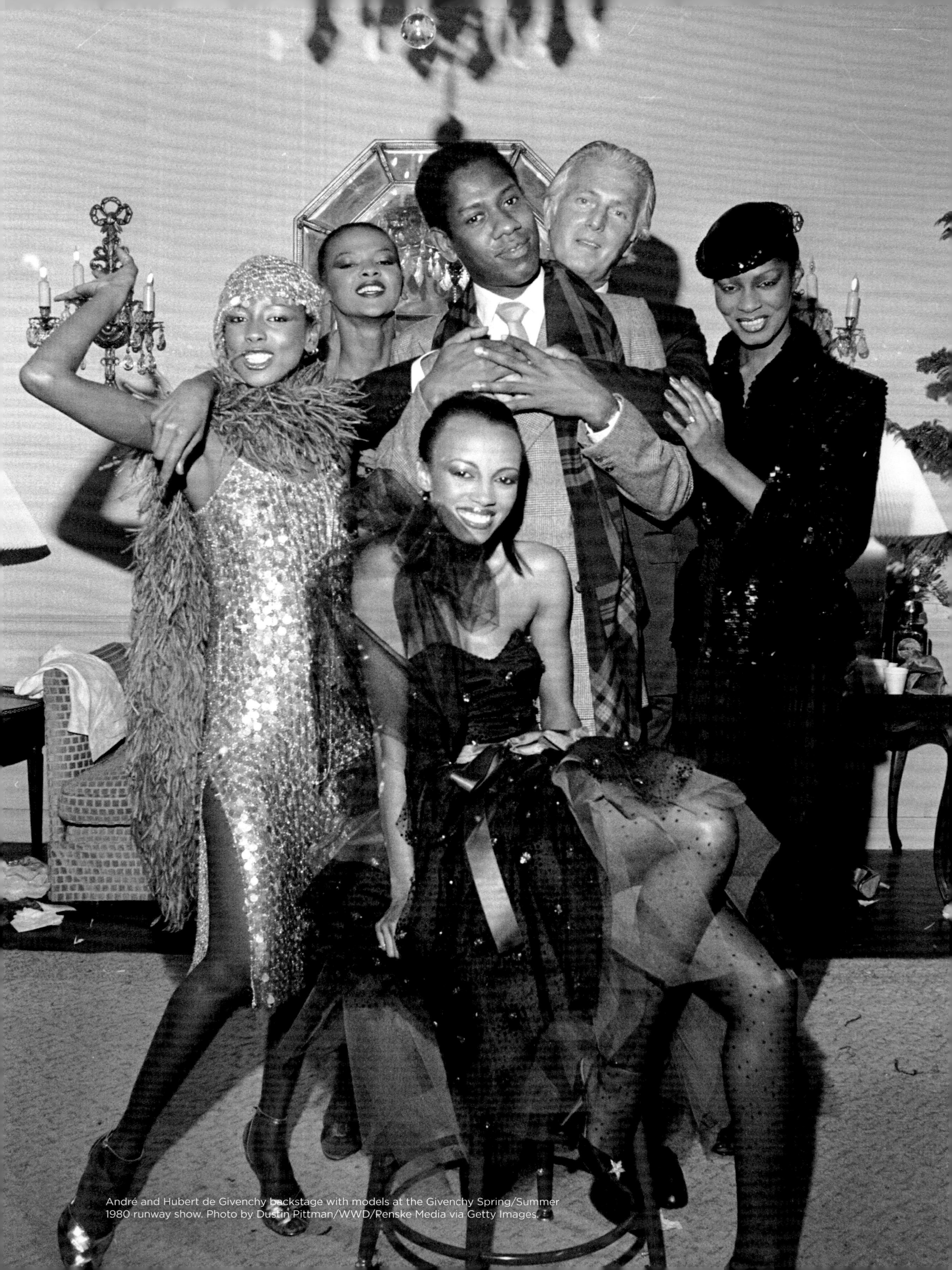

André and Hubert de Givenchy backstage with models at the Givenchy Spring/Summer 1980 runway show. Photo by Dustin Pittman/WWD/Penske Media via Getty Images.

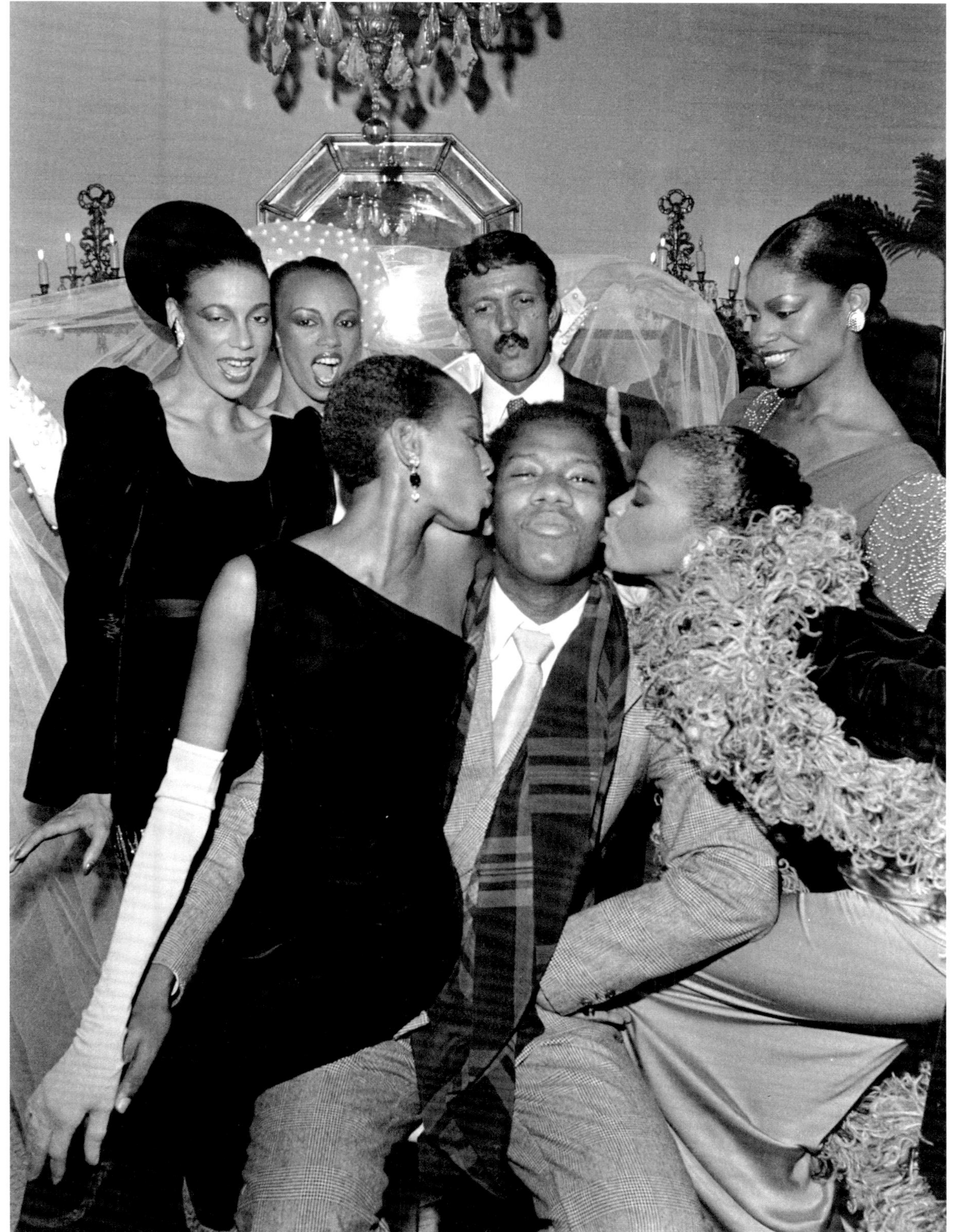

André backstage with models at the Givenchy Spring/Summer 1980 runway show. Photo by Dustin Pittman/WWD/Penske Media via Getty Images.

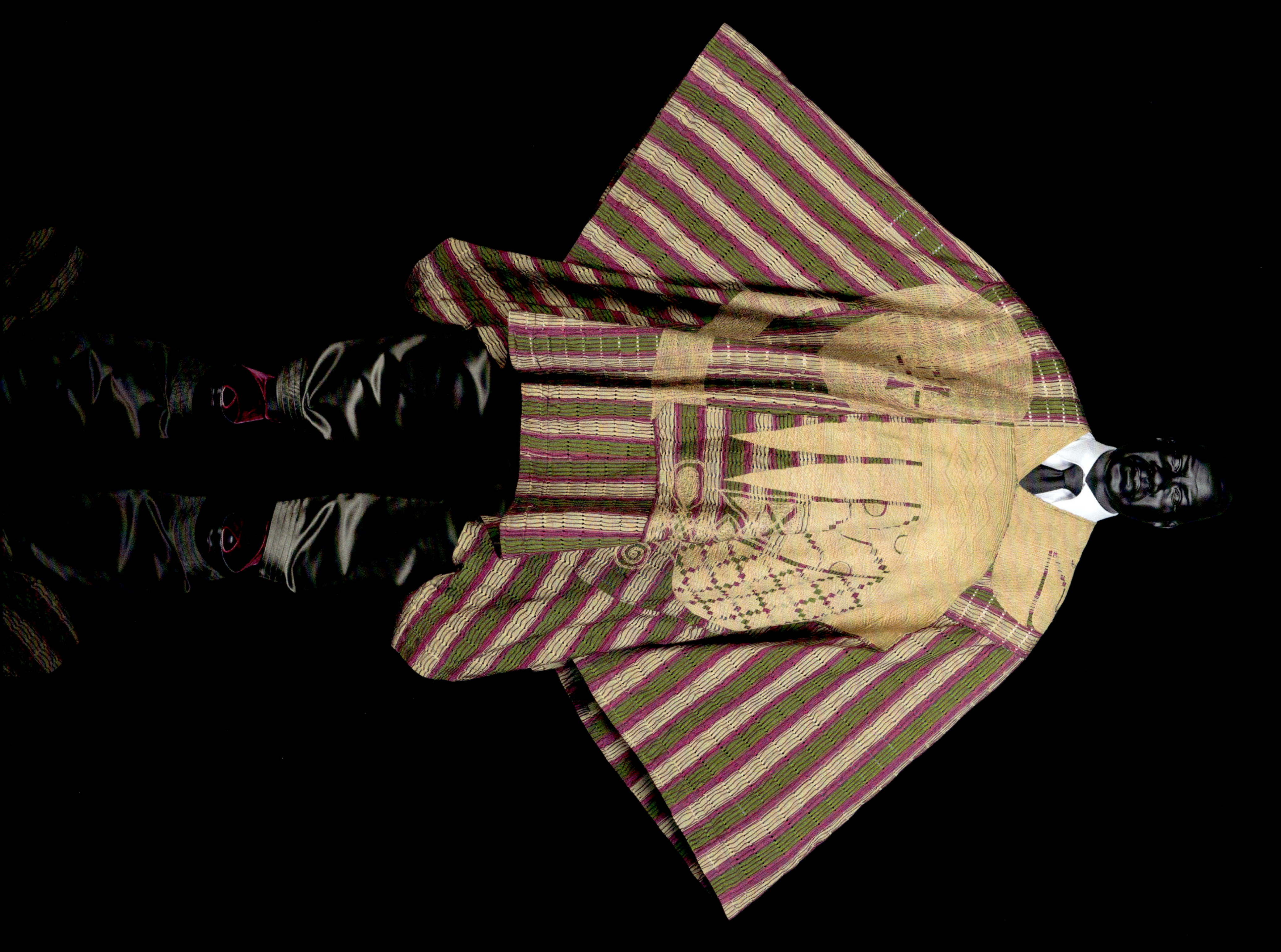

“

André’s **representation** inspired an entire generation.

”

CARLOS NAZARIO

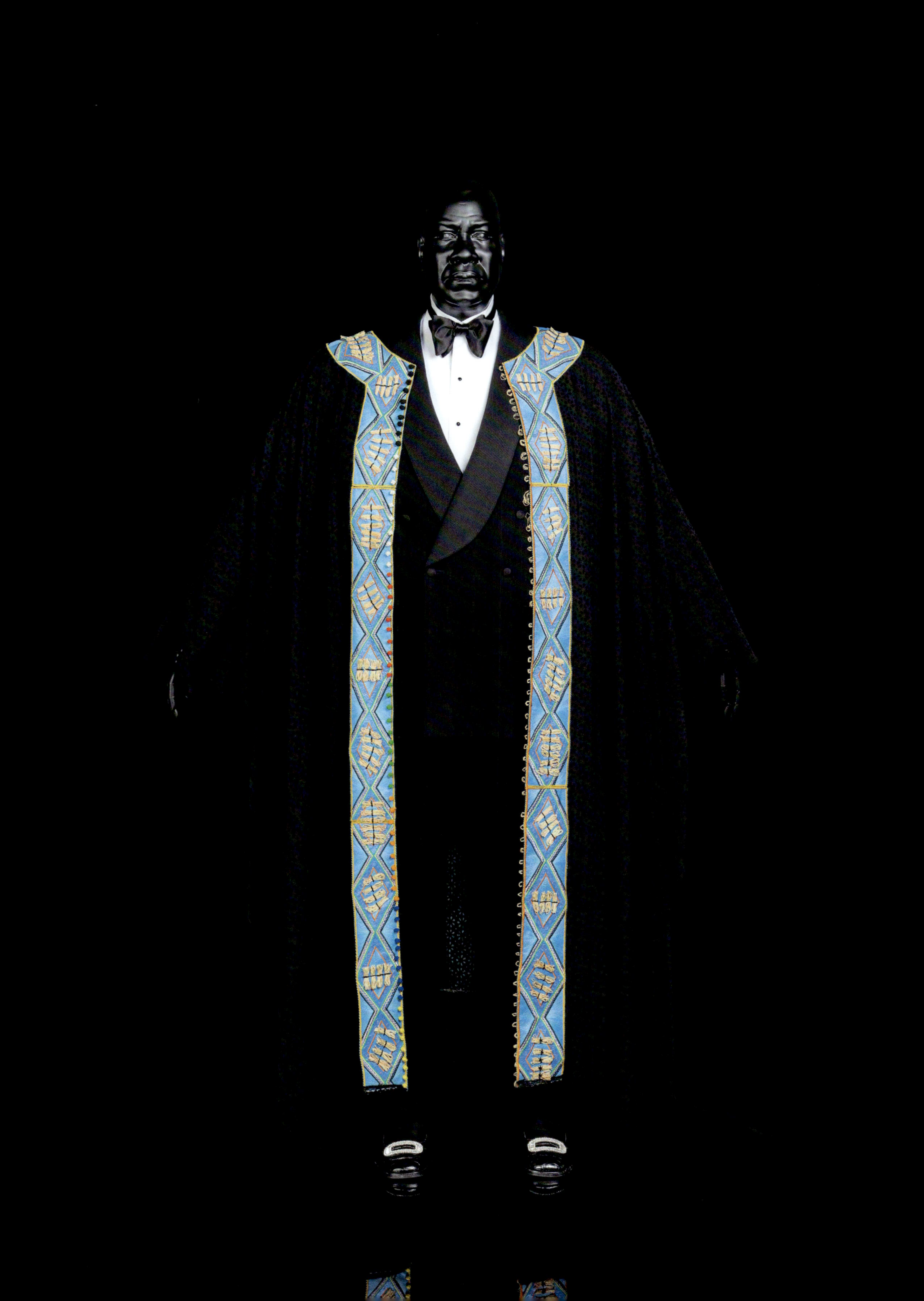

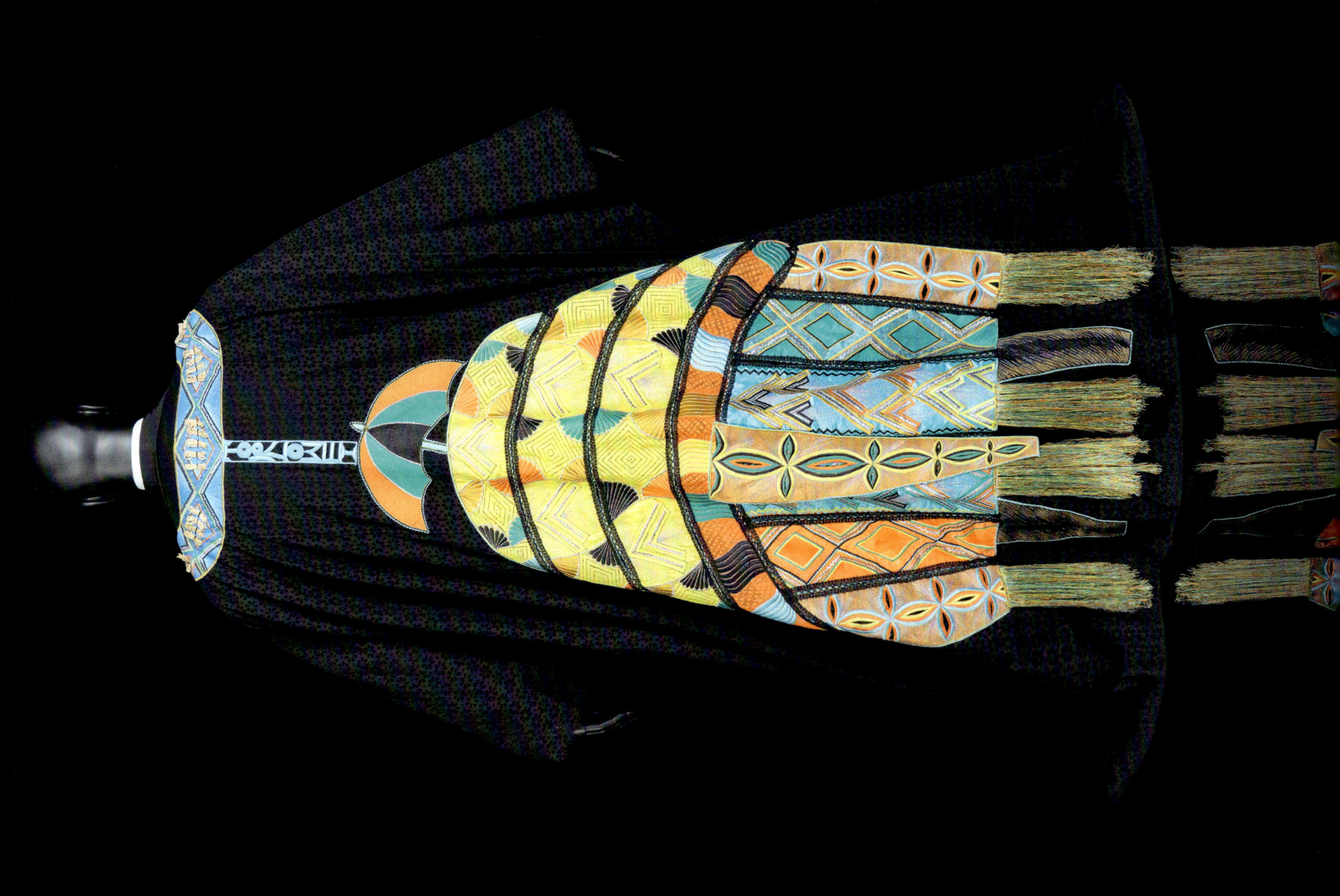

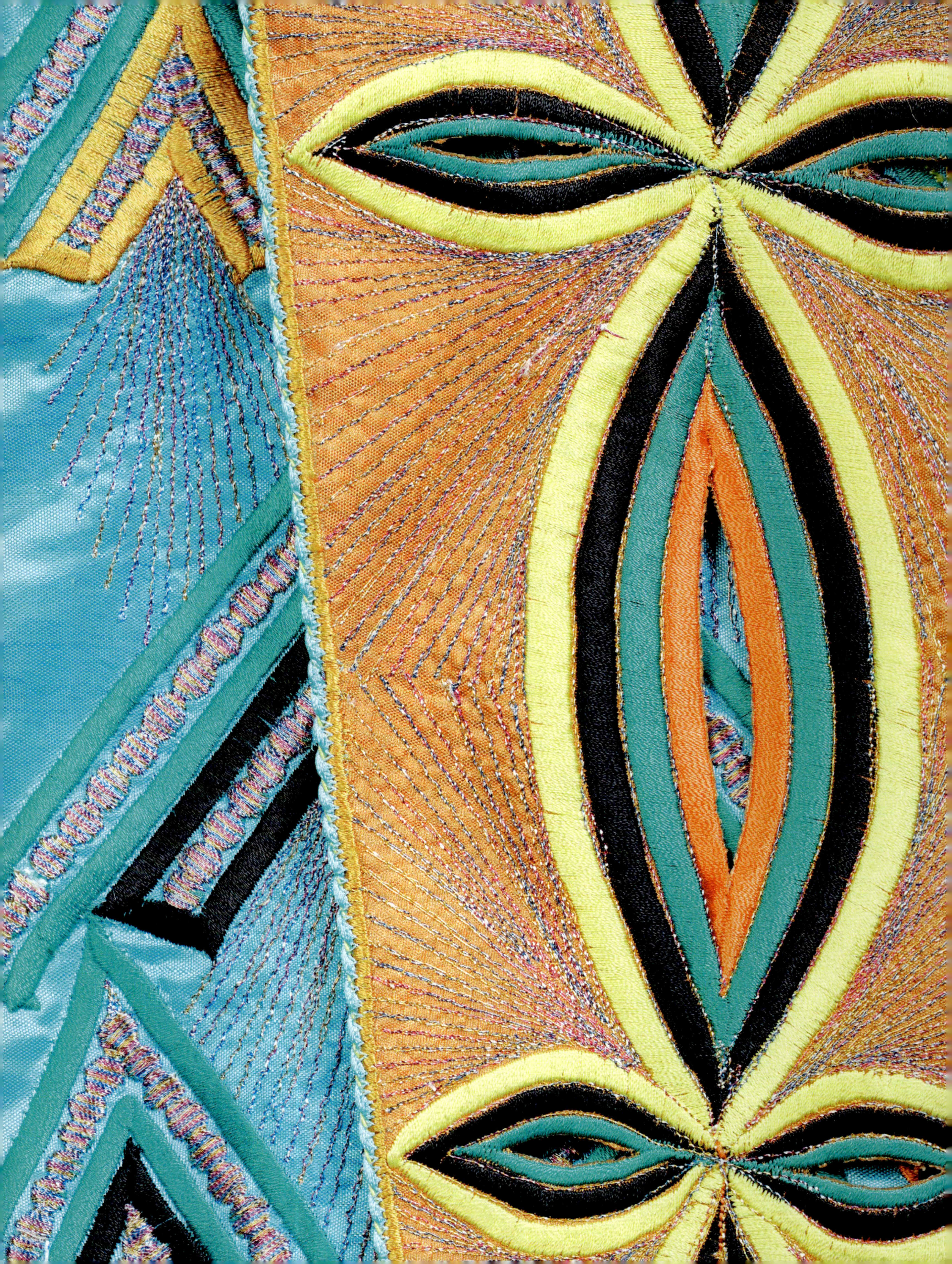

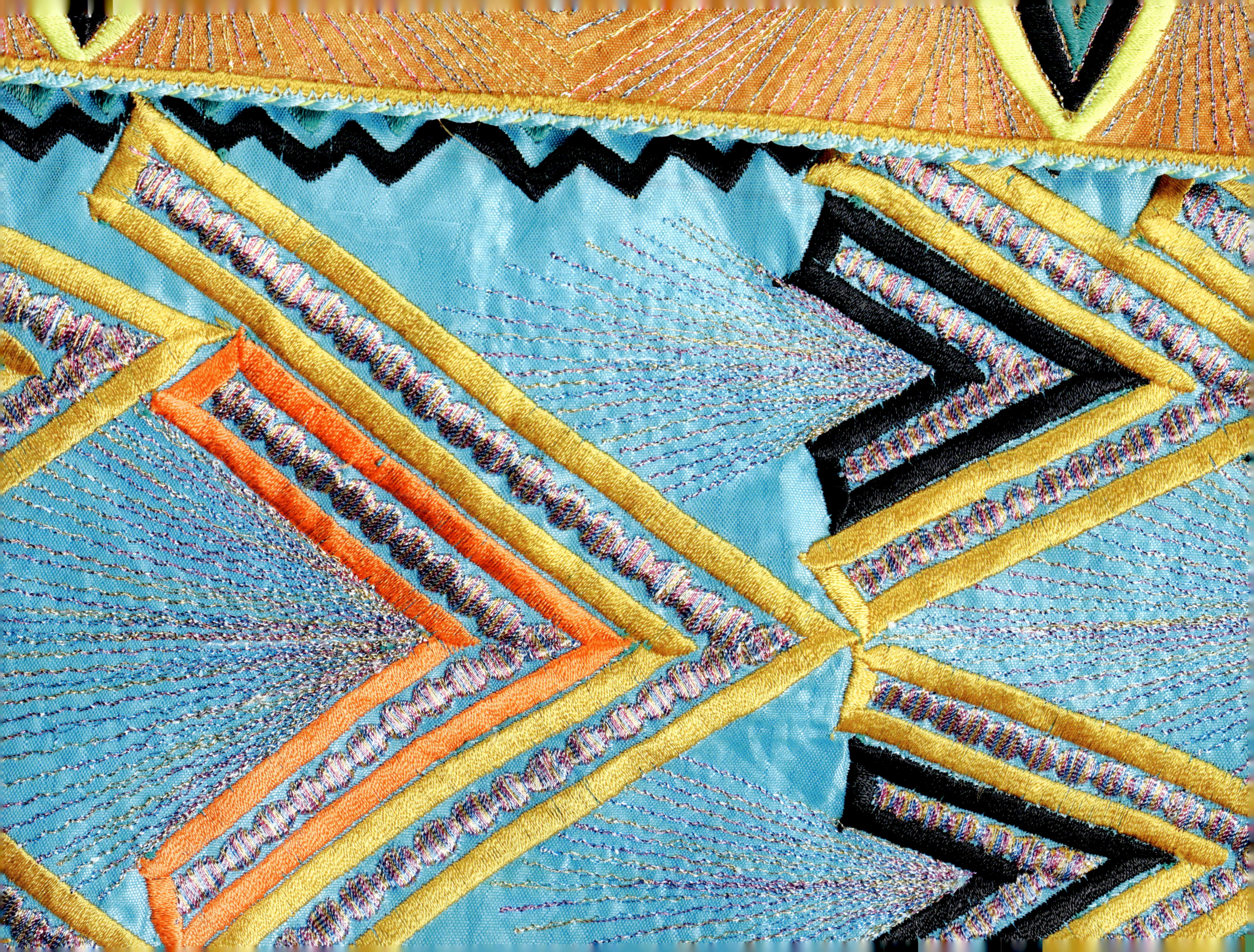

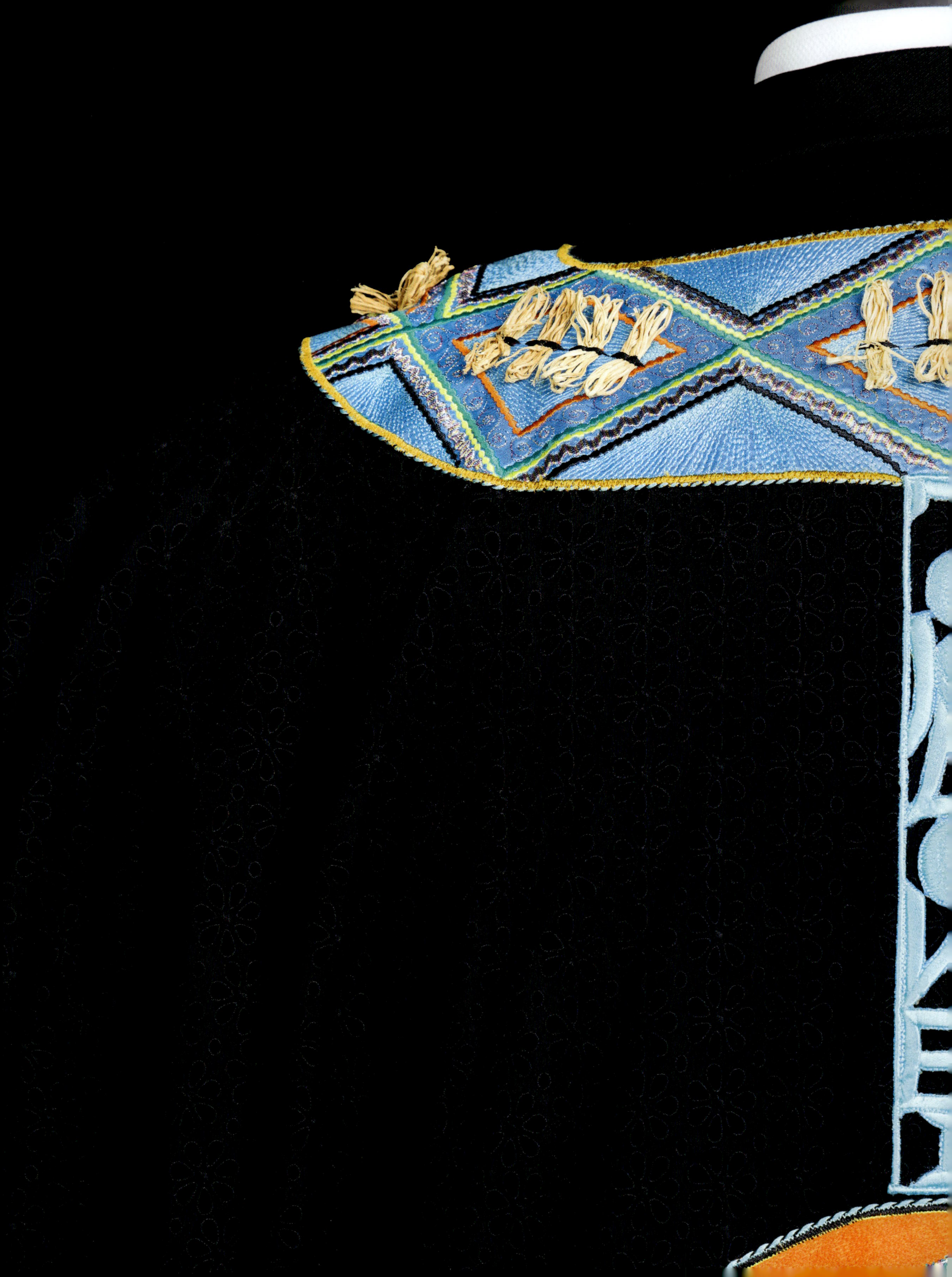

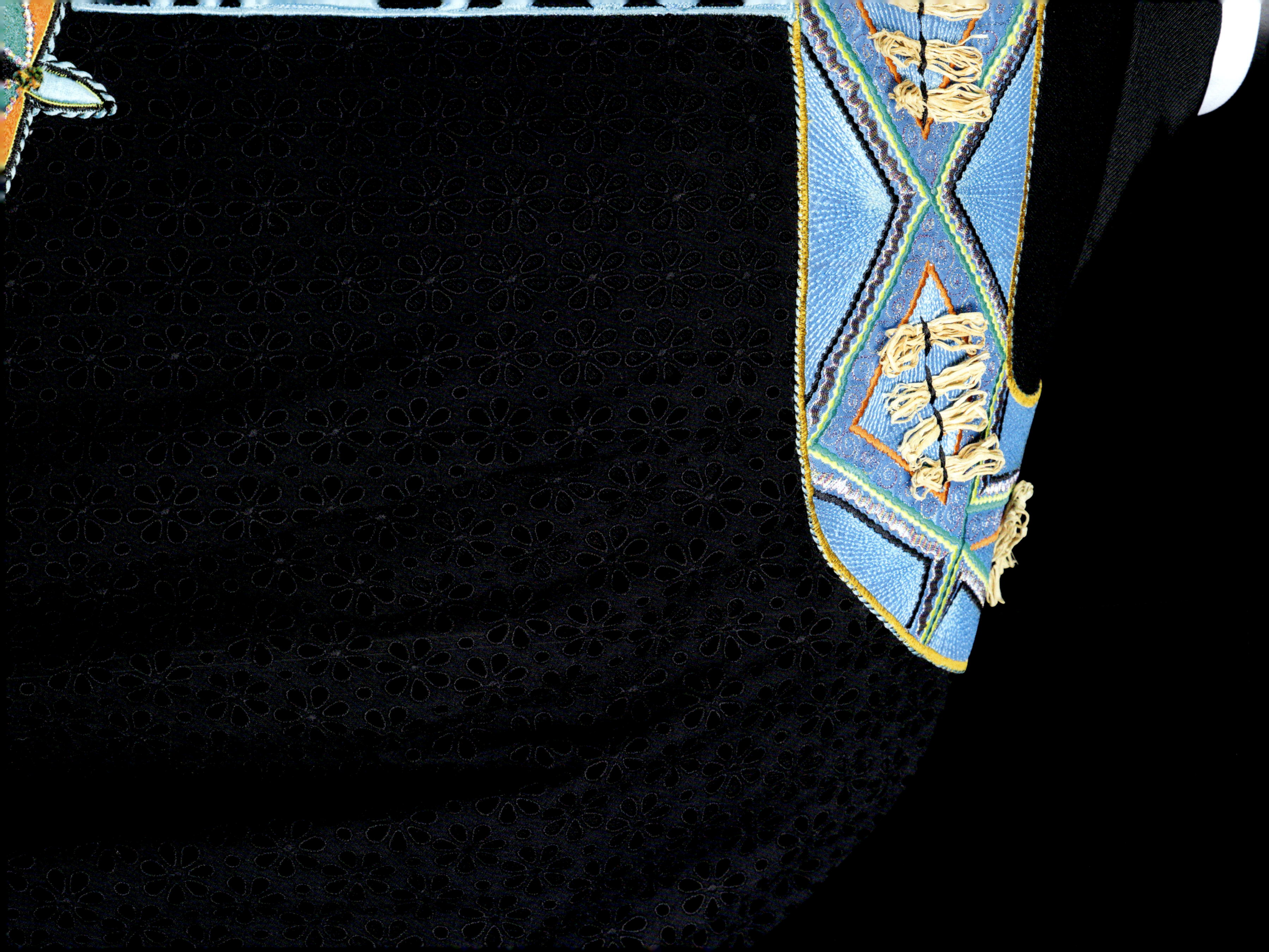

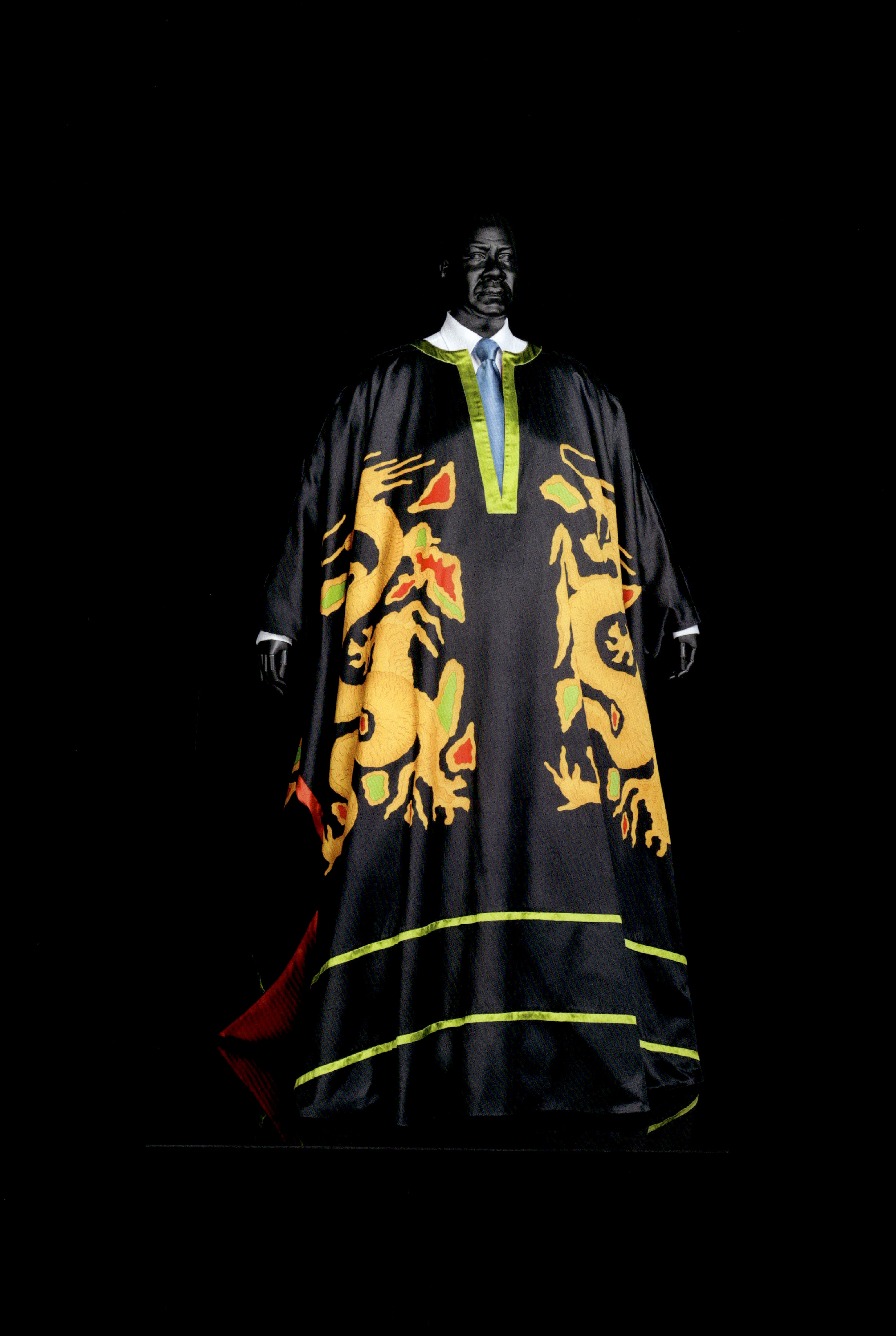

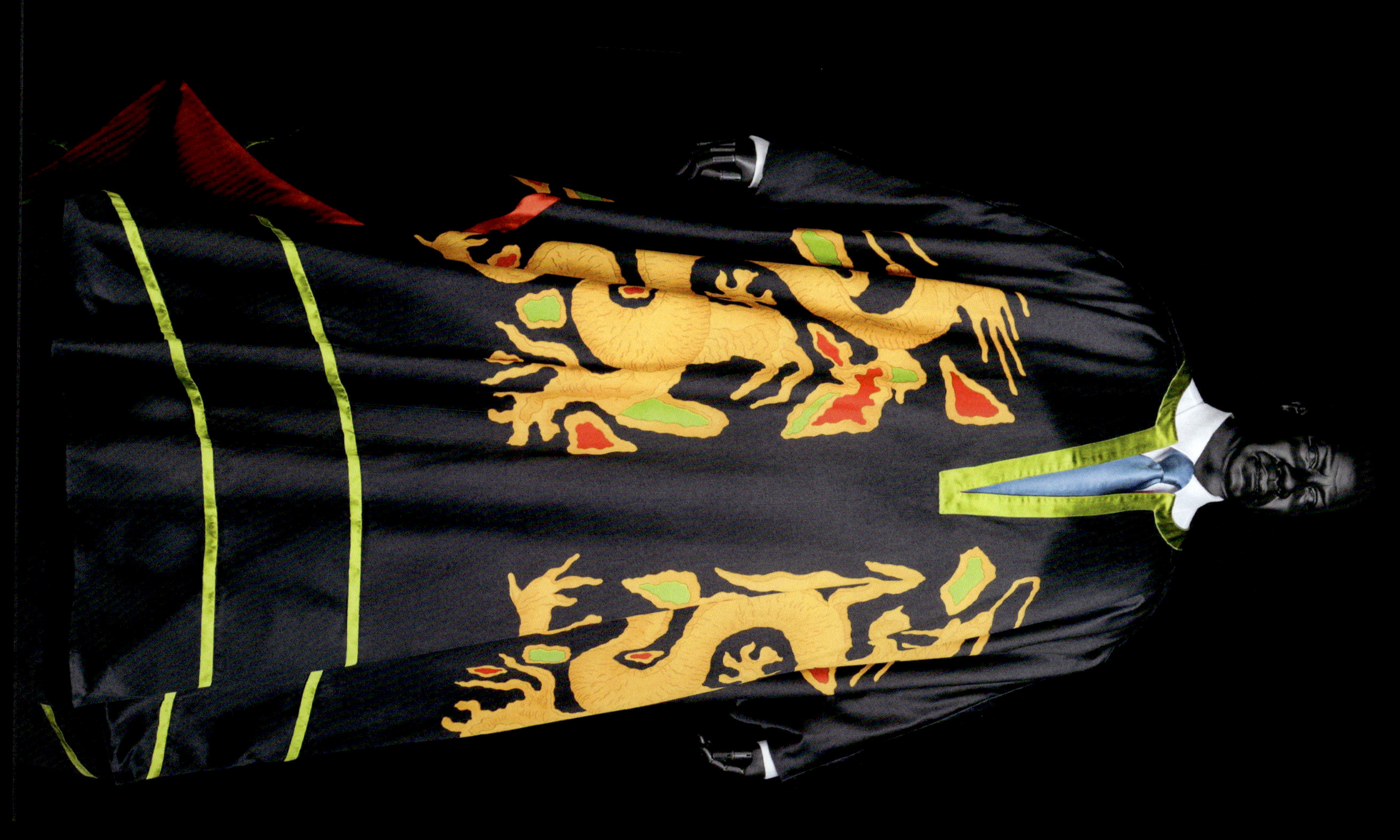

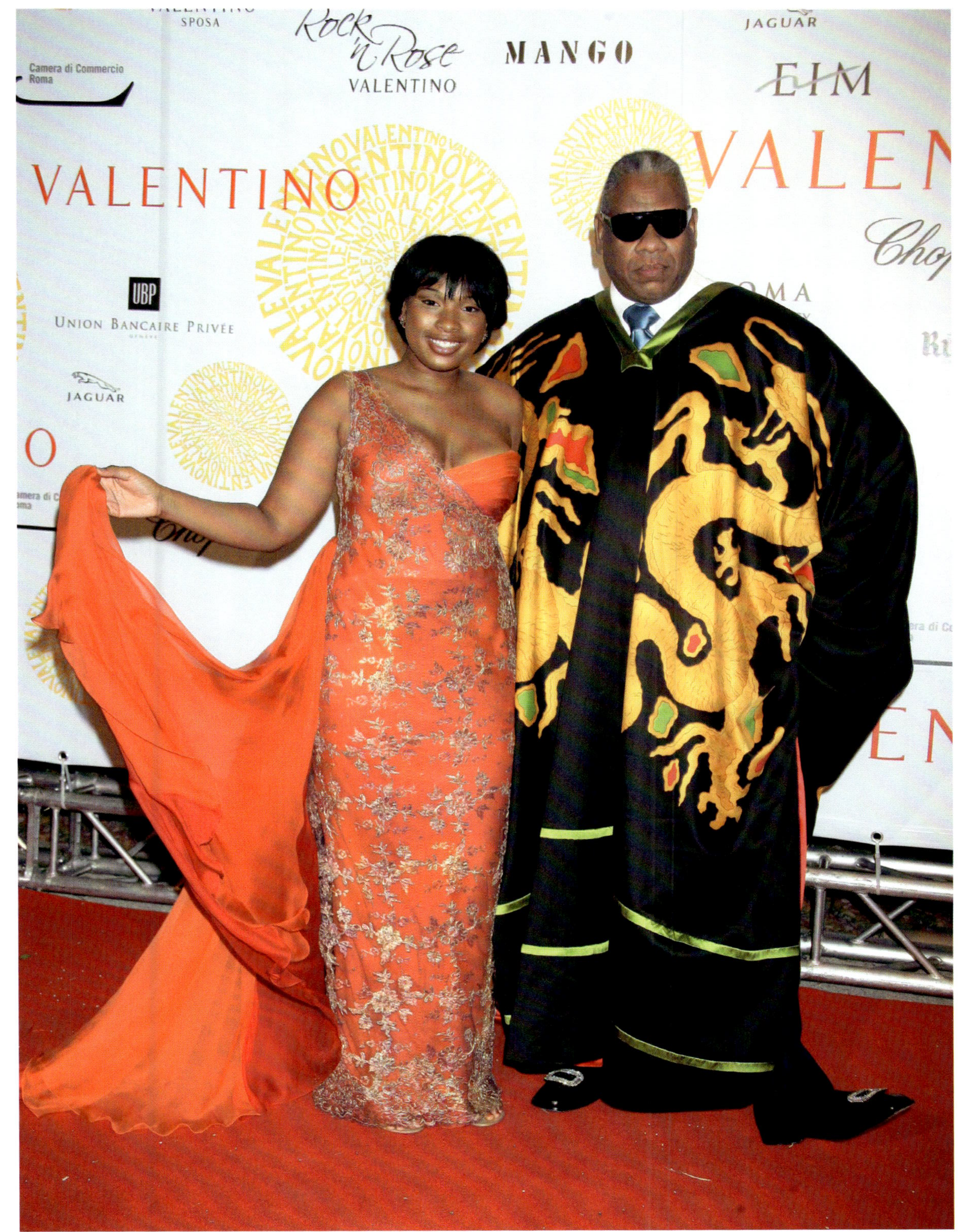

André and Jennifer Hudson at Villa Borghese in Rome for the forty-fifth anniversary of Valentino, 2007. Photo by Stephane Cardinale/Corbis via Getty Images.

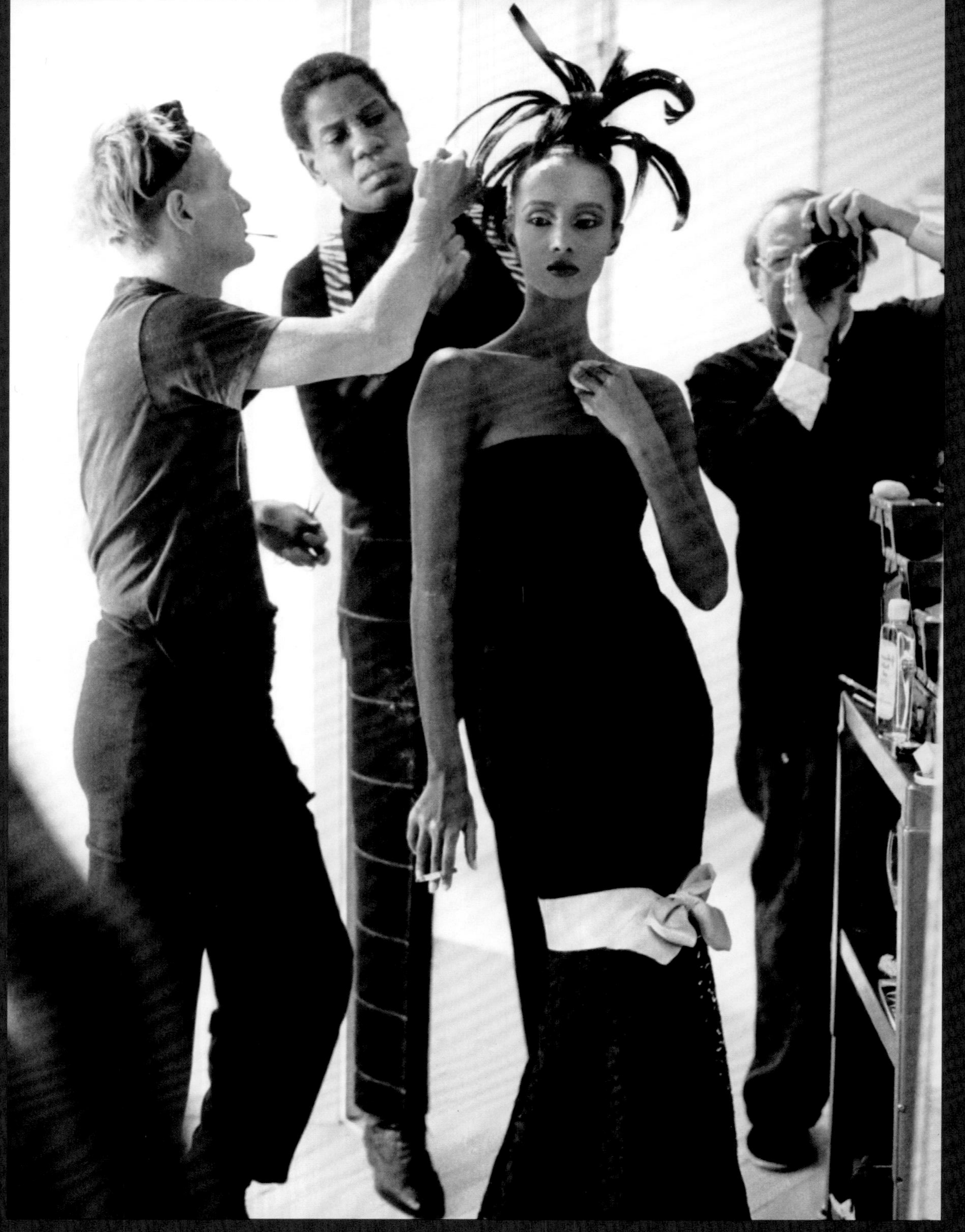

André, 1986. Photo by Arthur Elgort/Trunk Archive.

“

I am of the opinion that we have not yet **heard** fully the **importance** of André Leon Talley.

”

CONSTANCE WHITE

“

When André **shined his light** on you, you really felt like, even in this fashion world of misfits, there was a **place for you**.

”

DEREK BLASBERG

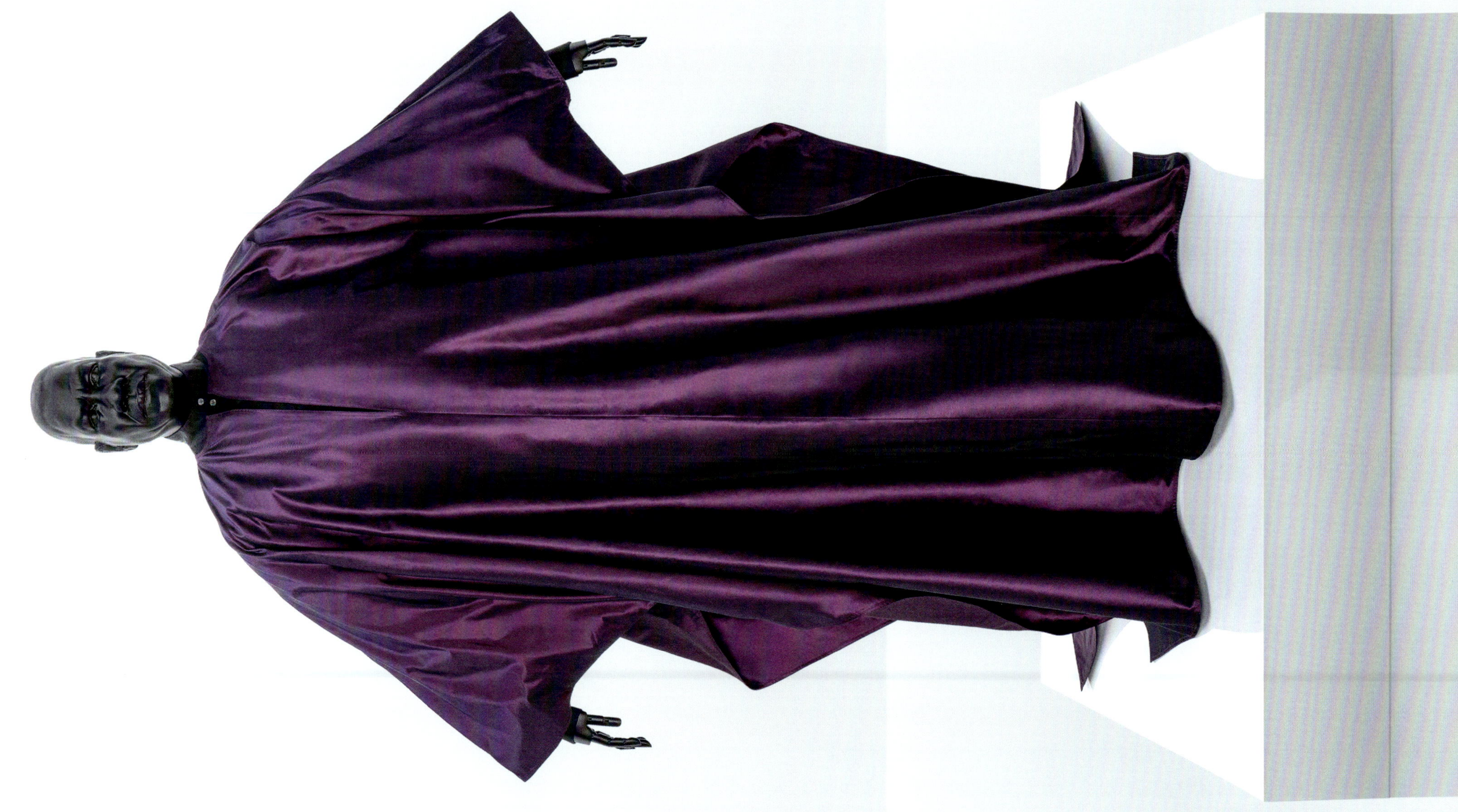

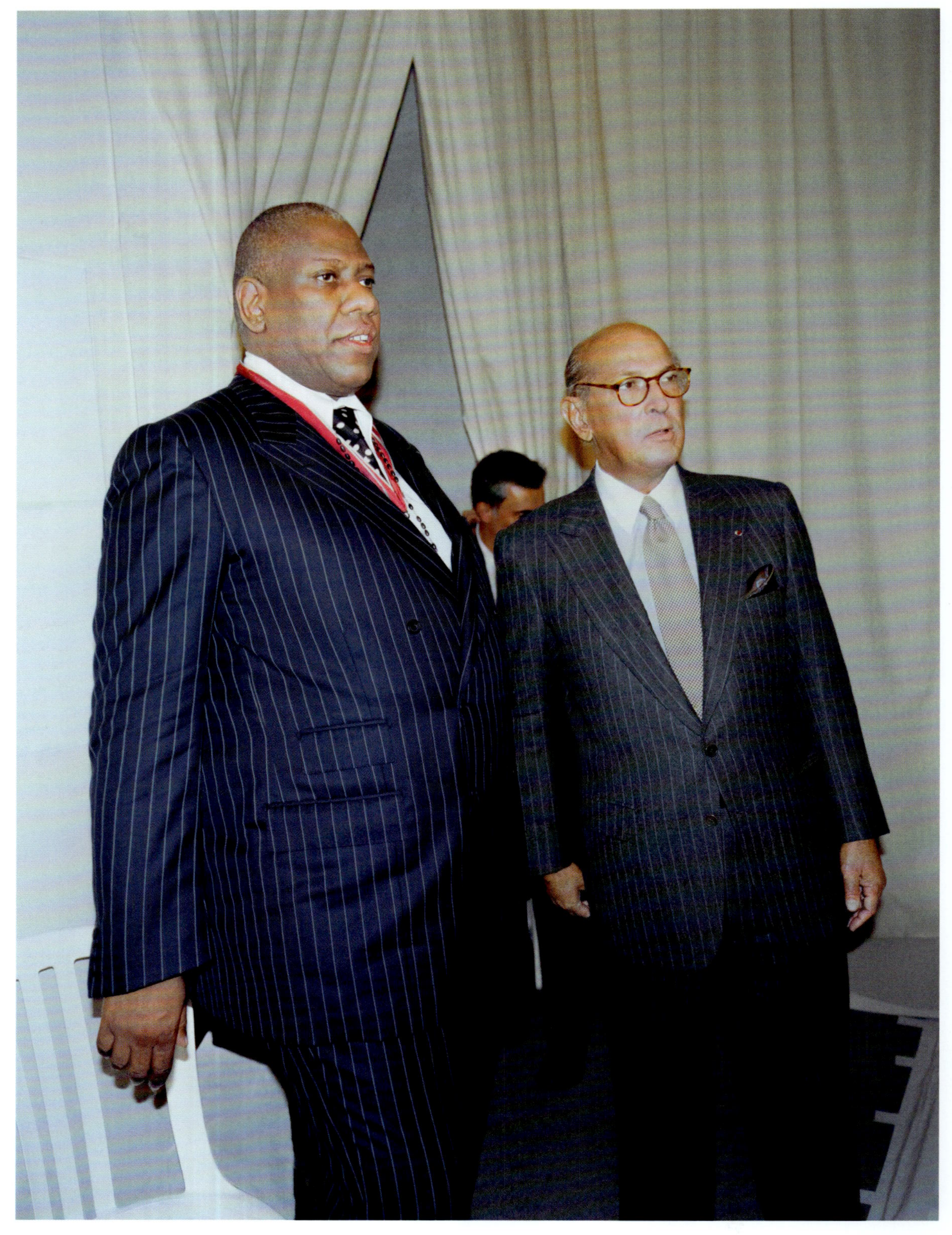

André and Oscar de la Renta backstage at the Balmain Spring/Summer 2002 haute couture runway show in Paris. Photo by Robert Fairer.

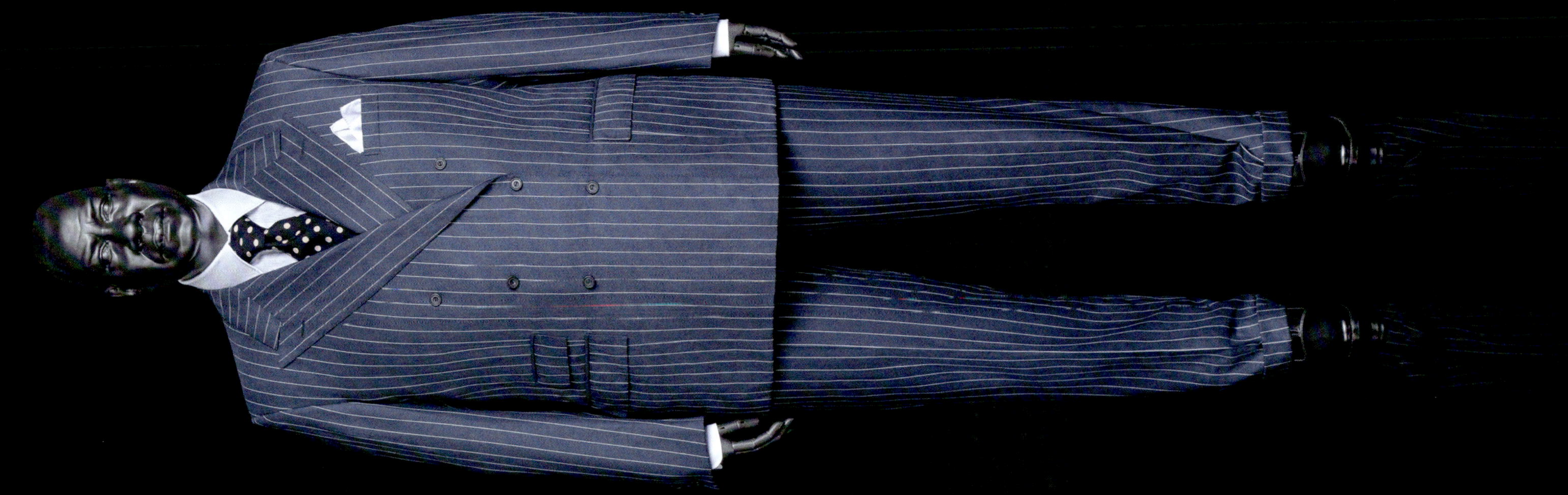

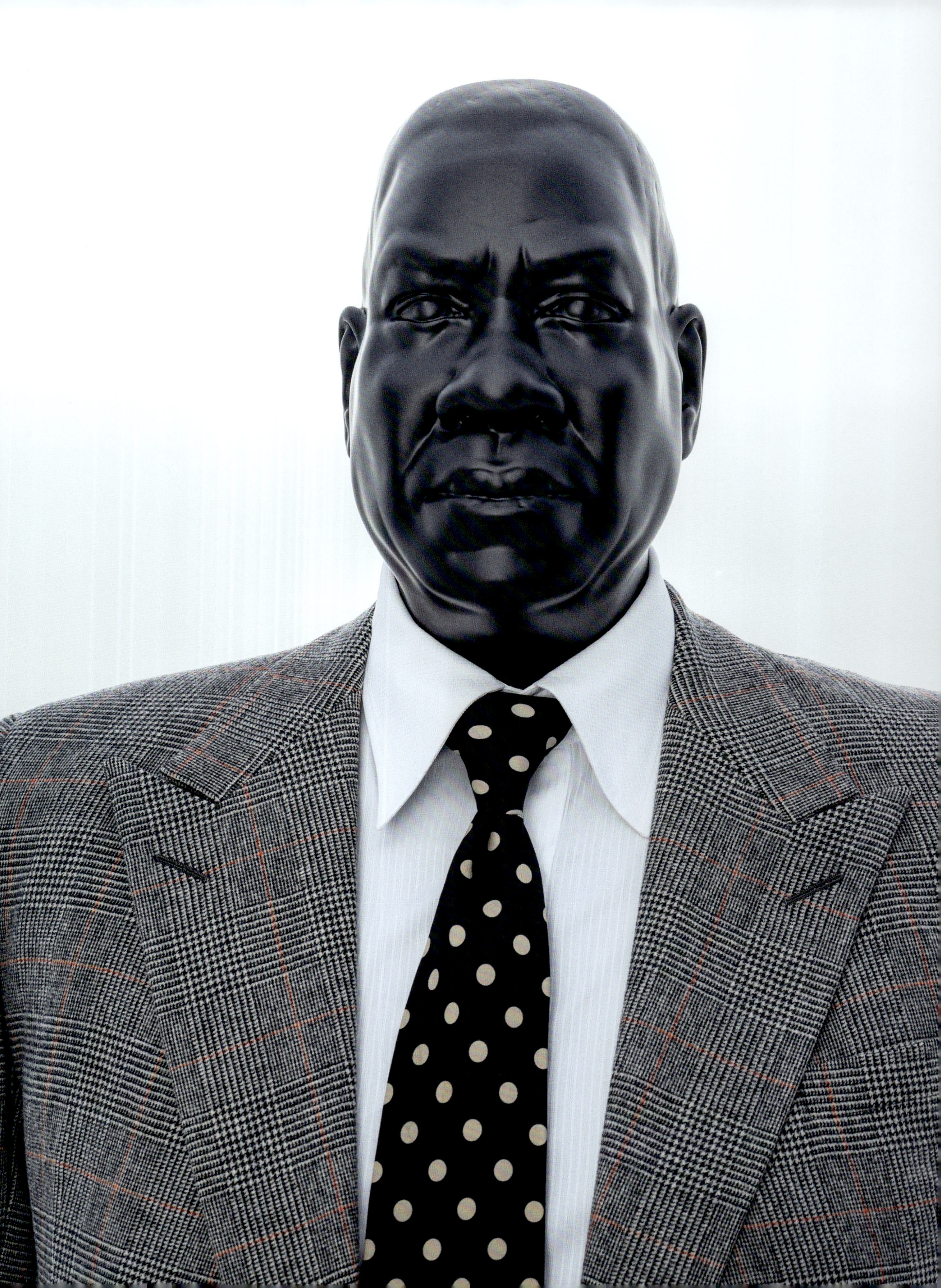

H. Huntsman & Sons suit

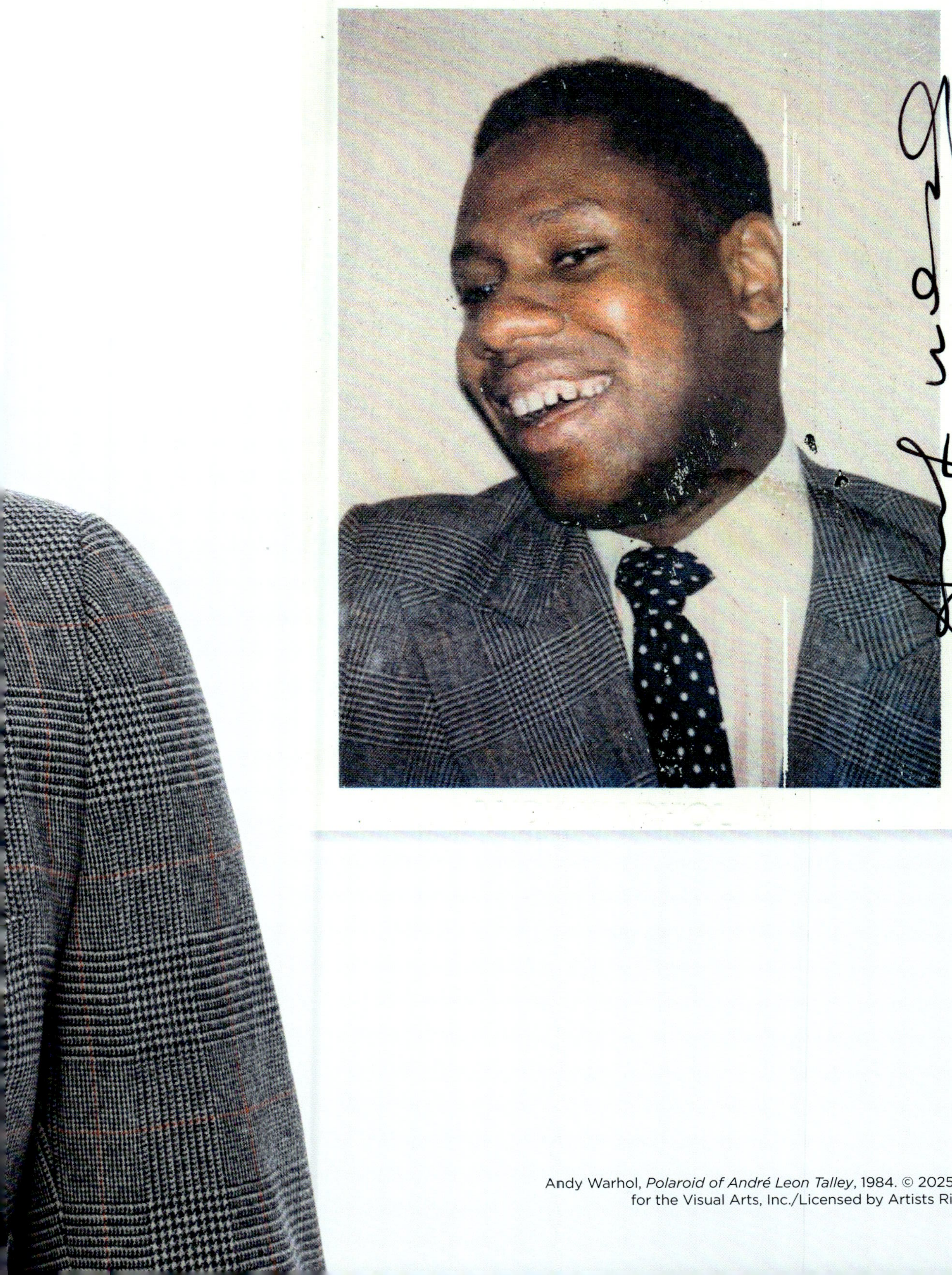

Andy Warhol, *Polaroid of André Leon Talley*, 1984. © 2025 The Andy Warhol Foundation for the Visual Arts, Inc./Licensed by Artists Rights Society (ARS), New York.

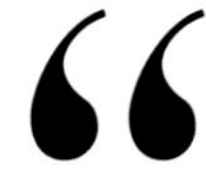

I had the pleasure of meeting André shortly after his arrival in New York. From the outset, it was evident that he possessed a **profound** passion for fashion and a deep understanding of the industry, largely shaped by his invaluable experience working alongside Mrs. Vreeland. His tireless dedication was **remarkable**; he was always the first to arrive and the last to leave, approaching every task with unwavering determination. Through his hard work and relentless pursuit of **excellence**, he transformed himself from a student into a true scholar of fashion.

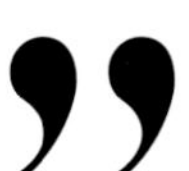

NORMA KAMALI

Norma Kamali sleeping bag coat and UGG boots

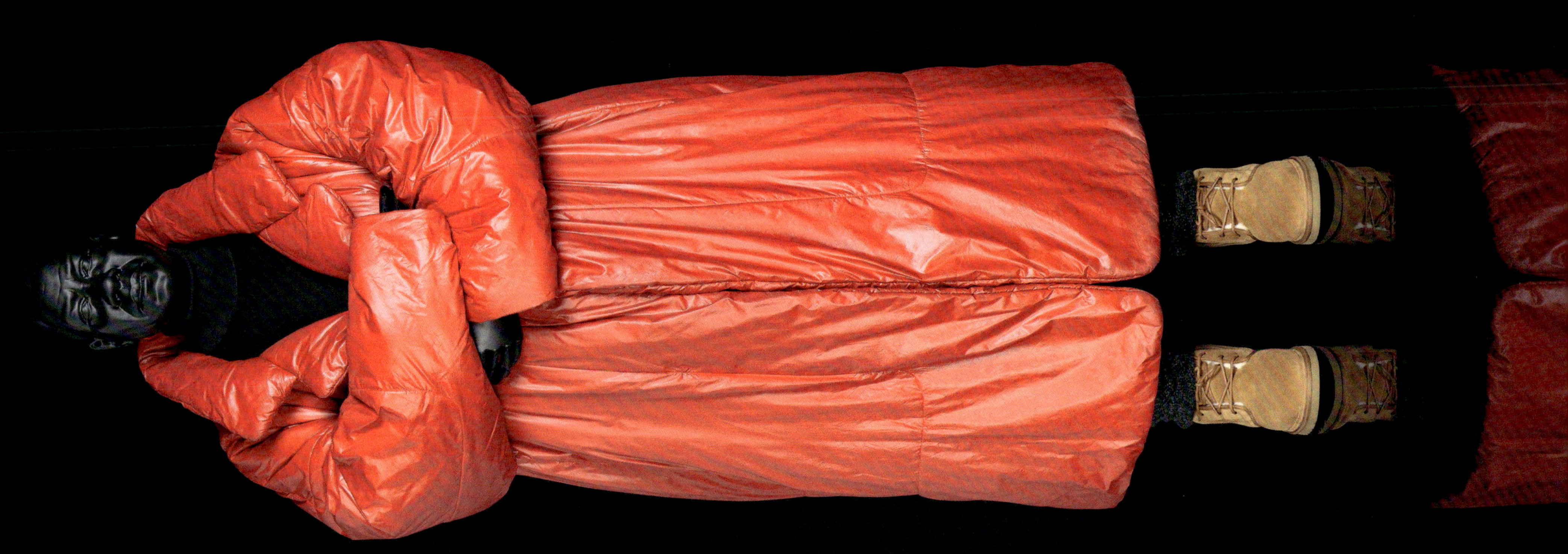

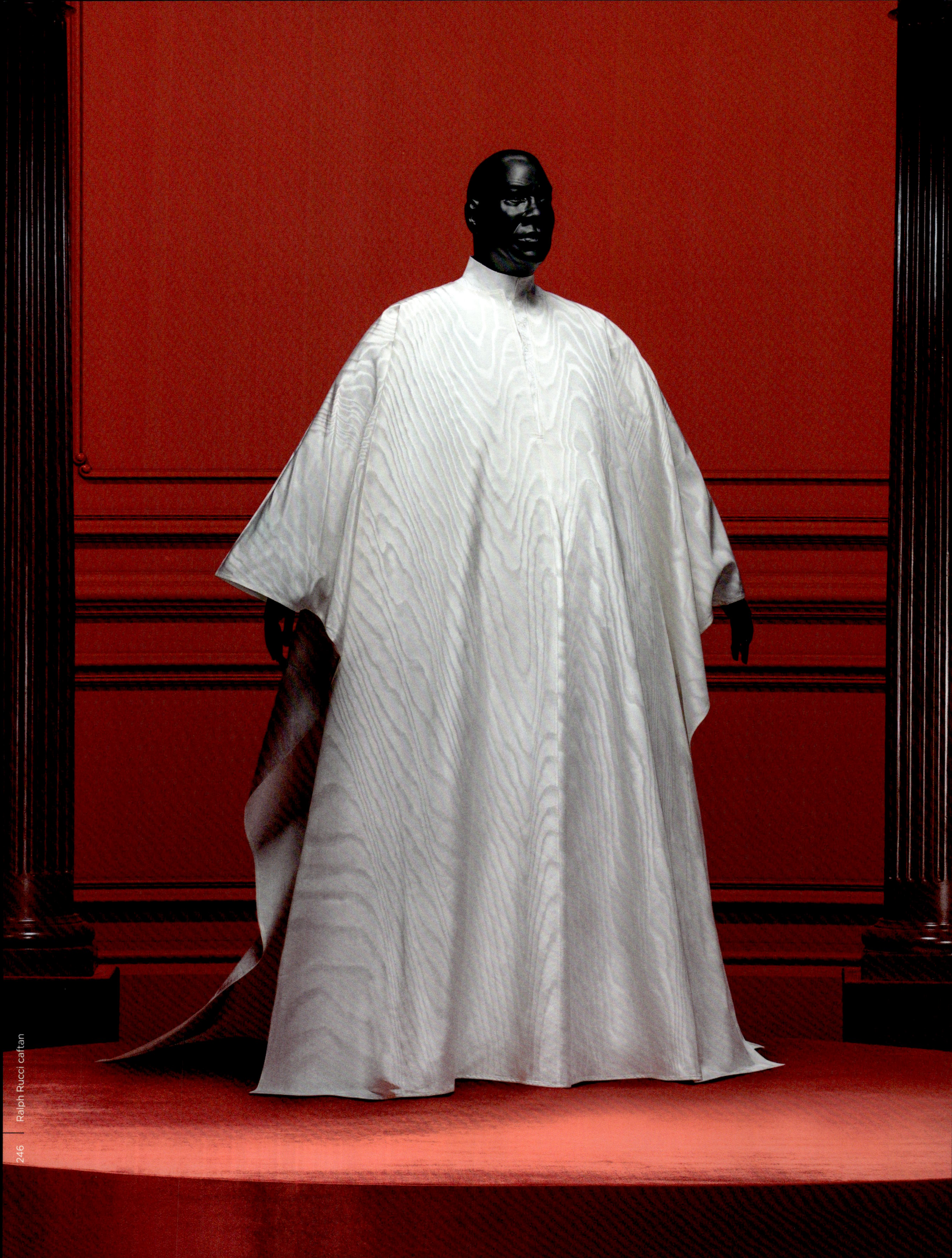

Ralph Rucci caftan

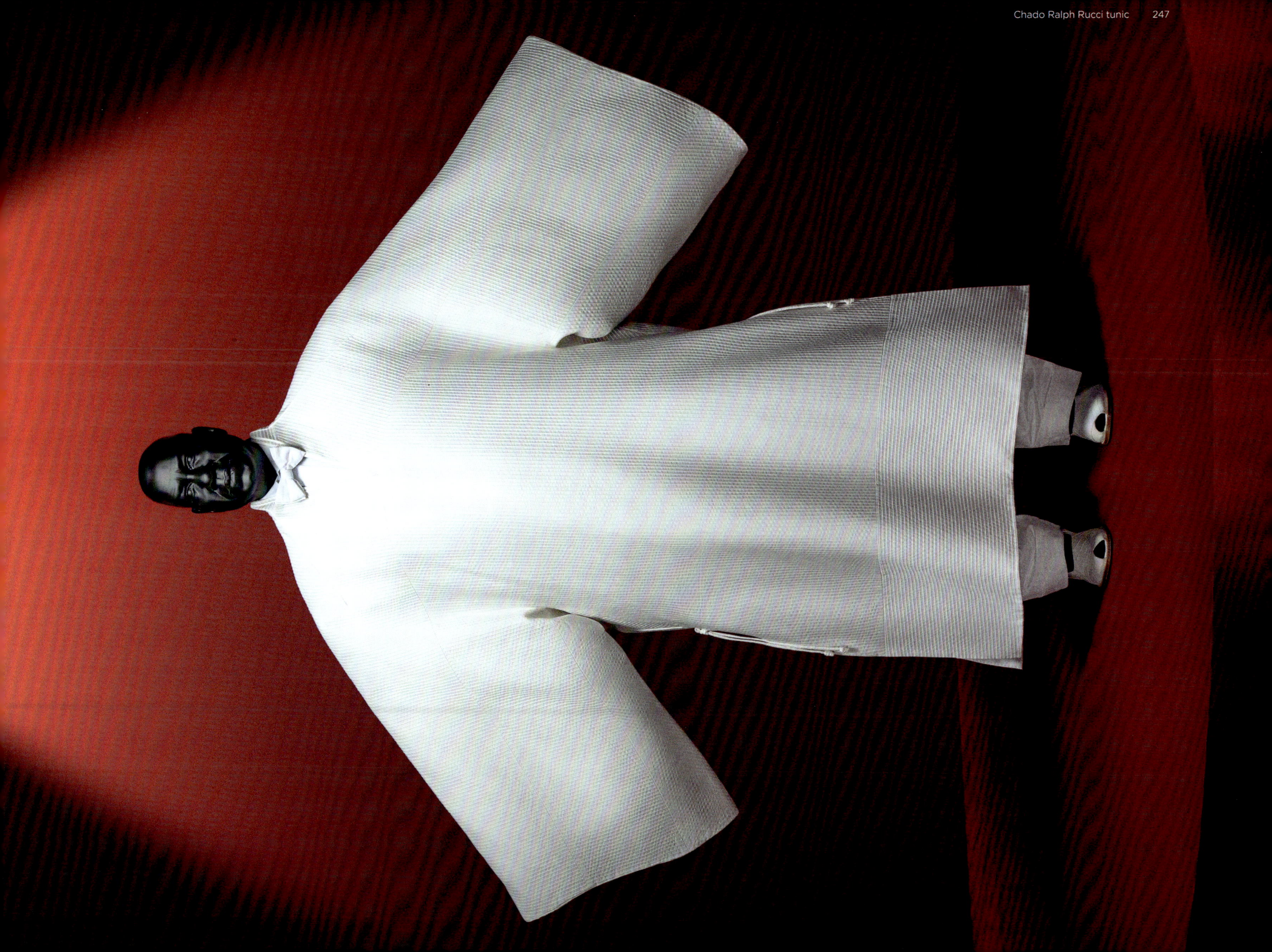

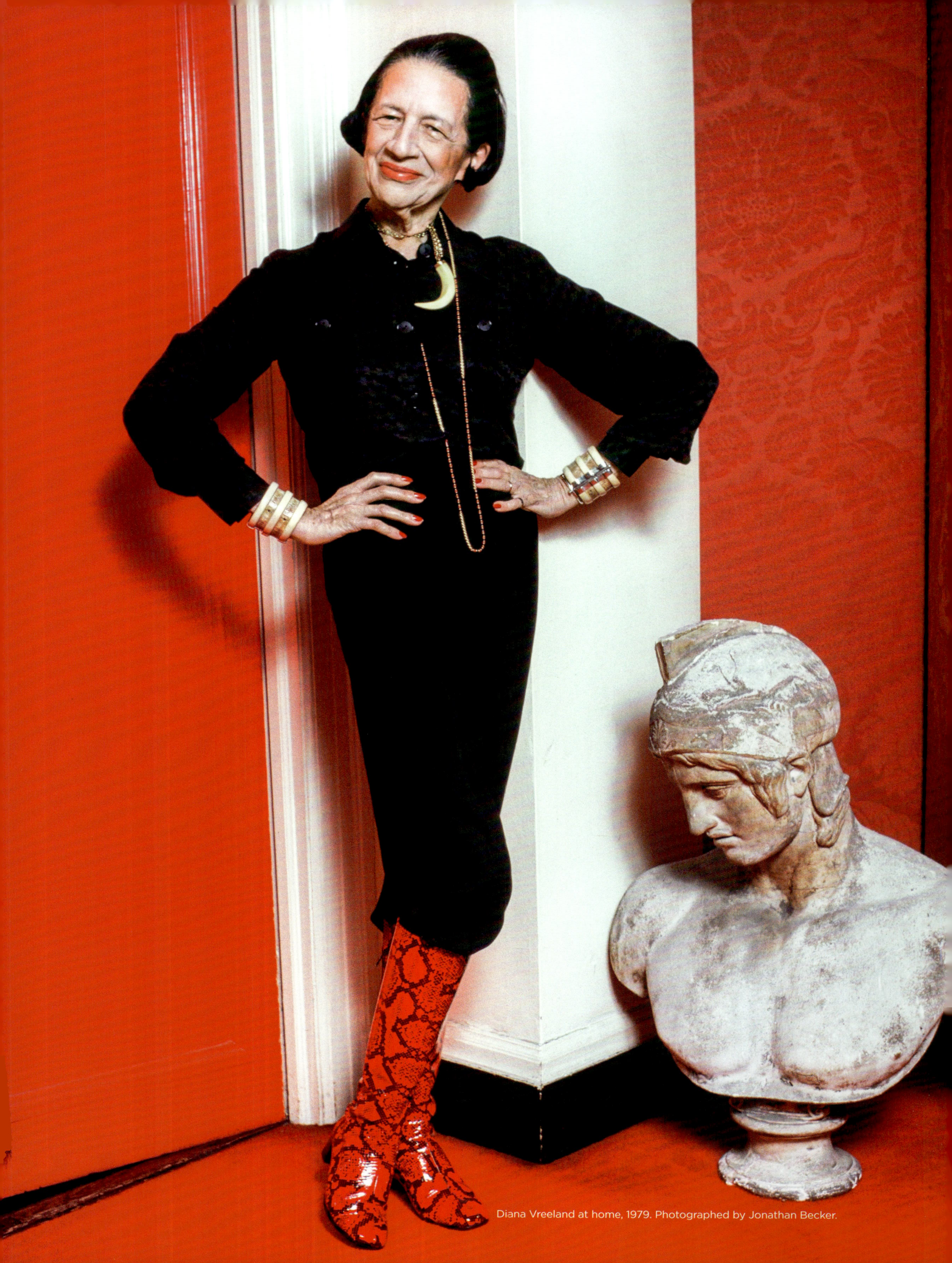

Diana Vreeland at home, 1979. Photographed by Jonathan Becker.

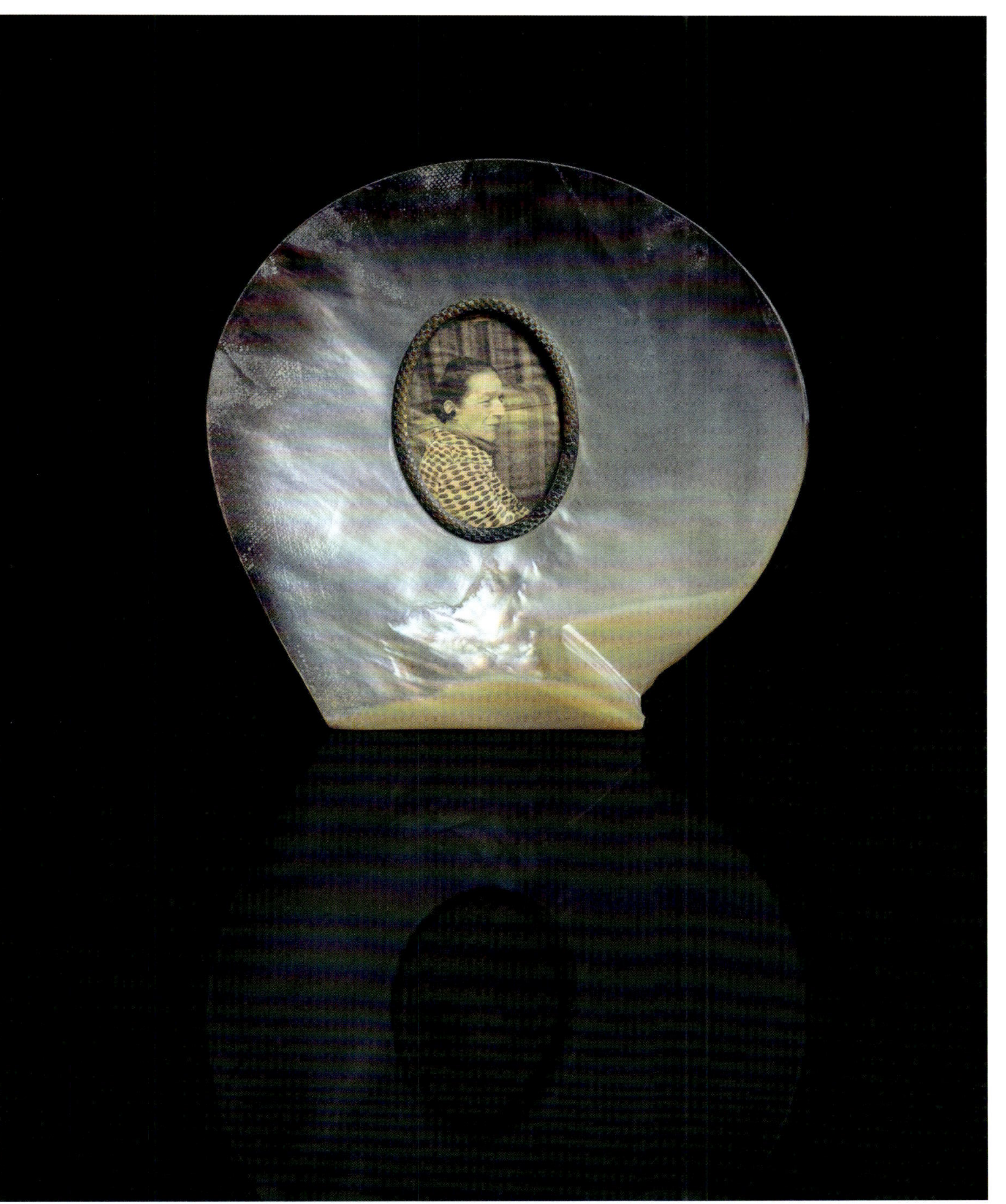

André's personal framed photo of Diana Vreeland

EMPRESS OF FASHION

Diana Vreeland was an extraordinary influence on André's life, second only to his grandmother. Renowned for her inimitable style and fashion intellect, she began her career at *Harper's Bazaar* in 1936. As editor in chief of *Vogue* in the 1960s, Vreeland embraced new ideals of beauty with eccentric, captivating editorials. In 1971 she became special consultant to the Costume Institute at The Metropolitan Museum of Art, taking on André as her beloved apprentice. She remained a devoted companion to André until her passing in 1989.

LOUIS XIV, EAT YOUR HEART OUT!

André’s friend Maureen Dowd, a columnist for *The New York Times*, commissioned this painting by Vietnamese artist Tuyen Vu Huy based on a 1701 portrait of Louis XIV by Baroque painter Hyacinthe Rigaud. The artist’s work uniquely blends fashion and history to explore themes of identity, like André’s own oeuvre as a cultural documentarian.

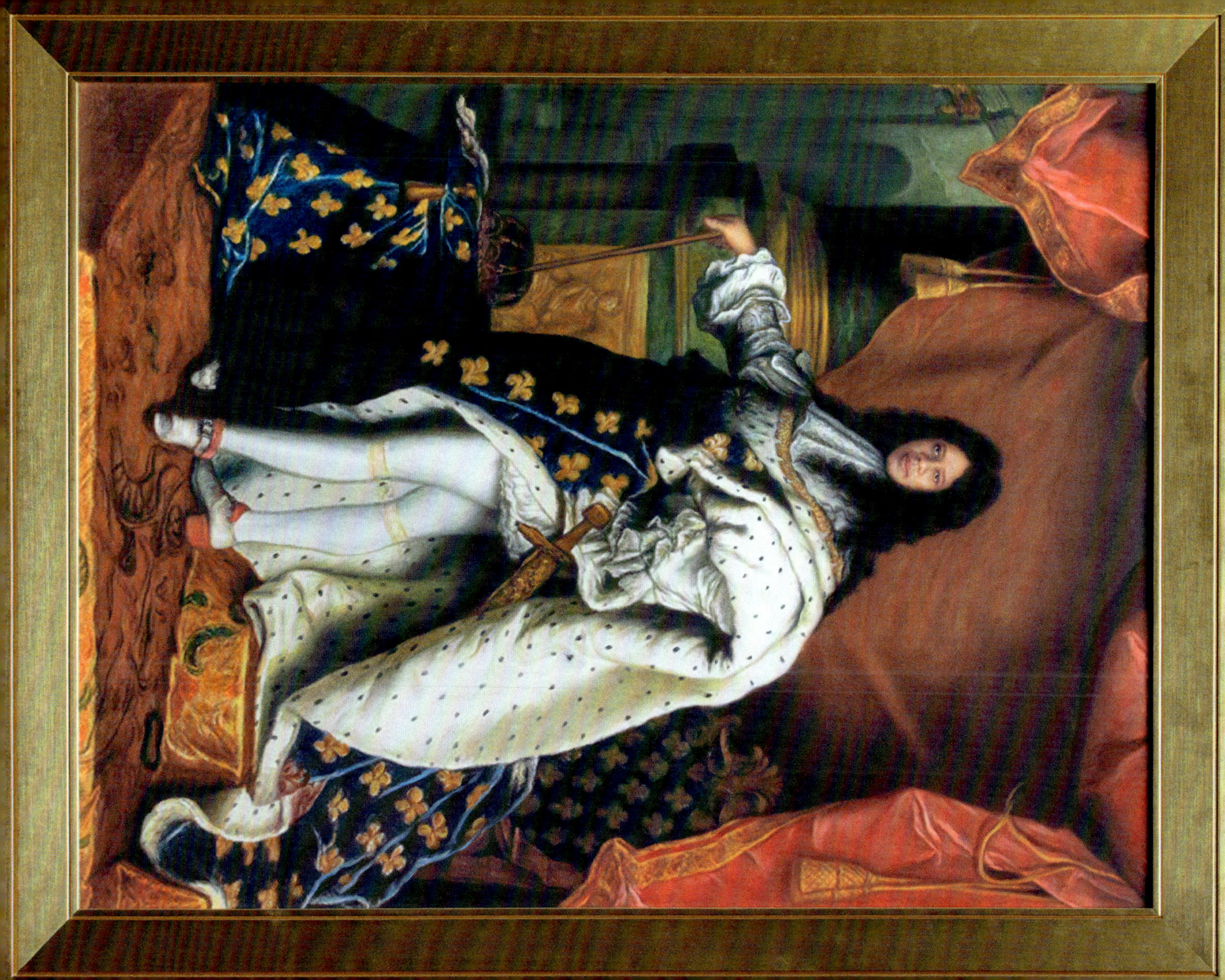

LIFE WITH ANDRÉ

Robert Fairer

"Robert, have you ever been to Rome?"

"Yes, André, just once . . . when I was a boy. I was a choral scholar and I came to the Vatican to sing before the pope."

That was the only time I ever saw André truly surprised. He squealed with delight as we sat on the landscaped terrace of a penthouse overlooking the terracotta rooftops of Rome. Then he roared with laughter. André was into "moments" and especially magnificent ones. Later he was invited to speak at the Oxford Union Society in England and he wrote to me, "it was one of the biggest moments of my entire LIFE! AND I HAVE HAD SOME MAJOR BIG MOMENTS!"

We had a super connection. I was his favorite "married, straight, white, male photographer" and over many years, we enjoyed assignments together around the world. Everything about our *Vogue* shoots unfolded like being on the set of a great movie. He was the film director and everyone took their cue from him. When André walked into the room, things started to happen. Everyone wanted to please, nothing was impossible. Louis Vuitton flagship store windows were dismantled because he wanted THAT trunk in the shot. With a wave of his arm, shop assistants ran to keep up with his rapid-fire commands, seeking the ultimate in beauty, opulence, and style: "It's for *VOGUE*."

The Ritz in Paris with Miuccia, Karl, or Valentino; Palm Beach with FLOTUS; Café de Flore lunching with supermodels—wherever we went people on the streets stopped in their tracks, wanting to say hello, to thank him for his inspirational example and shake his hand. Our work covered the zeitgeist, the Golden Age of Fashion, documenting and recording the established and the new at a portrait sitting, a couture atelier fitting, a grand hotel backdrop—or shooting behind the scenes with Marc Jacobs at Louis Vuitton, Karl Lagerfeld at Chanel, or John Galliano at Dior. André's voice cutting through the clamor of a backstage in full flow: "Robert, did you get the dress?"

"Yes, André," I would reply.

"Well follow her, follow her!" he would laugh. The models loved André's presence backstage.

The assignments and the downtime I spent with André remain the very pinnacle of everything that I hoped for in my career. He was Manhattan, Paris, and Rome. He was a Fashion Superhero personified: elegance, presence, strikingly beautiful and, indeed, behind the capes and suits, a kind, humble, and hugely supportive man who spoke fondly of my wife Vanessa, my mother and children, always happy to receive any "News please!"

André lived for the next big thing, and his staccato superlatives and energetic enthusiasm for a dress, a girl, or a look—all brilliantly placed and historically referenced on the spot—and his excitement at other people's success are the memories that run around my head. There really are no words that can put across the affection that I feel toward him: his need for good manners, the discipline instilled, of making sure "every dress and photograph tells a story" and the everlasting gift of knowing and working with one of the greatest men in fashion.

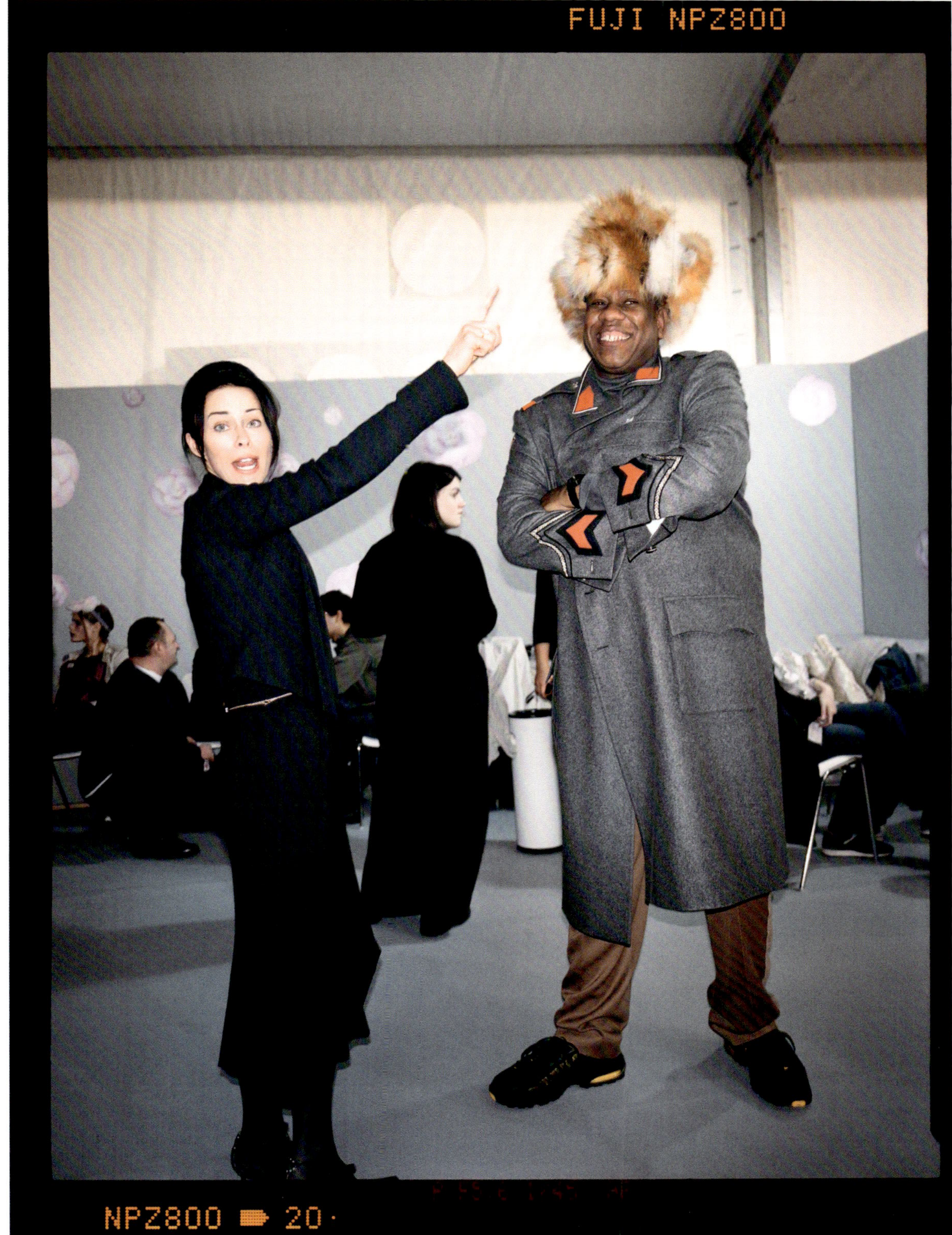

André with Amanda, Lady Harlech, backstage at the Chanel Spring/Summer 2002 haute couture runway show in Paris. Photo by Robert Fairer.

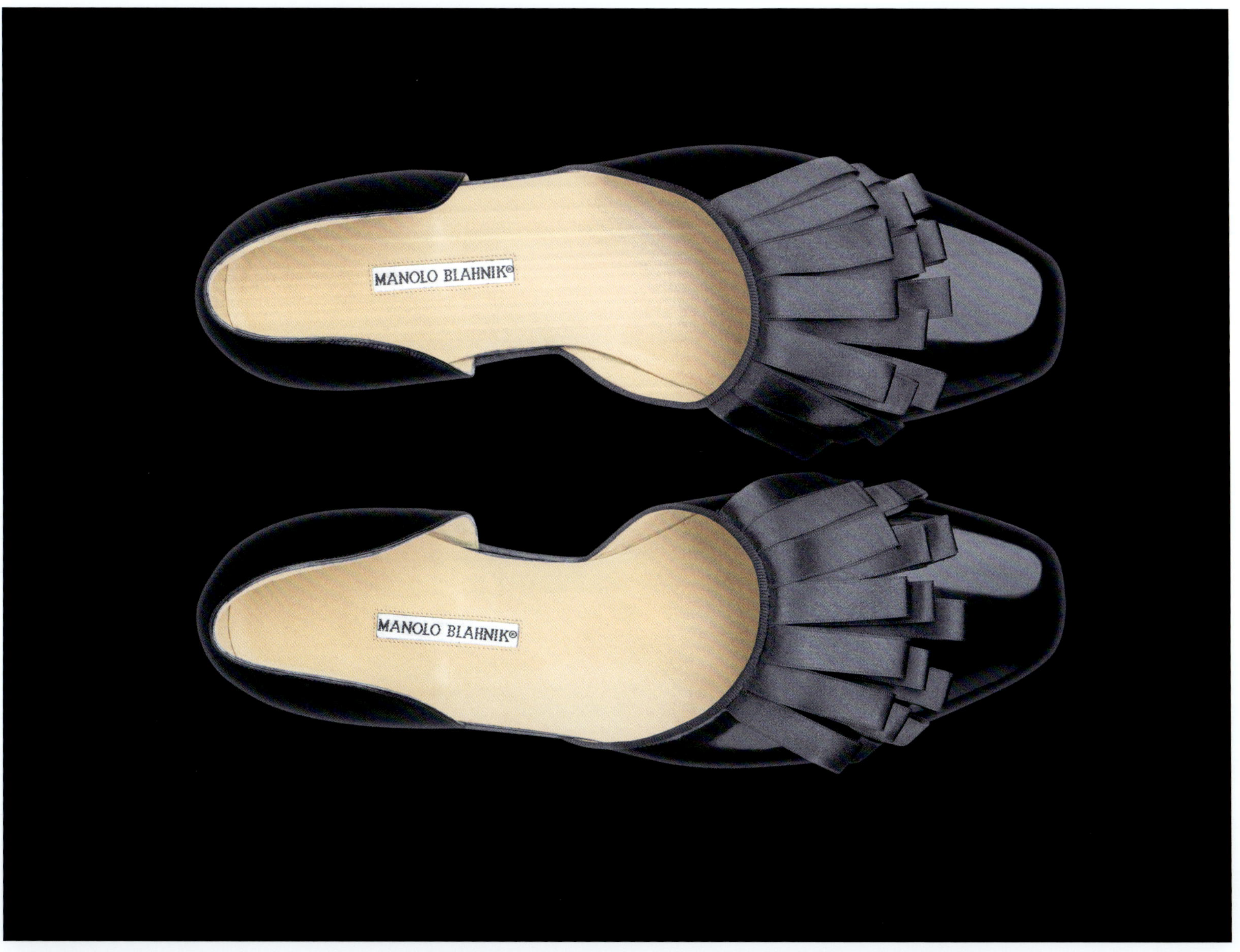
MANOLO BLAHNIK®
MANOLO BLAHNIK®

“

What **can I say** about André?
He’s the only one. The **only one**.

”

MANOLO BLAHNIK

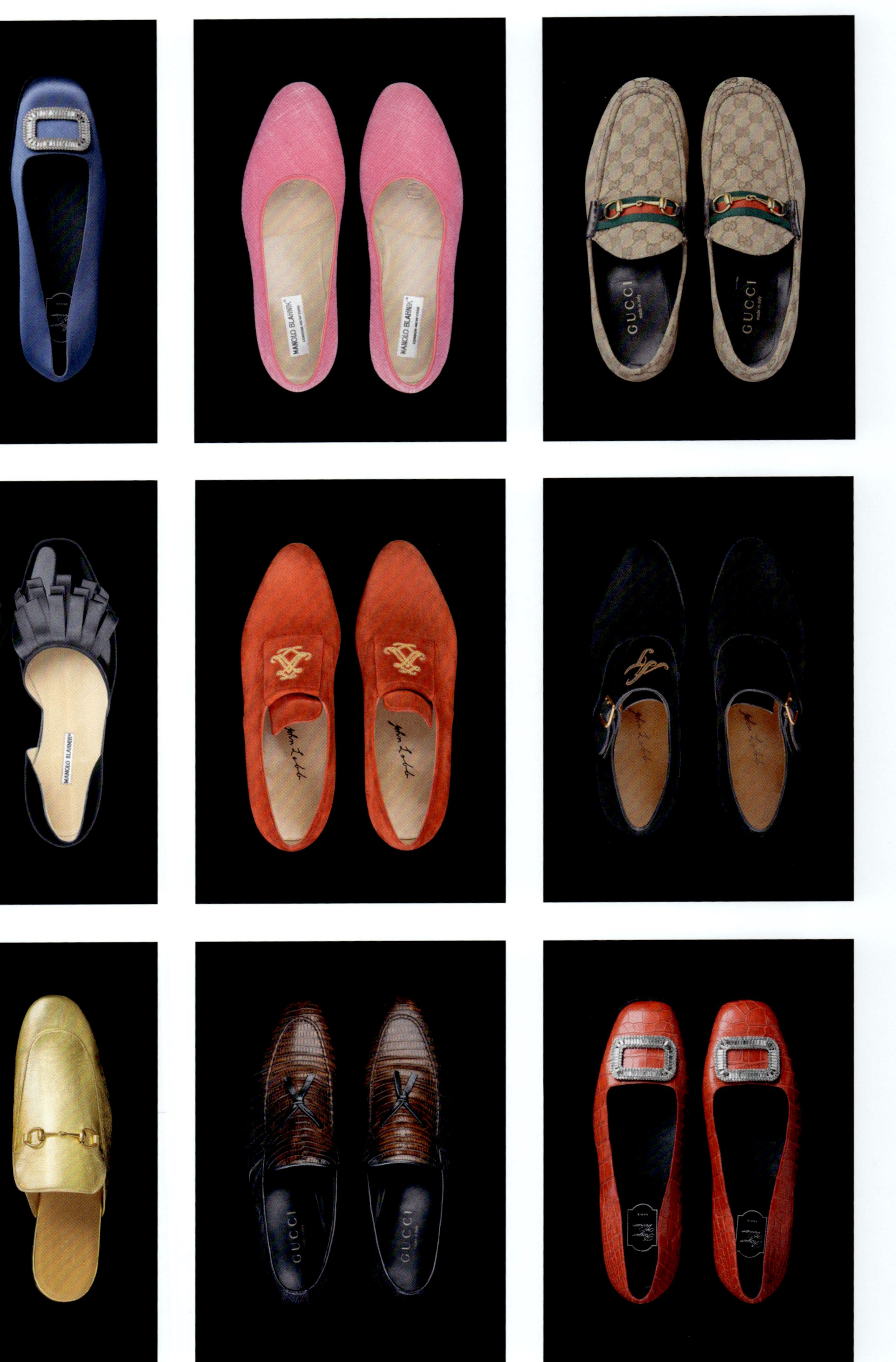

Left to right, above: Roger Vivier, Manolo Blahnik, Gucci; center: Manolo Blahnik, John Lobb, John Lobb; below: Gucci, Gucci, Roger Vivier

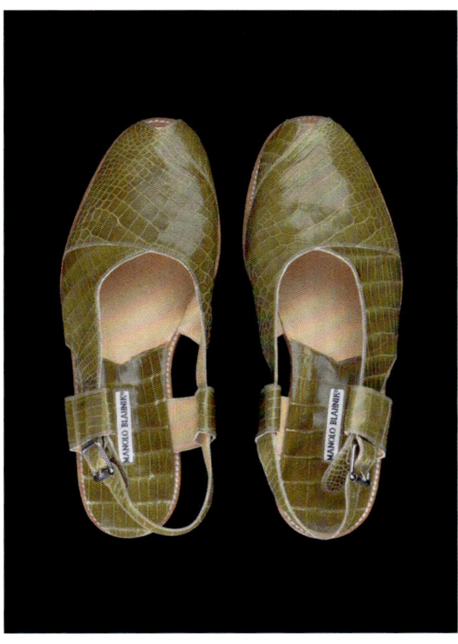

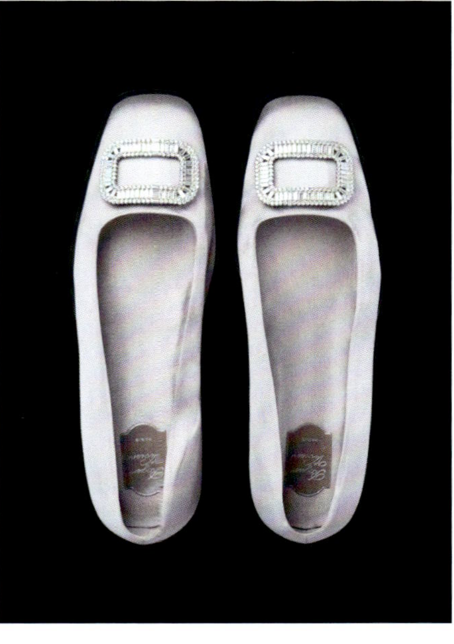

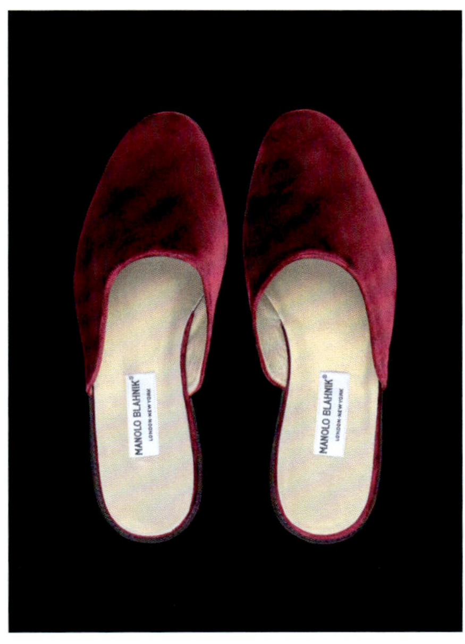

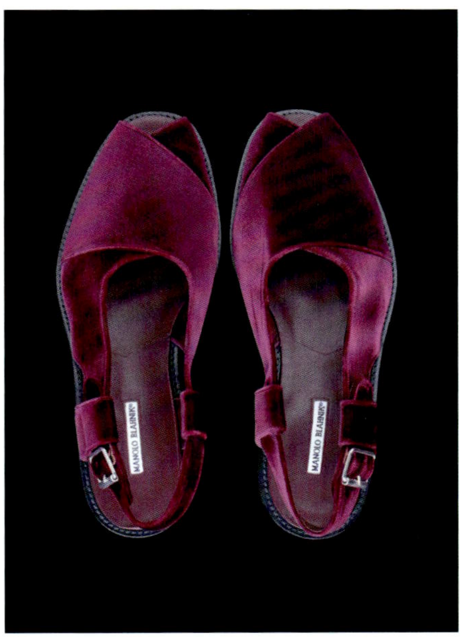

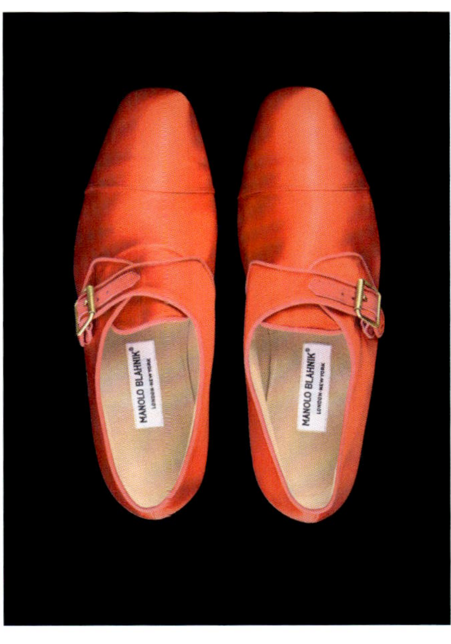

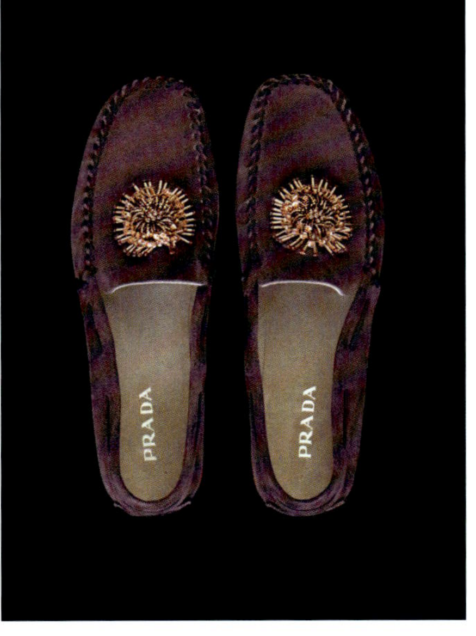

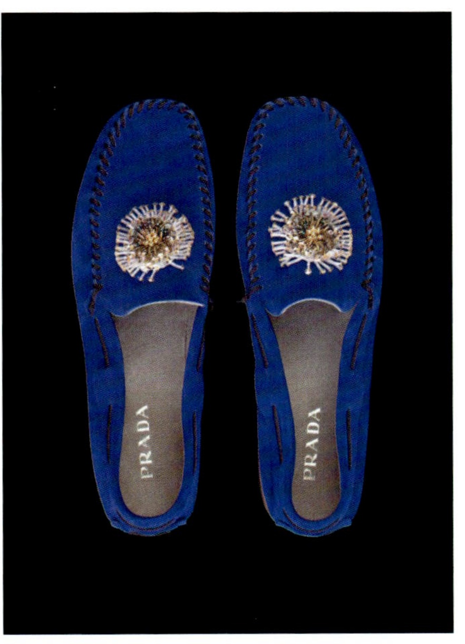

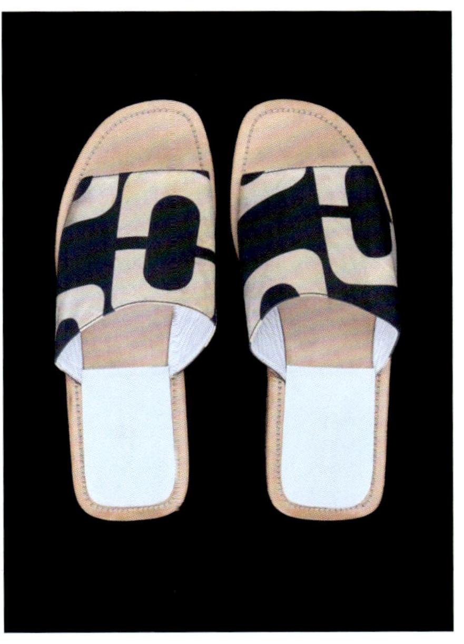

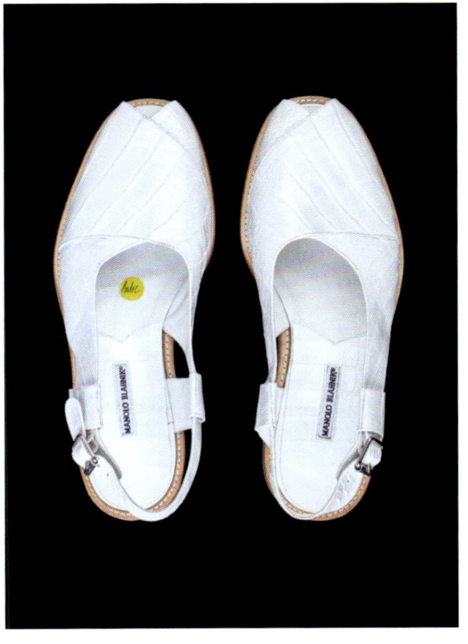

Left to right, above: Manolo Blahnik, Roger Vivier, Manolo Blahnik; center: Manolo Blahnik, Manolo Blahnik, Prada; below: Prada, Manolo Blahnik, Manolo Blahnik

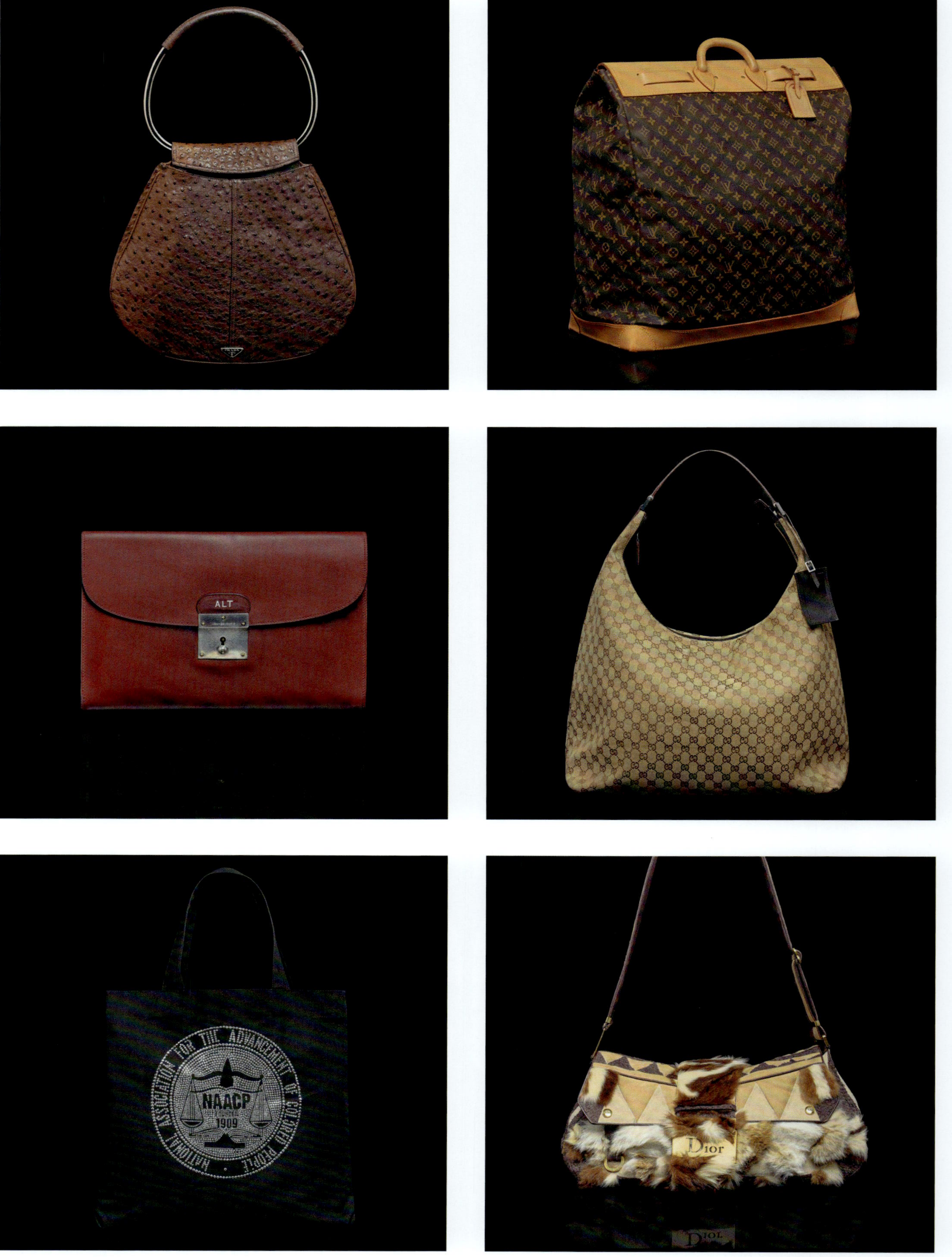

Left to right, above: Prada, Louis Vuitton; center: Hermès, Fendi; below: National Association for the Advancement of Colored People, Dior

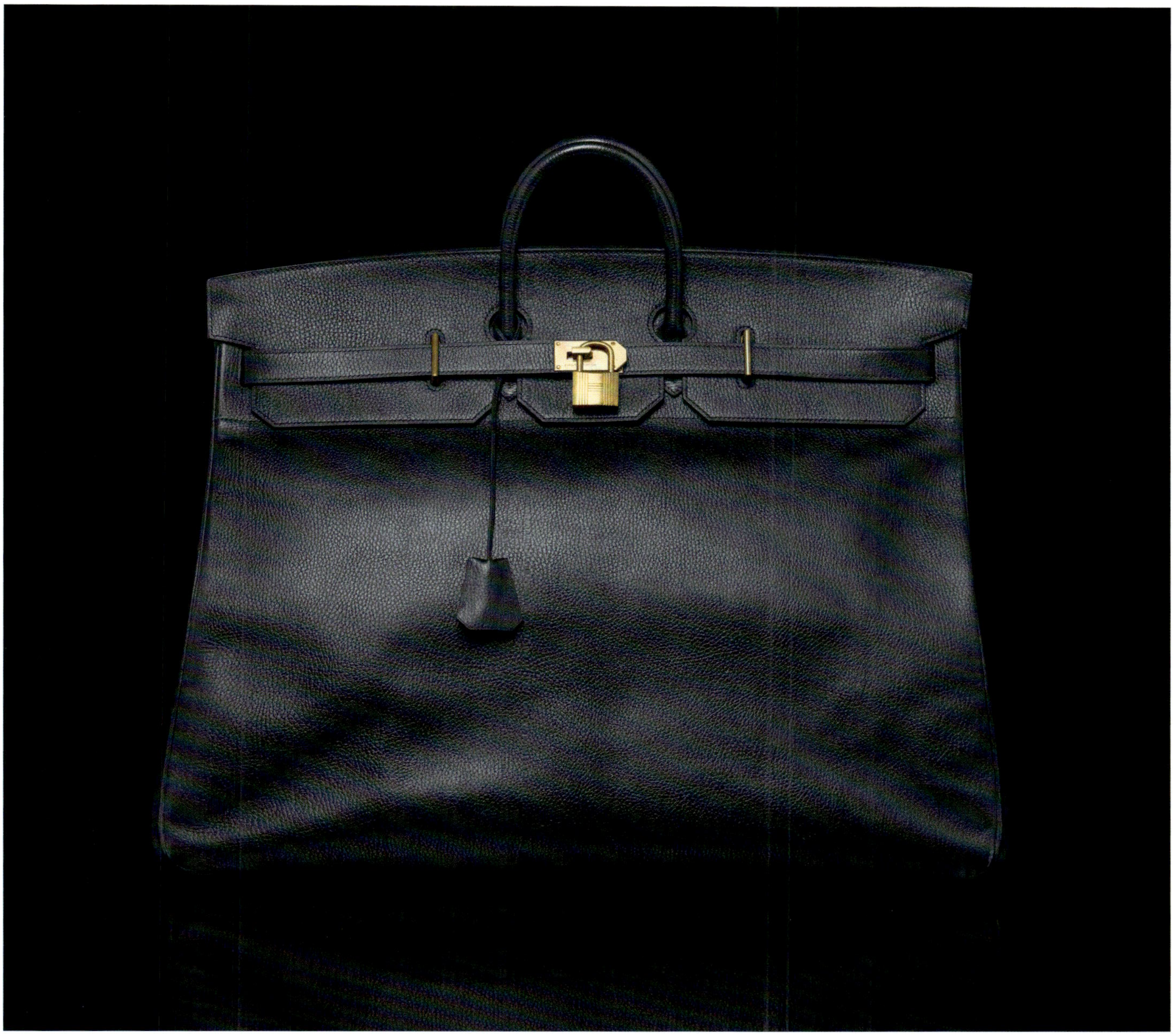

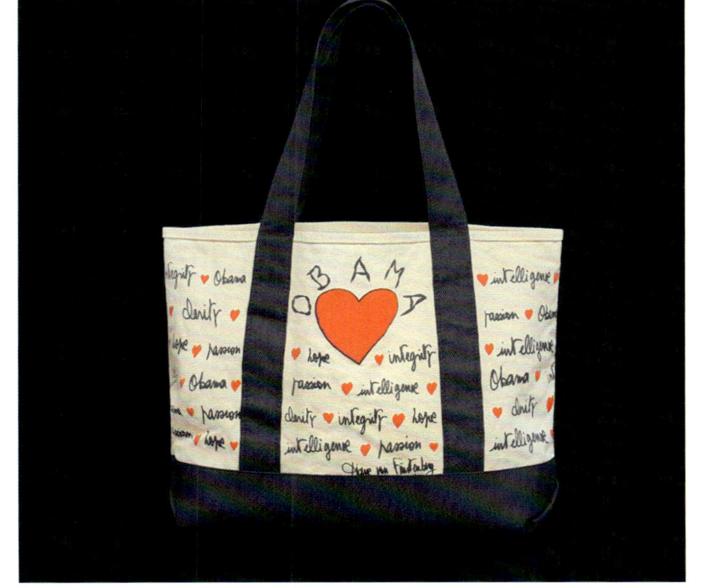

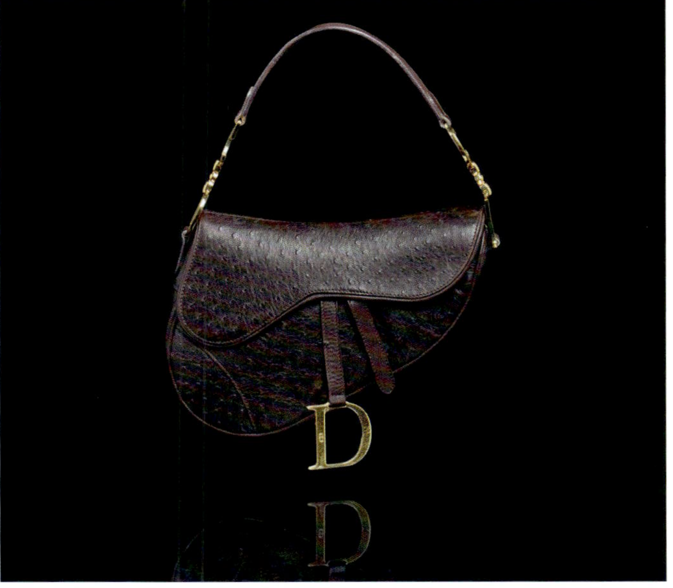

Above: Hermès; below: Diane von Furstenberg, Dior

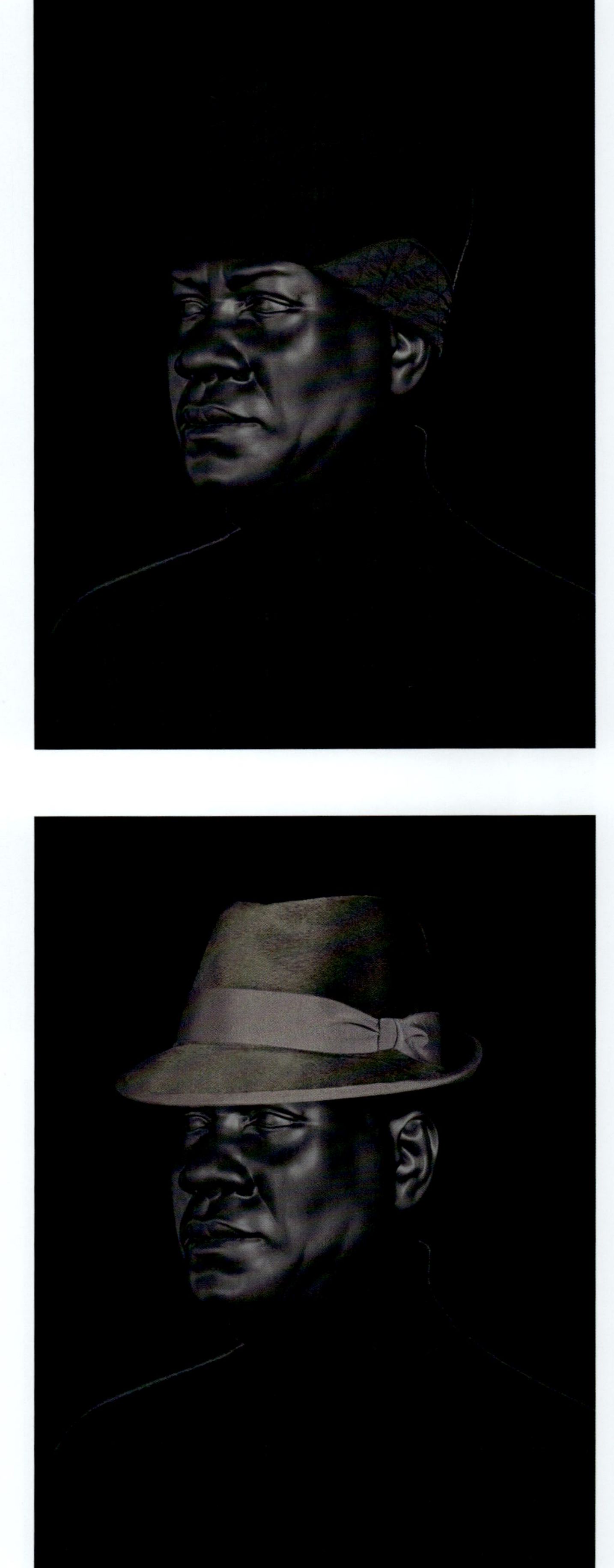

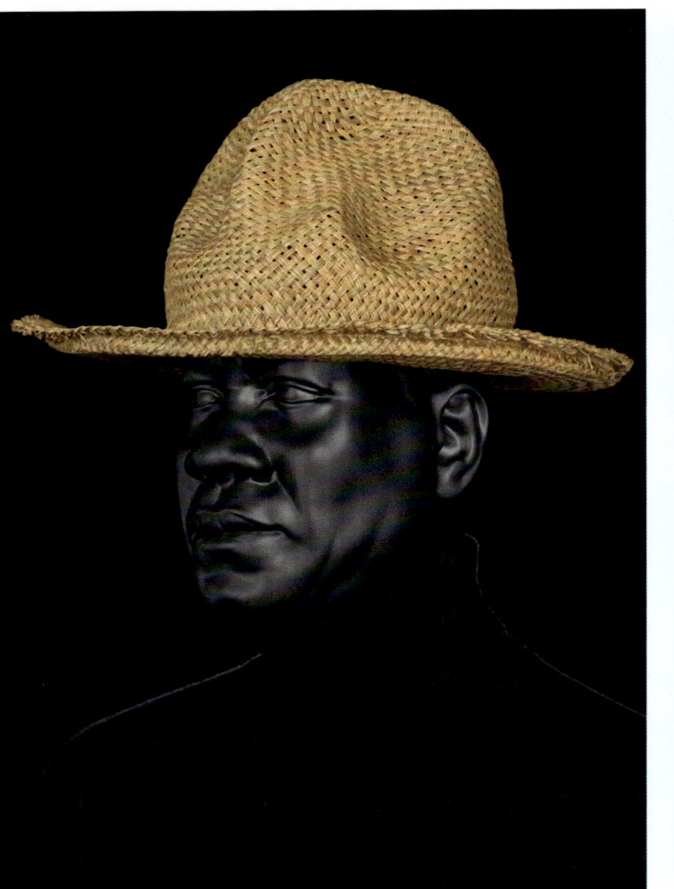

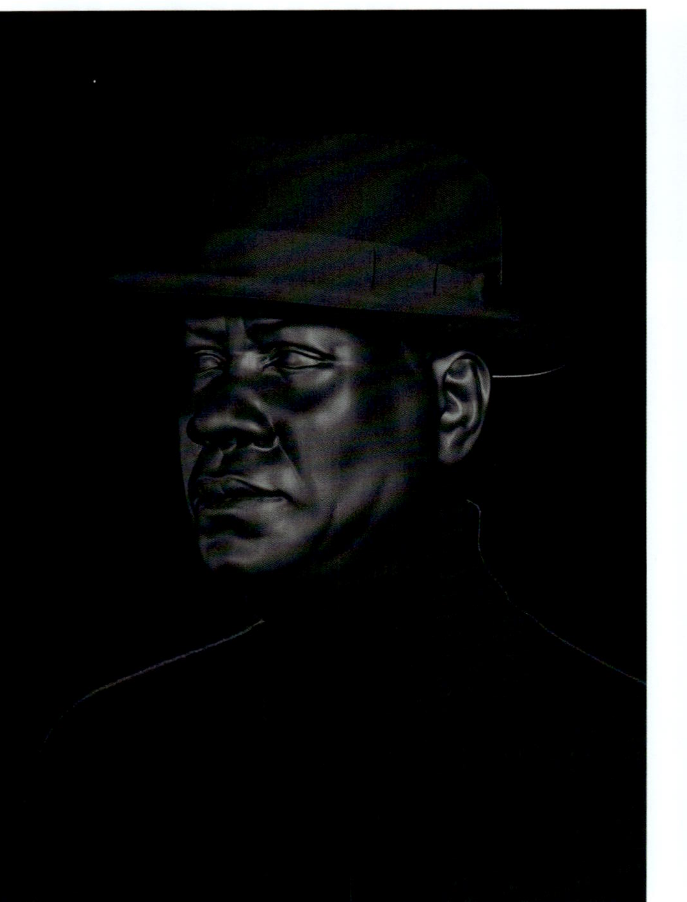

Left to right, above: Vivienne Westwood, Comme des Garçons Homme Plus; below: Lock & Co. Hatters, Rod Keenan

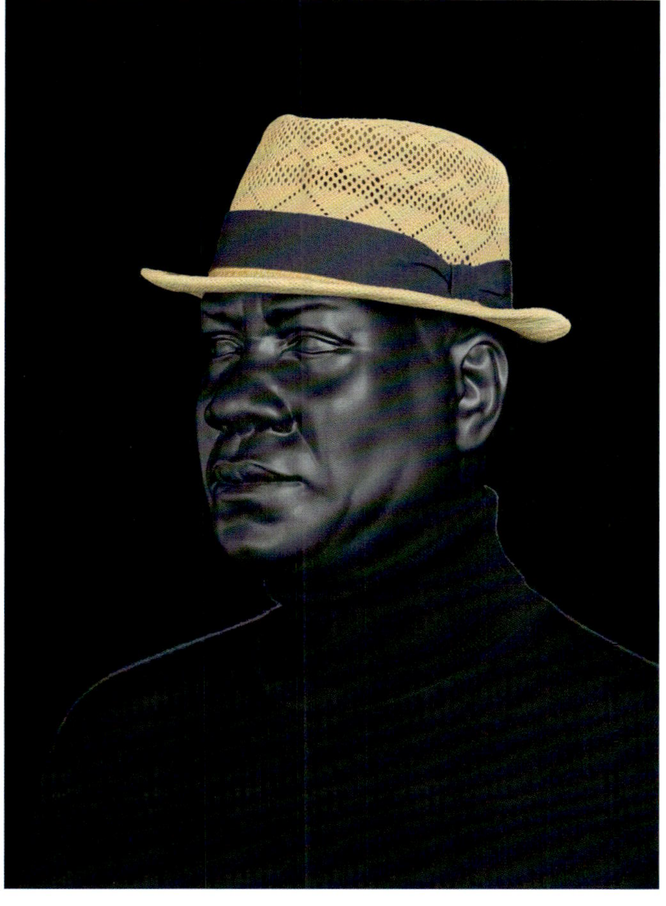
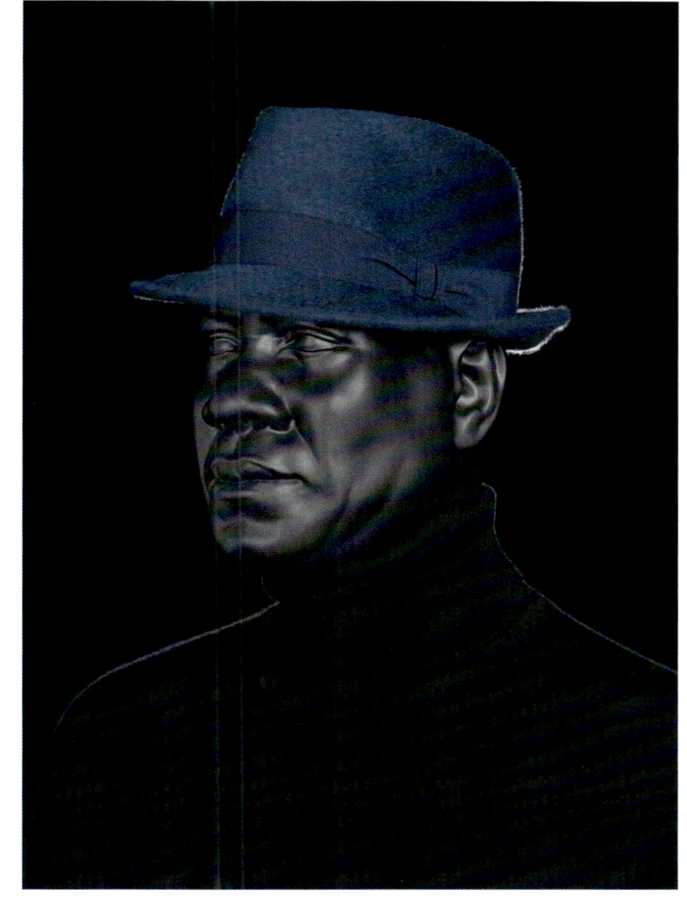
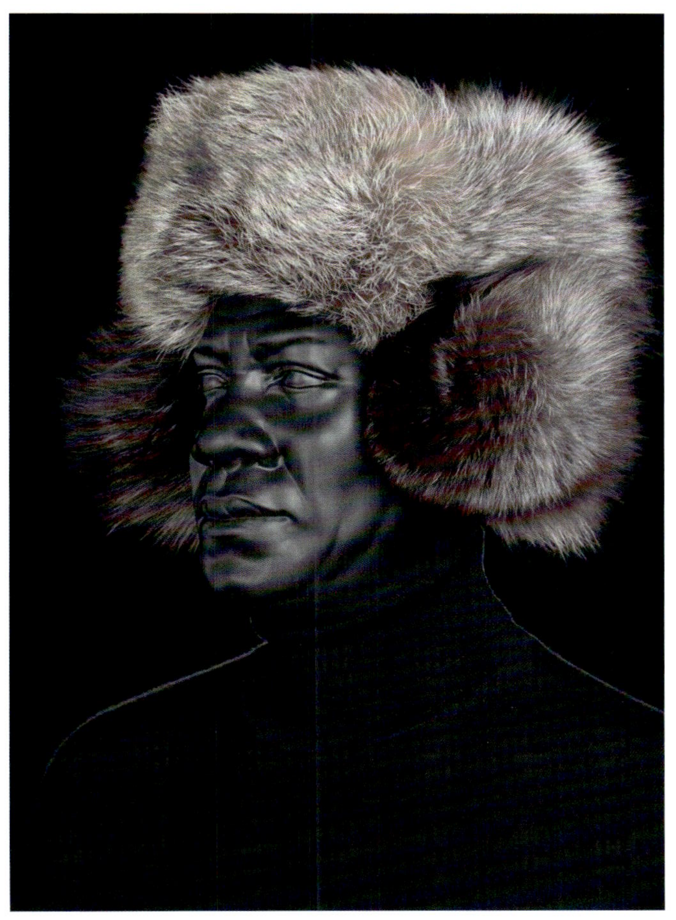
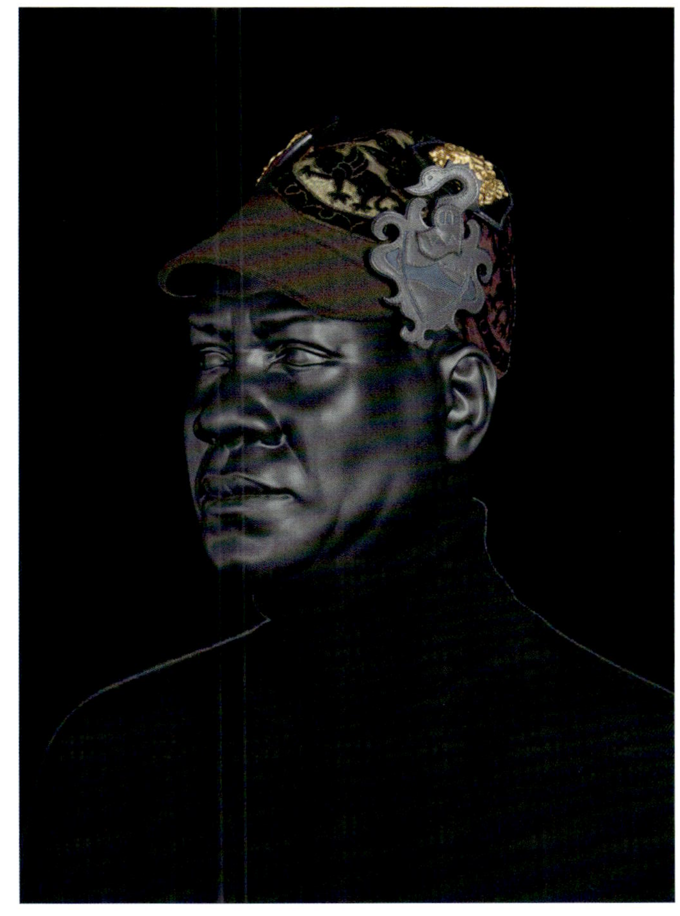

Left to right, above: Rod Keenan, Rod Keenan; below: Podium, Miu Miu

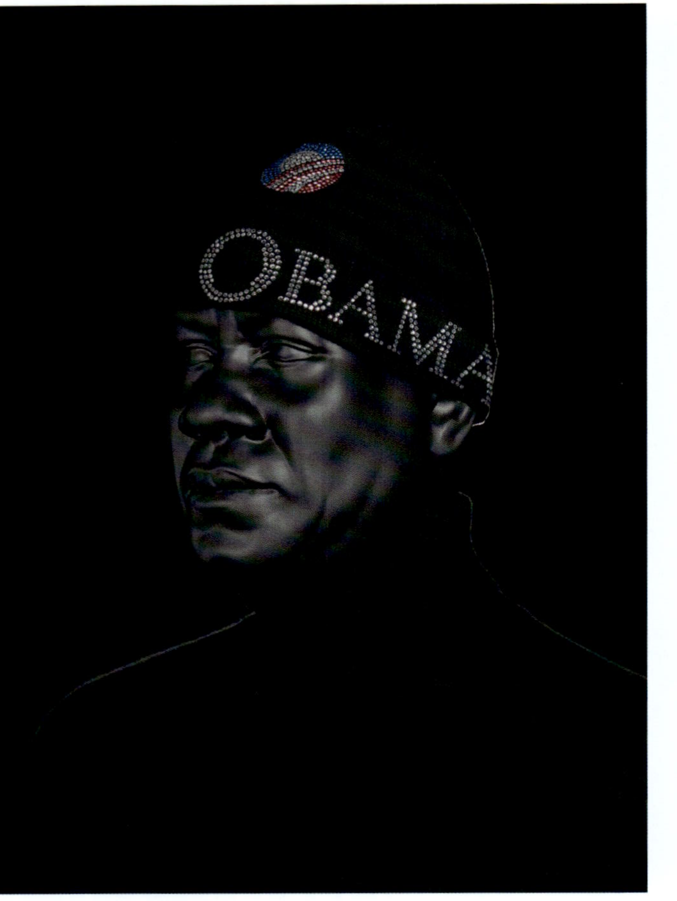

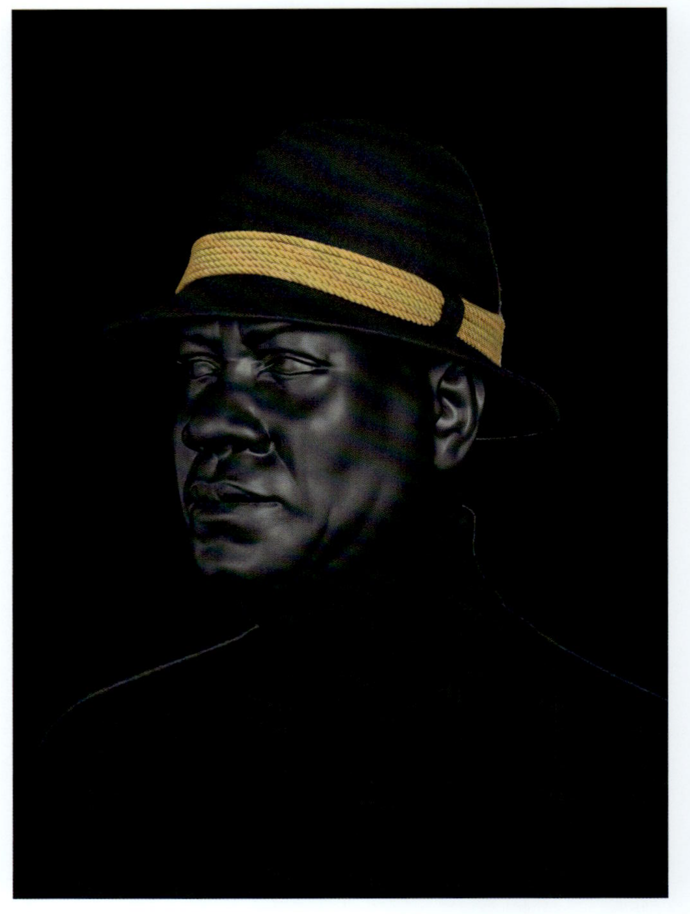

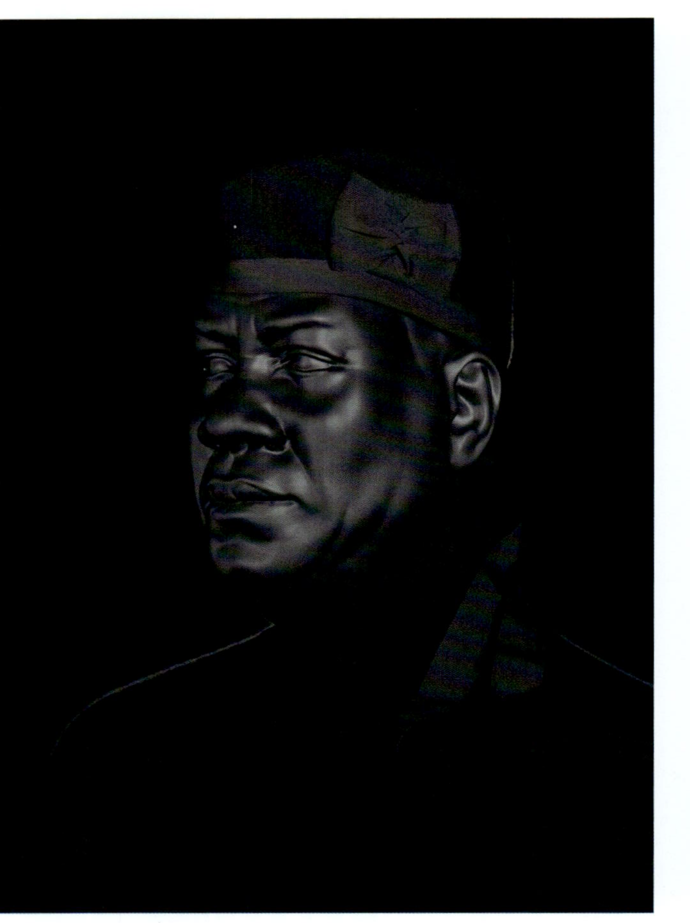

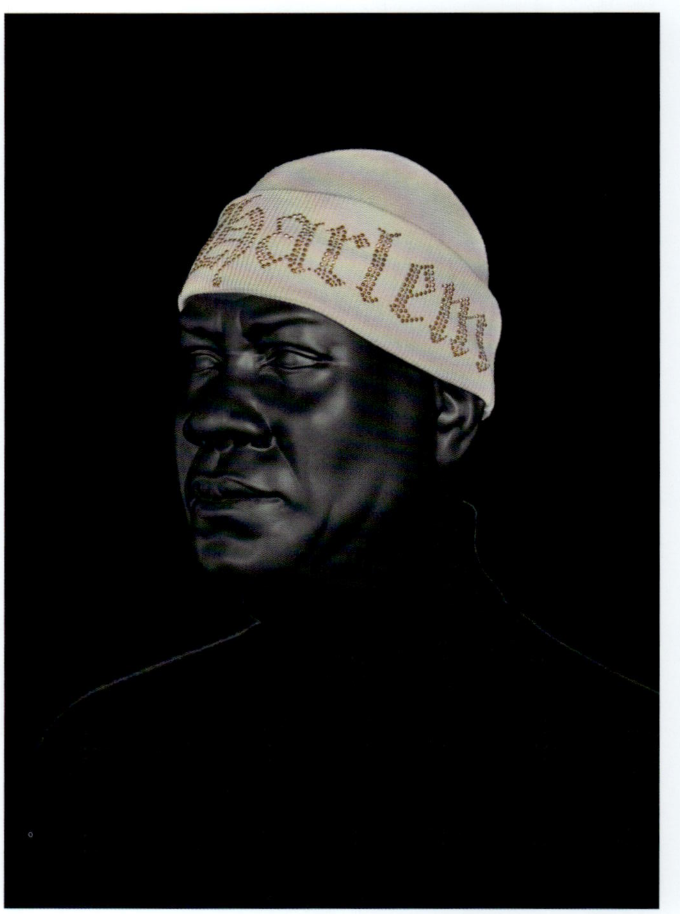

Left to right, above: City Lab, Hutkönig Regensburg; below: no label, City Lab

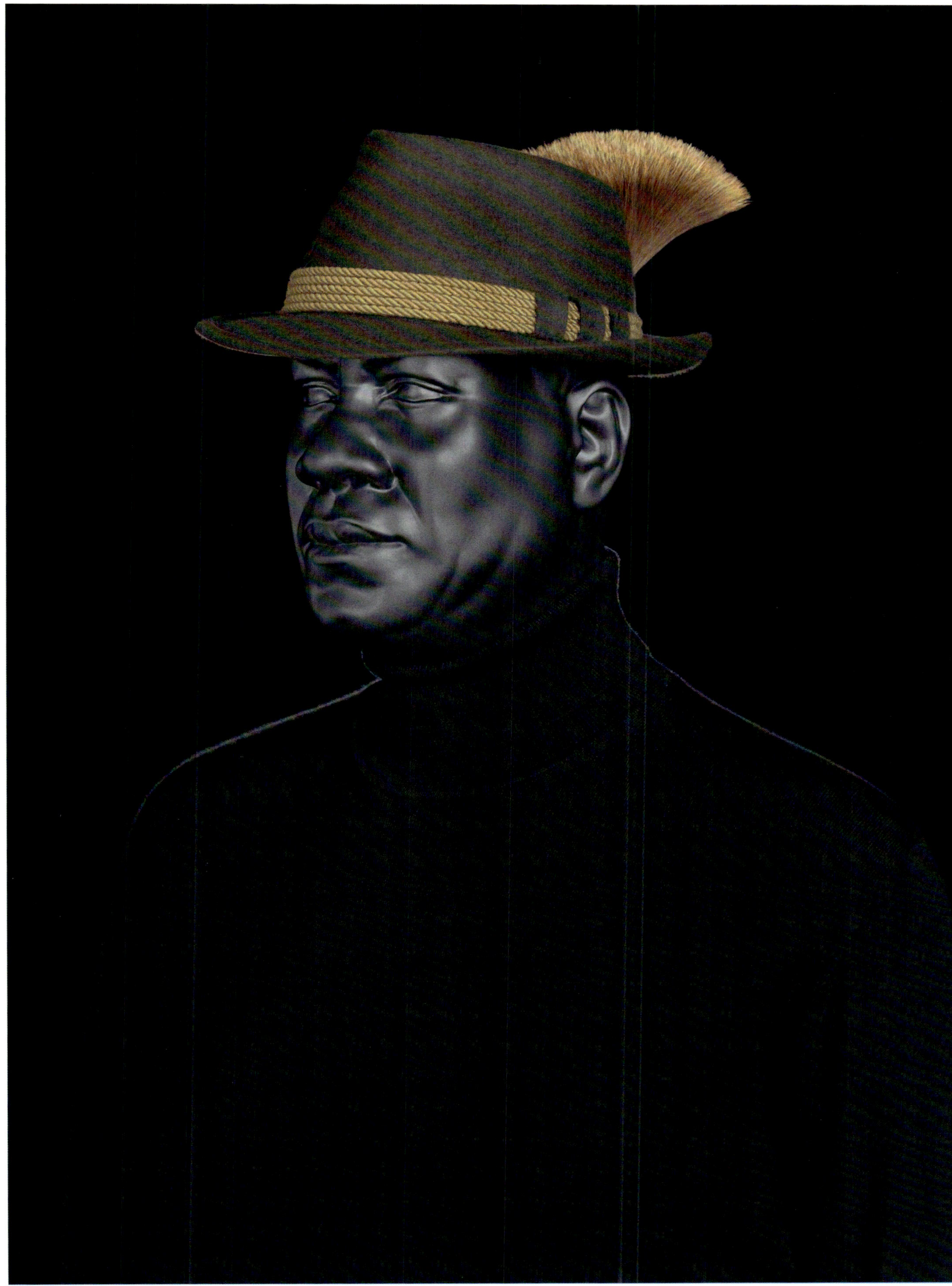

Hutkönig Regensburg

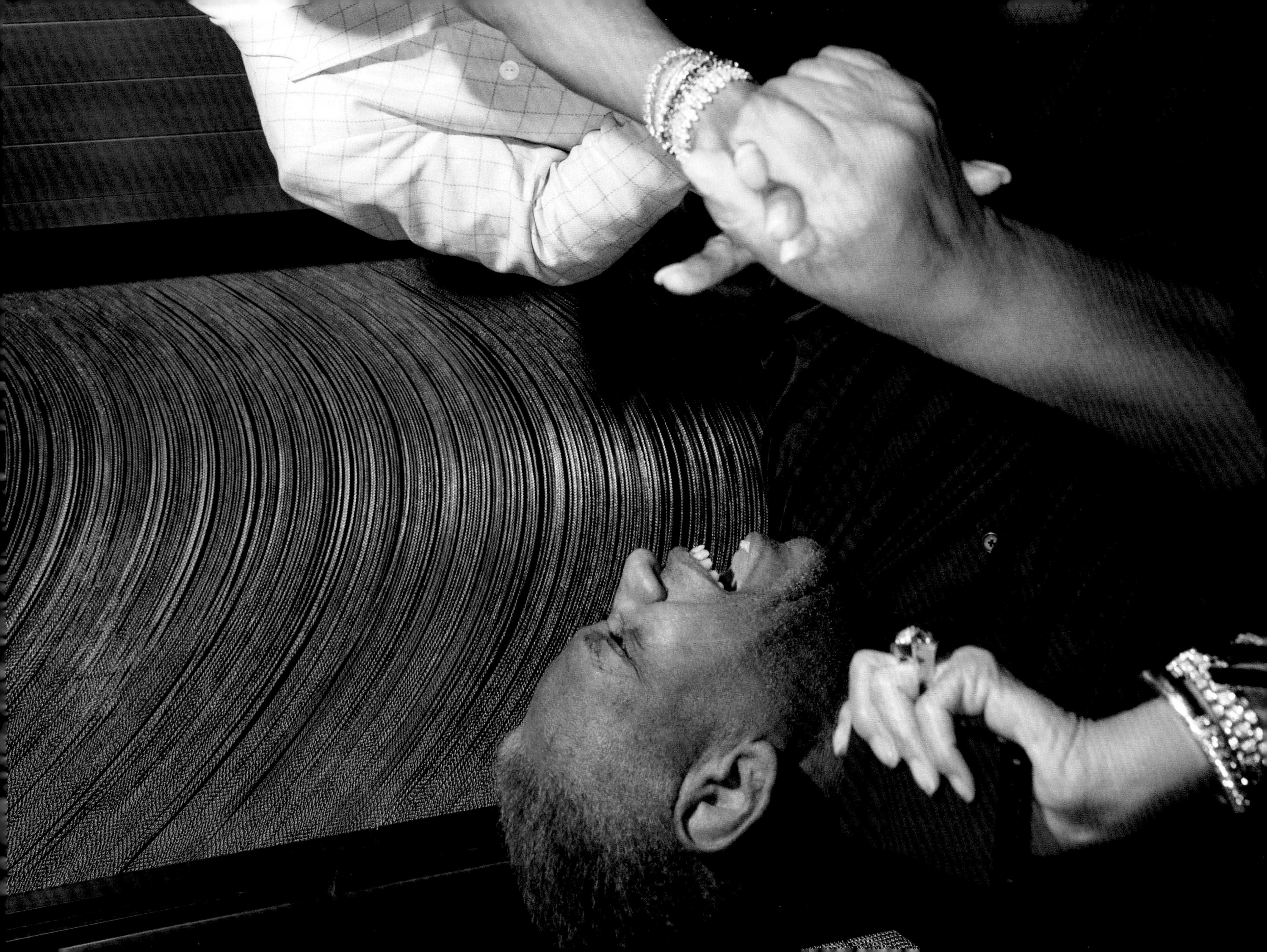

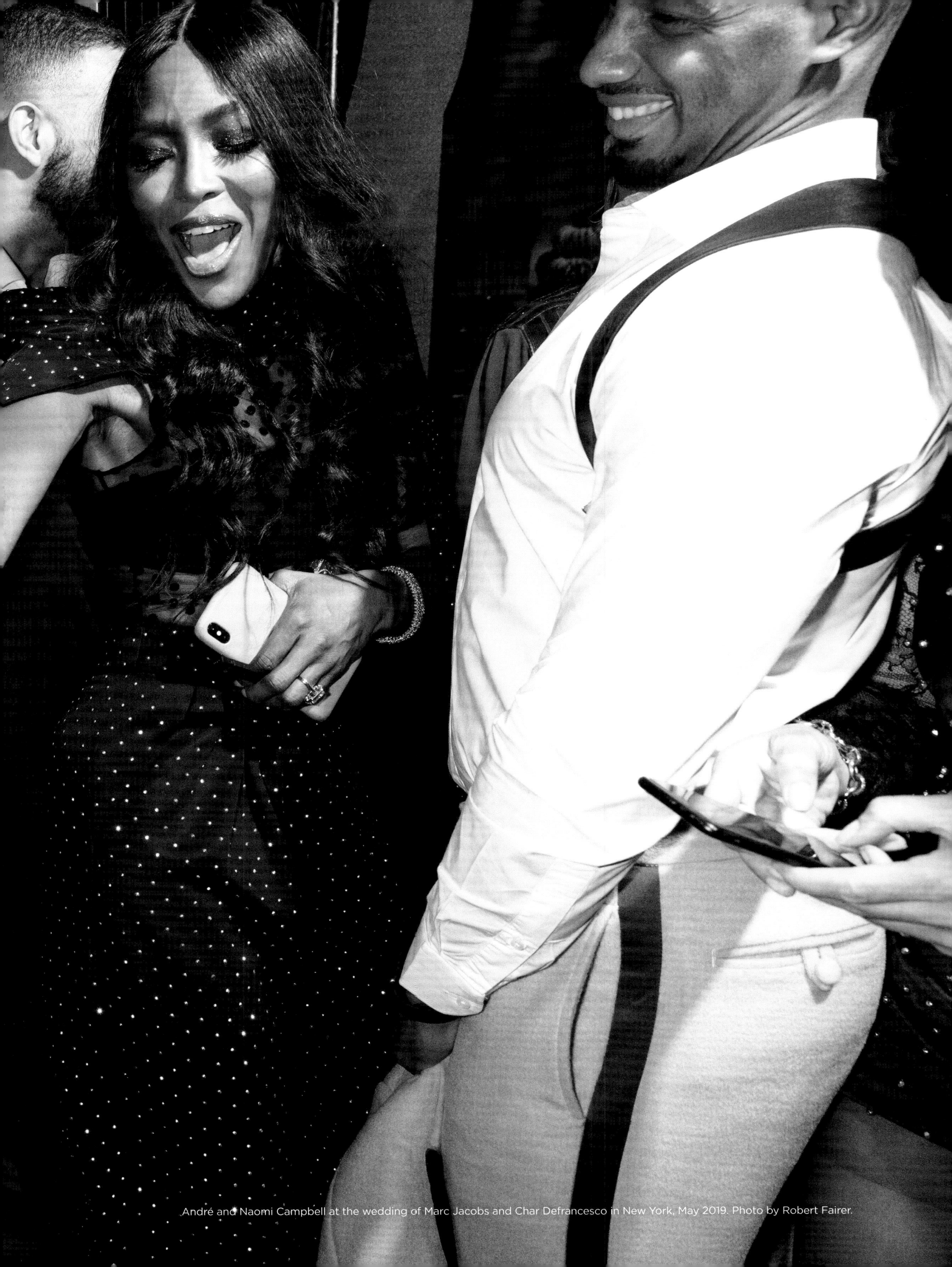

André and Naomi Campbell at the wedding of Marc Jacobs and Char Defrancesco in New York, May 2019. Photo by Robert Fairer.

CATALOGUE OF GARMENTS

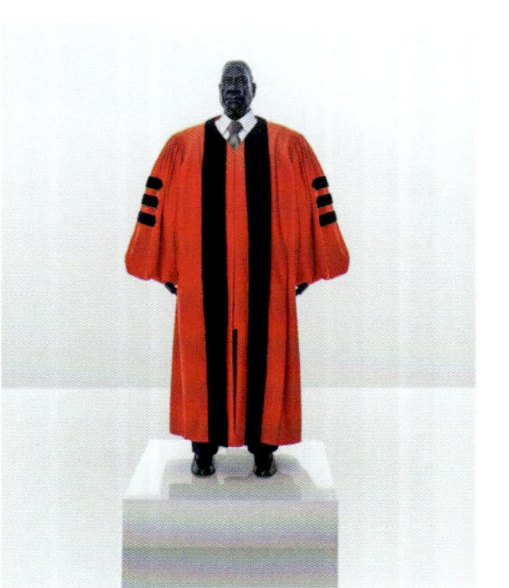

Page 31
SCAD ACADEMIC GOWN

In 2000, André was recognized with the SCAD Lifetime Achievement Award. In 2001, this honor was renamed the André Leon Talley Lifetime Achievement Award, which he bestowed on many of his colleagues in fashion, inviting them to SCAD to share their practices and insights with students through lectures, master classes, and exhibitions of their work at the SCAD Museum of Art and later SCAD FASH Museum of Fashion + Film. In 2008, SCAD presented André with an honorary doctorate of humanities. The three velvet stripes on the sleeves of his SCAD academic gown signify the highest level of academic achievement.

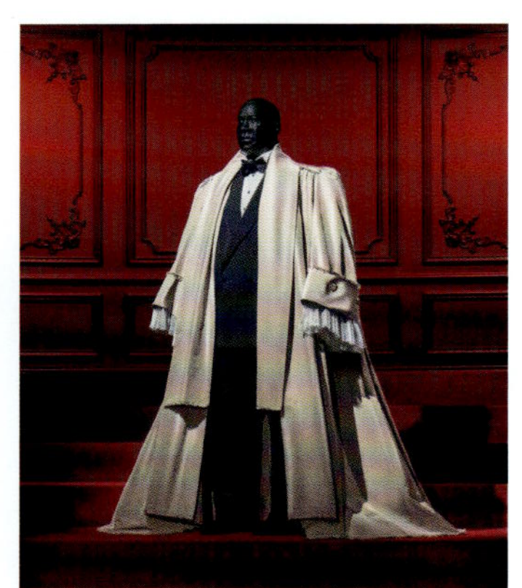

Page 32
CHANEL BY KARL LAGERFELD TAUPE SILK FAILLE COAT AND ARMANI TUXEDO

André wore this Chanel by Karl Lagerfeld coat and Armani tuxedo to the 2004 Met Gala for the exhibition opening of *Dangerous Liaisons: Fashion and Furniture in the Eighteenth Century*. Many of the garments André wore to the Met Gala were exclusively designed for him by Lagerfeld during his tenure at Chanel. Lagerfeld, who shared André's love of eighteenth-century art, design, and culture, created this silk faille haute couture coat using vintage buttons from 1790 found at the designer's favorite antique jewelry dealer in Paris and bought as a surprise for André.

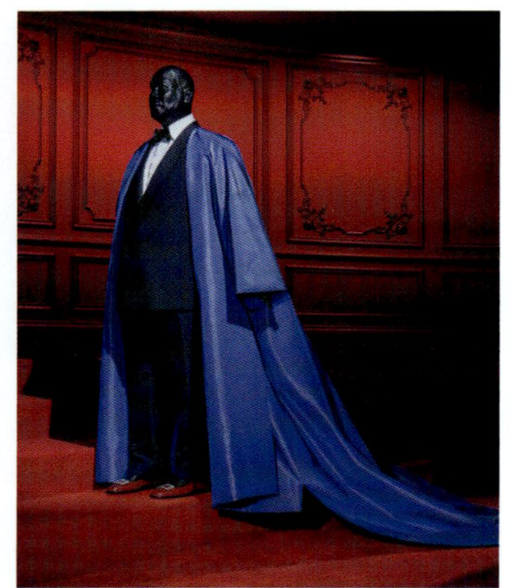

Page 38
NICOLAS GHESQUIÈRE FOR BALENCIAGA LE CORBUSIER BLUE SILK FAILLE COAT AND RALPH LAUREN SUIT WITH CHARVET SHIRT

Nicolas Ghesquière designed this French silk faille *manteau de cour* in Le Corbusier blue for André during the designer's tenure at Balenciaga. For the 2011 Met Gala and exhibition opening of *Alexander McQueen: Savage Beauty*, André paired the dramatic coat with his favorite midnight blue Ralph Lauren dinner suit with shawl collar, a Charvet shirt and bow tie, and Roger Vivier evening shoes in framboise—and placed himself at the top of his own "Best Dressed" list for *Vogue*.

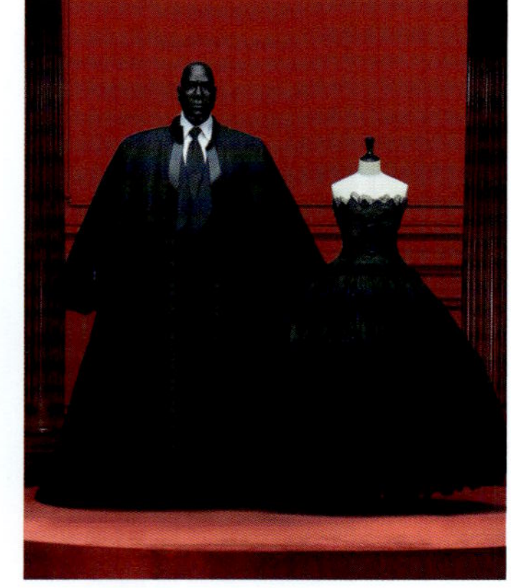

Page 40
AT LEFT, BLACK SILK TAFFETA COAT BY UNKNOWN DESIGNER; AT RIGHT, CHANEL HAUTE COUTURE GOWN

André wore this garment to the 2005 Met Gala for the exhibition opening of *House of Chanel*. He was joined on the red carpet by art dealer and socialite Pat Altschul, whose Chanel haute couture gown was later featured in the exhibition *Little Black Dress*, curated by André for the SCAD Museum of Art, and the accompanying catalogue.

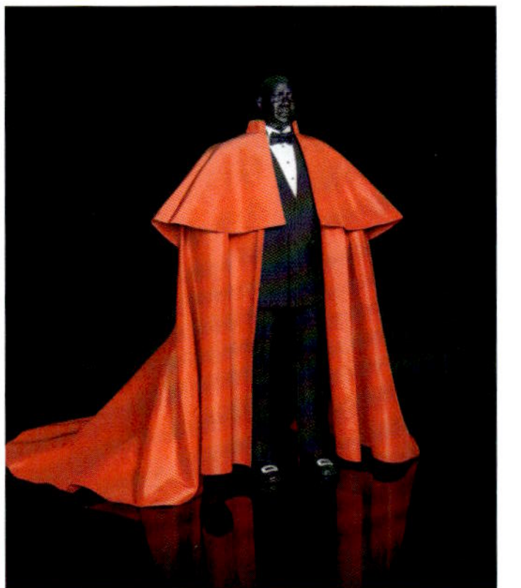

Page 42
CHANEL BY KARL LAGERFELD SCARLET SILK TAFFETA CAPE

For André, the cape was not just a regal garment but "a moment," in which the wearer stands, walks, and behaves differently. This silk taffeta cape, designed by Karl Lagerfeld for Chanel, was inspired by a garment worn by actor Merle Oberon in the 1934 film *The Scarlet Pimpernel*, set in eighteenth-century France. Lagerfeld designed a similar-style cape for André's ensemble at the 2007 Met Gala.

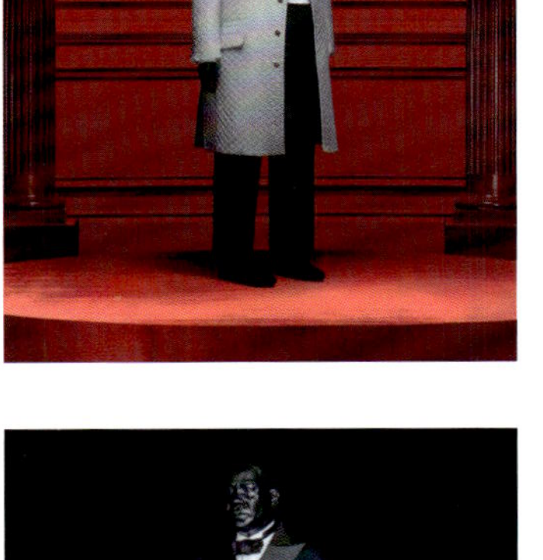

Page 44
VERSACE GRAY QUILTED SATIN COAT

André became friends with Gianni Versace while "running around" Paris covering fashion shows for *Women's Wear Daily*. Following the designer's tragic murder, André wore this Versace coat, symbolically adorned with brooches and diamond pins on the lapel over his heart, to the 1997 Met Gala for the exhibition opening of the Costume Institute's Gianni Versace retrospective.

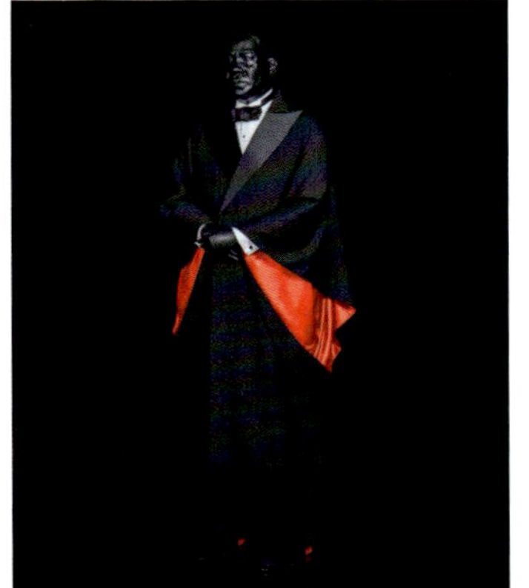

Page 49
BLACK AND RED KIMONO BY UNKNOWN DESIGNER

The most common type of men's kimono, the *montsuki*, is typically made of black silk and worn over traditional Japanese clothing known as *hakama*. André was particularly fond of kimono-style garments, made for him by many of his favorite designers including Ralph Rucci, Tom Ford, and Karl Lagerfeld.

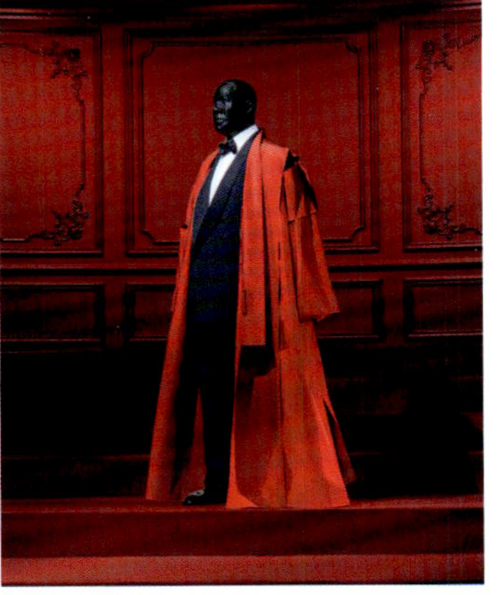

Page 51
TOM FORD RED SILK TAFFETA KIMONO

André wore this Tom Ford silk taffeta kimono to the 2015 Met Gala for the exhibition opening of *China: Through the Looking Glass*, famously interviewing Rihanna in her iconic gold Guo Pei couture gown with a royal court train. Preparing to interview Ford with his guest Rita Ora, André was surprised when the designer reversed roles, asking "Who are you wearing?"—to which André exclaimed "Tom Ford!"

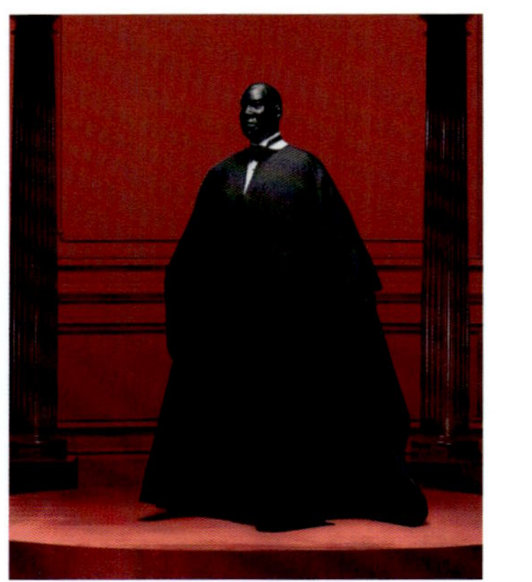

Page 53
RALPH RUCCI BLACK SILK TAFFETA CAFTAN

Ralph Rucci designed many caftans for André, who appreciated the designer's skill for achieving both drama and comfort. Rucci in particular paid careful attention to André's desire to dress with splendor—and to be admired for it.

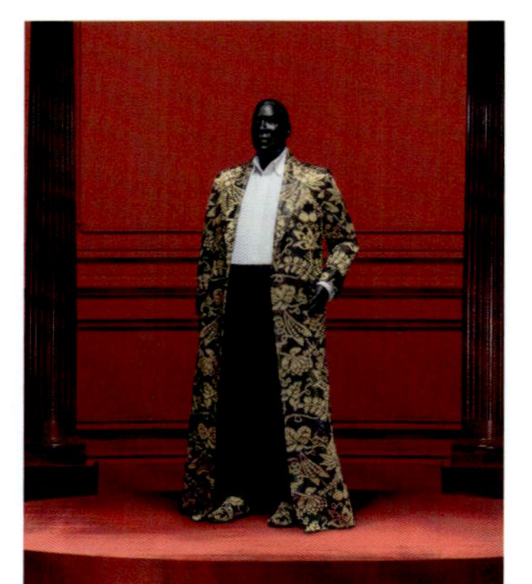

Page 55
TOM FORD FOR GUCCI EMBROIDERED LEATHER COAT

André was enamored with the court capes and ceremonial coats designed for him by Tom Ford, describing them as brilliant looks he felt privileged to wear. He donned this coat for the 1999 Met Gala and exhibition opening of *Rock Style*.

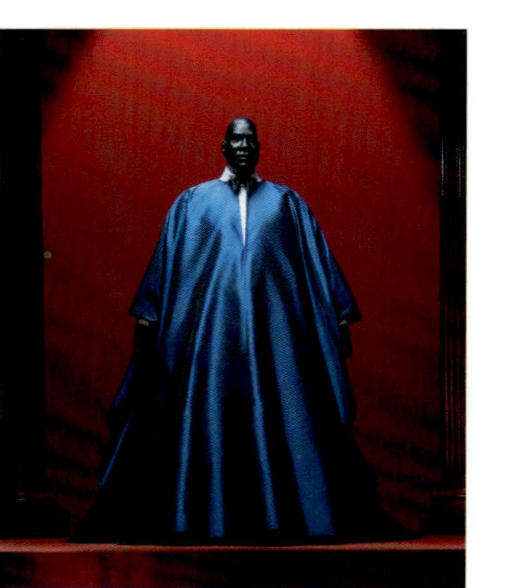

Page 61
RALPH RUCCI SAPPHIRE SILK TAFFETA CAFTAN

André wore this sumptuous Ralph Rucci silk caftan on several occasions but perhaps most proudly to the opening of SCAD's exhibition *Little Black Dress*, which he originally curated for the SCAD Museum of Art and reenvisioned at the Mona Bismarck American Center during Paris Couture Week in 2013.

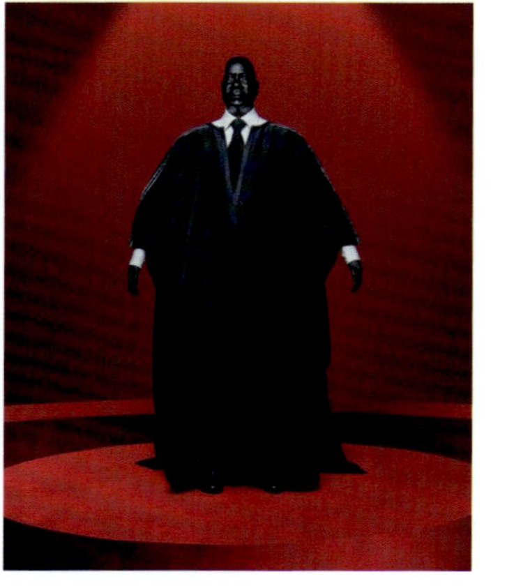

Page 63
ISABEL TOLEDO CAFTAN

André wore this Isabel Toledo caftan to the 2009 Met Gala for the exhibition opening of *The Model as Muse: Embodying Fashion*. André was longtime friends with Isabel and her husband Ruben Toledo, whom he met in the mid-1970s while working together at The Metropolitan Museum of Art's Costume Institute with Diana Vreeland. As a testament to their shared history, André invited the Toledos to SCAD to receive his namesake André Leon Talley Award in 2009. In 2012, the Toledos were named honorary chairs of the university's scholarship fundraising gala SCAD Seen. SCAD, in turn, hosted the first posthumous exhibition of Isabel's designs at SCAD FASH Lacoste in 2022 and at the SCAD Museum of Art in 2024.

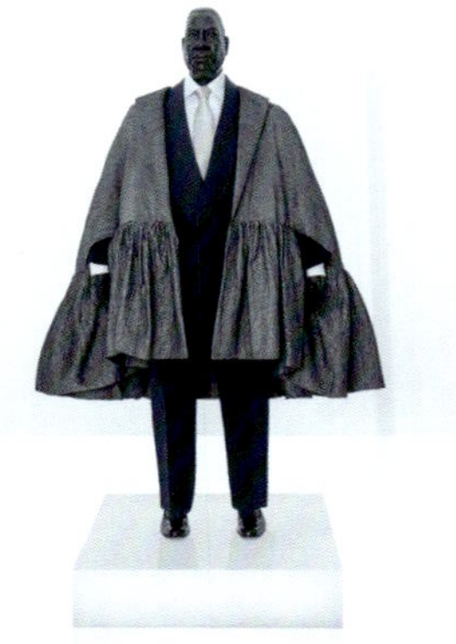

Page 64

NICOLAS GHESQUIÈRE FOR BALENCIAGA GRAY SILK CLOQUÉ CAPE

During his tenure at Balenciaga, Nicolas Ghesquière designed five capes for André in the Spanish style, reminiscent of house founder Cristóbal Balenciaga's oeuvre. André wore this silk cloqué Balenciaga cape to the 2006 Met Gala for the exhibition opening of *AngloMania: Tradition and Transgression in British Fashion*.

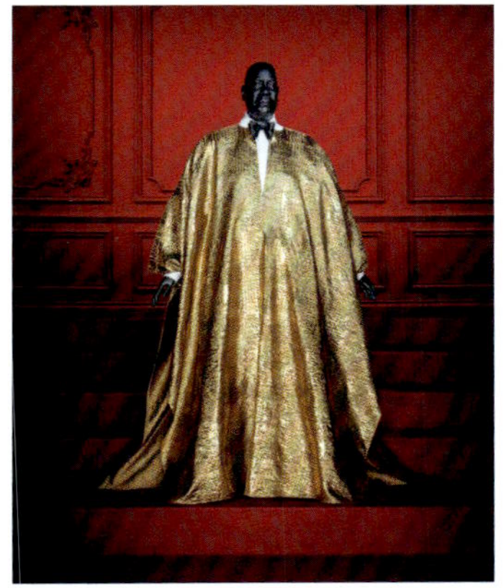

Page 68

RALPH RUCCI CAFTAN

After André's passing, Ralph Rucci recounted how André would stand during long fittings, as ever in his element, holding court on the process of couture. André connected deeply with Rucci's design philosophy as both favored garments with rigor and impact, dazzling in the details—like this caftan André wore for the Chanel "Paris-Dallas" 2013–14 Métiers d'Art runway show.

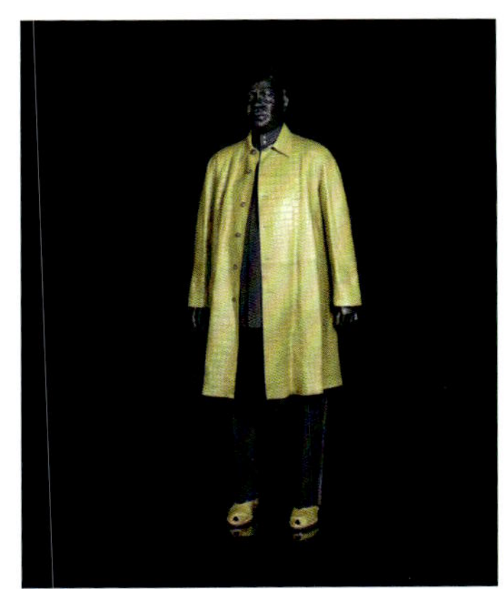

Page 70

PRADA CROCODILE BALMACAAN AND RALPH LAUREN TROUSERS

André was devoted to the art of the letter, articulating his love or critique of each collection in impeccably penned personal notes to the designers. Like many others, Miuccia Prada looked forward to receiving his honest reviews, anticipating an interesting point of view whether he liked the collection or not. André paired this Prada balmacaan with Ralph Lauren trousers for the Vera Wang Spring/Summer 2011 runway show.

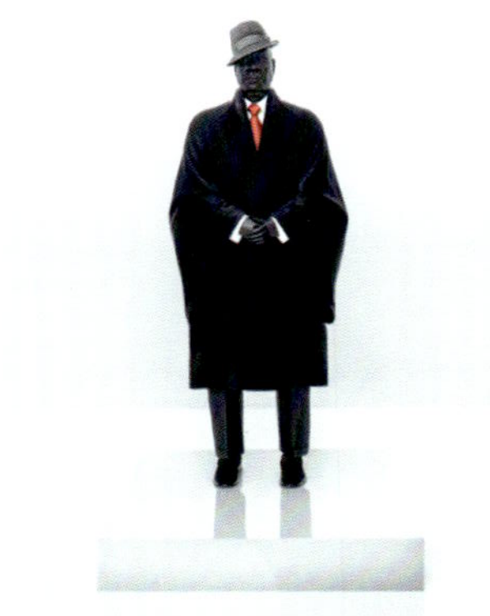

Page 73

RALPH RUCCI BLACK SILK TAFFETA TUNIC AND ROD KEENAN HAT

Ralph Rucci famously designed dozens of custom garments for André "in one fell swoop." Created from expensive silks, including a magnificent Italian couture silk from textile manufacturer Taroni, these garments became the foundation of André's wardrobe.

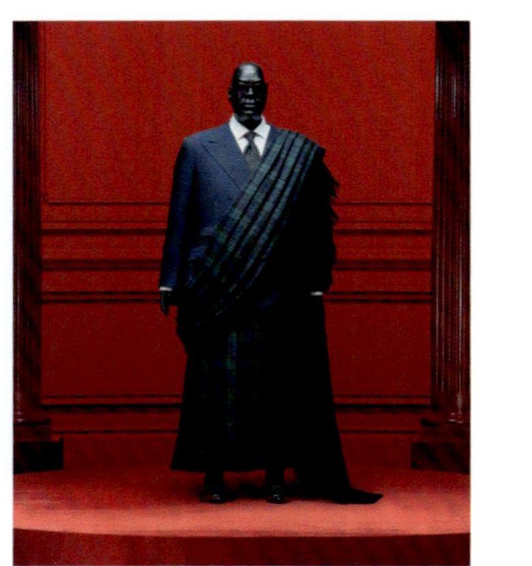

PAGE 76

21ST CENTURY KILTS BY HOWIE NICHOLSBY BLACK WATCH TARTAN KILT AND H. HUNTSMAN & SONS SUIT

Cofounded in 2003 by Sir Sean Connery and Dr. Geoffrey Scott Carroll, Dressed to Kilt is one of the highest profile benefit fashion shows in the world. In 2004 André was personally invited to attend the show by Connery and styled by Howie Nicholsby, the innovative designer and founder of 21st Century Kilts.

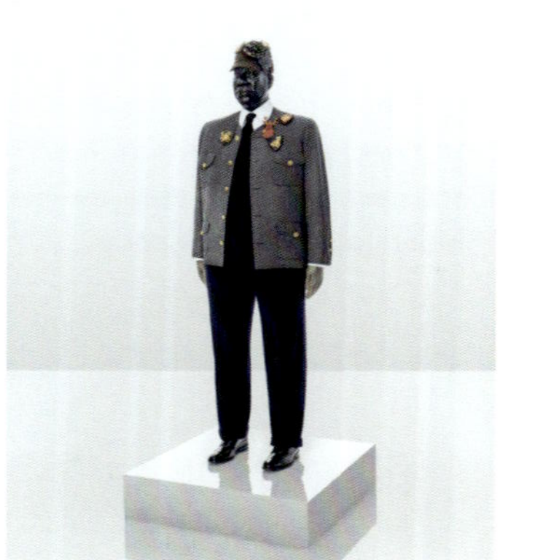

Page 79

CHANEL JACKET WITH MIU MIU BROOCHES AND MIU MIU HAT

André took creative license in this unusual pairing of two iconic designers and personal friends, Karl Lagerfeld for Chanel and Miuccia Prada for Miu Miu, which he wore to a special screening of the film *The Pursuit of Happyness* at Beekman Theatre in New York. André invited both designers to SCAD to receive his namesake André Leon Talley Award in 2002 and 2003, respectively.

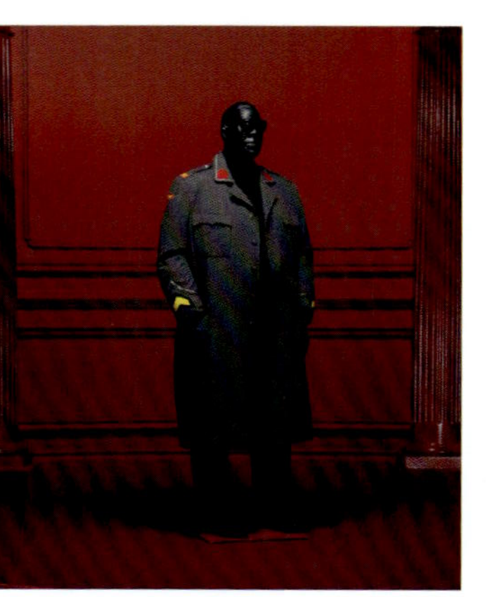

Page 81

JOHN GALLIANO FOR DIOR COAT

This coat was designed by John Galliano during his tenure as creative director of Dior from 1997 to 2011. In Galliano, an often controversial figure, André saw a true poet, declaring that no one would repeat what Galliano achieved at Dior.

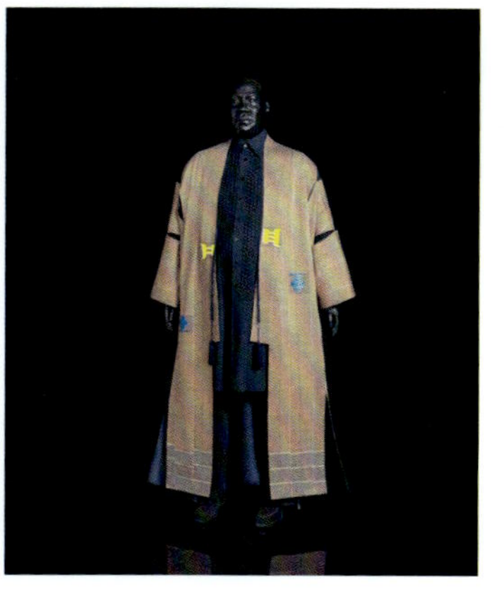

Page 84

TOM FORD KIMONO, DIOR HAUTE COUTURE SHIRT, AND CHADO RALPH RUCCI TROUSERS

Tom Ford created many custom garments for André, some simple caftans in taffeta and cotton poplin for lounging at home and other more formal capes and kimonos for various public appearances. André paired this ensemble for the Marc Jacobs Spring/Summer 2017 runway show.

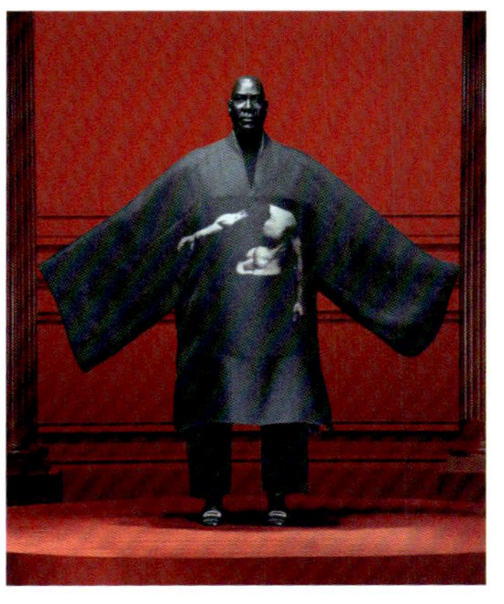

Page 87
CHADO RALPH RUCCI SILKSCREENED TUNIC

For his Chado Ralph Rucci Spring/Summer 2010 collection, the designer presented prints inspired by choreographer Pina Bausch, who had recently passed. Images of dancers from Bausch's company were silkscreened onto many of the garments, as well as two custom looks for André, one of which he wore to attend the Chado Ralph Rucci Fall/Winter 2010 runway show.

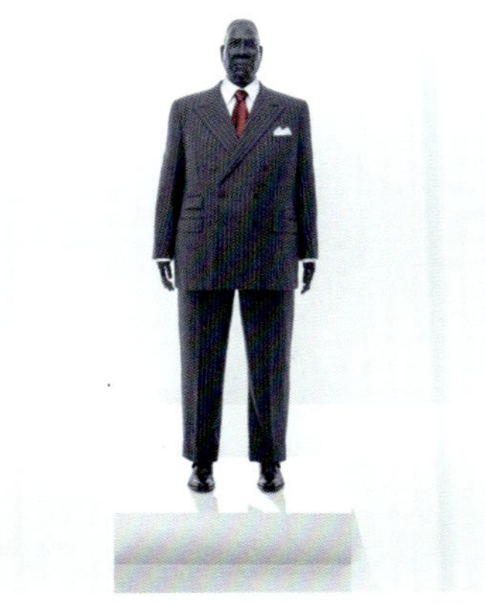

Page 91
H. HUNTSMAN & SONS SUIT

This banker's gray three-piece suit was custom-made for André's cameo appearance in the first *Sex and the City* movie and was one of his favorite bespoke garments from H. Huntsman & Sons.

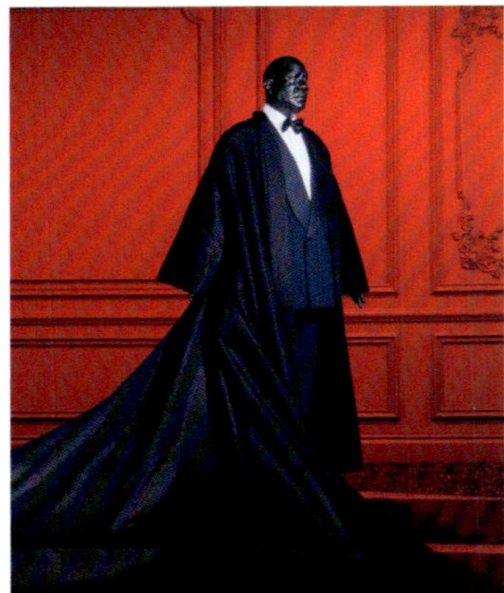

Page 95
RICCARDO TISCI FOR GIVENCHY BLACK SILK COAT WITH TRAIN

Featuring an opulent nearly 30-foot train, this coat was designed by Riccardo Tisci during his tenure as creative director of Givenchy from 2005 to 2017. Tisci's elegantly contemporary execution of the Romantic aesthetic lent itself to this piece, which André wore to attend the Chanel Cruise Collection 2012–13 runway show amid the grand French Baroque style of the Palace of Versailles.

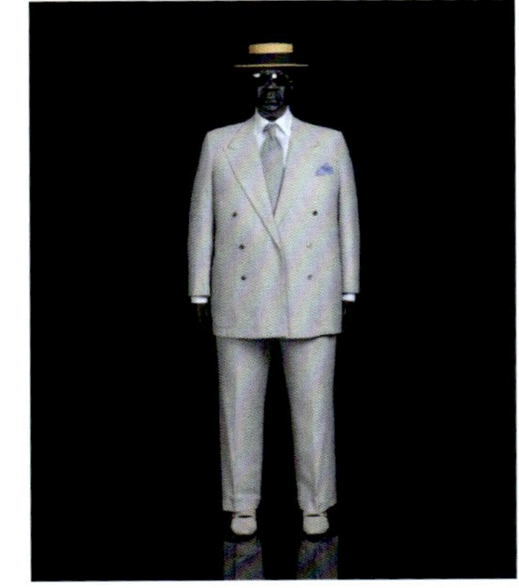

Page 99
RICHARD ANDERSON BLUE AND WHITE DOUBLE-BREASTED SEERSUCKER SUIT
WITH ALEX HITZ TIE AND NO LABEL BOATER HAT

André wore this bespoke seersucker suit by veteran Savile Row tailor Richard Anderson to the Chanel Spring/Summer 1992 couture runway show.

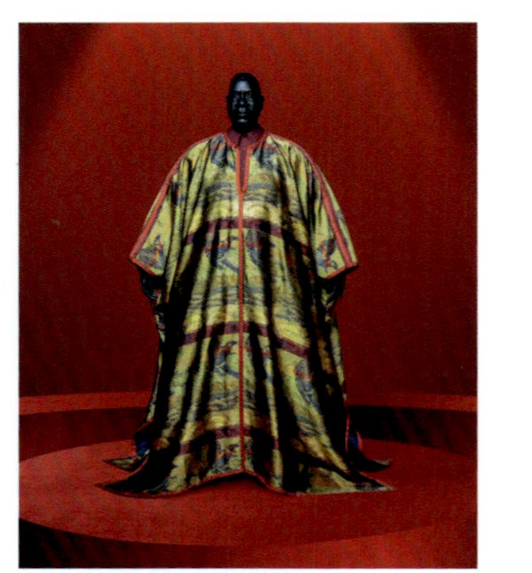

Page 100
GUCCI X DAPPER DAN REVERSIBLE GOLD BROCADE CAFTAN

For the premiere of the documentary film *The Gospel According to André* by Kate Novack, André chose a reversible caftan by Harlem fashion icon Daniel Day, also known as Dapper Dan, in collaboration with Gucci. The caftan, which features a gold and crimson Chinese brocade on one side and a deep blue brocade with leaping tigers on the other side, took three fittings to perfect. André was especially proud to wear this garment by a Black designer who he felt was finally beginning to receive proper due and respect from what André dubbed the "cruel beast" of the fashion world. André wore this look to many subsequent events, including screenings at the Tribeca Film Festival and Los Angeles County Museum of Art, a cocktail party in his honor at the Montclair Film Festival, and even an appearance on *Late Night with Seth Meyers*. André was also featured in this garment in an article by Vanessa Friedman on Dapper Dan for *The New York Times*.

Page 108
PRADA BLACK LEATHER FRINGE COAT AND CHARVET SHIRT AND TIE

André wore this Prada leather fringe coat to the Chanel Fall/Winter 2007 runway show at the Grand Palais in Paris.

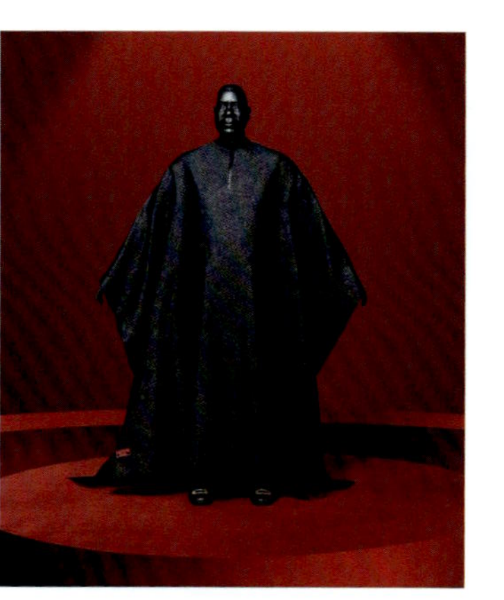

Page 110
DAPPER DAN CAFTAN

This garment is held in the personal collection of Black Fashion Fair founder Antoine Gregory. For Gregory, André was an important model of how to make one's own life as he paved the way for future generations of Black creatives. Gregory has, in turn, developed his own unique platform dedicated to celebrating and amplifying the work of Black designers, artists, and creators.

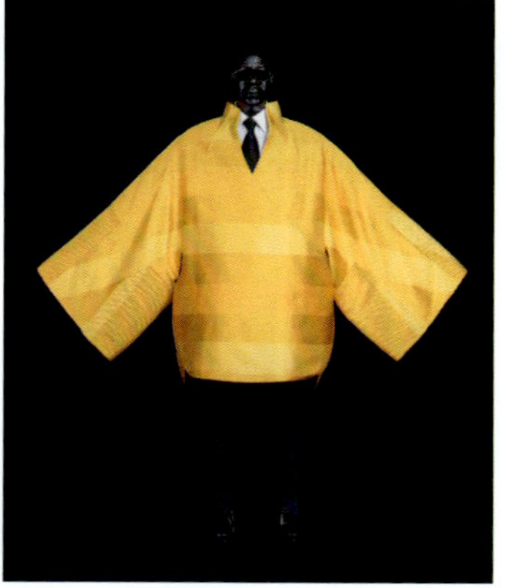

Page 114
CHADO RALPH RUCCI TRAPUNTO TUNIC

Ralph Rucci's "samurai warrior" trapunto garments were inspired by the exhibition *Art of the Samurai: Japanese Arms and Armor, 1156–1868* at The Metropolitan Museum of Art in 2009. André was likewise inspired by the exhibition, originating a shift in his personal style.

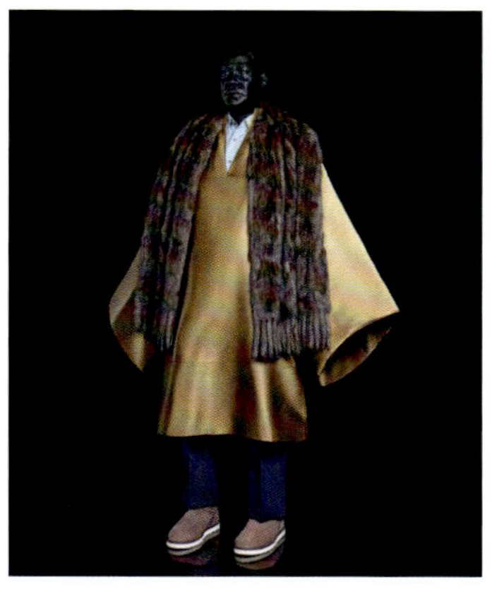

Page 117
RALPH RUCCI TUNIC AND UGG BOOTS

André paired this luxurious Ralph Rucci tunic with his beloved UGG boots for the Stella McCartney Fall/Winter 2012 runway show at Paris City Hall. He prided Rucci's expert technique on cutting his own dashing image: "Louis XIV, eat your heart out."

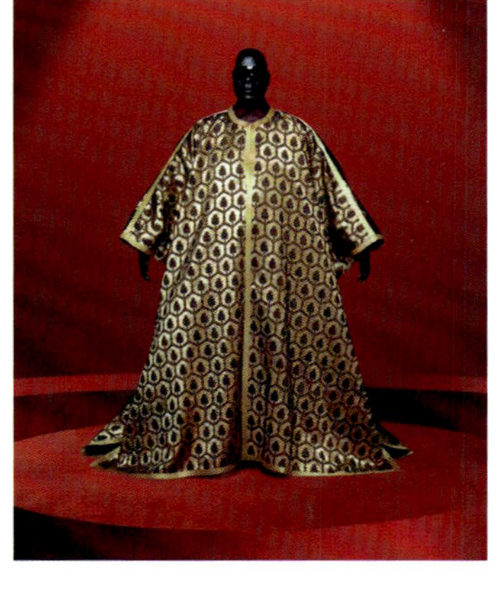

Page 118
GUCCI X DAPPER DAN GOLD BROCADE CAFTAN

André wore this Gucci x Dapper Dan caftan during his visit to Lagos, Nigeria, with Naomi Campbell for ARISE Fashion Week in 2019. André felt a divine calling to visit Africa, attending Easter service at the Cathedral Church of Christ with Nduka Obaigbena, the duke of Owa Kingdom and founding chairman and editor in chief of *ARISE Magazine*, before the Lagos debut of Kate Novack's documentary *The Gospel According to André*.

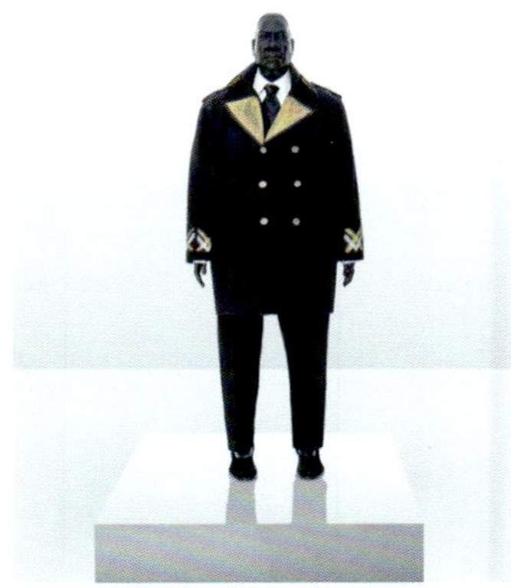

Page 126
BABY PHAT BEDAZZLED DENIM COAT

With the slogan "New American Dream" bedazzled across its back, this garment—designed by former Chanel model Kimora Lee Simmons for her Baby Phat label, an offshoot of her then-husband and Def Jam cofounder Russell Simmons's Phat Farm brand—signified the ascendance and promise of hip-hop culture in the sea change of American politics and society, signaled by the election of Barack Obama and other challenges to the mainstream status quo. André proudly wore this coat to the 2008 CFDA/Vogue Fashion Fund in New York.

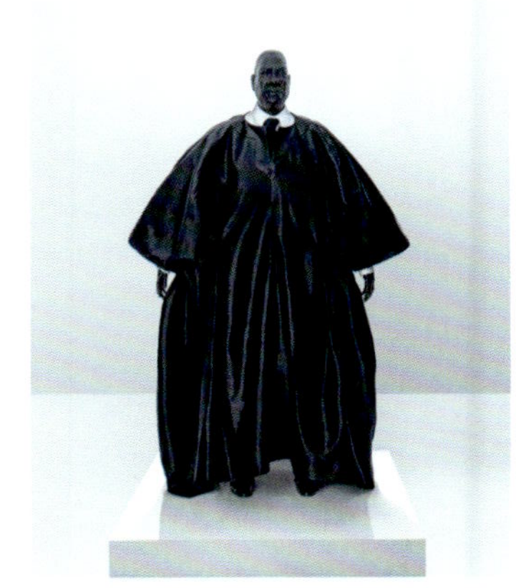

Page 131
VIVIENNE WESTWOOD SILK TAFFETA CAFTAN

André met Vivienne Westwood in the early 1980s at a runway show in Paris. The show was delayed as Westwood was still sewing backstage, perfecting her finishing touches on the garments, which intrigued André, leading him to deem her his "kind of lady."

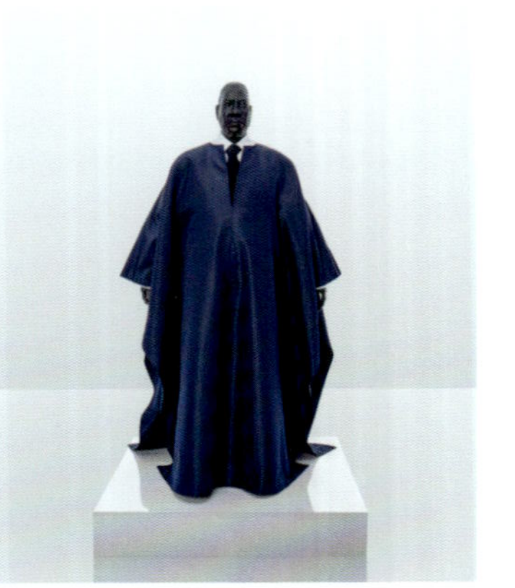

Page 132
RALPH RUCCI BLUE SILK TAFFETA CAFTAN

André wore this Ralph Rucci look to the tenth annual Style Awards during New York Fashion Week in 2013, where he presented Zac Posen with the Designer of the Year Award. André had previously invited Posen to SCAD in 2004, honoring the emerging designer with the freshly deemed André Leon Talley New Look Award. Posen was also named an honorary chair of the university's scholarship fundraising gala SCAD Seen in 2014.

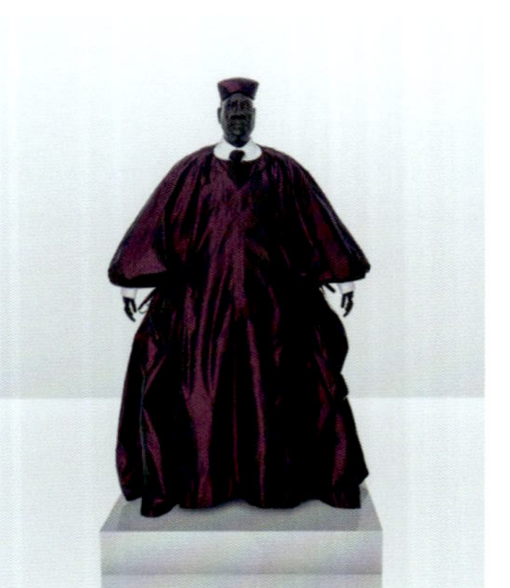

Page 133
VIVIENNE WESTWOOD SILK TAFFETA CAFTAN

André admired Vivienne Westwood's bold originality and innovation, describing her as the figurehead of a new movement in fashion. In 2015, he invited Westwood to SCAD to receive his namesake André Leon Talley Award and collaborated with the designer on an exhibition of her work, *Dress Up Story—1990 Until Now*, at the SCAD Museum of Art.

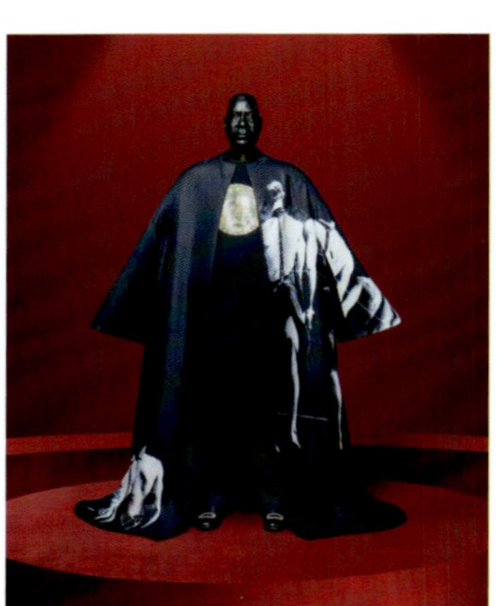

Page 138
CHADO RALPH RUCCI SILKSCREENED CAFTAN AND NAACP T-SHIRT

The longer version of two Chado Ralph Rucci looks the designer made for André based on his Spring/Summer 2010 collection, this garment similarly features silkscreened images of dancers from choreographer Pina Bausch's company, created after her passing. The caftan is paired here with a T-shirt bearing the crest of the National Association for the Advancement of Colored People, an American civil rights organization formed in 1909 as an interracial endeavor to advance justice for African Americans. André wore this T-shirt to the opening of the Costume Institute exhibition *American Woman: Fashioning a National Identity* at the 2010 Met Gala paired with a Ralph Rucci samurai robe.

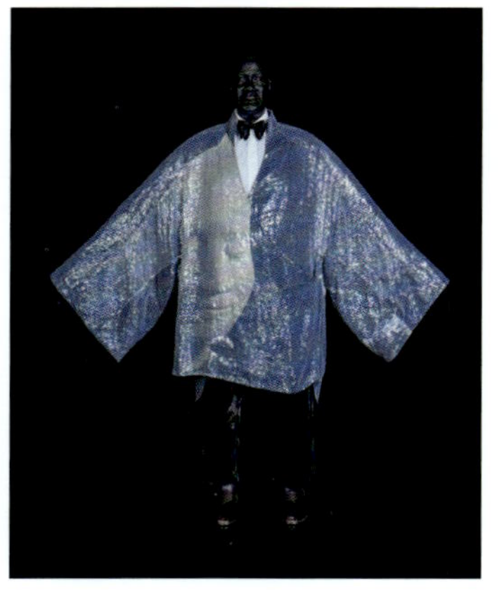

Page 142
CHADO RALPH RUCCI TUNIC

In 1994, Ralph Rucci renamed his fashion house Chado Ralph Rucci, referencing the deeply cultural and philosophical practice of the Japanese tea ceremony and alluding to the elements and values he strives for in his work: purity, respect, harmony, and tranquility. André admired Rucci's integrity, lauding his approach to combining exuberance with restraint within a visual pantheon spanning classical antiquity, Parisian haute couture, contemporary art, and global aesthetics.

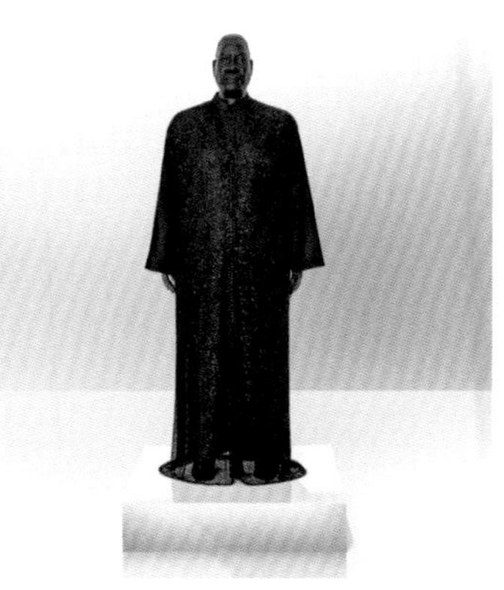

Page 147

NO LABEL BEADED VEST

For the Balenciaga Spring/Summer 2014 runway show during Paris Fashion Week, André wore this dazzling paillette-encrusted black vest with a simple black cotton shirt from tailors in Barbés, an African neighborhood in the city. The head tailor, Monsieur Sy from Nigeria, created several shirts for André, who also sourced similar garments from Au Fil d'Or, the largest souk in Marrakech, owned by ancestors of Monsieur Boujima, the artisan who made the passementerie for Yves Saint Laurent's collections in the 1980s.

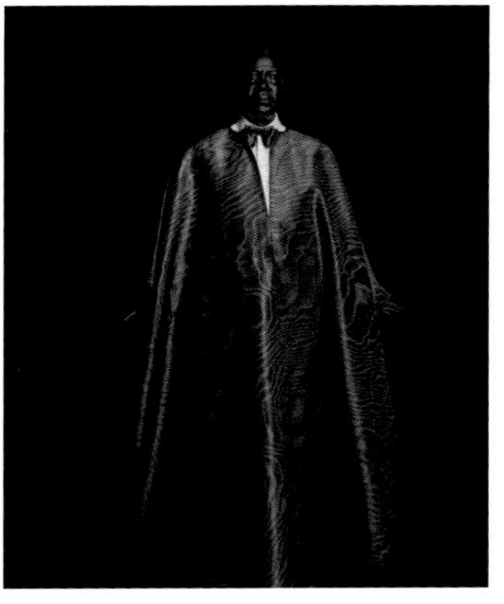

Page 148

RALPH RUCCI CHOCOLATE BROWN TARONI SILK MOIRÉ CAFTAN

André wore this Ralph Rucci caftan to the *Wall Street Journal Magazine*'s 2013 Innovator of the Year Awards, held at The Museum of Modern Art, where designer Valentino Garavani was honored among other visionaries in fashion, art, design, architecture, entertainment, technology, and humanitarianism.

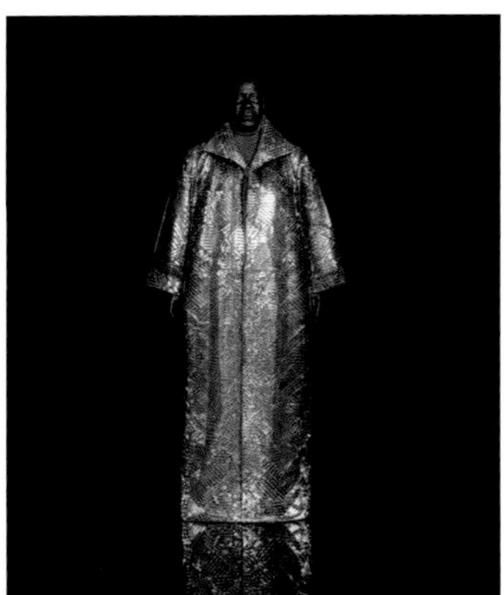

Page 153

FENDI LASER-CUT LEATHER COAT

André met Karl Lagerfeld at the Plaza Hotel in New York in 1975 and they remained close friends for decades. The laser-cut motif on this coat, which André wore to the All Hallow's Eve Party that Lagerfeld hosted for Fendi's eightieth anniversary in 2005, is reminiscent of an archival pattern by the designer from 1969 during his longtime partnership with the brand from 1965 to 2019.

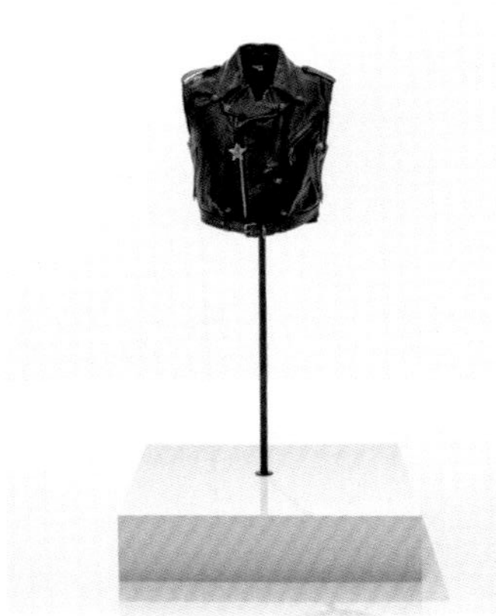

Page 156

BROOKS LEATHER SPORTSWEAR VEST WITH CHROME HEARTS ACCESSORIES

Brooks Leather Sportswear has been an American staple since 1959. André often wore this vest under his pinstriped suits and other tailored jackets, putting his own unique sartorial spin on the three-piece suit, including for the 1991 American Foundation for AIDS Research Benefit honoring Madonna. The vest is embellished with accessories by the brand Chrome Hearts, established in 1988.

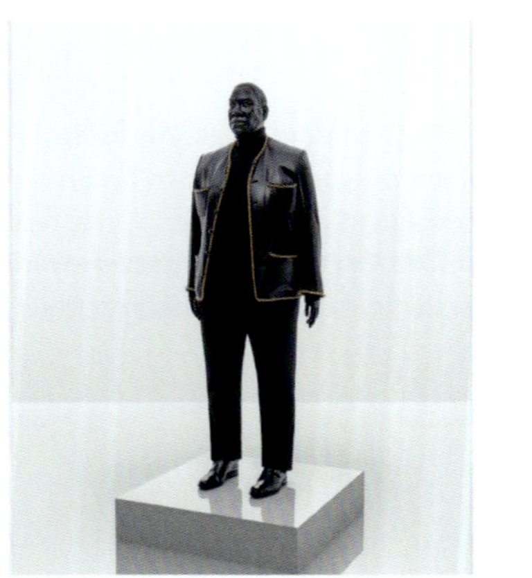

Page 163
CHANEL LEATHER JACKET WITH GOLD CHAIN

During his tenure as creative director at Chanel, Karl Lagerfeld made many couture jackets, capes, and caftans for André, who, aside from Lagerfeld himself, was privileged to wear the only custom Chanel menswear for many years. André wore this jacket as he sat front row for the Chanel Spring/Summer 2007 runway show during Paris Fashion Week.

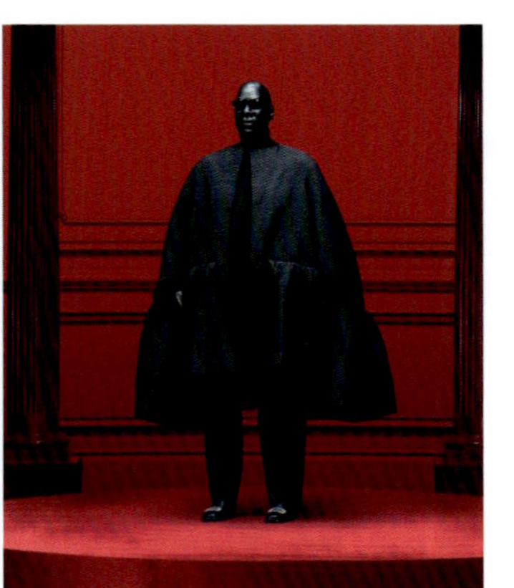

Page 164
NICOLAS GHESQUIÈRE FOR BALENCIAGA BLACK SILK CLOQUÉ RUFFLED CAPE

André wore this ruffled garment—one of five custom capes designed for him by Nicolas Ghesquière during his tenure as creative director at Balenciaga from 1997 to 2012—for the CFDA/Vogue Fashion Fund party at the Gramercy Park Hotel in 2006.

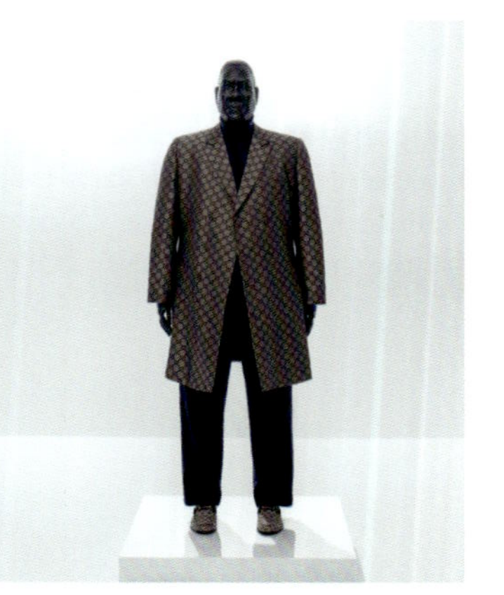

Page 169
TOM FORD FOR GUCCI COAT

Working with the brand as a womenswear designer since 1990, Tom Ford became creative director of Gucci in 1994. In 1998, Ford redesigned the Gucci logo, as seen here, giving the brand a bold new look while paying homage to its timeless tradition of innovation. André wore this coat for the opening of the Gucci storefront on Fifth Avenue in 2000 and invited Ford to SCAD to receive his namesake André Leon Talley Award in 2005.

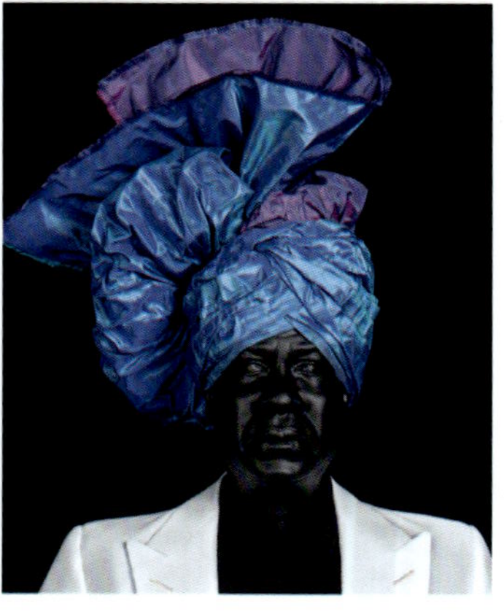

Page 171
YVES SAINT LAURENT MAJORELLE BLUE SILK TAFFETA TURBAN

This magnificent Yves Saint Laurent turban in Majorelle blue silk taffeta references the designer's deep appreciation for the cultural heritage of his youth in Oran, Algeria, and later his beloved Marrakech. Saint Laurent featured turbans in both haute couture and ready-to-wear collections, and they became one of the designer's signature styles. From the early 1960s until the end of his career, Saint Laurent reimagined the turban with contemporary elegance in various silhouettes. While specific details of the occasion for which André donned this turban are unknown, the grand scale and craftsmanship suggest it was created exclusively for him.

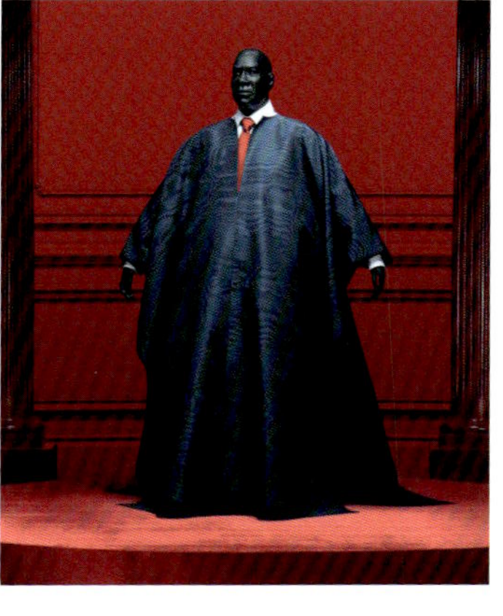

Page 175
RALPH RUCCI NAVY BLUE TAFFETA CAFTAN

André wore this Ralph Rucci caftan to the Ulyana Sergeenko Fall/Winter 2013 haute couture runway show during Paris Fashion Week. He became friends with Sergeenko—citing her as his “favorite person in Moscow, outside of Naomi Campbell”—during his time working for the Russian publication *Numéro*, directing an editorial featuring her designs with photographer Jonathan Becker on location at SCAD in 2013.

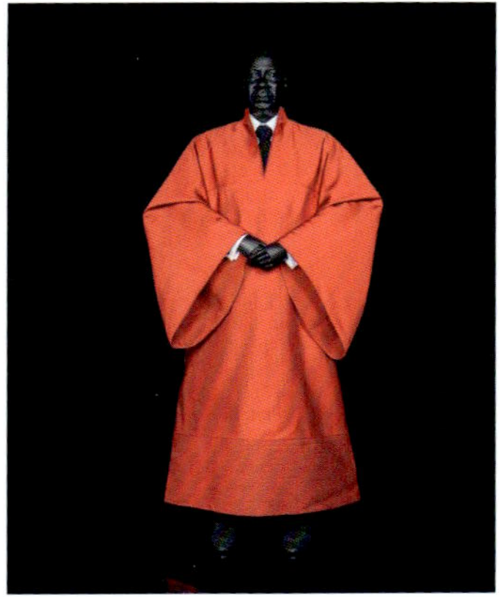

Page 177
RALPH RUCCI RED SILK TUNIC

Ralph Rucci fashioned this kimono-inspired tunic for André in red Taroni silk with trapunto stitching on the sleeves, patterned from his Fall/Winter 2011 ready-to-wear collection.

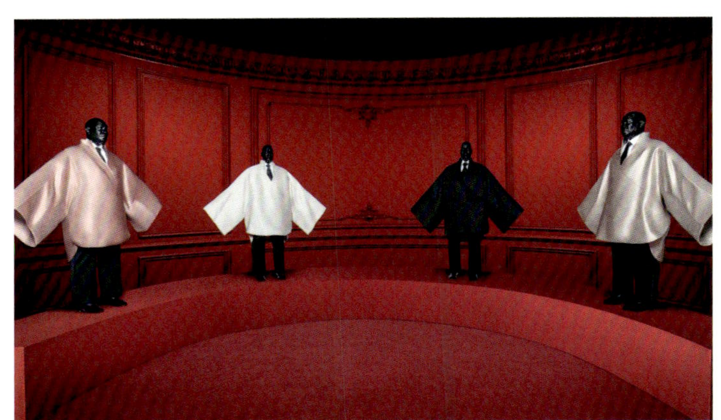

Page 178
RALPH RUCCI TUNICS

André frequently referred to his Ralph Rucci garments, including these “samurai warrior” trapunto tunics, as his armor, a reflection of his experiences as “the only one” in most circles of the fashion world.

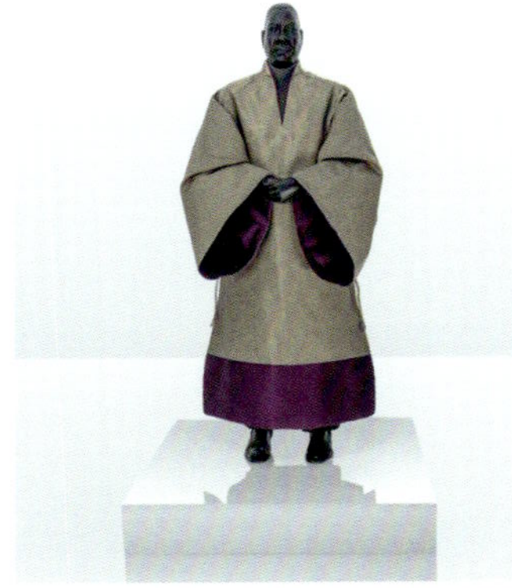

Page 185
RALPH RUCCI TARONI SILK MOIRÉ AND TRAPUNTO SILK FAILLE TUNIC

André wore this Mandarin-style garment, one of Ralph Rucci’s favorite custom designs, to the Élysée Palace where Anna Wintour was awarded the Légion d’Honneur from the French government in 2011. In 2020, André was in turn honored with the Chevalier de l’Ordre des Arts et des Lettres for his contributions to culture in France and throughout the world.

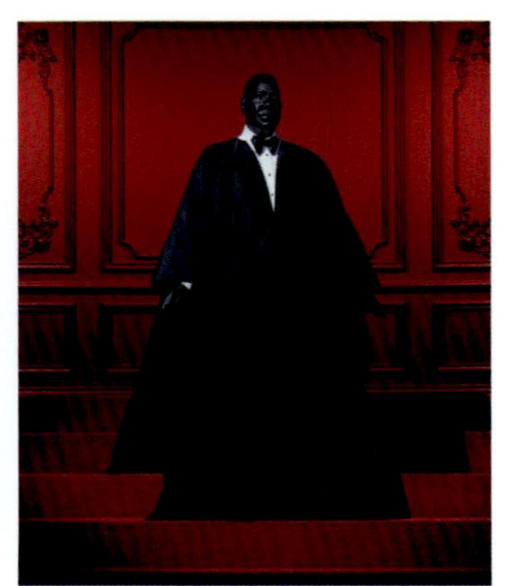

Page 186
RALPH RUCCI BLACK SILK CAFTAN

In 2012, André invited Ralph Rucci to SCAD to receive his namesake André Leon Talley Award—honoring the designer's exquisite attention to craft and impact on expanding notions of contemporary fashion—and curated an exhibition of Rucci's work, *Looking Back to the Future: Ralph Rucci Evolved*, for the SCAD Museum of Art. Rucci was also named an honorary chair of the university's scholarship fundraising gala SCAD Seen in 2013.

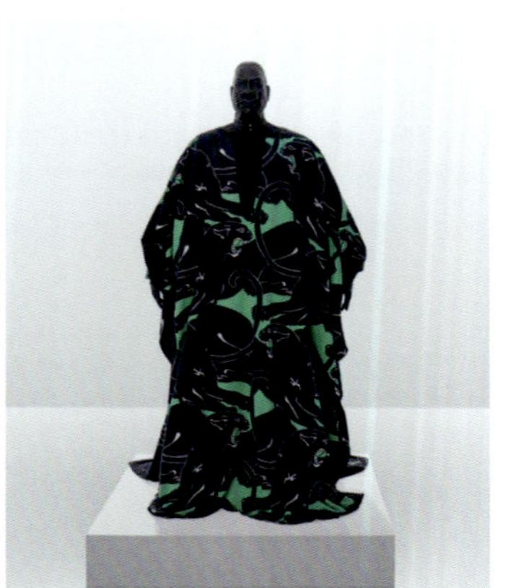

Page 188
VALENTINO CAFTAN IN AN ARCHIVAL PRINT ON COTTON AND GIANFRANCO FERRÉ SHIRT

Valentino Garavani designed two custom caftans for André to wear to the three-day celebration of the marriage of Kim Kardashian to Kanye West. Valentino's longtime friend and muse Carlos Souza coordinated two vintage couture fabrics from the Valentino archive—one in green cotton with black jaguars and another in a Chinese dragon motif. "It's a dialogue and a process," André reflected on the garments' creation, recalling the adventure of selecting the fabric in Rome and rushing straight to the atelier.

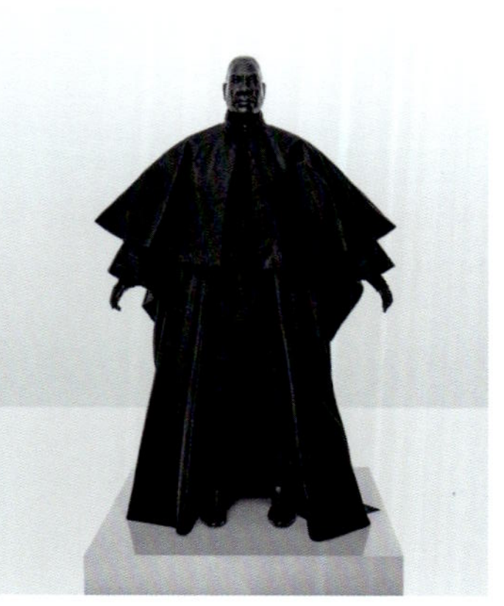

Page 191
LL CAPE

A deeply spiritual person, André wore this ecclesiastical cape to the 2018 Met Gala for the exhibition opening of *Heavenly Bodies: Fashion and the Catholic Imagination*. Asked about his grand style of capes and caftans by journalist Audie Cornish in an interview for NPR later that year, André responded that he dressed "for the drama of who I am."

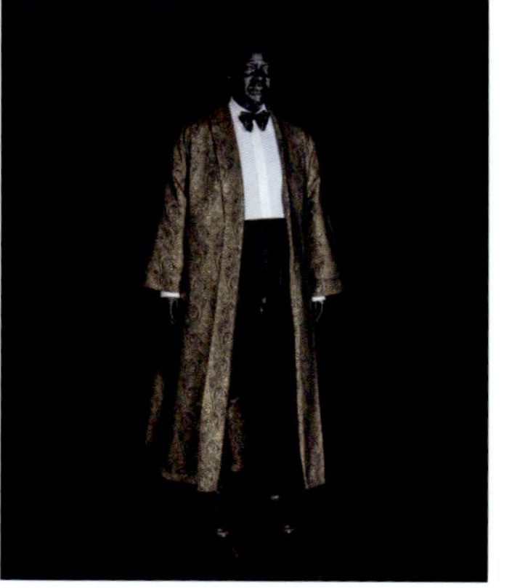

Page 194
VERSACE SILK BROCADE COAT

André spent many weekends with Gianni Versace and his partner Antonio D'Amico at Lake Como "whiling away in our dressing gowns and binging on movies long into the evening."

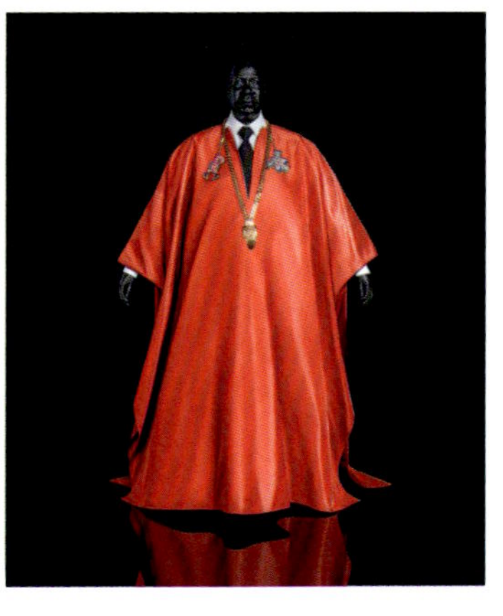

Page 196
RALPH RUCCI CAFTAN WITH DIANE VON FURSTENBERG ZODIAC CHARMS AND ACCESSOCRAFT NYC CHAIN

After André's passing, Ralph Rucci reflected that his larger-than-life approach to personal style was "the very pinnacle of life for André." Here, a Ralph Rucci caftan is paired with zodiac charms by Diane von Furstenberg representing André (Libra) and Anna Wintour (Scorpio).

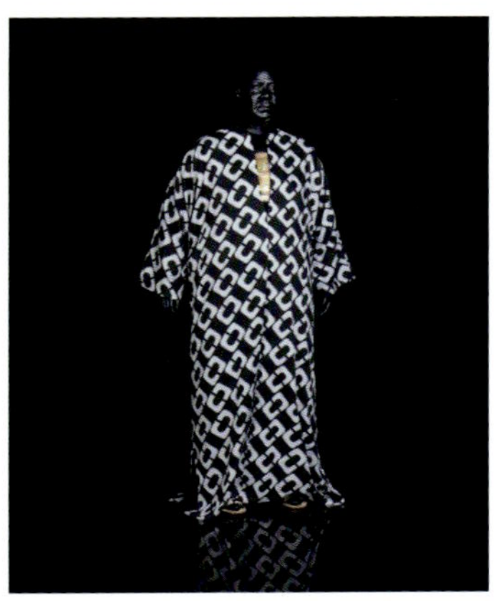

Page 203
DIANE VON FURSTENBERG CAFTAN IN AN ARCHIVAL PRINT ON COTTON

André shared a friendship with Diane von Furstenberg spanning more than forty-five years. He invited the designer to SCAD in 2010 to receive his namesake André Leon Talley Award and curated an exhibition of her work, *Diane von Furstenberg: Journey of a Dress*, for the university's Gutstein Gallery. The designer frequently made caftans for André using original silkscreened fabrics from her archive, including this pattern, which she also fashioned into a small elephant trinket.

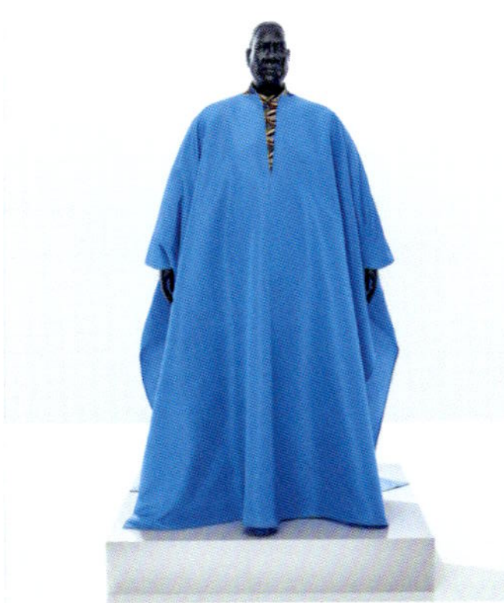

Page 207
RALPH RUCCI SILK TAFFETA CAFTAN WITH DEMESTIK BY REUBEN REUEL TUNIC IN AN AFRICAN PRINT

During a trip to North Africa and specifically Morocco, André was inspired by the men he saw in what he deemed the "indigenous dress of the Black man" and made a decision to begin wearing caftans instead of suits.

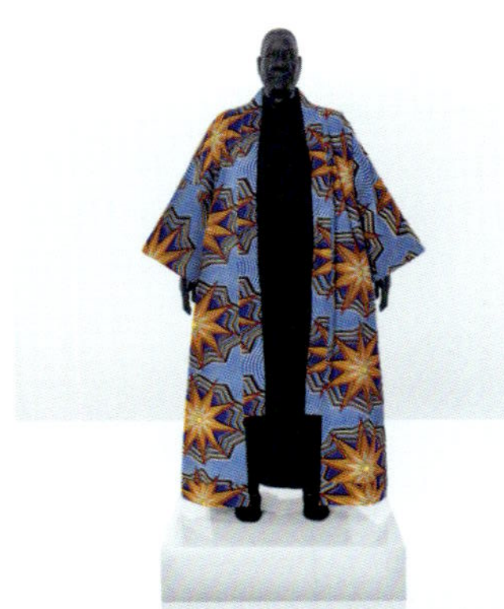

Page 210
DEMESTIK BY REUBEN REUEL KIMONO IN AN AFRICAN PRINT

André met designer Reuben Reuel, creative director of Demestik, at a St. Louis Fashion Fund event hosted by cofounder Susan Sherman. He wore this Demestik kimono to the Vivienne Westwood x Juergen Teller exhibition opening during New York Fashion Week 2017.

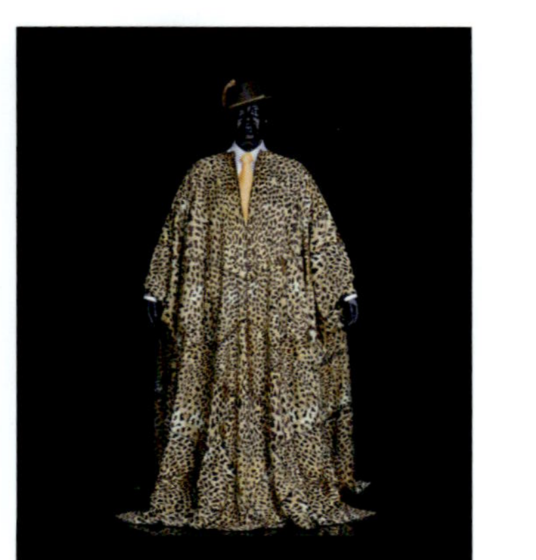

Page 212
TOM FORD FOR YVES SAINT LAURENT CAFTAN AND HUTKÖNIG REGENSBURG HAT

The first haute couture show André attended was Yves Saint Laurent in 1978, sparking a friendship that lasted until the designer's passing in 2008. During his tenure as the creative director of the house from 2000 to 2004, Tom Ford created this custom caftan, paired here with a Hutkönig Regensburg hat, for André from a look worn by Liya Kebede in the Spring/Summer 2002 collection. The Hutkönig company was founded in Regensburg, Germany, in 1875. In 1975, André was sent to St. Emmeram Palace to interview Princess von Thurn und Taxis, developing a close friendship and even referring to her as his surrogate sister.

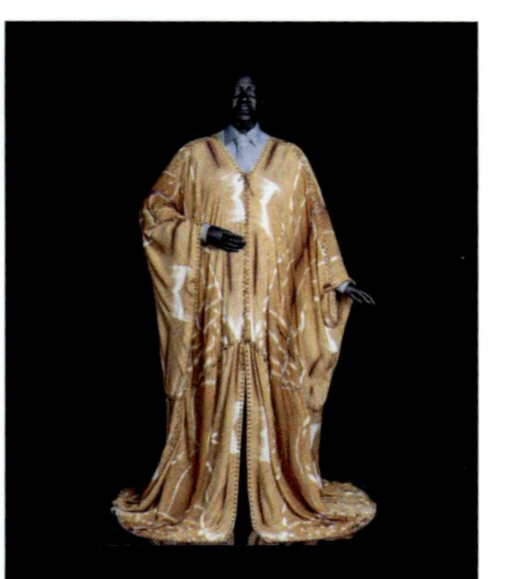

Page 216
TOM FORD FOR YVES SAINT LAURENT CAFTAN

Tom Ford designed this caftan for André from his first collection at Yves Saint Laurent for Spring/Summer 2002.

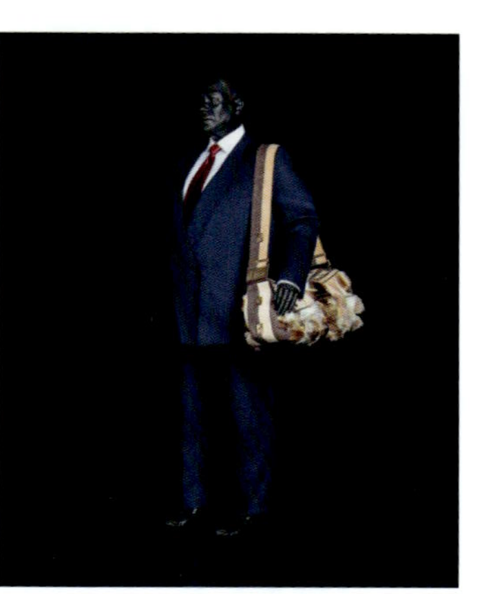

Page 221
H. HUNTSMAN & SONS SUIT

André was always in rarefied air in his suits by H. Huntsman & Sons, which he began wearing exclusively during his years as a fashion editor in Paris. Based in London, the Savile Row tailor has a long history dressing the British royalty and European elite. André enjoyed discussions of the craft during his fittings and was especially amused to select an "explosive" Schiaparelli pink lining for this suit.

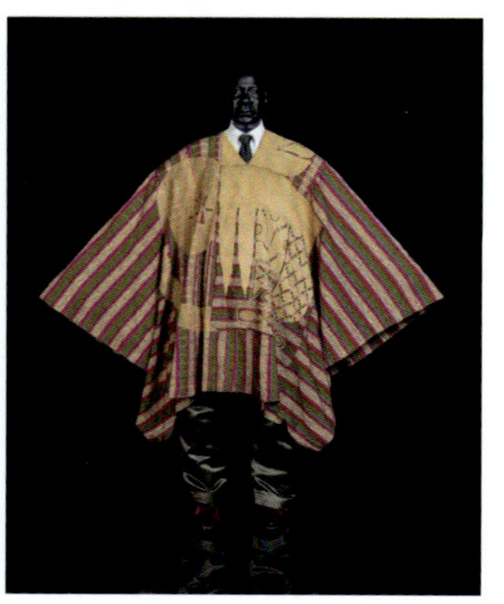

Page 226
ASO OKE AGBADA

Aso oke is a prestige textile created by Yoruba weavers in southwestern Nigeria that is fashioned into clothing for celebratory and ceremonial occasions such as *agbadas*, traditional male robes worn by the Yoruba people of West Africa. André visited Nigeria with model Naomi Campbell in 2019.

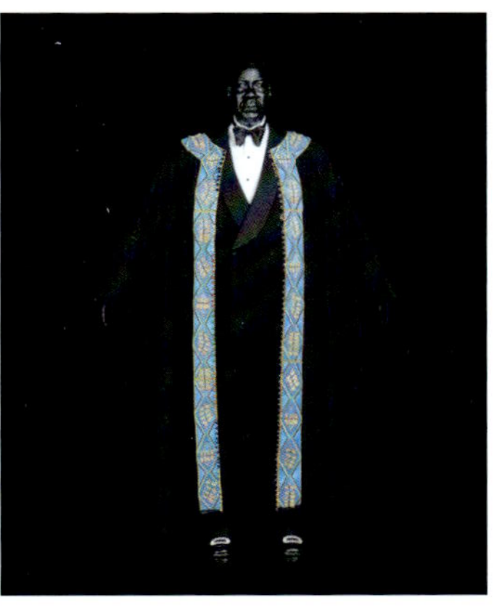

Page 228
PATIENCE TORLOWEI BLACK AGBADA

André met Nigerian designer Patience Torlowei at a panel discussion in Lagos. Impressed by her work in luxury womenswear, he commissioned this custom *agbada*. The back of the robe includes a representation of an *adenla*, a beaded crown worn only by a Yoruba king who can trace his ancestry to Oduduwa, the first ruler of Ile-Ife, the sacred home of all Yoruba people.

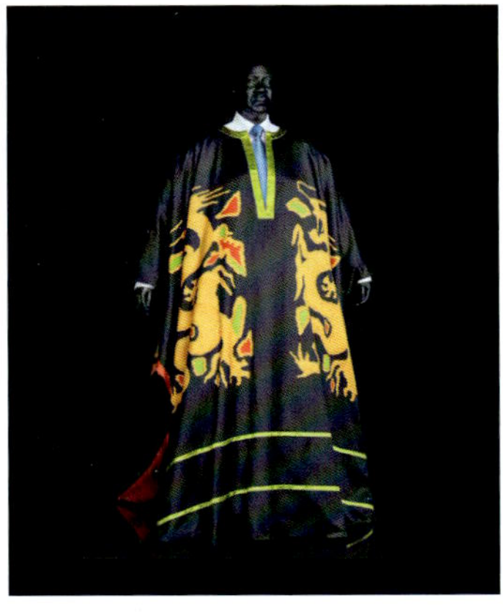

Page 234
VALENTINO CAFTAN IN A VINTAGE ARCHIVAL PRINT

André wore this caftan in a vintage archival print designed by Valentino for the forty-fifth anniversary of the house and later to the pre-wedding celebration at the Palace of Versailles for Kim Kardashian's marriage to Kanye West.

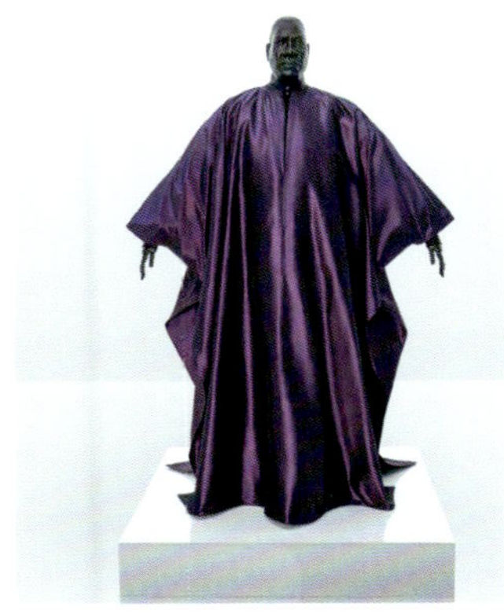

Page 239
CHADO RALPH RUCCI TAFFETA CAFTAN

André was quick to recognize Ralph Rucci's exceptional talent and laud his contributions to American couture. Their enduring friendship was rooted in profound admiration, creative synergy, and a commitment to supporting each other's prolific endeavors.

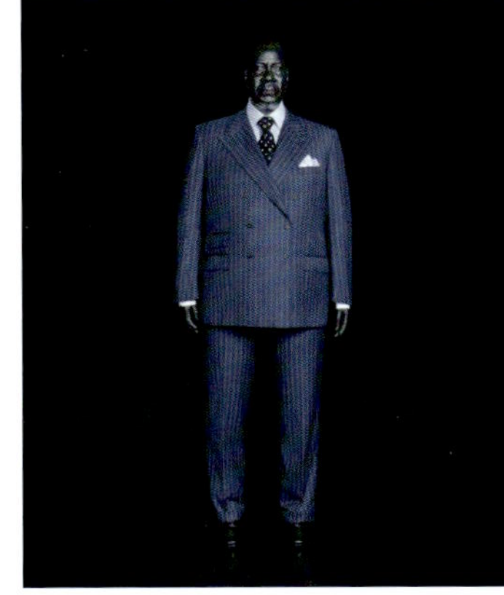

Page 241
H. HUNTSMAN & SONS SUIT

André commissioned this bespoke suit, featuring a lightweight raw silk in navy blue and vibrant red silk lining, from H. Huntsman & Sons in 2001. Epitomizing elegance and sophistication, the custom garment exemplifies H. Huntsman & Sons' signature craftsmanship and is testament to André's longstanding relationship with the Savile Row tailor.

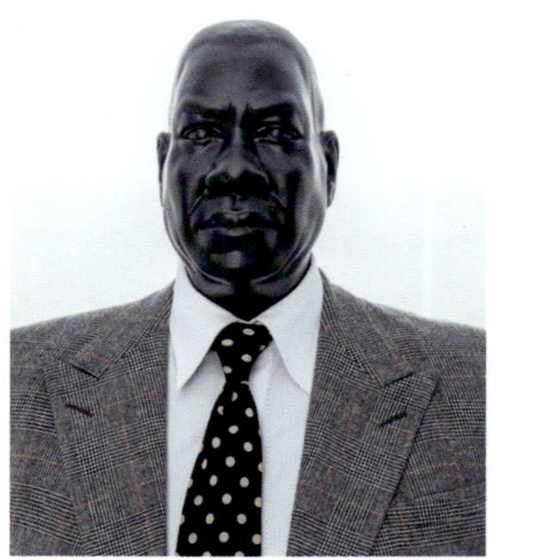

Page 242
H. HUNTSMAN & SONS SUIT

André was photographed in this H. Huntsman & Sons suit, an early example of his collaboration with the Savile Row tailor, by his former mentor Andy Warhol in 1984.

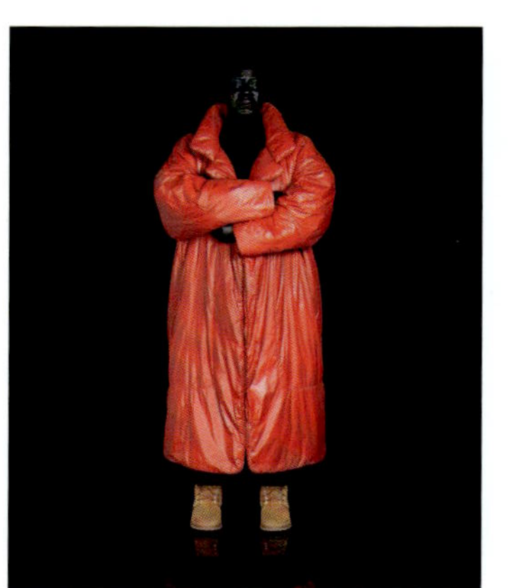

Page 245
NORMA KAMALI SLEEPING BAG COAT AND UGG BOOTS

Norma Kamali's now-iconic sleeping bag coat from the 2000s was hailed by André as "genius." The coat, which he affectionately referred to as his idea of "heaven on earth," became an instant staple in his wardrobe, worn devotedly until his passing. André's early adoration of UGG boots became a harbinger of the brand's later resurgence as a stylish collaborator in the fashion world.

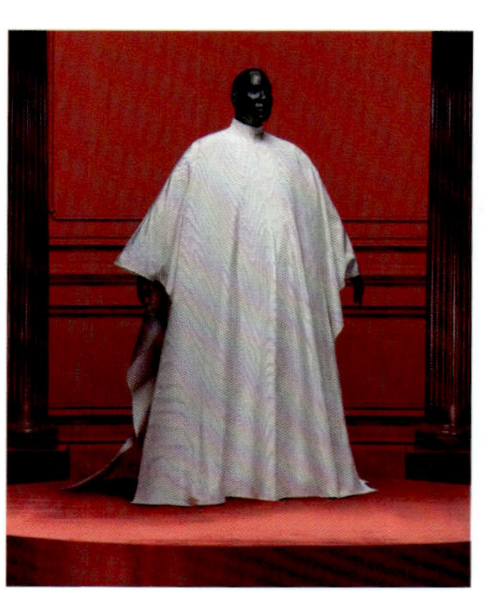

Page 246
RALPH RUCCI WHITE SILK MOIRÉ CAFTAN

Among the many caftans Ralph Rucci designed for André in royal jewel tones and majestic blacks, this look is fashioned in white Taroni silk. The perfect complement between the luxe moiré and the simplicity and purity of the garment's lines and volumes embodies André's belief in the timelessness of couture.

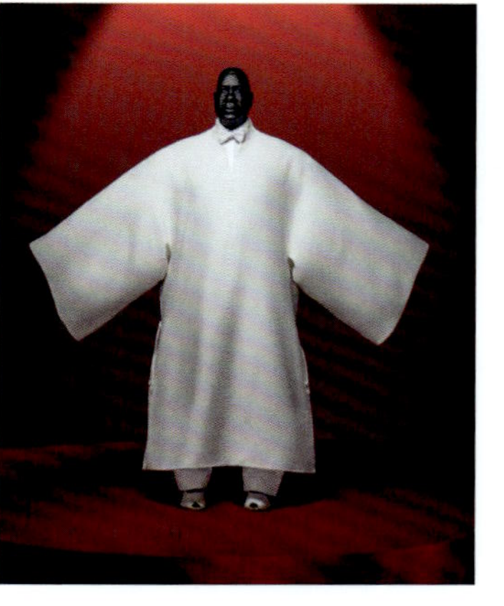

Page 247
CHADO RALPH RUCCI COTTON PIQUÉ TUNIC

Referencing the lines of a Shinto robe, this tunic in cotton piqué displays Ralph Rucci's elegant blending of couture techniques and luxury fabrics with contemporary technologies and more expected, even humble materials.

Please note: the majority of these garments were custom-designed for André and do not contain internal labels specifying the details of their textile composition. Made to measure, these bespoke creations reflect a high level of personalization and couture craftsmanship, which makes it difficult to verify the exact fiber content.

CONTRIBUTORS

Teri Agins

Teri Agins is an award-winning journalist, lecturer, consultant, and former senior special writer and "Ask Teri" columnist at *The Wall Street Journal*, where she developed and oversaw the paper's fashion industry beat for thirty years. She is the author of *Hijacking the Runway: How Celebrities Are Stealing the Spotlight from Fashion Designers* (Avery/Penguin Random House, 2014) and *The End of Fashion: How Marketing Changed the Clothing Business Forever* (William Morrow/HarperCollins, 1999). Agins has written for *The New York Times*, *Vogue*, *Essence*, *The Oprah Magazine*, *Town & Country*, *Allure*, *Elle*, *Fortune*, and *Harper's Bazaar* and appeared on *The Oprah Winfrey Show*, *Project Runway*, *The View*, *Full Frontal Fashion*, and *The Today Show*, as well as on CNN, CNBC, and National Public Radio. Agins also appeared in the documentary films *Victoria's Secret: Angels and Demons* (2022) and *The United States of Elie Tahari* (2021). She has received honors from the Council of Fashion Designers of America, the Accessories Council, Columbia University, the University of Missouri, the University of Georgia, and the Newswomen's Club of New York. She is a graduate of Wellesley College and earned an M.A. from the University of Missouri School of Journalism.

Jonathan Becker

A lifelong New Yorker, Jonathan Becker has photographed the most celebrated figures in modern culture. Renowned for his empathetic, richly contextual portraits for the world's top fashion and lifestyle publications, he began his career as a photographer for *Interview* and *Town & Country* before serving as a longtime contributor to *Vanity Fair* and *Vogue*. He has published six books of photographs, including *Bright Young Things: New York* and *Bright Young Things: London* with Brooke de Ocampo (Assouline, 2000 and 2003), *Studios by the Sea: Artists on Long Island's East End* with Bob Colacello (Abrams, 2002), and *Jonathan Becker: 30 Years at Vanity Fair* (Assouline, 2012). His photobiography *Jonathan Becker: Lost Time* (Phaidon), edited by Mark Holborn, was released in 2024.

Allen Cooley

Known for his ability to capture depth, elegance, and emotion in a single frame, Allen Cooley is an Atlanta-based photographer whose striking imagery blends technical precision and rich storytelling. For more than two decades, he has been a trusted creative partner for editorial and commercial campaigns with major beauty and fashion brands. Through his studio practice combining classic portraiture and contemporary aesthetics, Cooley's work reflects a deep reverence for culture, identity, and visual excellence. He received his M.F.A. in photography from the Savannah College of Art and Design in 2009.

Robert Fairer

Robert Fairer is a British photographer renowned for vibrant, dynamic images embodying the energy, chaos, and beauty behind the scenes of the world's top runway shows. Fairer gained prominence in the 1990s for his singular visual narratives characterized by vivid use of color, movement, and spontaneity. He began working closely with *Harper's Bazaar* in 1997 and American *Vogue* in 2001, exclusively documenting backstage at womenswear shows by major designers such as Alexander McQueen, John Galliano, and Karl Lagerfeld, accompanied by his then-editor André Leon Talley. Fairer's work offers an unfiltered, intimate look at high fashion, capturing the essence of the creative process while highlighting the emotions of models, designers, and stylists just moments before garments hit the runway. His iconic photos have become an essential visual archive of fashion history and continue to offer an authentic glimpse into the fast-paced and glamorous world of haute couture and ready-to-wear in the zeitgeist of the '90s and 2000s.

Tom Ford

Tom Ford is an internationally acclaimed American fashion designer, entrepreneur, and filmmaker. Ford joined Gucci in 1990 before becoming creative director of the brand in 1994. Under Ford's leadership, Gucci became one of the largest and most profitable luxury brands in the world. In 1999, Ford became vice chairman of Gucci Group and also served as creative director and chief designer of Yves Saint Laurent. In 2005, he announced the creation of the Tom Ford brand. Ford's success in the fashion industry has been recognized with honors including seven Council of Fashion Designers of America Awards, among them the prestigious Geoffrey Beene Lifetime Achievement Award; an unprecedented twenty-four FiFi Awards from The Fragrance Foundation including the Lifetime Achievement Award; and the Outstanding Achievement Award from the British Fashion Council. Ford served as chairman of the CFDA from 2019 to 2022, overseeing various diversity, equity, and inclusion initiatives. In 2009, he wrote, produced, and directed the Academy Award–nominated film *A Single Man*. Ford's second film, *Nocturnal Animals*, premiered at the Venice Film Festival, winning the Grand Jury Prize, and went on to receive three Golden Globe nominations and one win, nine BAFTA nominations, and an Academy Award nomination. Ford is currently concentrating on film projects in development via his production company Fade to Black.

Antoine Gregory

Antoine Gregory is a visionary fashion advocate, creative director, and founder of Black Fashion Fair—a platform dedicated to celebrating and amplifying the work of Black designers, artists, and creators. A graduate of the Fashion Institute of Technology with a background in fashion and art history, Gregory has emerged as a leading voice in fashion, championing diversity, equity, and authentic representation. His work has been featured in *The New York Times*, *Vogue*, *Essence*, and *Harper's Bazaar*, bridging fashion, art, and culture to create space and opportunities for Black creatives while reshaping an industry long resistant to inclusion. Gregory has collaborated with cultural institutions such as the Brooklyn Museum and the Baltimore Museum of Art, challenging traditional notions of space within these establishments and expanding audiences. Known for his innovative approach and unwavering commitment to Black excellence, Gregory continues to push boundaries, solidifying his legacy as a transformative force in fashion.

Rafael Brauer Gomes

Since 2015, Rafael Brauer Gomes has served as the creative director of SCAD FASH museums in Atlanta and Lacoste, France. Under his leadership, the museums have become global authorities in fashion, costume, and design exhibitions—renowned for innovative presentations that blend art, fashion, and culture. With a forward-thinking and educational curatorial approach, Brauer Gomes oversees every aspect of exhibition development, creating experiences that engage students, scholars, creatives, and international audiences. Since the museum's opening, Brauer Gomes has curated more than 50 major exhibitions across SCAD's locations in Savannah, Atlanta, and Lacoste—many of which have received critical acclaim, industry awards, and national tours. These exhibitions have reinforced SCAD's leadership in fashion curation and design education.

Prior to SCAD, Brauer Gomes spent more than a decade as head of archives at Vivienne Westwood, working closely with the designer. There, he gained rare insights into fashion exhibition-making and the global fashion industry, contributing to major exhibitions at institutions such as the Victoria and Albert Museum in London, the Palace of Versailles, and MoMu in Antwerp. A polyglot with a diverse cultural background, Brauer Gomes brings a global sensibility and deep knowledge of fashion history to every project. His cross-cultural fluency and scholarly contributions continue to shape the discourse of fashion exhibition-making, positioning SCAD FASH as a leading institution for innovation and exchange.

Carmela Spinelli

Carmela Spinelli is a fashion historian and academic with more than twenty years of experience in the design industry and higher education. During her thirteen-year tenure at the Savannah College of Art and Design, she served as chair of the university's top-ranked fashion program and led global recruitment initiatives. She frequently hosts workshops and conversations on fashion, beauty, branding, and exhibition design around the world at institutions such as the Musée des Arts Décoratifs in Paris; the Asian Civilisations Museum in Singapore; the Bowers Museum in Santa Ana, California; and the Brooklyn Museum in New York. Spinelli previously served as associate chair of fashion and accessory design at Parsons School of Design. Prior to joining academia, she held executive roles at Celine and Saks Fifth Avenue.

Diane von Furstenberg

Diane von Furstenberg is a fashion designer and philanthropist who has dedicated her life to empowering women. As founder of her eponymous brand and creator of the iconic wrap dress, von Furstenberg defined freedom for generations of women. She established the DVF Awards in 2010 to honor and empower women leaders worldwide. She is the author of several books including *Diane: A Signature Life* (Simon & Schuster, 2009), *The Woman I Wanted to Be* (Simon & Schuster, 2015), and *Own It: The Secret to Life* (Phaidon, 2021). Von Furstenberg was inducted into the National Women's Hall of Fame in 2019 and received the Chevalier de la Légion d'Honneur from the French government in 2020, as well as the Commandeur de l'Ordre de la Couronne from her native Belgium in 2021, among other honors. She serves on the boards of Vital Voices and the Council of Fashion Designers of America. In 2023, she was the subject of *Woman Before Fashion*, an exhibition dedicated to her life and career at the Fashion & Lace Museum in Brussels and Skirball Cultural Center in Los Angeles. In 2024, she was the subject of the documentary *Diane von Furstenberg: Woman in Charge*, which premiered as the opening selection at Tribeca Festival before streaming internationally.

Darren Walker

Darren Walker is president of the Ford Foundation, a $16 billion international social justice philanthropy. Under his leadership, the Ford Foundation became the first nonprofit in U.S. history to issue a $1 billion designated social bond to stabilize nonprofit organizations in the wake of COVID-19. Before joining the Ford Foundation, Walker served as vice president of the Rockefeller Foundation. Previously, he was COO of Harlem's Abyssinian Development Corporation. Walker cofounded both the U.S. Impact Investing Alliance and the Presidents' Council on Disability Inclusion in Philanthropy. In 2022, he was named Commandeur de l'Ordre des Arts et des Lettres by the French government for leadership in the arts. In 2023, he was appointed by Queen Elizabeth II to the Order of the British Empire for services to U.K./U.S. relations. He serves on many boards, including the National Gallery of Art, Carnegie Hall, the High Line, the Smithsonian National Museum of African American History and Culture, Committee to Protect Journalists, Ralph Lauren, Bloomberg, and PepsiCo. In 2024, President Joe Biden awarded Walker the National Humanities Medal, which honors individuals or groups whose work has deepened the nation's engagement with the arts and humanities.

Paula Wallace

Paula Wallace founded SCAD in 1978 and is one of the longest-serving women presidents in the history of U.S. higher education. Since being named CEO in 2000, she has more than tripled enrollment, elevated the SCAD alumni employment rate to 99 percent, and led the creation of new SCAD locations in the U.S. and Europe, as well as the online learning platform SCADnow. As the world's most comprehensive university for creative professions, SCAD currently enrolls more than 18,600 students.

Wallace's impact on the creative industries is vast. In addition to leading the development of more than one hundred academic degree programs, she created the SCAD Savannah Film Festival, the world's largest university-run film festival, as well as signature events SCAD TVfest, SCAD AnimationFest, SCAD deFINE ART, and the SCAD FASHION show, each specially designed to launch the careers of SCAD students. Wallace has also led the creation of four university museums on two continents, including SCAD FASH Museum of Fashion + Film in Atlanta, SCAD FASH Lacoste, and the SCAD Museum of Art in Savannah, widely recognized as the top teaching museums in the world. In 2025, she received the Presidential Citizens Medal, the second-highest civilian award in the U.S. Wallace has also been named an honorary member of the American Institute of Architects and a Chevalier dans l'Ordre des Palmes Académiques by the French Embassy to the U.S., among other recognitions including the National Trust for Historic Preservation's highest honor, the Louise du Pont Crowninshield Award.

Anna Wintour

Anna Wintour has held the position of *Vogue* editor in chief since 1988 and was named U.S. artistic director of Condé Nast in 2013. In 2019, she was appointed global content advisor of Condé Nast. During her tenure at Condé Nast, Wintour has been actively involved in philanthropic fundraising, particularly for The Metropolitan Museum of Art's Costume Institute, for which she has raised more than $400 million, and serves as an elective trustee of the institution. She is also a founding committee member for the New York-Presbyterian Center for Youth Mental Health, which focuses on anxiety disorders in people aged sixteen to twenty-eight. She is the recipient of numerous awards for her leadership and charitable efforts, including the Council of Fashion Designers of America Lifetime Achievement Award and the Award of Courage from the American Foundation for AIDS Research. In 2009, President Barack Obama appointed Wintour to the President's Committee on the Arts and Humanities. In 2011, she was awarded the Légion d'Honneur by French president Nicolas Sarkozy. In 2017, for her service to British journalism and fashion, Wintour was named Dame Commander (DBE) of the Order of the British Empire by Queen Elizabeth II.

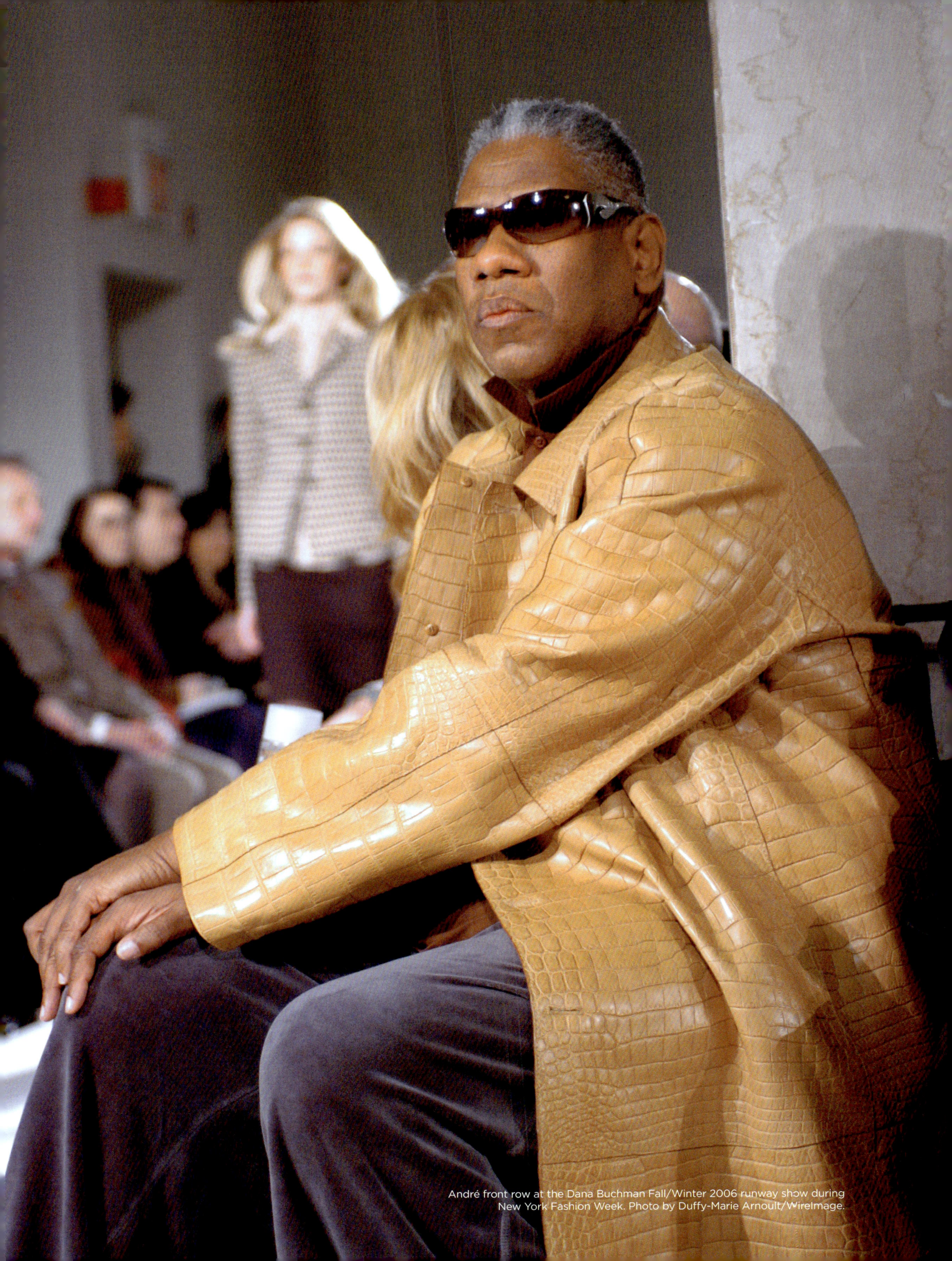

André front row at the Dana Buchman Fall/Winter 2006 runway show during New York Fashion Week. Photo by Duffy-Marie Arnoult/WireImage.

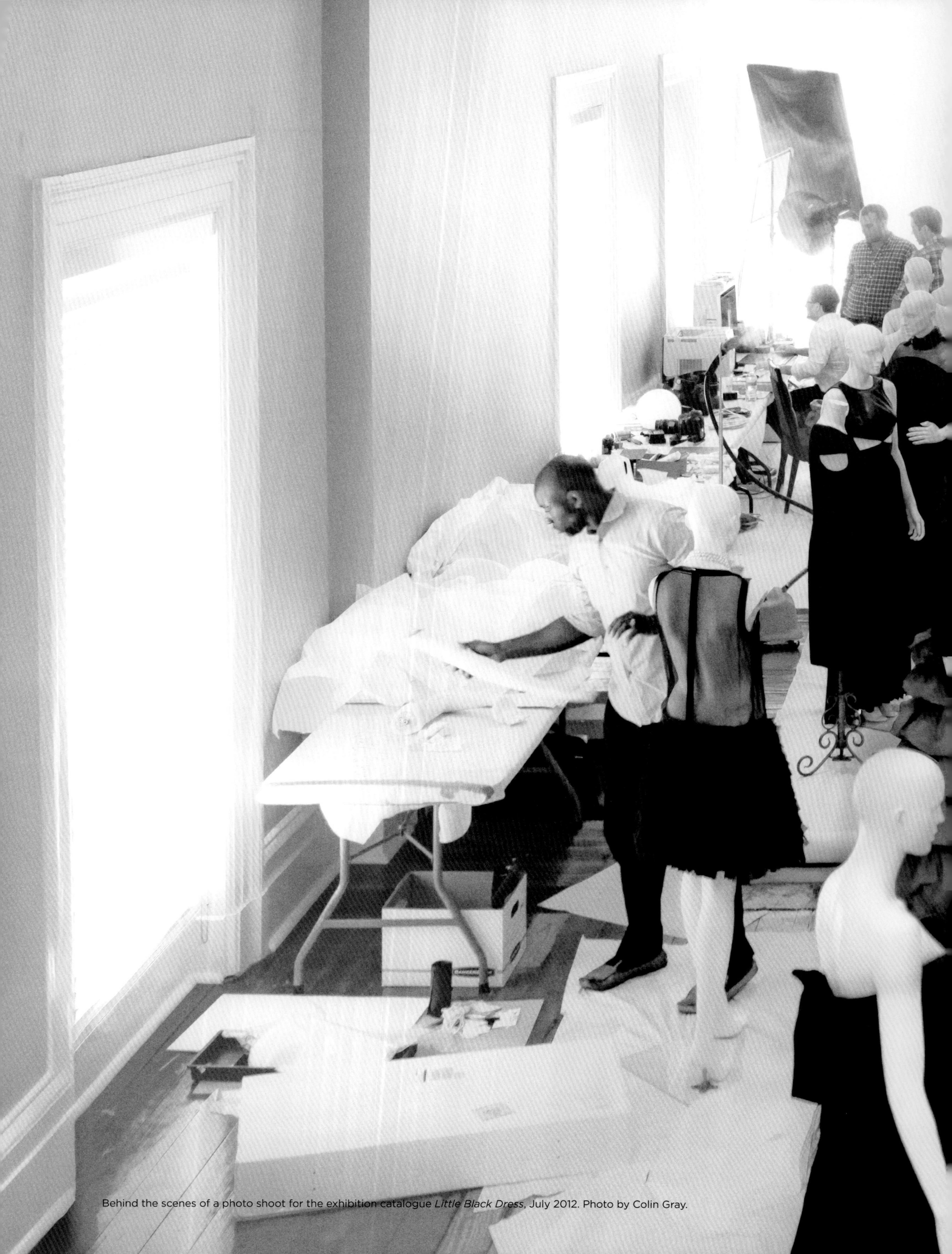

Behind the scenes of a photo shoot for the exhibition catalogue *Little Black Dress*, July 2012. Photo by Colin Gray.

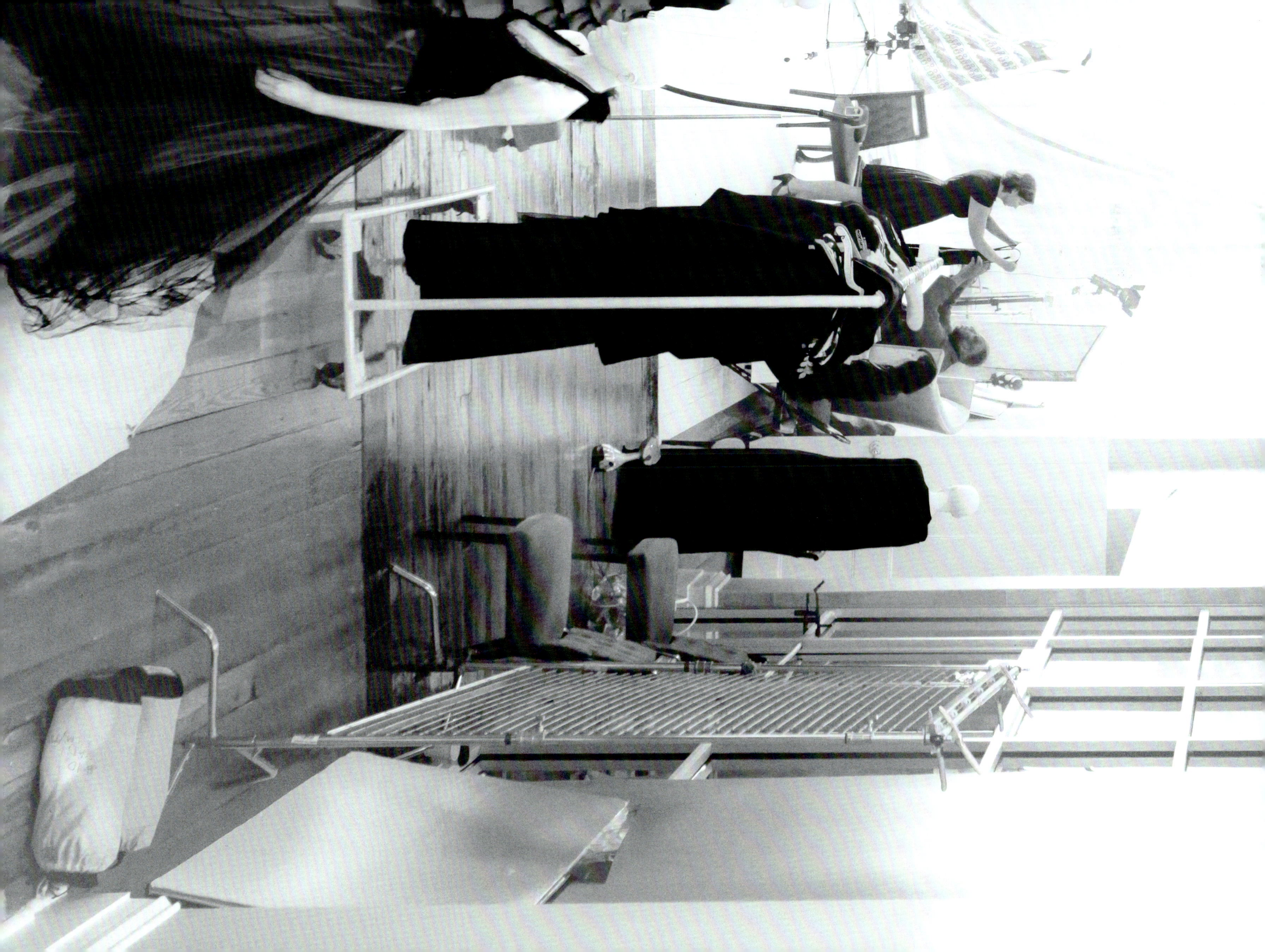

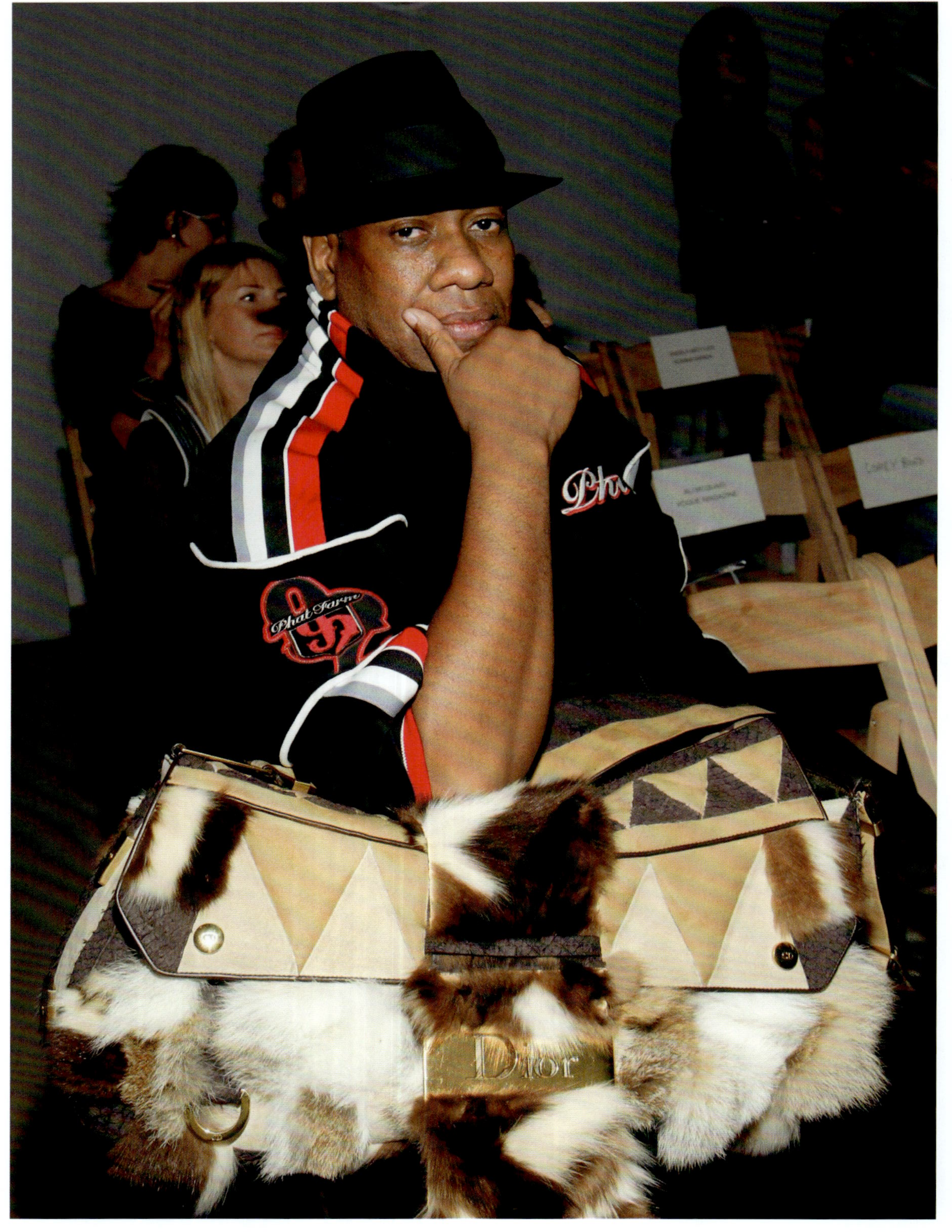

André attending the Zang Toi Spring/Summer 2004 runway show during New York Fashion Week. Photo by Evan Agostini/Getty Images.

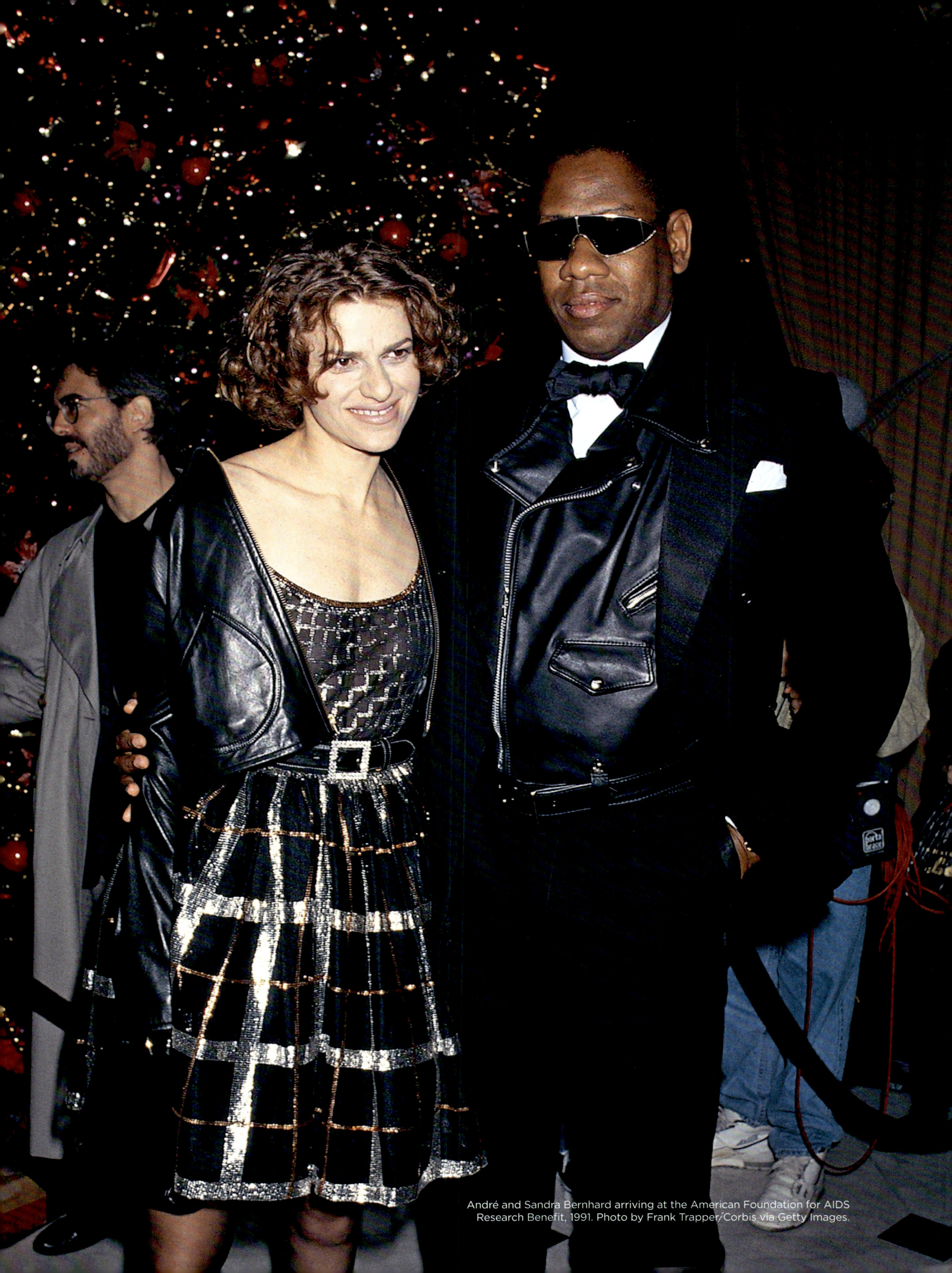

André and Sandra Bernhard arriving at the American Foundation for AIDS Research Benefit, 1991. Photo by Frank Trapper/Corbis via Getty Images.

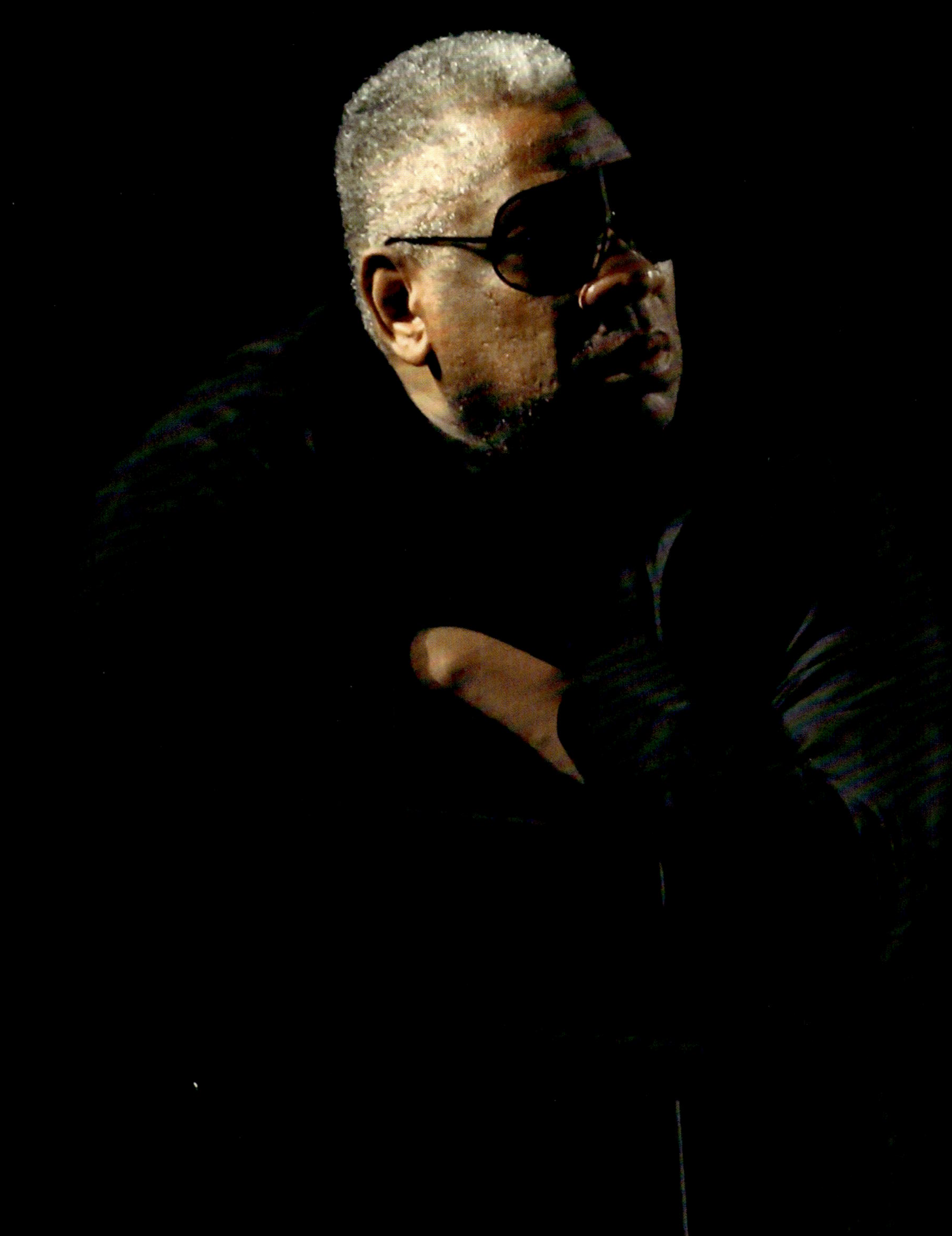

André at the Prabal Gurung Spring/Summer 2016 runway show during New York Fashion Week. Photo by Astrid Stawiarz/Getty Images for NYFW: The Shows.

ANDRÉ LEON TALLEY

1948-2022

ACKNOWLEDGMENTS

This catalogue and its accompanying exhibitions in Atlanta and Savannah united many hands, hearts, and minds. I am especially grateful to Rafael Brauer Gomes, creative director of SCAD FASH museums, for his thoughtful curation of this project that holds such meaning for so many of us. I extend deep gratitude to SCAD FASH executive director Alex Delotch Davis and SCAD executive director of museum operations Megan Tatom for their steadfast support and leadership as well as to our exhibitions team, including Kimberly Coulton, Madison Govedich, Summer Orndorff, Stephanie Ray, Emily Smith, Ariel Stark, and Jessie Ward, among others, for their meticulous attention to showcasing this collection.

I extend great appreciation to Antoine Gregory, whose creative vision has guided this catalogue from the very beginning, as we connected on this collaboration just a few months after André's passing. Thank you for honoring us with your expertise and spirit. I am also grateful to our SCAD University Press team including executive director Chris Miller as well as Sarah Kramer, Maria Silena Luque, Jennifer McCarn, Mariel Morris, James Toftness, Rosa Triolo, and Kevin Whitworth, who devoted their time and talents to shaping every page, as well as our publishing partner Rizzoli Electa.

I offer much gratitude to SCAD alum Allen Cooley (M.F.A., photography, 2009), whose photographs capture the essence of André's sartorial elegance, and to the SCAD photography and production team including senior creative director of visual media Siobhan Bonnouvrier, Omar Acevedo, Colin Gray, Alex Lacey, Alex Neumann, Yani Pedroza, Anna Robertson, Aman Shakya, True Skalde, Allison Smith, Hadley Stambaugh, and Jenny Upperman for their dedication to achieving such striking imagery, as well as to our image retoucher, SCAD alum David Field (B.F.A., photography, 2005).

Thank you to our technical sewing team including Fiorella Alvarado, Daniela Gutierrez Arreguin, Deidra David, Jessica Rubinstein Ekerman, Karen Laporte, Luz Valenzuela Taracena, and Shrutee Tokekar.

I am also grateful to Stephen Hayes for the sculptural artistry of custom forms in André's visage, adding a dramatic and uniquely personal touch to the garment displays. I offer further gratitude to SCAD general counsel Hannah Flower for her invaluable insight and to fashion scholar Carmela Spinelli for her research on the historical and cultural significance of this collection.

My appreciation extends to our esteemed contributors, André's friends and colleagues, whose warmth and love resonate throughout these pages: Teri Agins, Jonathan Becker, Manolo Blahnik, Derek Blasberg, Mariah Carey, Pat Cleveland, Dapper Dan, Robert and Vanessa Fairer, Tom Ford, Diane von Furstenberg, Bethann Hardison, Carolina Herrera, Norma Kamali, Kimora Lee Simmons, Carlos Nazario, Zac Posen, Lauren Santo Domingo, Zach Stafford, Darren Walker, Vera Wang, Veronica Webb, Constance White, and Anna Wintour.

To SCAD President and Founder Paula Wallace, my eternal gratitude for first welcoming André into our fold and nurturing such a profound connection. Your leadership envisioning and guiding our premier fashion exhibitions program and conceiving this project has been transformative. You have my enduring admiration and respect. Most of all, I am deeply indebted to André himself, who placed his trust in our team—generously giving his time, sharing his knowledge, and collaborating with us to bring so many exhibitions to life. Ultimately, he honored us with the greatest expression of that trust by gifting this collection to SCAD, confident that we would carry on his legacy with care and purpose.

Kari Herrin
Head of SCAD museums and exhibitions

This catalogue is published on the occasion of the exhibition *André Leon Talley: Style Is Forever*, organized by SCAD FASH Museum of Fashion + Film and the SCAD Museum of Art and curated by Rafael Brauer Gomes, creative director of SCAD FASH museums.

SCAD FASH Museum of Fashion + Film
1600 Peachtree Street
Atlanta, Georgia 30309
scadfash.org

SCAD Museum of Art
601 Turner Boulevard
Savannah, Georgia 31401
scadmoa.org

First published in the United States of America in 2025 by
Rizzoli Electa, a division of Rizzoli International Publications, Inc.
49 West 27th Street
New York, New York 10001
rizzoliusa.com

Publisher: Charles Miers
Associate Publisher: Margaret Chace
Senior Editor: Loren Olson
Proofreader: Marian Appellof
Production Manager: Kaija Markoe

Visit us online
Instagram: @RizzoliBooks
Facebook.com/RizzoliNewYork
Youtube.com/user/RizzoliNY

ISBN: 978-0-8478-7441-5
Library of Congress Control Number: 2025936474

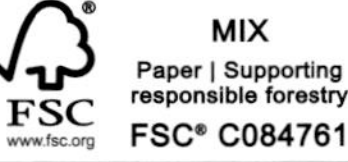

Printed in Italy
2025 2026 2027 2028 / 10 9 8 7 6 5 4 3 2 1

The authorized representative in the EU for product safety and compliance is Mondadori Libri S.p.A., via Gian Battista Vico 42, Milan, Italy, 20123.
mondadori.it

Published in association with
Savannah College of Art and Design
scad.edu

Produced by SCAD University Press

Garment photography by Allen Cooley
Back cover photo by Pari Dukovic/Trunk Archive
Photo retouching by David Field and Colin Gray

SCAD
Paula Wallace, president and founder
Kari Herrin, senior vice president for brand experience and head of SCAD museums and exhibitions

Exhibitions
Kimberly Coulton, visitation and operations coordinator
Alex Delotch Davis, executive director of SCAD FASH Museum of Fashion + Film and Atlanta exhibitions
Rafael Brauer Gomes, creative director of SCAD FASH museums
Madison Govedich, operations manager
Marcos Hernandez-Chavez, art preparator
Julie Mullenix, art preparator
Summer Orndorff, head registrar
Stephanie Ray, education and programs manager
Emily Smith, assistant director of fashion exhibitions
Ariel Stark, assistant director of fashion exhibitions and operations
Megan Tatom, executive director of museum operations
Jessie Ward, collections manager

SCAD University Press
Sarah Kramer, editorial director
Maria Silena Luque, graphic designer
Jennifer McCarn, senior art director
Chris Miller, executive director
Mariel Morris, senior graphic designer
James Toftness, publications manager
Rosa Triolo, art director
Kevin Whitworth, production manager